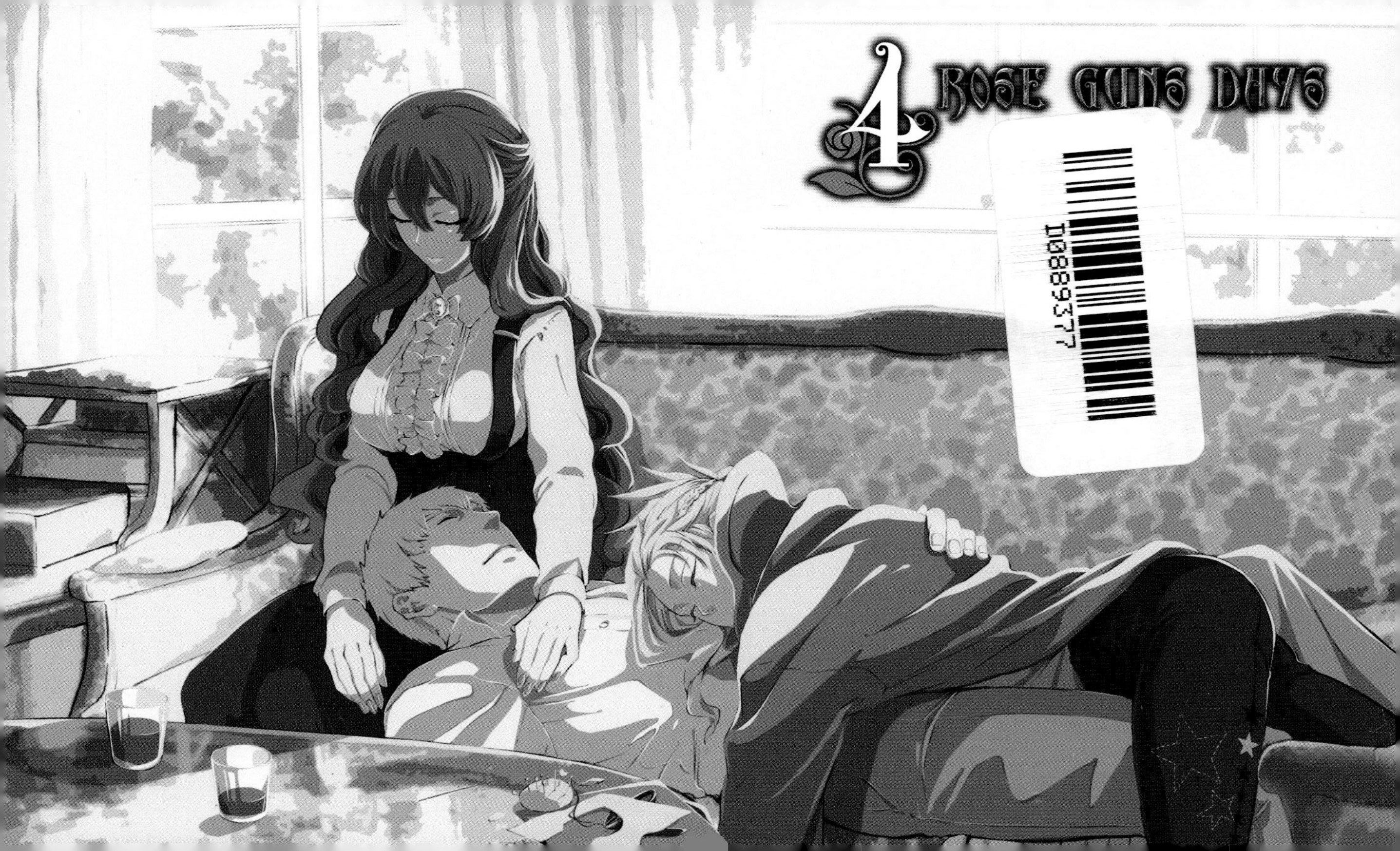
4
ROSE GUNS DAYS

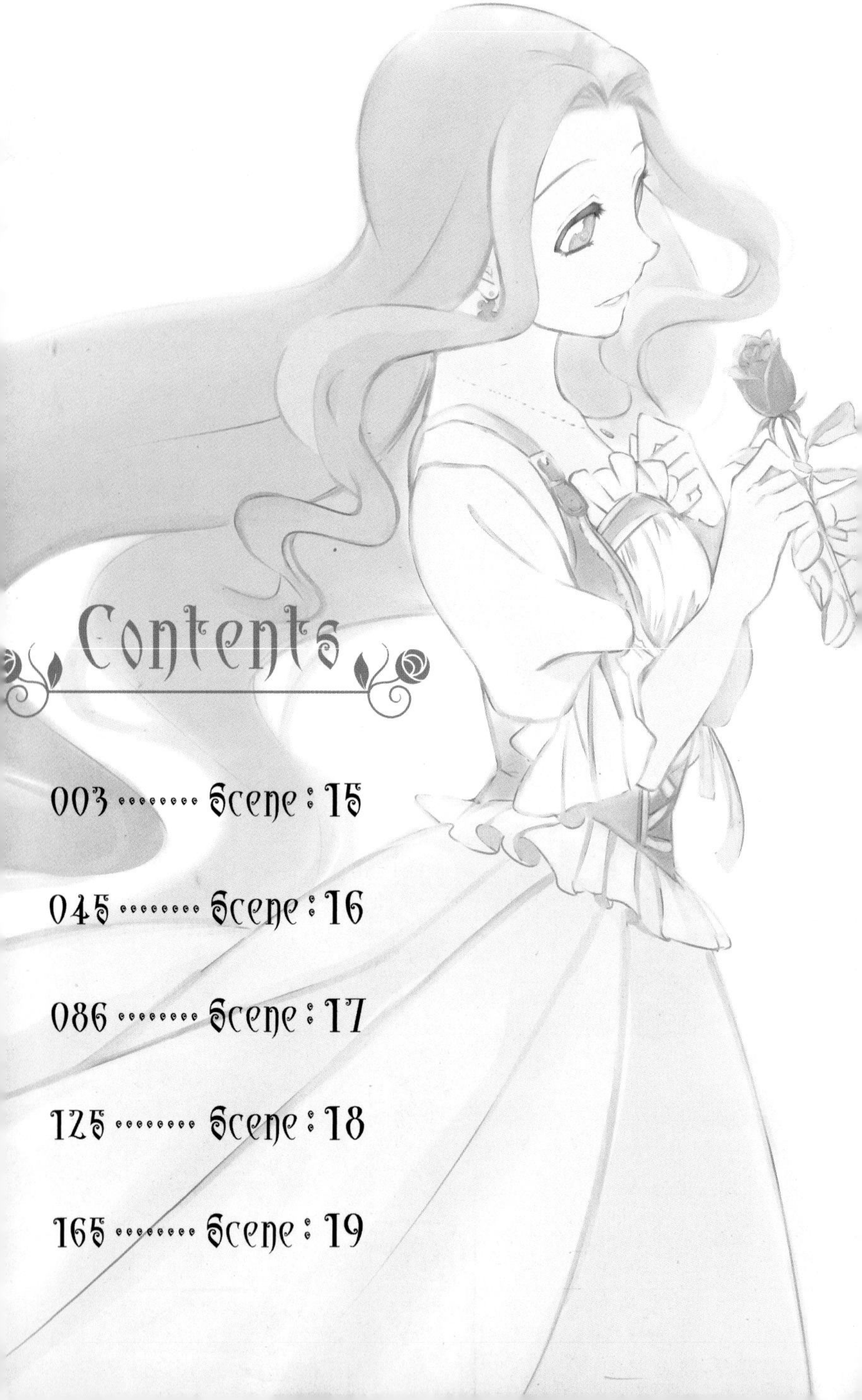

Contents

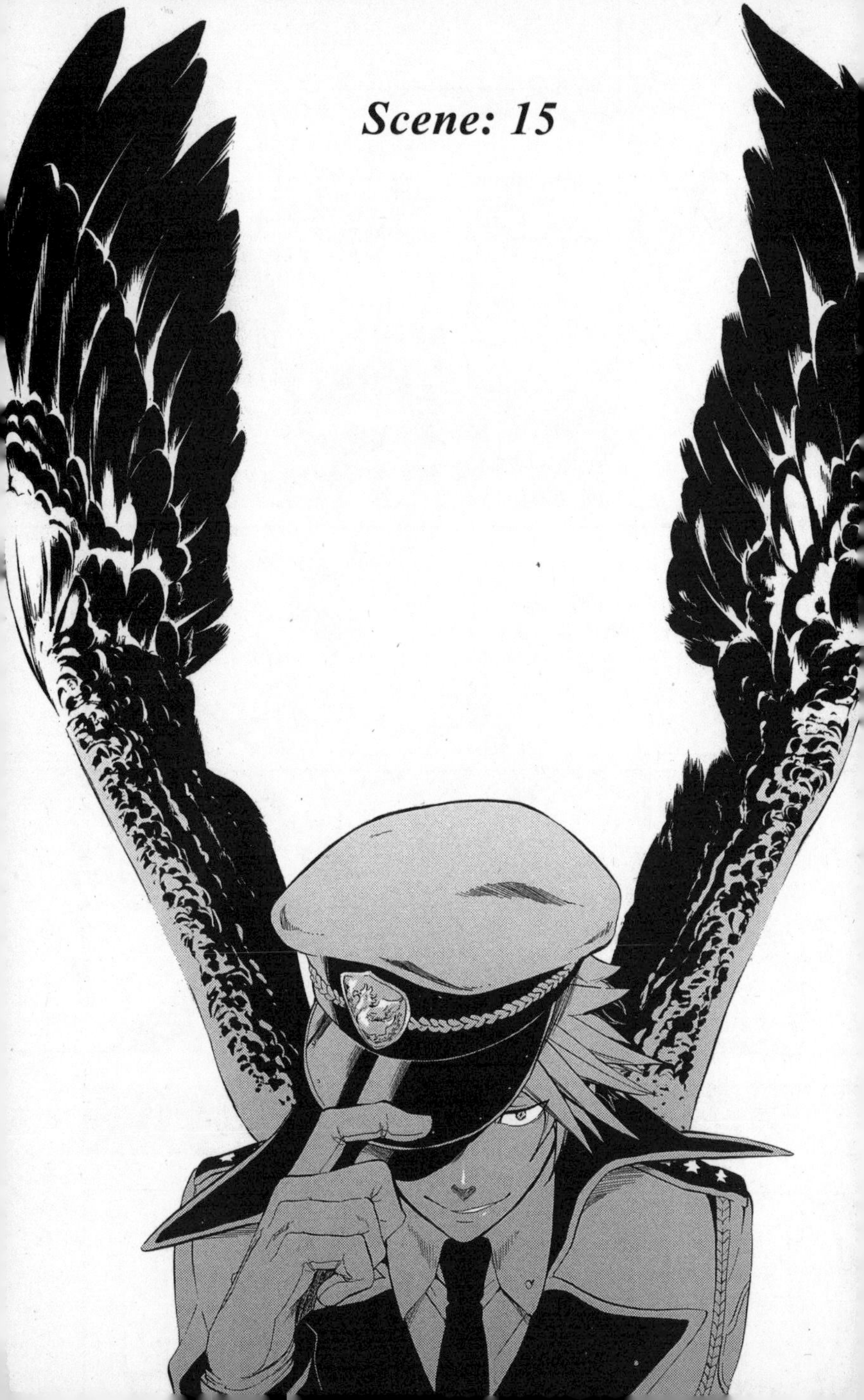
Scene: 15

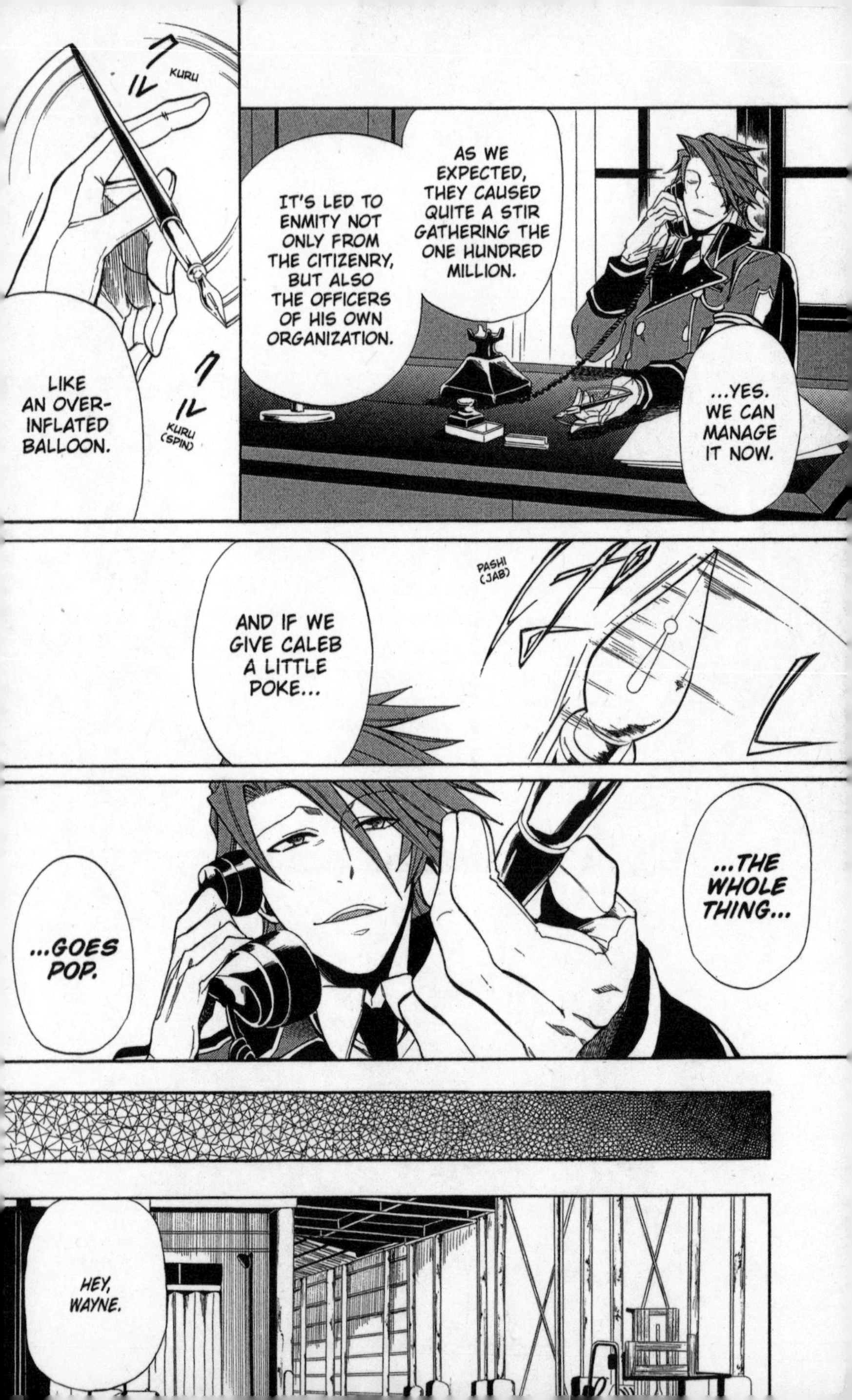
AS WE EXPECTED, THEY CAUSED QUITE A STIR GATHERING THE ONE HUNDRED MILLION.
IT'S LED TO ENMITY NOT ONLY FROM THE CITIZENRY, BUT ALSO THE OFFICERS OF HIS OWN ORGANIZATION.
...YES. WE CAN MANAGE IT NOW.
KURU
LIKE AN OVER-INFLATED BALLOON.
KURU (SPIN)
PASHI (JAB)
AND IF WE GIVE CALEB A LITTLE POKE...
...THE WHOLE THING...
...GOES POP.
HEY, WAYNE.

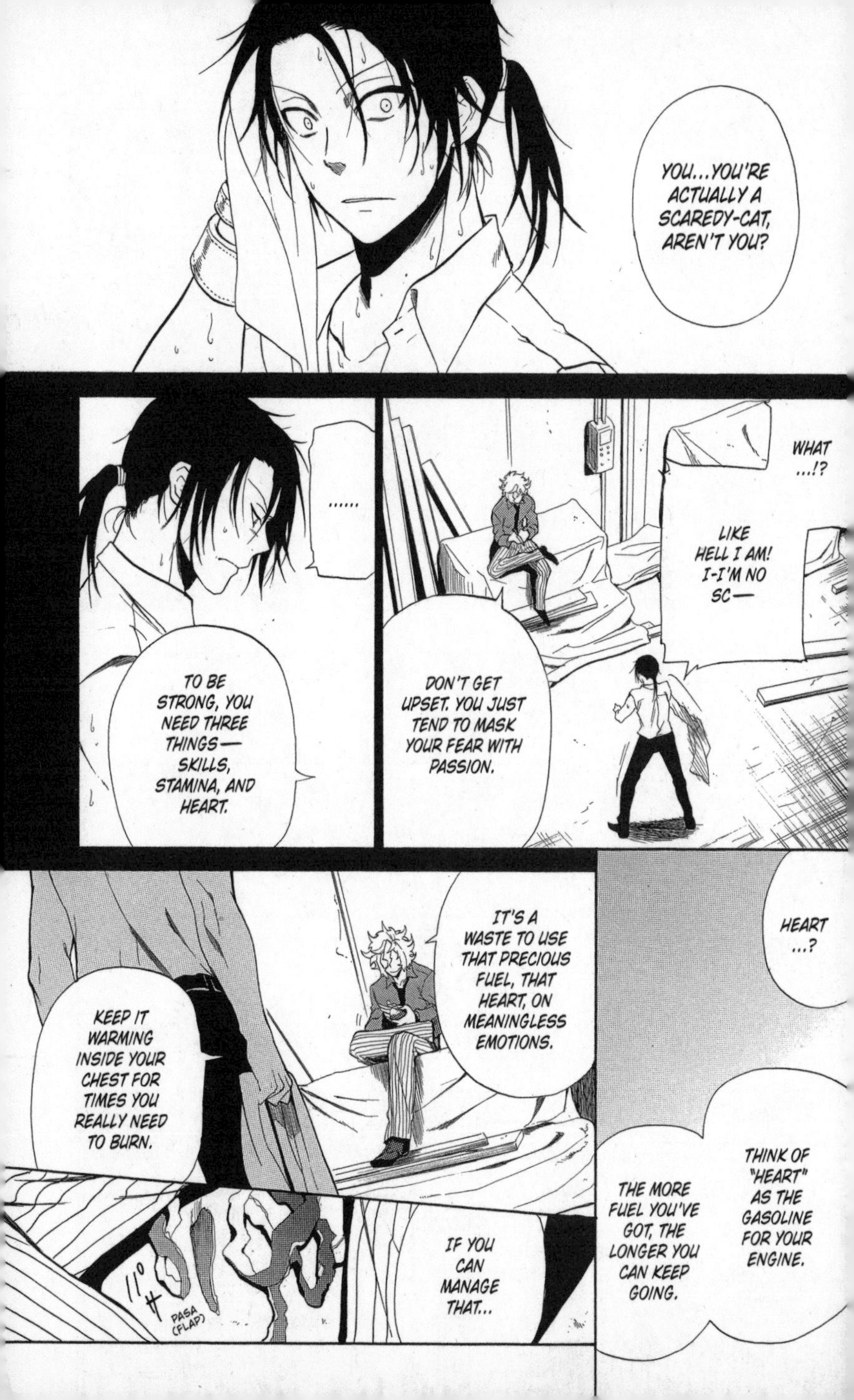
YOU...YOU'RE ACTUALLY A SCAREDY-CAT, AREN'T YOU?
WHAT ...!?
LIKE HELL I AM! I-I'M NO SC—
DON'T GET UPSET. YOU JUST TEND TO MASK YOUR FEAR WITH PASSION.
......
TO BE STRONG, YOU NEED THREE THINGS— SKILLS, STAMINA, AND HEART.
HEART ...?
THINK OF "HEART" AS THE GASOLINE FOR YOUR ENGINE.
THE MORE FUEL YOU'VE GOT, THE LONGER YOU CAN KEEP GOING.
IT'S A WASTE TO USE THAT PRECIOUS FUEL, THAT HEART, ON MEANINGLESS EMOTIONS.
KEEP IT WARMING INSIDE YOUR CHEST FOR TIMES YOU REALLY NEED TO BURN.
IF YOU CAN MANAGE THAT...
PASA (FLAP)

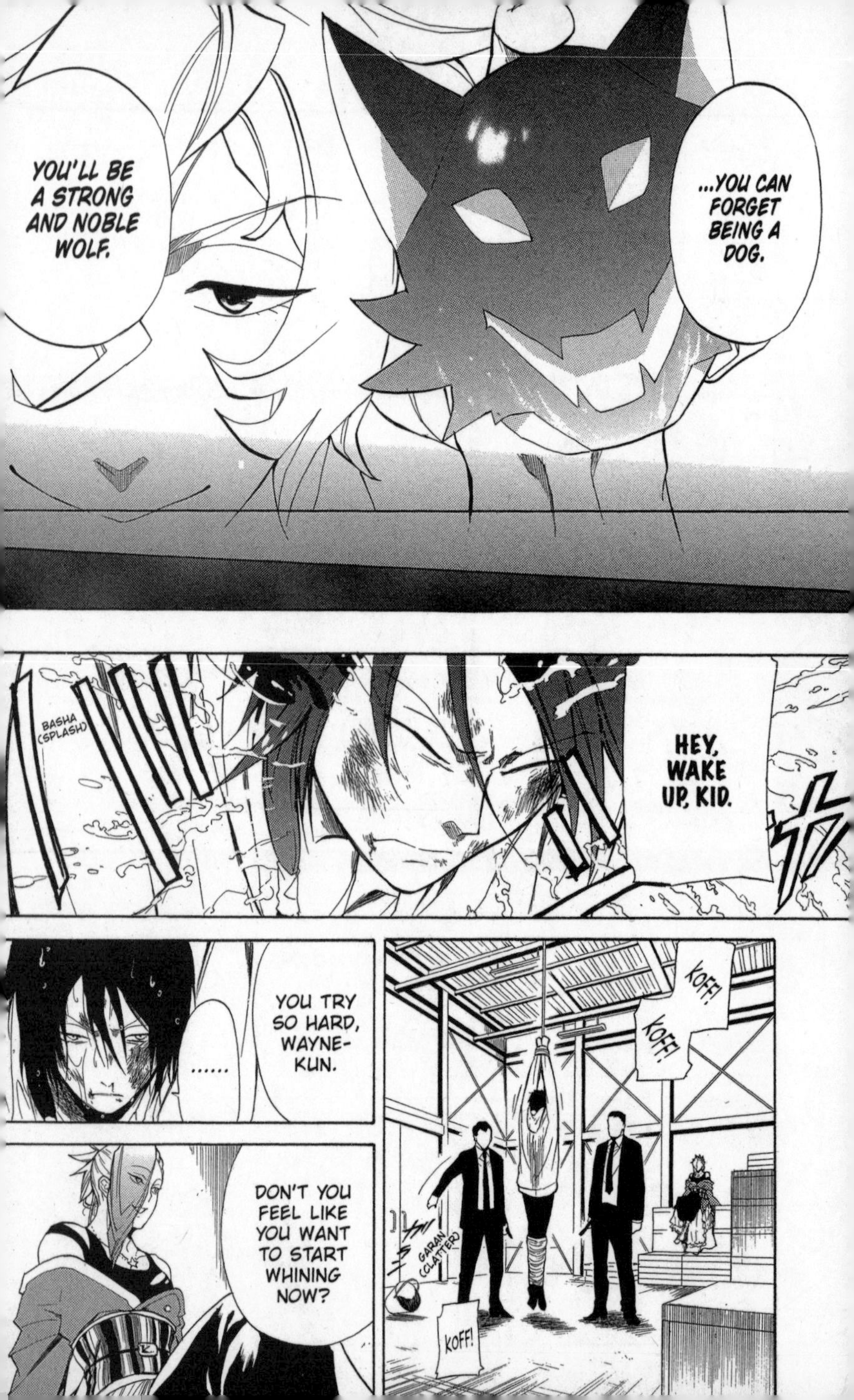
...YOU CAN FORGET BEING A DOG.
YOU'LL BE A STRONG AND NOBLE WOLF.
HEY, WAKE UP, KID.
BASHA (SPLASH)
KOFF!
KOFF!
GARAN (CLATTER)
KOFF!
YOU TRY SO HARD, WAYNE-KUN.
......
DON'T YOU FEEL LIKE YOU WANT TO START WHINING NOW?

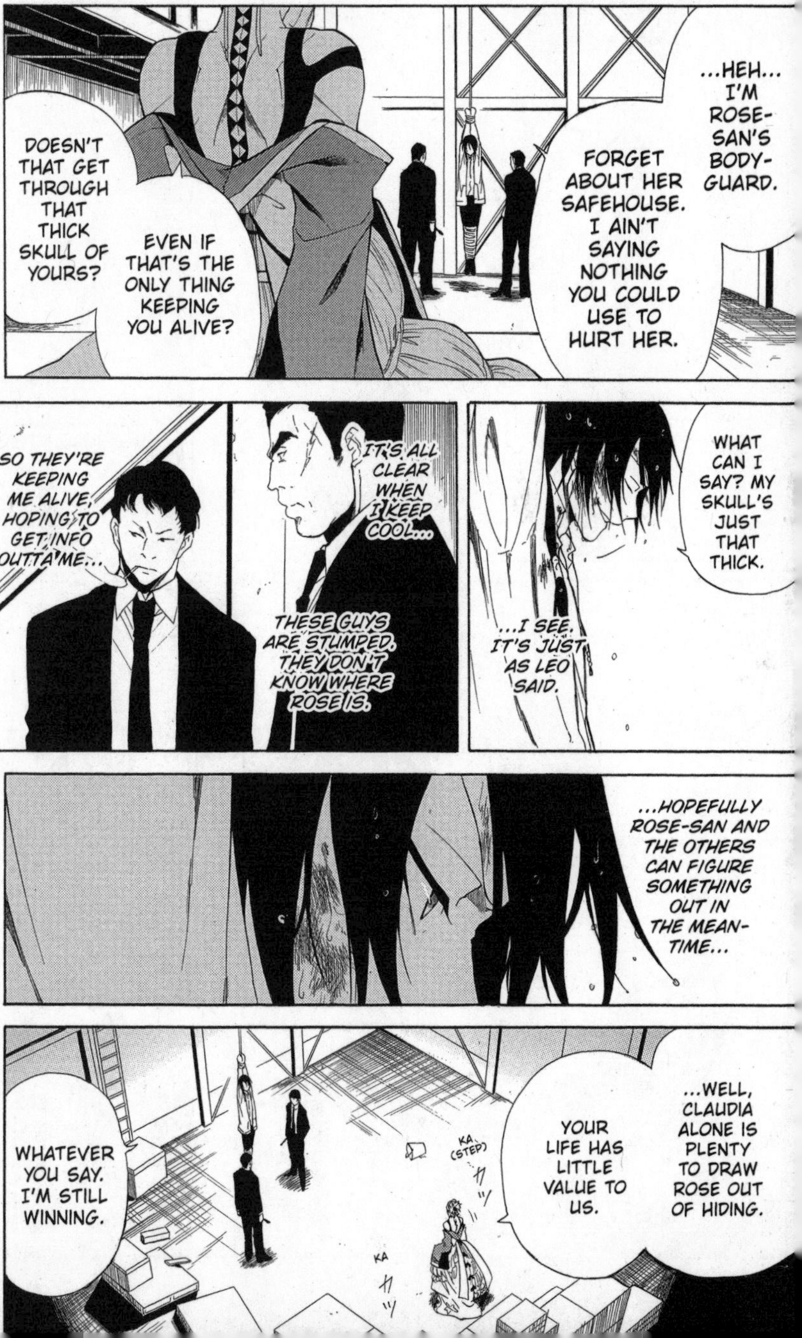
...HEH... I'M ROSE-SAN'S BODY-GUARD.
FORGET ABOUT HER SAFEHOUSE. I AIN'T SAYING NOTHING YOU COULD USE TO HURT HER.
EVEN IF THAT'S THE ONLY THING KEEPING YOU ALIVE?
DOESN'T THAT GET THROUGH THAT THICK SKULL OF YOURS?
WHAT CAN I SAY? MY SKULL'S JUST THAT THICK.
...I SEE. IT'S JUST AS LEO SAID.
IT'S ALL CLEAR WHEN I KEEP COOL...
THESE GUYS ARE STUMPED. THEY DON'T KNOW WHERE ROSE IS.
SO THEY'RE KEEPING ME ALIVE, HOPING TO GET INFO OUTTA ME...
...HOPEFULLY ROSE-SAN AND THE OTHERS CAN FIGURE SOMETHING OUT IN THE MEAN-TIME...
...WELL, CLAUDIA ALONE IS PLENTY TO DRAW ROSE OUT OF HIDING.
YOUR LIFE HAS LITTLE VALUE TO US.
KA (STEP)
KA
WHATEVER YOU SAY. I'M STILL WINNING.

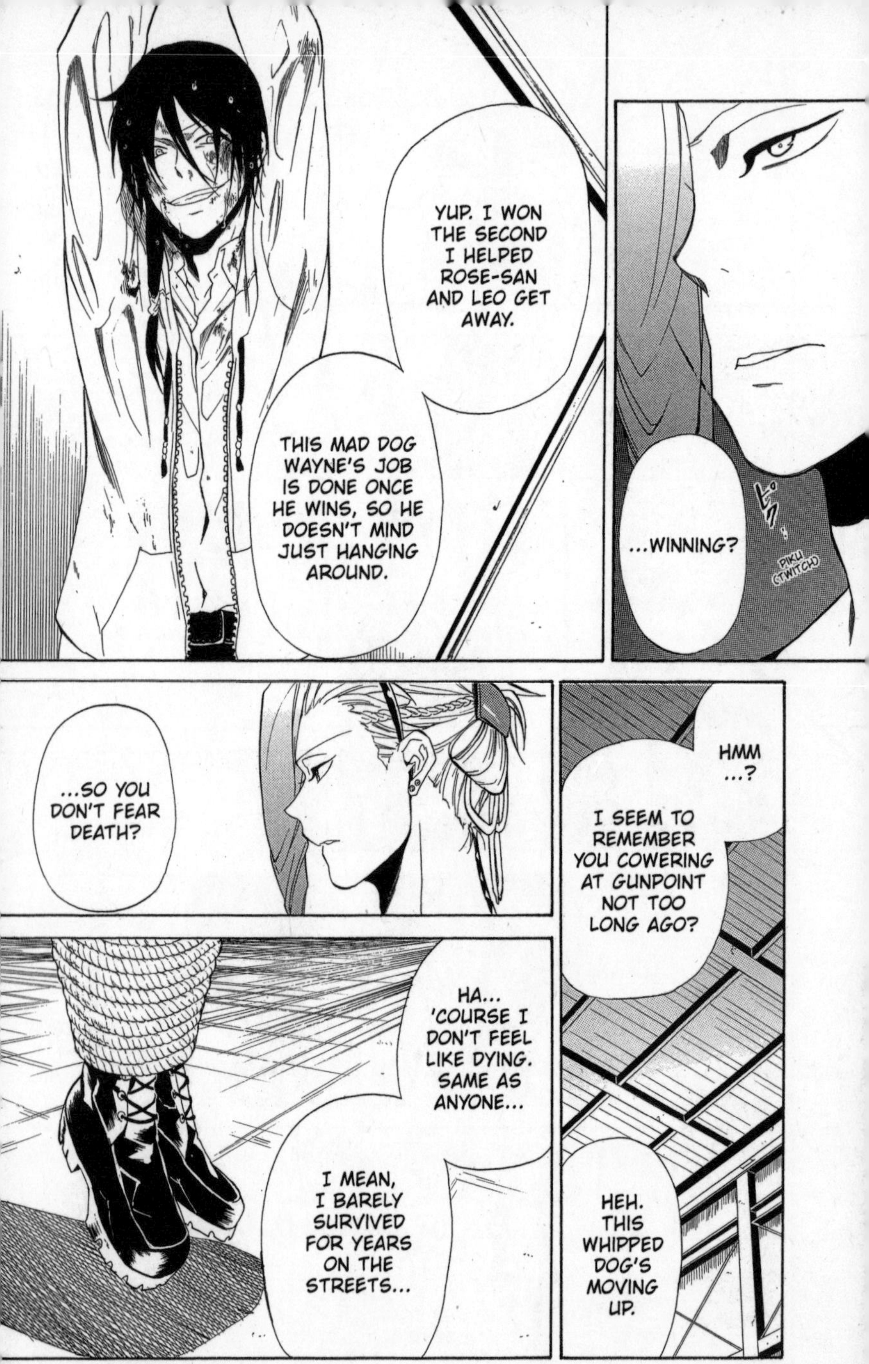
YUP. I WON THE SECOND I HELPED ROSE-SAN AND LEO GET AWAY.
THIS MAD DOG WAYNE'S JOB IS DONE ONCE HE WINS, SO HE DOESN'T MIND JUST HANGING AROUND.
...WINNING?
PIKU (TWITCH)
...SO YOU DON'T FEAR DEATH?
HMM ...?
I SEEM TO REMEMBER YOU COWERING AT GUNPOINT NOT TOO LONG AGO?
HA... 'COURSE I DON'T FEEL LIKE DYING. SAME AS ANYONE...
I MEAN, I BARELY SURVIVED FOR YEARS ON THE STREETS...
HEH. THIS WHIPPED DOG'S MOVING UP.

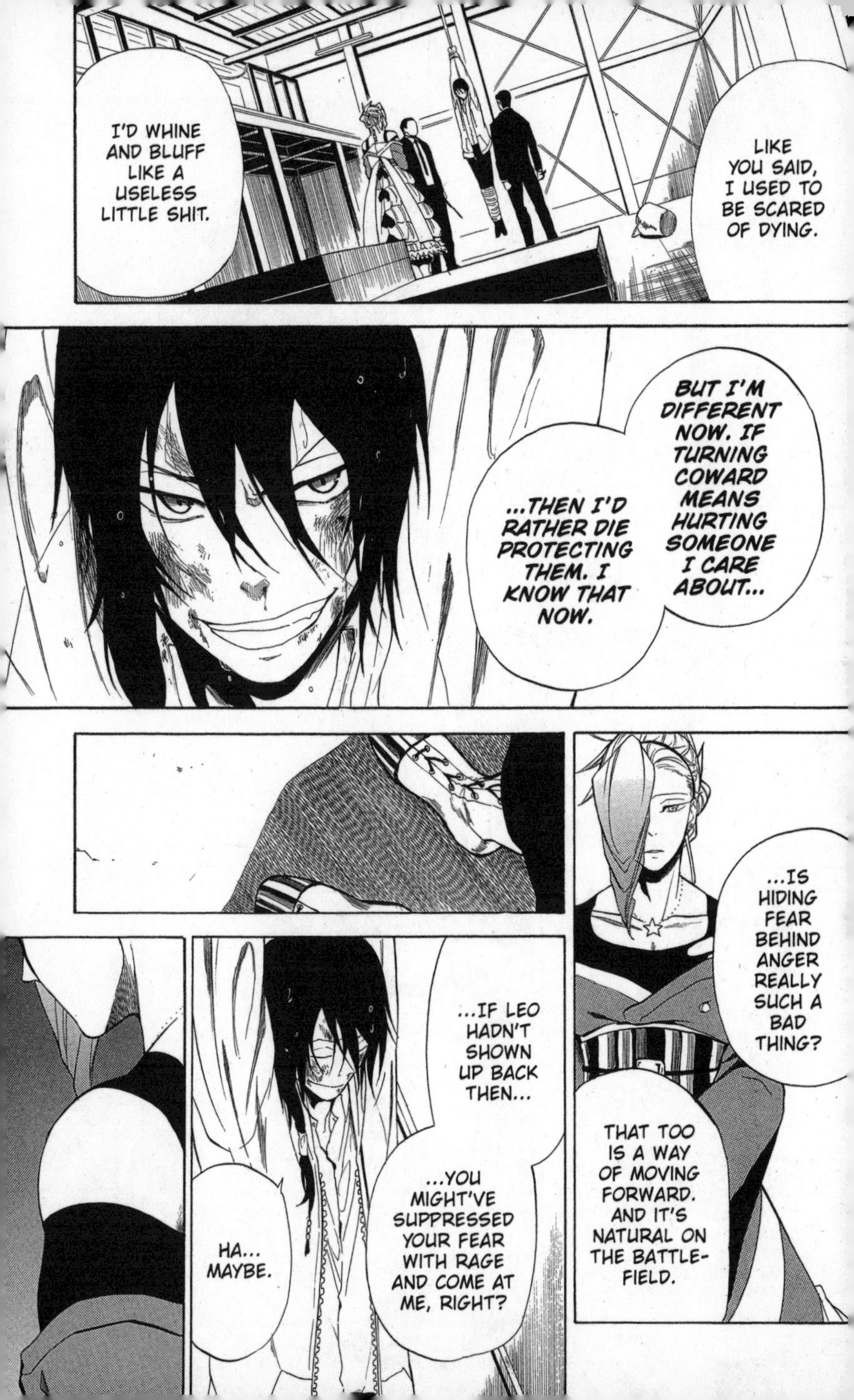
LIKE YOU SAID, I USED TO BE SCARED OF DYING.
I'D WHINE AND BLUFF LIKE A USELESS LITTLE SHIT.
BUT I'M DIFFERENT NOW. IF TURNING COWARD MEANS HURTING SOMEONE I CARE ABOUT...
...THEN I'D RATHER DIE PROTECTING THEM. I KNOW THAT NOW.
...IS HIDING FEAR BEHIND ANGER REALLY SUCH A BAD THING?
THAT TOO IS A WAY OF MOVING FORWARD. AND IT'S NATURAL ON THE BATTLE-FIELD.
...IF LEO HADN'T SHOWN UP BACK THEN...
...YOU MIGHT'VE SUPPRESSED YOUR FEAR WITH RAGE AND COME AT ME, RIGHT?
HA... MAYBE.

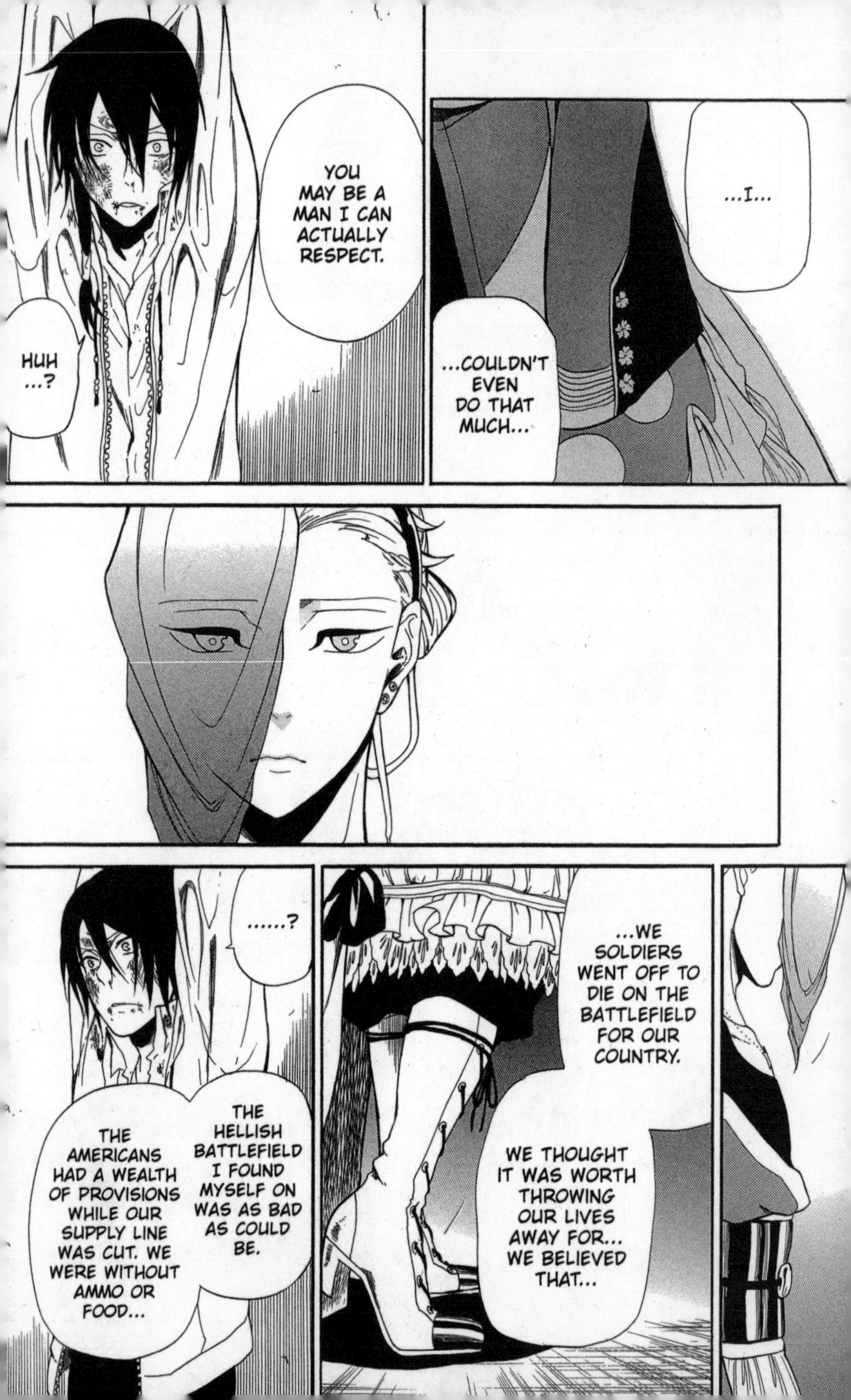
...I...
...COULDN'T EVEN DO THAT MUCH...
YOU MAY BE A MAN I CAN ACTUALLY RESPECT.
HUH ...?
...WE SOLDIERS WENT OFF TO DIE ON THE BATTLEFIELD FOR OUR COUNTRY.
WE THOUGHT IT WAS WORTH THROWING OUR LIVES AWAY FOR... WE BELIEVED THAT...
......?
THE HELLISH BATTLEFIELD I FOUND MYSELF ON WAS AS BAD AS COULD BE.
THE AMERICANS HAD A WEALTH OF PROVISIONS WHILE OUR SUPPLY LINE WAS CUT. WE WERE WITHOUT AMMO OR FOOD...

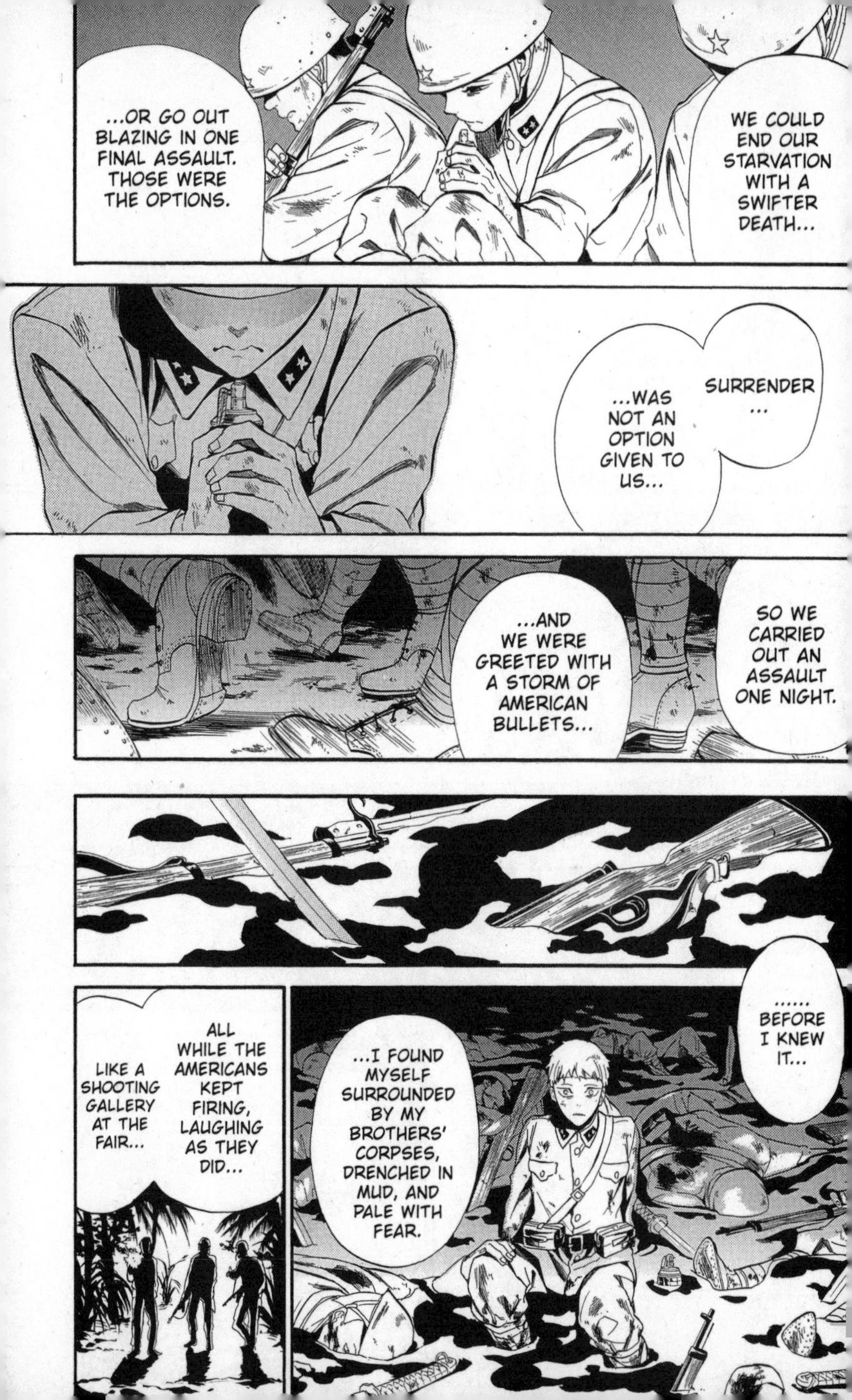
WE COULD END OUR STARVATION WITH A SWIFTER DEATH...
...OR GO OUT BLAZING IN ONE FINAL ASSAULT. THOSE WERE THE OPTIONS.
SURRENDER ...
...WAS NOT AN OPTION GIVEN TO US...
SO WE CARRIED OUT AN ASSAULT ONE NIGHT.
...AND WE WERE GREETED WITH A STORM OF AMERICAN BULLETS...
...... BEFORE I KNEW IT...
...I FOUND MYSELF SURROUNDED BY MY BROTHERS' CORPSES, DRENCHED IN MUD, AND PALE WITH FEAR.
ALL WHILE THE AMERICANS KEPT FIRING, LAUGHING AS THEY DID...
LIKE A SHOOTING GALLERY AT THE FAIR...

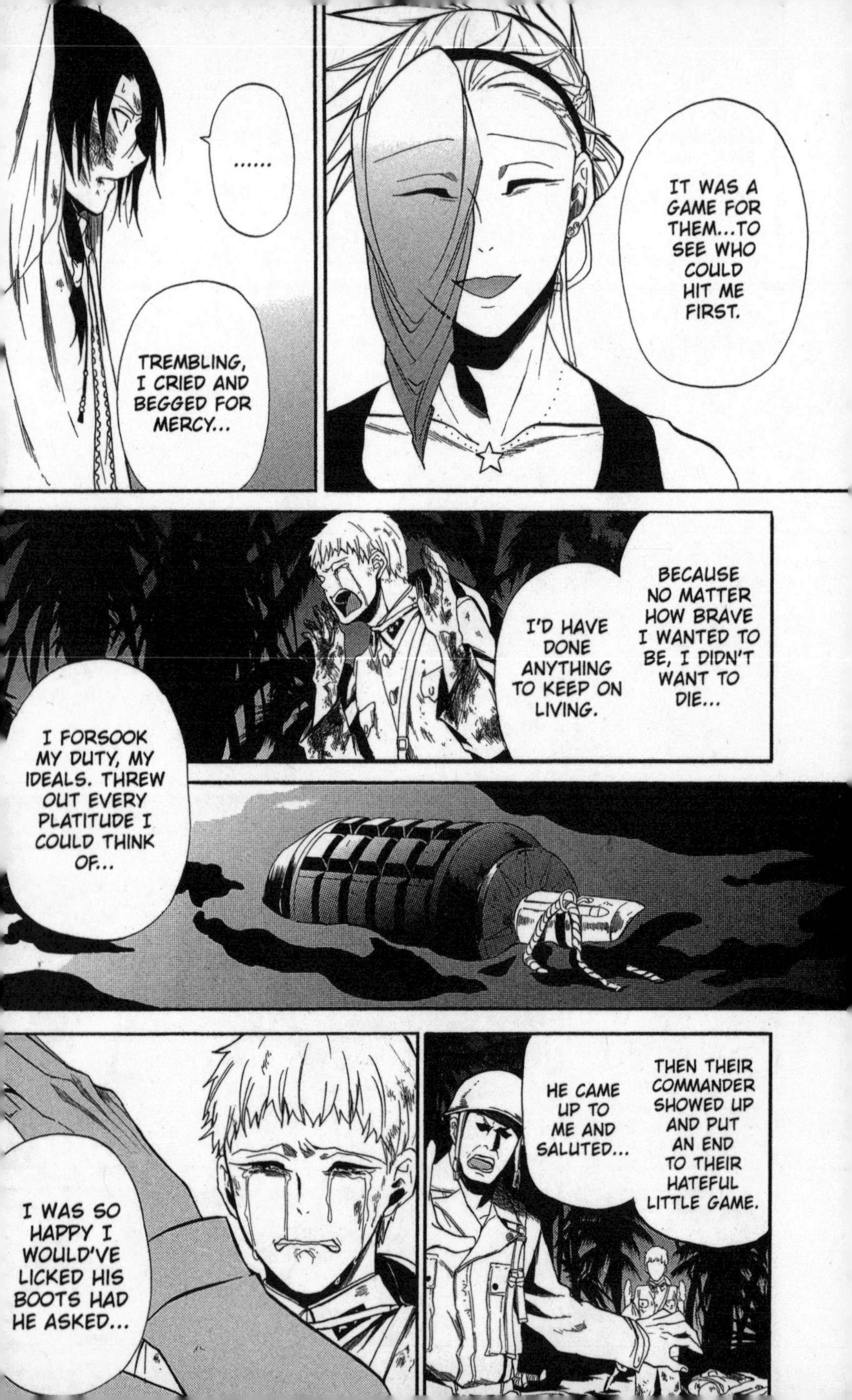
IT WAS A GAME FOR THEM...TO SEE WHO COULD HIT ME FIRST.
......
TREMBLING, I CRIED AND BEGGED FOR MERCY...
BECAUSE NO MATTER HOW BRAVE I WANTED TO BE, I DIDN'T WANT TO DIE...
I'D HAVE DONE ANYTHING TO KEEP ON LIVING.
I FORSOOK MY DUTY, MY IDEALS. THREW OUT EVERY PLATITUDE I COULD THINK OF...
THEN THEIR COMMANDER SHOWED UP AND PUT AN END TO THEIR HATEFUL LITTLE GAME.
HE CAME UP TO ME AND SALUTED...
I WAS SO HAPPY I WOULD'VE LICKED HIS BOOTS HAD HE ASKED...

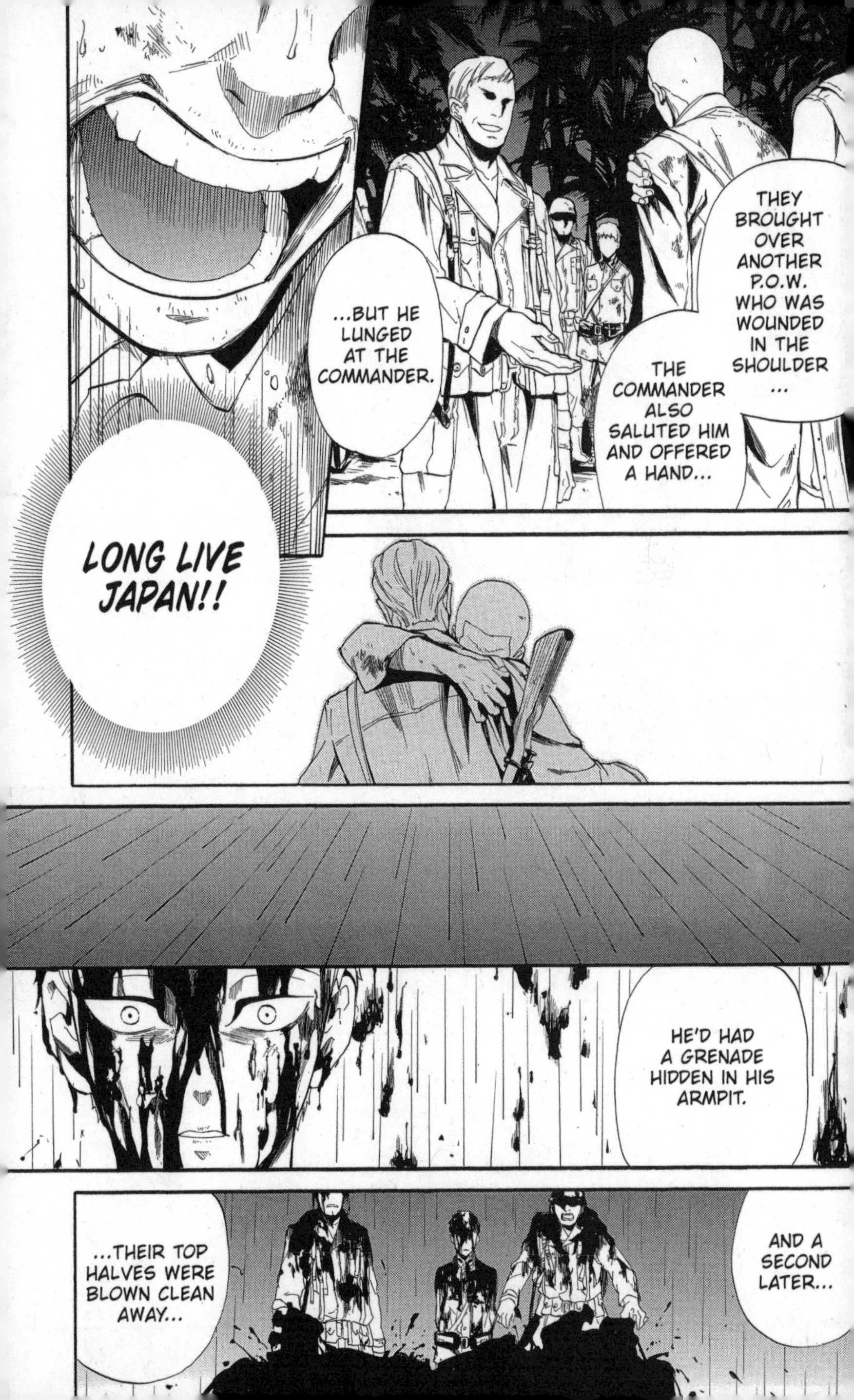
THEY BROUGHT OVER ANOTHER P.O.W. WHO WAS WOUNDED IN THE SHOULDER...
THE COMMANDER ALSO SALUTED HIM AND OFFERED A HAND...
...BUT HE LUNGED AT THE COMMANDER.
LONG LIVE JAPAN!!
HE'D HAD A GRENADE HIDDEN IN HIS ARMPIT.
AND A SECOND LATER...
...THEIR TOP HALVES WERE BLOWN CLEAN AWAY...

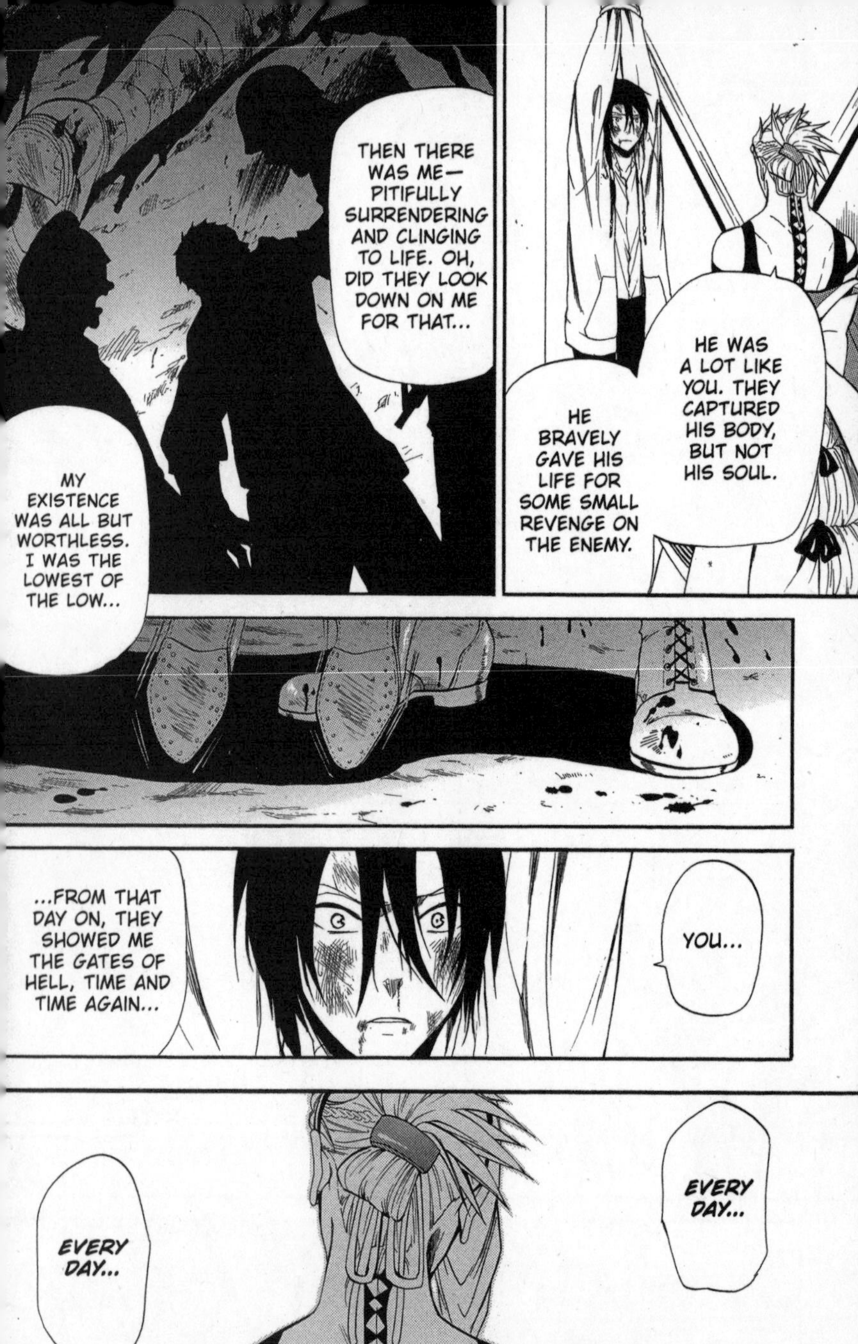
HE WAS A LOT LIKE YOU. THEY CAPTURED HIS BODY, BUT NOT HIS SOUL.
HE BRAVELY GAVE HIS LIFE FOR SOME SMALL REVENGE ON THE ENEMY.
THEN THERE WAS ME—PITIFULLY SURRENDERING AND CLINGING TO LIFE. OH, DID THEY LOOK DOWN ON ME FOR THAT...
MY EXISTENCE WAS ALL BUT WORTHLESS. I WAS THE LOWEST OF THE LOW...
YOU...
...FROM THAT DAY ON, THEY SHOWED ME THE GATES OF HELL, TIME AND TIME AGAIN...
EVERY DAY...
EVERY DAY...

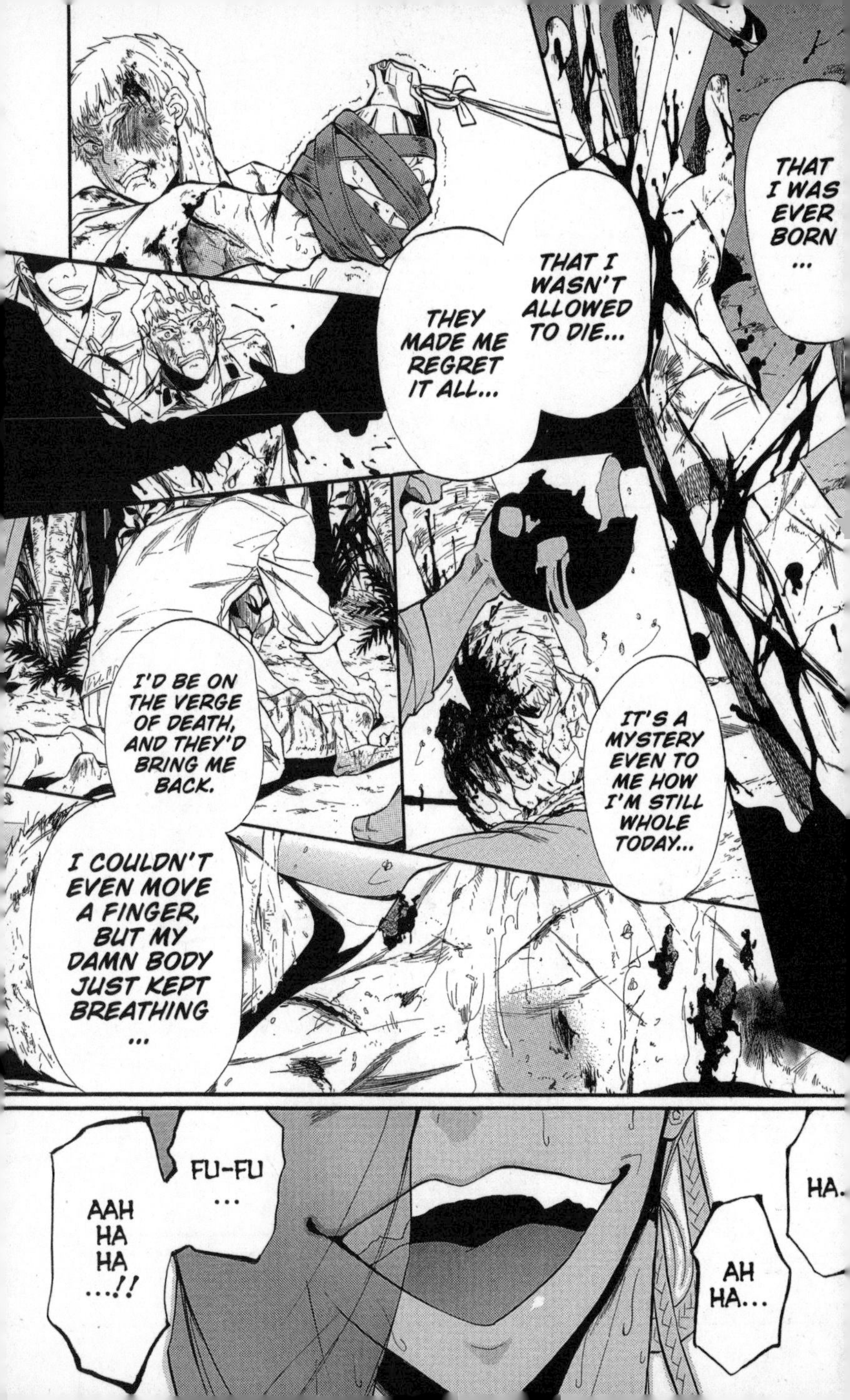
THAT I WAS EVER BORN ...
THAT I WASN'T ALLOWED TO DIE...
THEY MADE ME REGRET IT ALL...
IT'S A MYSTERY EVEN TO ME HOW I'M STILL WHOLE TODAY...
I'D BE ON THE VERGE OF DEATH, AND THEY'D BRING ME BACK.
I COULDN'T EVEN MOVE A FINGER, BUT MY DAMN BODY JUST KEPT BREATHING ...
HA.
AH HA...
FU-FU ...
AAH HA HA ...!!

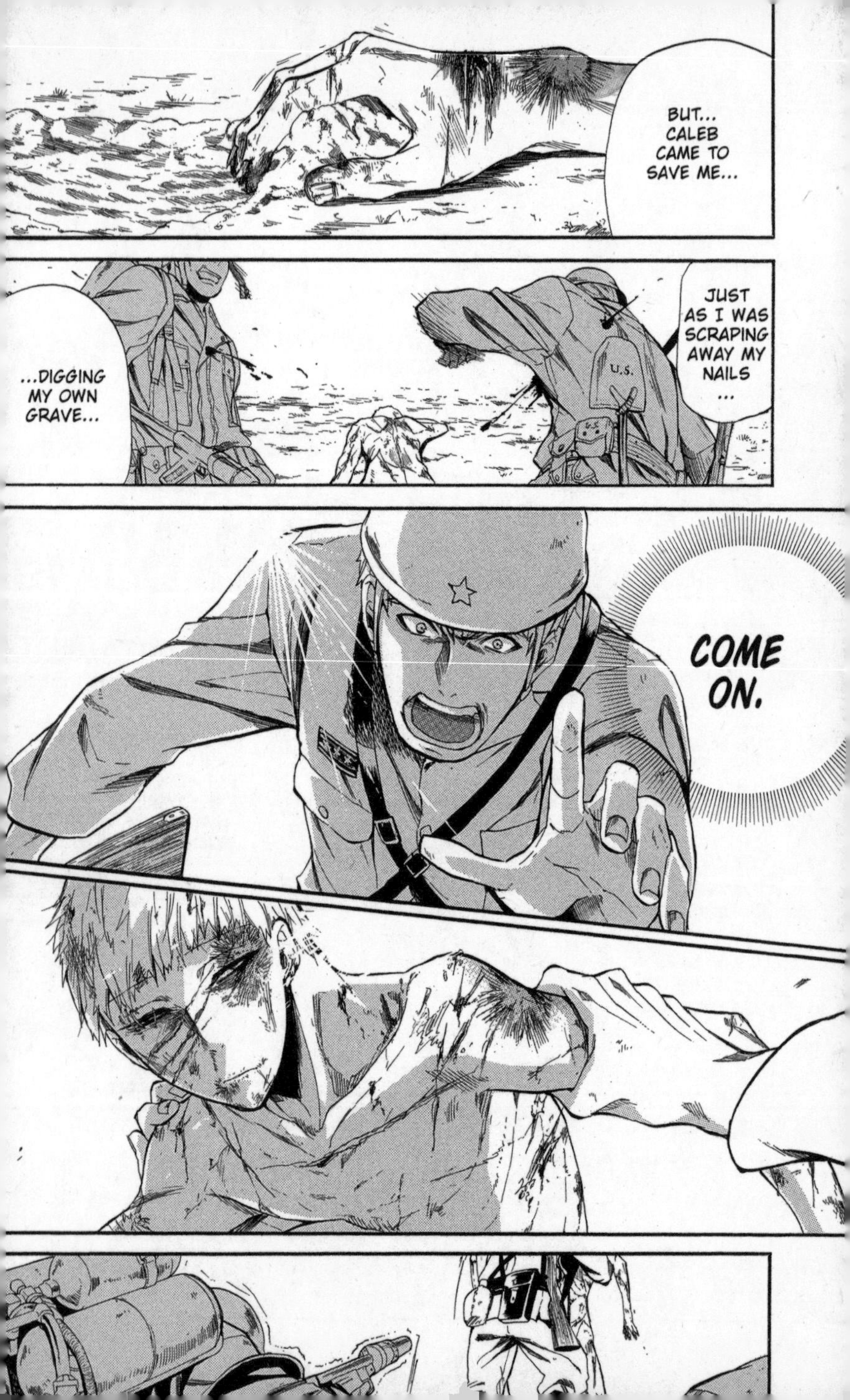
BUT... CALEB CAME TO SAVE ME...
JUST AS I WAS SCRAPING AWAY MY NAILS ...
...DIGGING MY OWN GRAVE...
COME ON.

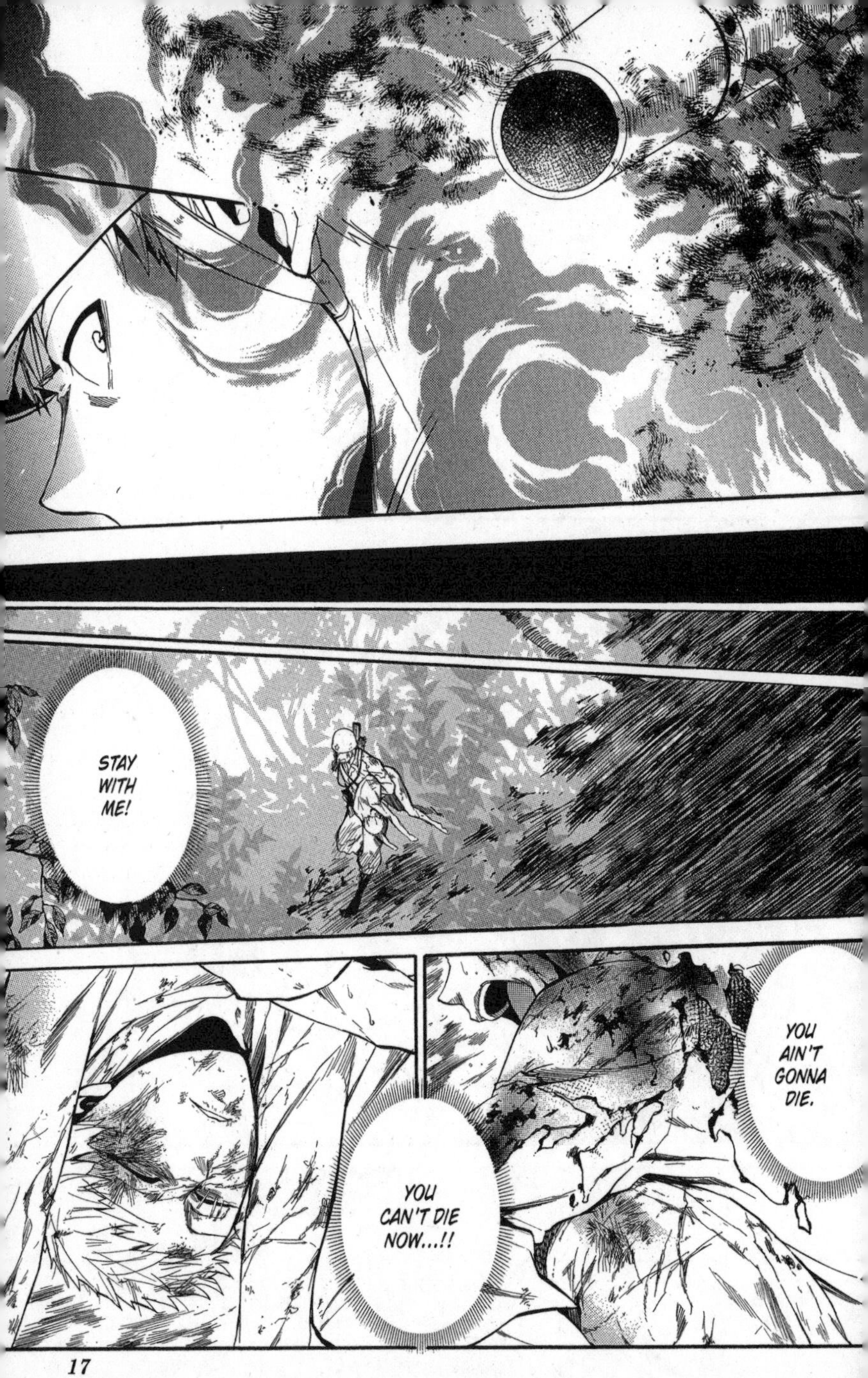
STAY WITH ME!
YOU AIN'T GONNA DIE.
YOU CAN'T DIE NOW...!!

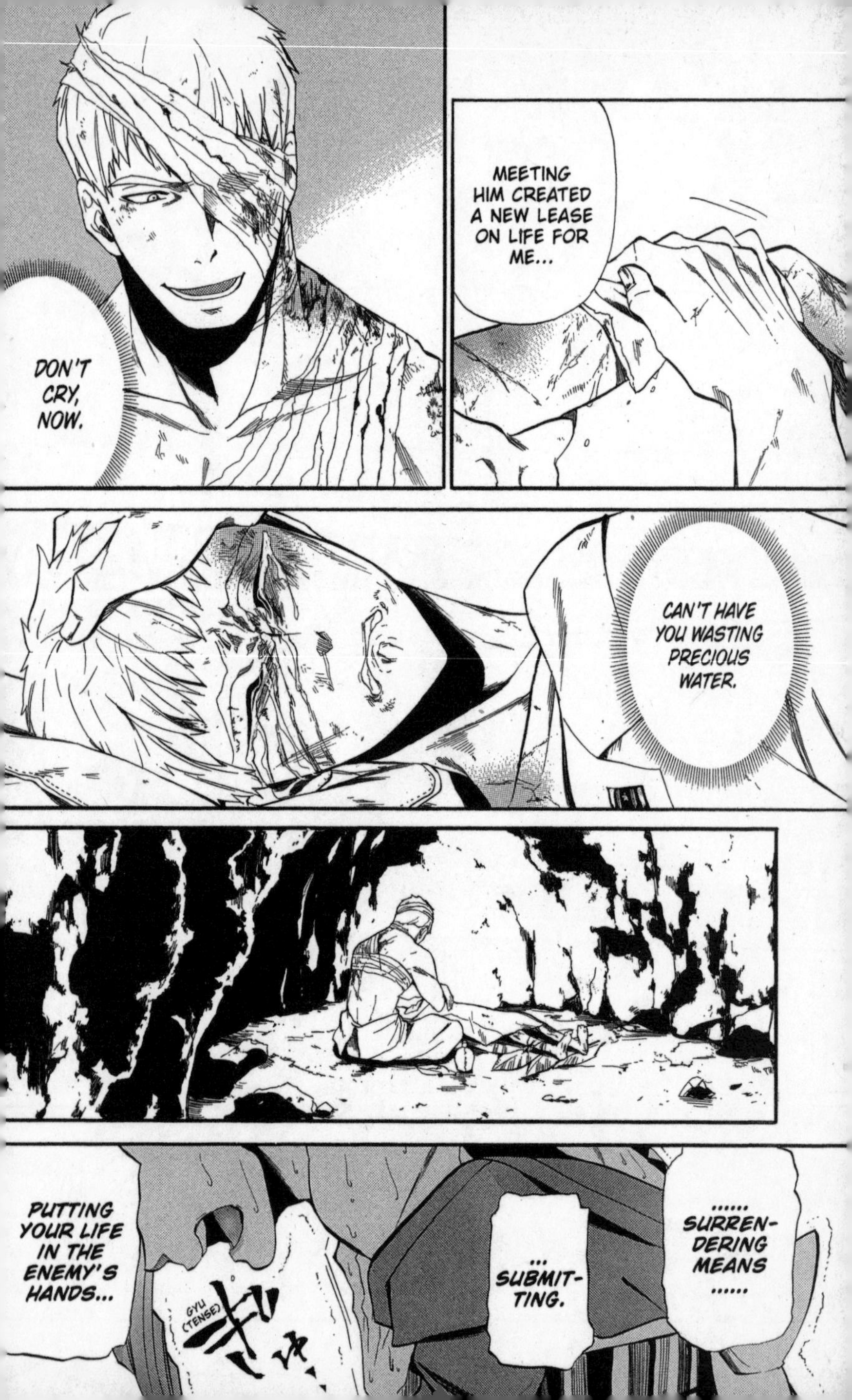
MEETING HIM CREATED A NEW LEASE ON LIFE FOR ME...
DON'T CRY, NOW.
CAN'T HAVE YOU WASTING PRECIOUS WATER.
...... SURREN-DERING MEANS ......
... SUBMIT-TING.
GYU (TENSE)
PUTTING YOUR LIFE IN THE ENEMY'S HANDS...

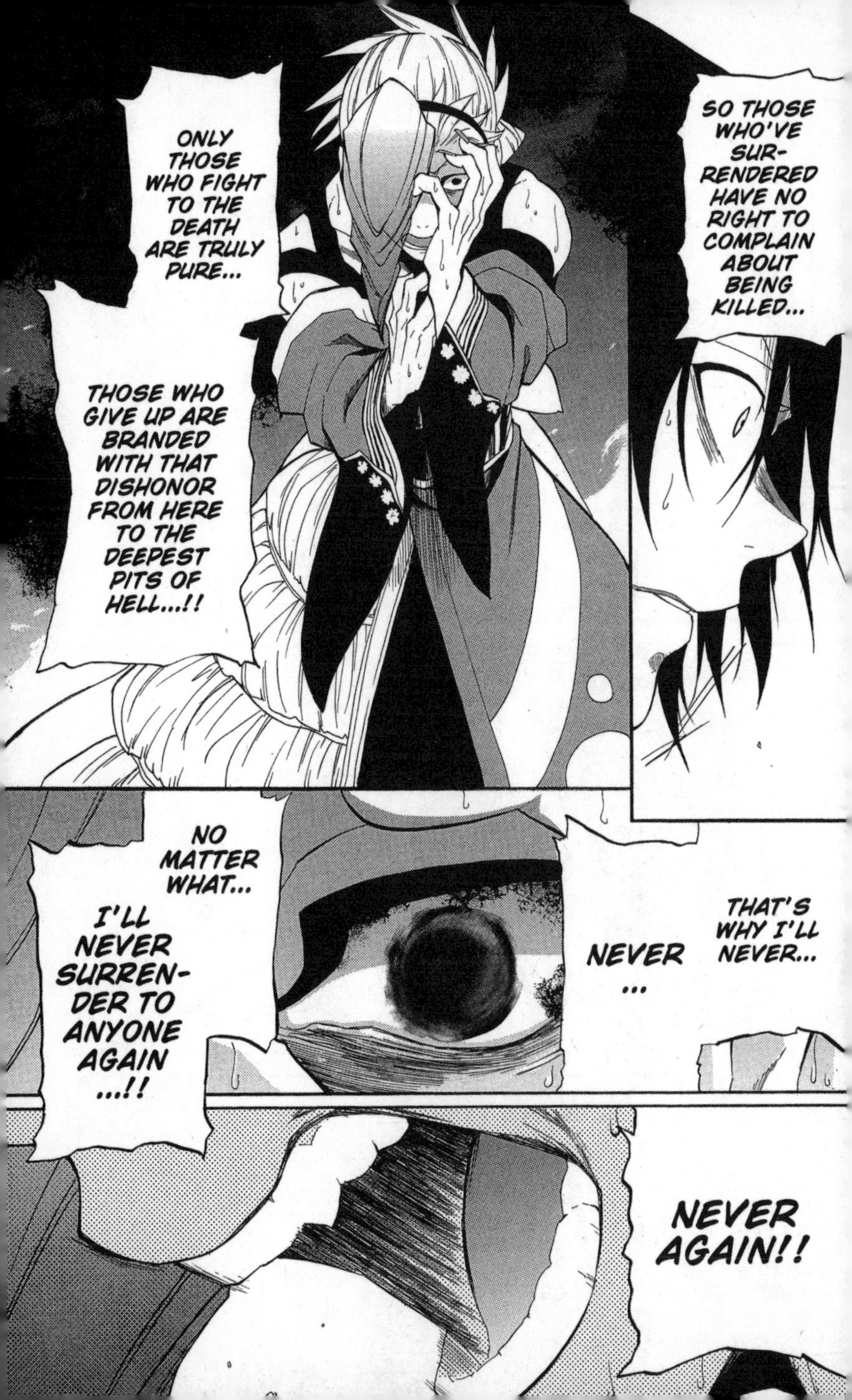
SO THOSE WHO'VE SURRENDERED HAVE NO RIGHT TO COMPLAIN ABOUT BEING KILLED...
ONLY THOSE WHO FIGHT TO THE DEATH ARE TRULY PURE...
THOSE WHO GIVE UP ARE BRANDED WITH THAT DISHONOR FROM HERE TO THE DEEPEST PITS OF HELL...!!
THAT'S WHY I'LL NEVER...
NEVER ...
NO MATTER WHAT...
I'LL NEVER SURRENDER TO ANYONE AGAIN ...!!
NEVER AGAIN!!

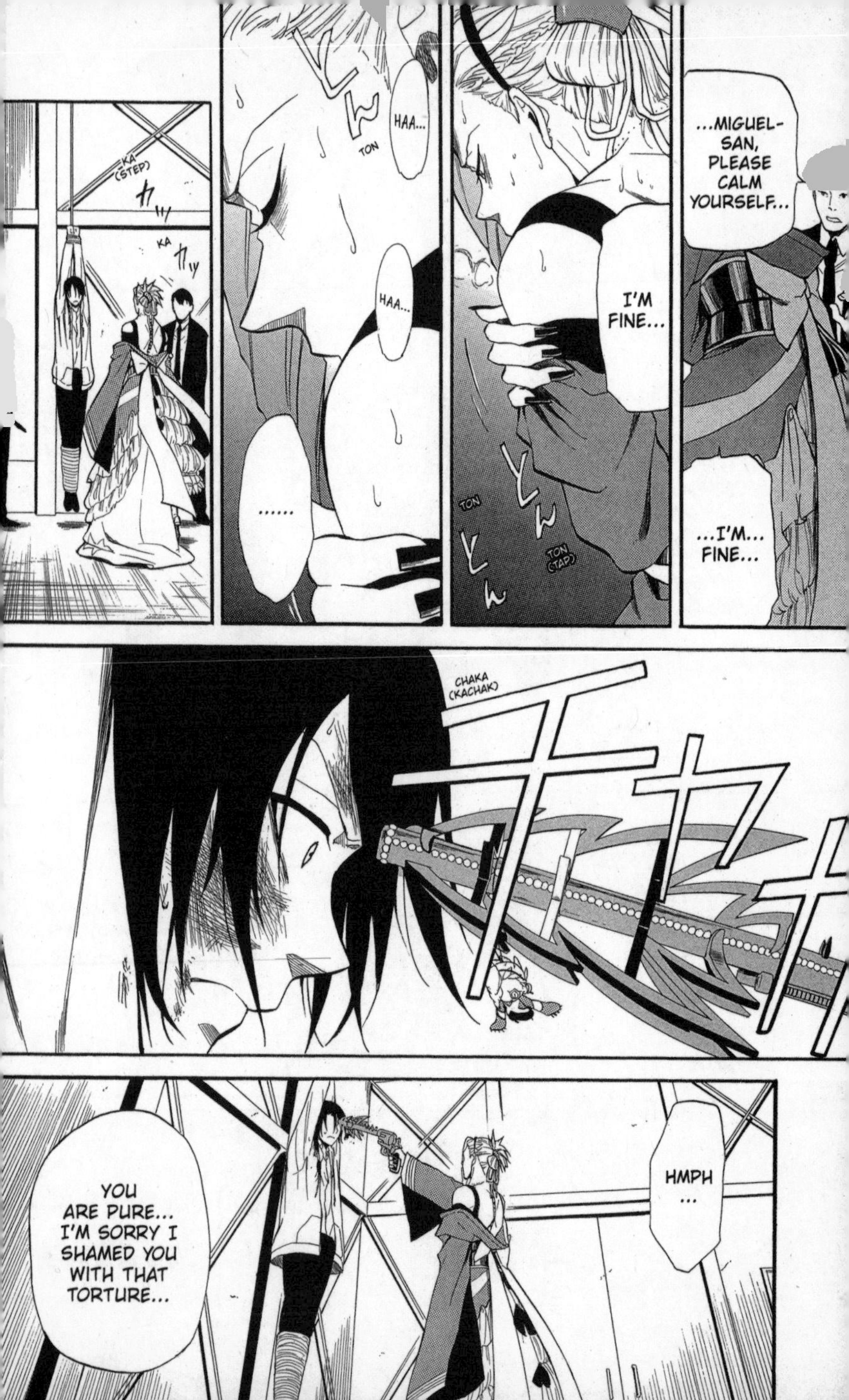
...MIGUEL-SAN, PLEASE CALM YOURSELF...
...I'M... FINE...
I'M FINE...
TON
TON (TAP)
HAA...
TON
HAA...
......
KA (STEP)
KA
CHAKA (KACHAK)
HMPH...
YOU ARE PURE... I'M SORRY I SHAMED YOU WITH THAT TORTURE...

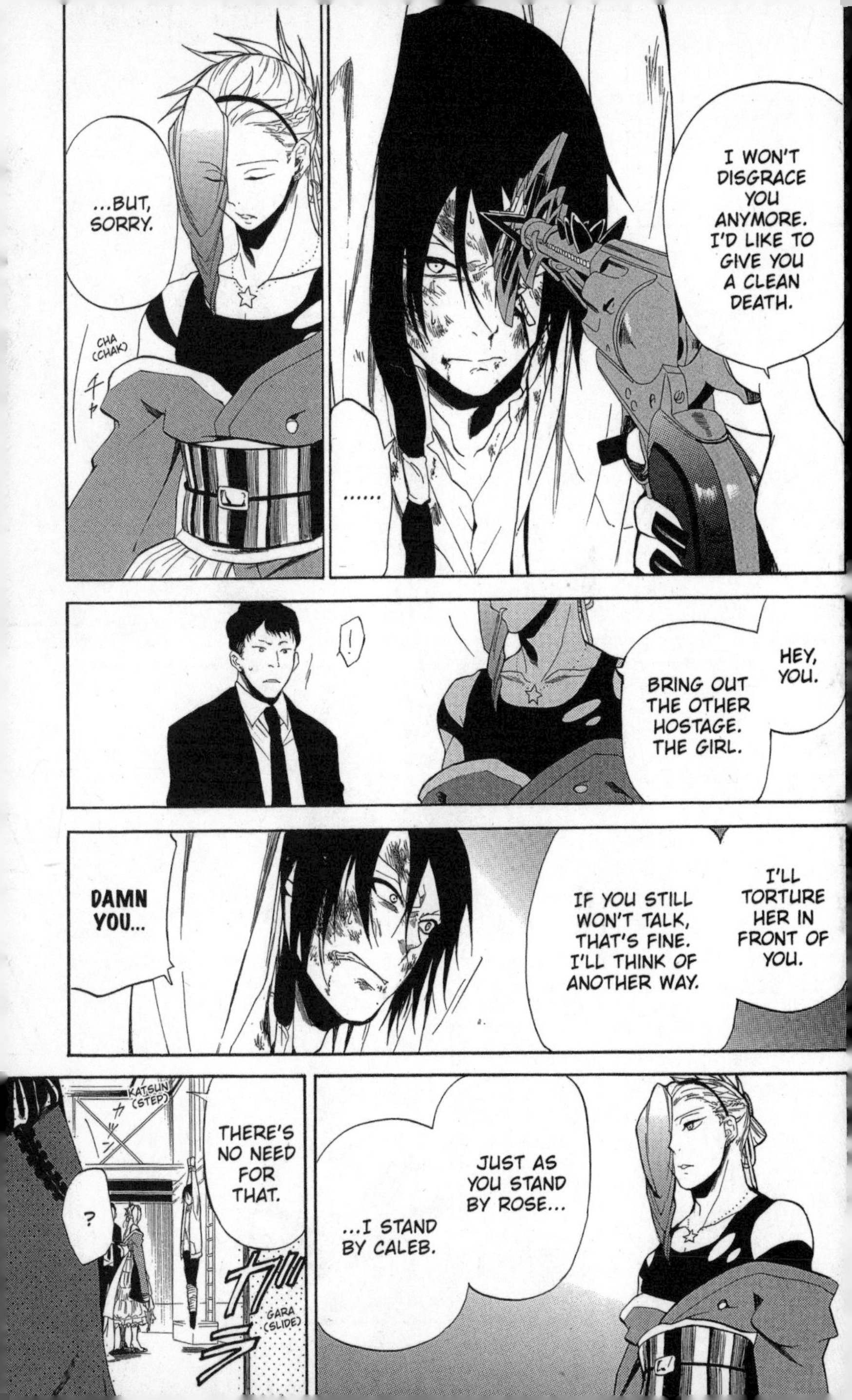
I WON'T DISGRACE YOU ANYMORE. I'D LIKE TO GIVE YOU A CLEAN DEATH.
......
...BUT, SORRY.
CHA (CHAK)
HEY, YOU.
BRING OUT THE OTHER HOSTAGE. THE GIRL.
!
I'LL TORTURE HER IN FRONT OF YOU.
IF YOU STILL WON'T TALK, THAT'S FINE. I'LL THINK OF ANOTHER WAY.
DAMN YOU...
JUST AS YOU STAND BY ROSE...
...I STAND BY CALEB.
THERE'S NO NEED FOR THAT.
KATSUN (STEP)
GARA (SLIDE)
?

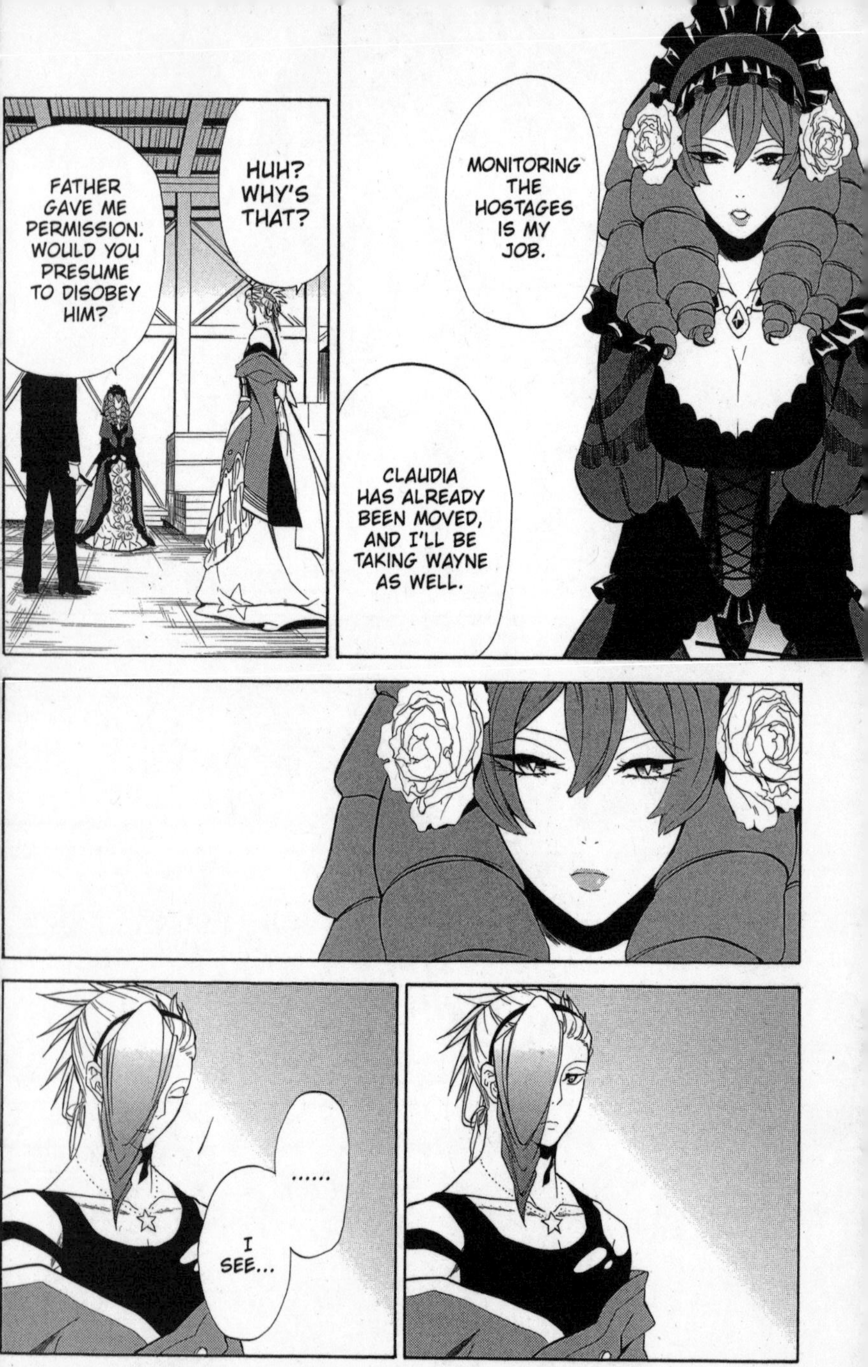
MONITORING THE HOSTAGES IS MY JOB.
CLAUDIA HAS ALREADY BEEN MOVED, AND I'LL BE TAKING WAYNE AS WELL.
HUH? WHY'S THAT?
FATHER GAVE ME PERMISSION. WOULD YOU PRESUME TO DISOBEY HIM?
......
I SEE...

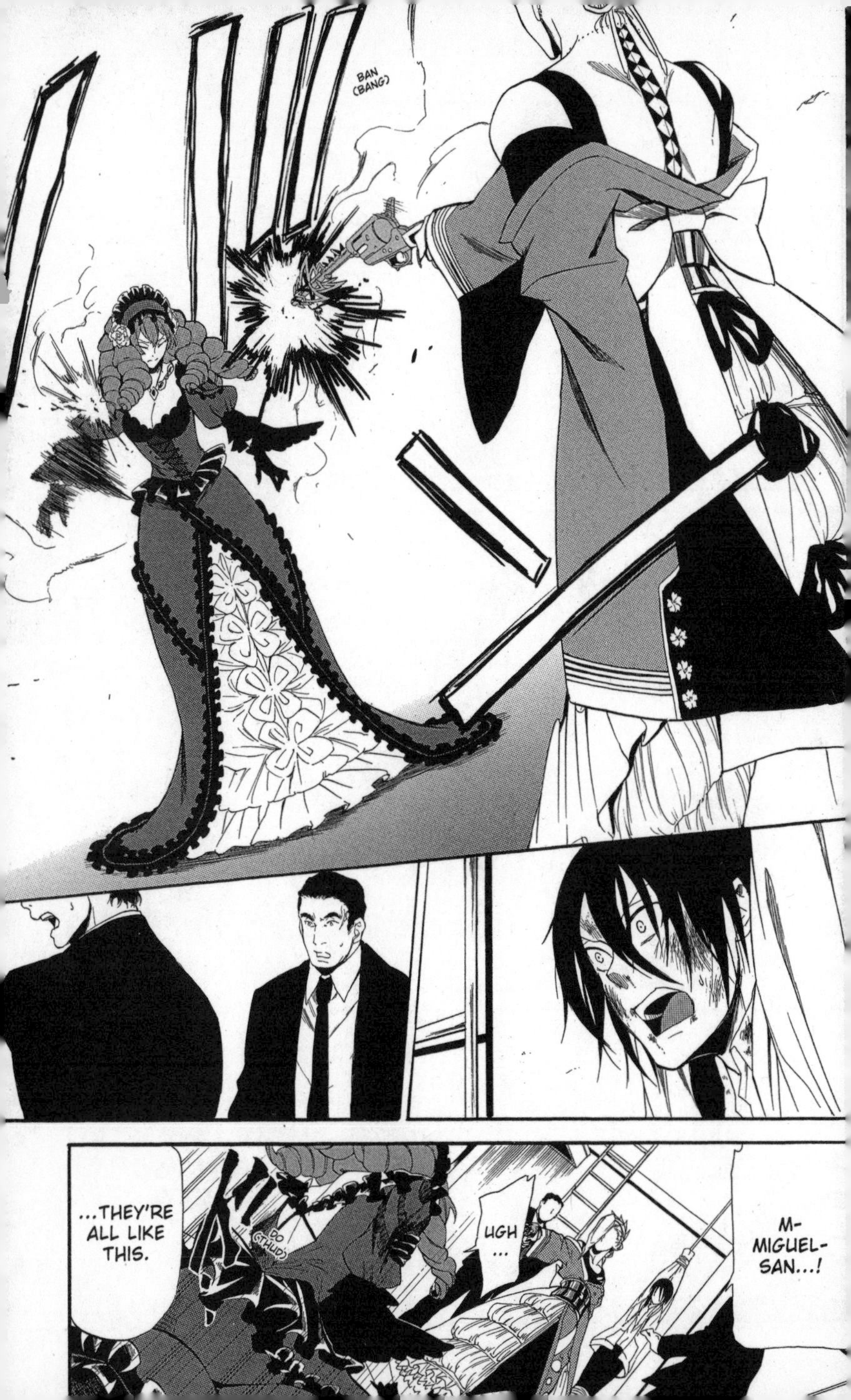
BAN (BANG)
M-MIGUEL-SAN...!
UGH ...
DO (THUD)
...THEY'RE ALL LIKE THIS.

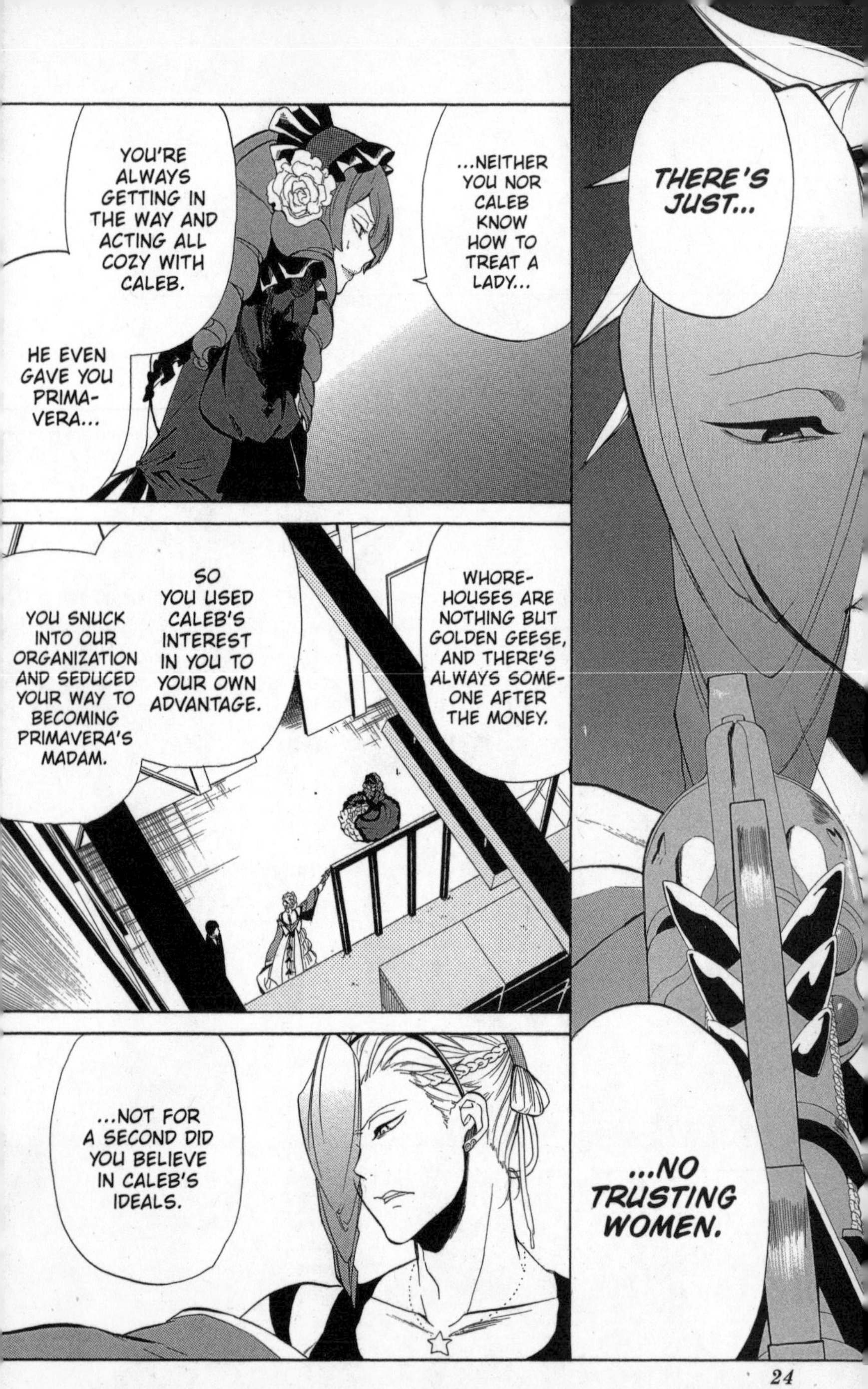
THERE'S JUST...
...NO TRUSTING WOMEN.
...NEITHER YOU NOR CALEB KNOW HOW TO TREAT A LADY...
YOU'RE ALWAYS GETTING IN THE WAY AND ACTING ALL COZY WITH CALEB.
HE EVEN GAVE YOU PRIMA-VERA...
WHORE-HOUSES ARE NOTHING BUT GOLDEN GEESE, AND THERE'S ALWAYS SOME-ONE AFTER THE MONEY.
SO YOU USED CALEB'S INTEREST IN YOU TO YOUR OWN ADVANTAGE.
YOU SNUCK INTO OUR ORGANIZATION AND SEDUCED YOUR WAY TO BECOMING PRIMAVERA'S MADAM.
...NOT FOR A SECOND DID YOU BELIEVE IN CALEB'S IDEALS.

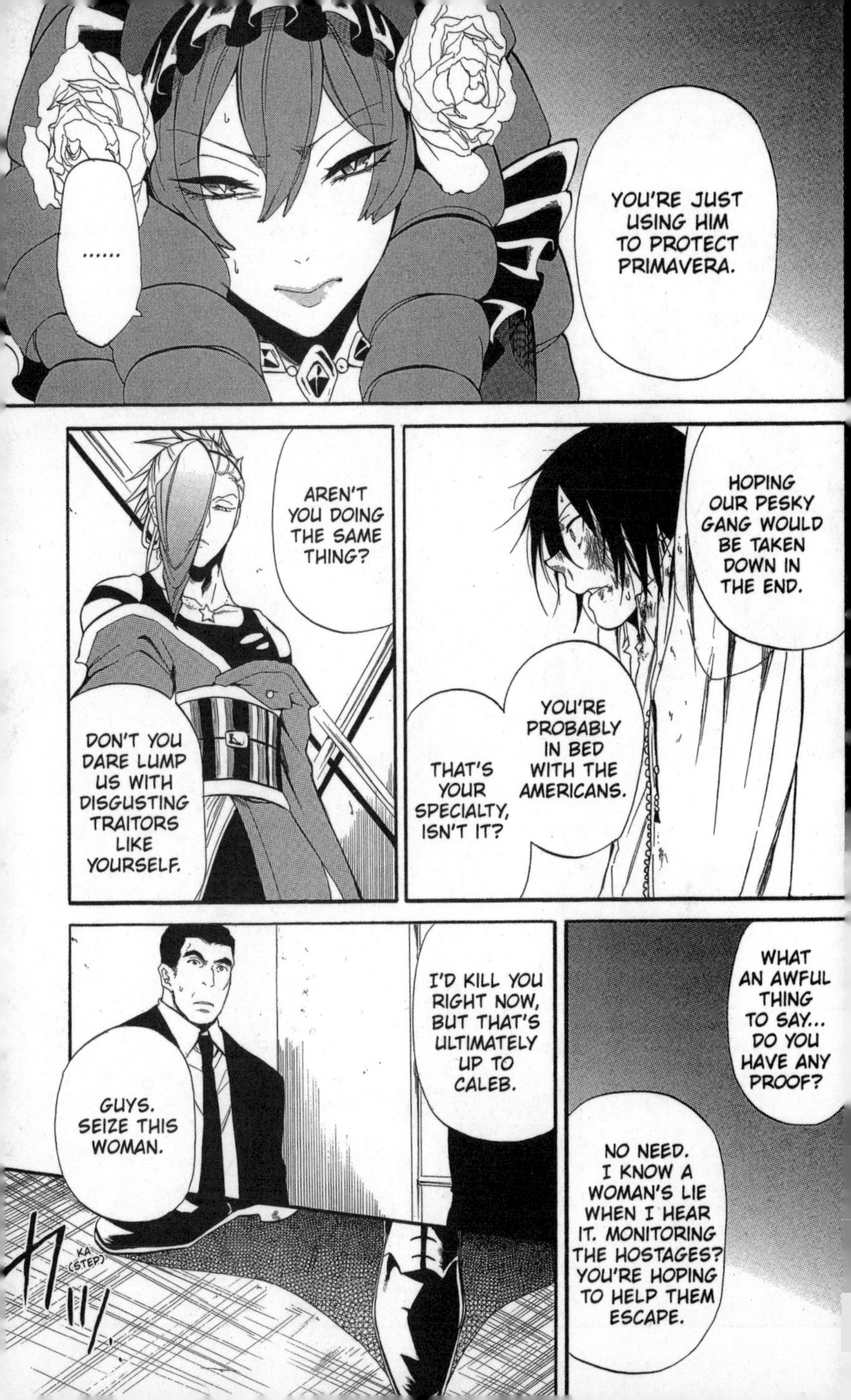
YOU'RE JUST USING HIM TO PROTECT PRIMAVERA.
......
HOPING OUR PESKY GANG WOULD BE TAKEN DOWN IN THE END.
YOU'RE PROBABLY IN BED WITH THE AMERICANS.
THAT'S YOUR SPECIALTY, ISN'T IT?
AREN'T YOU DOING THE SAME THING?
DON'T YOU DARE LUMP US WITH DISGUSTING TRAITORS LIKE YOURSELF.
WHAT AN AWFUL THING TO SAY... DO YOU HAVE ANY PROOF?
NO NEED. I KNOW A WOMAN'S LIE WHEN I HEAR IT. MONITORING THE HOSTAGES? YOU'RE HOPING TO HELP THEM ESCAPE.
I'D KILL YOU RIGHT NOW, BUT THAT'S ULTIMATELY UP TO CALEB.
GUYS. SEIZE THIS WOMAN.
KA (STEP)

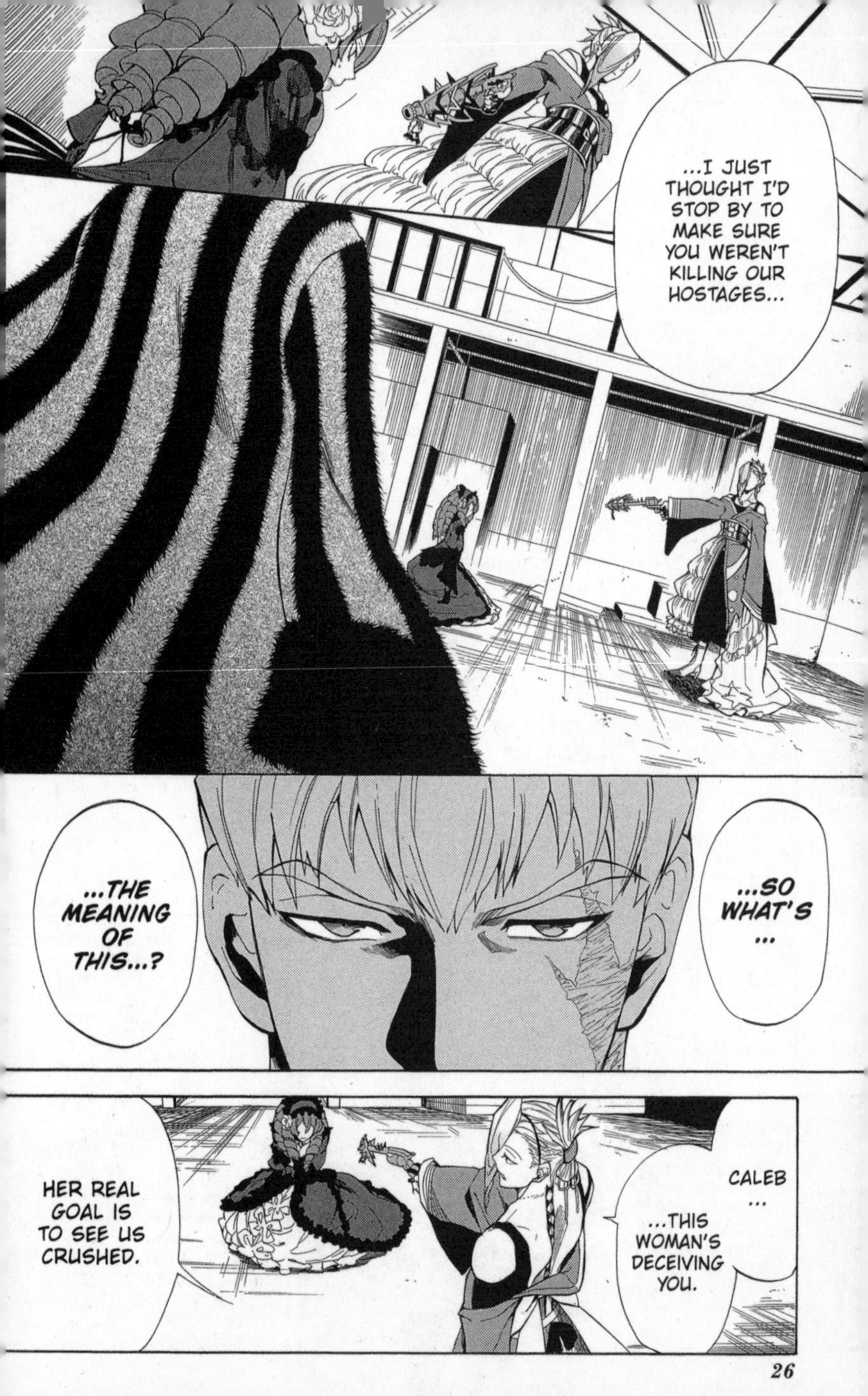
...I JUST THOUGHT I'D STOP BY TO MAKE SURE YOU WEREN'T KILLING OUR HOSTAGES...
...SO WHAT'S ...
...THE MEANING OF THIS...?
CALEB ...
...THIS WOMAN'S DECEIVING YOU.
HER REAL GOAL IS TO SEE US CRUSHED.

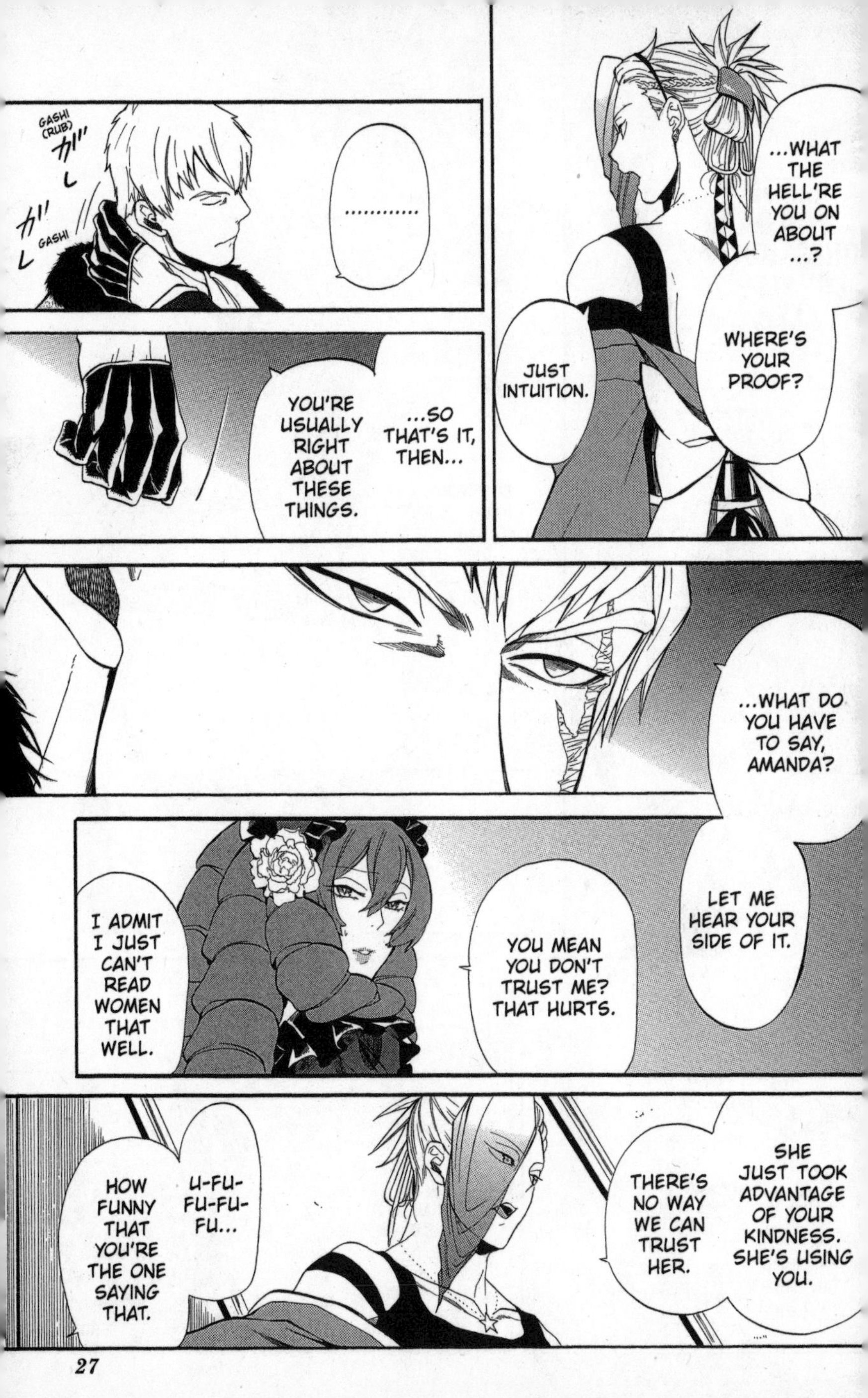
...WHAT THE HELL'RE YOU ON ABOUT ...?
WHERE'S YOUR PROOF?
JUST INTUITION.
GASHI (RUB) ガシ
ガシ GASHI
....
...SO THAT'S IT, THEN...
YOU'RE USUALLY RIGHT ABOUT THESE THINGS.
...WHAT DO YOU HAVE TO SAY, AMANDA?
LET ME HEAR YOUR SIDE OF IT.
YOU MEAN YOU DON'T TRUST ME? THAT HURTS.
I ADMIT I JUST CAN'T READ WOMEN THAT WELL.
SHE JUST TOOK ADVANTAGE OF YOUR KINDNESS. SHE'S USING YOU.
THERE'S NO WAY WE CAN TRUST HER.
U-FU-FU-FU-FU...
HOW FUNNY THAT YOU'RE THE ONE SAYING THAT.

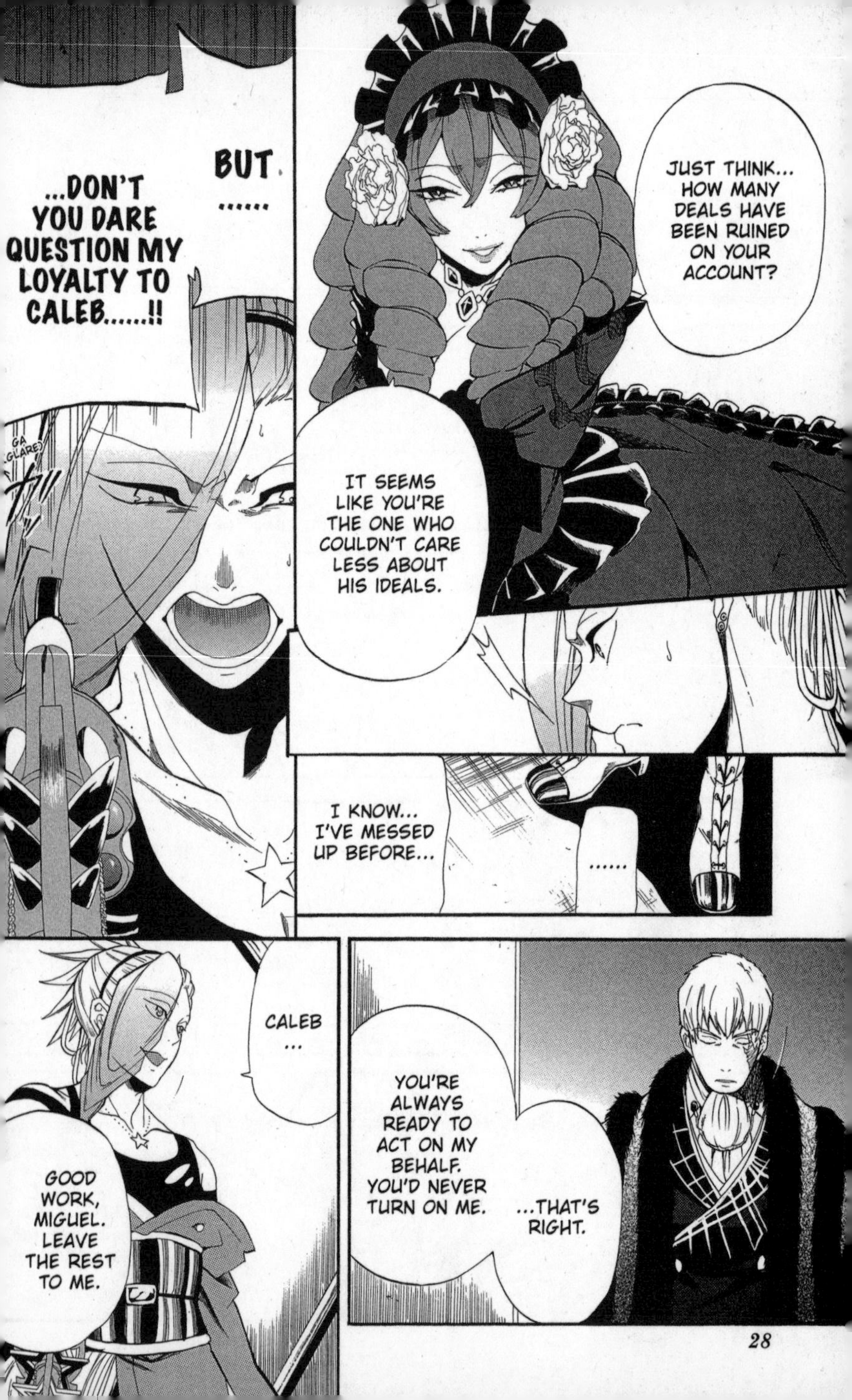
JUST THINK... HOW MANY DEALS HAVE BEEN RUINED ON YOUR ACCOUNT?
IT SEEMS LIKE YOU'RE THE ONE WHO COULDN'T CARE LESS ABOUT HIS IDEALS.
I KNOW... I'VE MESSED UP BEFORE...
......
BUT ......
...DON'T YOU DARE QUESTION MY LOYALTY TO CALEB......!!
GA (GLARE)
YOU'RE ALWAYS READY TO ACT ON MY BEHALF. YOU'D NEVER TURN ON ME.
...THAT'S RIGHT.
CALEB ...
GOOD WORK, MIGUEL. LEAVE THE REST TO ME.

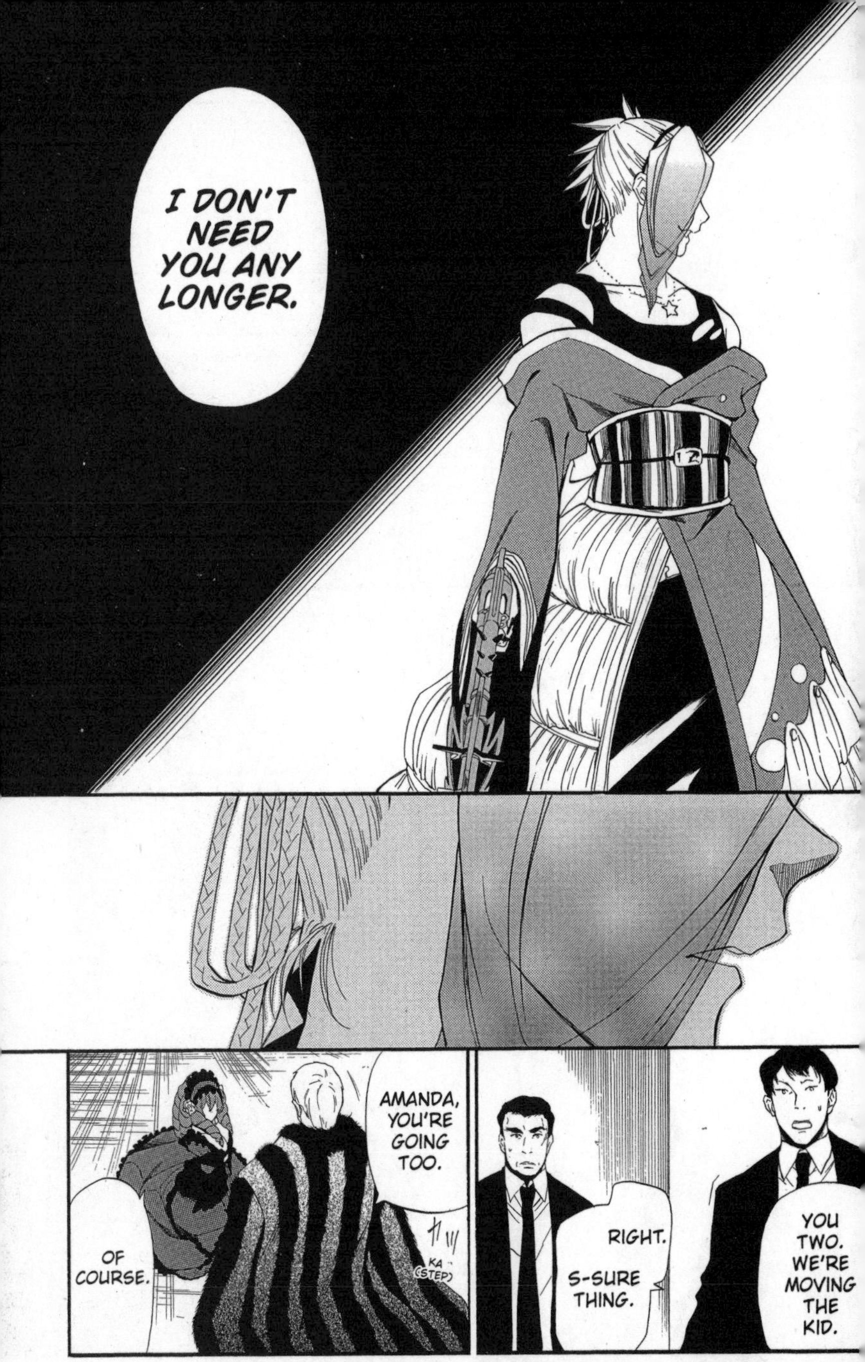
I DON'T NEED YOU ANY LONGER.
YOU TWO. WE'RE MOVING THE KID.
RIGHT.
S-SURE THING.
AMANDA, YOU'RE GOING TOO.
KA (STEP)
OF COURSE.

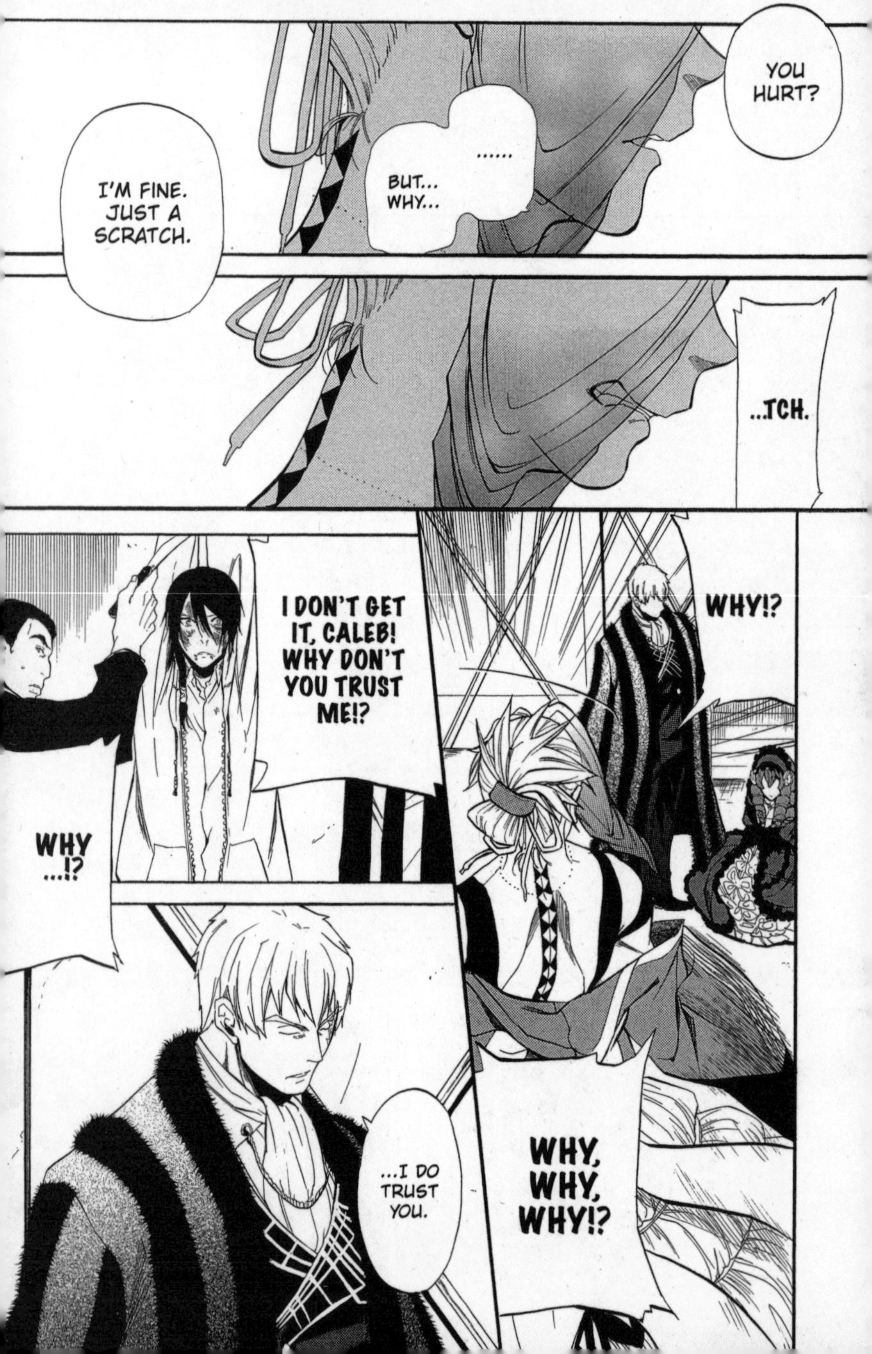
YOU HURT?
......
BUT... WHY...
I'M FINE. JUST A SCRATCH.
...TCH.
WHY!?
I DON'T GET IT, CALEB! WHY DON'T YOU TRUST ME!?
WHY ...!?
WHY, WHY, WHY!?
...I DO TRUST YOU.

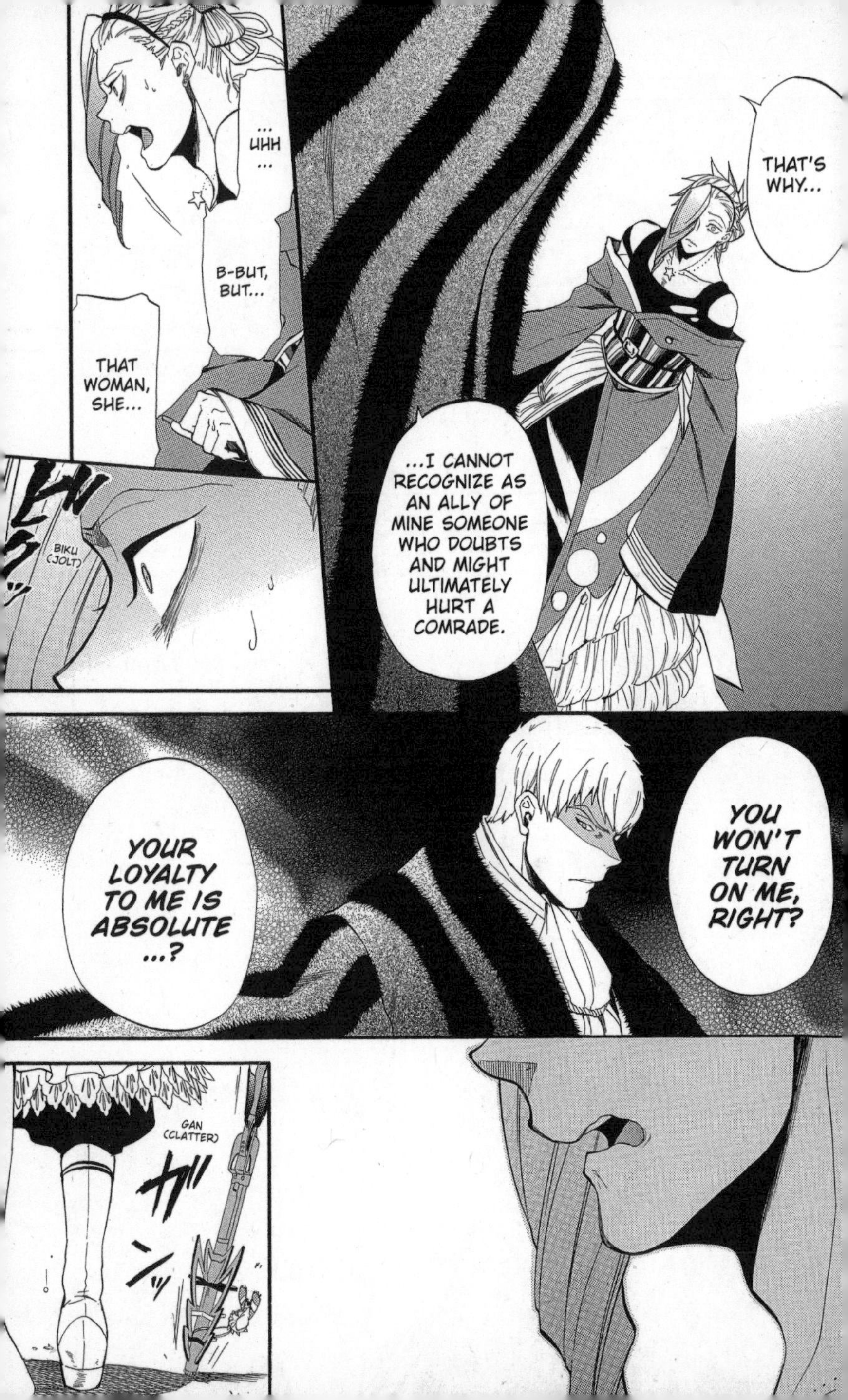
THAT'S WHY...
...I CANNOT RECOGNIZE AS AN ALLY OF MINE SOMEONE WHO DOUBTS AND MIGHT ULTIMATELY HURT A COMRADE.
...UHH...
B-BUT, BUT...
THAT WOMAN, SHE...
BIKU (JOLT)
YOU WON'T TURN ON ME, RIGHT?
YOUR LOYALTY TO ME IS ABSOLUTE...?
GAN (CLATTER)

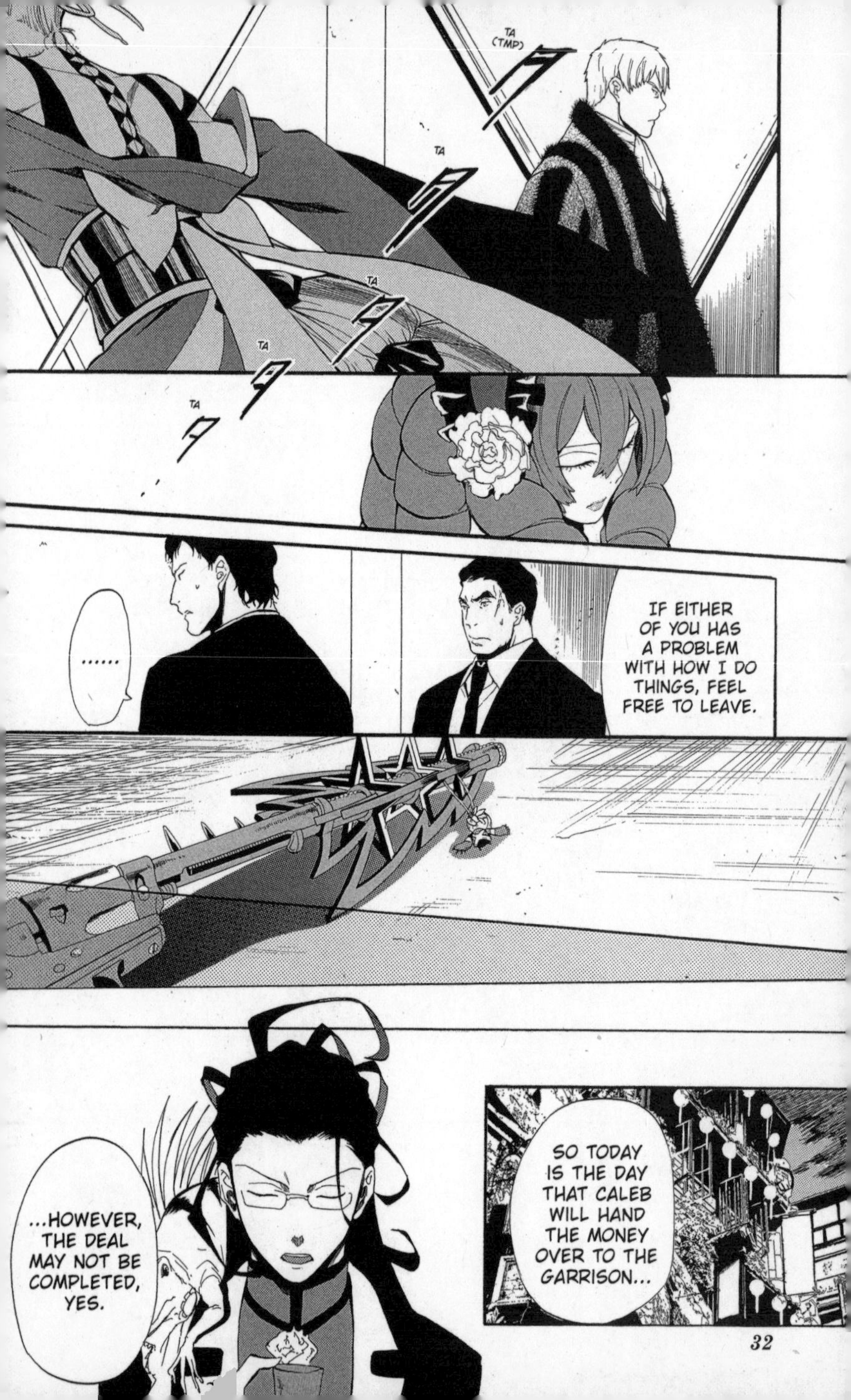
TA (TMP)
TA
TA
TA
TA
IF EITHER OF YOU HAS A PROBLEM WITH HOW I DO THINGS, FEEL FREE TO LEAVE.
......
SO TODAY IS THE DAY THAT CALEB WILL HAND THE MONEY OVER TO THE GARRISON...
...HOWEVER, THE DEAL MAY NOT BE COMPLETED, YES.

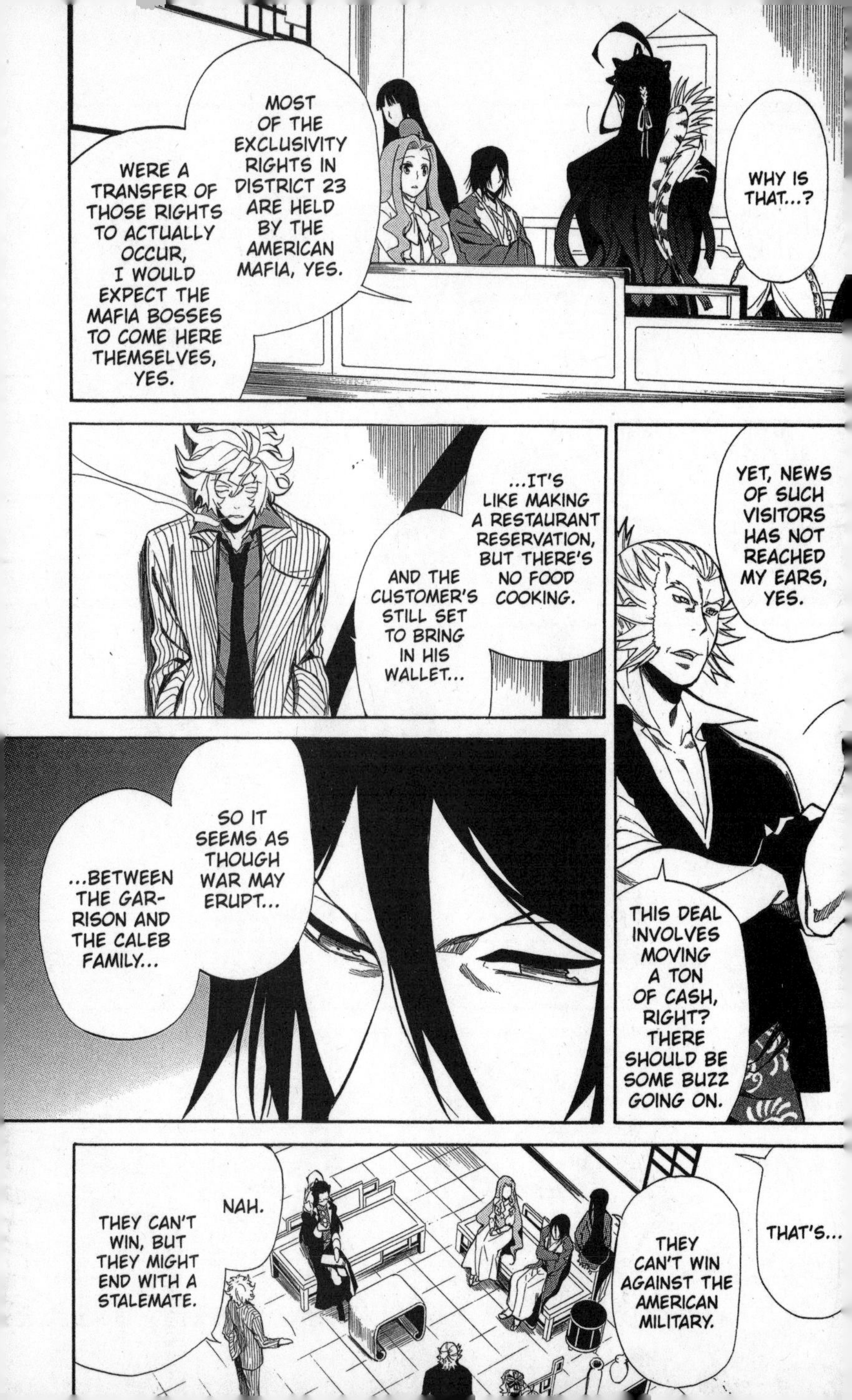
WHY IS THAT...?
MOST OF THE EXCLUSIVITY RIGHTS IN DISTRICT 23 ARE HELD BY THE AMERICAN MAFIA, YES.
WERE A TRANSFER OF THOSE RIGHTS TO ACTUALLY OCCUR, I WOULD EXPECT THE MAFIA BOSSES TO COME HERE THEMSELVES, YES.
YET, NEWS OF SUCH VISITORS HAS NOT REACHED MY EARS, YES.
THIS DEAL INVOLVES MOVING A TON OF CASH, RIGHT? THERE SHOULD BE SOME BUZZ GOING ON.
...IT'S LIKE MAKING A RESTAURANT RESERVATION, BUT THERE'S NO FOOD COOKING.
AND THE CUSTOMER'S STILL SET TO BRING IN HIS WALLET...
SO IT SEEMS AS THOUGH WAR MAY ERUPT...
...BETWEEN THE GAR-RISON AND THE CALEB FAMILY...
THAT'S...
THEY CAN'T WIN AGAINST THE AMERICAN MILITARY.
NAH.
THEY CAN'T WIN, BUT THEY MIGHT END WITH A STALEMATE.

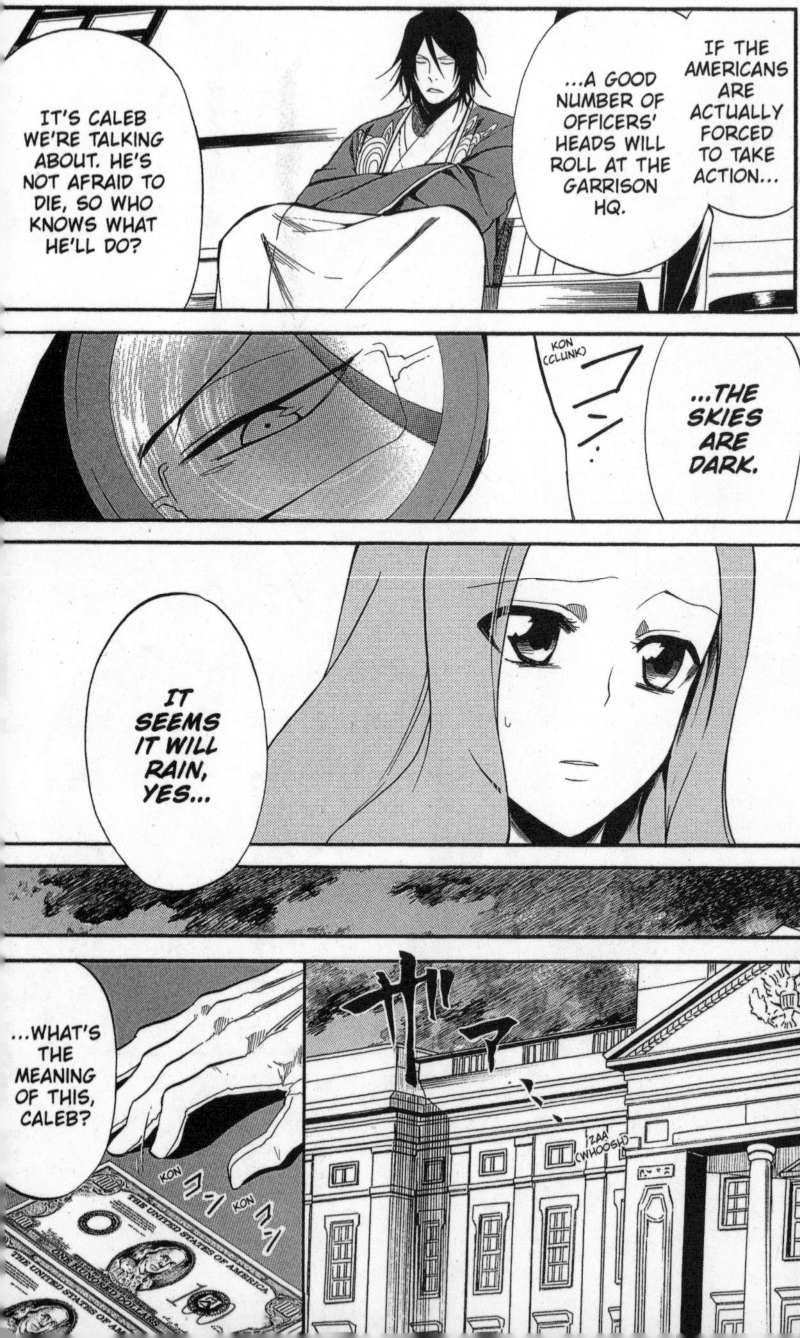
IF THE AMERICANS ARE ACTUALLY FORCED TO TAKE ACTION...
...A GOOD NUMBER OF OFFICERS' HEADS WILL ROLL AT THE GARRISON HQ.
IT'S CALEB WE'RE TALKING ABOUT. HE'S NOT AFRAID TO DIE, SO WHO KNOWS WHAT HE'LL DO?
...THE SKIES ARE DARK.
KON (CLUNK)
IT SEEMS IT WILL RAIN, YES...
ZAA (WHOOSH)
...WHAT'S THE MEANING OF THIS, CALEB?
KON
KON
THE UNITED STATES OF AMERICA

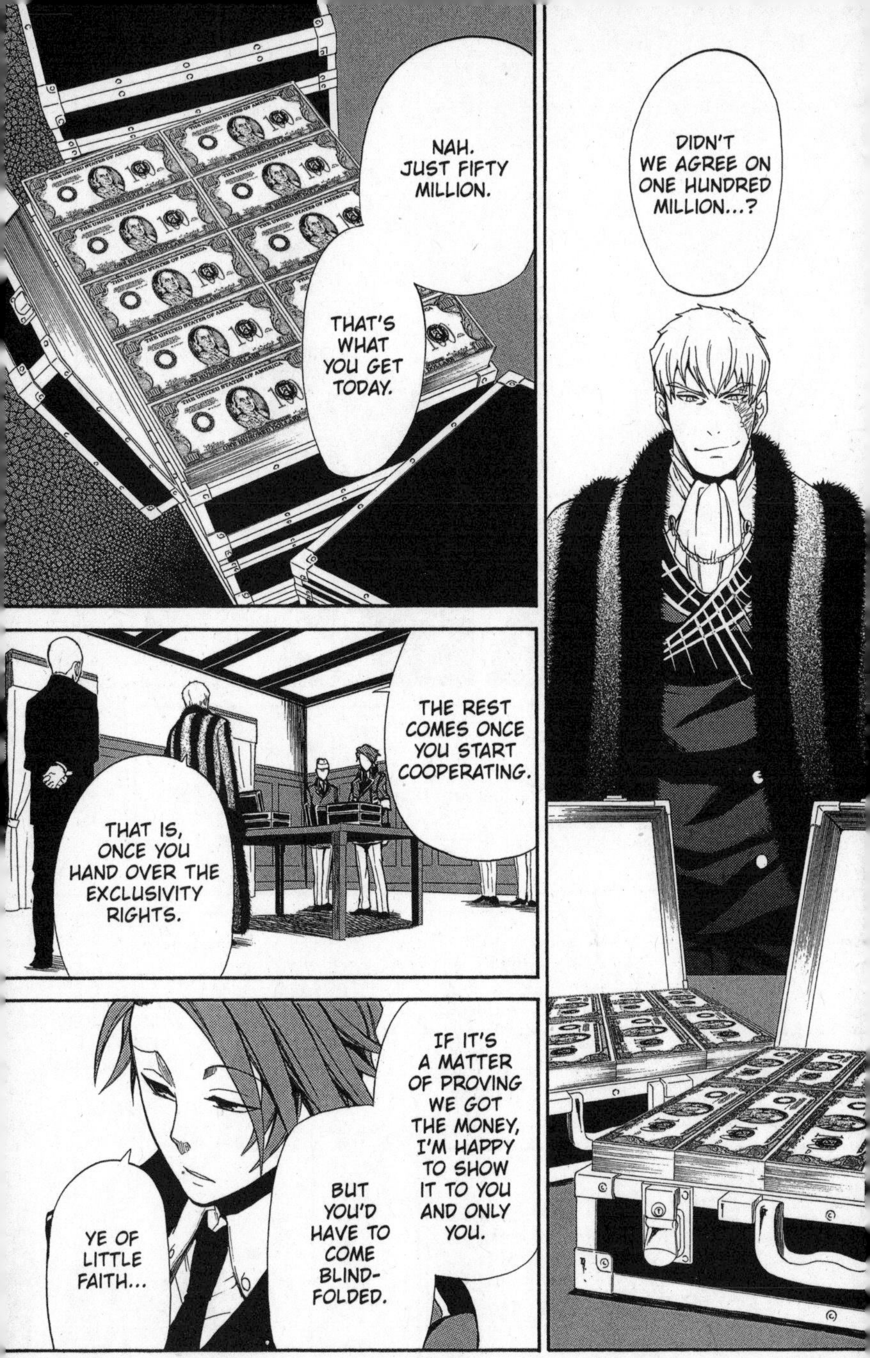
DIDN'T WE AGREE ON ONE HUNDRED MILLION...?
NAH. JUST FIFTY MILLION.
THAT'S WHAT YOU GET TODAY.
THE REST COMES ONCE YOU START COOPERATING.
THAT IS, ONCE YOU HAND OVER THE EXCLUSIVITY RIGHTS.
IF IT'S A MATTER OF PROVING WE GOT THE MONEY, I'M HAPPY TO SHOW IT TO YOU AND ONLY YOU.
BUT YOU'D HAVE TO COME BLIND-FOLDED.
YE OF LITTLE FAITH...

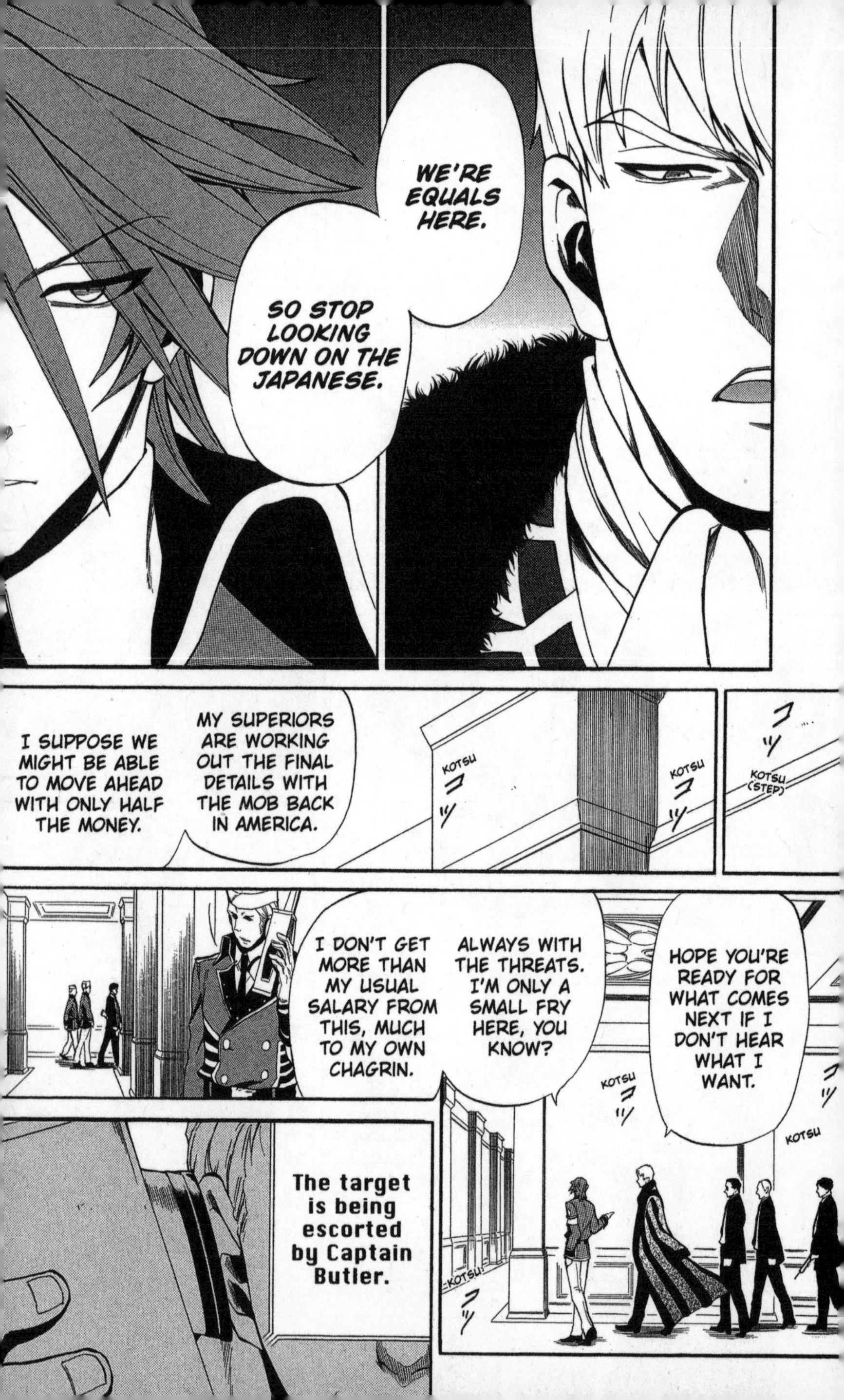
WE'RE EQUALS HERE.
SO STOP LOOKING DOWN ON THE JAPANESE.
KOTSU (STEP)
KOTSU
KOTSU
MY SUPERIORS ARE WORKING OUT THE FINAL DETAILS WITH THE MOB BACK IN AMERICA.
I SUPPOSE WE MIGHT BE ABLE TO MOVE AHEAD WITH ONLY HALF THE MONEY.
HOPE YOU'RE READY FOR WHAT COMES NEXT IF I DON'T HEAR WHAT I WANT.
KOTSU
KOTSU
KOTSU
ALWAYS WITH THE THREATS. I'M ONLY A SMALL FRY HERE, YOU KNOW?
I DON'T GET MORE THAN MY USUAL SALARY FROM THIS, MUCH TO MY OWN CHAGRIN.
The target is being escorted by Captain Butler.

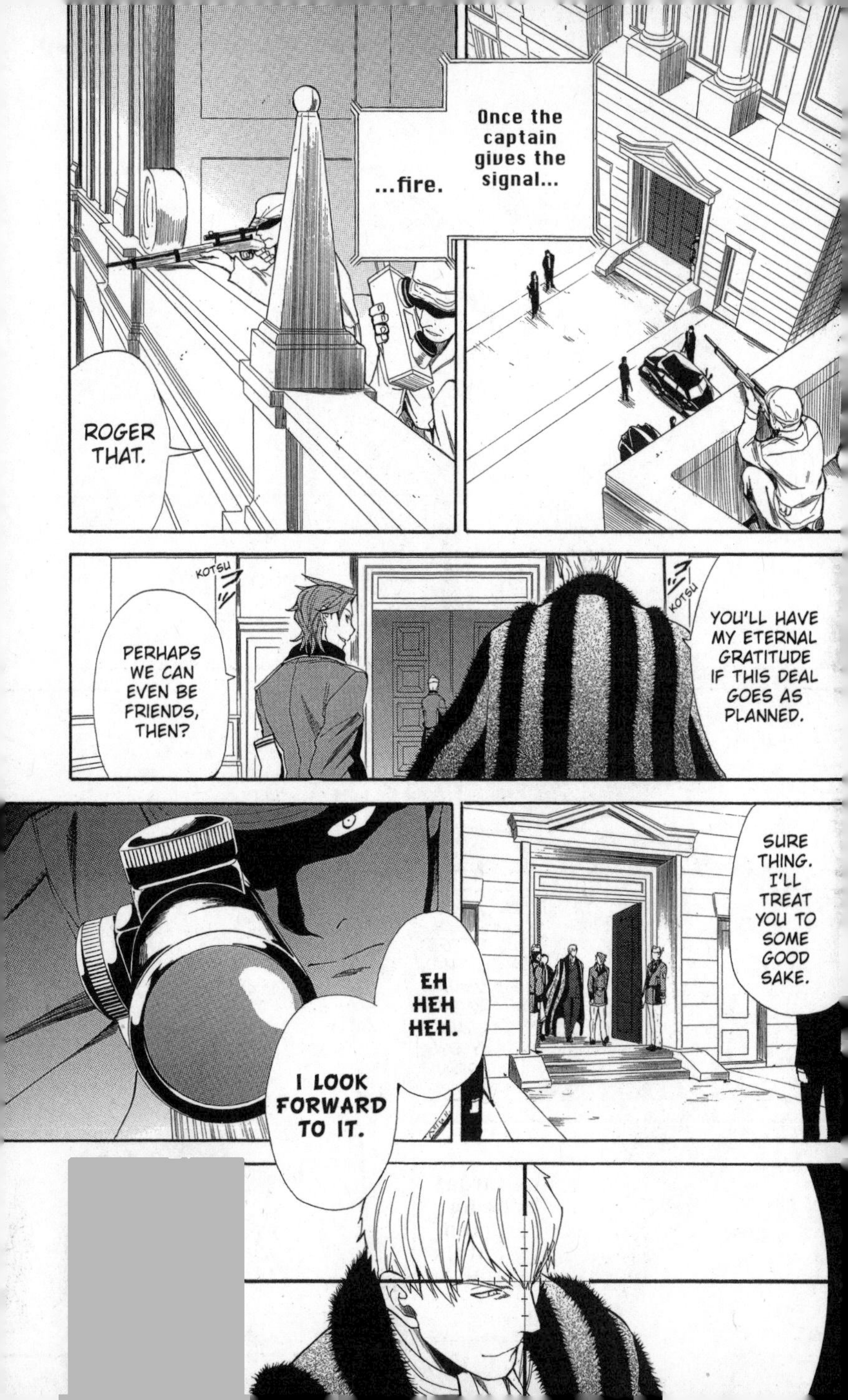
Once the captain gives the signal...
...fire.
ROGER THAT.
KOTSU
YOU'LL HAVE MY ETERNAL GRATITUDE IF THIS DEAL GOES AS PLANNED.
KOTSU
PERHAPS WE CAN EVEN BE FRIENDS, THEN?
SURE THING. I'LL TREAT YOU TO SOME GOOD SAKE.
EH HEH HEH.
I LOOK FORWARD TO IT.

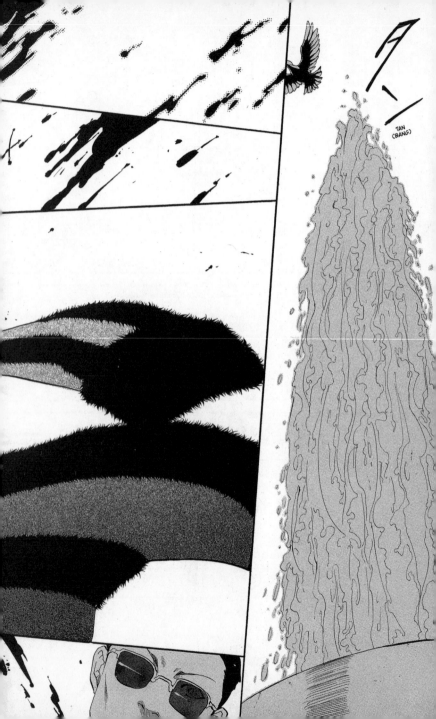

ターン
TAN
(BANG)

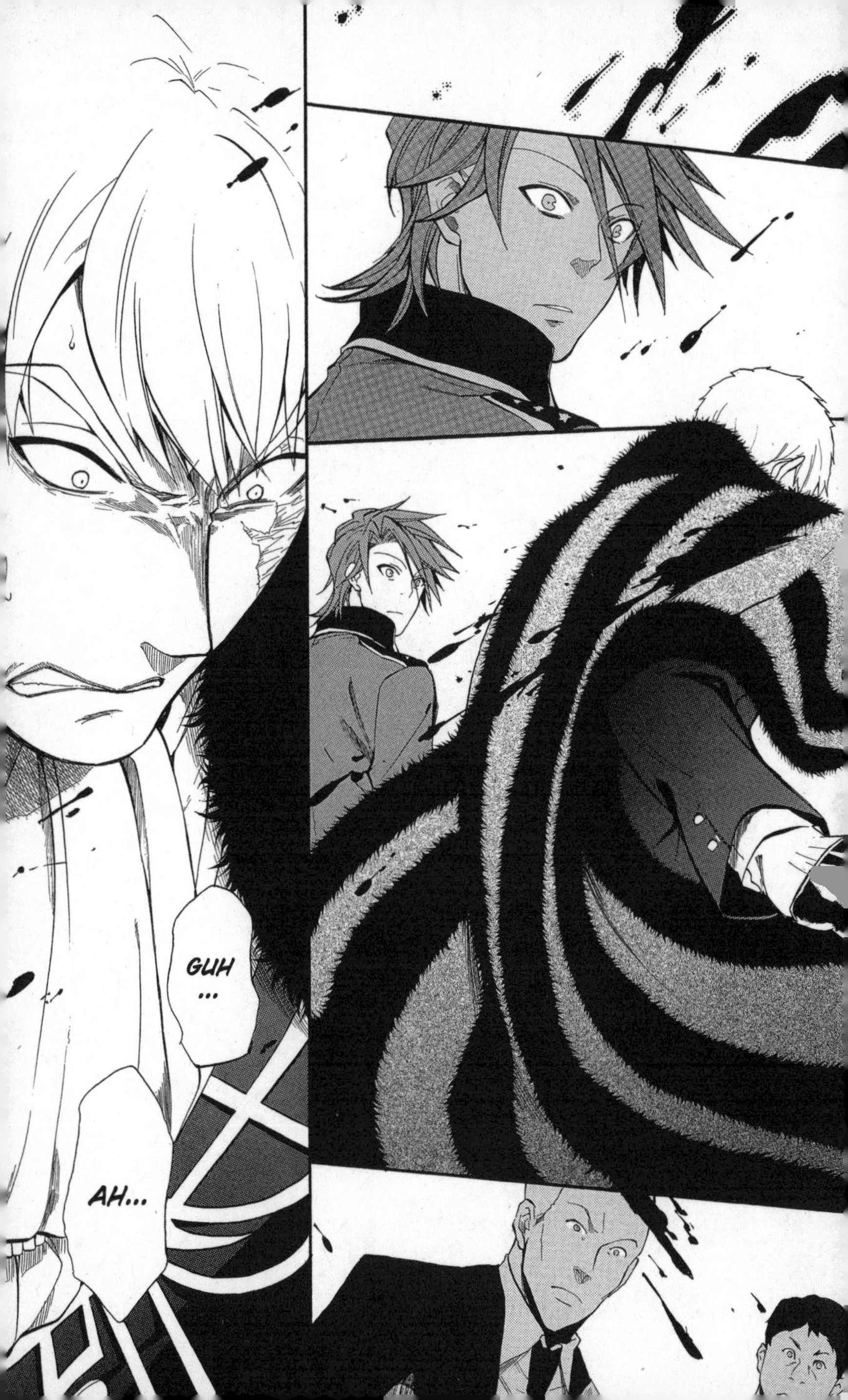
GUH
...
AH...

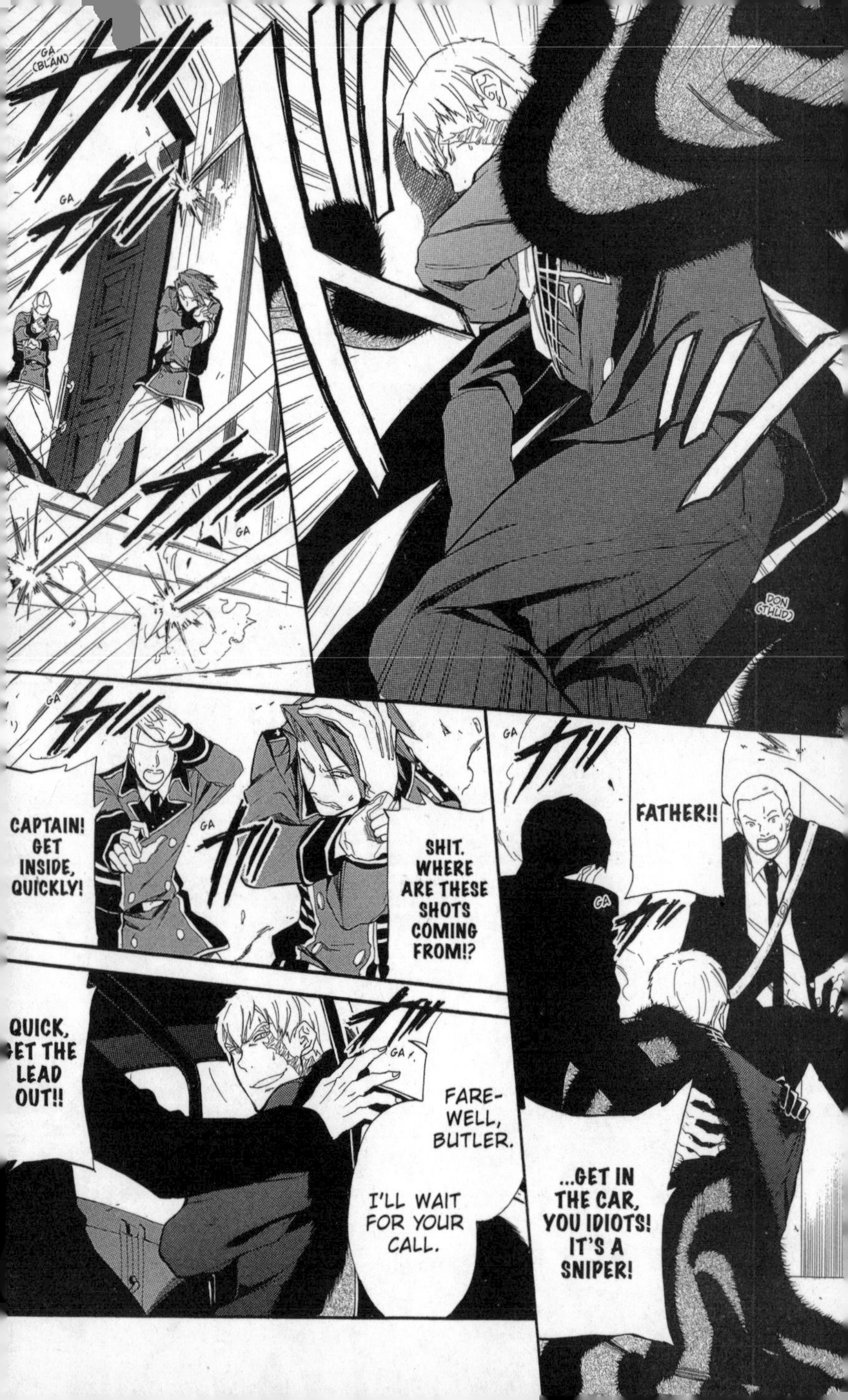
DON (THUD)
GA (BLAM)
GA
GA
GA
FATHER!!
GA
...GET IN THE CAR, YOU IDIOTS! IT'S A SNIPER!
GA
SHIT. WHERE ARE THESE SHOTS COMING FROM!?
GA
CAPTAIN! GET INSIDE, QUICKLY!
GA
FARE-WELL, BUTLER.
I'LL WAIT FOR YOUR CALL.
QUICK, GET THE LEAD OUT!!

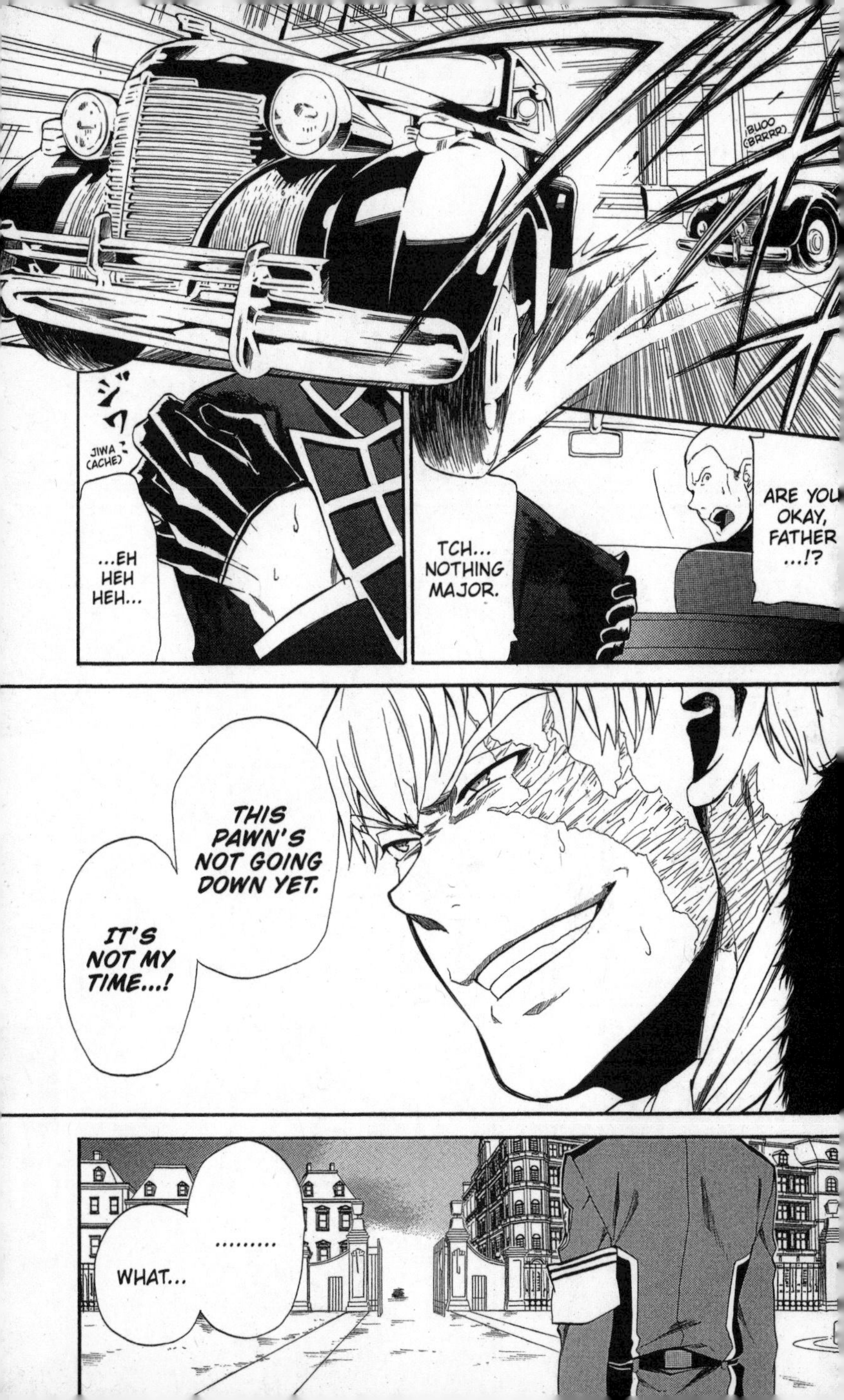
BUOO (BRRRR)
ARE YOU OKAY, FATHER ...!?
TCH... NOTHING MAJOR.
ジワ
JIWA (ACHE)
...EH HEH HEH...
THIS PAWN'S NOT GOING DOWN YET.
IT'S NOT MY TIME...!
....
WHAT...

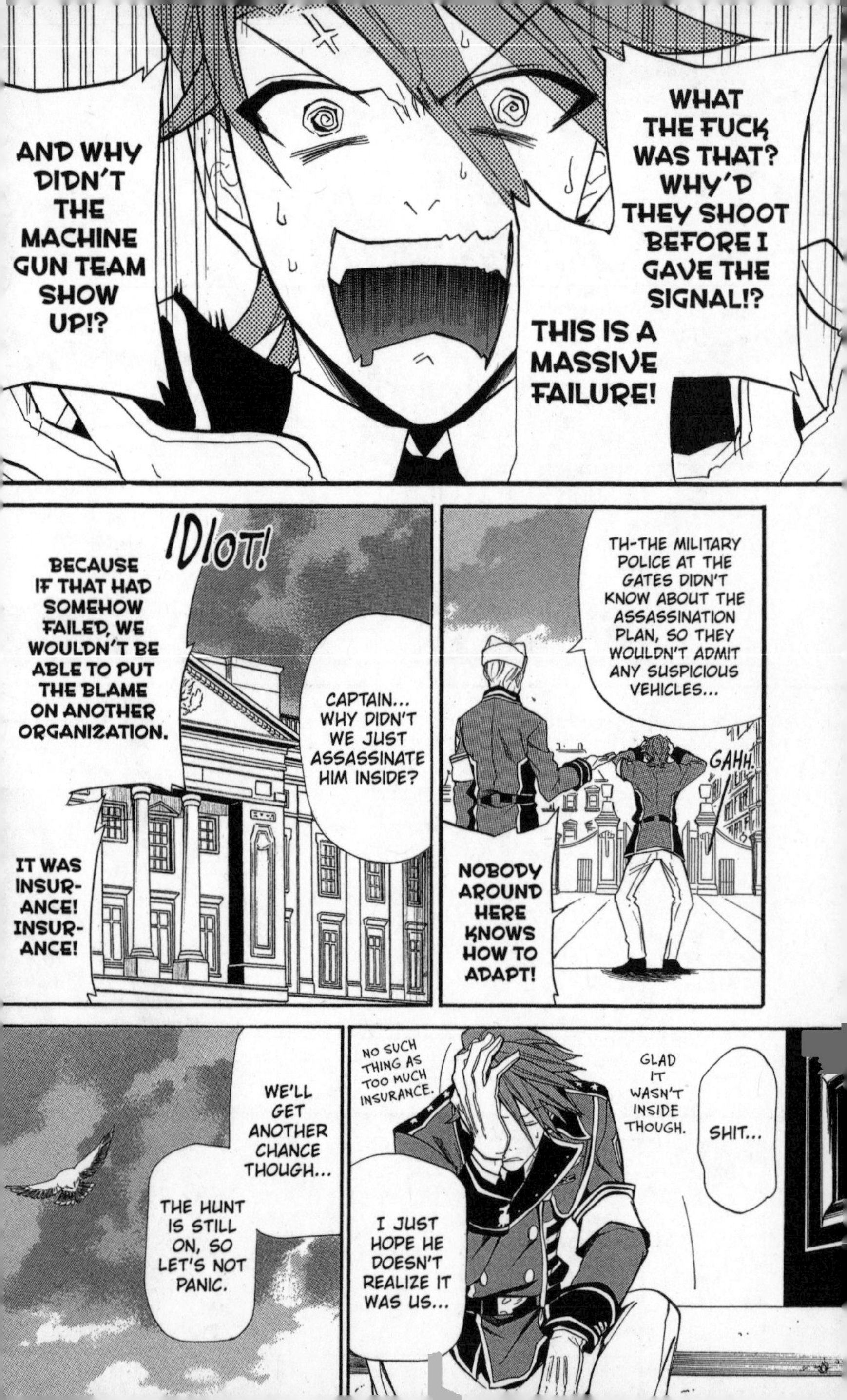
WHAT THE FUCK WAS THAT? WHY'D THEY SHOOT BEFORE I GAVE THE SIGNAL!?
THIS IS A MASSIVE FAILURE!
AND WHY DIDN'T THE MACHINE GUN TEAM SHOW UP!?
TH-THE MILITARY POLICE AT THE GATES DIDN'T KNOW ABOUT THE ASSASSINATION PLAN, SO THEY WOULDN'T ADMIT ANY SUSPICIOUS VEHICLES...
GAHH
NOBODY AROUND HERE KNOWS HOW TO ADAPT!
CAPTAIN... WHY DIDN'T WE JUST ASSASSINATE HIM INSIDE?
IDIOT!
BECAUSE IF THAT HAD SOMEHOW FAILED, WE WOULDN'T BE ABLE TO PUT THE BLAME ON ANOTHER ORGANIZATION.
IT WAS INSUR-ANCE! INSUR-ANCE!
SHIT...
GLAD IT WASN'T INSIDE THOUGH.
NO SUCH THING AS TOO MUCH INSURANCE.
I JUST HOPE HE DOESN'T REALIZE IT WAS US...
WE'LL GET ANOTHER CHANCE THOUGH...
THE HUNT IS STILL ON, SO LET'S NOT PANIC.

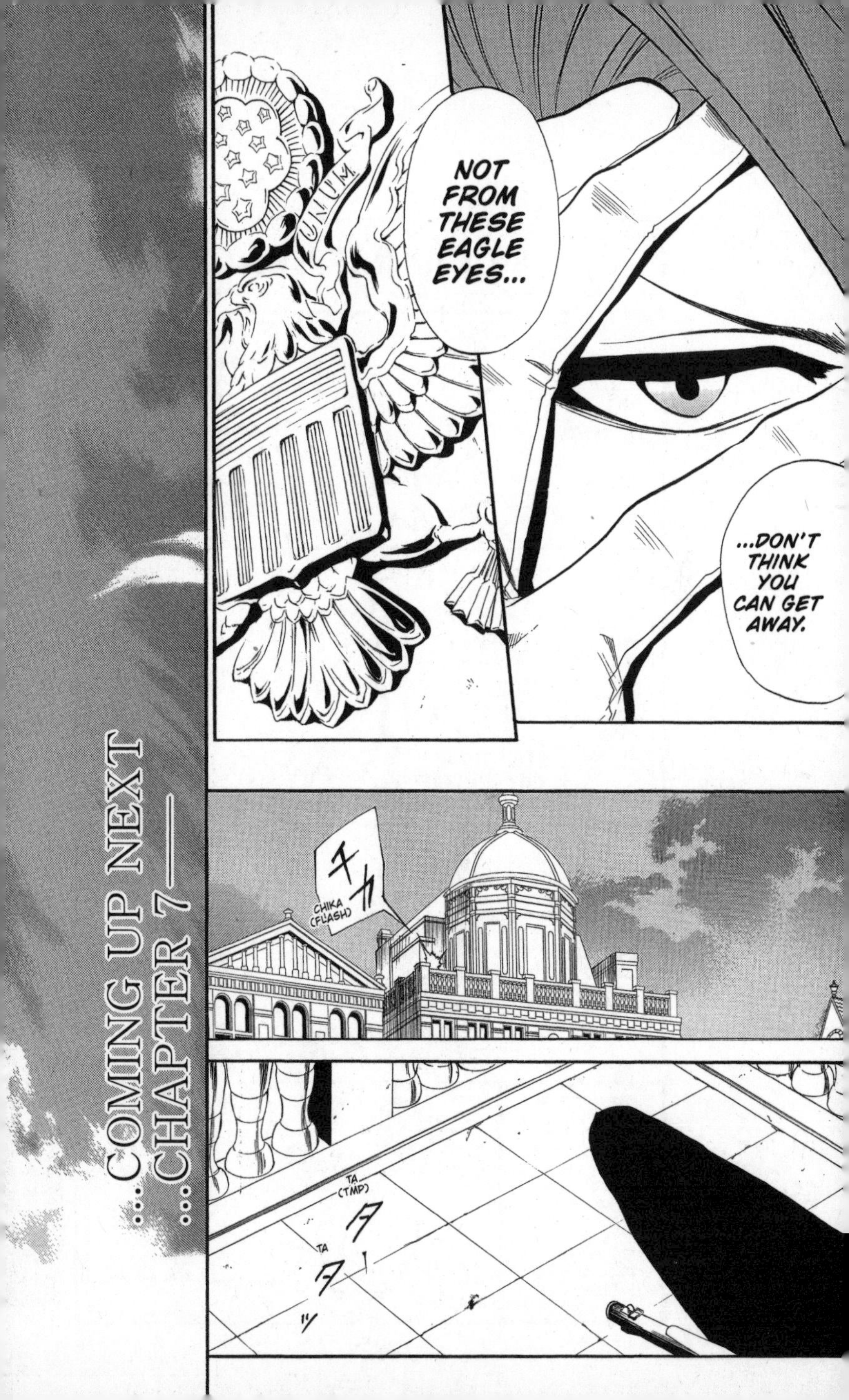
NOT FROM THESE EAGLE EYES...
...DON'T THINK YOU CAN GET AWAY.
UNUM
チカ
CHIKA (FLASH)
TA (TMP)
TA
...COMING UP NEXT
...CHAPTER 7—

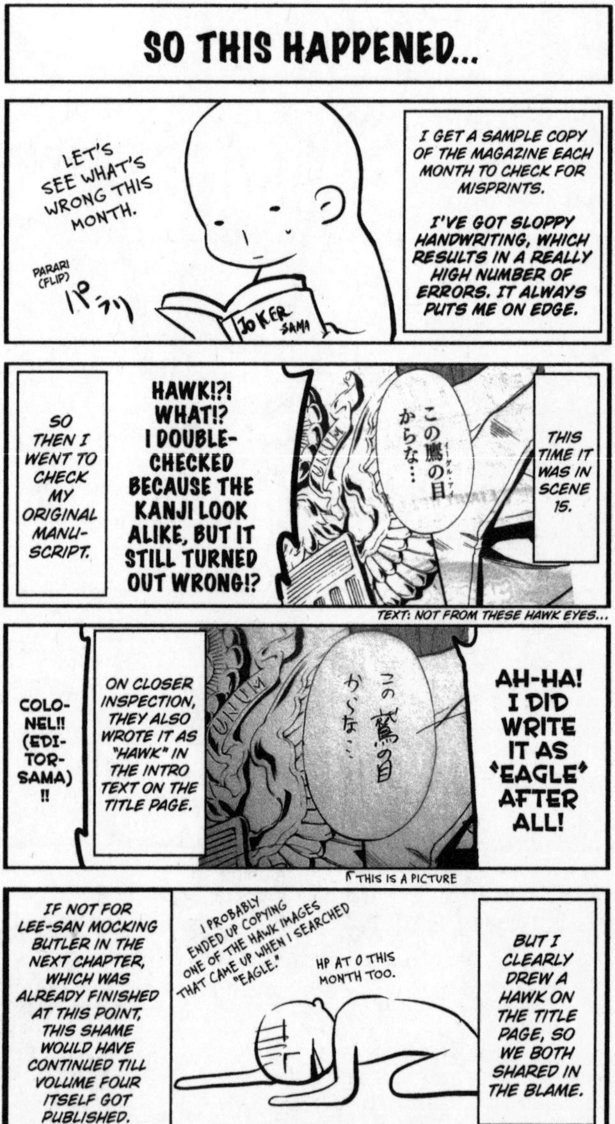
SO THIS HAPPENED...
I GET A SAMPLE COPY OF THE MAGAZINE EACH MONTH TO CHECK FOR MISPRINTS.
I'VE GOT SLOPPY HANDWRITING, WHICH RESULTS IN A REALLY HIGH NUMBER OF ERRORS. IT ALWAYS PUTS ME ON EDGE.
LET'S SEE WHAT'S WRONG THIS MONTH.
PARARI (FLIP)
パラリ
JOKER SAMA
THIS TIME IT WAS IN SCENE 15.
この鷹の目からな…
HAWK!?! WHAT!? I DOUBLE-CHECKED BECAUSE THE KANJI LOOK ALIKE, BUT IT STILL TURNED OUT WRONG!?
SO THEN I WENT TO CHECK MY ORIGINAL MANUSCRIPT.
TEXT: NOT FROM THESE HAWK EYES...
AH-HA! I DID WRITE IT AS "EAGLE" AFTER ALL!
この鷲の目からな…
ON CLOSER INSPECTION, THEY ALSO WROTE IT AS "HAWK" IN THE INTRO TEXT ON THE TITLE PAGE.
COLONEL!! (EDITOR-SAMA)!!
THIS IS A PICTURE
BUT I CLEARLY DREW A HAWK ON THE TITLE PAGE, SO WE BOTH SHARED IN THE BLAME.
HP AT 0 THIS MONTH TOO.
I PROBABLY ENDED UP COPYING ONE OF THE HAWK IMAGES THAT CAME UP WHEN I SEARCHED "EAGLE."
IF NOT FOR LEE-SAN MOCKING BUTLER IN THE NEXT CHAPTER, WHICH WAS ALREADY FINISHED AT THIS POINT, THIS SHAME WOULD HAVE CONTINUED TILL VOLUME FOUR ITSELF GOT PUBLISHED.

I'M SO SORRY.

I'M SO VERY GRATEFUL TO LEE-SAN.

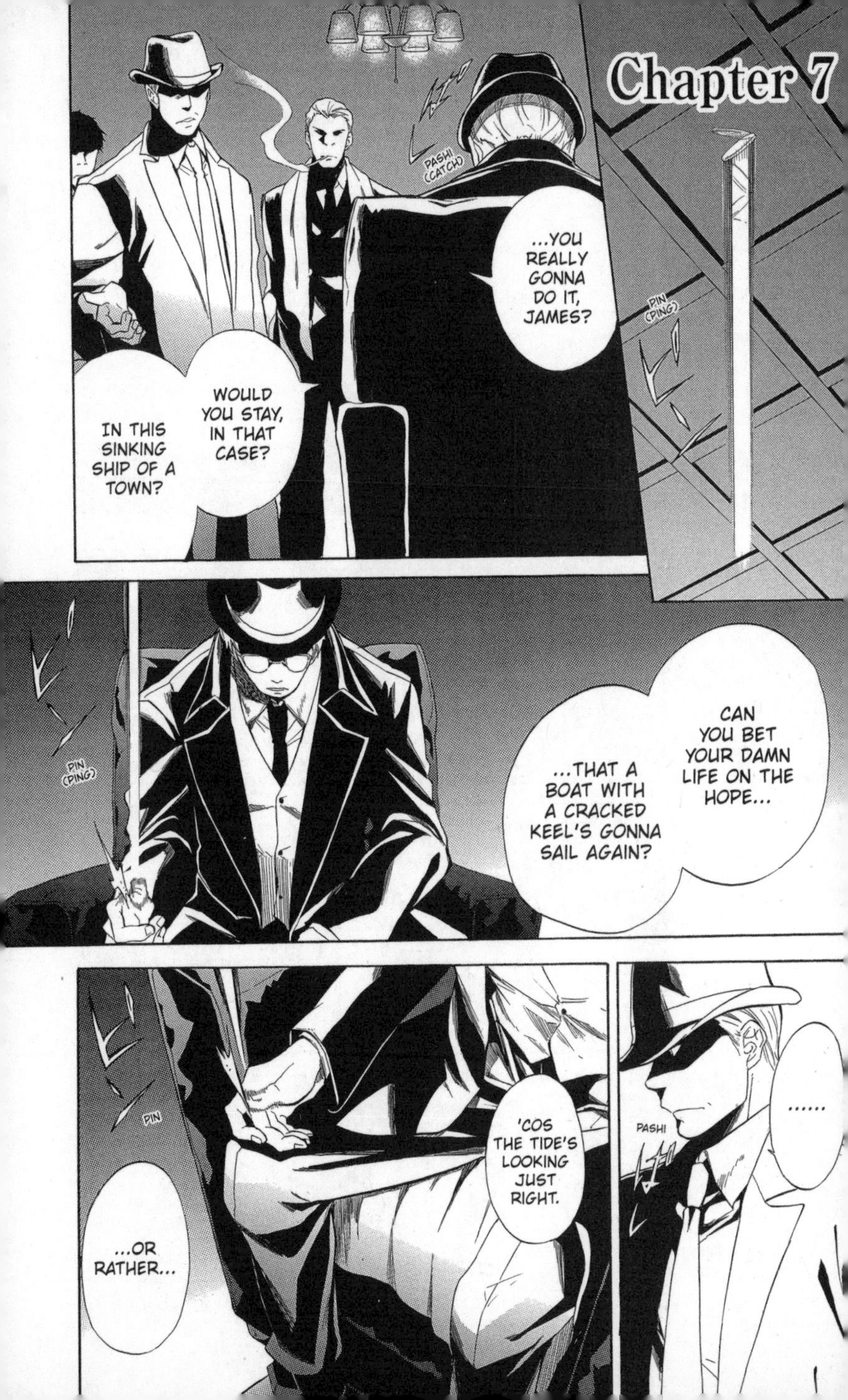
Chapter 7
PASHI (CATCH)
...YOU REALLY GONNA DO IT, JAMES?
PIN (PING)
WOULD YOU STAY, IN THAT CASE?
IN THIS SINKING SHIP OF A TOWN?
CAN YOU BET YOUR DAMN LIFE ON THE HOPE...
...THAT A BOAT WITH A CRACKED KEEL'S GONNA SAIL AGAIN?
PIN (PING)
......
PASHI
'COS THE TIDE'S LOOKING JUST RIGHT.
PIN
...OR RATHER...

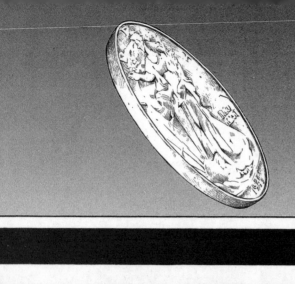

...IT'S A GOOD TIME TO PLACE A BET...
Scene: 16
...YEAH. THAT'S GOOD.
HOW ABOUT THE HOSTAGES?
Just like you said.
GOTCHA. ...RIGHT.
LATER, THEN.
CHIN (DING)

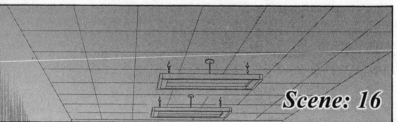

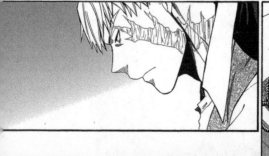

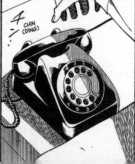

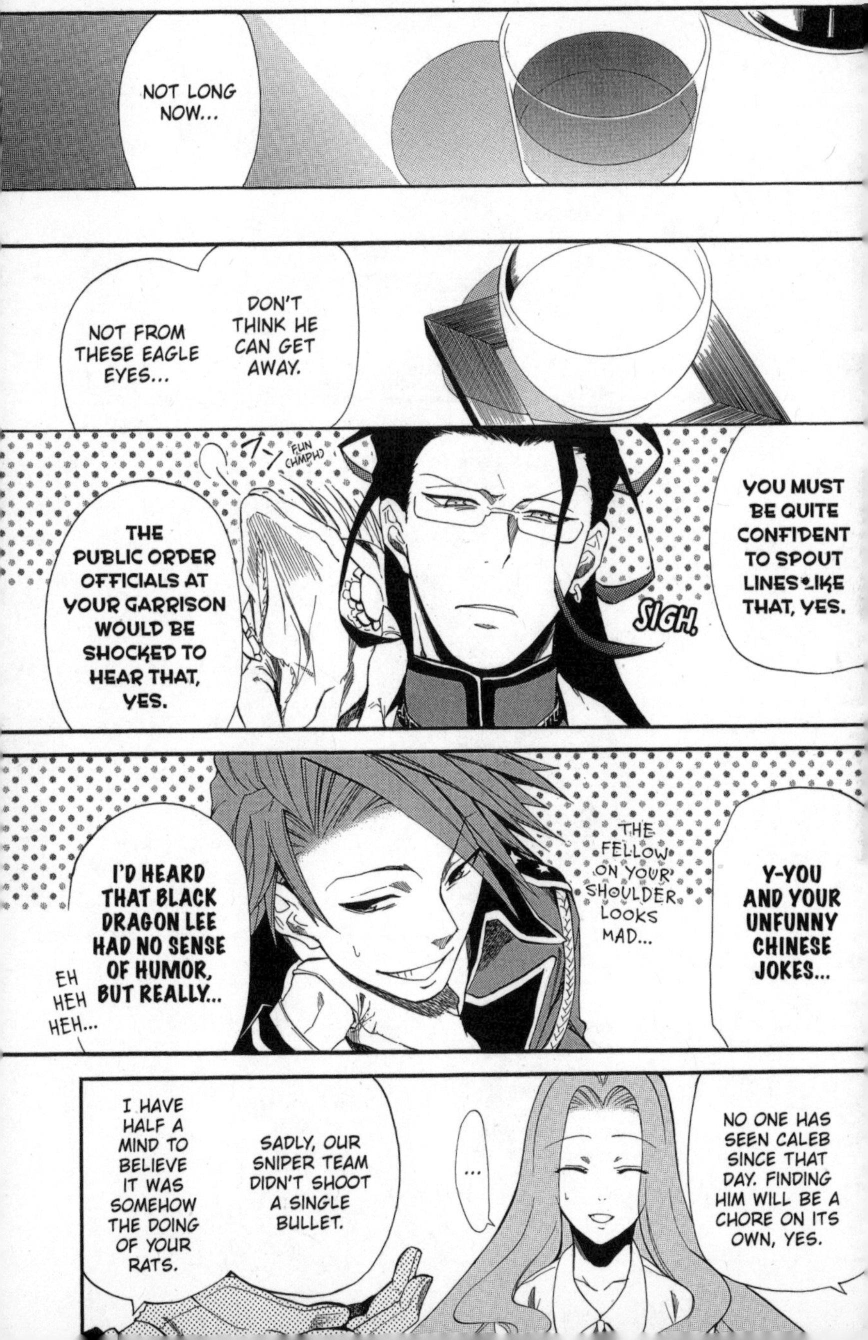
NOT LONG NOW...
DON'T THINK HE CAN GET AWAY.
NOT FROM THESE EAGLE EYES...
YOU MUST BE QUITE CONFIDENT TO SPOUT LINES LIKE THAT, YES.
SIGH.
FUN CHMPH
THE PUBLIC ORDER OFFICIALS AT YOUR GARRISON WOULD BE SHOCKED TO HEAR THAT, YES.
Y-YOU AND YOUR UNFUNNY CHINESE JOKES...
THE FELLOW ON YOUR SHOULDER LOOKS MAD...
I'D HEARD THAT BLACK DRAGON LEE HAD NO SENSE OF HUMOR, BUT REALLY...
EH HEH HEH...
NO ONE HAS SEEN CALEB SINCE THAT DAY. FINDING HIM WILL BE A CHORE ON ITS OWN, YES.
...
SADLY, OUR SNIPER TEAM DIDN'T SHOOT A SINGLE BULLET.
I HAVE HALF A MIND TO BELIEVE IT WAS SOMEHOW THE DOING OF YOUR RATS.

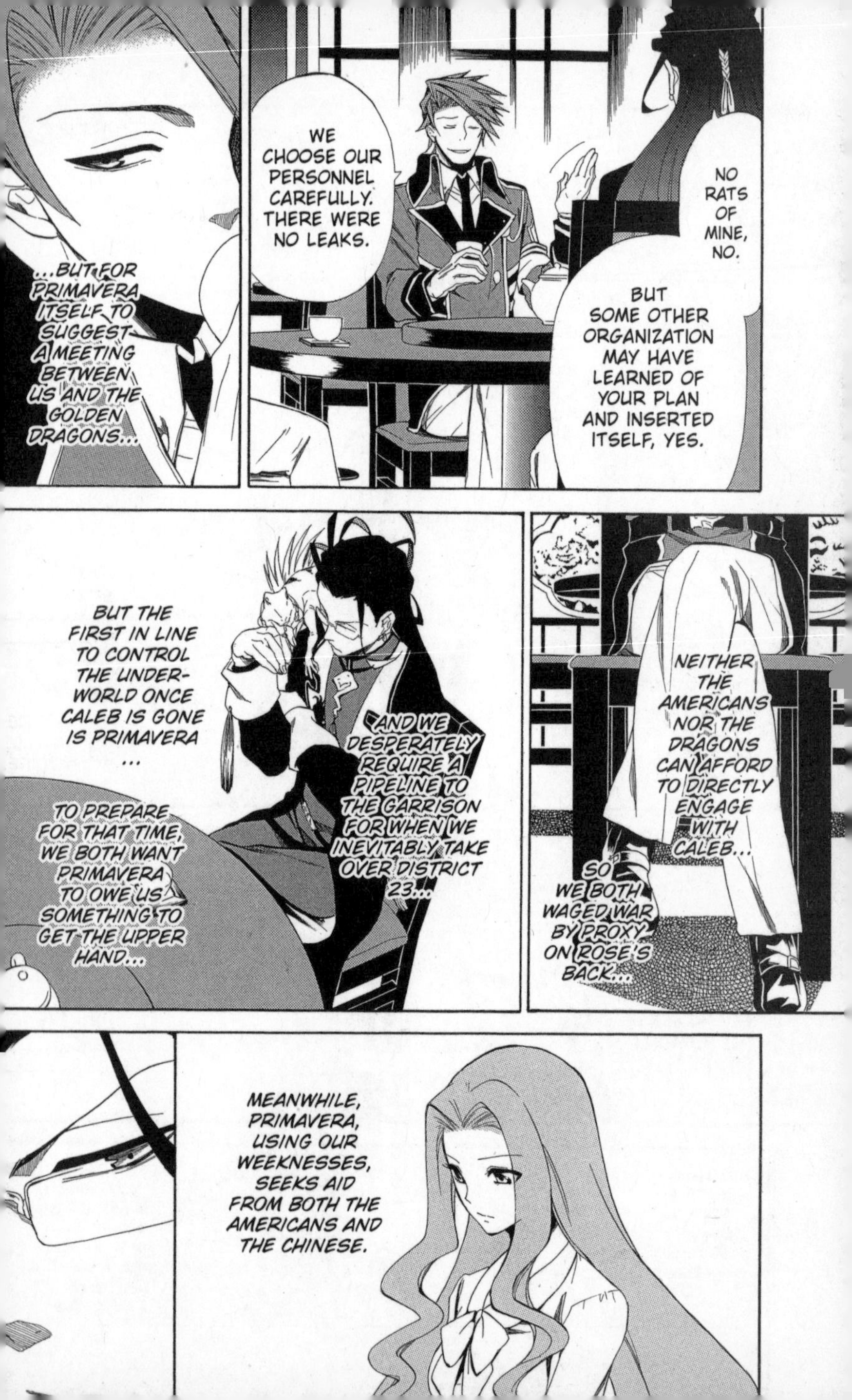
WE CHOOSE OUR PERSONNEL CAREFULLY. THERE WERE NO LEAKS.
NO RATS OF MINE, NO.
BUT SOME OTHER ORGANIZATION MAY HAVE LEARNED OF YOUR PLAN AND INSERTED ITSELF, YES.
...BUT FOR PRIMAVERA ITSELF TO SUGGEST A MEETING BETWEEN US AND THE GOLDEN DRAGONS...
NEITHER THE AMERICANS NOR THE DRAGONS CAN AFFORD TO DIRECTLY ENGAGE WITH CALEB...
SO WE BOTH WAGED WAR BY PROXY ON ROSE'S BACK...
BUT THE FIRST IN LINE TO CONTROL THE UNDER-WORLD ONCE CALEB IS GONE IS PRIMAVERA ...
AND WE DESPERATELY REQUIRE A PIPELINE TO THE GARRISON FOR WHEN WE INEVITABLY TAKE OVER DISTRICT 23...
TO PREPARE FOR THAT TIME, WE BOTH WANT PRIMAVERA TO OWE US SOMETHING TO GET THE UPPER HAND...
MEANWHILE, PRIMAVERA, USING OUR WEEKNESSES, SEEKS AID FROM BOTH THE AMERICANS AND THE CHINESE.

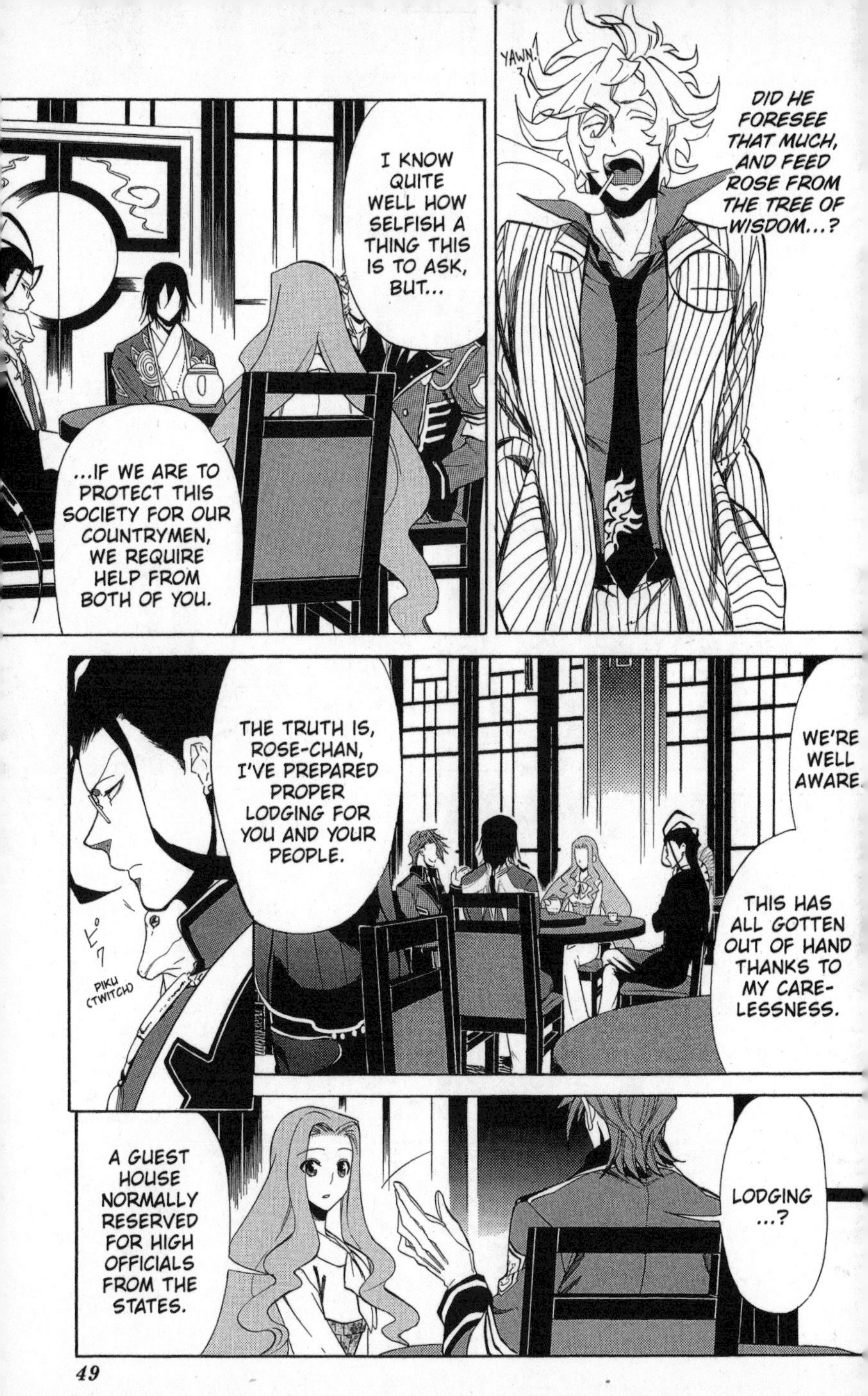
YAWN!
DID HE FORESEE THAT MUCH, AND FEED ROSE FROM THE TREE OF WISDOM...?
I KNOW QUITE WELL HOW SELFISH A THING THIS IS TO ASK, BUT...
...IF WE ARE TO PROTECT THIS SOCIETY FOR OUR COUNTRYMEN, WE REQUIRE HELP FROM BOTH OF YOU.
WE'RE WELL AWARE.
THIS HAS ALL GOTTEN OUT OF HAND THANKS TO MY CARE-LESSNESS.
THE TRUTH IS, ROSE-CHAN, I'VE PREPARED PROPER LODGING FOR YOU AND YOUR PEOPLE.
ピク
PIKU (TWITCH)
LODGING ...?
A GUEST HOUSE NORMALLY RESERVED FOR HIGH OFFICIALS FROM THE STATES.

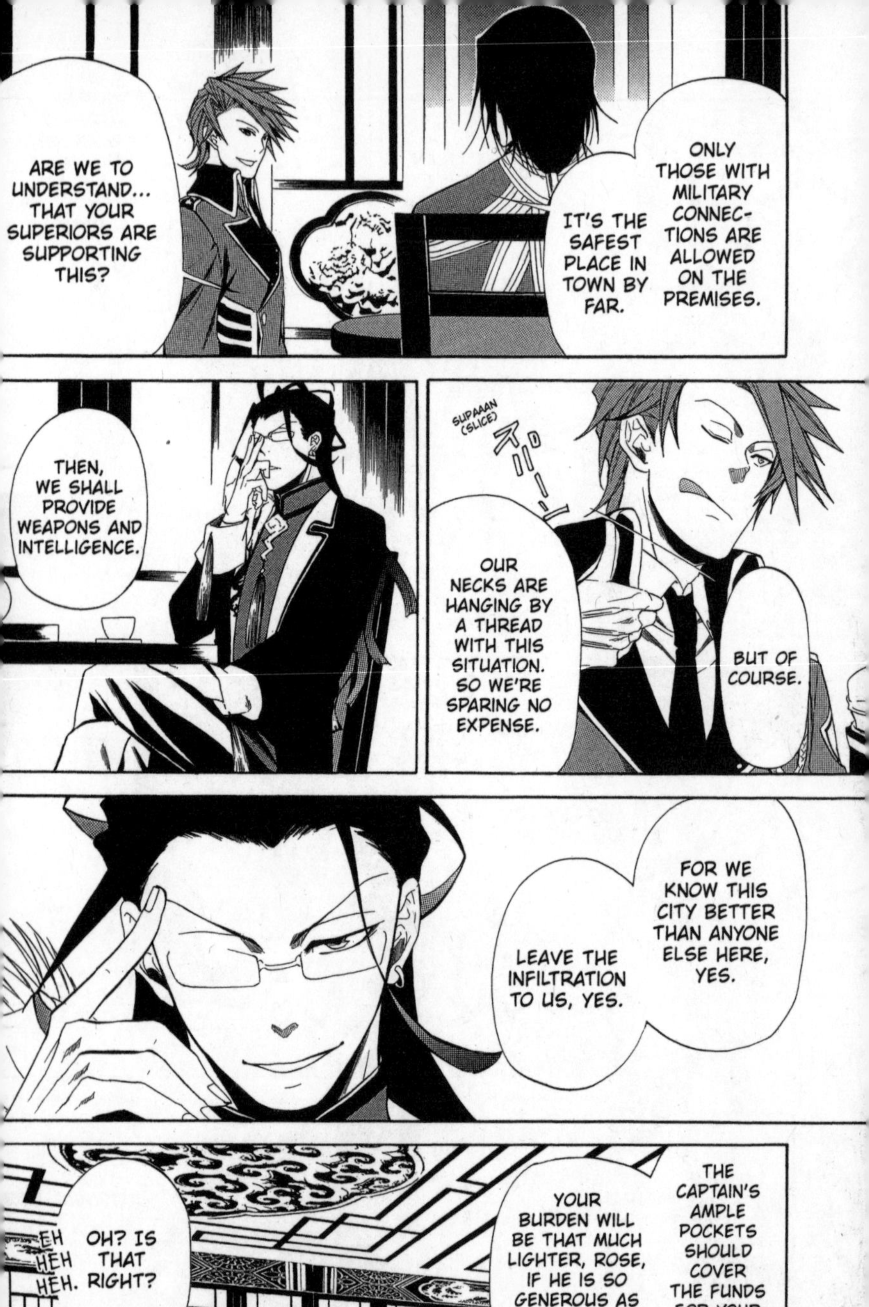
ONLY THOSE WITH MILITARY CONNEC-TIONS ARE ALLOWED ON THE PREMISES.
IT'S THE SAFEST PLACE IN TOWN BY FAR.
ARE WE TO UNDERSTAND... THAT YOUR SUPERIORS ARE SUPPORTING THIS?
SUPAAAN (SLICE)
BUT OF COURSE.
OUR NECKS ARE HANGING BY A THREAD WITH THIS SITUATION. SO WE'RE SPARING NO EXPENSE.
THEN, WE SHALL PROVIDE WEAPONS AND INTELLIGENCE.
FOR WE KNOW THIS CITY BETTER THAN ANYONE ELSE HERE, YES.
LEAVE THE INFILTRATION TO US, YES.
THE CAPTAIN'S AMPLE POCKETS SHOULD COVER THE FUNDS FOR YOUR WEAPONS.
YOUR BURDEN WILL BE THAT MUCH LIGHTER, ROSE, IF HE IS SO GENEROUS AS TO ASSIST, YES.
OH? IS THAT RIGHT?
EH HEH HEH.

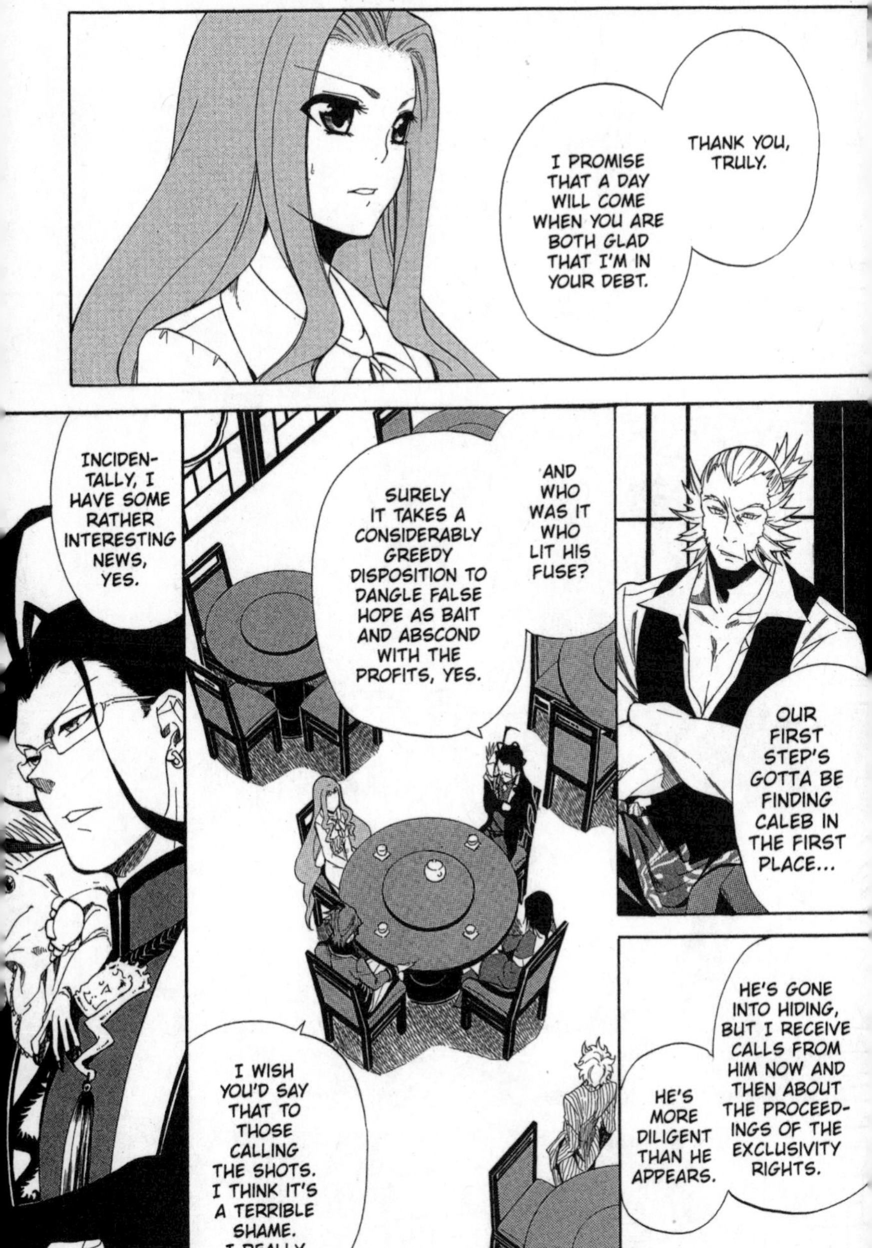
THANK YOU, TRULY.
I PROMISE THAT A DAY WILL COME WHEN YOU ARE BOTH GLAD THAT I'M IN YOUR DEBT.
OUR FIRST STEP'S GOTTA BE FINDING CALEB IN THE FIRST PLACE...
HE'S GONE INTO HIDING, BUT I RECEIVE CALLS FROM HIM NOW AND THEN ABOUT THE PROCEEDINGS OF THE EXCLUSIVITY RIGHTS.
HE'S MORE DILIGENT THAN HE APPEARS.
AND WHO WAS IT WHO LIT HIS FUSE?
SURELY IT TAKES A CONSIDERABLY GREEDY DISPOSITION TO DANGLE FALSE HOPE AS BAIT AND ABSCOND WITH THE PROFITS, YES.
I WISH YOU'D SAY THAT TO THOSE CALLING THE SHOTS. I THINK IT'S A TERRIBLE SHAME. I REALLY DO.
INCIDENTALLY, I HAVE SOME RATHER INTERESTING NEWS, YES.

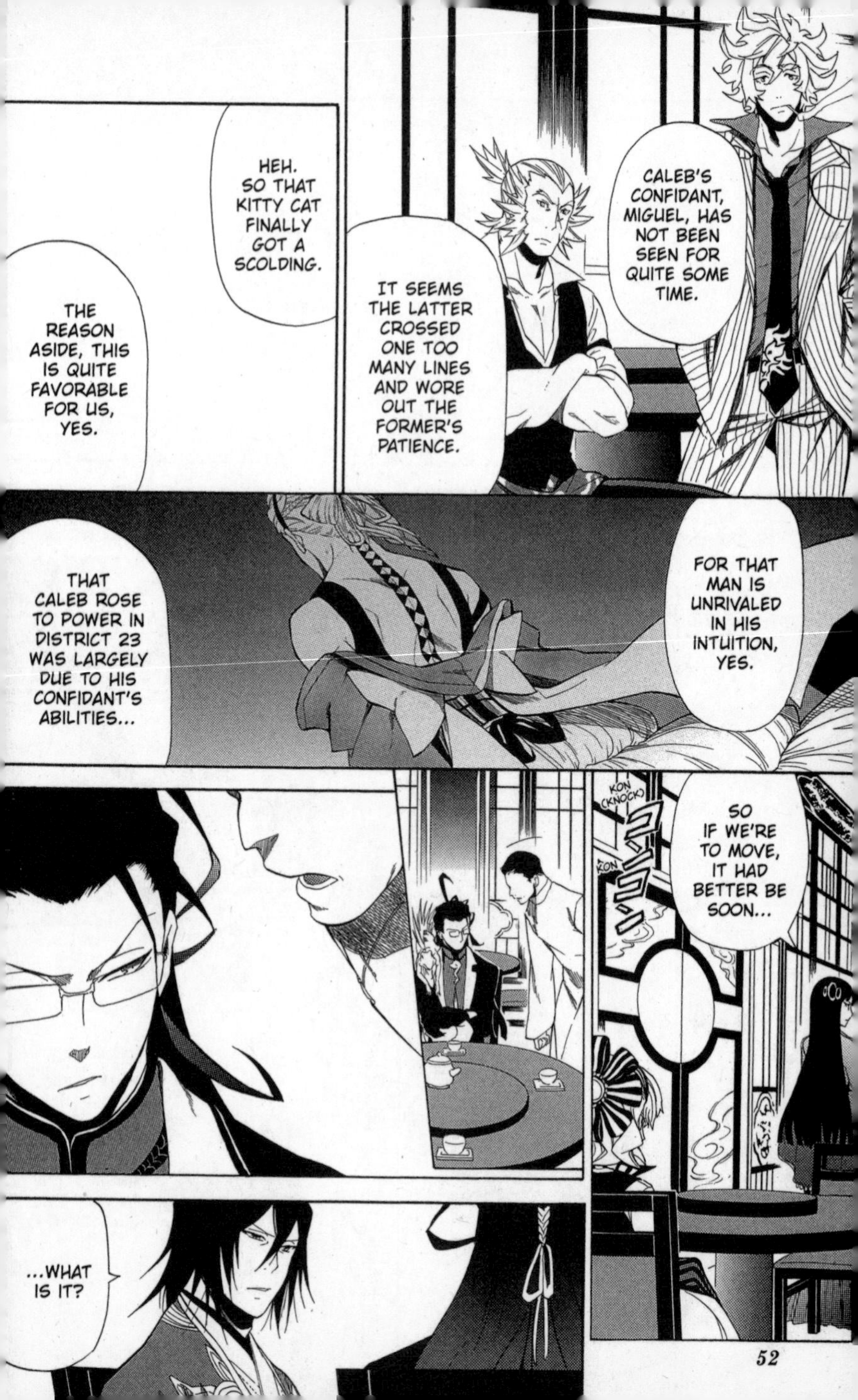
CALEB'S CONFIDANT, MIGUEL, HAS NOT BEEN SEEN FOR QUITE SOME TIME.
IT SEEMS THE LATTER CROSSED ONE TOO MANY LINES AND WORE OUT THE FORMER'S PATIENCE.
HEH. SO THAT KITTY CAT FINALLY GOT A SCOLDING.
THE REASON ASIDE, THIS IS QUITE FAVORABLE FOR US, YES.
FOR THAT MAN IS UNRIVALED IN HIS INTUITION, YES.
THAT CALEB ROSE TO POWER IN DISTRICT 23 WAS LARGELY DUE TO HIS CONFIDANT'S ABILITIES...
KON (KNOCK)
KON
SO IF WE'RE TO MOVE, IT HAD BETTER BE SOON...
...WHAT IS IT?

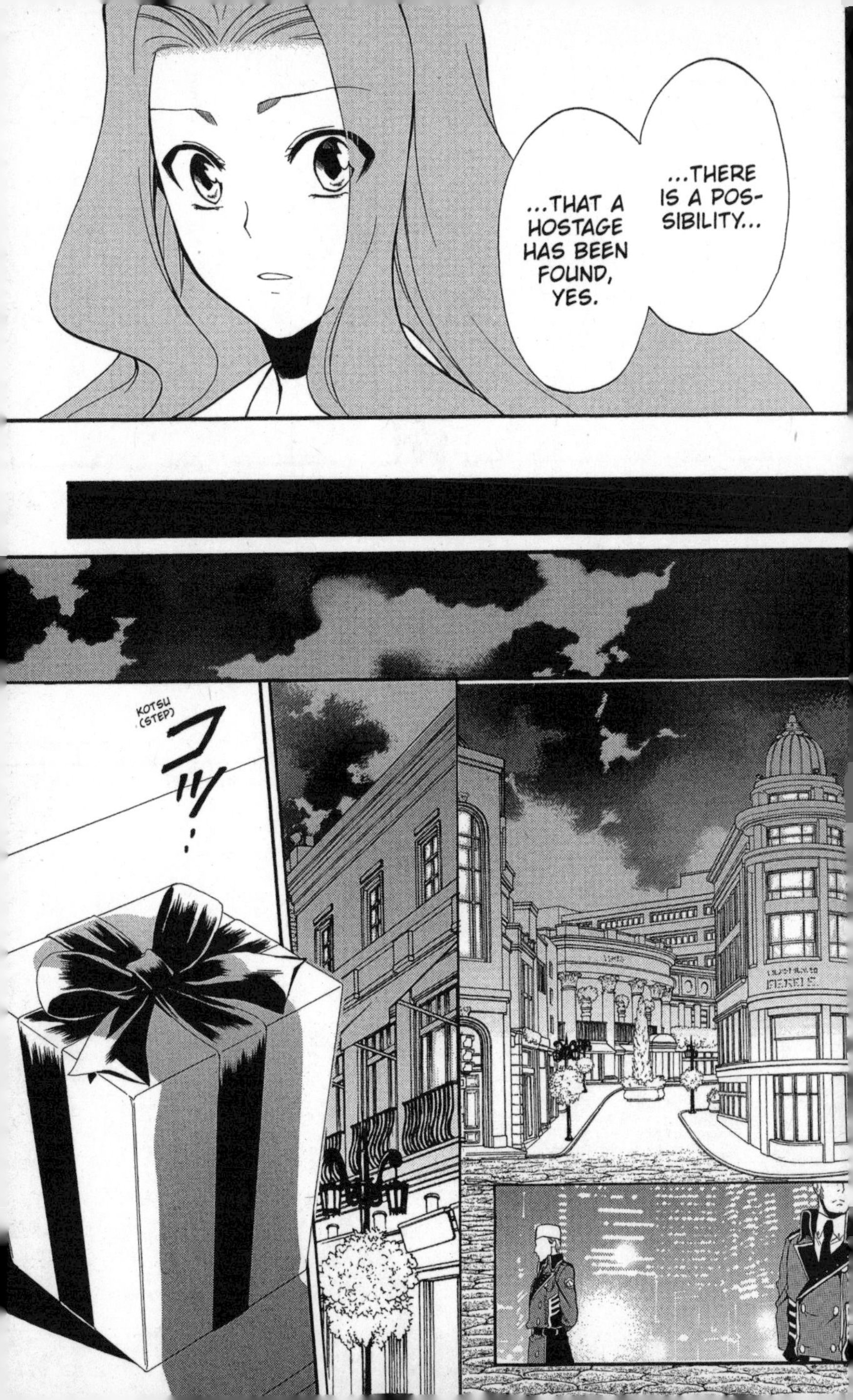
...THERE IS A POS-SIBILITY...
...THAT A HOSTAGE HAS BEEN FOUND, YES.
KOTSU (STEP)
コツ

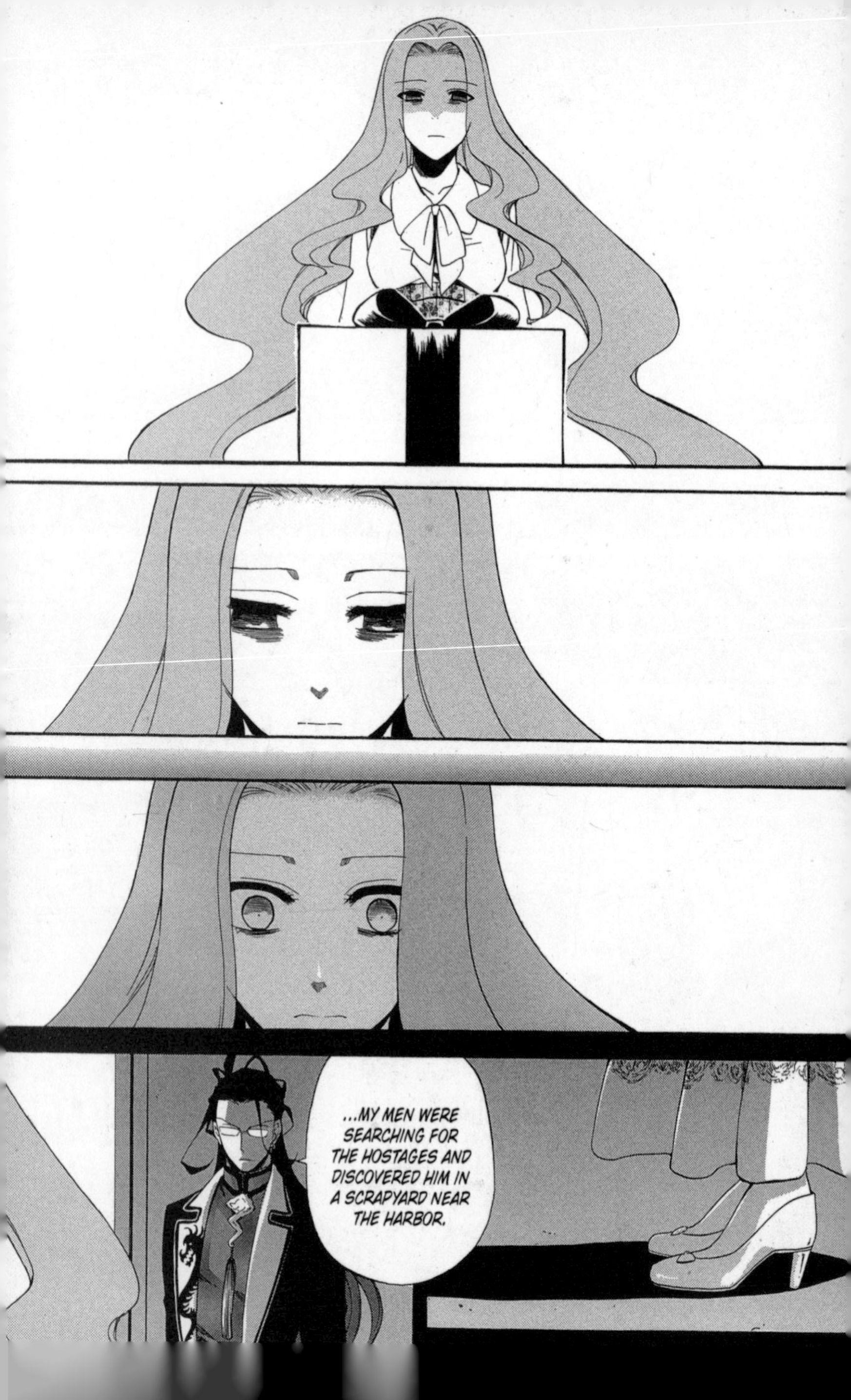
...MY MEN WERE SEARCHING FOR THE HOSTAGES AND DISCOVERED HIM IN A SCRAPYARD NEAR THE HARBOR.

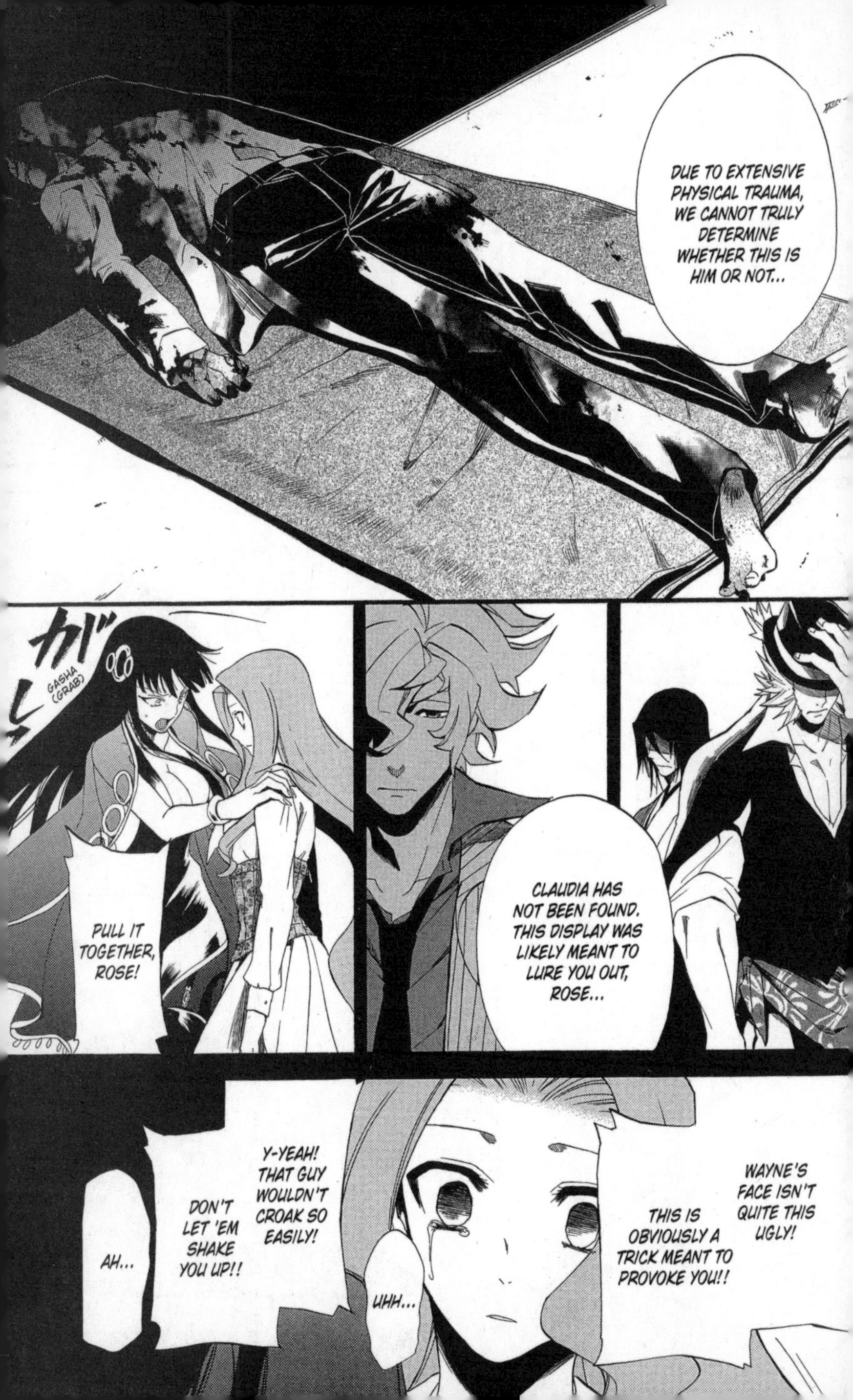
DUE TO EXTENSIVE PHYSICAL TRAUMA, WE CANNOT TRULY DETERMINE WHETHER THIS IS HIM OR NOT...
CLAUDIA HAS NOT BEEN FOUND. THIS DISPLAY WAS LIKELY MEANT TO LURE YOU OUT, ROSE...
GASHA (GRAB)
PULL IT TOGETHER, ROSE!
WAYNE'S FACE ISN'T QUITE THIS UGLY!
THIS IS OBVIOUSLY A TRICK MEANT TO PROVOKE YOU!!
UHH...
Y-YEAH! THAT GUY WOULDN'T CROAK SO EASILY!
DON'T LET 'EM SHAKE YOU UP!!
AH...

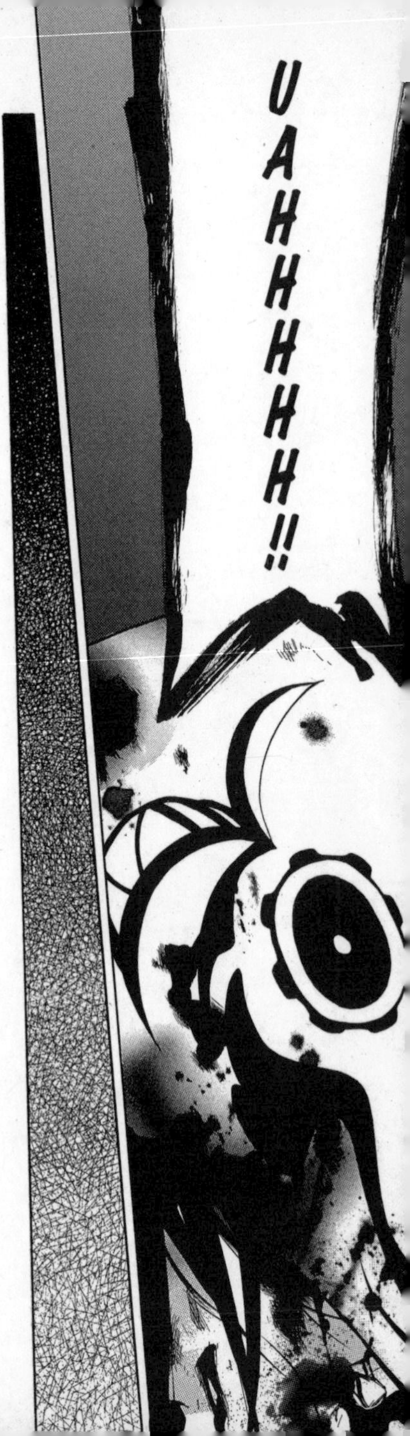
UAHHHHHHH!!

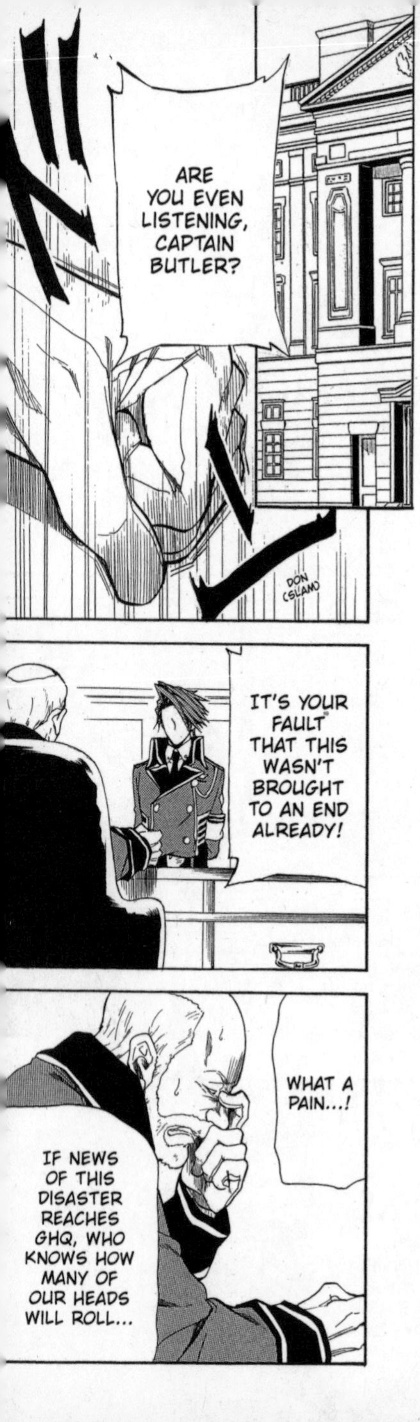
ARE YOU EVEN LISTENING, CAPTAIN BUTLER?
DON (SLAM)
IT'S YOUR FAULT THAT THIS WASN'T BROUGHT TO AN END ALREADY!
WHAT A PAIN...!
IF NEWS OF THIS DISASTER REACHES GHQ, WHO KNOWS HOW MANY OF OUR HEADS WILL ROLL...

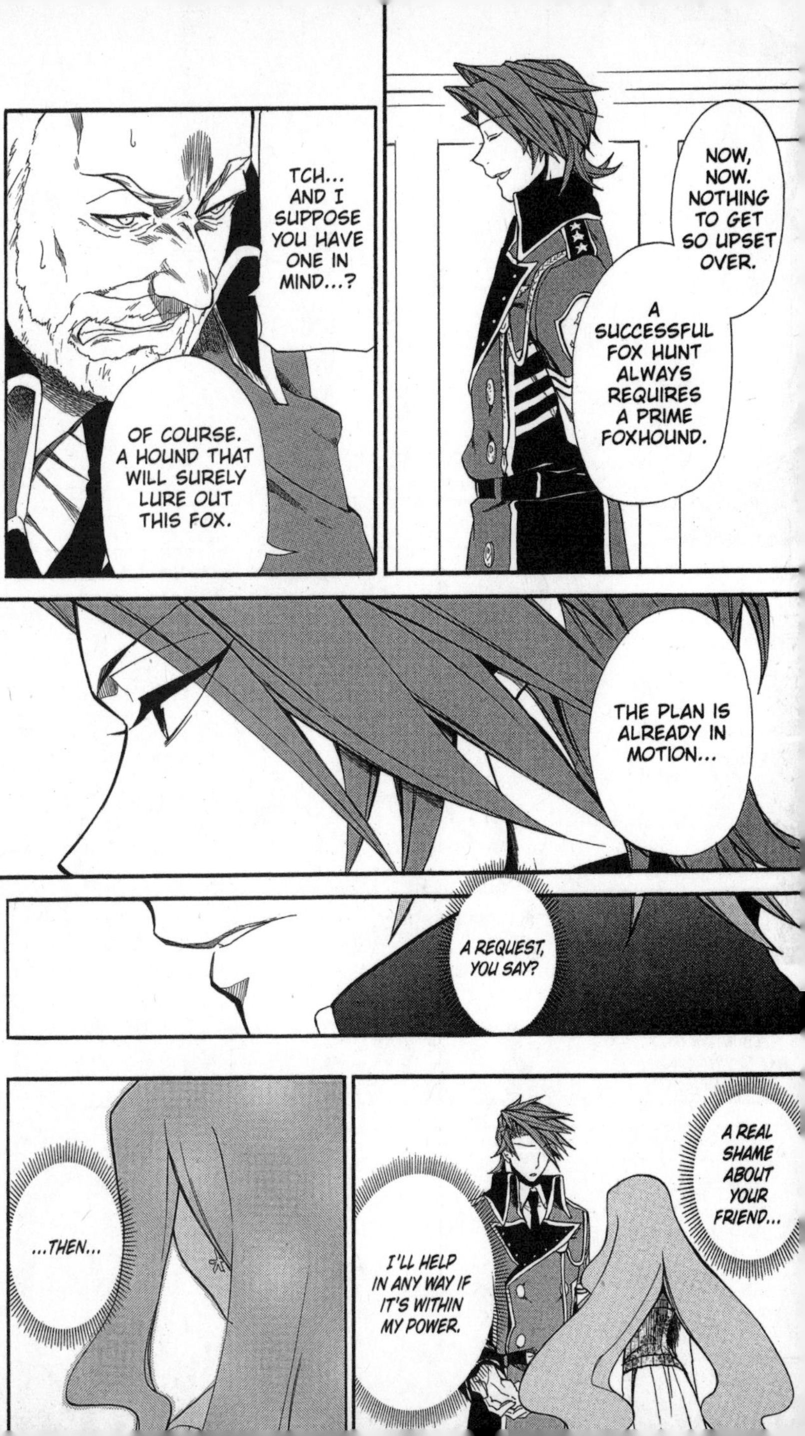
NOW, NOW. NOTHING TO GET SO UPSET OVER.
A SUCCESSFUL FOX HUNT ALWAYS REQUIRES A PRIME FOXHOUND.
TCH... AND I SUPPOSE YOU HAVE ONE IN MIND...?
OF COURSE. A HOUND THAT WILL SURELY LURE OUT THIS FOX.
THE PLAN IS ALREADY IN MOTION...
A REQUEST, YOU SAY?
A REAL SHAME ABOUT YOUR FRIEND...
I'LL HELP IN ANY WAY IF IT'S WITHIN MY POWER.
...THEN...

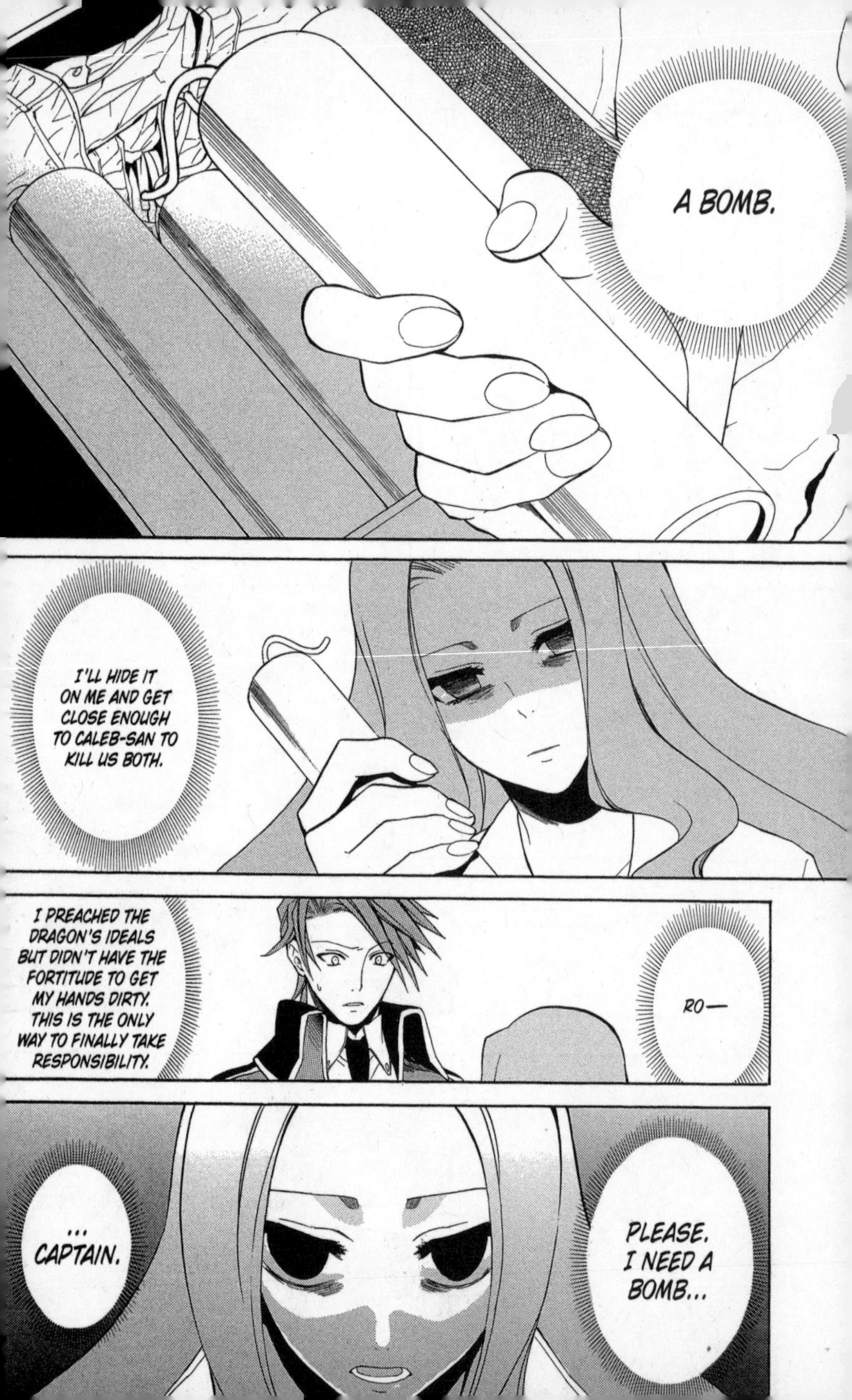
A BOMB.
I'LL HIDE IT ON ME AND GET CLOSE ENOUGH TO CALEB-SAN TO KILL US BOTH.
RO—
I PREACHED THE DRAGON'S IDEALS BUT DIDN'T HAVE THE FORTITUDE TO GET MY HANDS DIRTY. THIS IS THE ONLY WAY TO FINALLY TAKE RESPONSIBILITY.
PLEASE. I NEED A BOMB...
... CAPTAIN.

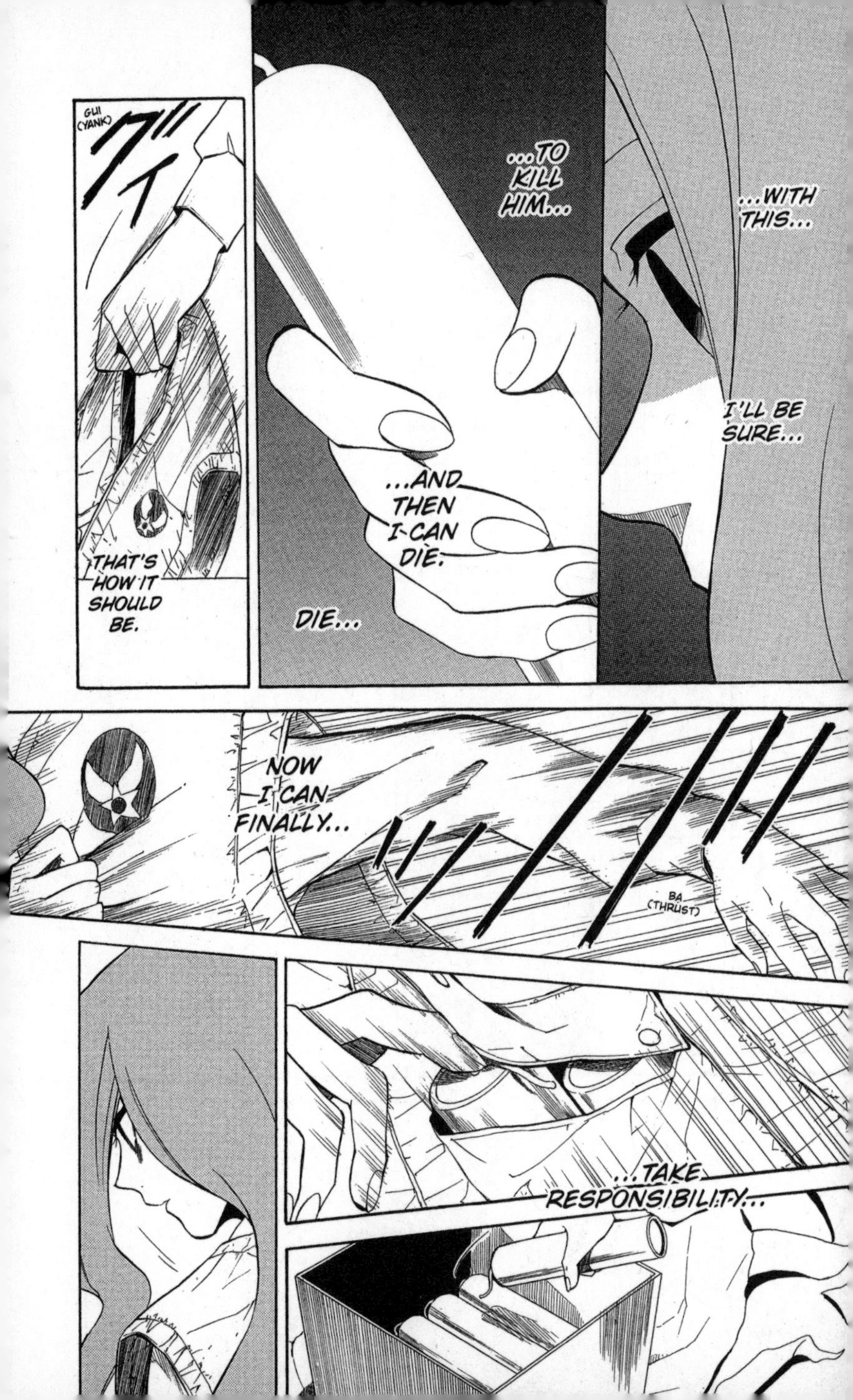
...WITH THIS...
I'LL BE SURE...
...TO KILL HIM...
...AND THEN I CAN DIE.
DIE...
GUI (YANK)
THAT'S HOW IT SHOULD BE.
NOW I CAN FINALLY...
BA (THRUST)
...TAKE RESPONSIBILITY...

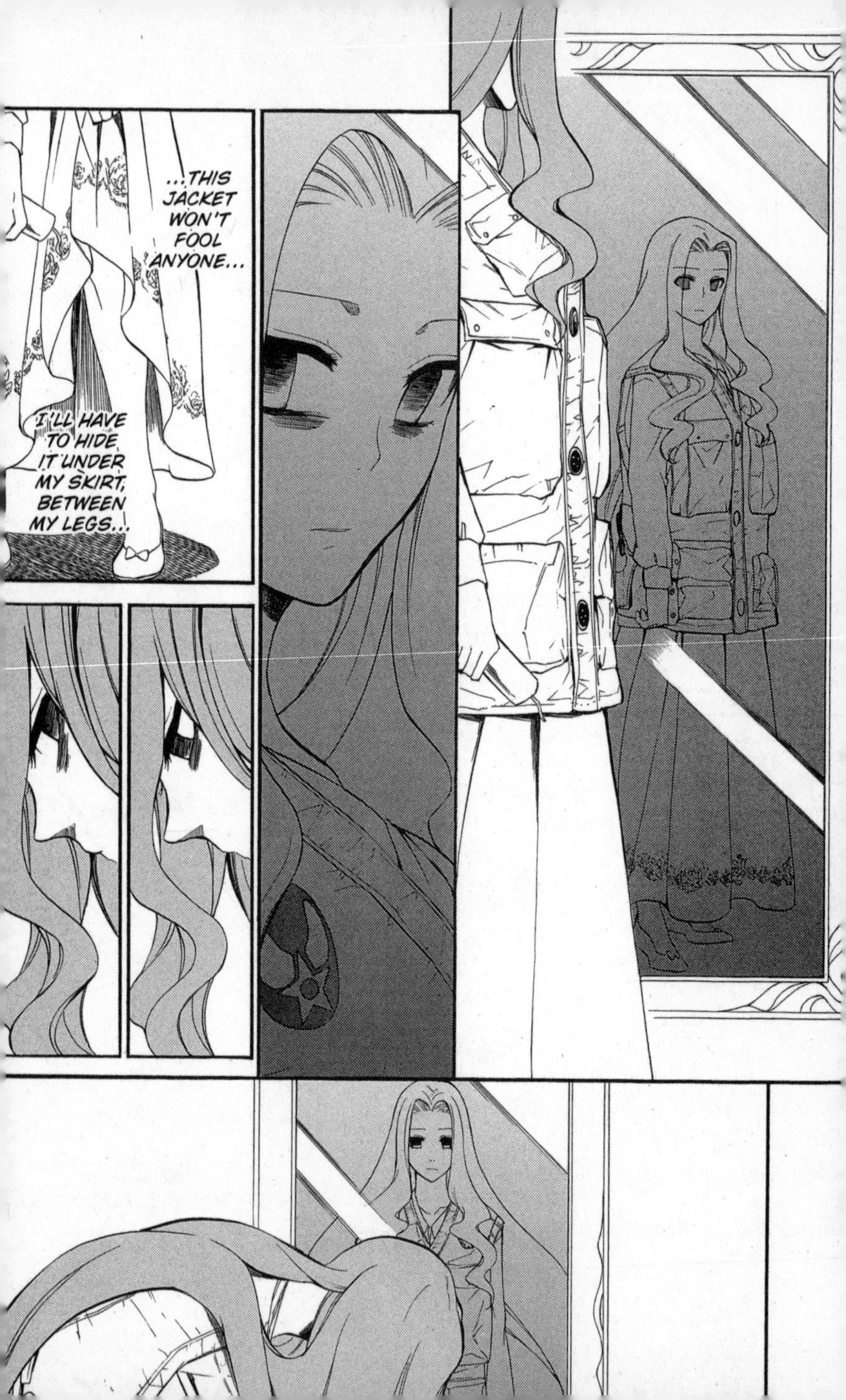
...THIS JACKET WON'T FOOL ANYONE...
I'LL HAVE TO HIDE IT UNDER MY SKIRT, BETWEEN MY LEGS...

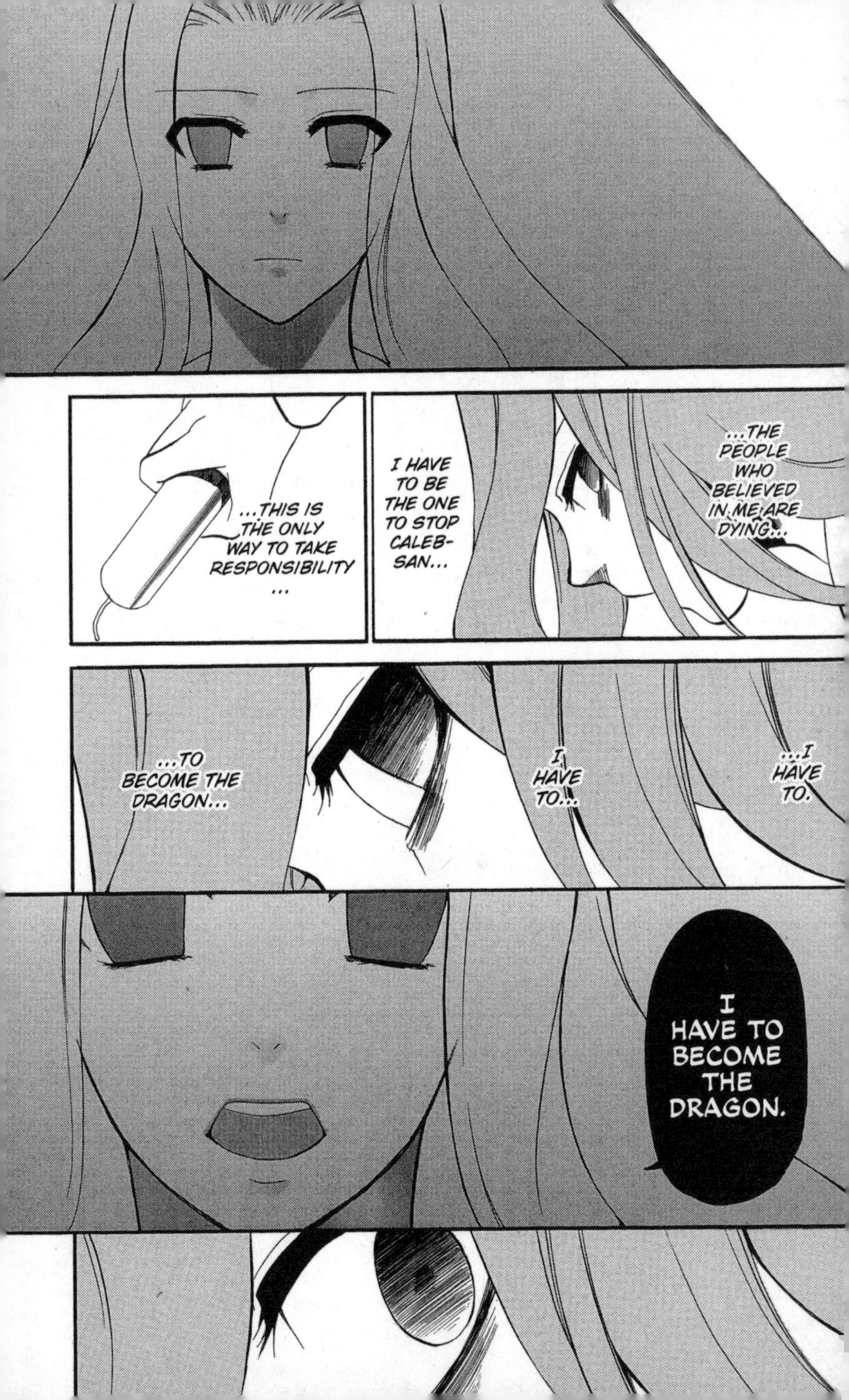
...THE PEOPLE WHO BELIEVED IN ME ARE DYING...
I HAVE TO BE THE ONE TO STOP CALEB-SAN...
...THIS IS THE ONLY WAY TO TAKE RESPONSIBILITY ...
...I HAVE TO.
I HAVE TO...
...TO BECOME THE DRAGON...
I HAVE TO BECOME THE DRAGON.

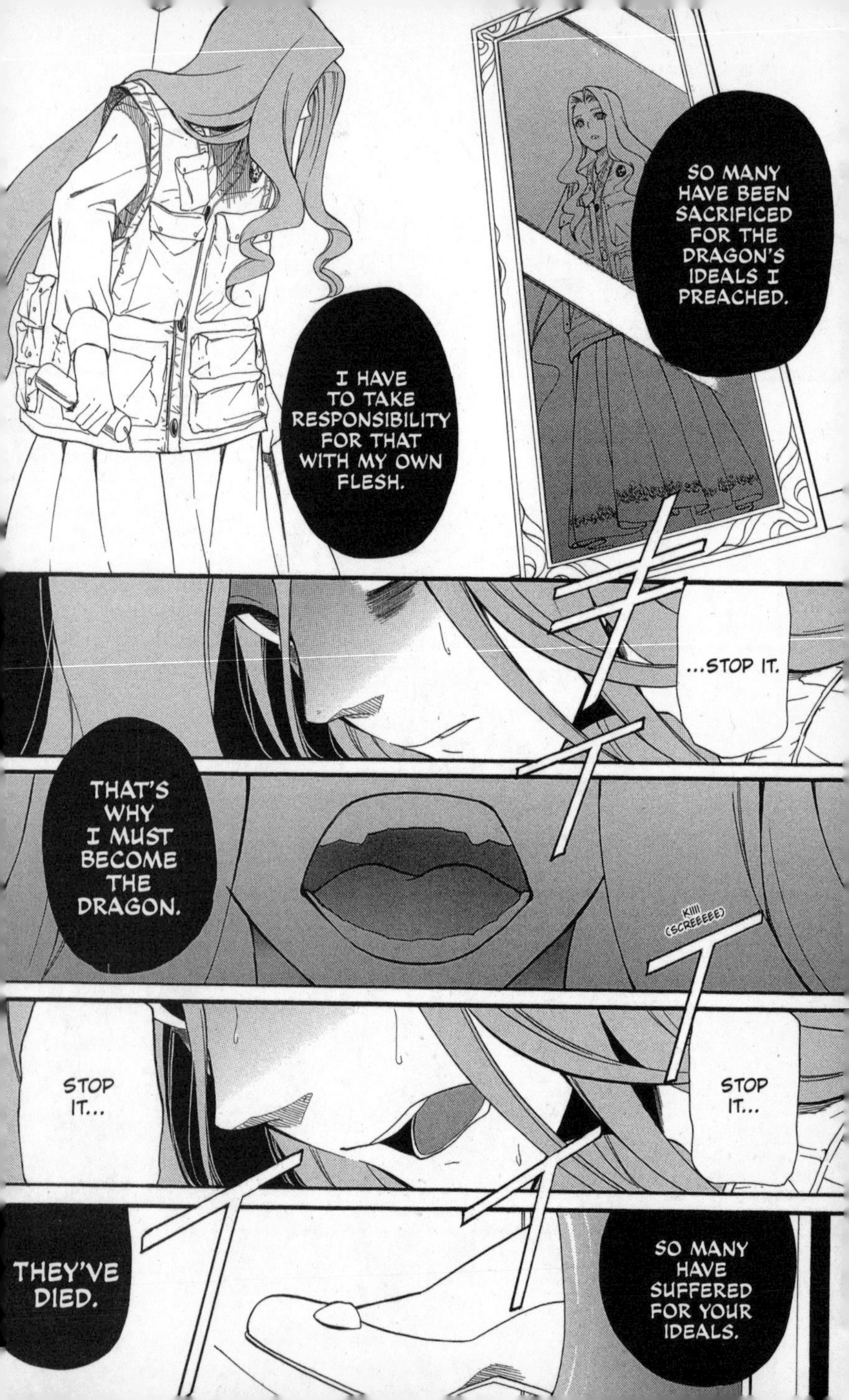
SO MANY HAVE BEEN SACRIFICED FOR THE DRAGON'S IDEALS I PREACHED.
I HAVE TO TAKE RESPONSIBILITY FOR THAT WITH MY OWN FLESH.
...STOP IT.
THAT'S WHY I MUST BECOME THE DRAGON.
KIIII (SCREEEEEE)
STOP IT...
STOP IT...
SO MANY HAVE SUFFERED FOR YOUR IDEALS.
THEY'VE DIED.

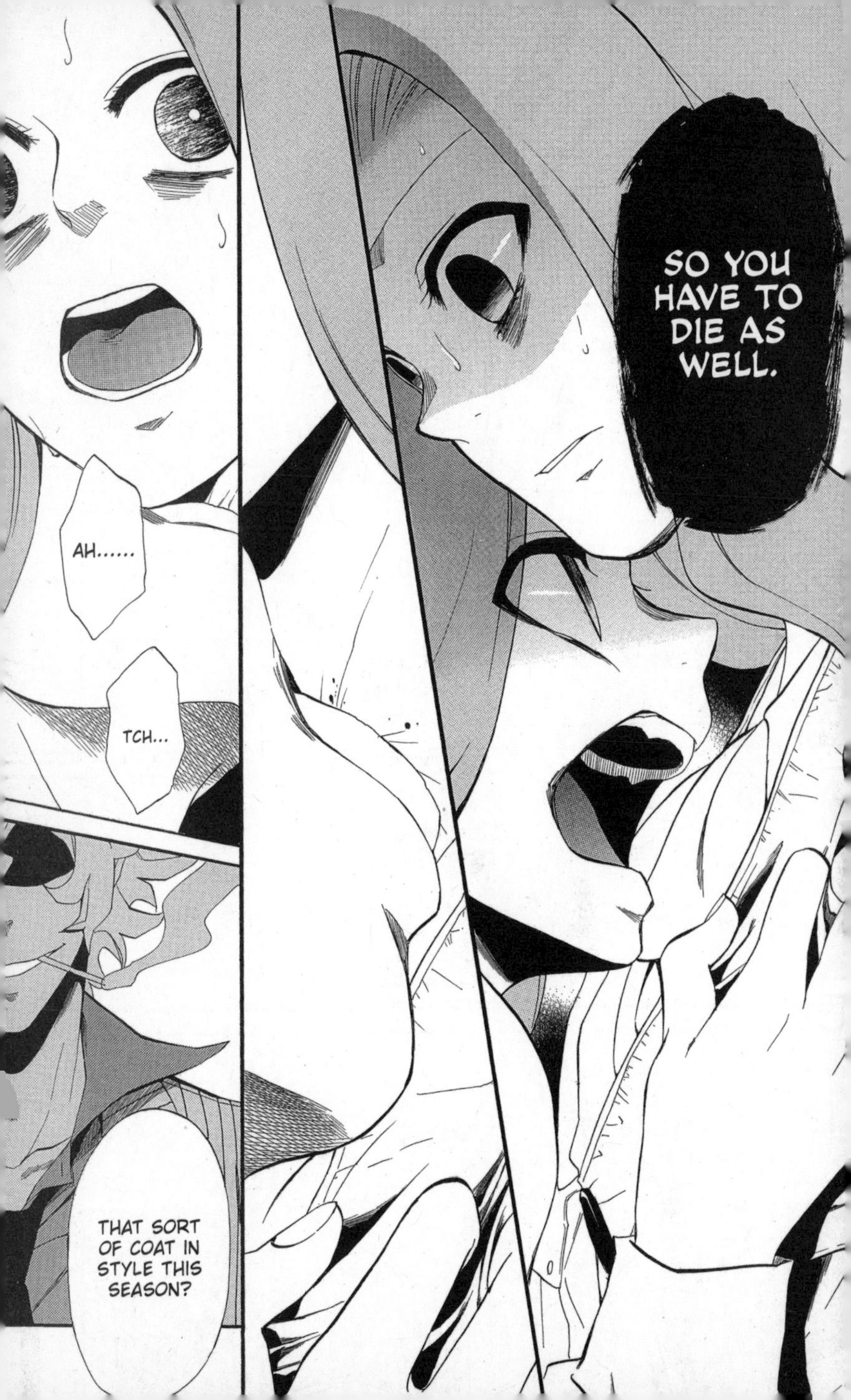
SO YOU HAVE TO DIE AS WELL.
AH......
TCH...
THAT SORT OF COAT IN STYLE THIS SEASON?

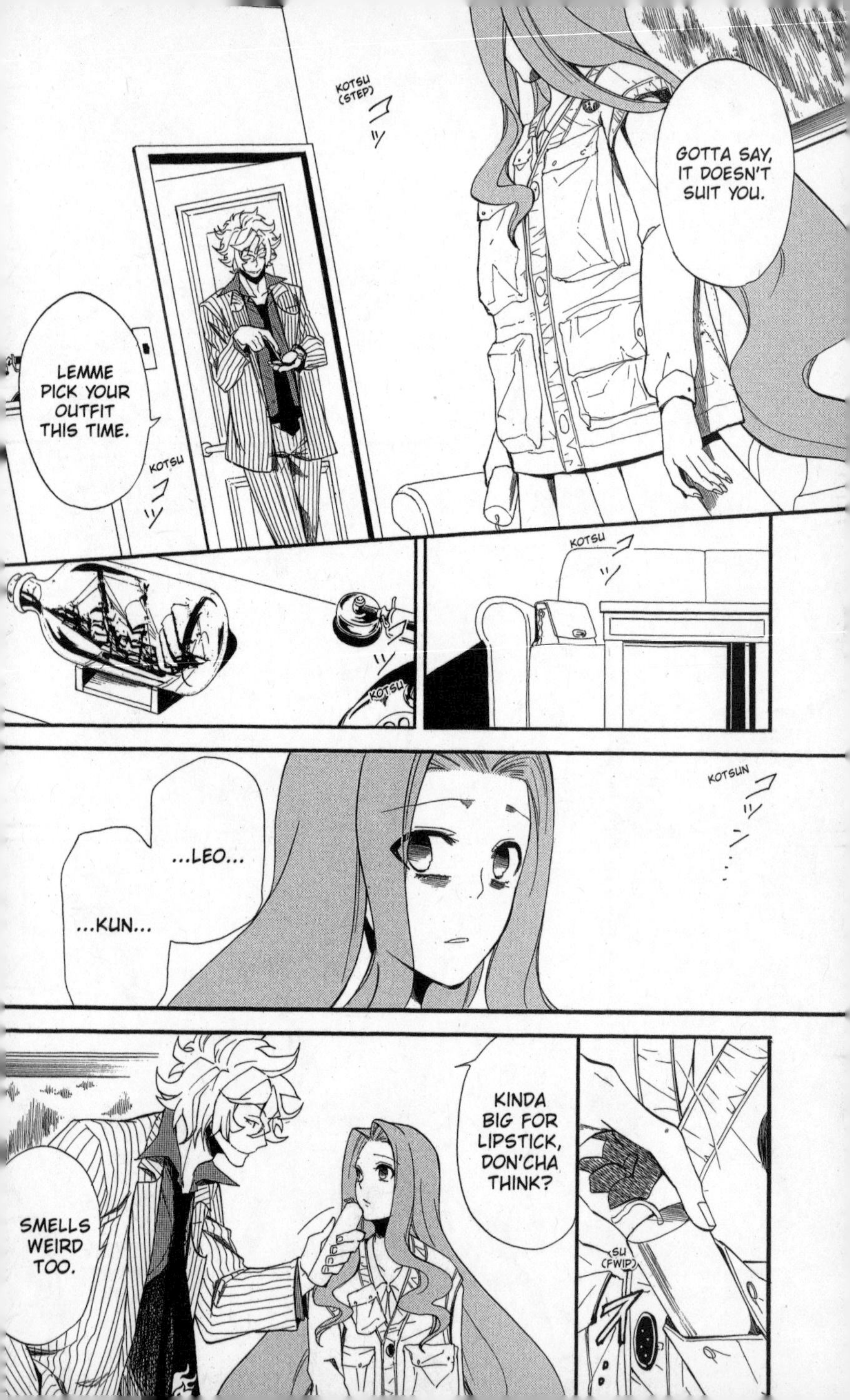
GOTTA SAY, IT DOESN'T SUIT YOU.
KOTSU (STEP)
LEMME PICK YOUR OUTFIT THIS TIME.
KOTSU
KOTSU
KOTSU
KOTSUN
...LEO...
...KUN...
SU (FWIP)
KINDA BIG FOR LIPSTICK, DON'CHA THINK?
SMELLS WEIRD TOO.

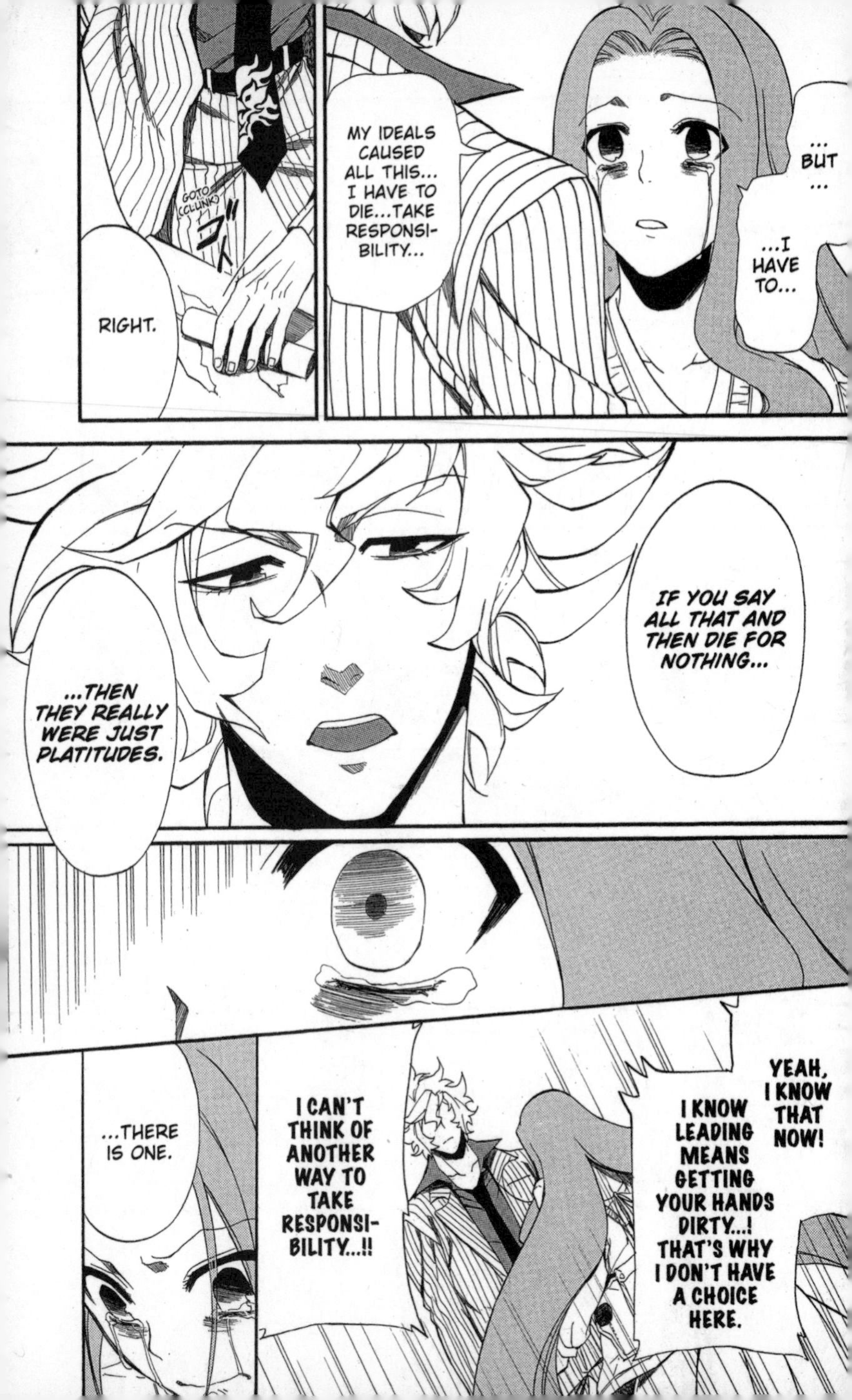
...BUT...
...I HAVE TO...
MY IDEALS CAUSED ALL THIS... I HAVE TO DIE...TAKE RESPONSI-BILITY...
GOTO (CLUNK)
RIGHT.
IF YOU SAY ALL THAT AND THEN DIE FOR NOTHING...
...THEN THEY REALLY WERE JUST PLATITUDES.
YEAH, I KNOW THAT NOW!
I KNOW LEADING MEANS GETTING YOUR HANDS DIRTY...! THAT'S WHY I DON'T HAVE A CHOICE HERE.
I CAN'T THINK OF ANOTHER WAY TO TAKE RESPONSI-BILITY...!!
...THERE IS ONE.

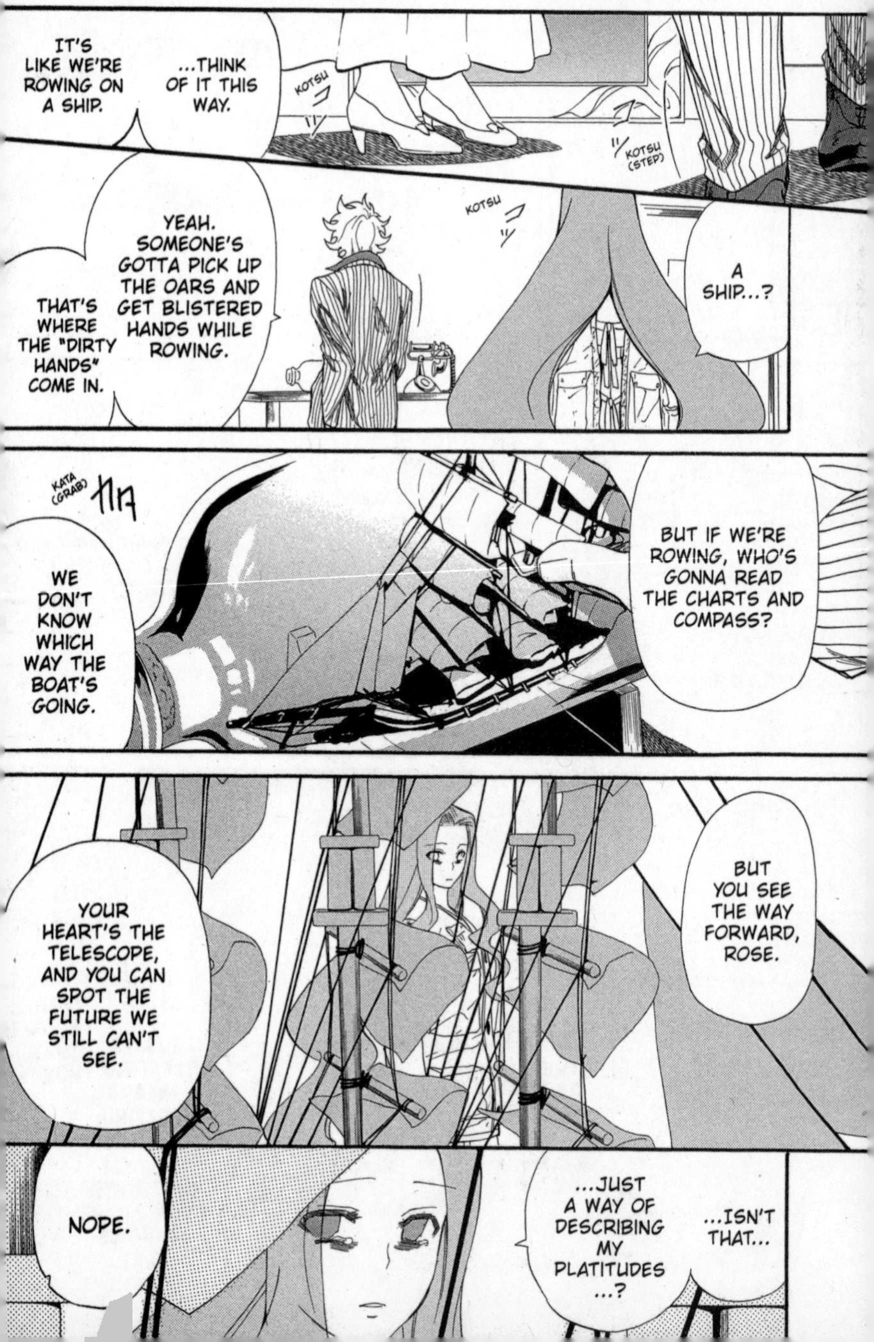
KOTSU (STEP)
KOTSU
...THINK OF IT THIS WAY.
IT'S LIKE WE'RE ROWING ON A SHIP.
A SHIP...?
KOTSU
YEAH. SOMEONE'S GOTTA PICK UP THE OARS AND GET BLISTERED HANDS WHILE ROWING.
THAT'S WHERE THE "DIRTY HANDS" COME IN.
BUT IF WE'RE ROWING, WHO'S GONNA READ THE CHARTS AND COMPASS?
KATA (GRAB)
WE DON'T KNOW WHICH WAY THE BOAT'S GOING.
BUT YOU SEE THE WAY FORWARD, ROSE.
YOUR HEART'S THE TELESCOPE, AND YOU CAN SPOT THE FUTURE WE STILL CAN'T SEE.
...ISN'T THAT...
...JUST A WAY OF DESCRIBING MY PLATITUDES ...?
NOPE.

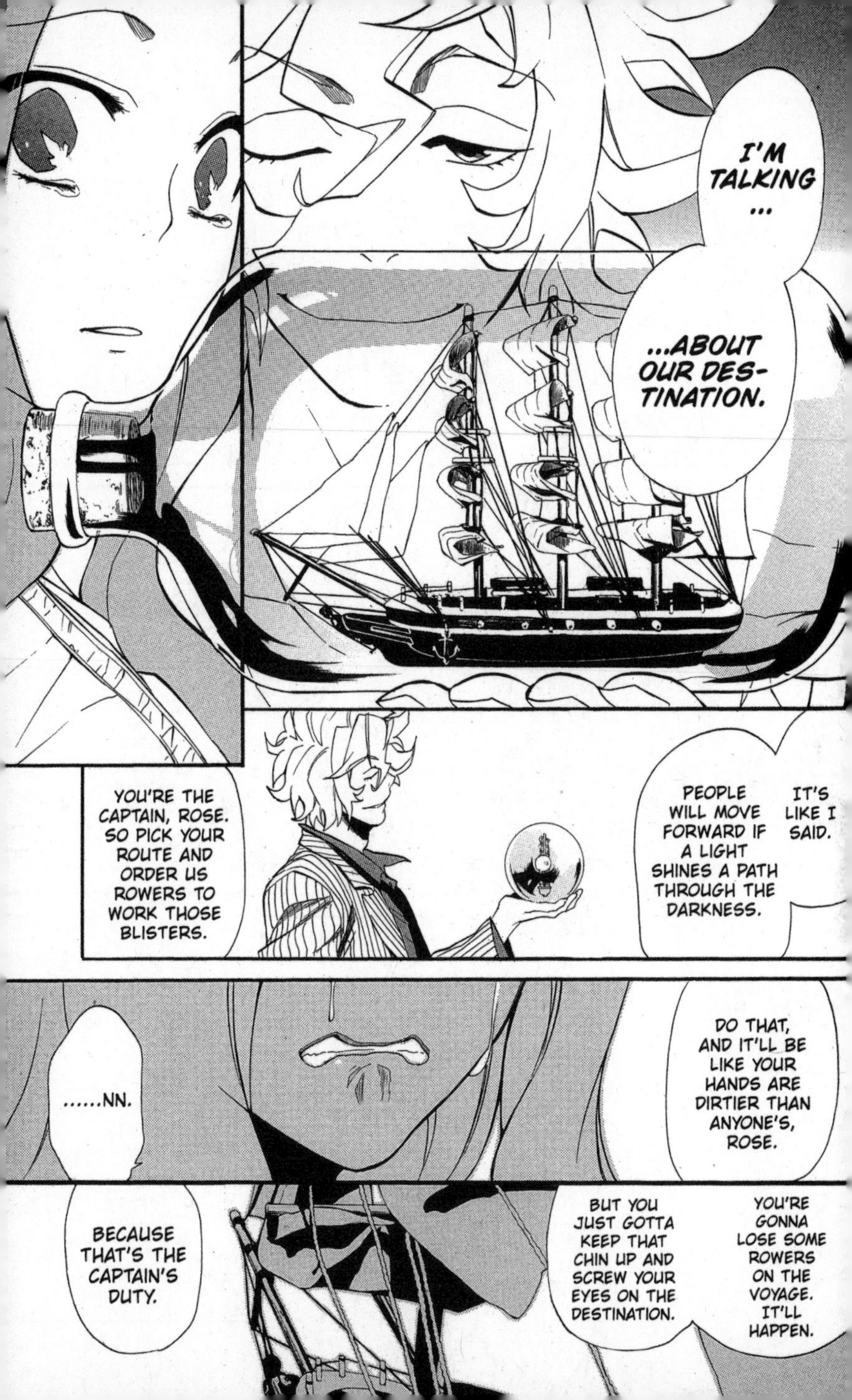
I'M TALKING ...
...ABOUT OUR DESTINATION.
IT'S LIKE I SAID.
PEOPLE WILL MOVE FORWARD IF A LIGHT SHINES A PATH THROUGH THE DARKNESS.
YOU'RE THE CAPTAIN, ROSE. SO PICK YOUR ROUTE AND ORDER US ROWERS TO WORK THOSE BLISTERS.
DO THAT, AND IT'LL BE LIKE YOUR HANDS ARE DIRTIER THAN ANYONE'S, ROSE.
......NN.
YOU'RE GONNA LOSE SOME ROWERS ON THE VOYAGE. IT'LL HAPPEN.
BUT YOU JUST GOTTA KEEP THAT CHIN UP AND SCREW YOUR EYES ON THE DESTINATION.
BECAUSE THAT'S THE CAPTAIN'S DUTY.

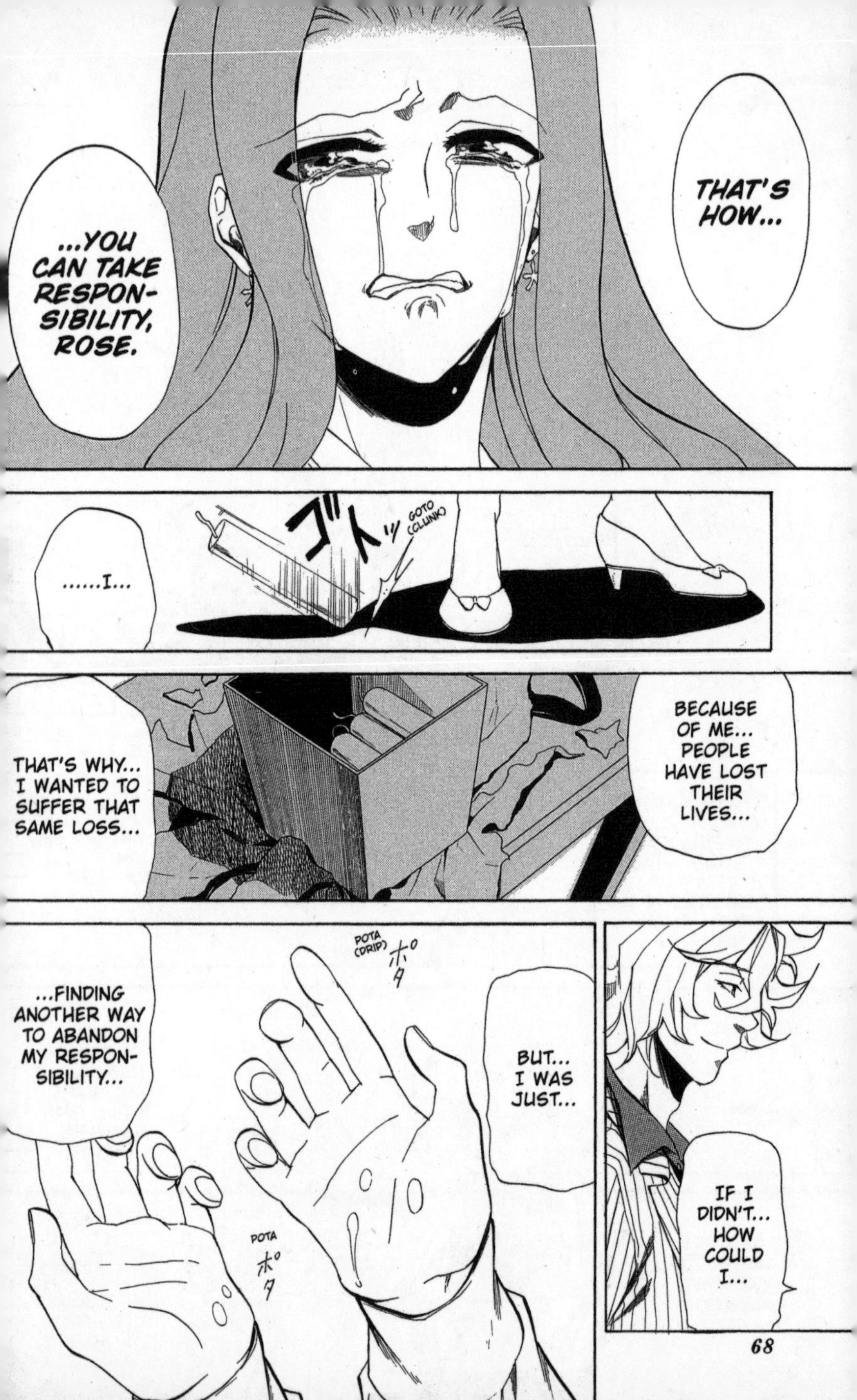
THAT'S HOW...
...YOU CAN TAKE RESPON-SIBILITY, ROSE.
GOTO (CLUNK)
......I...
BECAUSE OF ME... PEOPLE HAVE LOST THEIR LIVES...
THAT'S WHY... I WANTED TO SUFFER THAT SAME LOSS...
IF I DIDN'T... HOW COULD I...
POTA (DRIP)
BUT... I WAS JUST...
...FINDING ANOTHER WAY TO ABANDON MY RESPON-SIBILITY...
POTA

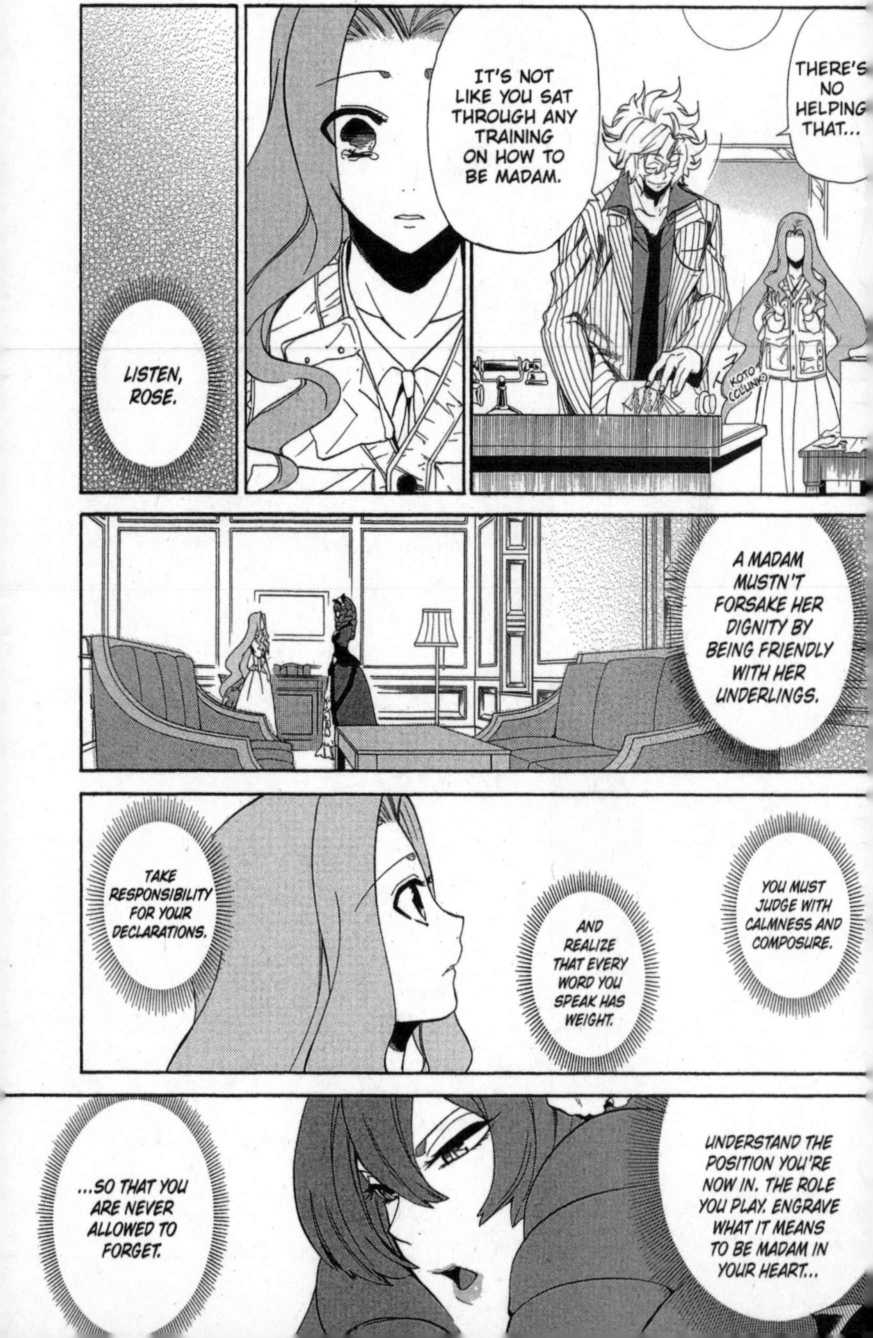
THERE'S NO HELPING THAT...
KOTO (CLUNK)
IT'S NOT LIKE YOU SAT THROUGH ANY TRAINING ON HOW TO BE MADAM.
LISTEN, ROSE.
A MADAM MUSTN'T FORSAKE HER DIGNITY BY BEING FRIENDLY WITH HER UNDERLINGS.
YOU MUST JUDGE WITH CALMNESS AND COMPOSURE.
AND REALIZE THAT EVERY WORD YOU SPEAK HAS WEIGHT.
TAKE RESPONSIBILITY FOR YOUR DECLARATIONS.
UNDERSTAND THE POSITION YOU'RE NOW IN. THE ROLE YOU PLAY. ENGRAVE WHAT IT MEANS TO BE MADAM IN YOUR HEART...
...SO THAT YOU ARE NEVER ALLOWED TO FORGET.

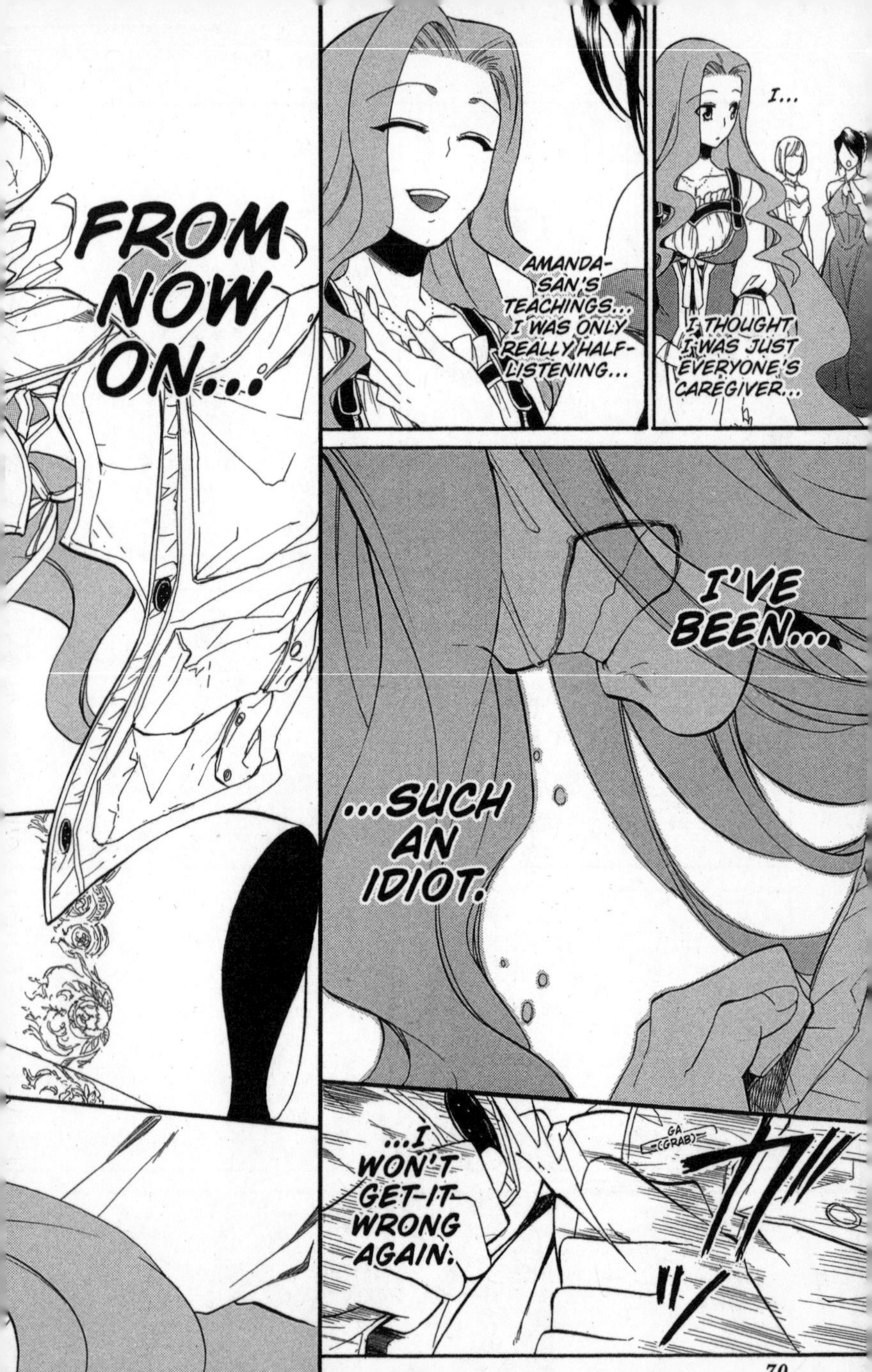
I...
I THOUGHT I WAS JUST EVERYONE'S CAREGIVER...
AMANDA-SAN'S TEACHINGS... I WAS ONLY REALLY HALF-LISTENING...
I'VE BEEN...
...SUCH AN IDIOT.
GA (GRAB)
...I WON'T GET IT WRONG AGAIN.
FROM NOW ON...

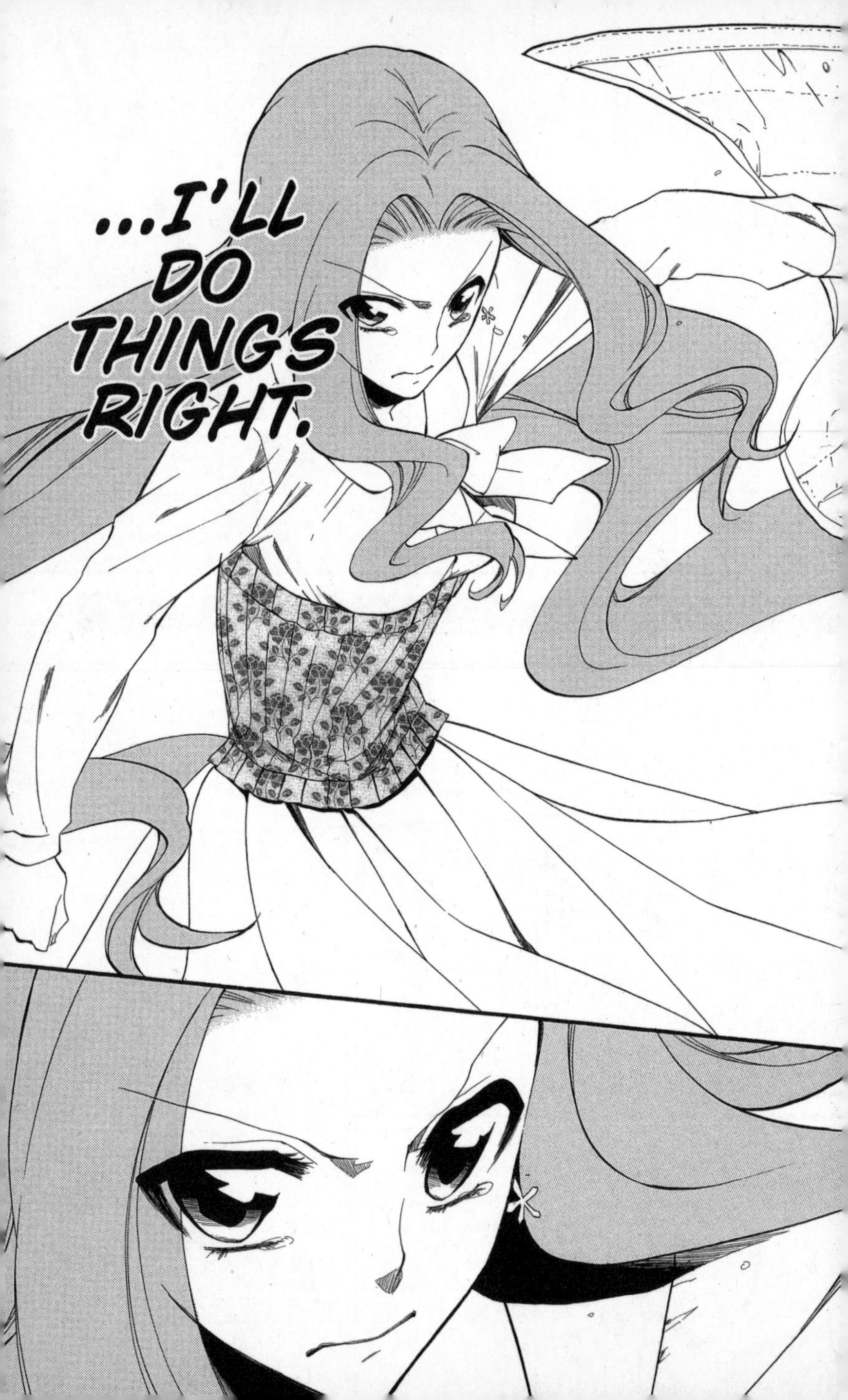
...I'LL DO THINGS RIGHT.

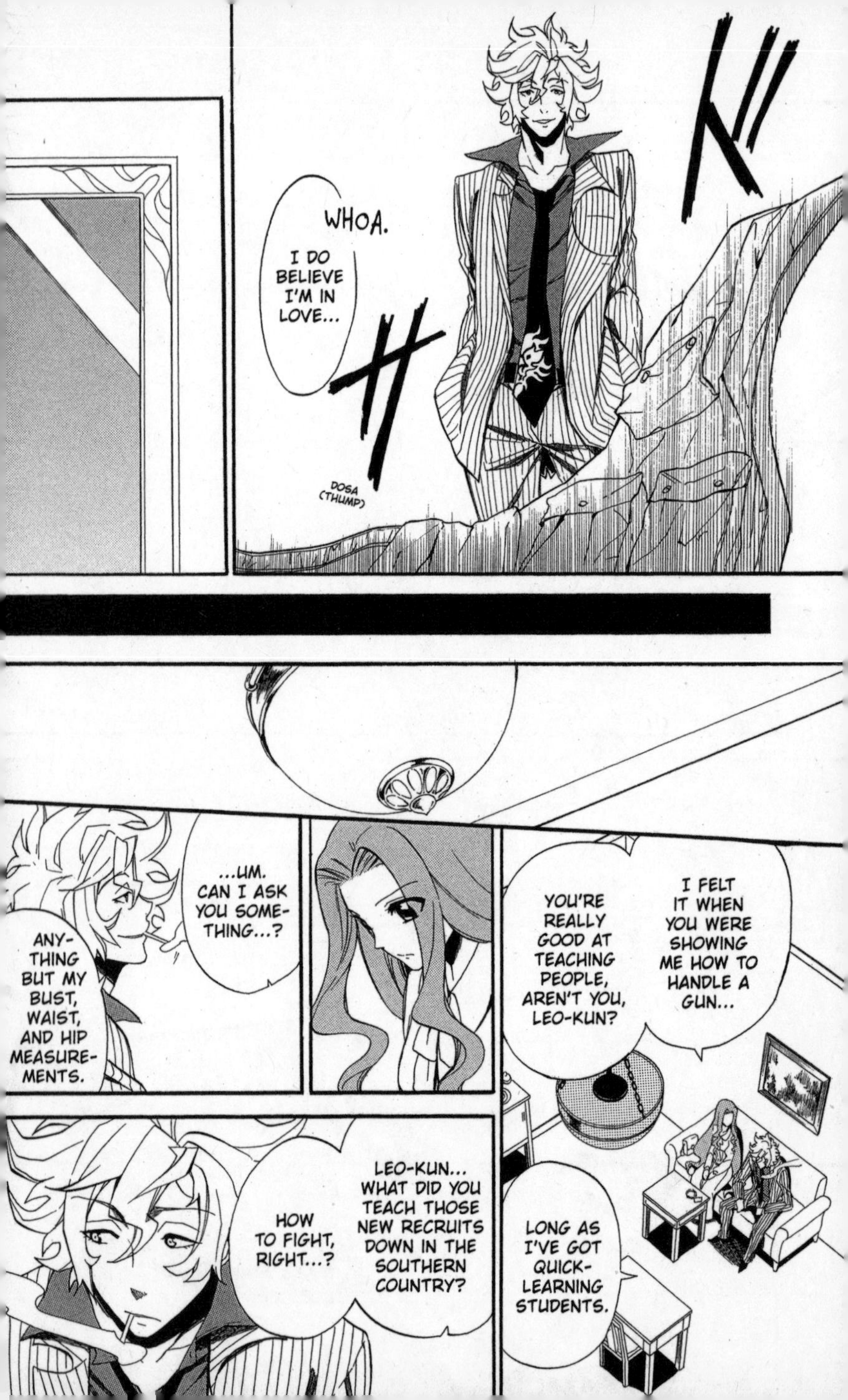
WHOA.
I DO BELIEVE I'M IN LOVE...
DOSA (THUMP)
I FELT IT WHEN YOU WERE SHOWING ME HOW TO HANDLE A GUN...
YOU'RE REALLY GOOD AT TEACHING PEOPLE, AREN'T YOU, LEO-KUN?
LONG AS I'VE GOT QUICK-LEARNING STUDENTS.
...UM. CAN I ASK YOU SOMETHING...?
ANYTHING BUT MY BUST, WAIST, AND HIP MEASUREMENTS.
LEO-KUN... WHAT DID YOU TEACH THOSE NEW RECRUITS DOWN IN THE SOUTHERN COUNTRY?
HOW TO FIGHT, RIGHT...?

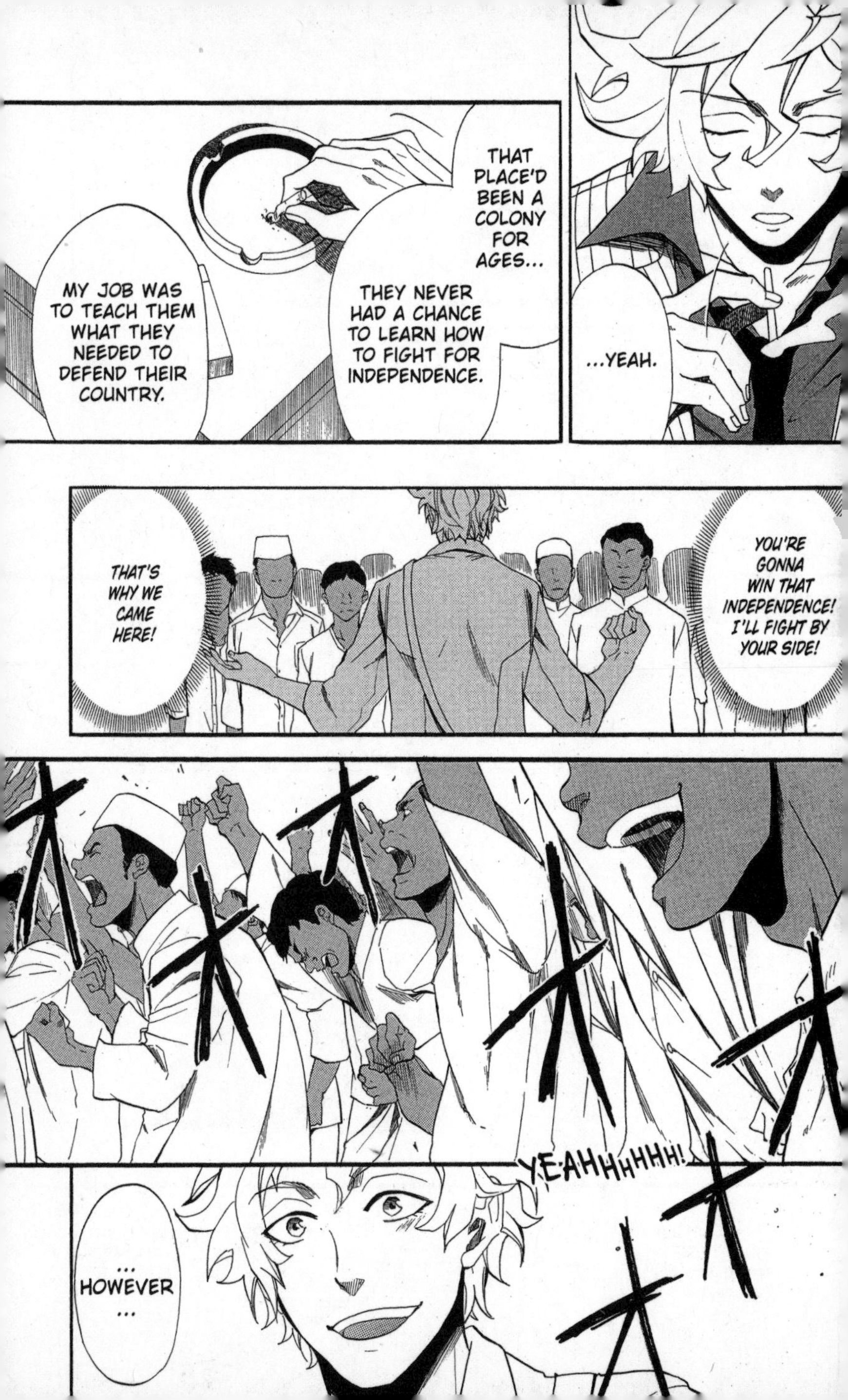
...YEAH.
THAT PLACE'D BEEN A COLONY FOR AGES...
THEY NEVER HAD A CHANCE TO LEARN HOW TO FIGHT FOR INDEPENDENCE.
MY JOB WAS TO TEACH THEM WHAT THEY NEEDED TO DEFEND THEIR COUNTRY.
YOU'RE GONNA WIN THAT INDEPENDENCE! I'LL FIGHT BY YOUR SIDE!
THAT'S WHY WE CAME HERE!
YEAHHHHHH!
...HOWEVER...

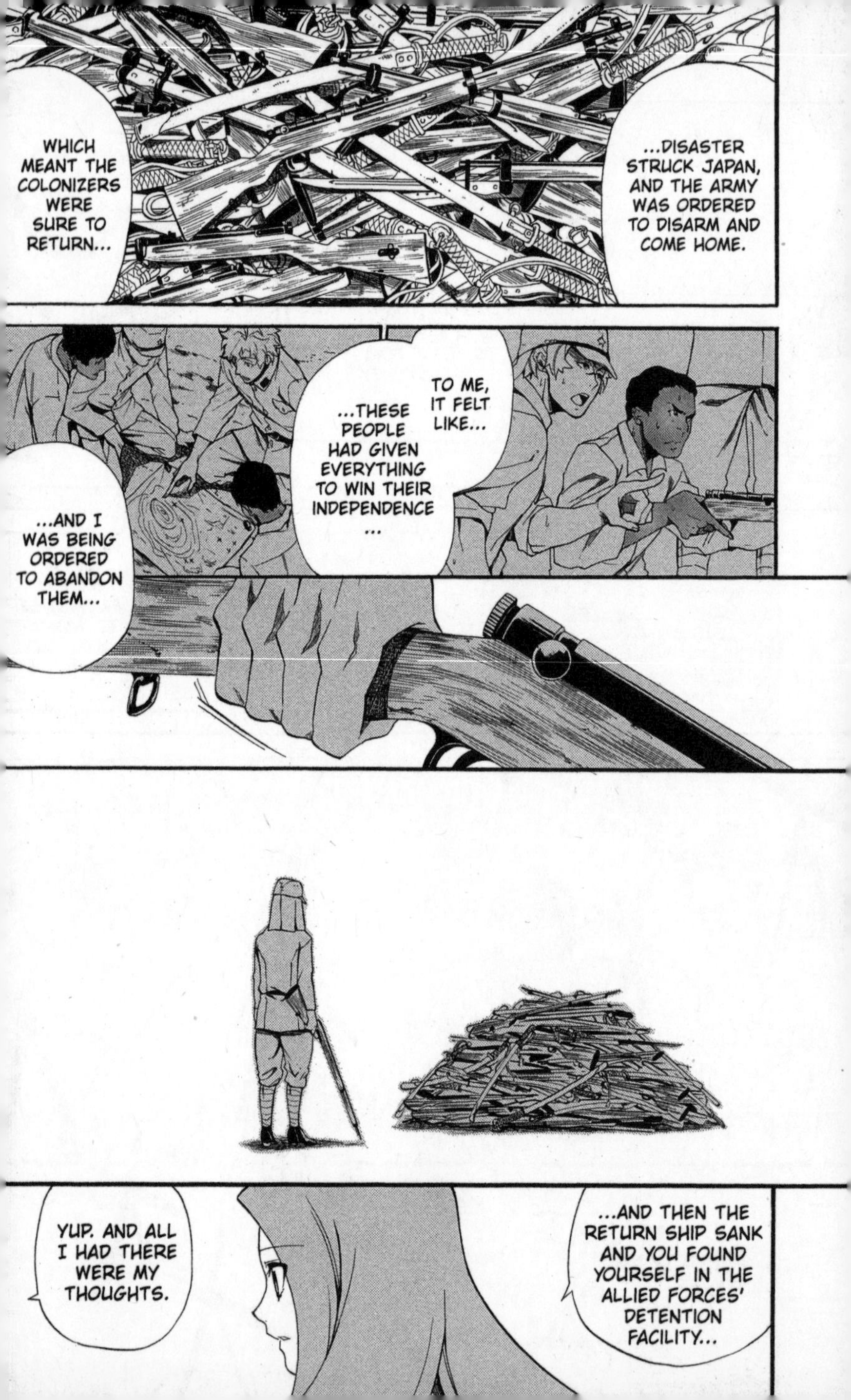
...DISASTER STRUCK JAPAN, AND THE ARMY WAS ORDERED TO DISARM AND COME HOME.
WHICH MEANT THE COLONIZERS WERE SURE TO RETURN...
TO ME, IT FELT LIKE...
...THESE PEOPLE HAD GIVEN EVERYTHING TO WIN THEIR INDEPENDENCE ...
...AND I WAS BEING ORDERED TO ABANDON THEM...
...AND THEN THE RETURN SHIP SANK AND YOU FOUND YOURSELF IN THE ALLIED FORCES' DETENTION FACILITY...
YUP. AND ALL I HAD THERE WERE MY THOUGHTS.

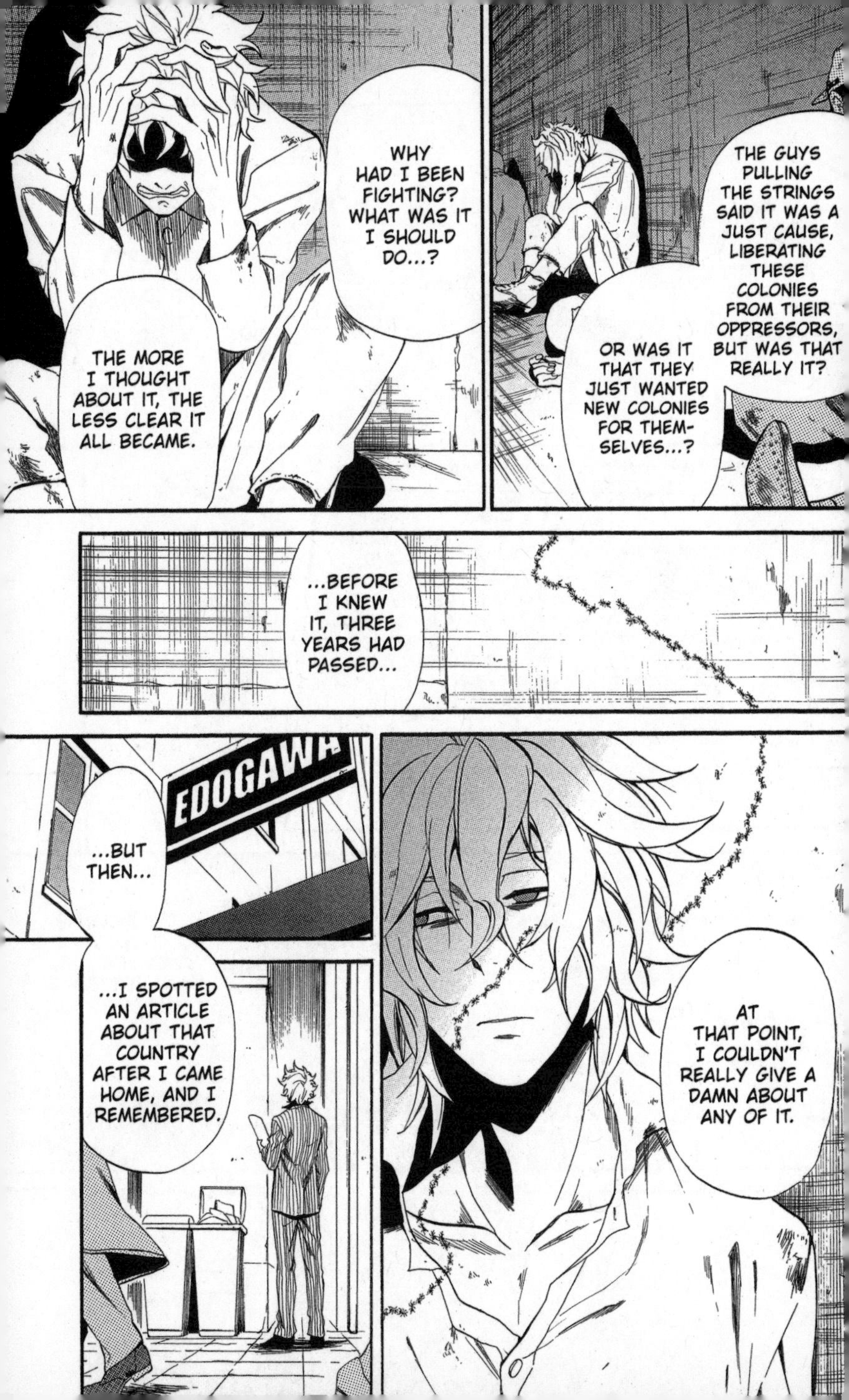
THE GUYS PULLING THE STRINGS SAID IT WAS A JUST CAUSE, LIBERATING THESE COLONIES FROM THEIR OPPRESSORS, BUT WAS THAT REALLY IT?
OR WAS IT THAT THEY JUST WANTED NEW COLONIES FOR THEMSELVES...?
WHY HAD I BEEN FIGHTING? WHAT WAS IT I SHOULD DO...?
THE MORE I THOUGHT ABOUT IT, THE LESS CLEAR IT ALL BECAME.
...BEFORE I KNEW IT, THREE YEARS HAD PASSED...
AT THAT POINT, I COULDN'T REALLY GIVE A DAMN ABOUT ANY OF IT.
EDOGAWA
...BUT THEN...
...I SPOTTED AN ARTICLE ABOUT THAT COUNTRY AFTER I CAME HOME, AND I REMEMBERED.

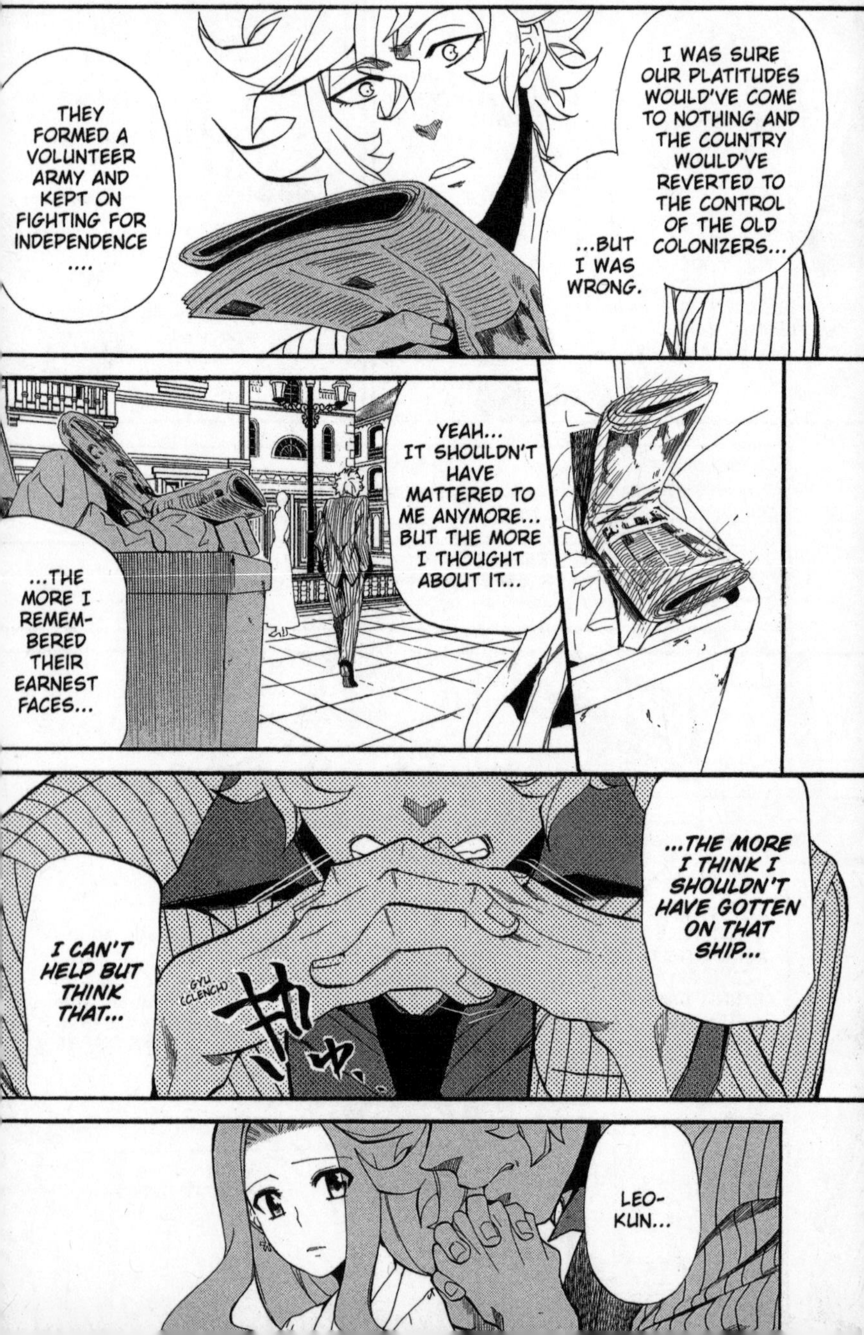
I WAS SURE OUR PLATITUDES WOULD'VE COME TO NOTHING AND THE COUNTRY WOULD'VE REVERTED TO THE CONTROL OF THE OLD COLONIZERS...
...BUT I WAS WRONG.
THEY FORMED A VOLUNTEER ARMY AND KEPT ON FIGHTING FOR INDEPENDENCE....
YEAH... IT SHOULDN'T HAVE MATTERED TO ME ANYMORE... BUT THE MORE I THOUGHT ABOUT IT...
...THE MORE I REMEMBERED THEIR EARNEST FACES...
...THE MORE I THINK I SHOULDN'T HAVE GOTTEN ON THAT SHIP...
GYU (CLENCH)
I CAN'T HELP BUT THINK THAT...
LEO-KUN...

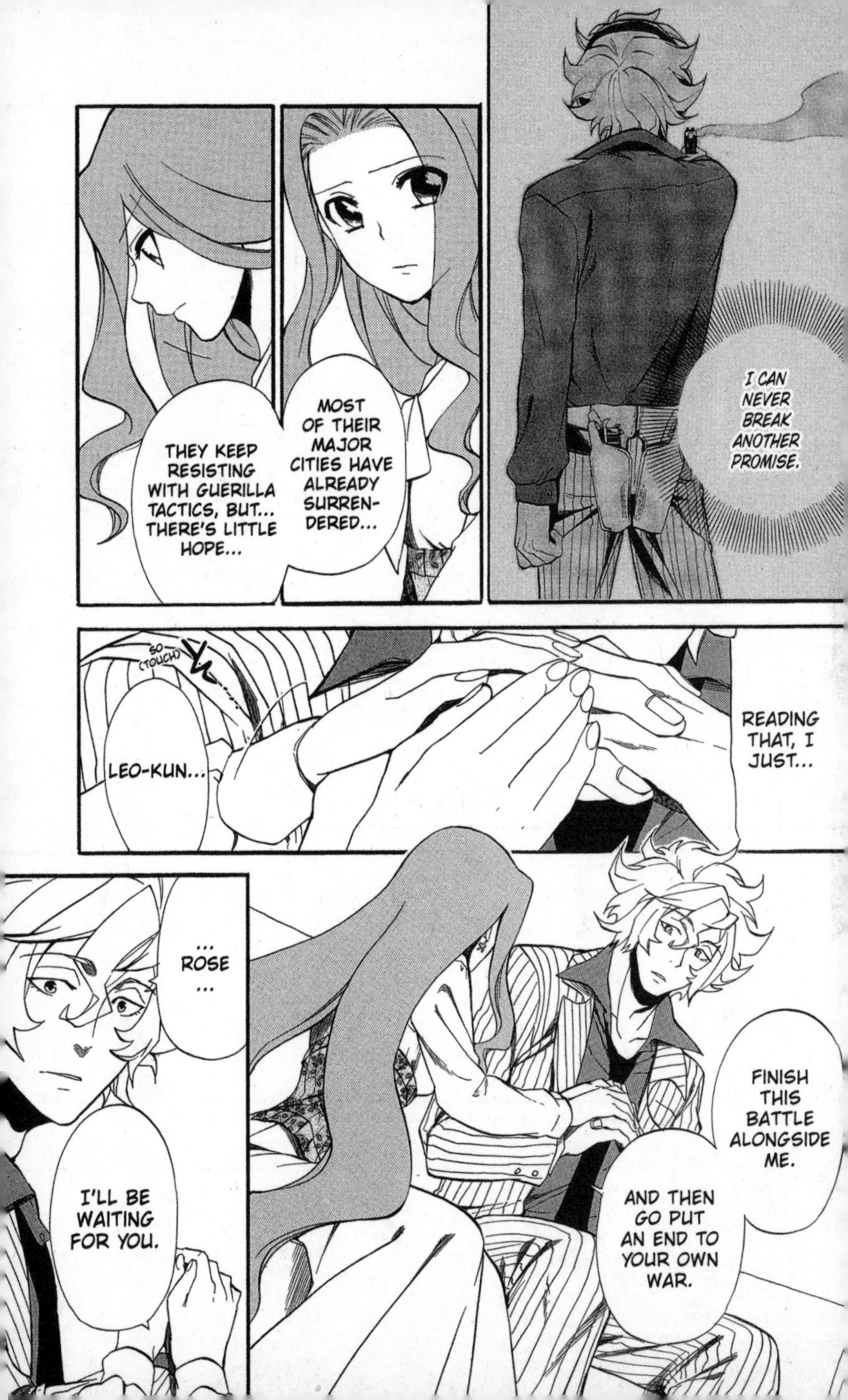
I CAN NEVER BREAK ANOTHER PROMISE.
MOST OF THEIR MAJOR CITIES HAVE ALREADY SURRENDERED...
THEY KEEP RESISTING WITH GUERILLA TACTICS, BUT... THERE'S LITTLE HOPE...
READING THAT, I JUST...
SO- (TOUCH)
LEO-KUN...
FINISH THIS BATTLE ALONGSIDE ME.
AND THEN GO PUT AN END TO YOUR OWN WAR.
... ROSE ...
I'LL BE WAITING FOR YOU.

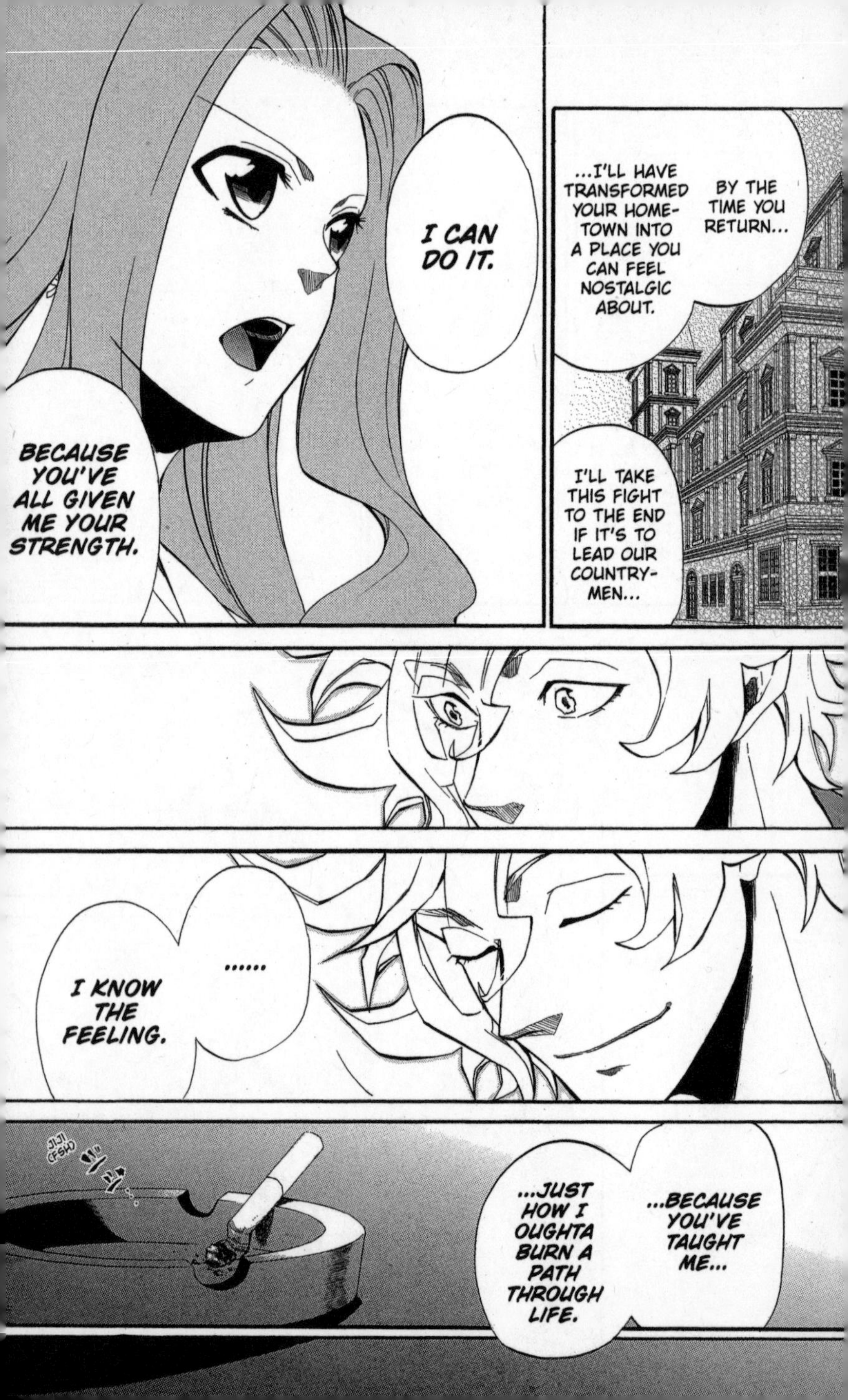
BY THE TIME YOU RETURN...
...I'LL HAVE TRANSFORMED YOUR HOME-TOWN INTO A PLACE YOU CAN FEEL NOSTALGIC ABOUT.
I'LL TAKE THIS FIGHT TO THE END IF IT'S TO LEAD OUR COUNTRY-MEN...
I CAN DO IT.
BECAUSE YOU'VE ALL GIVEN ME YOUR STRENGTH.
......
I KNOW THE FEELING.
...BECAUSE YOU'VE TAUGHT ME...
...JUST HOW I OUGHTA BURN A PATH THROUGH LIFE.
JIJI (FSH)

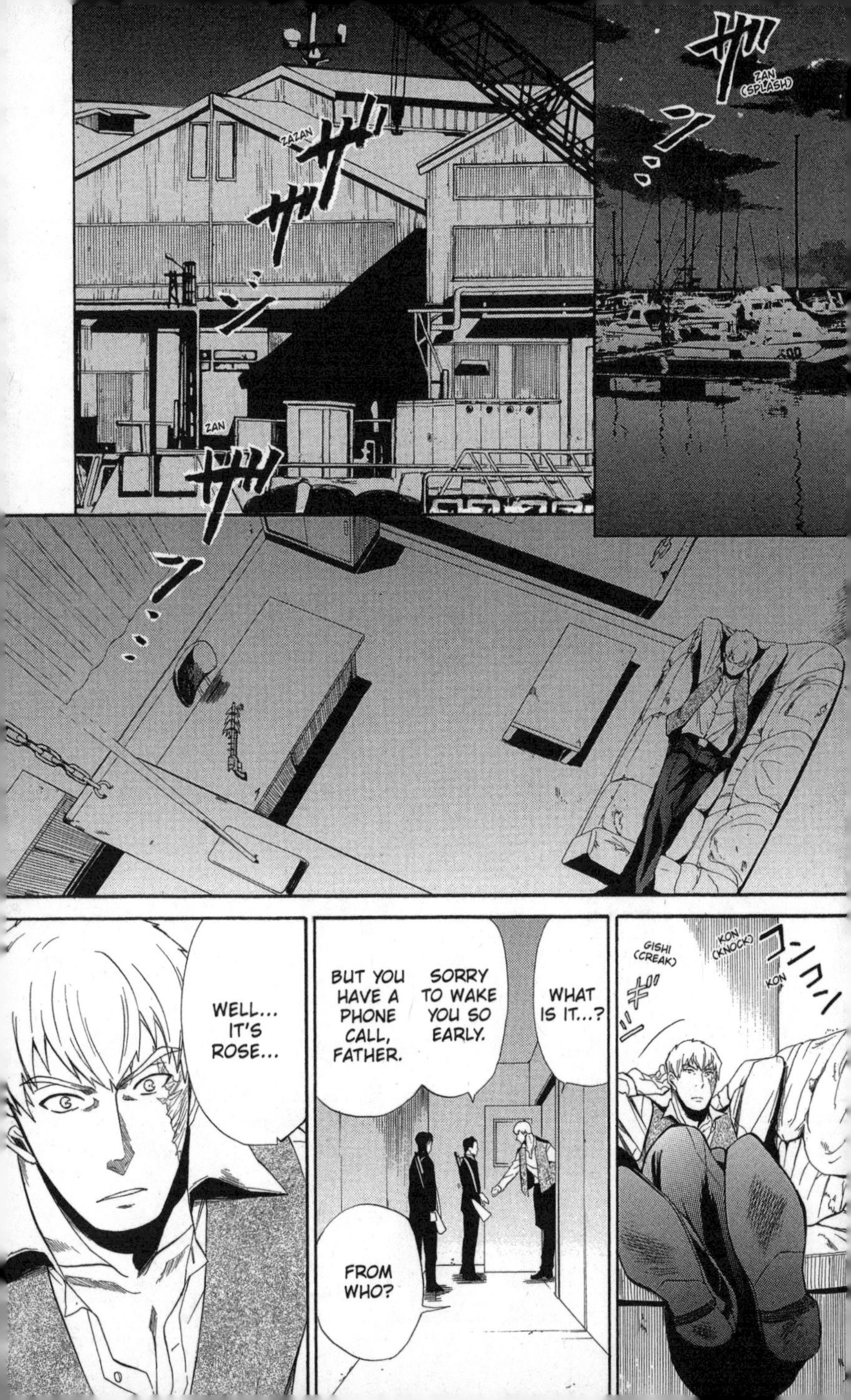
ZAN
(SPLASH)
ZAZAN
ZAN
KON
(KNOCK)
KON
GISHI
(CREAK)
WHAT IS IT...?
SORRY TO WAKE YOU SO EARLY.
BUT YOU HAVE A PHONE CALL, FATHER.
FROM WHO?
WELL... IT'S ROSE...

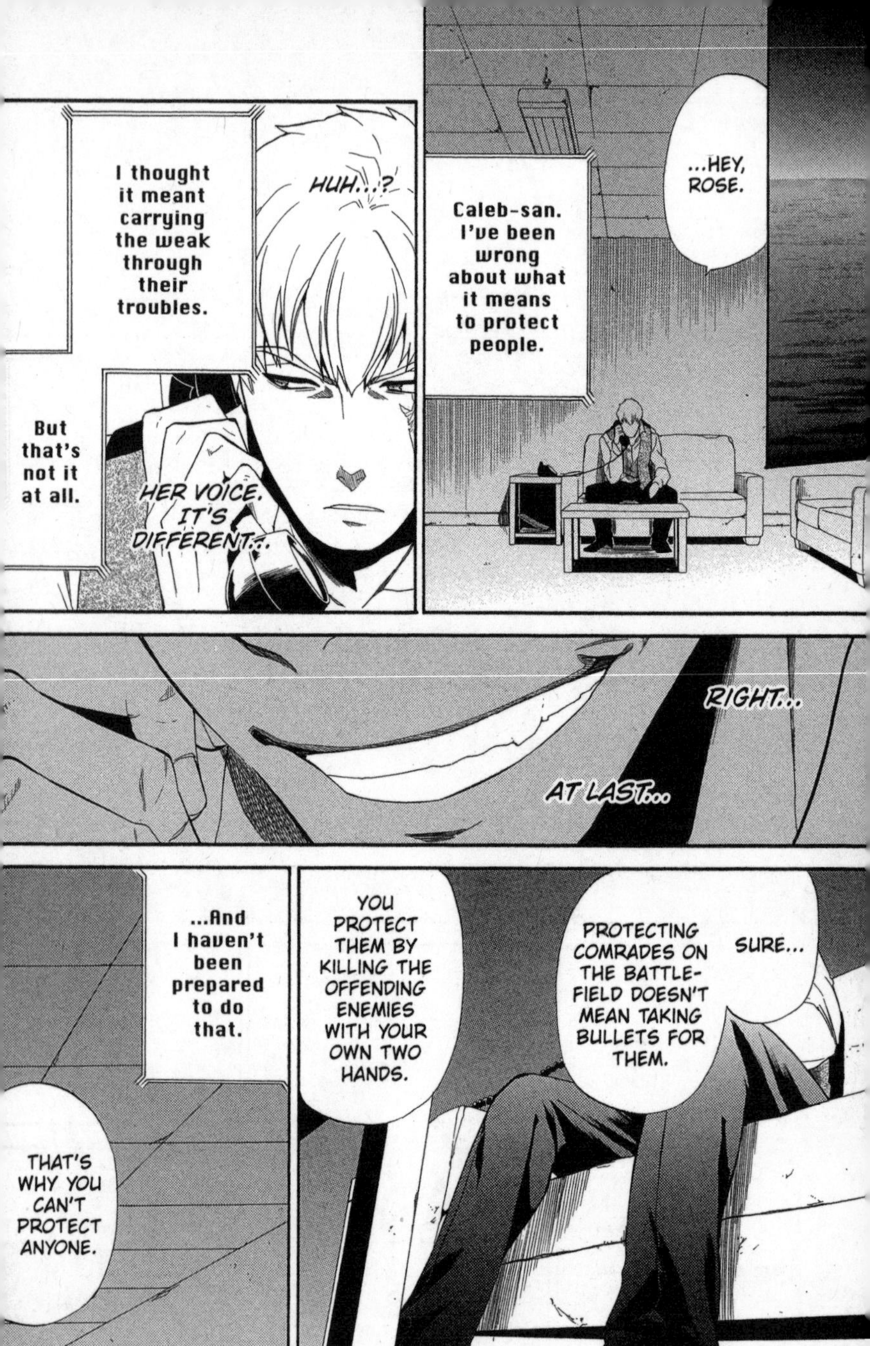
...HEY, ROSE.
Caleb-san. I've been wrong about what it means to protect people.
HUH...?
I thought it meant carrying the weak through their troubles.
HER VOICE. IT'S DIFFERENT...
But that's not it at all.
RIGHT...
AT LAST...
SURE...
PROTECTING COMRADES ON THE BATTLE-FIELD DOESN'T MEAN TAKING BULLETS FOR THEM.
YOU PROTECT THEM BY KILLING THE OFFENDING ENEMIES WITH YOUR OWN TWO HANDS.
...And I haven't been prepared to do that.
THAT'S WHY YOU CAN'T PROTECT ANYONE.

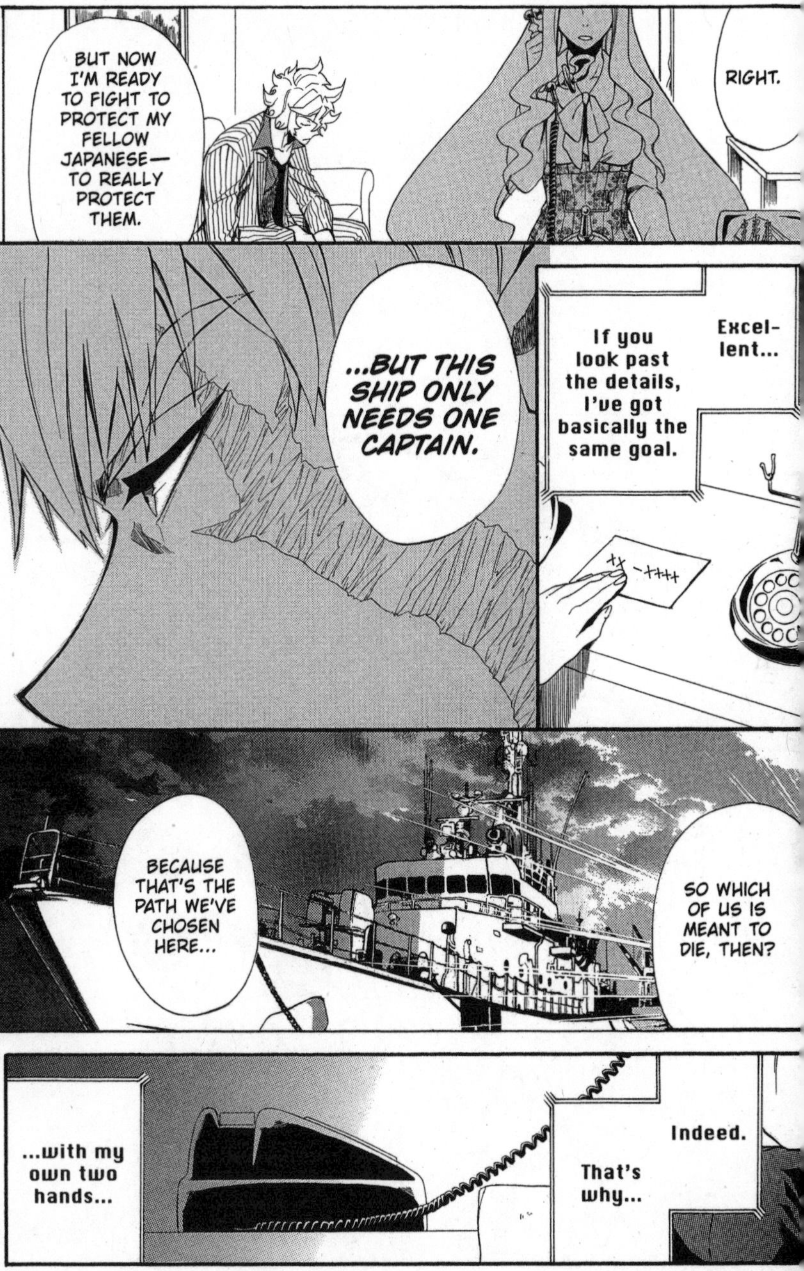
RIGHT.
BUT NOW I'M READY TO FIGHT TO PROTECT MY FELLOW JAPANESE—TO REALLY PROTECT THEM.
Excel-lent...
If you look past the details, I've got basically the same goal.
...BUT THIS SHIP ONLY NEEDS ONE CAPTAIN.
SO WHICH OF US IS MEANT TO DIE, THEN?
BECAUSE THAT'S THE PATH WE'VE CHOSEN HERE...
Indeed.
That's why...
...with my own two hands...

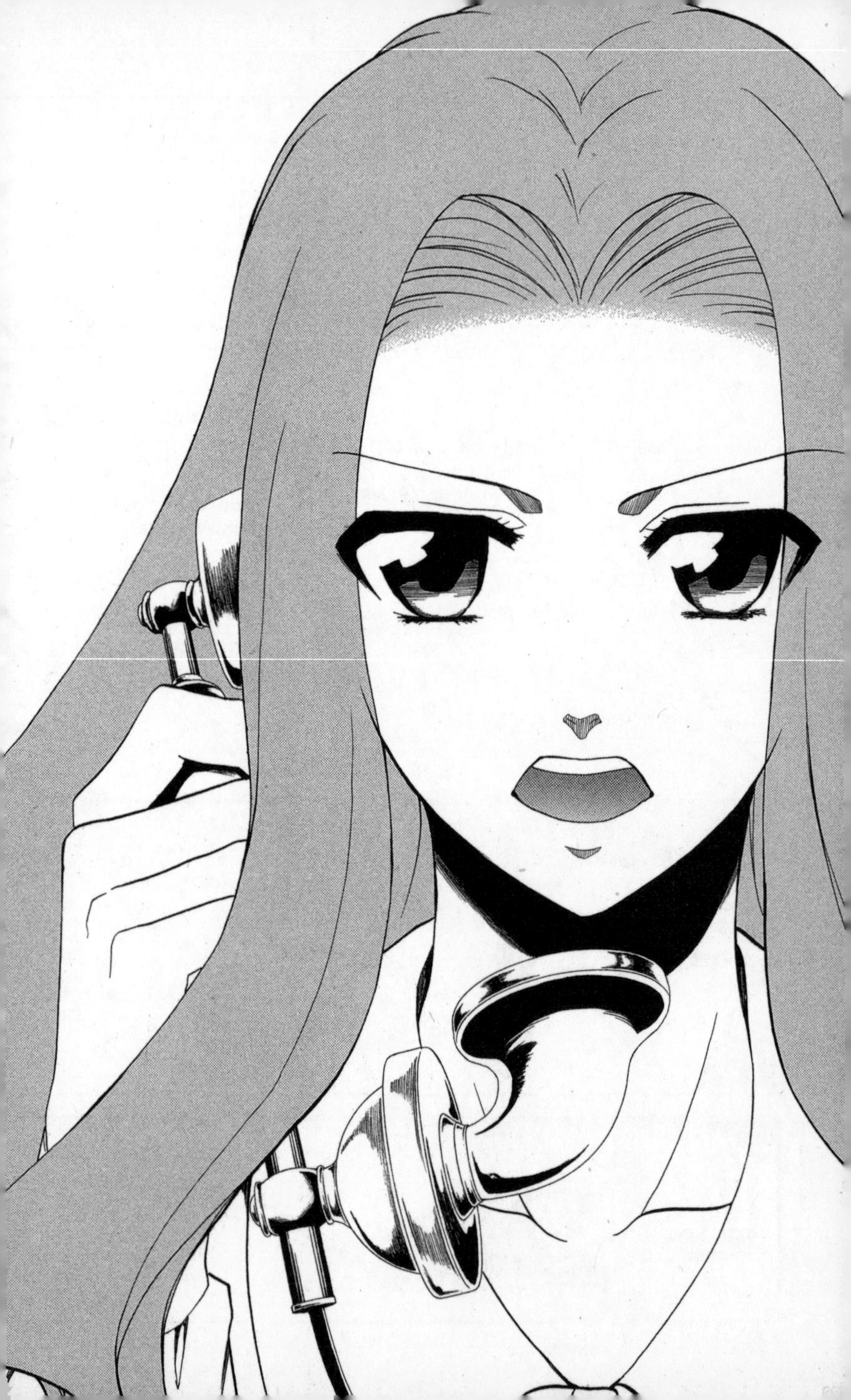

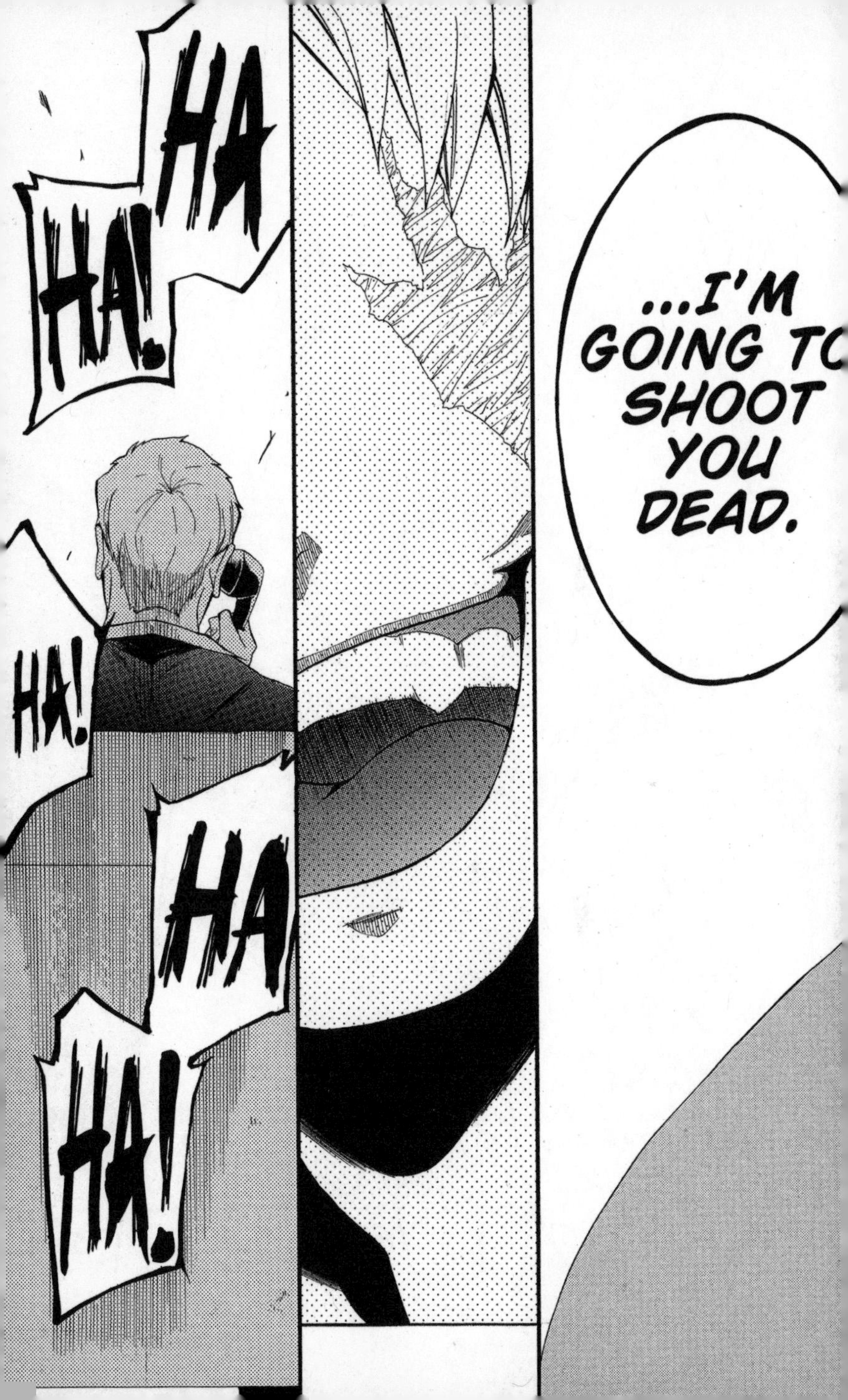
...I'M GOING TO SHOOT YOU DEAD.
HA
HA!
HA!
HA
HA!

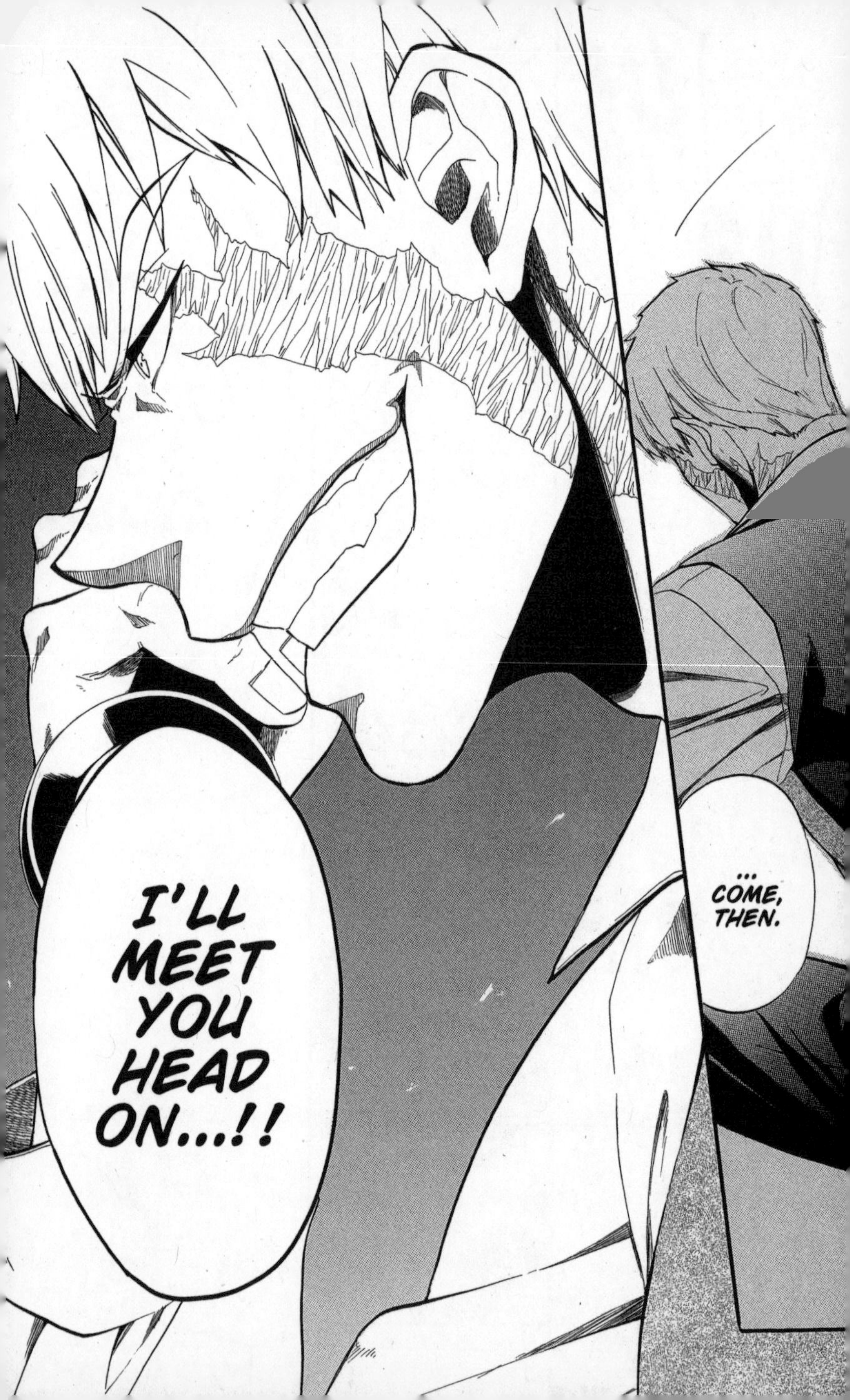
...COME, THEN.
I'LL MEET YOU HEAD ON...!!

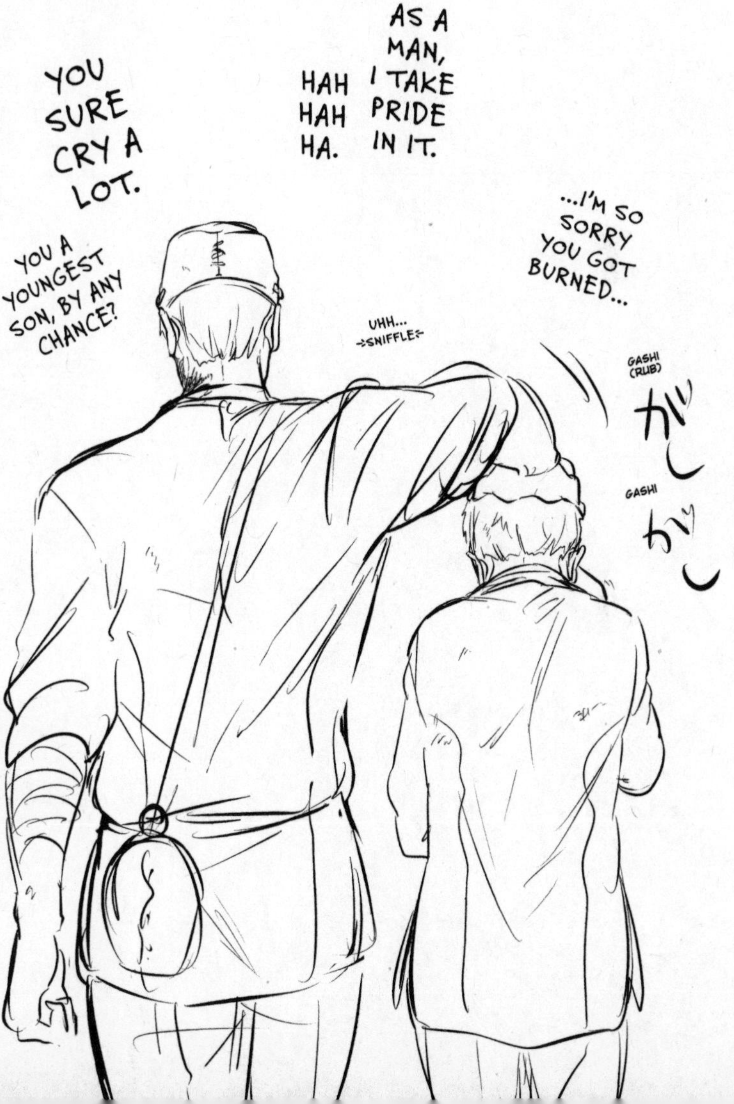
AS A MAN, I TAKE PRIDE IN IT.
HAH HAH HA.
YOU SURE CRY A LOT.
...I'M SO SORRY YOU GOT BURNED...
GASHI (RUB)
がし
GASHI
がし
UHH... -SNIFFLE-
YOU A YOUNGEST SON, BY ANY CHANCE?

Scene: 17

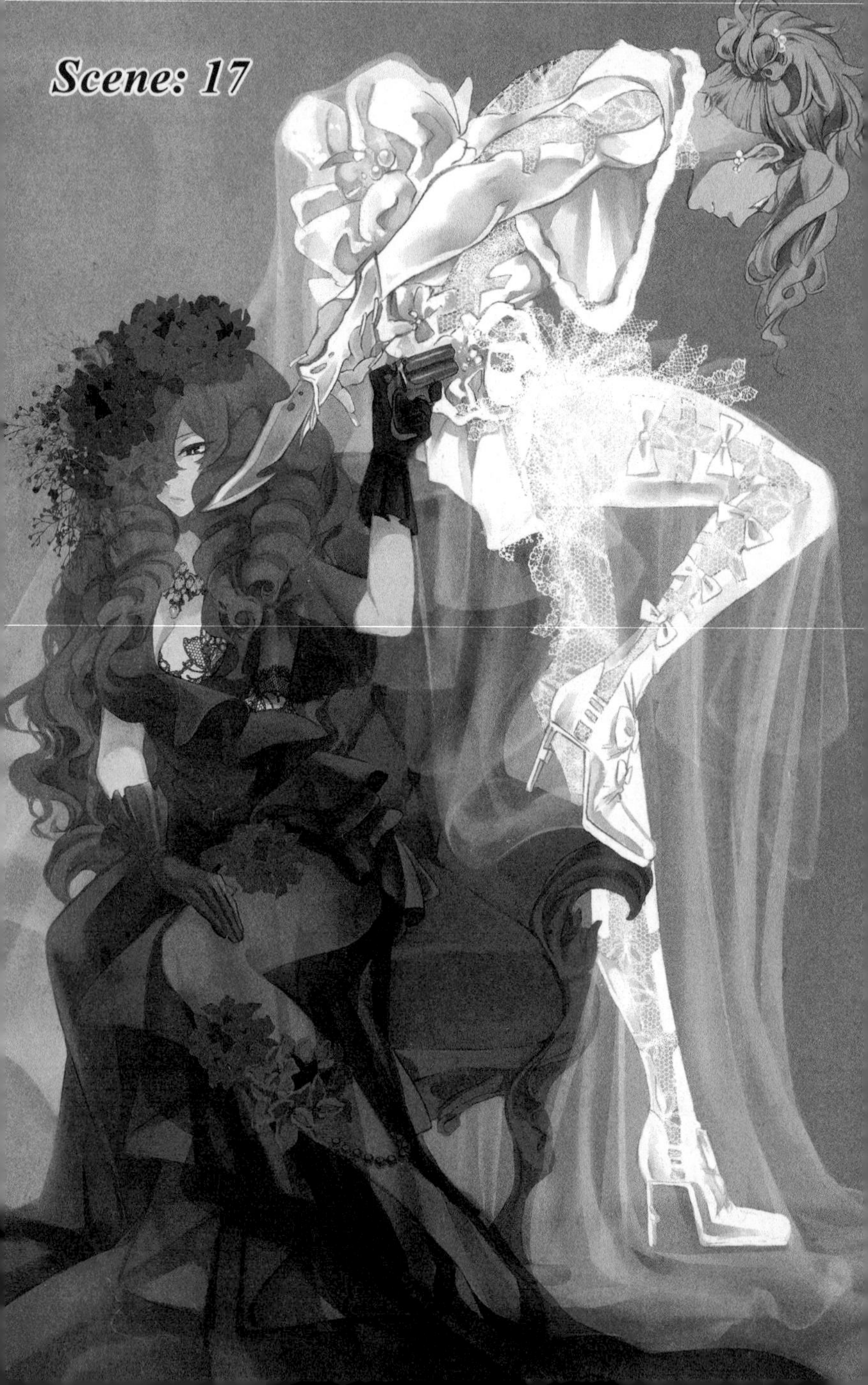

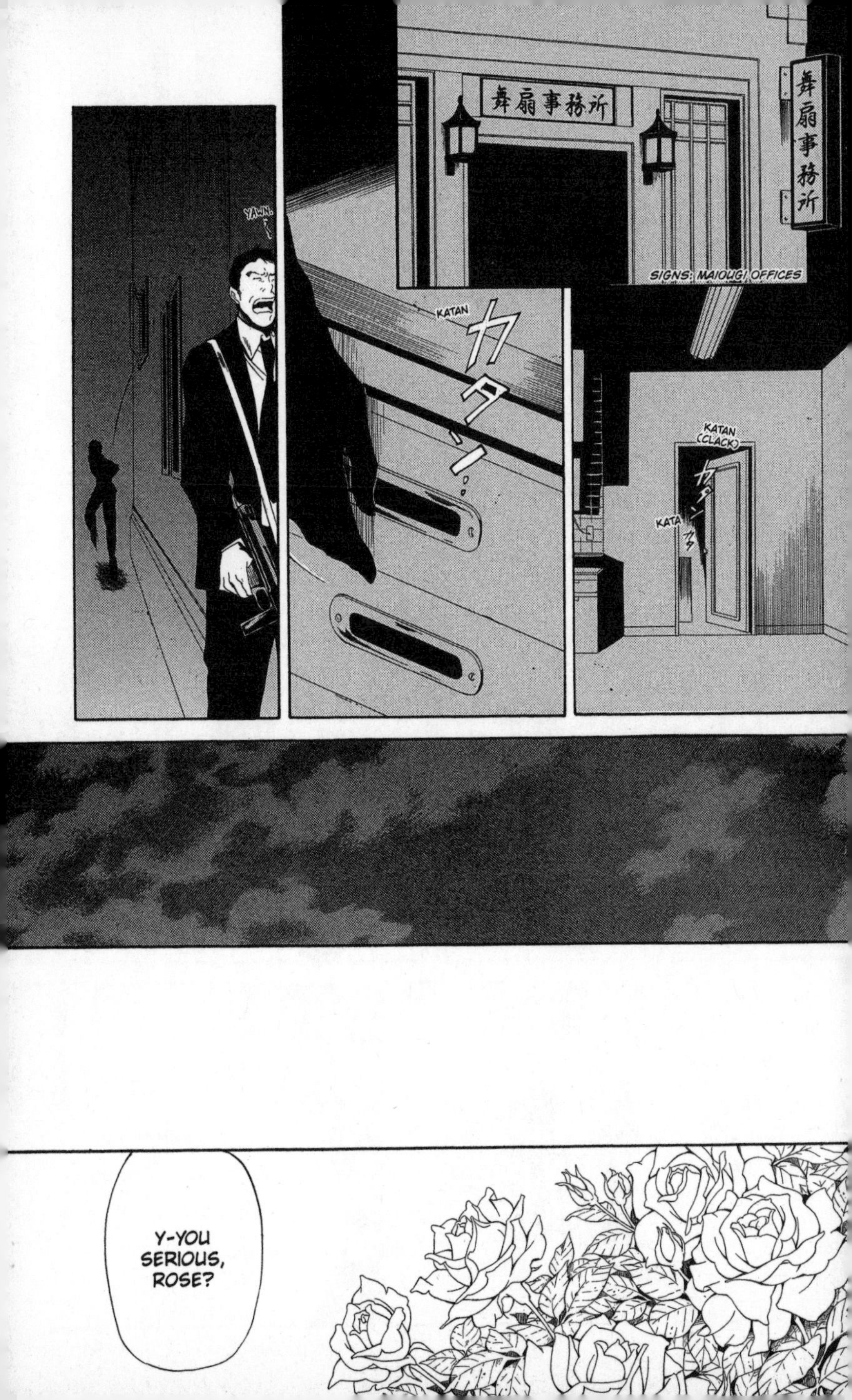
舞扇事務所
舞扇事務所
SIGNS: MAIOUGI OFFICES
KATAN (CLACK)
カタン
KATA
カタ
KATAN
カタン!
YAWN.
Y-YOU SERIOUS, ROSE?

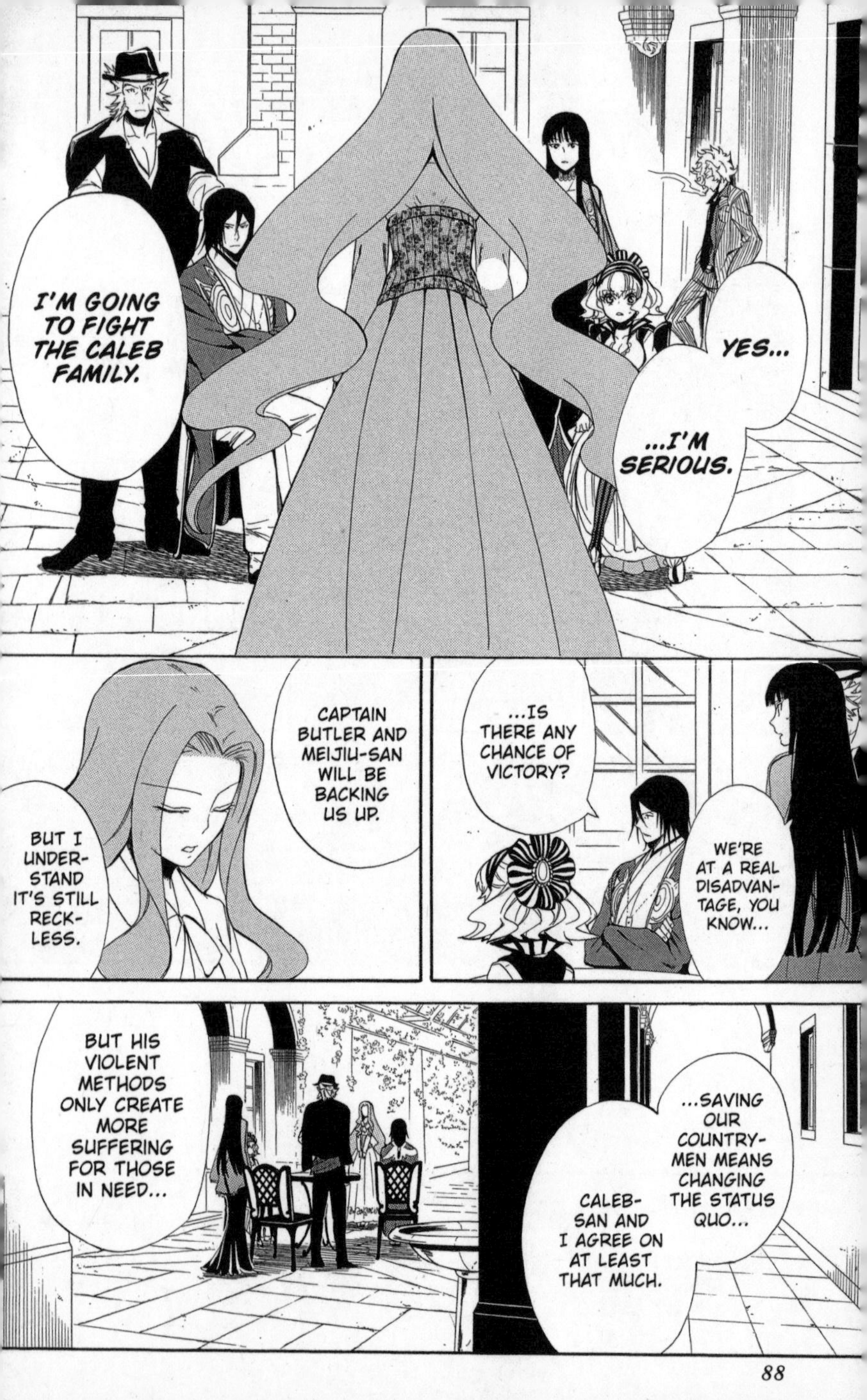
YES... ...I'M SERIOUS.
I'M GOING TO FIGHT THE CALEB FAMILY.
...IS THERE ANY CHANCE OF VICTORY?
WE'RE AT A REAL DISADVANTAGE, YOU KNOW...
CAPTAIN BUTLER AND MEIJIU-SAN WILL BE BACKING US UP.
BUT I UNDERSTAND IT'S STILL RECKLESS.
...SAVING OUR COUNTRYMEN MEANS CHANGING THE STATUS QUO...
CALEB-SAN AND I AGREE ON AT LEAST THAT MUCH.
BUT HIS VIOLENT METHODS ONLY CREATE MORE SUFFERING FOR THOSE IN NEED...

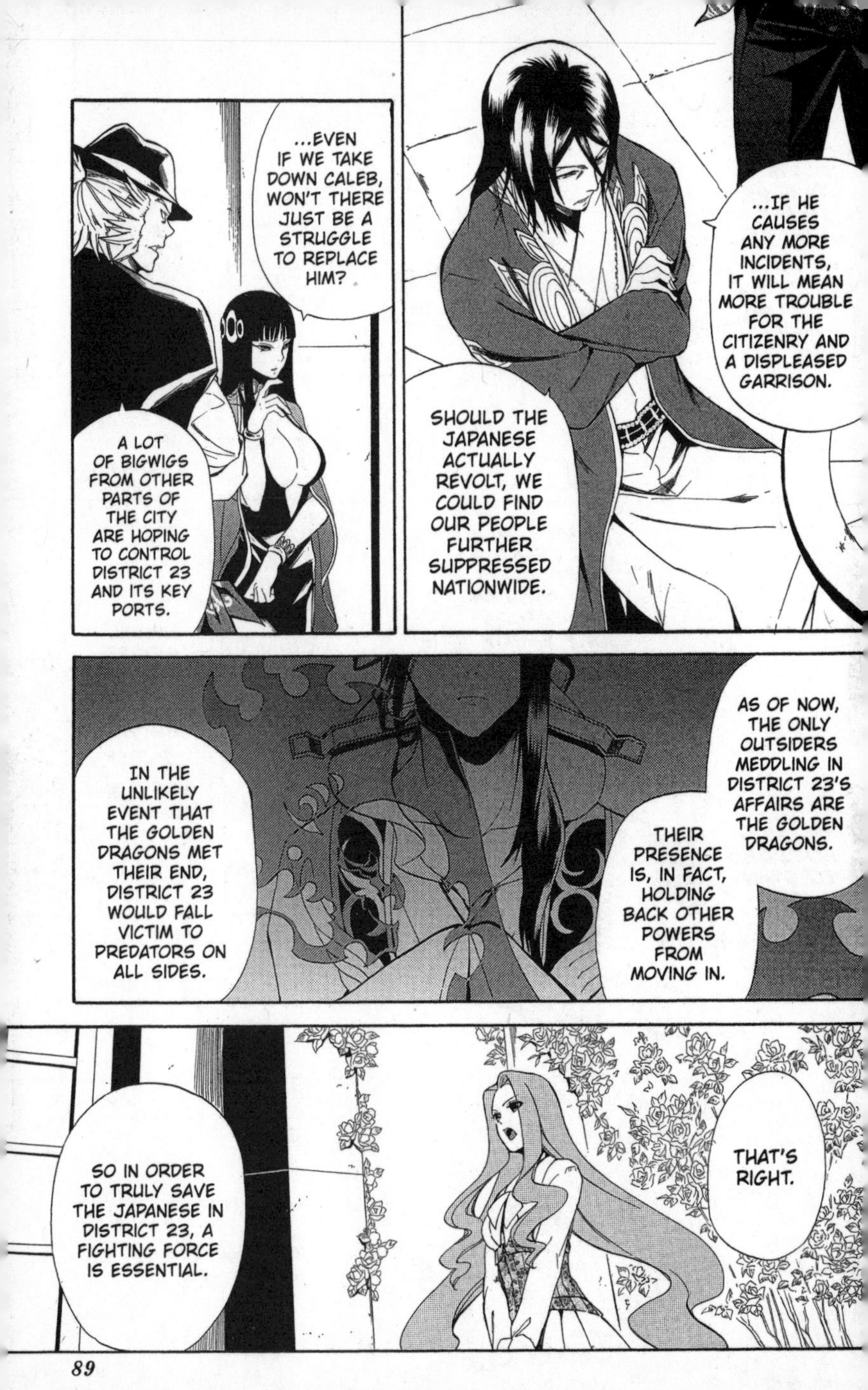
...IF HE CAUSES ANY MORE INCIDENTS, IT WILL MEAN MORE TROUBLE FOR THE CITIZENRY AND A DISPLEASED GARRISON.
SHOULD THE JAPANESE ACTUALLY REVOLT, WE COULD FIND OUR PEOPLE FURTHER SUPPRESSED NATIONWIDE.
...EVEN IF WE TAKE DOWN CALEB, WON'T THERE JUST BE A STRUGGLE TO REPLACE HIM?
A LOT OF BIGWIGS FROM OTHER PARTS OF THE CITY ARE HOPING TO CONTROL DISTRICT 23 AND ITS KEY PORTS.
AS OF NOW, THE ONLY OUTSIDERS MEDDLING IN DISTRICT 23'S AFFAIRS ARE THE GOLDEN DRAGONS.
THEIR PRESENCE IS, IN FACT, HOLDING BACK OTHER POWERS FROM MOVING IN.
IN THE UNLIKELY EVENT THAT THE GOLDEN DRAGONS MET THEIR END, DISTRICT 23 WOULD FALL VICTIM TO PREDATORS ON ALL SIDES.
THAT'S RIGHT.
SO IN ORDER TO TRULY SAVE THE JAPANESE IN DISTRICT 23, A FIGHTING FORCE IS ESSENTIAL.

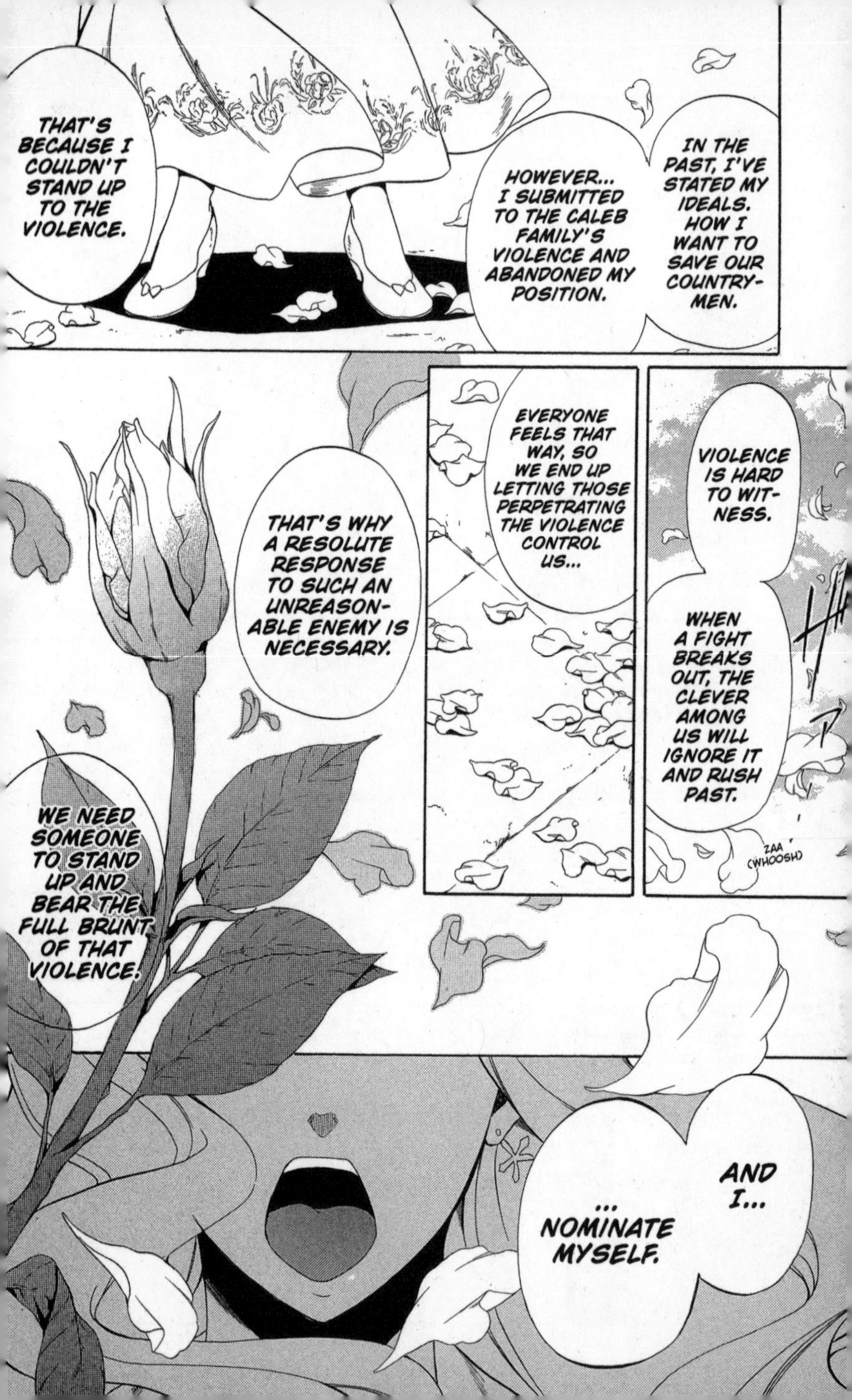
IN THE PAST, I'VE STATED MY IDEALS. HOW I WANT TO SAVE OUR COUNTRYMEN.
HOWEVER... I SUBMITTED TO THE CALEB FAMILY'S VIOLENCE AND ABANDONED MY POSITION.
THAT'S BECAUSE I COULDN'T STAND UP TO THE VIOLENCE.
VIOLENCE IS HARD TO WITNESS.
WHEN A FIGHT BREAKS OUT, THE CLEVER AMONG US WILL IGNORE IT AND RUSH PAST.
ZAA (WHOOSH)
EVERYONE FEELS THAT WAY, SO WE END UP LETTING THOSE PERPETRATING THE VIOLENCE CONTROL US...
THAT'S WHY A RESOLUTE RESPONSE TO SUCH AN UNREASONABLE ENEMY IS NECESSARY.
WE NEED SOMEONE TO STAND UP AND BEAR THE FULL BRUNT OF THAT VIOLENCE.
AND I...
...NOMINATE MYSELF.

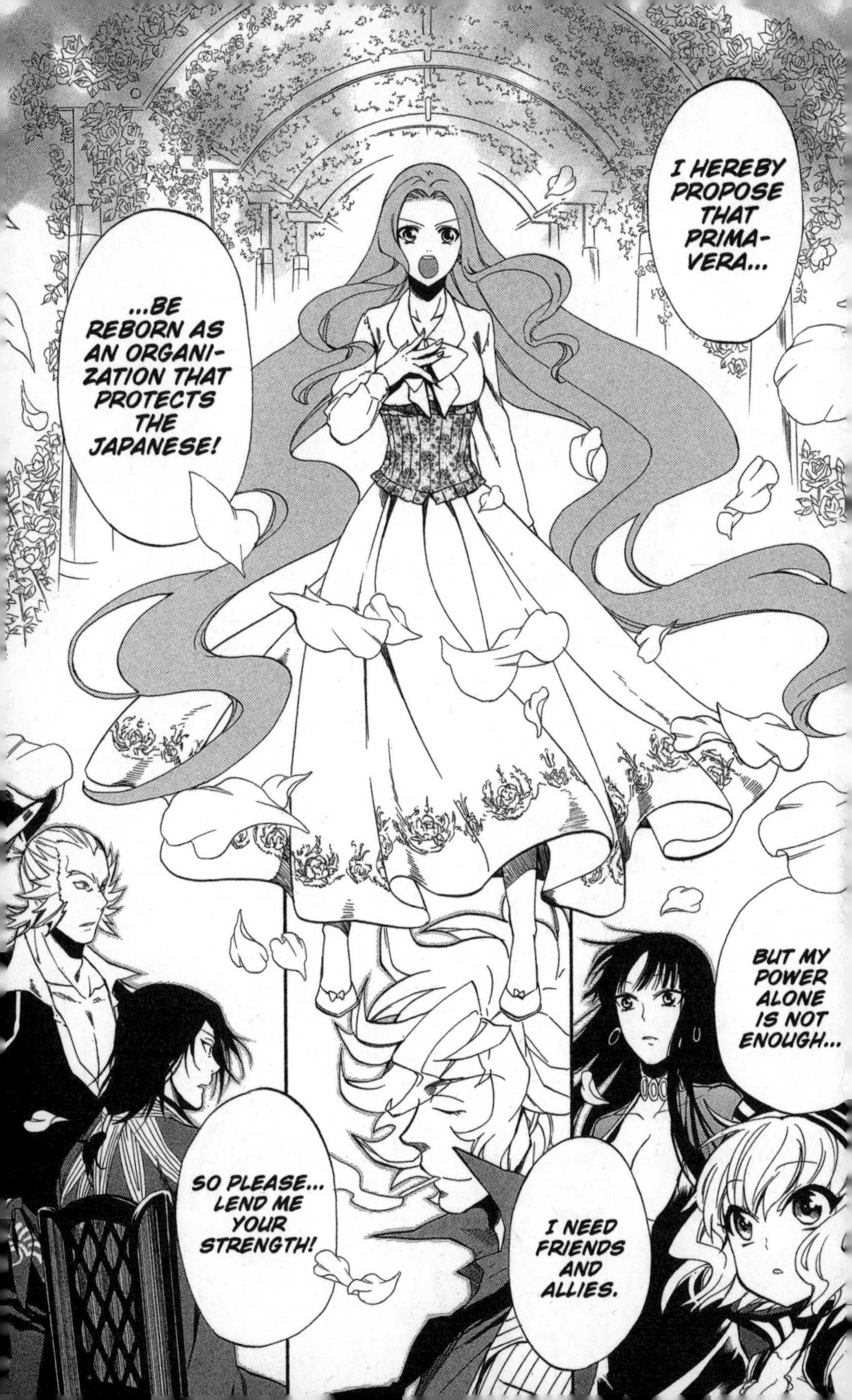
I HEREBY PROPOSE THAT PRIMA-VERA...
...BE REBORN AS AN ORGANI-ZATION THAT PROTECTS THE JAPANESE!
BUT MY POWER ALONE IS NOT ENOUGH...
I NEED FRIENDS AND ALLIES.
SO PLEASE... LEND ME YOUR STRENGTH!

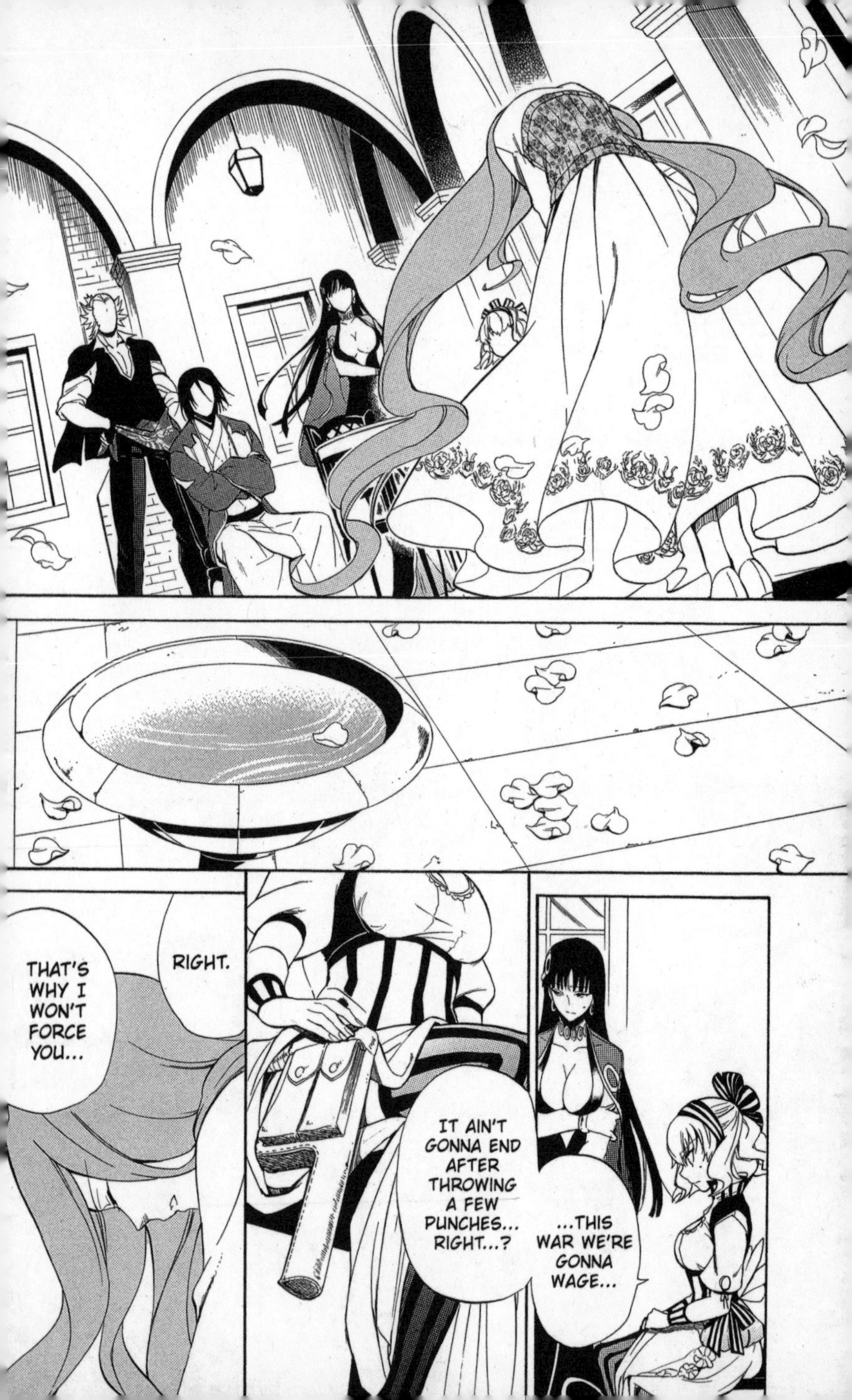
...THIS WAR WE'RE GONNA WAGE...
IT AIN'T GONNA END AFTER THROWING A FEW PUNCHES... RIGHT...?
RIGHT.
THAT'S WHY I WON'T FORCE YOU...

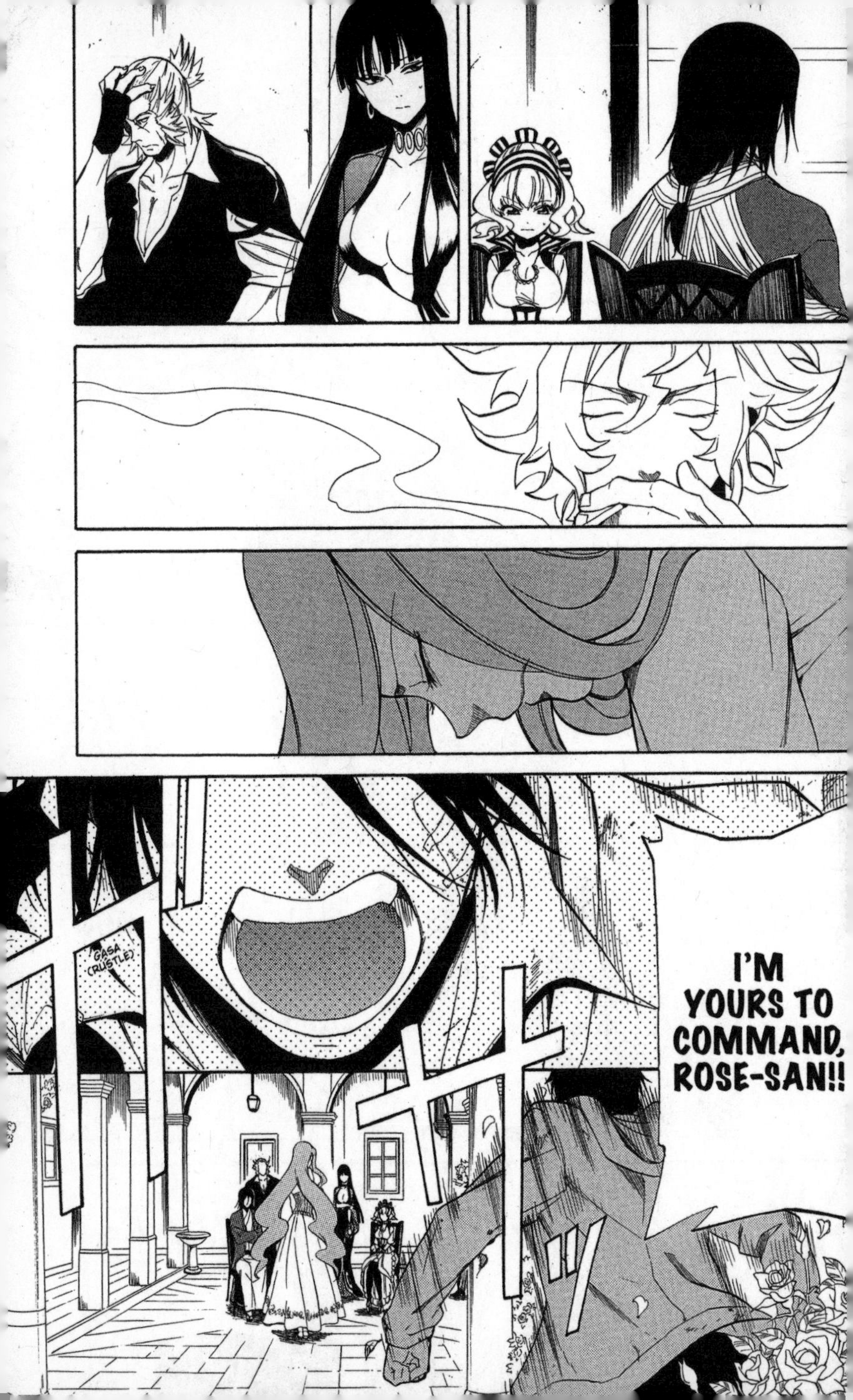
I'M YOURS TO COMMAND, ROSE-SAN!!
GASA (RUSTLE)

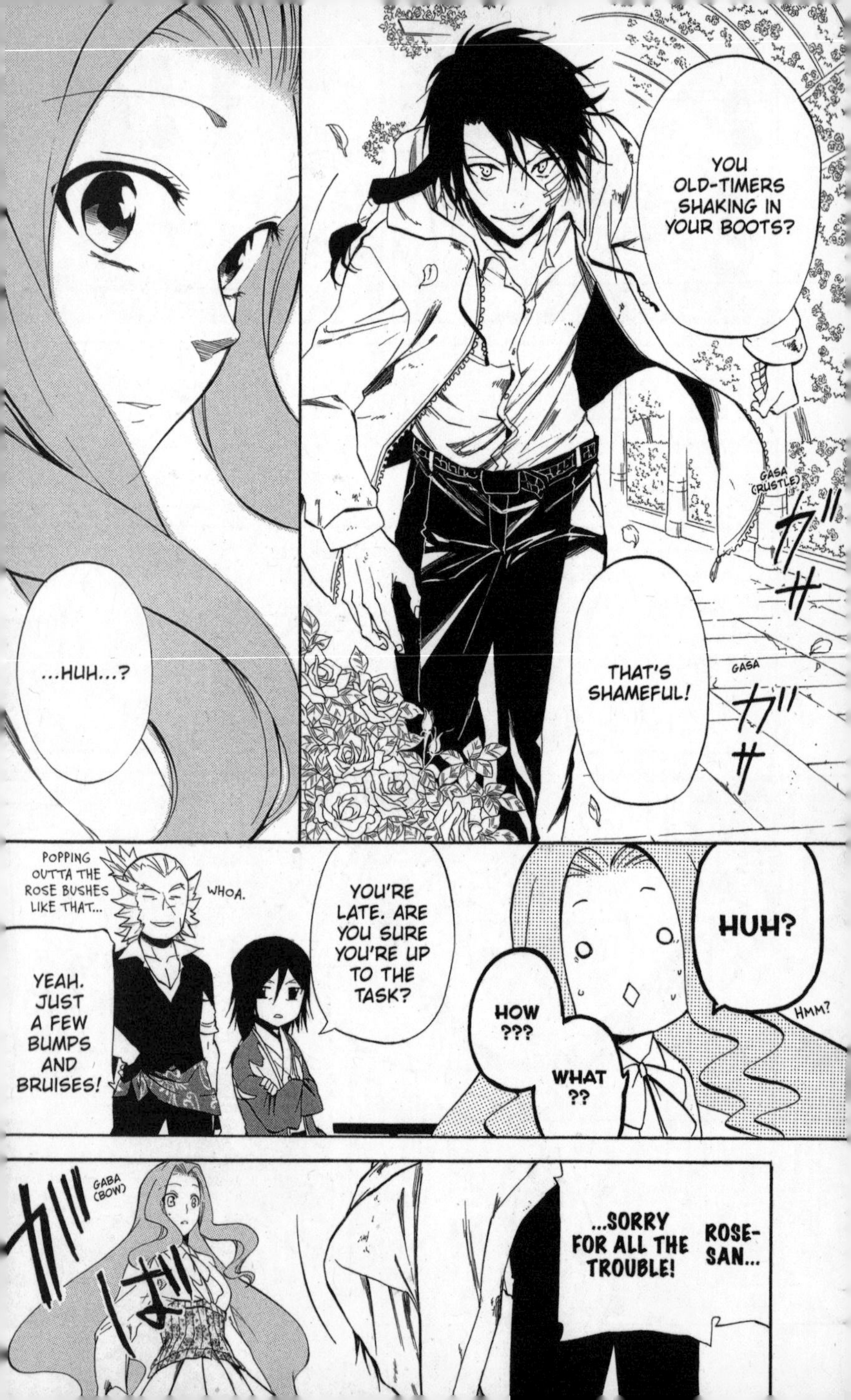
YOU OLD-TIMERS SHAKING IN YOUR BOOTS?
GASA (RUSTLE)
THAT'S SHAMEFUL!
GASA
...HUH...?
HUH?
HMM?
HOW ???
WHAT ??
YOU'RE LATE. ARE YOU SURE YOU'RE UP TO THE TASK?
WHOA.
POPPING OUTTA THE ROSE BUSHES LIKE THAT...
YEAH. JUST A FEW BUMPS AND BRUISES!
ROSE-SAN...
...SORRY FOR ALL THE TROUBLE!
GABA (BOW)

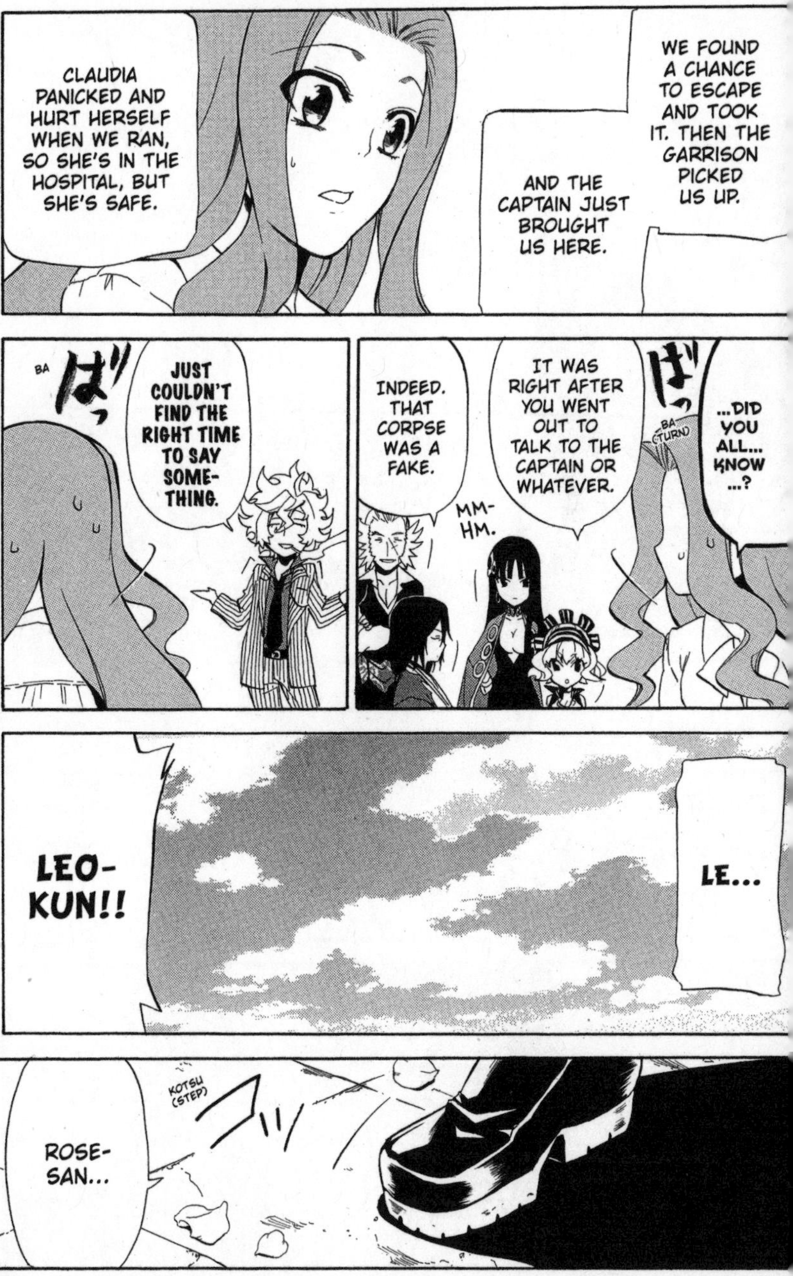
WE FOUND A CHANCE TO ESCAPE AND TOOK IT. THEN THE GARRISON PICKED US UP.
AND THE CAPTAIN JUST BROUGHT US HERE.
CLAUDIA PANICKED AND HURT HERSELF WHEN WE RAN, SO SHE'S IN THE HOSPITAL, BUT SHE'S SAFE.
BA (TURN)
...DID YOU ALL... KNOW ...?
IT WAS RIGHT AFTER YOU WENT OUT TO TALK TO THE CAPTAIN OR WHATEVER.
MM-HM.
INDEED. THAT CORPSE WAS A FAKE.
JUST COULDN'T FIND THE RIGHT TIME TO SAY SOME-THING.
BA
LE...
LEO-KUN!!
KOTSU (STEP)
ROSE-SAN...

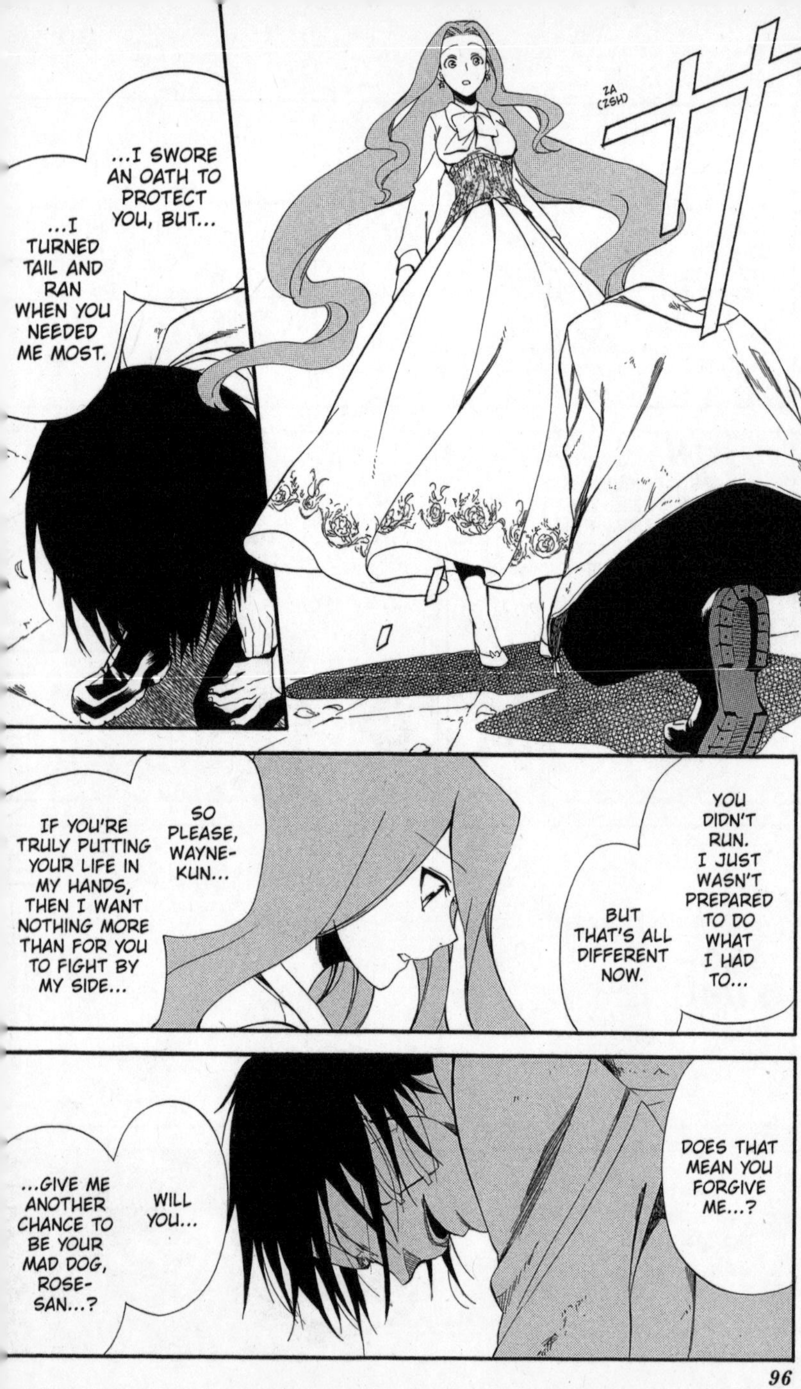
ZA (ZSH)
...I SWORE AN OATH TO PROTECT YOU, BUT...
...I TURNED TAIL AND RAN WHEN YOU NEEDED ME MOST.
YOU DIDN'T RUN. I JUST WASN'T PREPARED TO DO WHAT I HAD TO...
BUT THAT'S ALL DIFFERENT NOW.
SO PLEASE, WAYNE-KUN...
IF YOU'RE TRULY PUTTING YOUR LIFE IN MY HANDS, THEN I WANT NOTHING MORE THAN FOR YOU TO FIGHT BY MY SIDE...
DOES THAT MEAN YOU FORGIVE ME...?
WILL YOU...
...GIVE ME ANOTHER CHANCE TO BE YOUR MAD DOG, ROSE-SAN...?

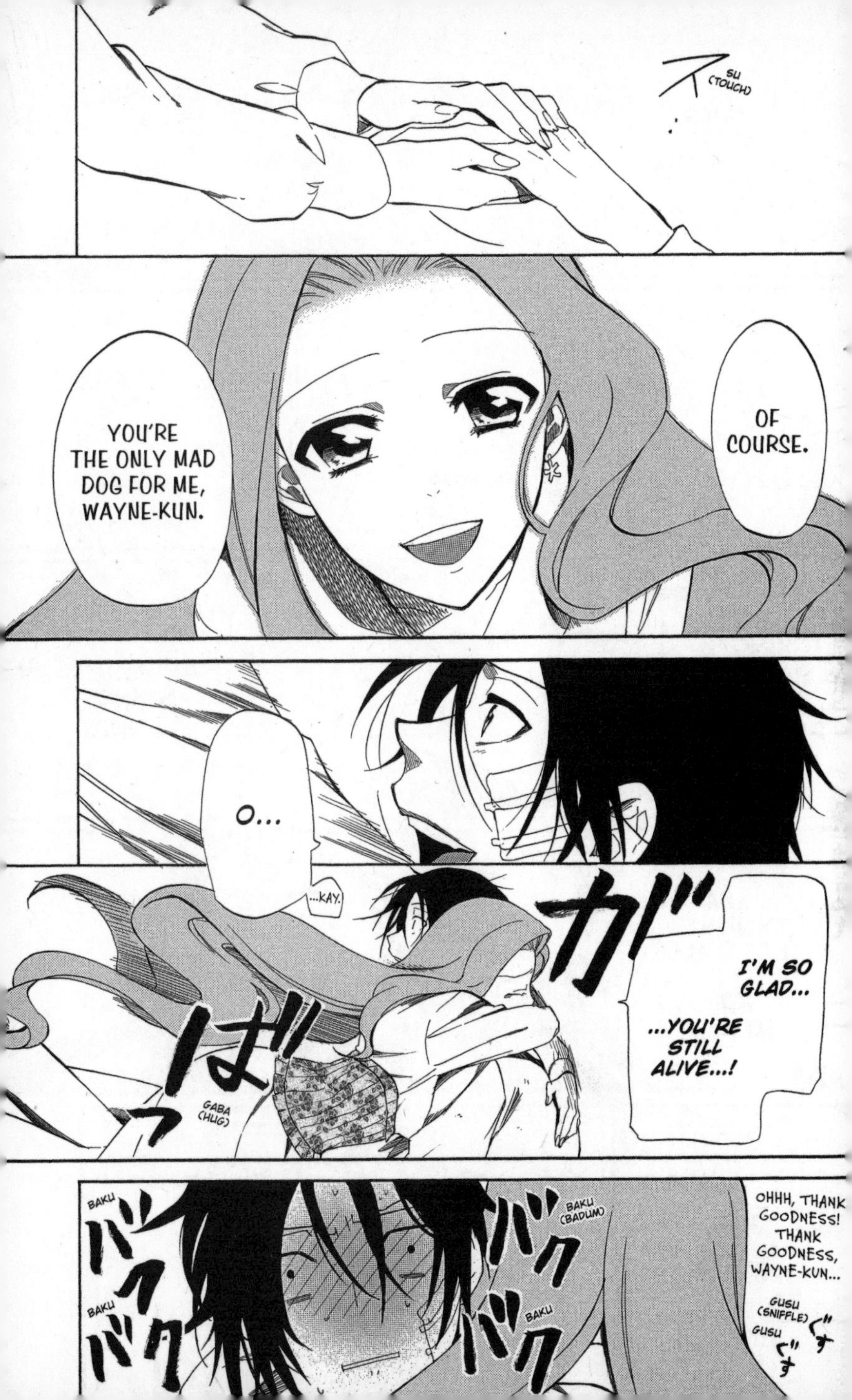
SU (TOUCH)
OF COURSE.
YOU'RE THE ONLY MAD DOG FOR ME, WAYNE-KUN.
O...
...KAY.
I'M SO GLAD...
...YOU'RE STILL ALIVE...!
GABA (HUG)
OHHH, THANK GOODNESS! THANK GOODNESS, WAYNE-KUN...
GUSU (SNIFFLE)
GUSU
BAKU (BADUM)
BAKU
BAKU
BAKU

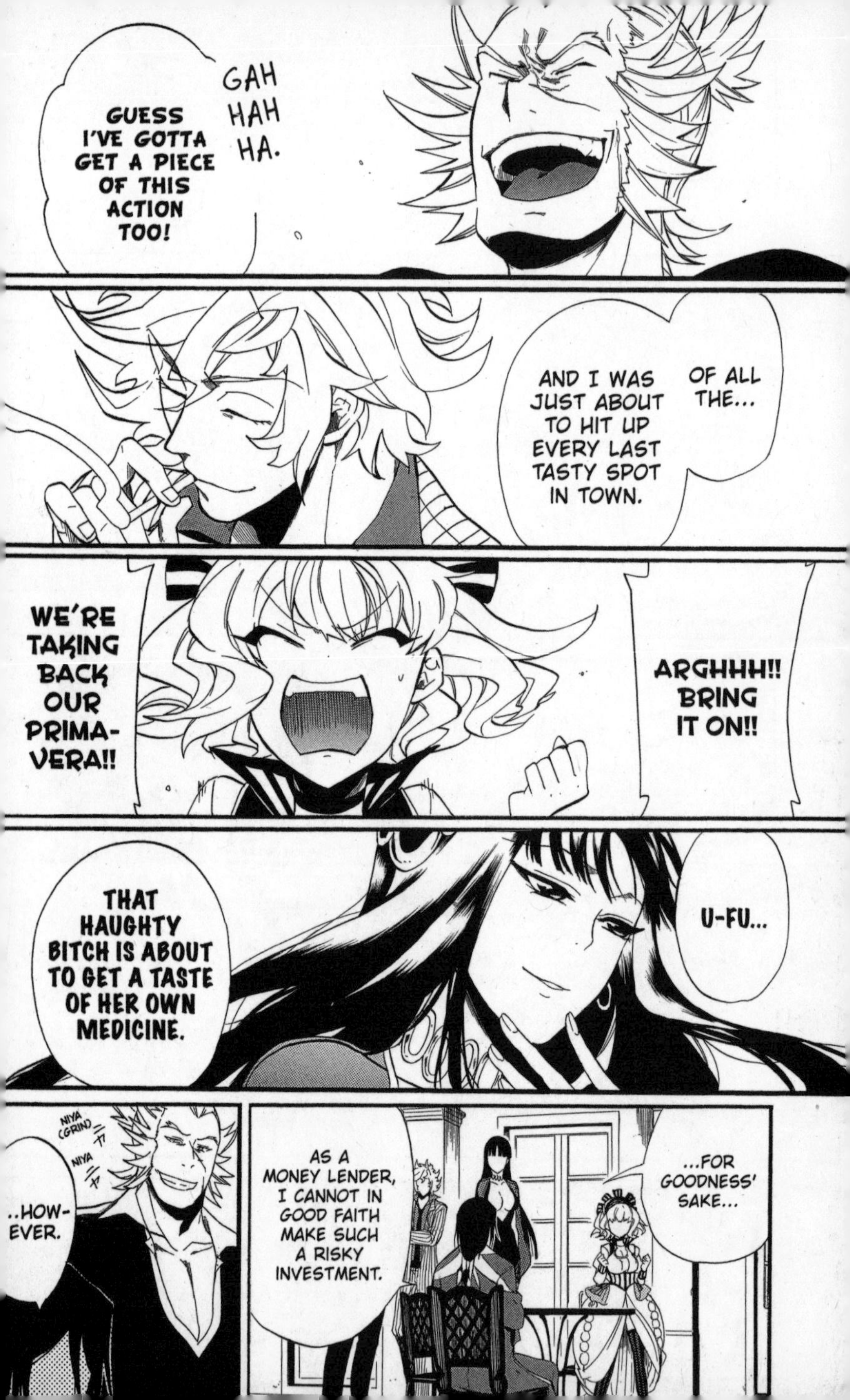
GAH HAH HA.
GUESS I'VE GOTTA GET A PIECE OF THIS ACTION TOO!
OF ALL THE...
AND I WAS JUST ABOUT TO HIT UP EVERY LAST TASTY SPOT IN TOWN.
ARGHHH!! BRING IT ON!!
WE'RE TAKING BACK OUR PRIMA-VERA!!
U-FU...
THAT HAUGHTY BITCH IS ABOUT TO GET A TASTE OF HER OWN MEDICINE.
...FOR GOODNESS' SAKE...
AS A MONEY LENDER, I CANNOT IN GOOD FAITH MAKE SUCH A RISKY INVESTMENT.
NIYA (GRIN)
NIYA
..HOW-EVER.

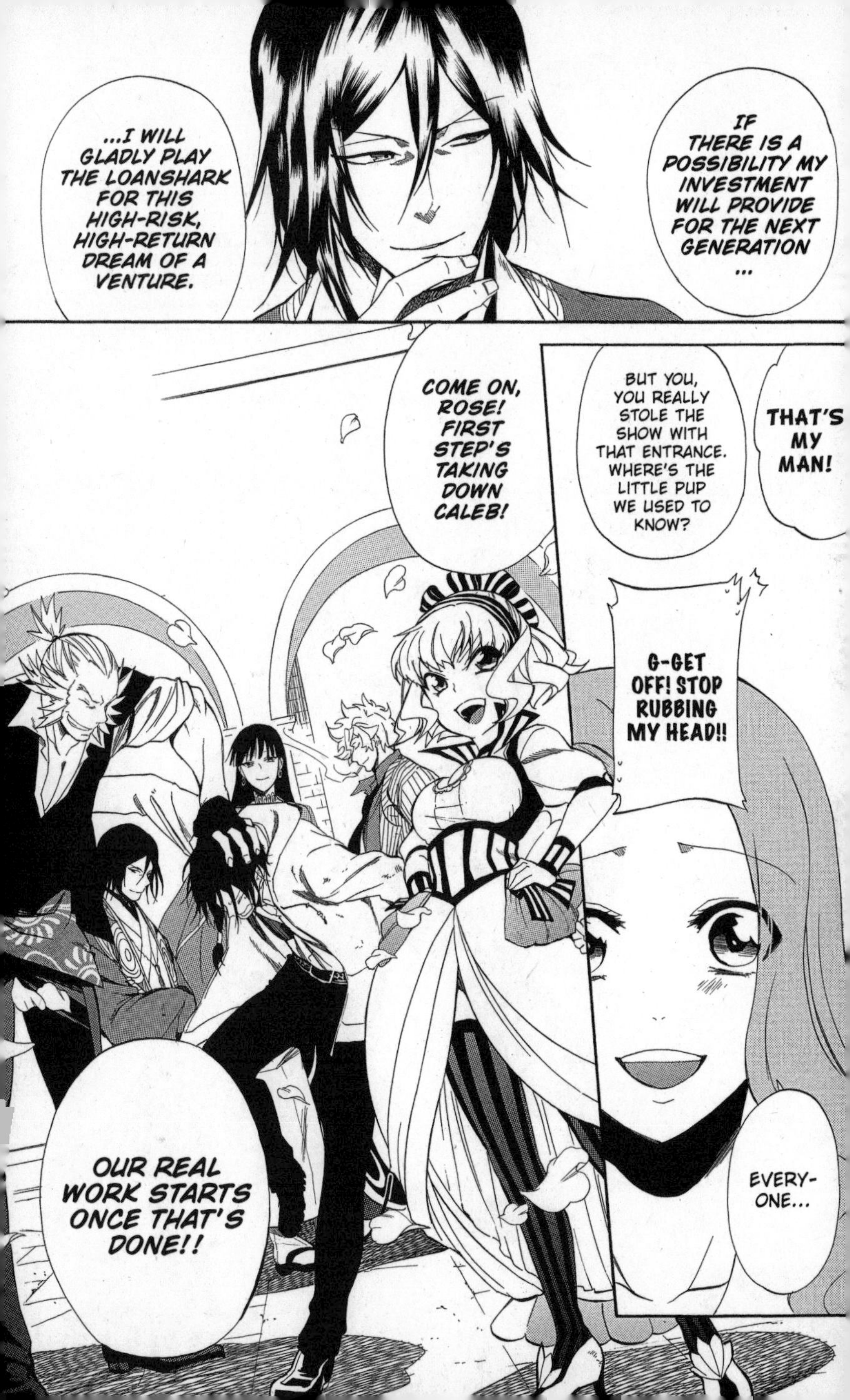
IF THERE IS A POSSIBILITY MY INVESTMENT WILL PROVIDE FOR THE NEXT GENERATION ...
...I WILL GLADLY PLAY THE LOANSHARK FOR THIS HIGH-RISK, HIGH-RETURN DREAM OF A VENTURE.
THAT'S MY MAN!
BUT YOU, YOU REALLY STOLE THE SHOW WITH THAT ENTRANCE. WHERE'S THE LITTLE PUP WE USED TO KNOW?
COME ON, ROSE! FIRST STEP'S TAKING DOWN CALEB!
G-GET OFF! STOP RUBBING MY HEAD!!
EVERY-ONE...
OUR REAL WORK STARTS ONCE THAT'S DONE!!

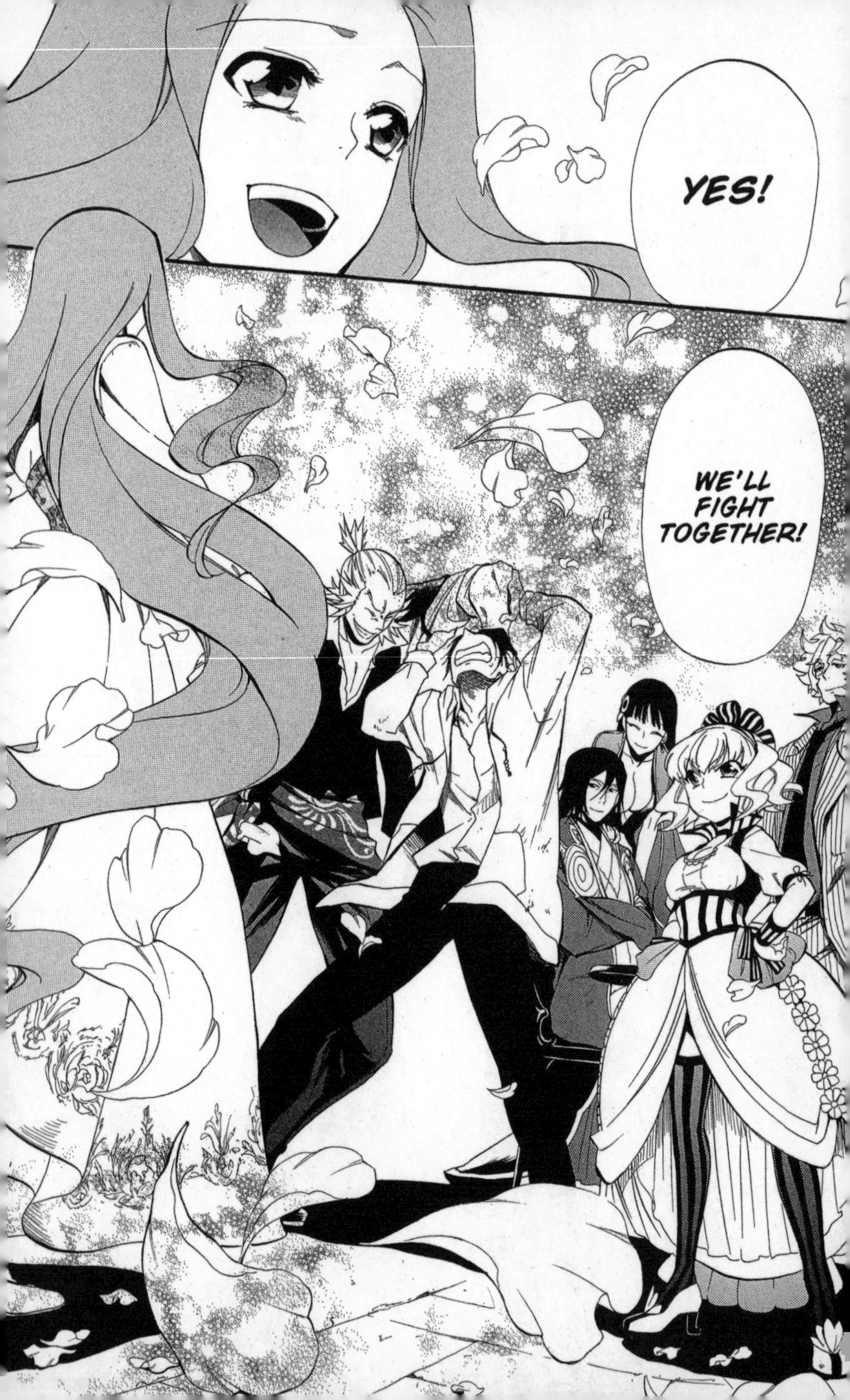
YES!
WE'LL FIGHT TOGETHER!

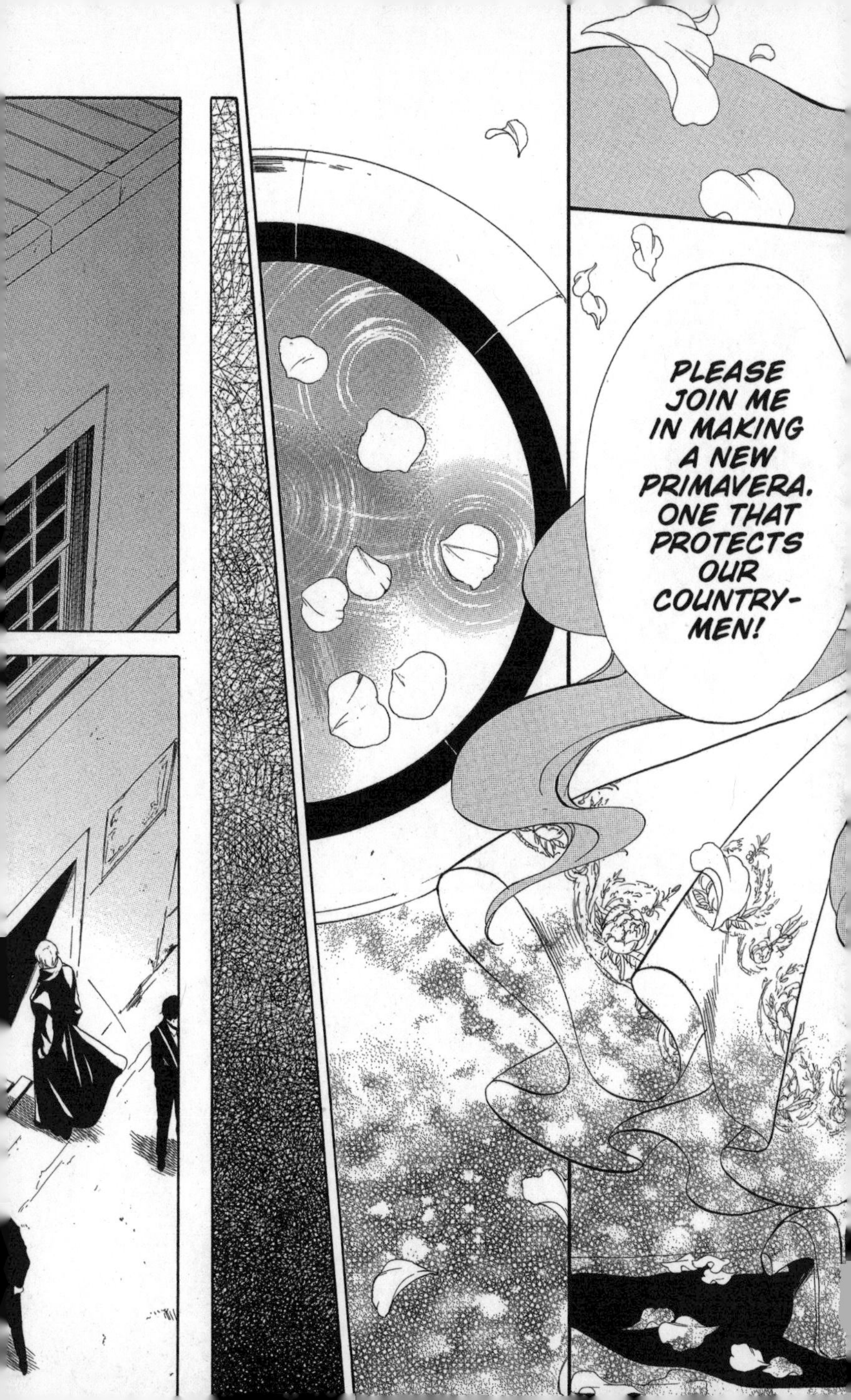
PLEASE JOIN ME IN MAKING A NEW PRIMAVERA. ONE THAT PROTECTS OUR COUNTRY-MEN!

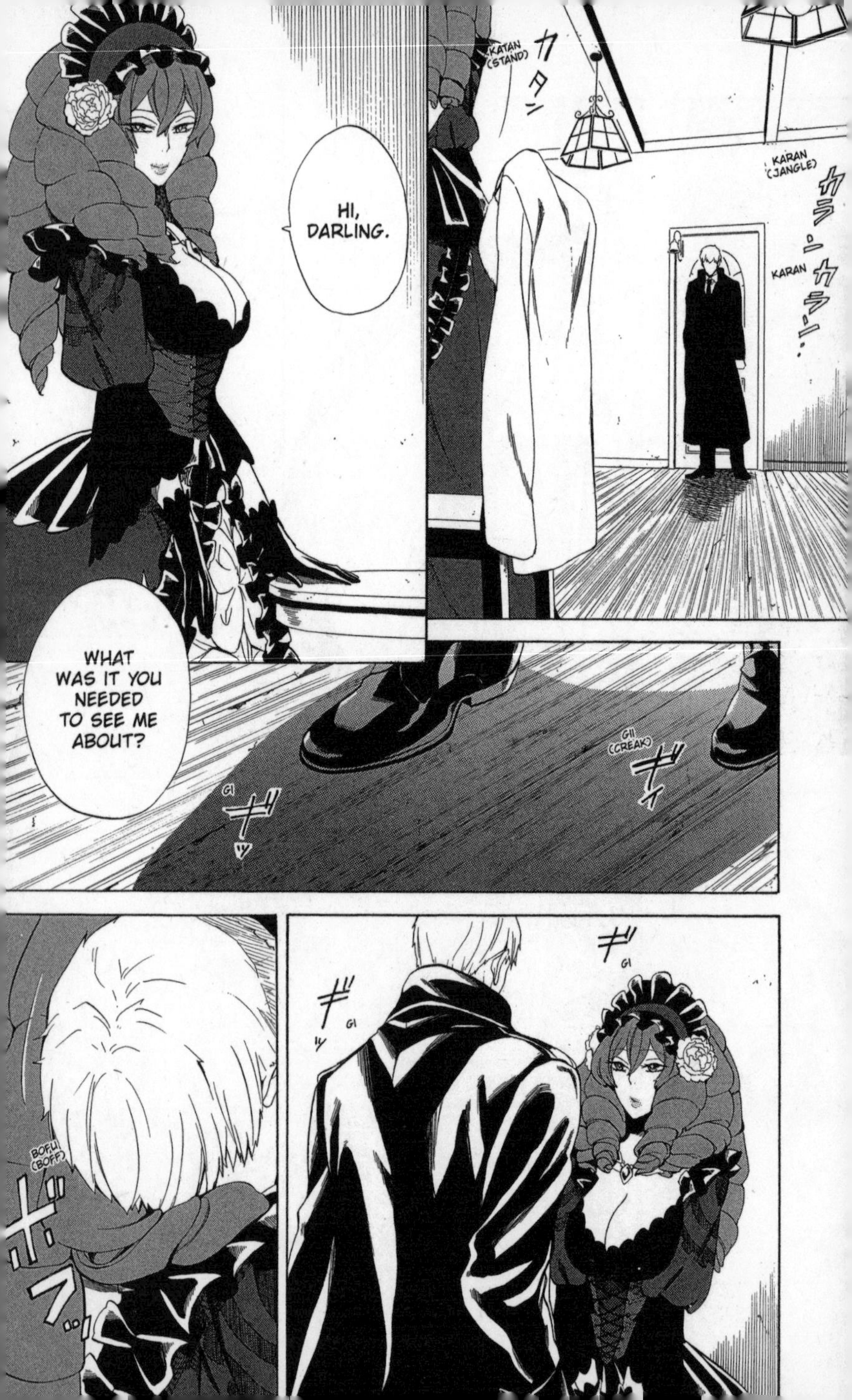
KATAN (STAND)
KARAN (JANGLE)
KARAN
HI, DARLING.
GII (CREAK)
WHAT WAS IT YOU NEEDED TO SEE ME ABOUT?
GI
GI
GI
BOFU (BOFF)

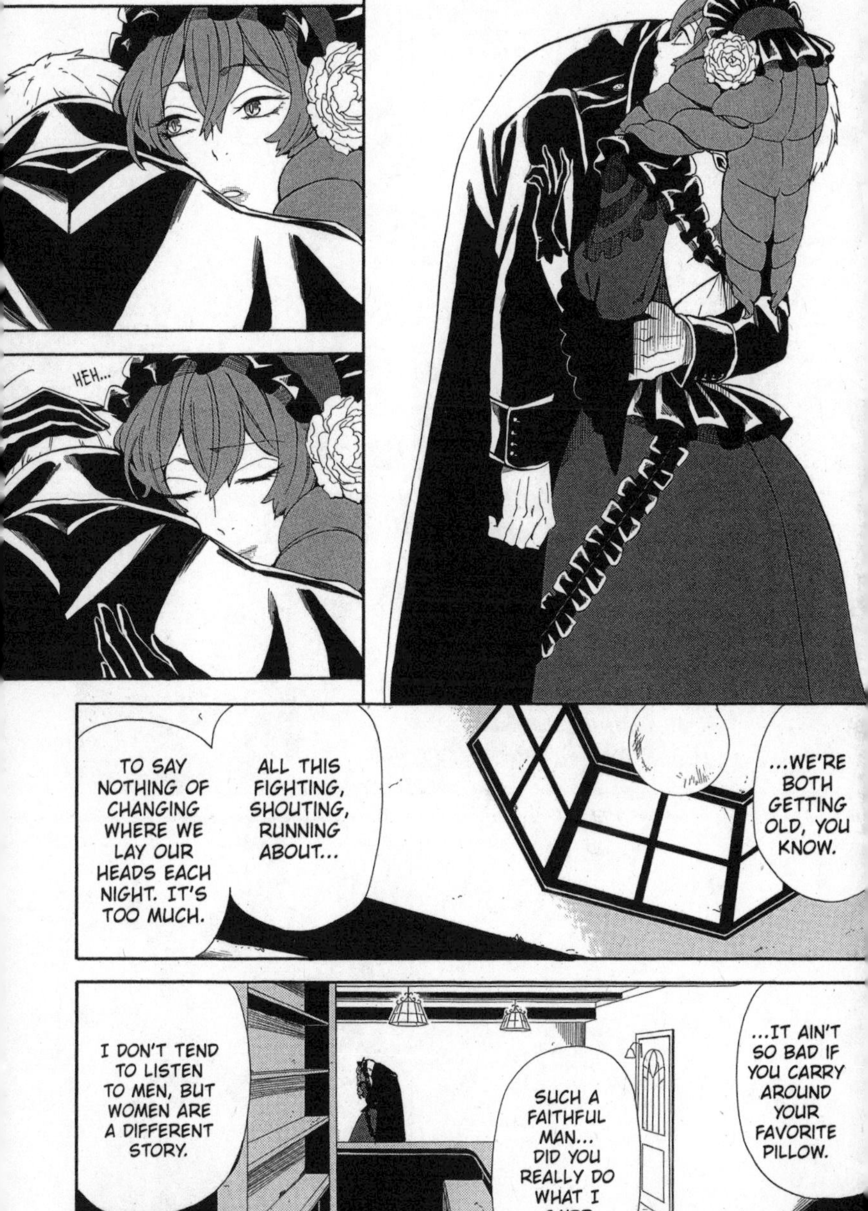
HEH...
...WE'RE BOTH GETTING OLD, YOU KNOW.
ALL THIS FIGHTING, SHOUTING, RUNNING ABOUT...
TO SAY NOTHING OF CHANGING WHERE WE LAY OUR HEADS EACH NIGHT. IT'S TOO MUCH.
...IT AIN'T SO BAD IF YOU CARRY AROUND YOUR FAVORITE PILLOW.
SUCH A FAITHFUL MAN... DID YOU REALLY DO WHAT I SAID?
I DON'T TEND TO LISTEN TO MEN, BUT WOMEN ARE A DIFFERENT STORY.

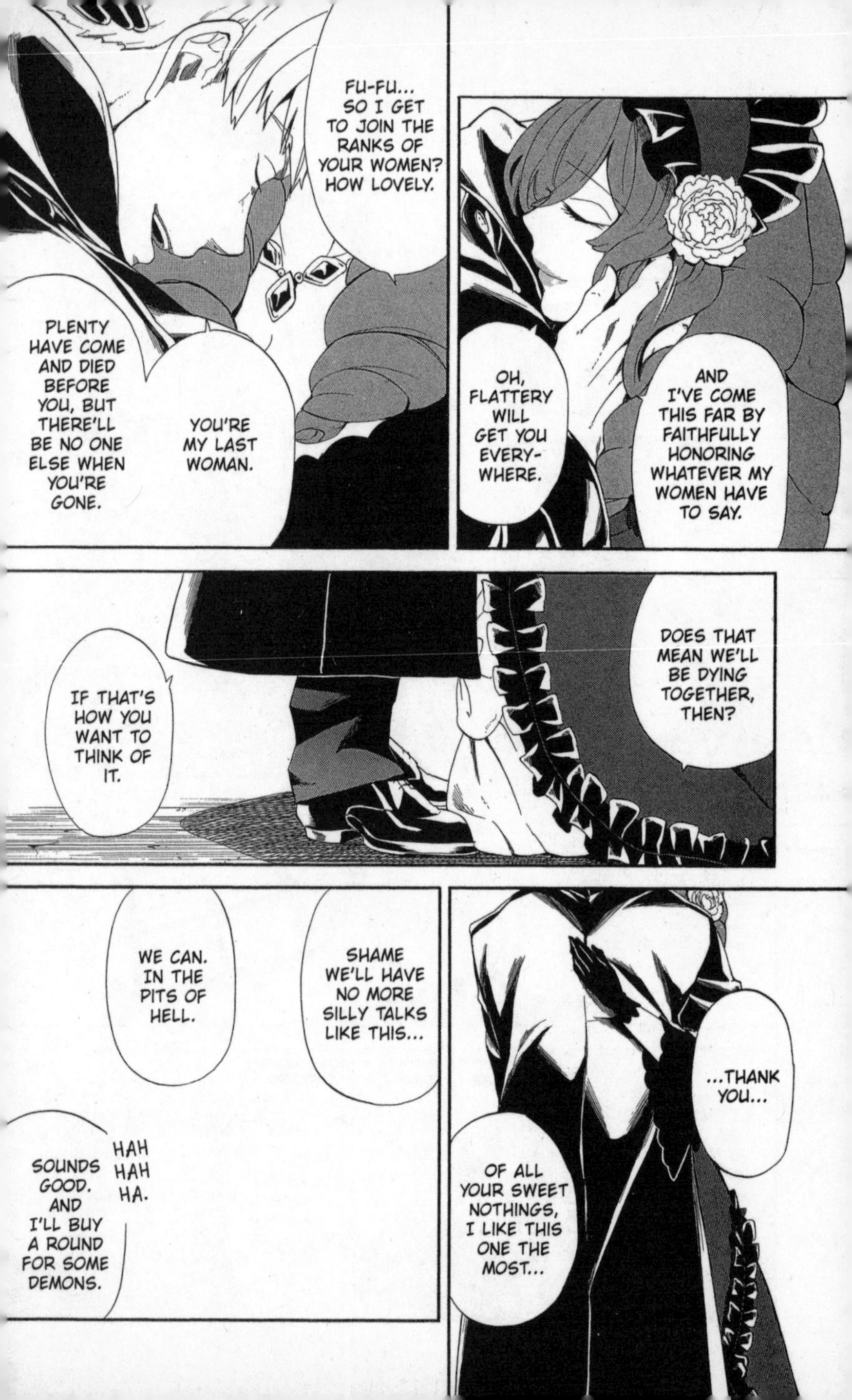
AND I'VE COME THIS FAR BY FAITHFULLY HONORING WHATEVER MY WOMEN HAVE TO SAY.
OH, FLATTERY WILL GET YOU EVERY-WHERE.
FU-FU... SO I GET TO JOIN THE RANKS OF YOUR WOMEN? HOW LOVELY.
YOU'RE MY LAST WOMAN.
PLENTY HAVE COME AND DIED BEFORE YOU, BUT THERE'LL BE NO ONE ELSE WHEN YOU'RE GONE.
DOES THAT MEAN WE'LL BE DYING TOGETHER, THEN?
IF THAT'S HOW YOU WANT TO THINK OF IT.
...THANK YOU...
OF ALL YOUR SWEET NOTHINGS, I LIKE THIS ONE THE MOST...
SHAME WE'LL HAVE NO MORE SILLY TALKS LIKE THIS...
WE CAN. IN THE PITS OF HELL.
HAH HAH HA.
SOUNDS GOOD. AND I'LL BUY A ROUND FOR SOME DEMONS.

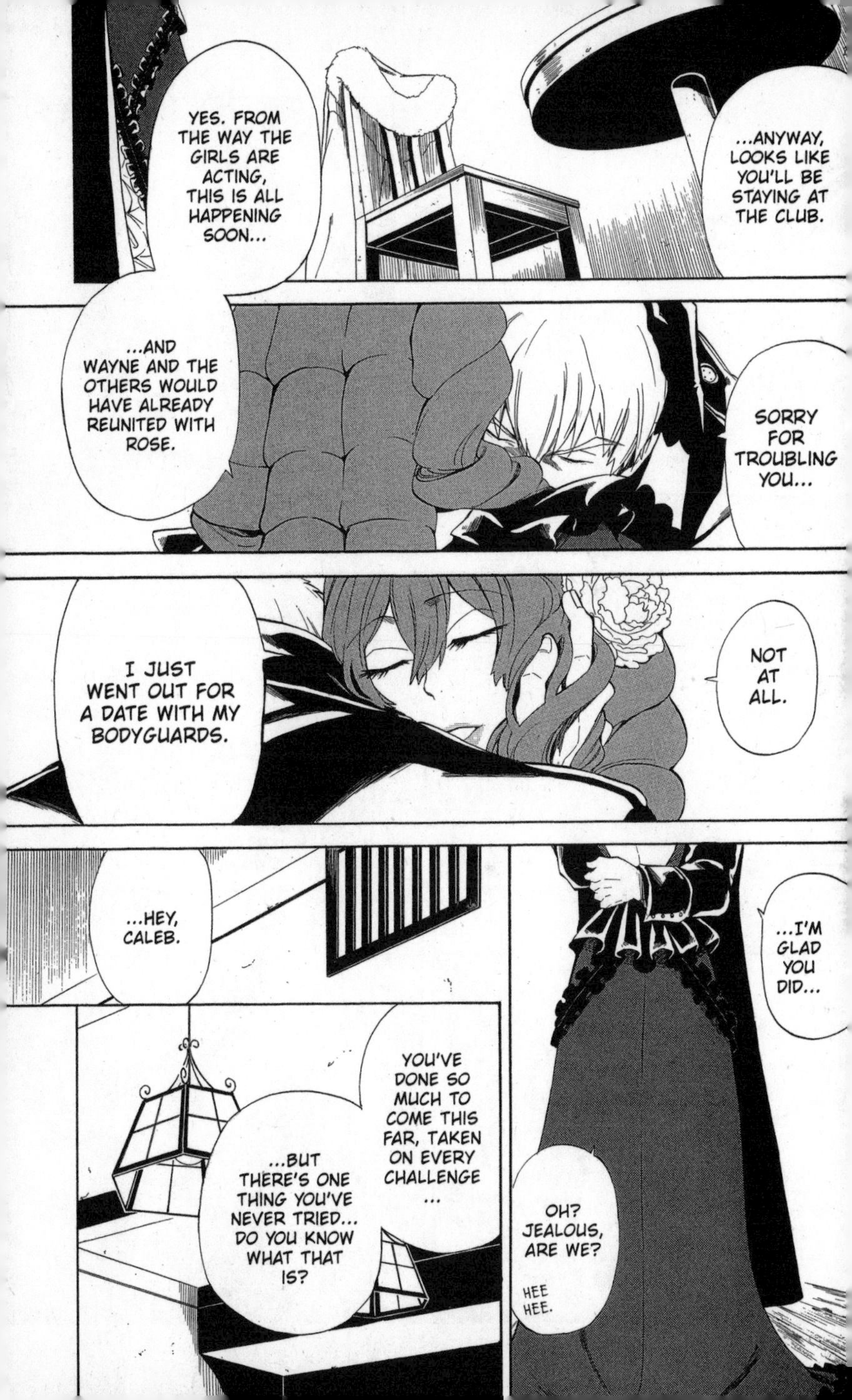
...ANYWAY, LOOKS LIKE YOU'LL BE STAYING AT THE CLUB.
YES. FROM THE WAY THE GIRLS ARE ACTING, THIS IS ALL HAPPENING SOON...
...AND WAYNE AND THE OTHERS WOULD HAVE ALREADY REUNITED WITH ROSE.
SORRY FOR TROUBLING YOU...
NOT AT ALL.
I JUST WENT OUT FOR A DATE WITH MY BODYGUARDS.
...I'M GLAD YOU DID...
OH? JEALOUS, ARE WE?
HEE HEE.
...HEY, CALEB.
YOU'VE DONE SO MUCH TO COME THIS FAR, TAKEN ON EVERY CHALLENGE ...
...BUT THERE'S ONE THING YOU'VE NEVER TRIED... DO YOU KNOW WHAT THAT IS?

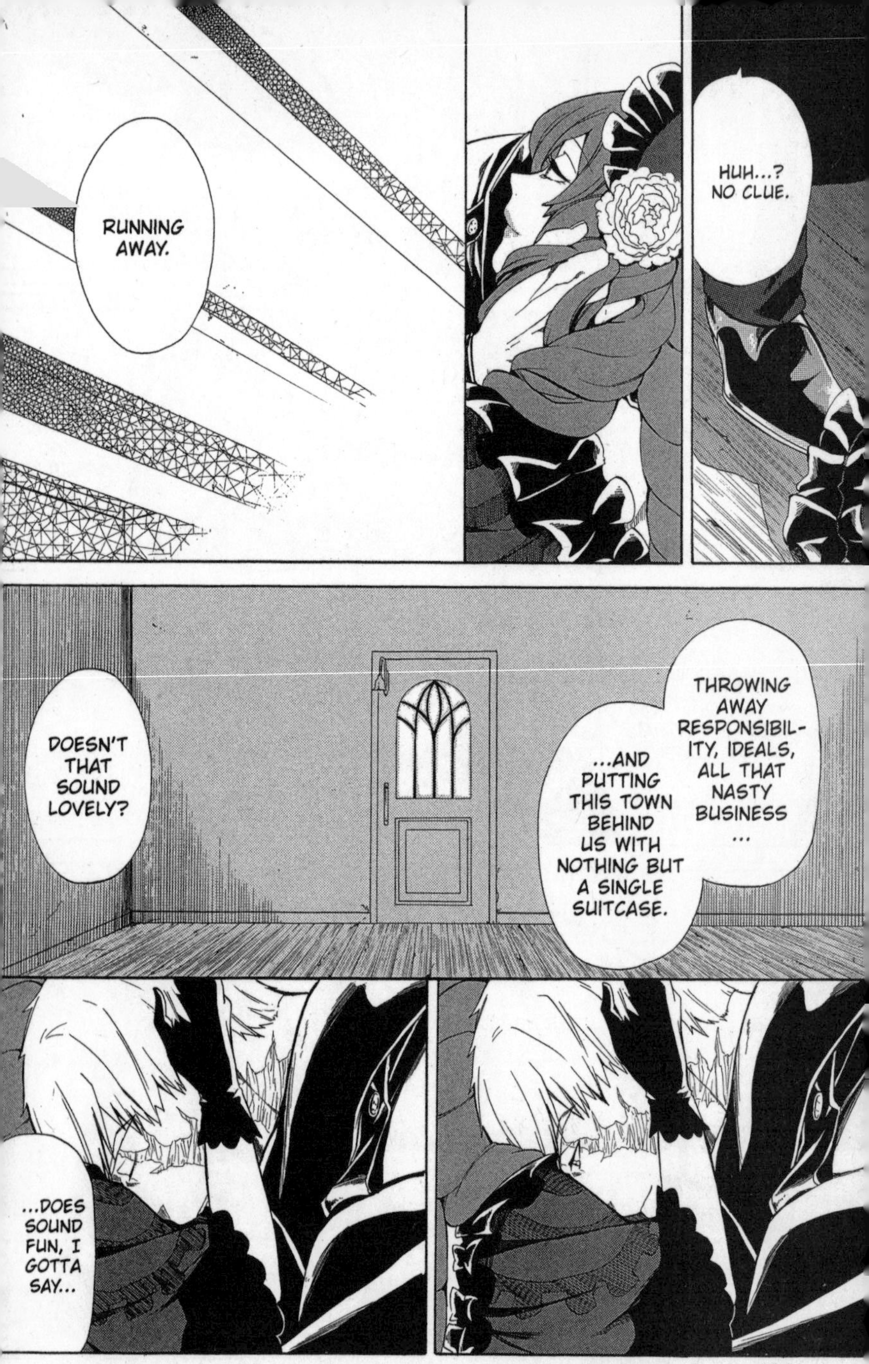
HUH...? NO CLUE.
RUNNING AWAY.
THROWING AWAY RESPONSIBILITY, IDEALS, ALL THAT NASTY BUSINESS...
...AND PUTTING THIS TOWN BEHIND US WITH NOTHING BUT A SINGLE SUITCASE.
DOESN'T THAT SOUND LOVELY?
...DOES SOUND FUN, I GOTTA SAY...

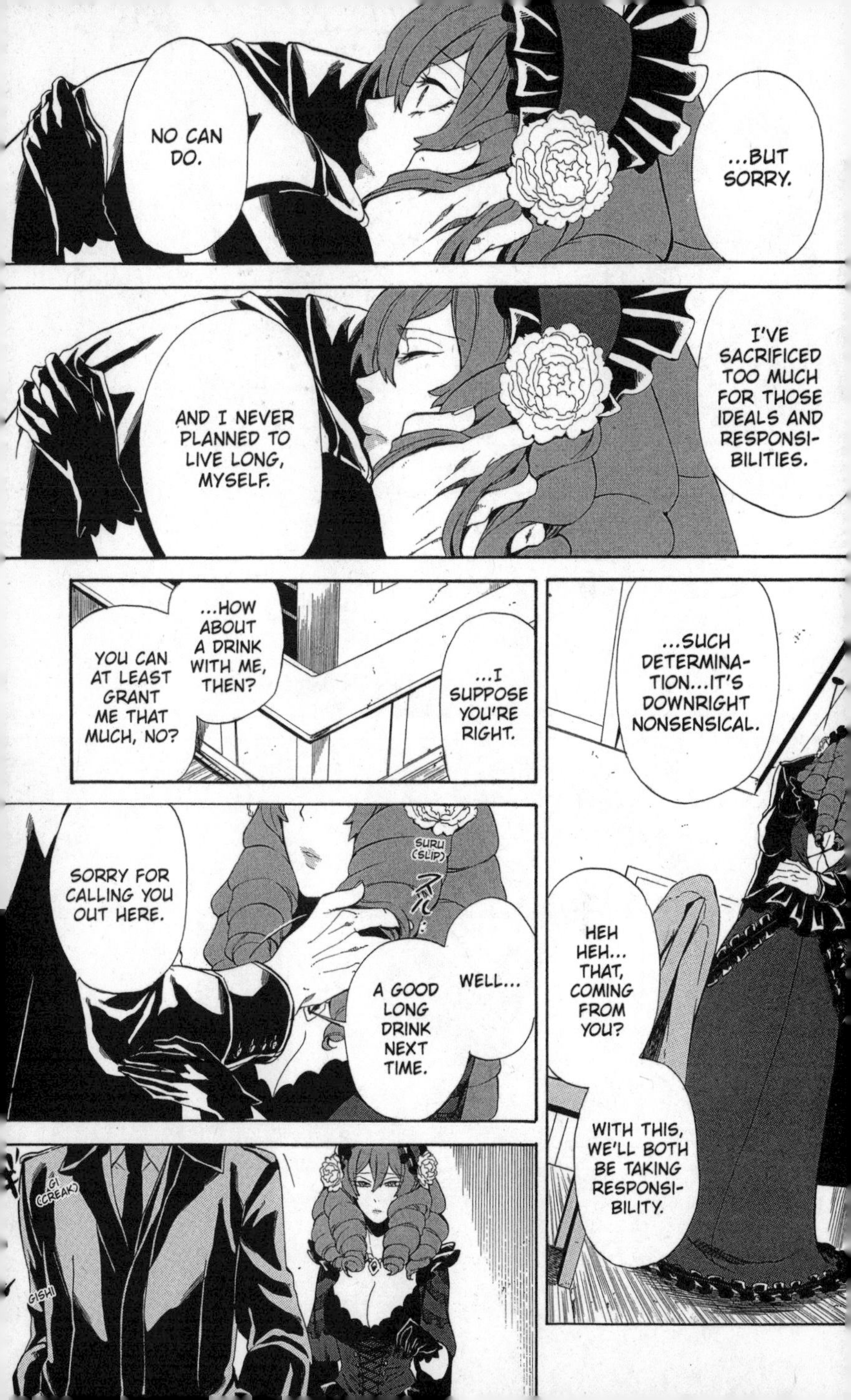
...BUT SORRY.
NO CAN DO.
I'VE SACRIFICED TOO MUCH FOR THOSE IDEALS AND RESPONSI-BILITIES.
AND I NEVER PLANNED TO LIVE LONG, MYSELF.
...SUCH DETERMINA-TION...IT'S DOWNRIGHT NONSENSICAL.
HEH HEH... THAT, COMING FROM YOU?
WITH THIS, WE'LL BOTH BE TAKING RESPONSI-BILITY.
...I SUPPOSE YOU'RE RIGHT.
...HOW ABOUT A DRINK WITH ME, THEN?
YOU CAN AT LEAST GRANT ME THAT MUCH, NO?
SURU (SLIP)
WELL...
A GOOD LONG DRINK NEXT TIME.
SORRY FOR CALLING YOU OUT HERE.
GI (CREAK)
GISHI

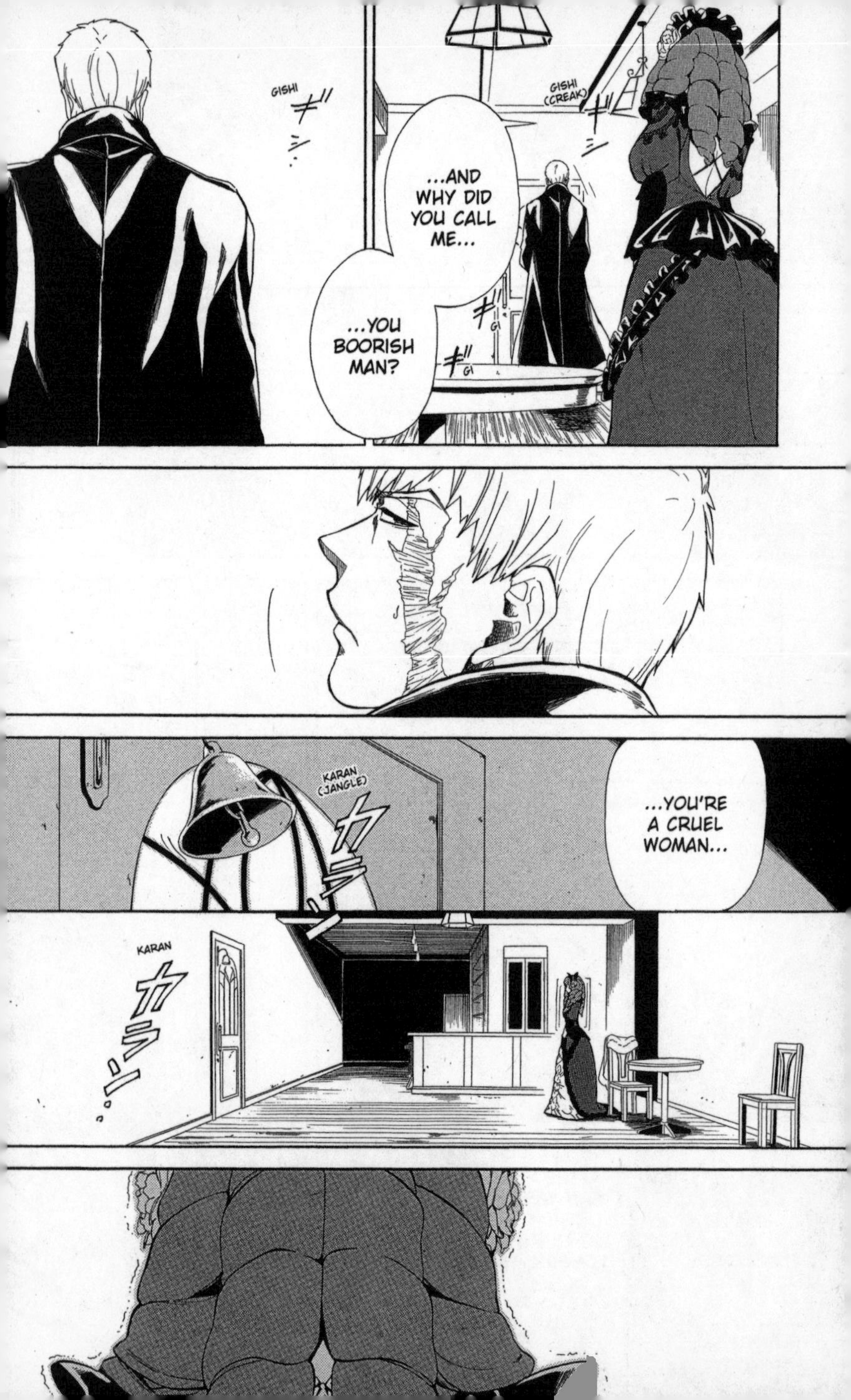
GISHI (CREAK)
...AND WHY DID YOU CALL ME...
...YOU BOORISH MAN?
GI
GI
GISHI
...YOU'RE A CRUEL WOMAN...
KARAN (JANGLE)
KARAN

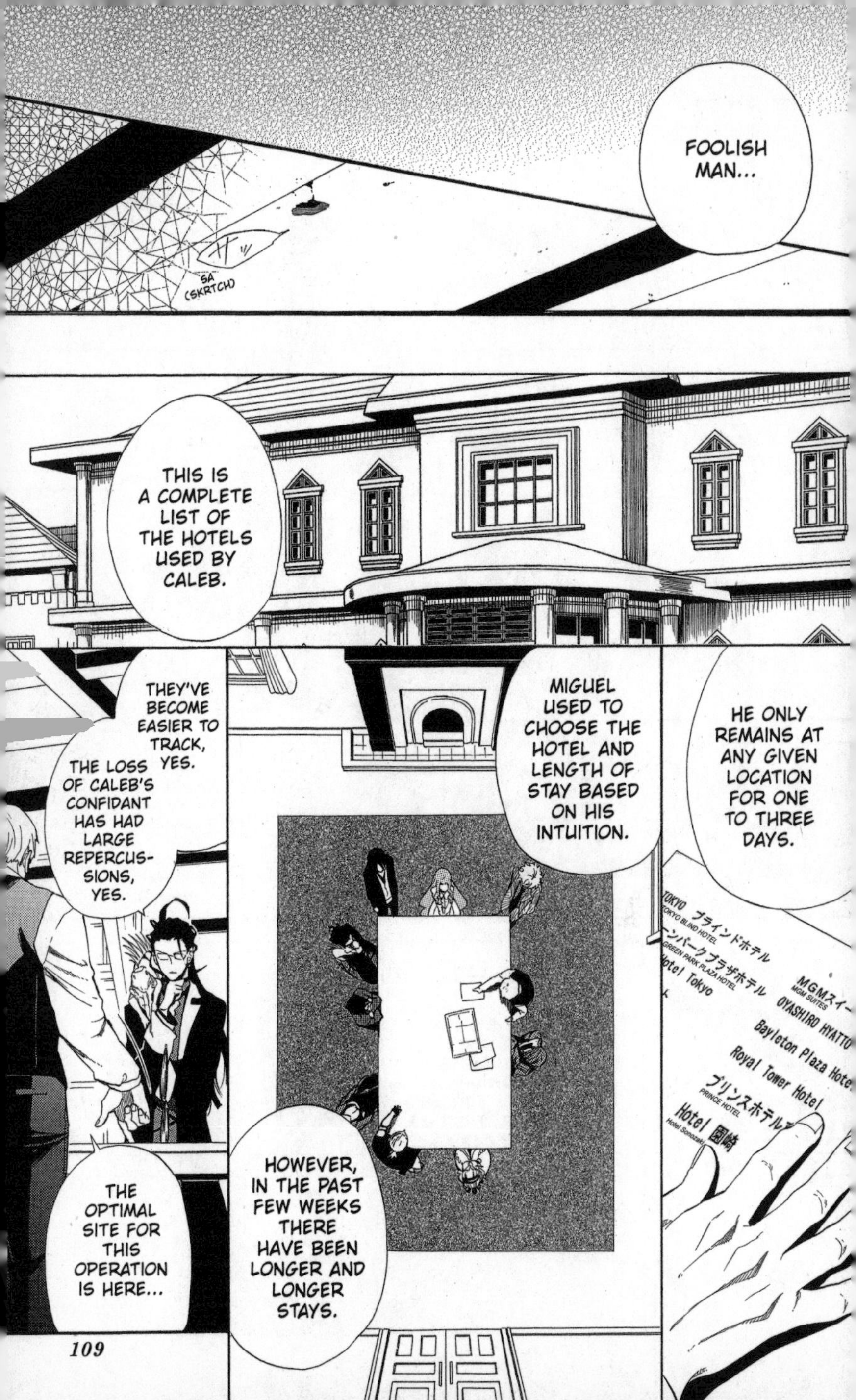
FOOLISH MAN...
SA (SKRTCH)
THIS IS A COMPLETE LIST OF THE HOTELS USED BY CALEB.
HE ONLY REMAINS AT ANY GIVEN LOCATION FOR ONE TO THREE DAYS.
TOKYO ブラインドホテル
TOKYO BLIND HOTEL
ーンパークプラザホテル
GREEN PARK PLAZA HOTEL
Hotel Tokyo
MGMスイー
MGM SUITES
OYASHIRO HYATT
Bayleton Plaza Hote
Royal Tower Hotel
プリンスホテル
PRINCE HOTEL
Hotel 園崎
Hotel Sonozaki
MIGUEL USED TO CHOOSE THE HOTEL AND LENGTH OF STAY BASED ON HIS INTUITION.
HOWEVER, IN THE PAST FEW WEEKS THERE HAVE BEEN LONGER AND LONGER STAYS.
THEY'VE BECOME EASIER TO TRACK, YES.
THE LOSS OF CALEB'S CONFIDANT HAS HAD LARGE REPERCUS-SIONS, YES.
THE OPTIMAL SITE FOR THIS OPERATION IS HERE...

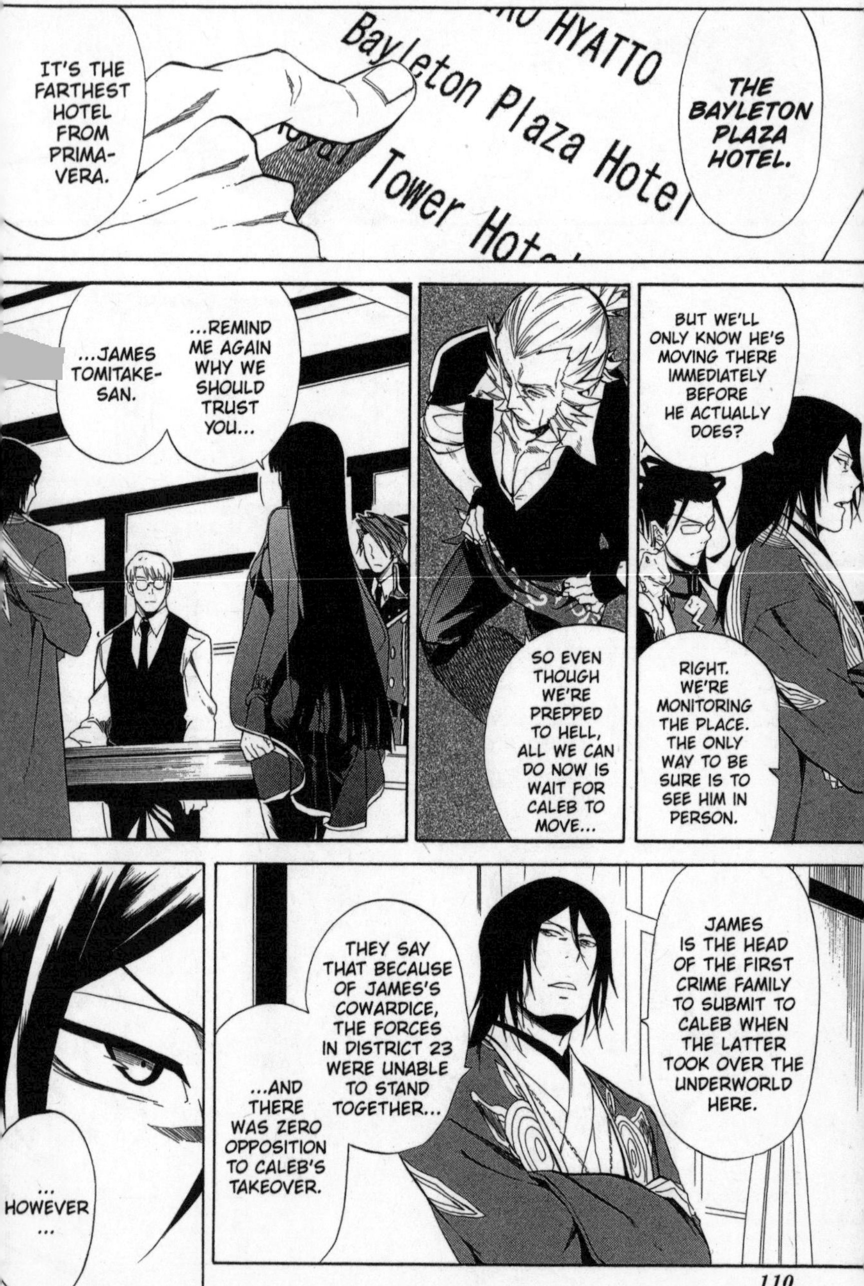
THE BAYLETON PLAZA HOTEL.
Bayleton Plaza Hotel
IT'S THE FARTHEST HOTEL FROM PRIMA-VERA.
BUT WE'LL ONLY KNOW HE'S MOVING THERE IMMEDIATELY BEFORE HE ACTUALLY DOES?
RIGHT. WE'RE MONITORING THE PLACE. THE ONLY WAY TO BE SURE IS TO SEE HIM IN PERSON.
SO EVEN THOUGH WE'RE PREPPED TO HELL, ALL WE CAN DO NOW IS WAIT FOR CALEB TO MOVE...
...REMIND ME AGAIN WHY WE SHOULD TRUST YOU...
...JAMES TOMITAKE-SAN.
JAMES IS THE HEAD OF THE FIRST CRIME FAMILY TO SUBMIT TO CALEB WHEN THE LATTER TOOK OVER THE UNDERWORLD HERE.
THEY SAY THAT BECAUSE OF JAMES'S COWARDICE, THE FORCES IN DISTRICT 23 WERE UNABLE TO STAND TOGETHER...
...AND THERE WAS ZERO OPPOSITION TO CALEB'S TAKEOVER.
...HOWEVER...

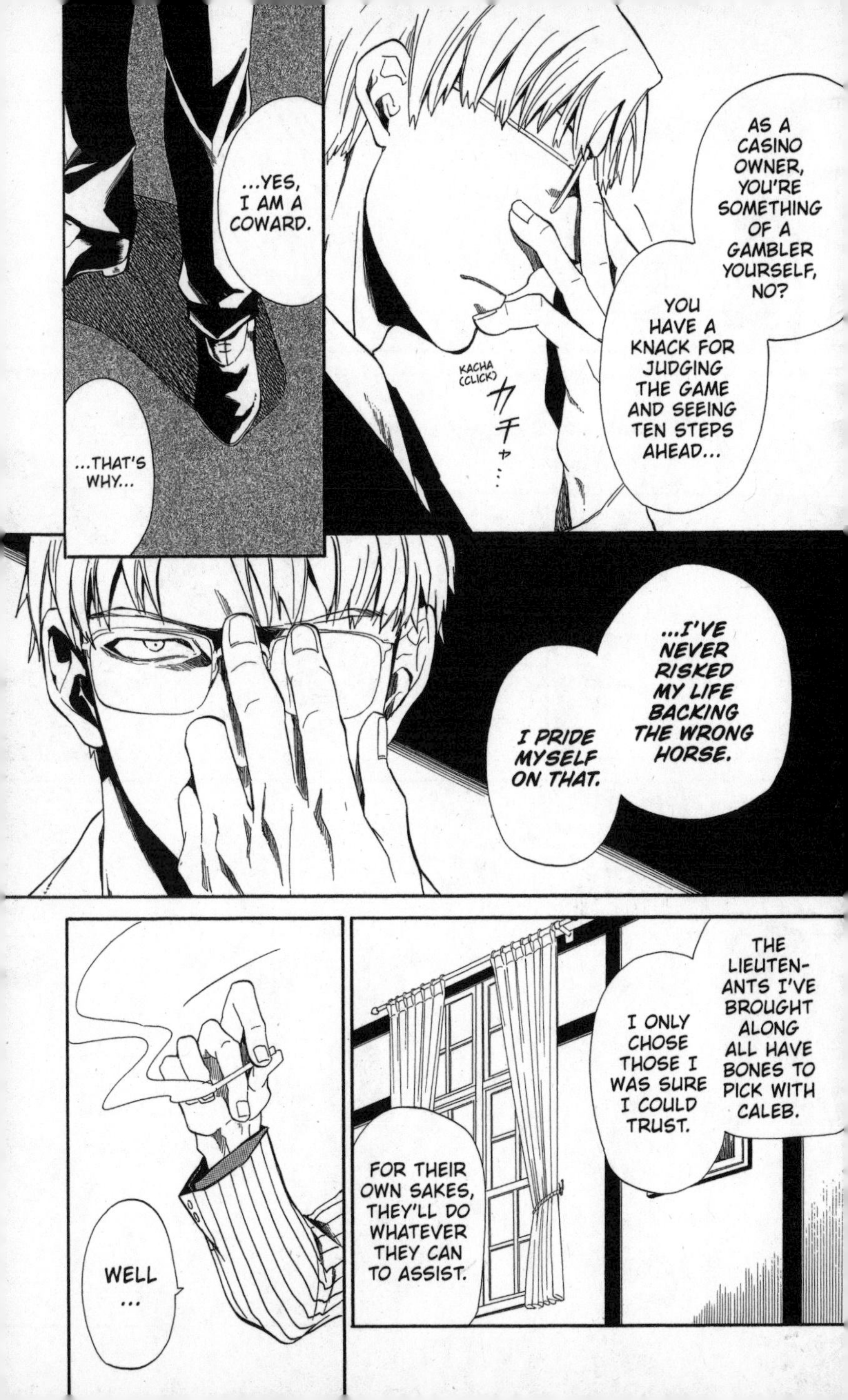
AS A CASINO OWNER, YOU'RE SOMETHING OF A GAMBLER YOURSELF, NO?
YOU HAVE A KNACK FOR JUDGING THE GAME AND SEEING TEN STEPS AHEAD...
KACHA (CLICK)
カチャ…
...YES, I AM A COWARD.
...THAT'S WHY...
...I'VE NEVER RISKED MY LIFE BACKING THE WRONG HORSE.
I PRIDE MYSELF ON THAT.
THE LIEUTEN-ANTS I'VE BROUGHT ALONG ALL HAVE BONES TO PICK WITH CALEB.
I ONLY CHOSE THOSE I WAS SURE I COULD TRUST.
FOR THEIR OWN SAKES, THEY'LL DO WHATEVER THEY CAN TO ASSIST.
WELL ...

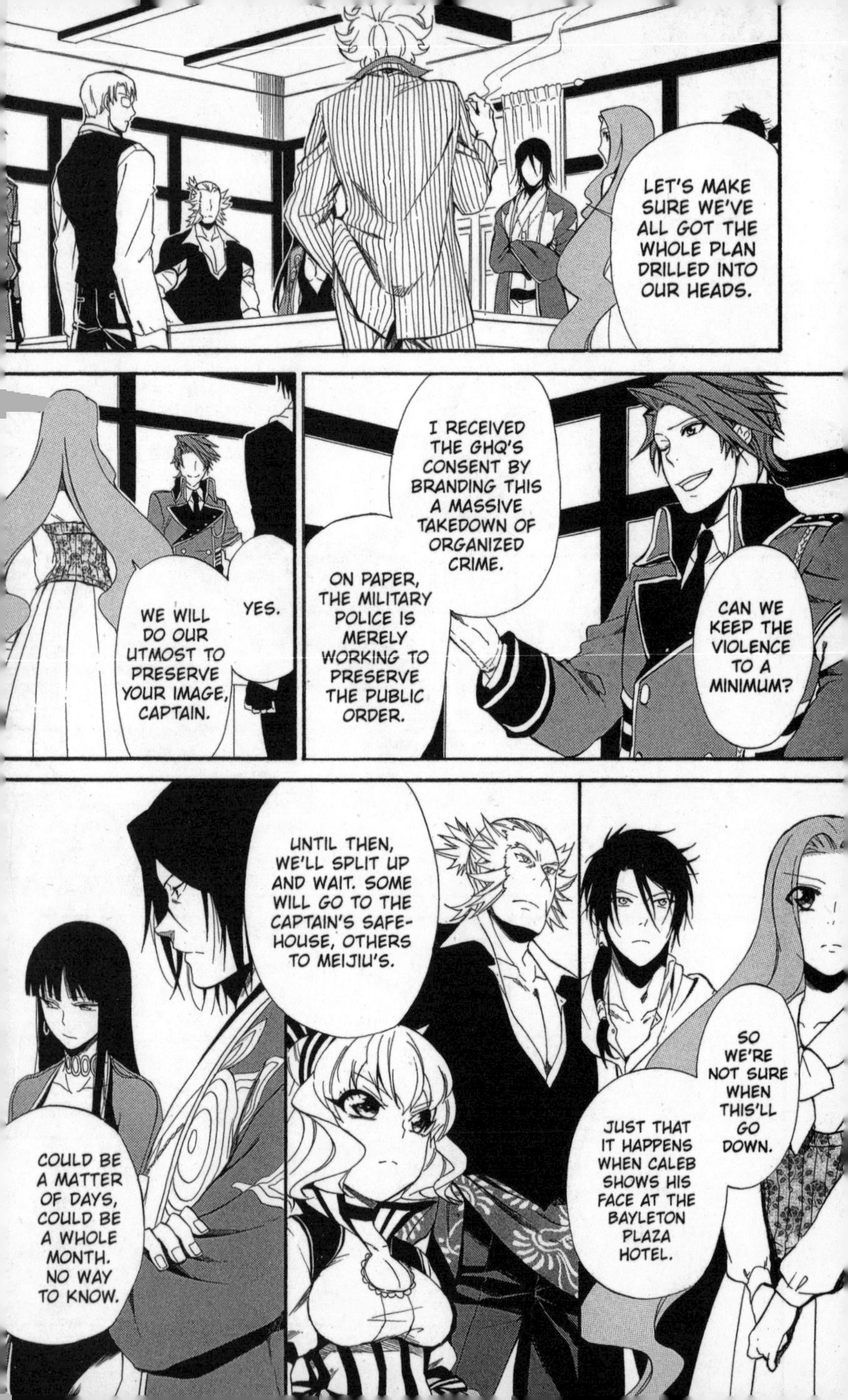
LET'S MAKE SURE WE'VE ALL GOT THE WHOLE PLAN DRILLED INTO OUR HEADS.
I RECEIVED THE GHQ'S CONSENT BY BRANDING THIS A MASSIVE TAKEDOWN OF ORGANIZED CRIME.
ON PAPER, THE MILITARY POLICE IS MERELY WORKING TO PRESERVE THE PUBLIC ORDER.
CAN WE KEEP THE VIOLENCE TO A MINIMUM?
YES.
WE WILL DO OUR UTMOST TO PRESERVE YOUR IMAGE, CAPTAIN.
SO WE'RE NOT SURE WHEN THIS'LL GO DOWN.
JUST THAT IT HAPPENS WHEN CALEB SHOWS HIS FACE AT THE BAYLETON PLAZA HOTEL.
UNTIL THEN, WE'LL SPLIT UP AND WAIT. SOME WILL GO TO THE CAPTAIN'S SAFE-HOUSE, OTHERS TO MEIJIU'S.
COULD BE A MATTER OF DAYS, COULD BE A WHOLE MONTH. NO WAY TO KNOW.

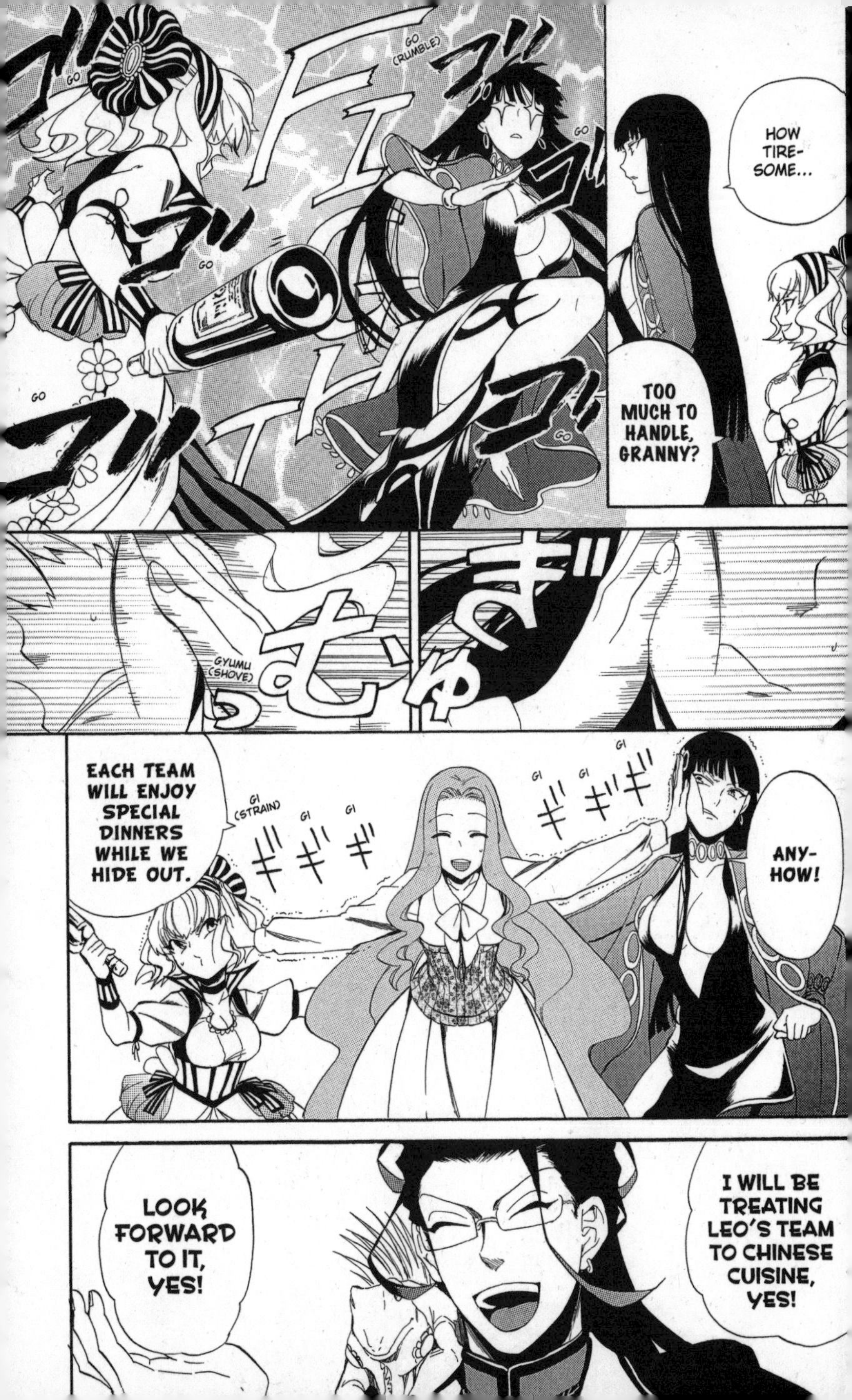
HOW TIRE-SOME...
TOO MUCH TO HANDLE, GRANNY?
GO (RUMBLE)
GO
GO
GO
GO
GO
GYUMU (SHOVE)
ANY-HOW!
GI GI GI
GI (STRAIN) GI GI
EACH TEAM WILL ENJOY SPECIAL DINNERS WHILE WE HIDE OUT.
I WILL BE TREATING LEO'S TEAM TO CHINESE CUISINE, YES!
LOOK FORWARD TO IT, YES!

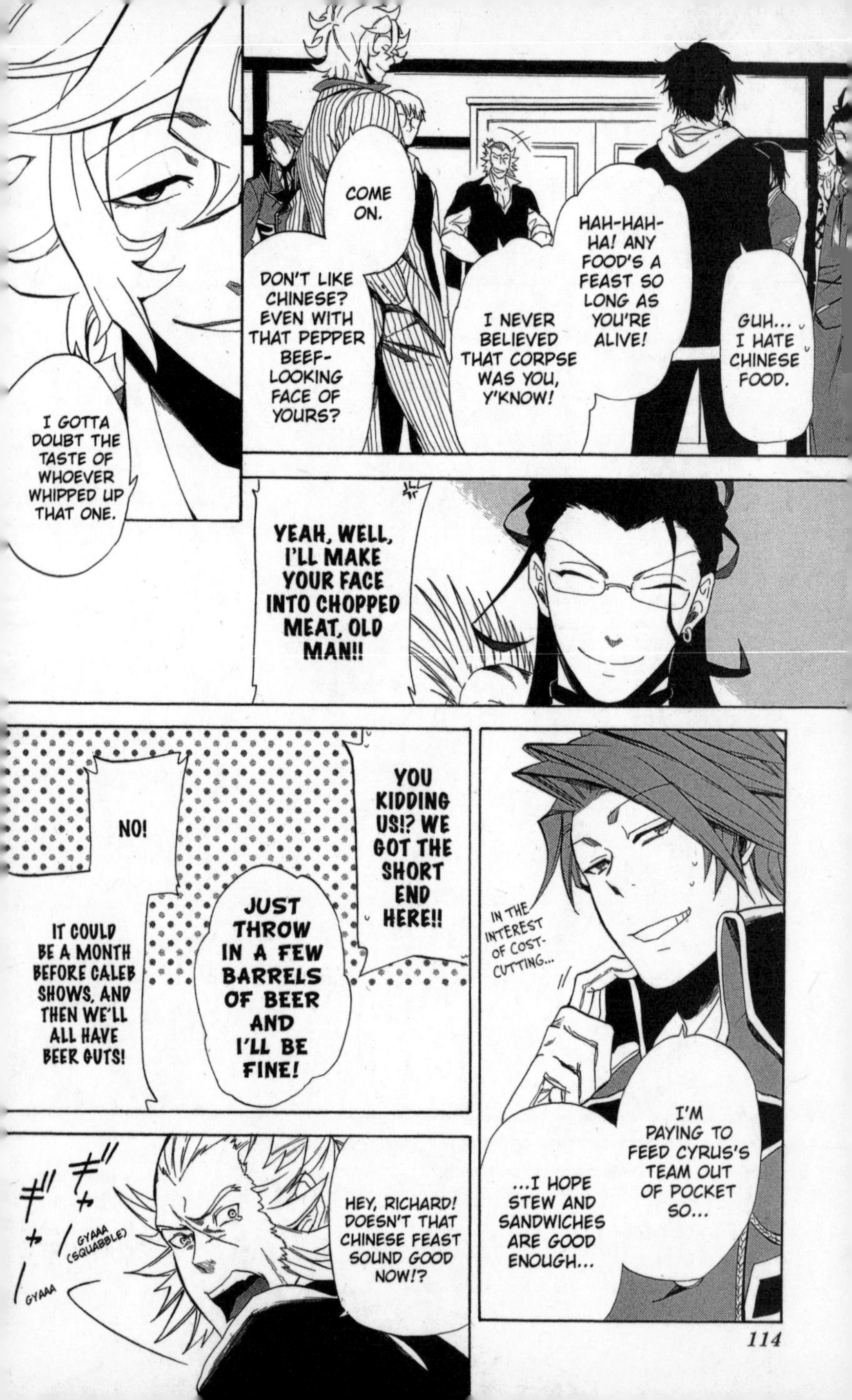
GUH... I HATE CHINESE FOOD.
HAH-HAH-HA! ANY FOOD'S A FEAST SO LONG AS YOU'RE ALIVE!
I NEVER BELIEVED THAT CORPSE WAS YOU, Y'KNOW!
COME ON.
DON'T LIKE CHINESE? EVEN WITH THAT PEPPER BEEF-LOOKING FACE OF YOURS?
I GOTTA DOUBT THE TASTE OF WHOEVER WHIPPED UP THAT ONE.
YEAH, WELL, I'LL MAKE YOUR FACE INTO CHOPPED MEAT, OLD MAN!!
IN THE INTEREST OF COST-CUTTING...
I'M PAYING TO FEED CYRUS'S TEAM OUT OF POCKET SO...
...I HOPE STEW AND SANDWICHES ARE GOOD ENOUGH...
YOU KIDDING US!? WE GOT THE SHORT END HERE!!
NO!
JUST THROW IN A FEW BARRELS OF BEER AND I'LL BE FINE!
IT COULD BE A MONTH BEFORE CALEB SHOWS, AND THEN WE'LL ALL HAVE BEER GUTS!
HEY, RICHARD! DOESN'T THAT CHINESE FEAST SOUND GOOD NOW!?
GYAAA (SQUABBLE)
GYAAA

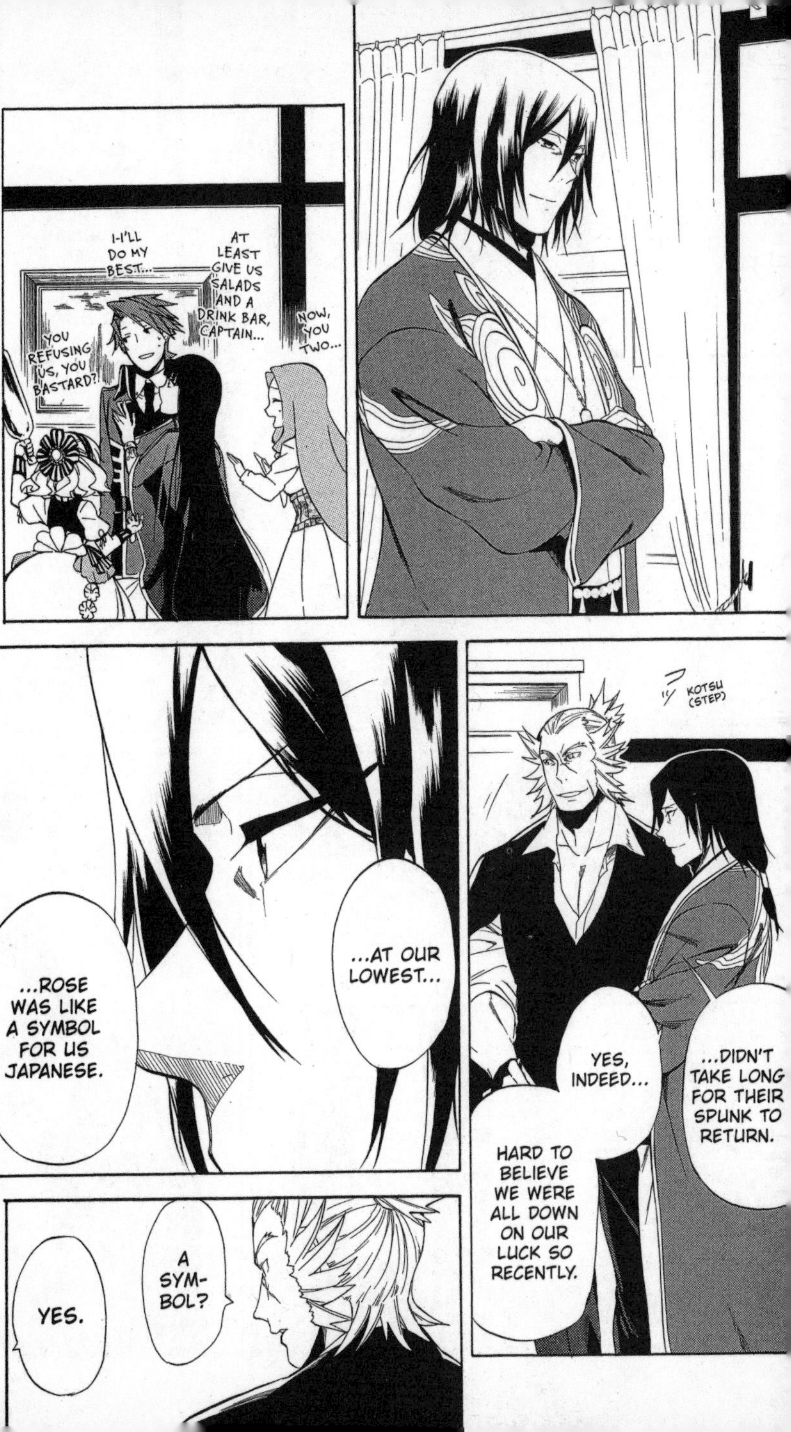
NOW, YOU TWO...
AT LEAST GIVE US SALADS AND A DRINK BAR, CAPTAIN...
I-I'LL DO MY BEST...
YOU REFUSING US, YOU BASTARD?!
KOTSU (STEP)
...DIDN'T TAKE LONG FOR THEIR SPUNK TO RETURN.
YES, INDEED...
HARD TO BELIEVE WE WERE ALL DOWN ON OUR LUCK SO RECENTLY.
...AT OUR LOWEST...
...ROSE WAS LIKE A SYMBOL FOR US JAPANESE.
A SYM-BOL?
YES.

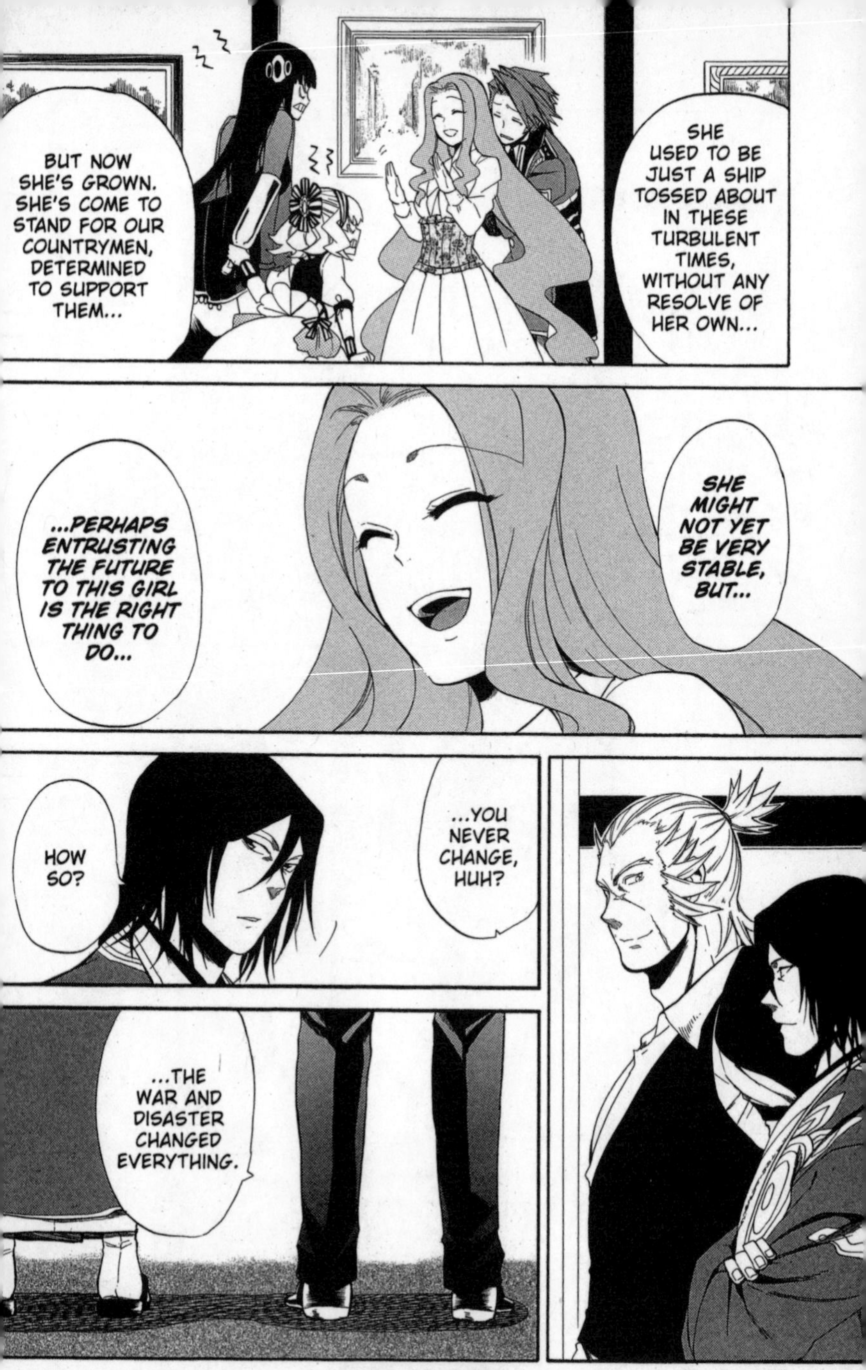
SHE USED TO BE JUST A SHIP TOSSED ABOUT IN THESE TURBULENT TIMES, WITHOUT ANY RESOLVE OF HER OWN...
BUT NOW SHE'S GROWN. SHE'S COME TO STAND FOR OUR COUNTRYMEN, DETERMINED TO SUPPORT THEM...
SHE MIGHT NOT YET BE VERY STABLE, BUT...
...PERHAPS ENTRUSTING THE FUTURE TO THIS GIRL IS THE RIGHT THING TO DO...
...YOU NEVER CHANGE, HUH?
HOW SO?
...THE WAR AND DISASTER CHANGED EVERYTHING.

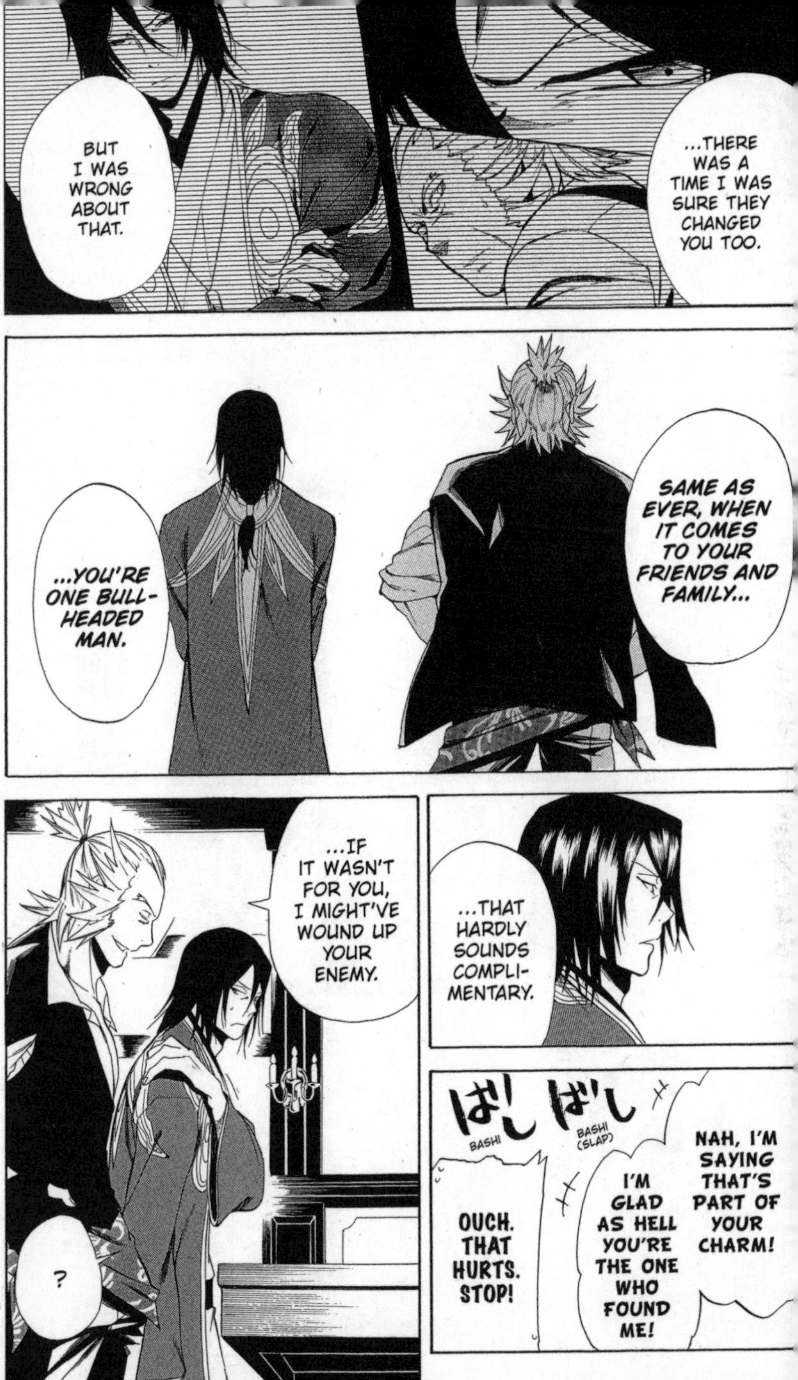
...THERE WAS A TIME I WAS SURE THEY CHANGED YOU TOO.
BUT I WAS WRONG ABOUT THAT.
SAME AS EVER, WHEN IT COMES TO YOUR FRIENDS AND FAMILY...
...YOU'RE ONE BULL-HEADED MAN.
...THAT HARDLY SOUNDS COMPLI-MENTARY.
ばしばし
BASHI BASHI (SLAP)
NAH, I'M SAYING THAT'S PART OF YOUR CHARM!
I'M GLAD AS HELL YOU'RE THE ONE WHO FOUND ME!
OUCH. THAT HURTS. STOP!
...IF IT WASN'T FOR YOU, I MIGHT'VE WOUND UP YOUR ENEMY.
?

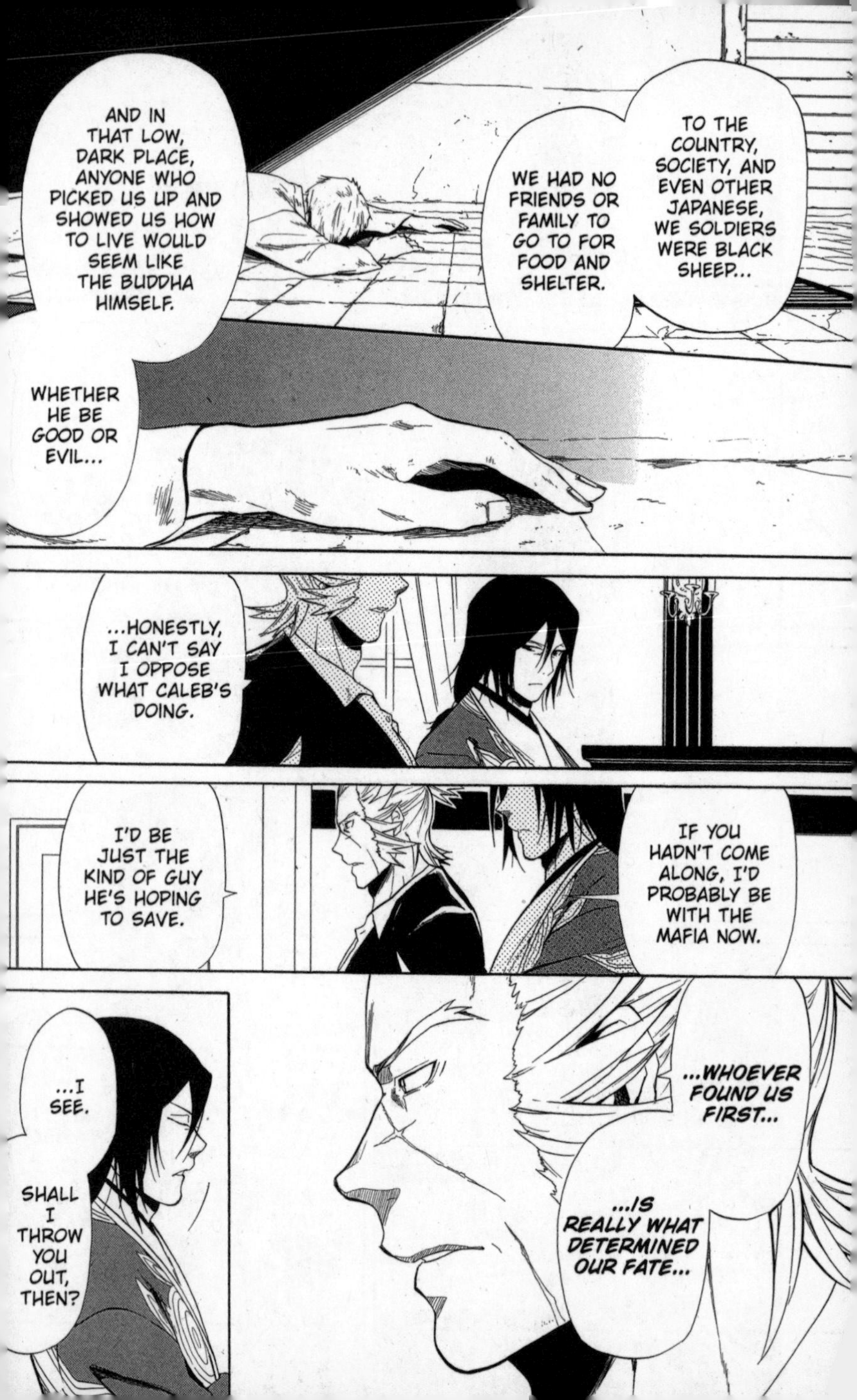
TO THE COUNTRY, SOCIETY, AND EVEN OTHER JAPANESE, WE SOLDIERS WERE BLACK SHEEP...
WE HAD NO FRIENDS OR FAMILY TO GO TO FOR FOOD AND SHELTER.
AND IN THAT LOW, DARK PLACE, ANYONE WHO PICKED US UP AND SHOWED US HOW TO LIVE WOULD SEEM LIKE THE BUDDHA HIMSELF.
WHETHER HE BE GOOD OR EVIL...
...HONESTLY, I CAN'T SAY I OPPOSE WHAT CALEB'S DOING.
IF YOU HADN'T COME ALONG, I'D PROBABLY BE WITH THE MAFIA NOW.
I'D BE JUST THE KIND OF GUY HE'S HOPING TO SAVE.
...WHOEVER FOUND US FIRST...
...IS REALLY WHAT DETERMINED OUR FATE...
...I SEE.
SHALL I THROW YOU OUT, THEN?

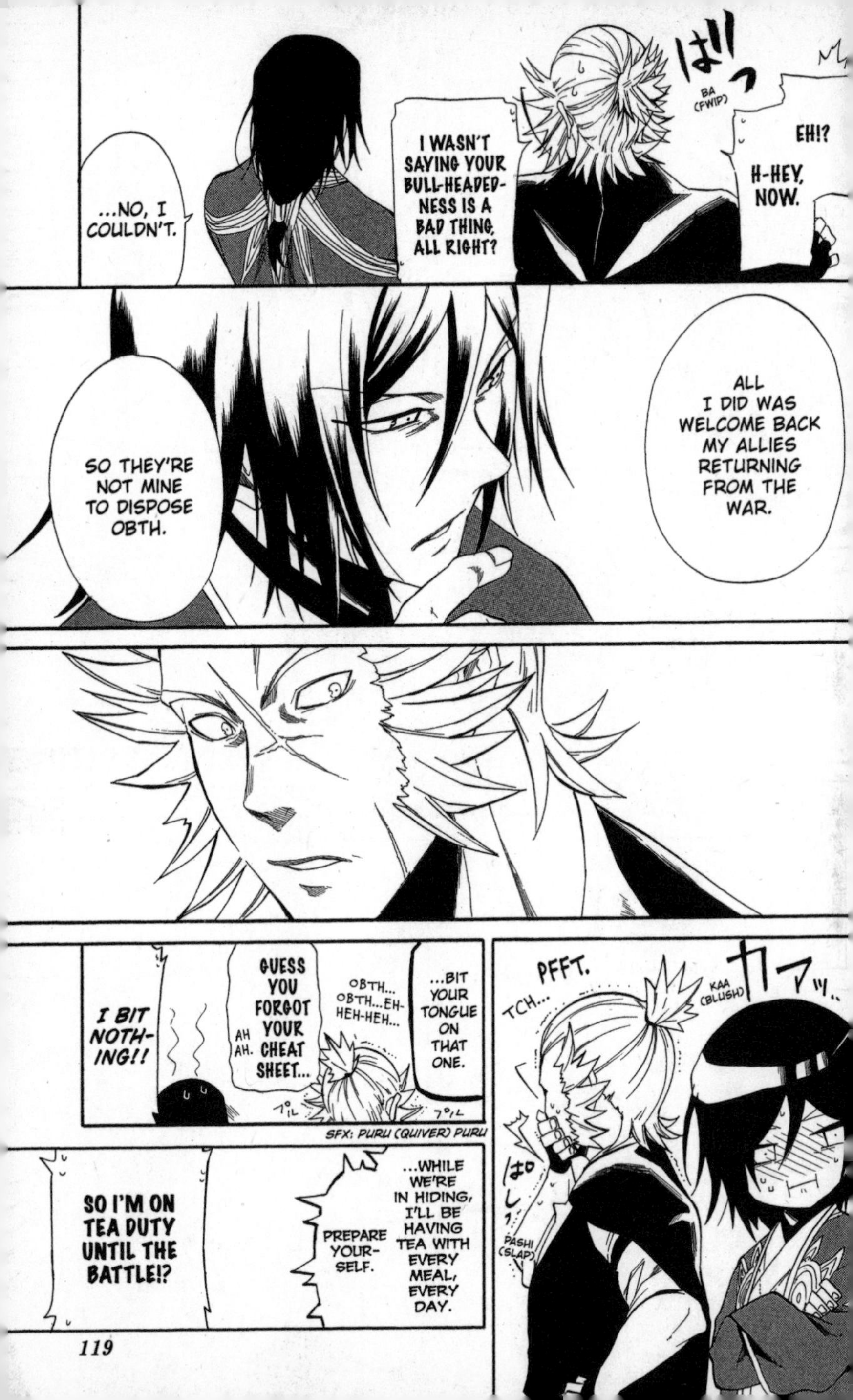
ばっ
BA (FWIP)
EH!?
H-HEY, NOW.
I WASN'T SAYING YOUR BULL-HEADEDNESS IS A BAD THING, ALL RIGHT?
...NO, I COULDN'T.
ALL I DID WAS WELCOME BACK MY ALLIES RETURNING FROM THE WAR.
SO THEY'RE NOT MINE TO DISPOSE OBTH.
カァッ..
KAA (BLUSH)
PFFT.
TCH...
はしっ
PASHI (SLAP)
...BIT YOUR TONGUE ON THAT ONE.
OBTH... OBTH...EH-HEH-HEH...
GUESS YOU FORGOT YOUR CHEAT SHEET...
AH AH.
I BIT NOTHING!!
SFX: PURU (QUIVER) PURU
...WHILE WE'RE IN HIDING, I'LL BE HAVING TEA WITH EVERY MEAL, EVERY DAY.
PREPARE YOURSELF.
SO I'M ON TEA DUTY UNTIL THE BATTLE!?

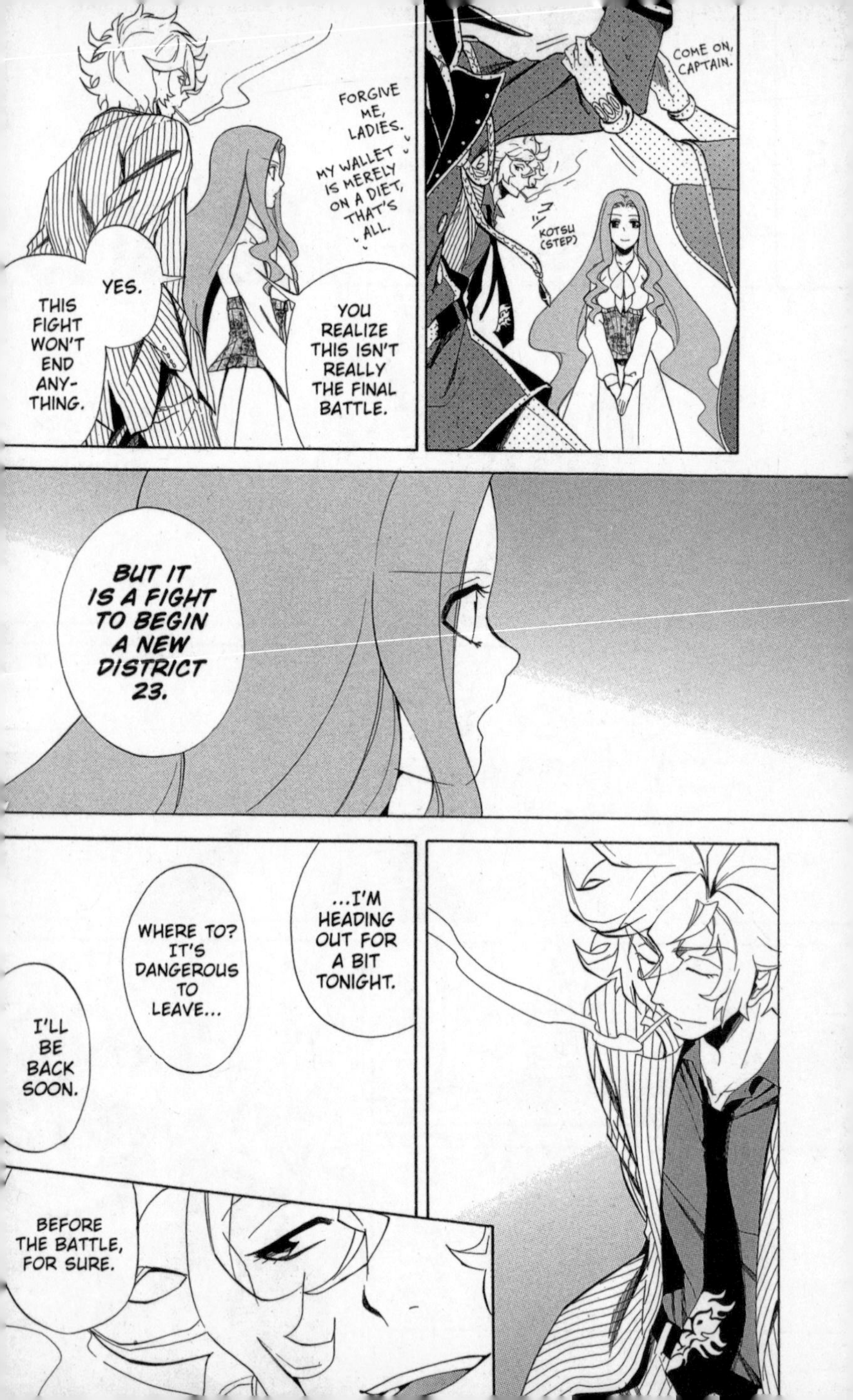
COME ON, CAPTAIN.
KOTSU (STEP)
FORGIVE ME, LADIES.
MY WALLET IS MERELY ON A DIET, THAT'S ALL.
YOU REALIZE THIS ISN'T REALLY THE FINAL BATTLE.
YES.
THIS FIGHT WON'T END ANYTHING.
BUT IT IS A FIGHT TO BEGIN A NEW DISTRICT 23.
...I'M HEADING OUT FOR A BIT TONIGHT.
WHERE TO? IT'S DANGEROUS TO LEAVE...
I'LL BE BACK SOON.
BEFORE THE BATTLE, FOR SURE.

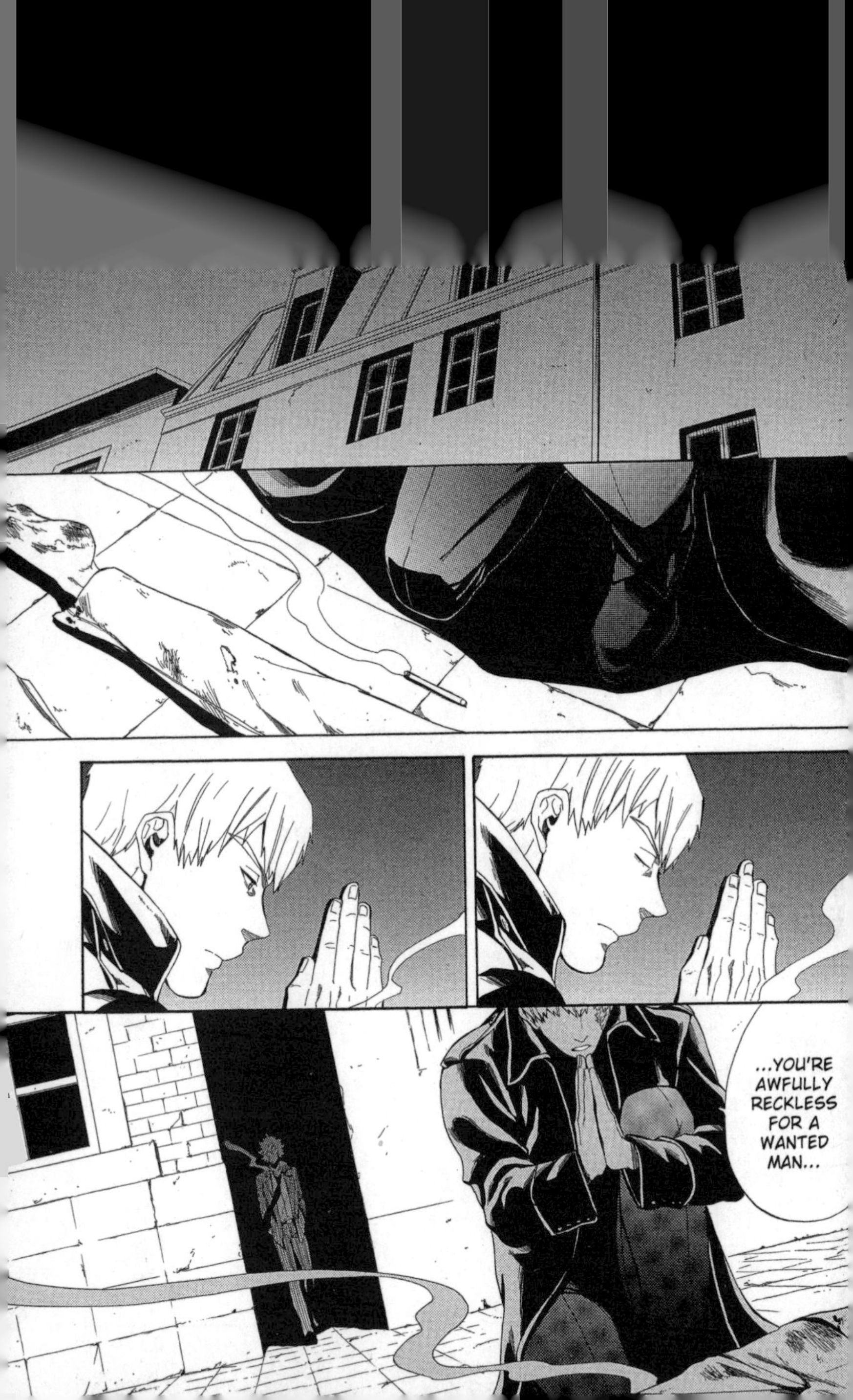
...YOU'RE AWFULLY RECKLESS FOR A WANTED MAN...

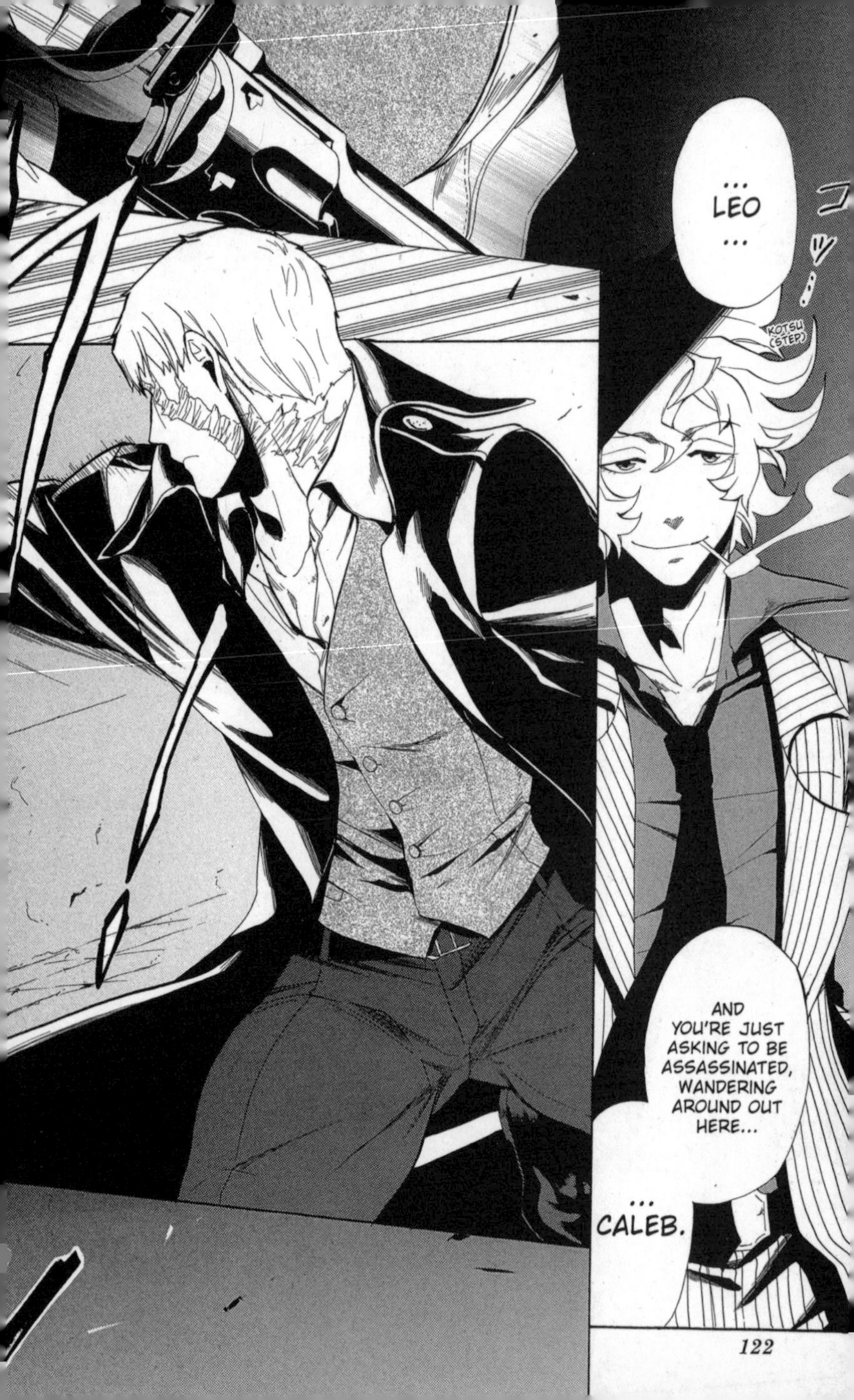
... LEO ...
コツ!
KOTSU (STEP)
AND YOU'RE JUST ASKING TO BE ASSASSINATED, WANDERING AROUND OUT HERE...
... CALEB.

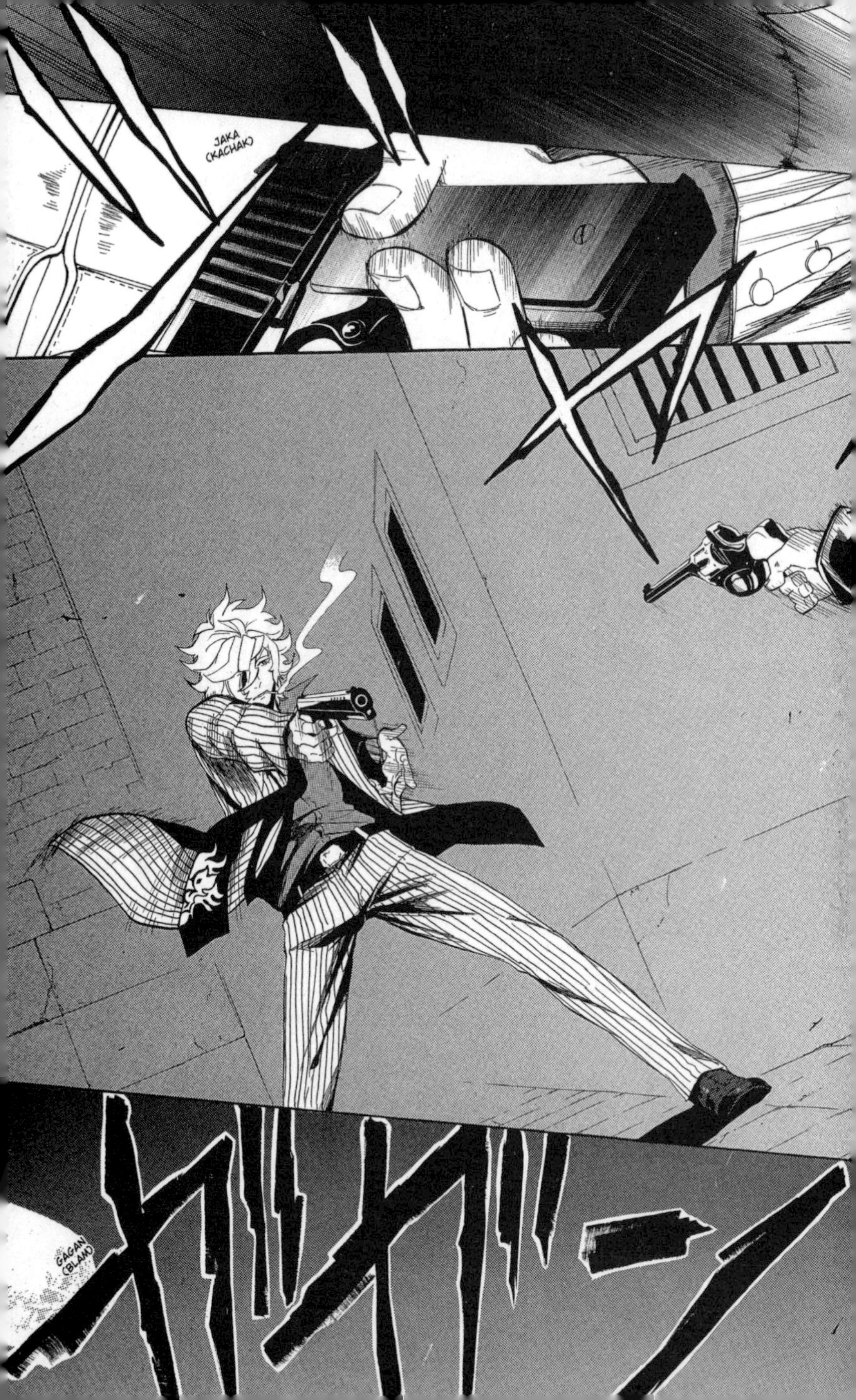
JAKA (KACHAK)
GAGAN (BLAM)

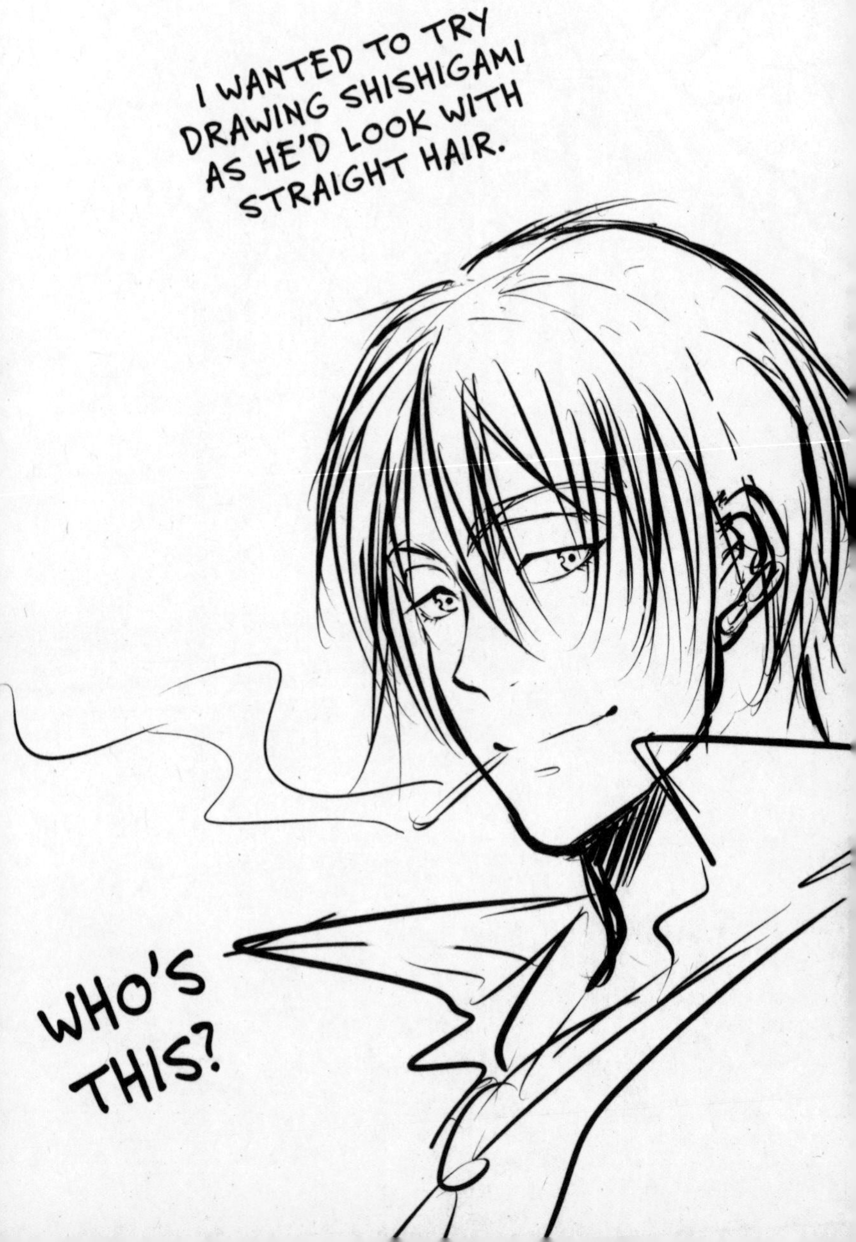
I WANTED TO TRY DRAWING SHISHIGAMI AS HE'D LOOK WITH STRAIGHT HAIR.
WHO'S THIS?

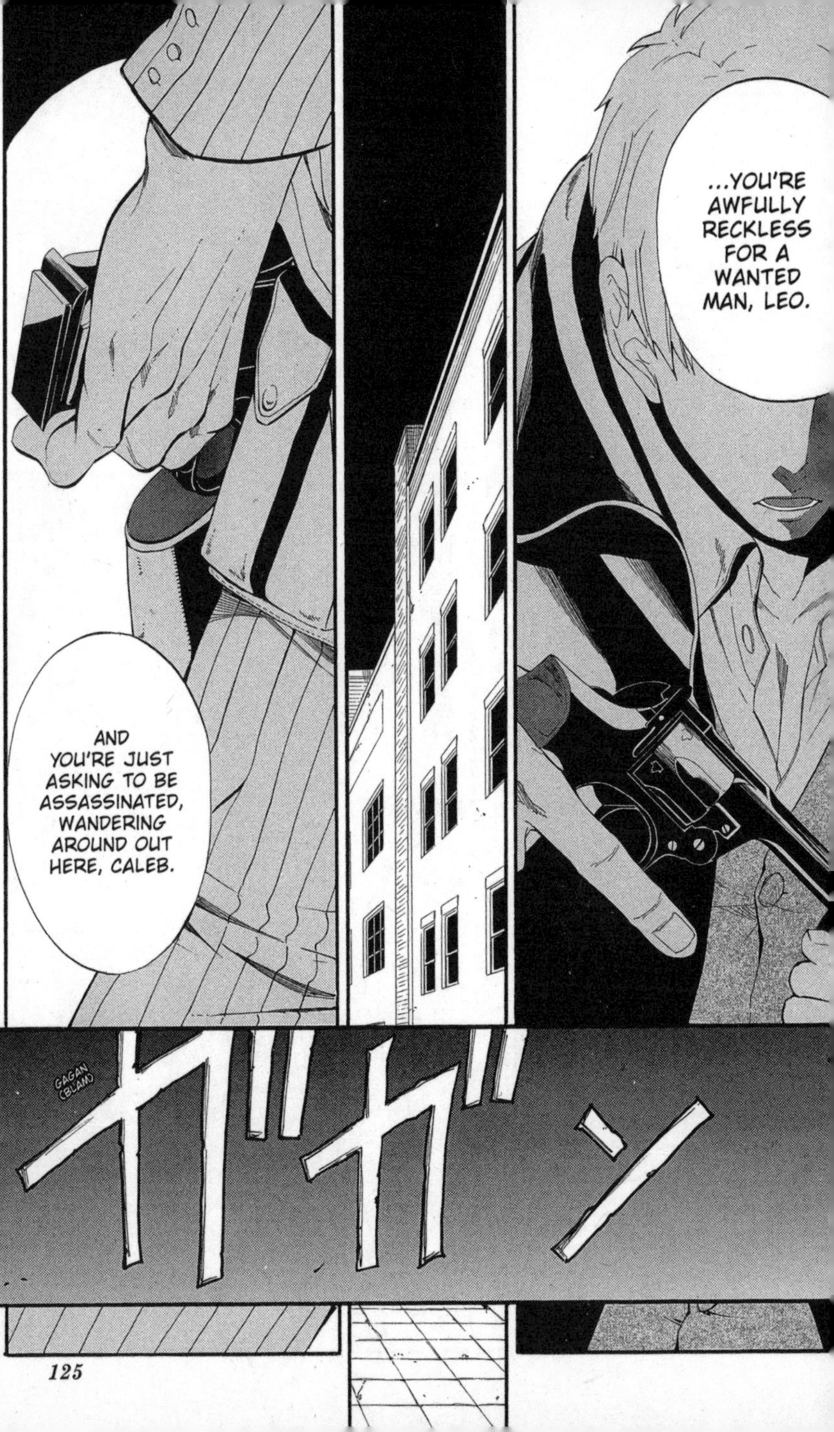
...YOU'RE AWFULLY RECKLESS FOR A WANTED MAN, LEO.
AND YOU'RE JUST ASKING TO BE ASSASSINATED, WANDERING AROUND OUT HERE, CALEB.
GAGAN (BLAM)

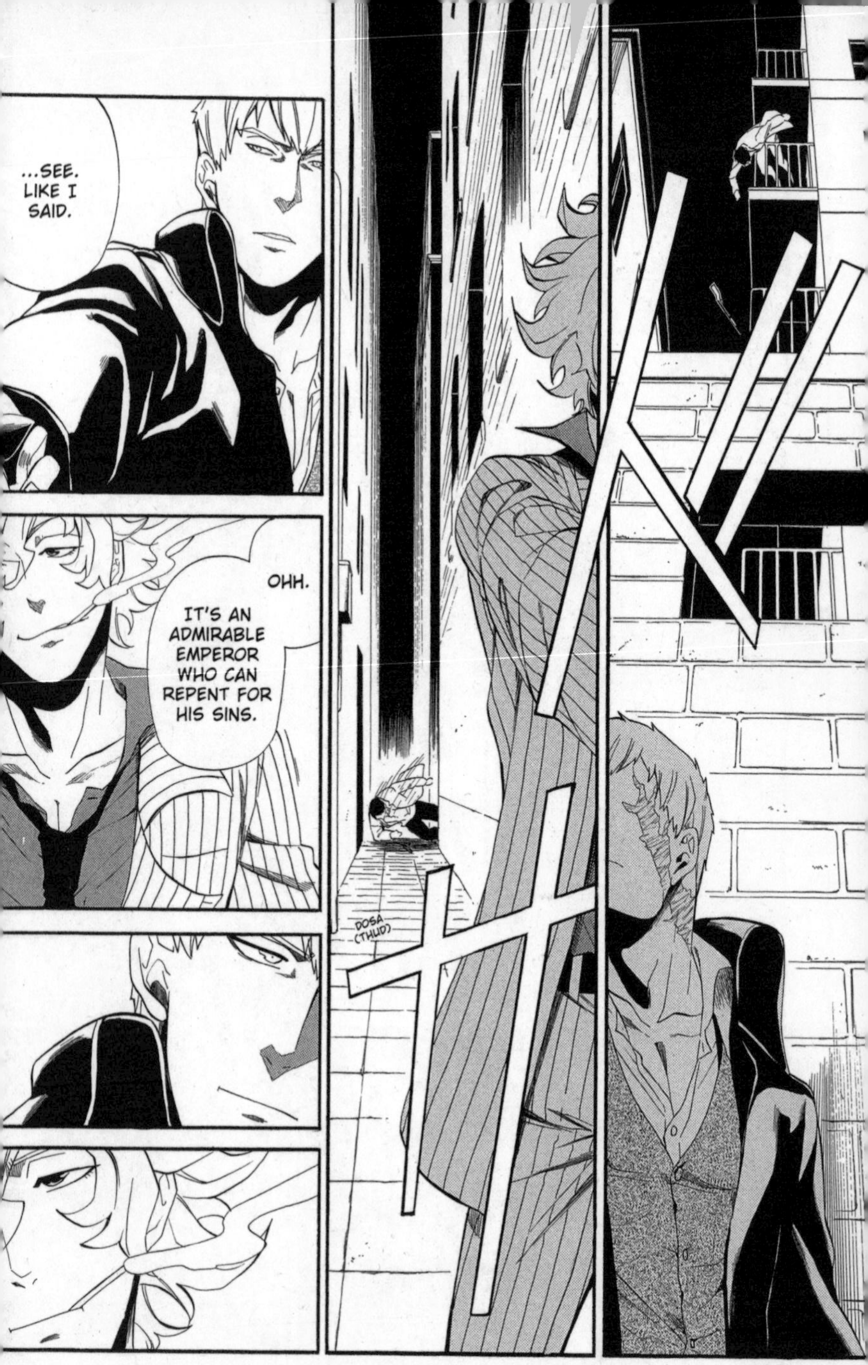
DOSA (THUD)
...SEE. LIKE I SAID.
OHH.
IT'S AN ADMIRABLE EMPEROR WHO CAN REPENT FOR HIS SINS.

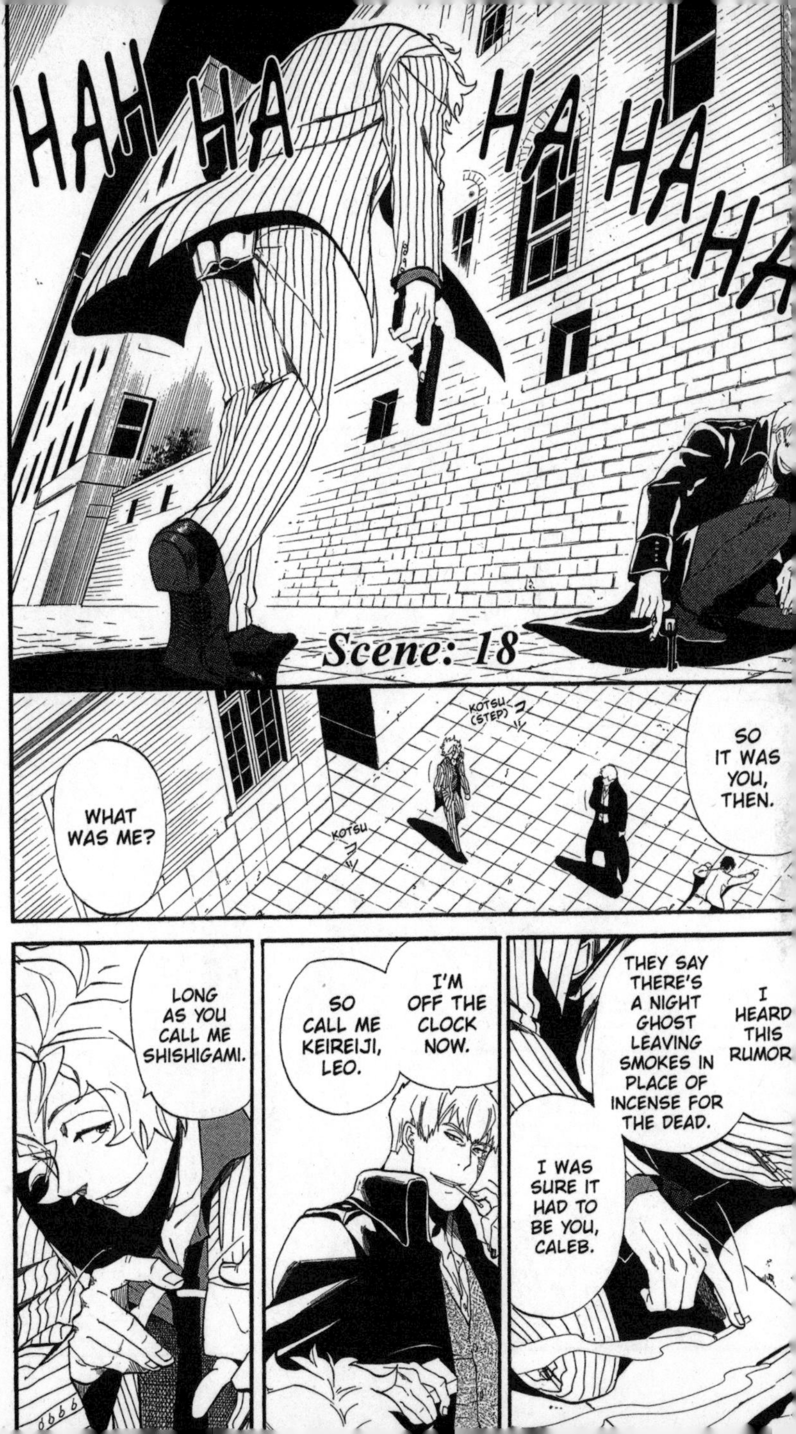
HAH HA HA HA HA HA
Scene: 18
KOTSU (STEP)
SO IT WAS YOU, THEN.
KOTSU
WHAT WAS ME?
I HEARD THIS RUMOR
THEY SAY THERE'S A NIGHT GHOST LEAVING SMOKES IN PLACE OF INCENSE FOR THE DEAD.
I WAS SURE IT HAD TO BE YOU, CALEB.
I'M OFF THE CLOCK NOW.
SO CALL ME KEIREIJI, LEO.
LONG AS YOU CALL ME SHISHIGAMI.

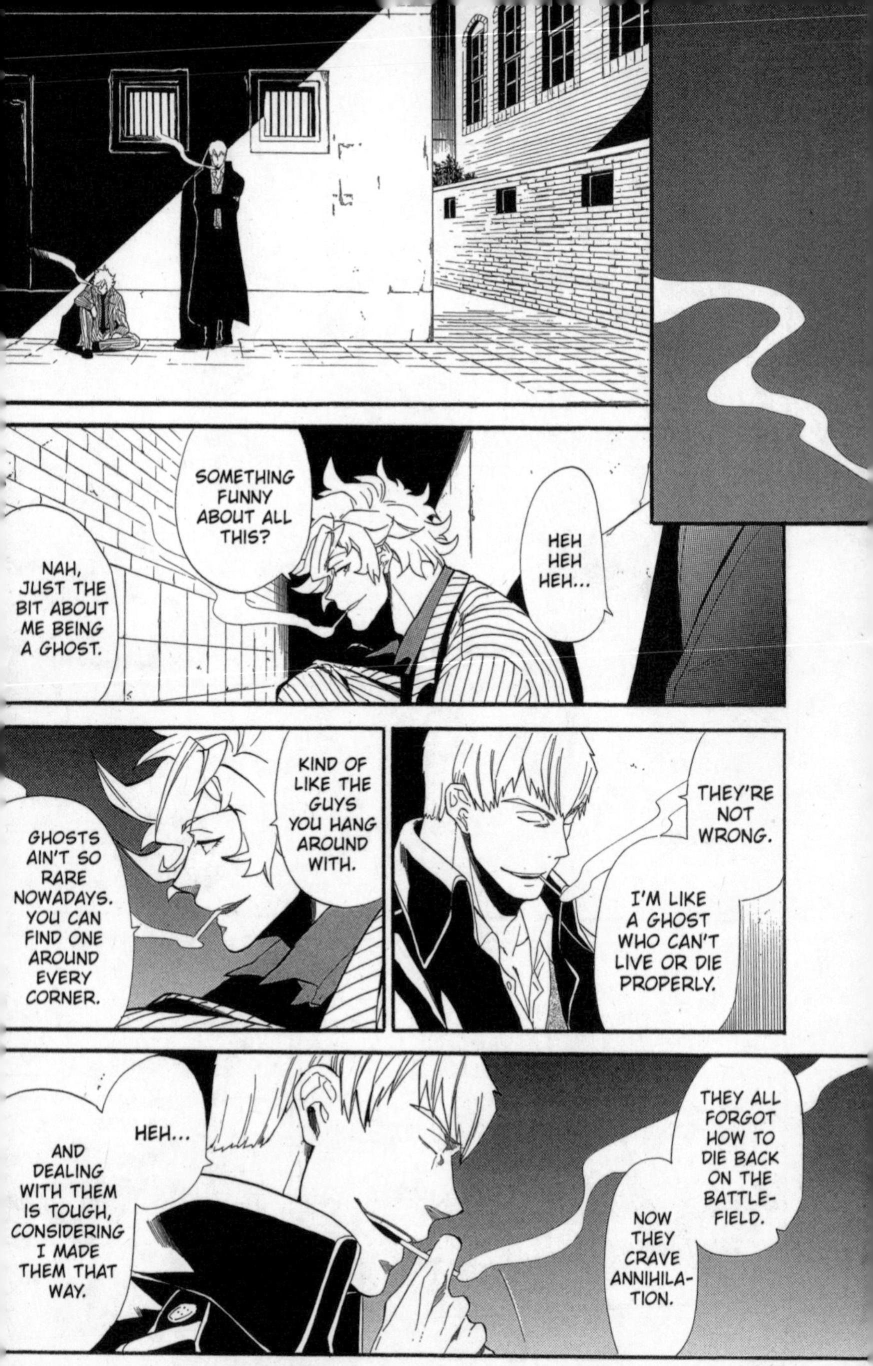
HEH HEH HEH...
SOMETHING FUNNY ABOUT ALL THIS?
NAH, JUST THE BIT ABOUT ME BEING A GHOST.
THEY'RE NOT WRONG.
I'M LIKE A GHOST WHO CAN'T LIVE OR DIE PROPERLY.
GHOSTS AIN'T SO RARE NOWADAYS. YOU CAN FIND ONE AROUND EVERY CORNER.
KIND OF LIKE THE GUYS YOU HANG AROUND WITH.
THEY ALL FORGOT HOW TO DIE BACK ON THE BATTLE-FIELD.
NOW THEY CRAVE ANNIHILA-TION.
HEH...
AND DEALING WITH THEM IS TOUGH, CONSIDERING I MADE THEM THAT WAY.

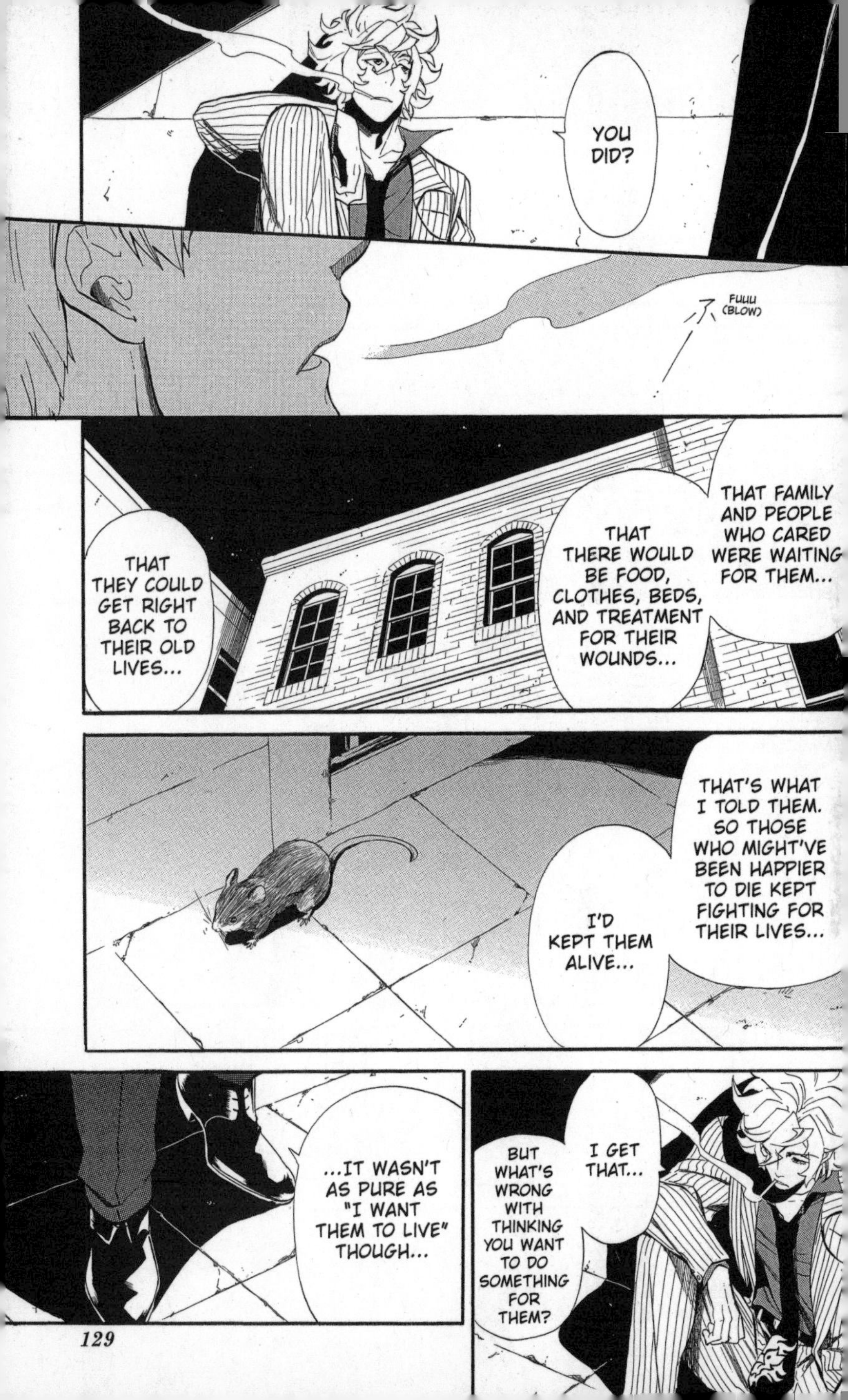
YOU DID?
FUUU (BLOW)
THAT FAMILY AND PEOPLE WHO CARED WERE WAITING FOR THEM...
THAT THERE WOULD BE FOOD, CLOTHES, BEDS, AND TREATMENT FOR THEIR WOUNDS...
THAT THEY COULD GET RIGHT BACK TO THEIR OLD LIVES...
THAT'S WHAT I TOLD THEM. SO THOSE WHO MIGHT'VE BEEN HAPPIER TO DIE KEPT FIGHTING FOR THEIR LIVES...
I'D KEPT THEM ALIVE...
I GET THAT...
BUT WHAT'S WRONG WITH THINKING YOU WANT TO DO SOMETHING FOR THEM?
...IT WASN'T AS PURE AS "I WANT THEM TO LIVE" THOUGH...

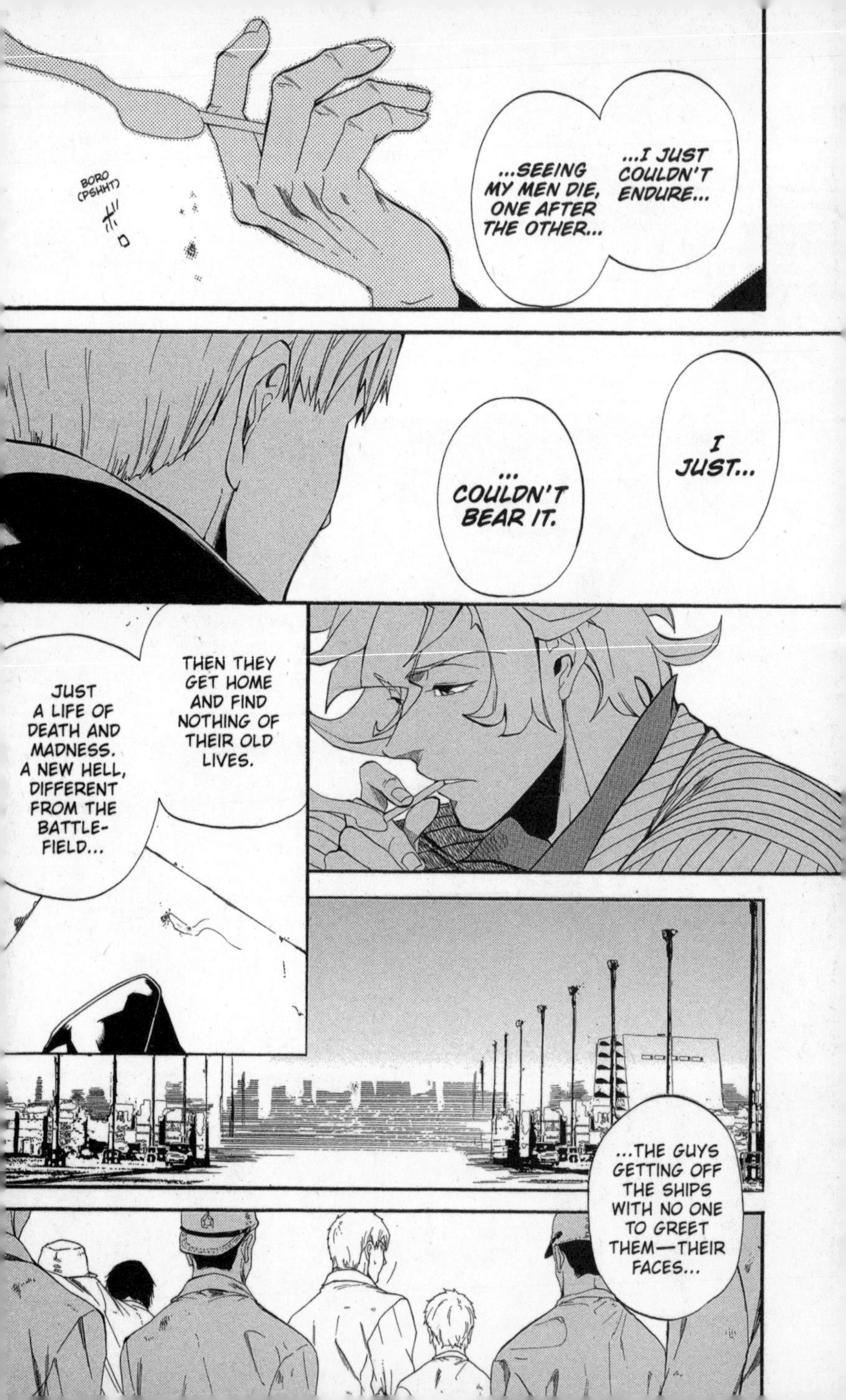
BORO (PSHHT)
...I JUST COULDN'T ENDURE...
...SEEING MY MEN DIE, ONE AFTER THE OTHER...
I JUST...
...COULDN'T BEAR IT.
...THE GUYS GETTING OFF THE SHIPS WITH NO ONE TO GREET THEM—THEIR FACES...
THEN THEY GET HOME AND FIND NOTHING OF THEIR OLD LIVES.
JUST A LIFE OF DEATH AND MADNESS. A NEW HELL, DIFFERENT FROM THE BATTLE-FIELD...

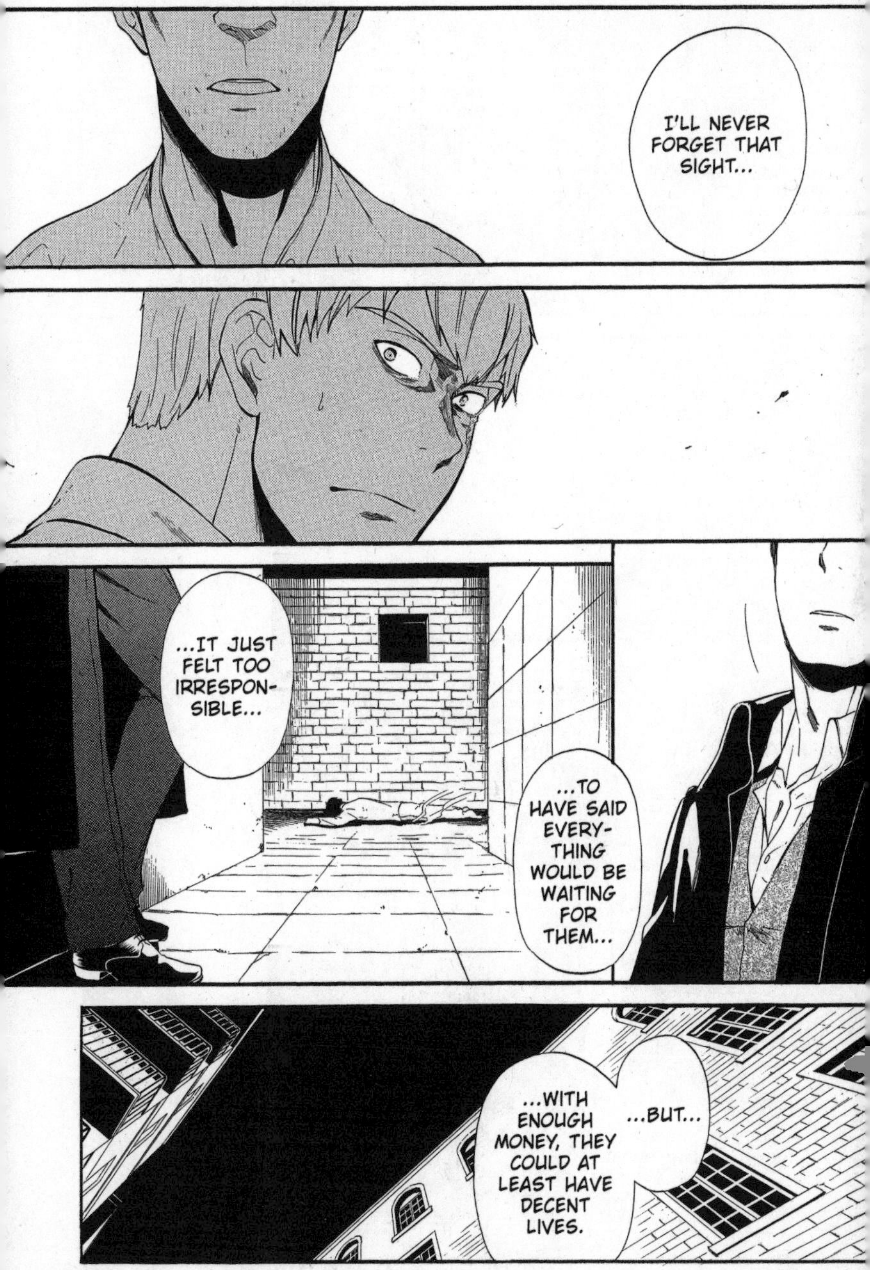
I'LL NEVER FORGET THAT SIGHT...
...TO HAVE SAID EVERY-THING WOULD BE WAITING FOR THEM...
...IT JUST FELT TOO IRRESPON-SIBLE...
...BUT...
...WITH ENOUGH MONEY, THEY COULD AT LEAST HAVE DECENT LIVES.

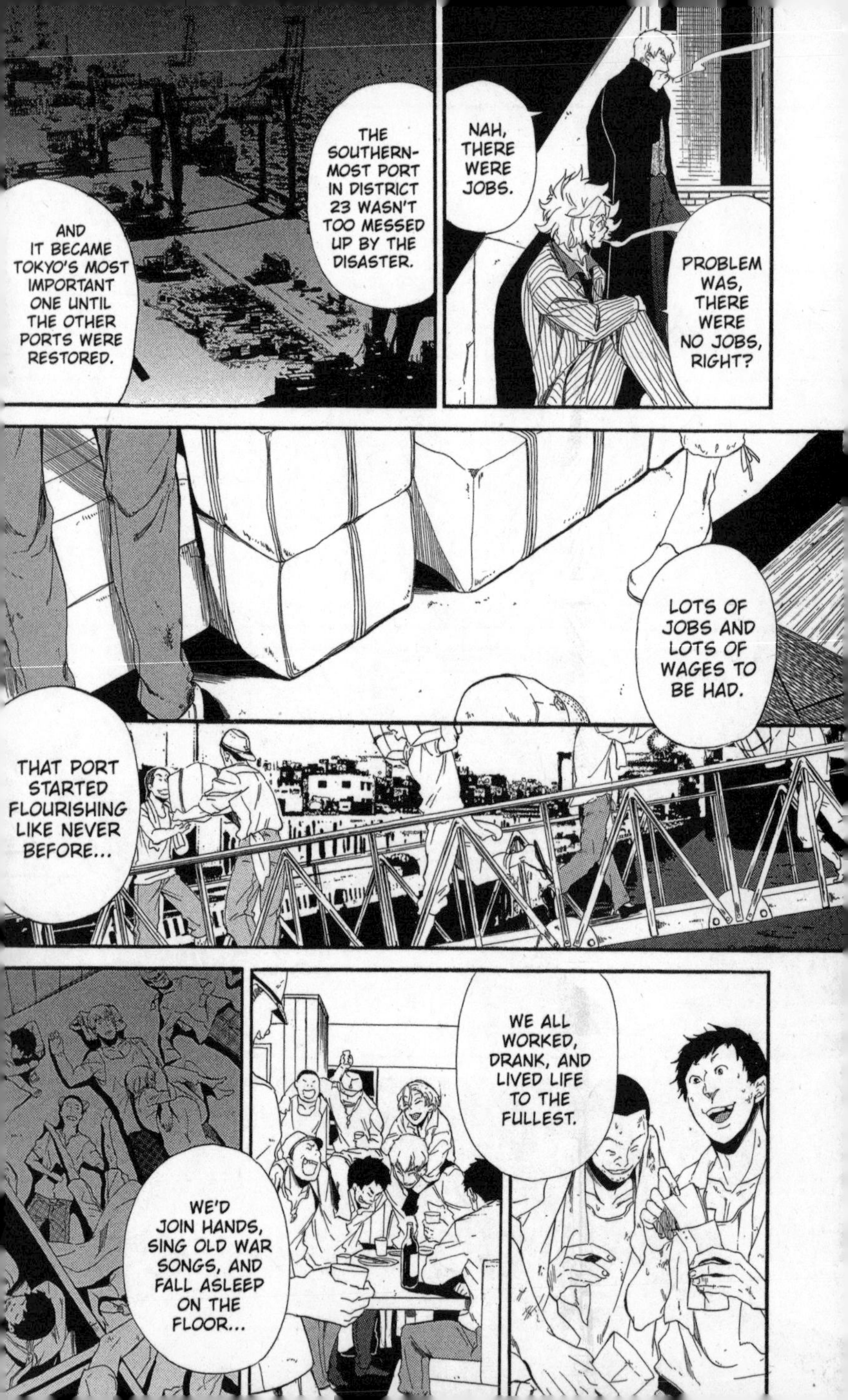
PROBLEM WAS, THERE WERE NO JOBS, RIGHT?
NAH, THERE WERE JOBS.
THE SOUTHERN-MOST PORT IN DISTRICT 23 WASN'T TOO MESSED UP BY THE DISASTER.
AND IT BECAME TOKYO'S MOST IMPORTANT ONE UNTIL THE OTHER PORTS WERE RESTORED.
LOTS OF JOBS AND LOTS OF WAGES TO BE HAD.
THAT PORT STARTED FLOURISHING LIKE NEVER BEFORE...
WE ALL WORKED, DRANK, AND LIVED LIFE TO THE FULLEST.
WE'D JOIN HANDS, SING OLD WAR SONGS, AND FALL ASLEEP ON THE FLOOR...

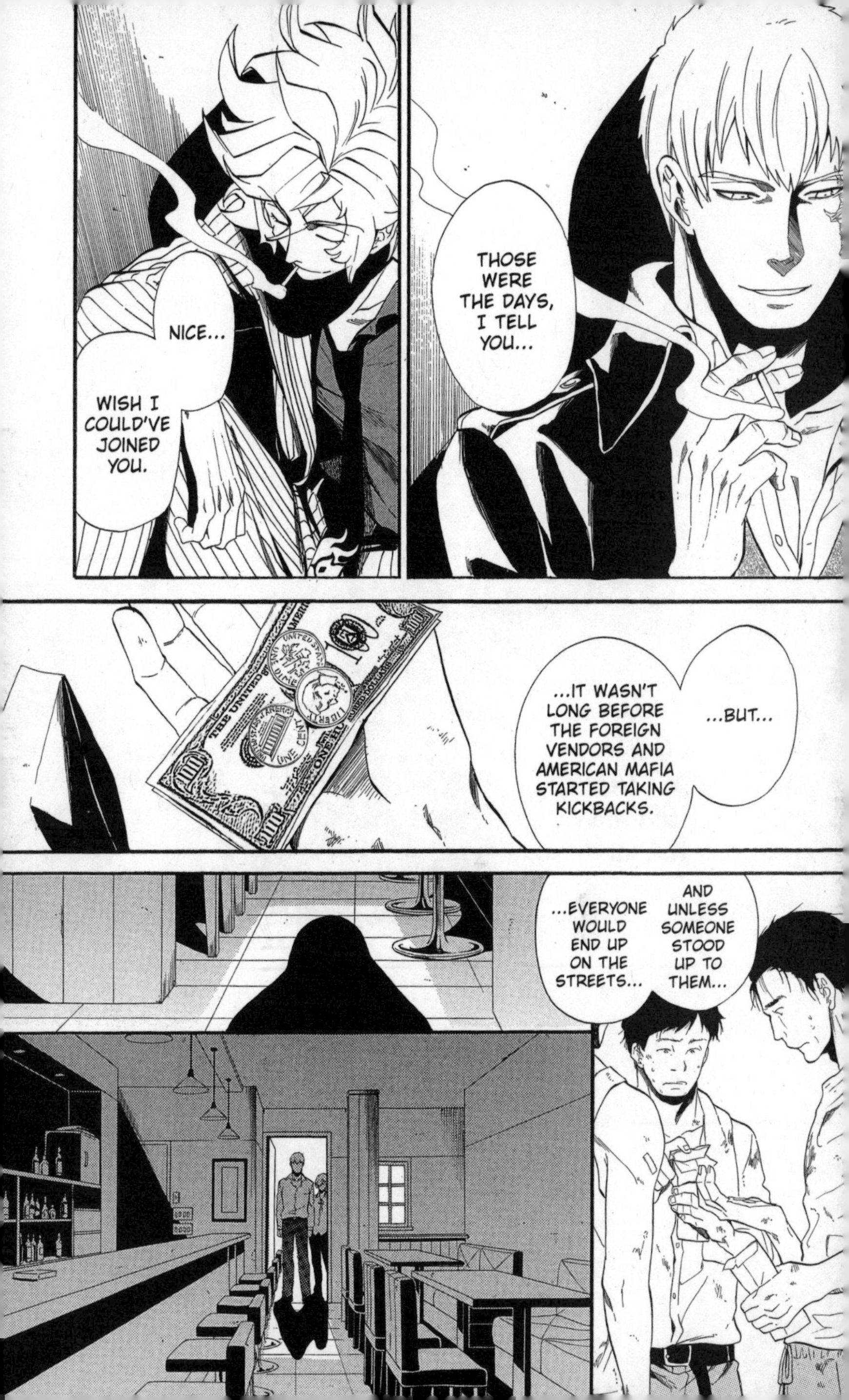
THOSE WERE THE DAYS, I TELL YOU...
NICE...
WISH I COULD'VE JOINED YOU.
...BUT...
...IT WASN'T LONG BEFORE THE FOREIGN VENDORS AND AMERICAN MAFIA STARTED TAKING KICKBACKS.
AND UNLESS SOMEONE STOOD UP TO THEM...
...EVERYONE WOULD END UP ON THE STREETS...

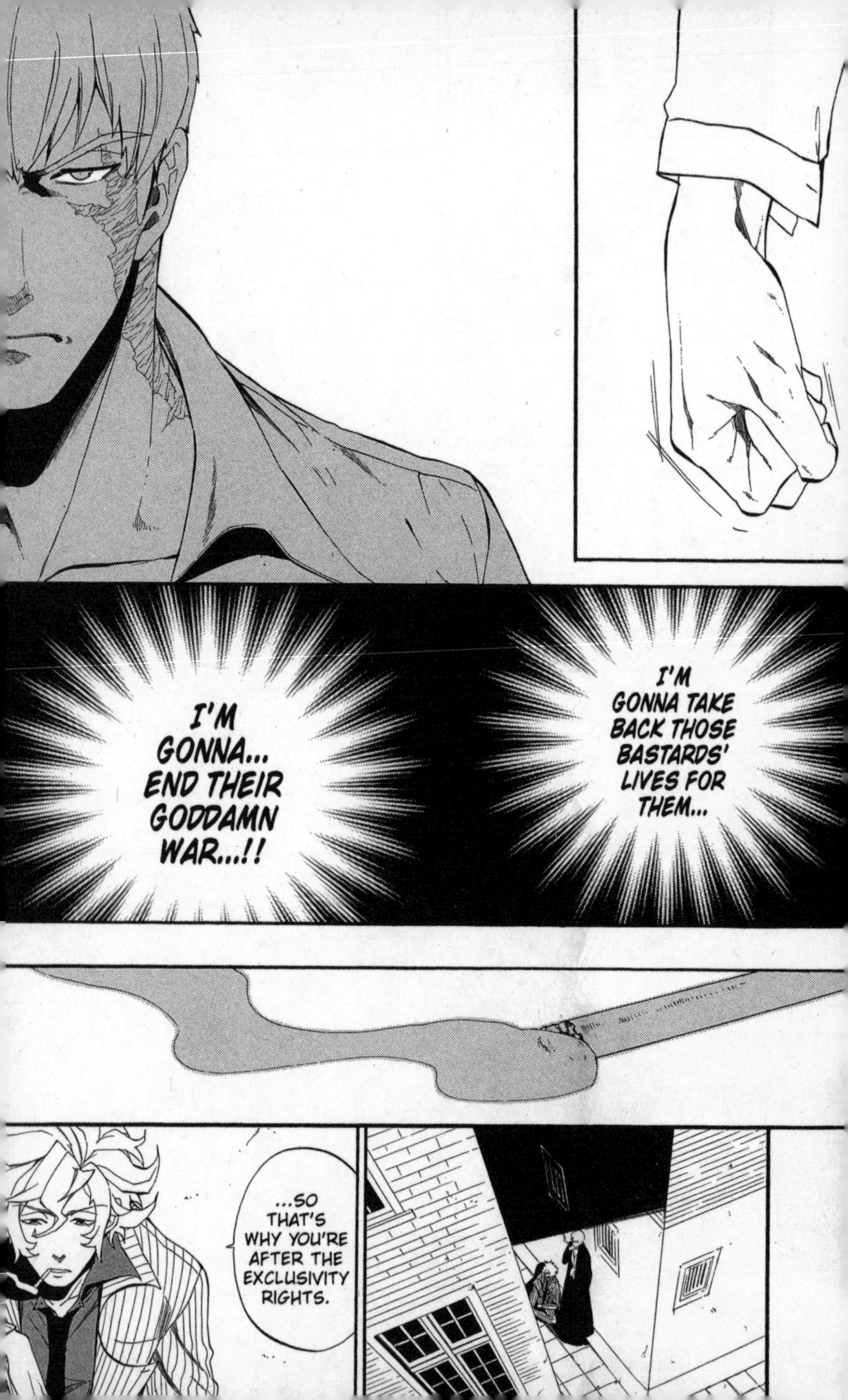
I'M GONNA TAKE BACK THOSE BASTARDS' LIVES FOR THEM...
I'M GONNA... END THEIR GODDAMN WAR...!!
...SO THAT'S WHY YOU'RE AFTER THE EXCLUSIVITY RIGHTS.

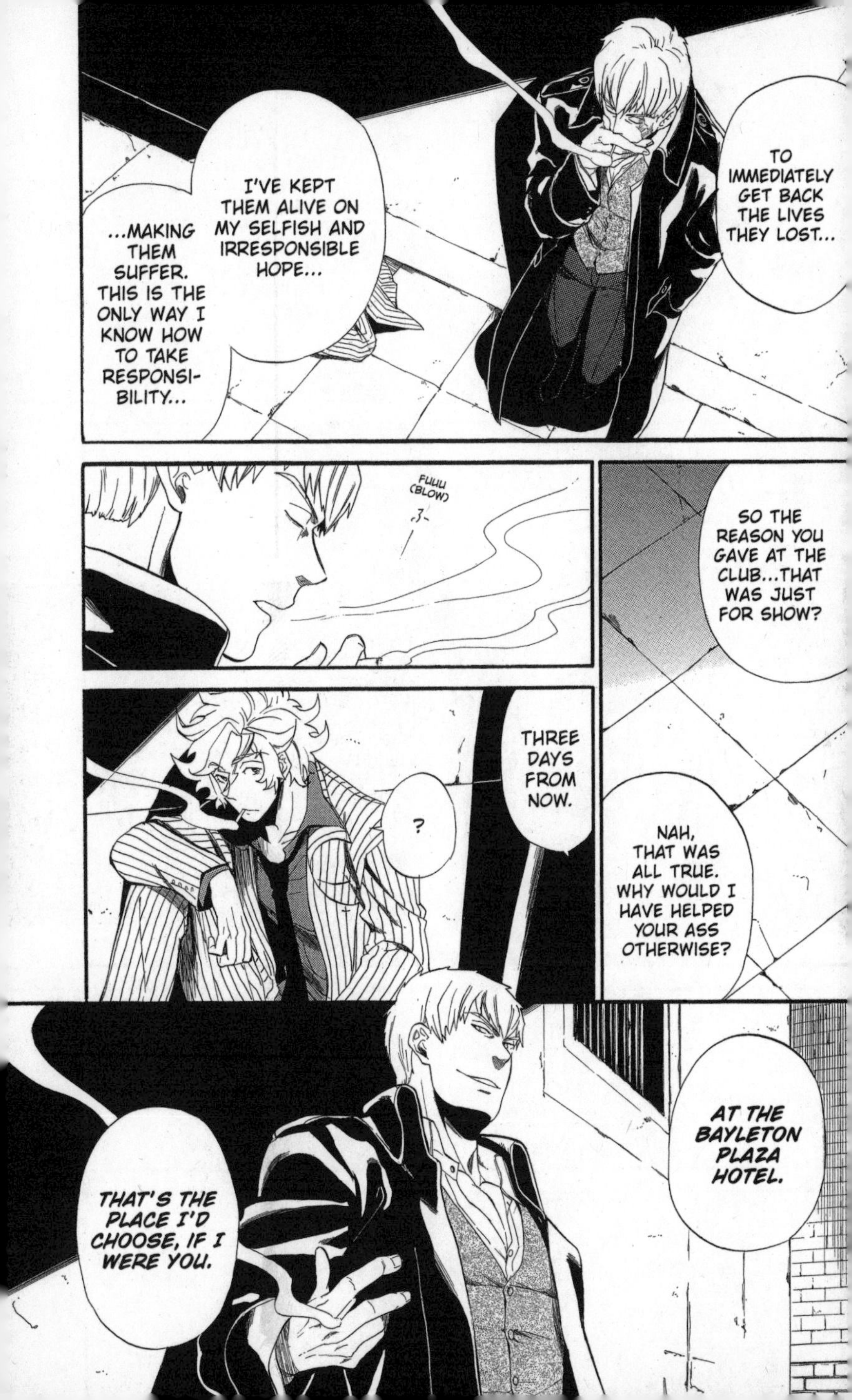

TO IMMEDIATELY GET BACK THE LIVES THEY LOST...
I'VE KEPT THEM ALIVE ON MY SELFISH AND IRRESPONSIBLE HOPE...
...MAKING THEM SUFFER. THIS IS THE ONLY WAY I KNOW HOW TO TAKE RESPONSI-BILITY...
SO THE REASON YOU GAVE AT THE CLUB...THAT WAS JUST FOR SHOW?
NAH, THAT WAS ALL TRUE. WHY WOULD I HAVE HELPED YOUR ASS OTHERWISE?
FUUU (BLOW)
THREE DAYS FROM NOW.
?
AT THE BAYLETON PLAZA HOTEL.
THAT'S THE PLACE I'D CHOOSE, IF I WERE YOU.

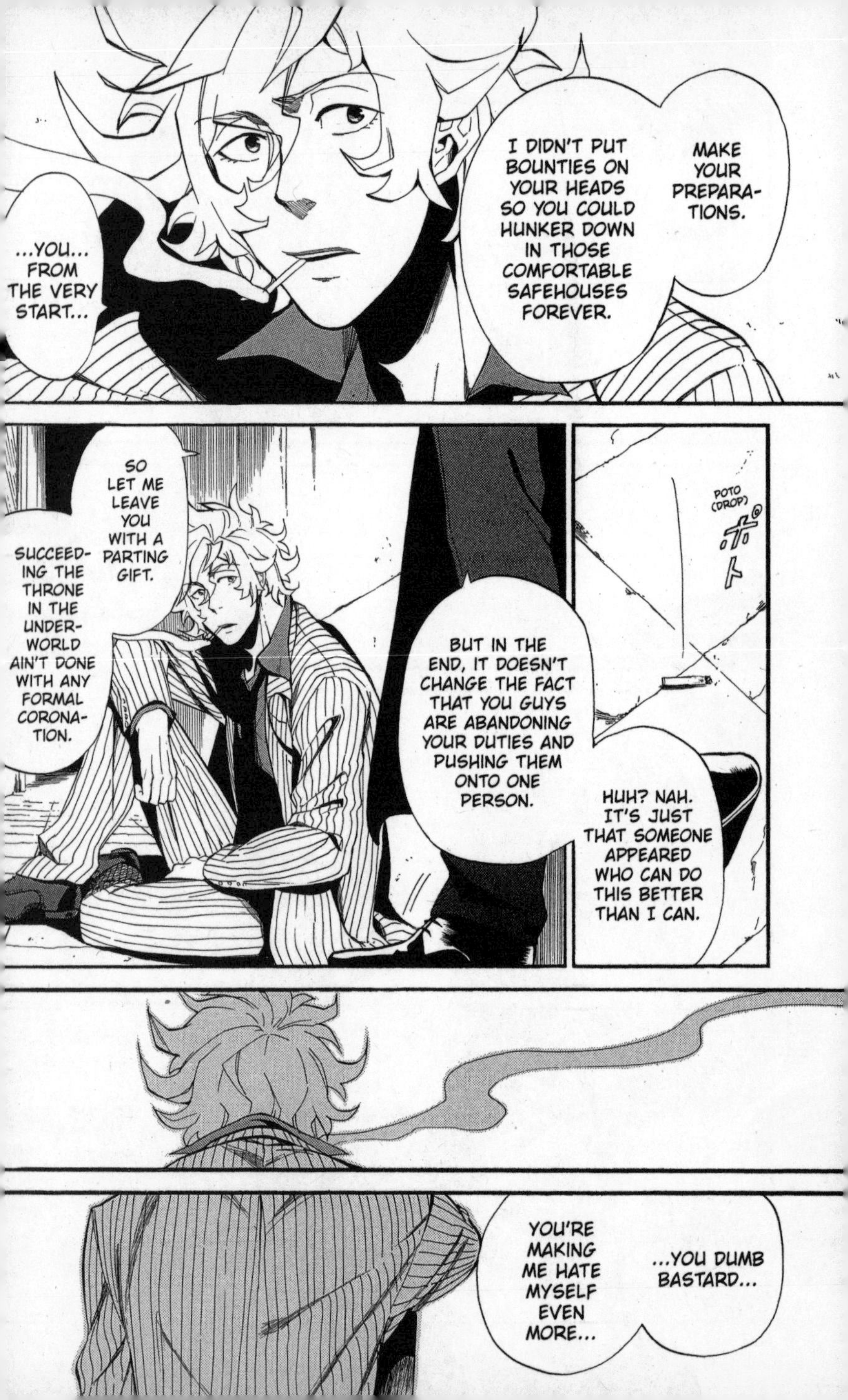
MAKE YOUR PREPARA-TIONS.
I DIDN'T PUT BOUNTIES ON YOUR HEADS SO YOU COULD HUNKER DOWN IN THOSE COMFORTABLE SAFEHOUSES FOREVER.
...YOU... FROM THE VERY START...
POTO (DROP)
ポト
BUT IN THE END, IT DOESN'T CHANGE THE FACT THAT YOU GUYS ARE ABANDONING YOUR DUTIES AND PUSHING THEM ONTO ONE PERSON.
HUH? NAH. IT'S JUST THAT SOMEONE APPEARED WHO CAN DO THIS BETTER THAN I CAN.
SO LET ME LEAVE YOU WITH A PARTING GIFT.
SUCCEED-ING THE THRONE IN THE UNDER-WORLD AIN'T DONE WITH ANY FORMAL CORONA-TION.
YOU'RE MAKING ME HATE MYSELF EVEN MORE...
...YOU DUMB BASTARD...

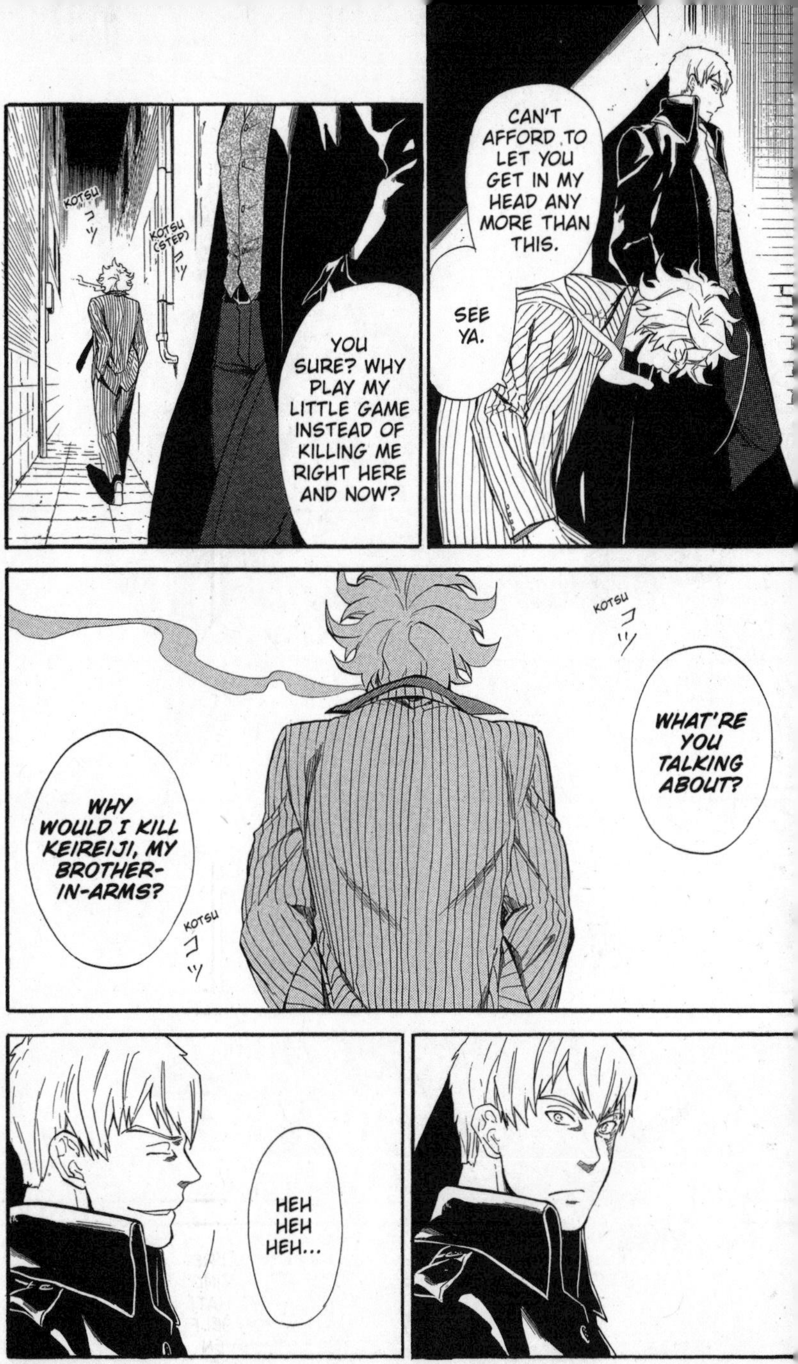
CAN'T AFFORD TO LET YOU GET IN MY HEAD ANY MORE THAN THIS.
SEE YA.
YOU SURE? WHY PLAY MY LITTLE GAME INSTEAD OF KILLING ME RIGHT HERE AND NOW?
KOTSU (STEP)
コッ
KOTSU
コッ
KOTSU
コッ
WHAT'RE YOU TALKING ABOUT?
WHY WOULD I KILL KEIREIJI, MY BROTHER-IN-ARMS?
KOTSU
コッ
HEH HEH HEH...

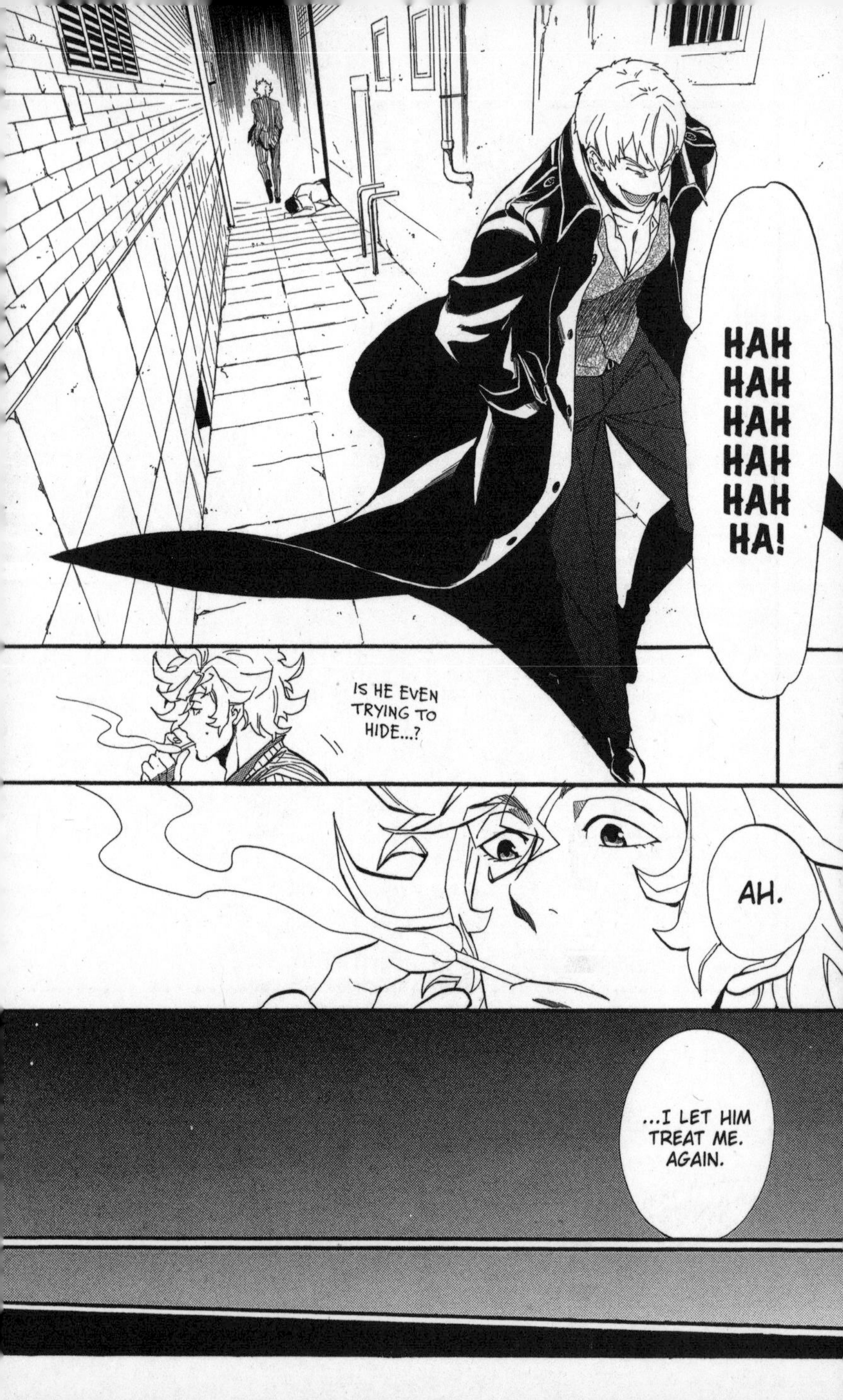
HAH HAH HAH HAH HAH HA!
IS HE EVEN TRYING TO HIDE...?
AH.
...I LET HIM TREAT ME. AGAIN.

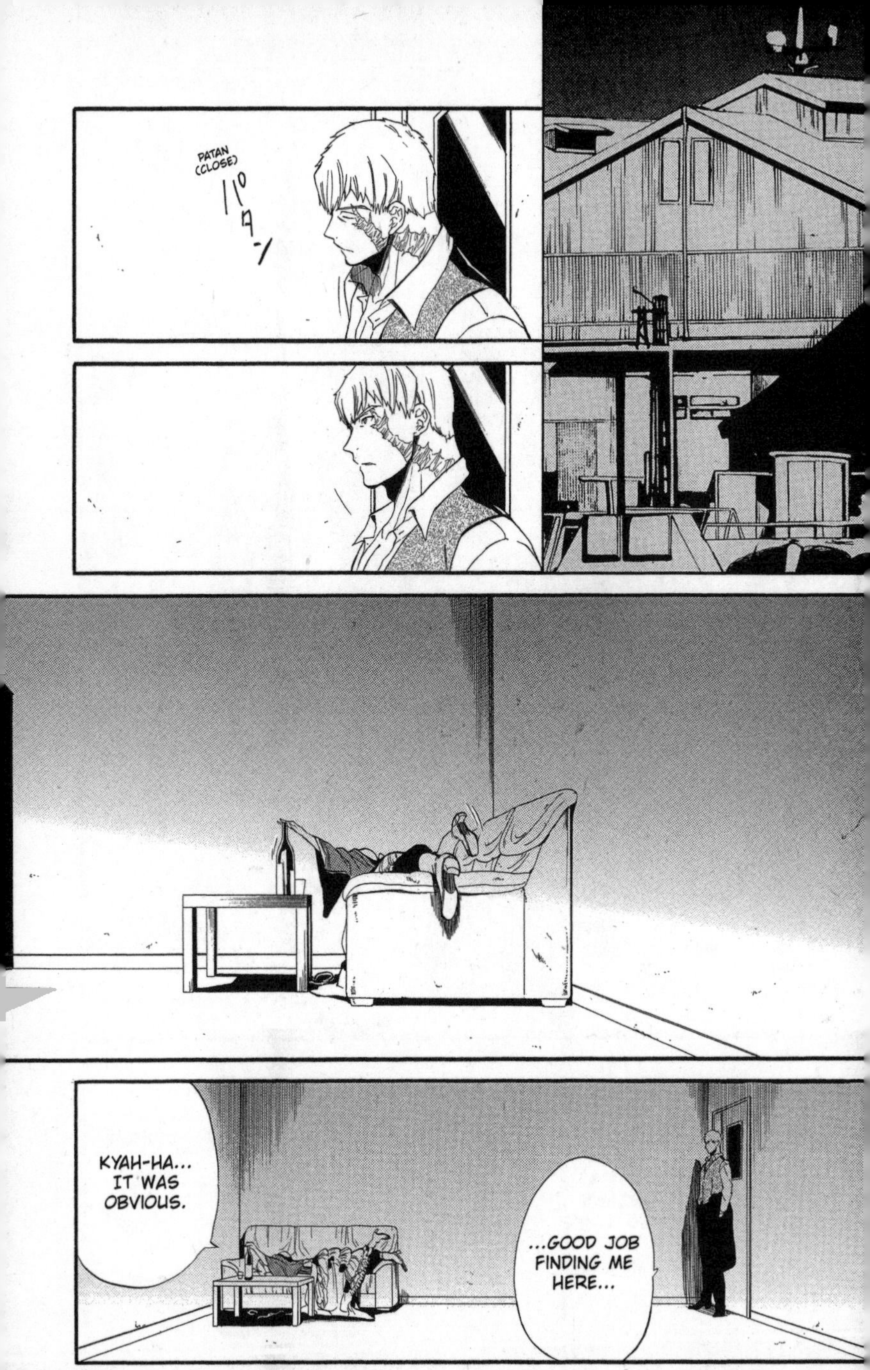
PATAN (CLOSE)
パタン
...GOOD JOB FINDING ME HERE...
KYAH-HA... IT WAS OBVIOUS.

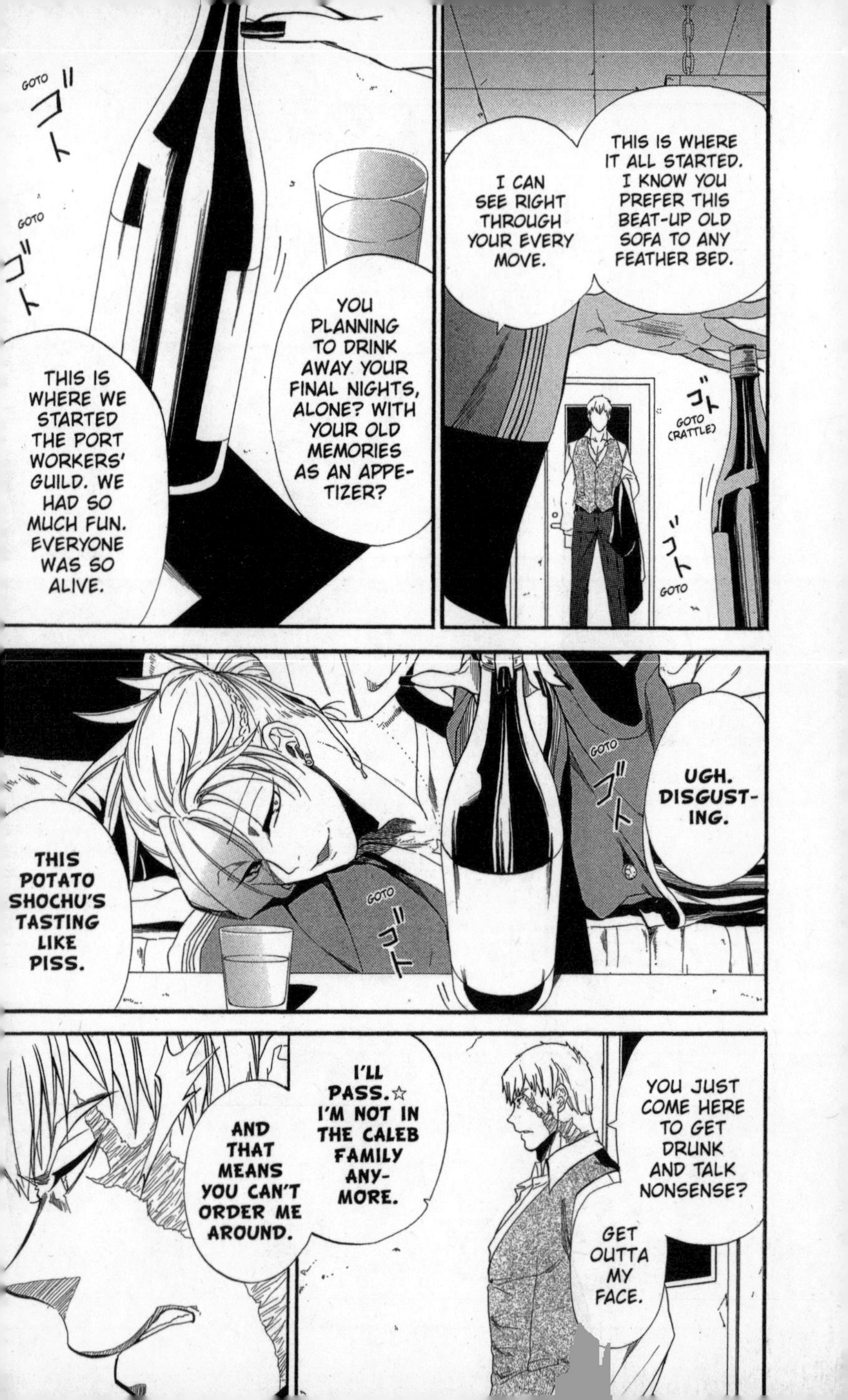
THIS IS WHERE IT ALL STARTED. I KNOW YOU PREFER THIS BEAT-UP OLD SOFA TO ANY FEATHER BED.
I CAN SEE RIGHT THROUGH YOUR EVERY MOVE.
ゴト GOTO (RATTLE)
ゴト GOTO
YOU PLANNING TO DRINK AWAY YOUR FINAL NIGHTS, ALONE? WITH YOUR OLD MEMORIES AS AN APPE-TIZER?
ゴト GOTO
ゴト GOTO
THIS IS WHERE WE STARTED THE PORT WORKERS' GUILD. WE HAD SO MUCH FUN. EVERYONE WAS SO ALIVE.
UGH. DISGUST-ING.
ゴト GOTO
ゴト GOTO
THIS POTATO SHOCHU'S TASTING LIKE PISS.
YOU JUST COME HERE TO GET DRUNK AND TALK NONSENSE?
GET OUTTA MY FACE.
I'LL PASS.☆ I'M NOT IN THE CALEB FAMILY ANY-MORE.
AND THAT MEANS YOU CAN'T ORDER ME AROUND.

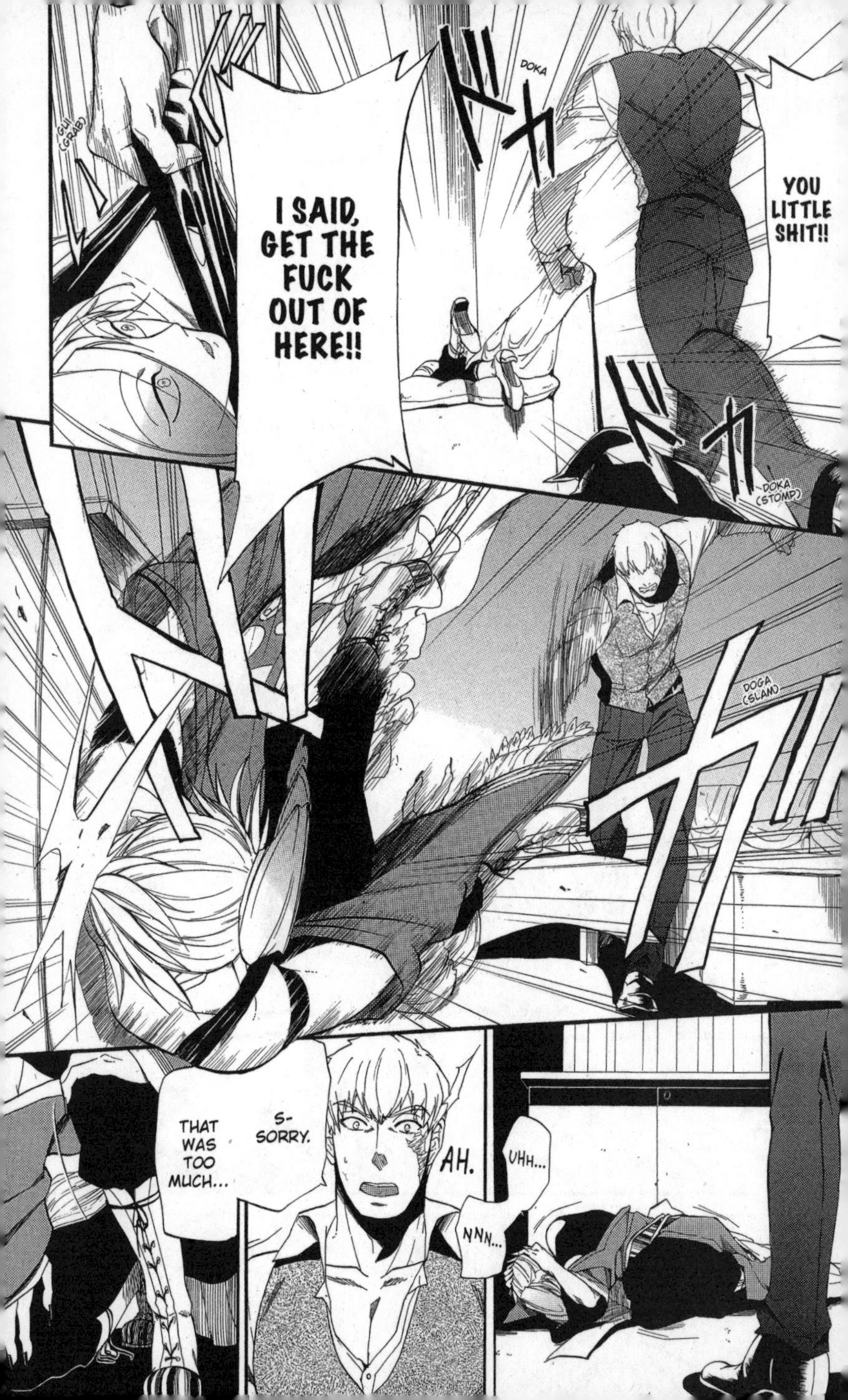
DOKA
YOU LITTLE SHIT!!
GUI (GRAB)
I SAID, GET THE FUCK OUT OF HERE!!
DOKA (STOMP)
DOGA (SLAM)
UHH...
NNN...
AH.
S-SORRY.
THAT WAS TOO MUCH...

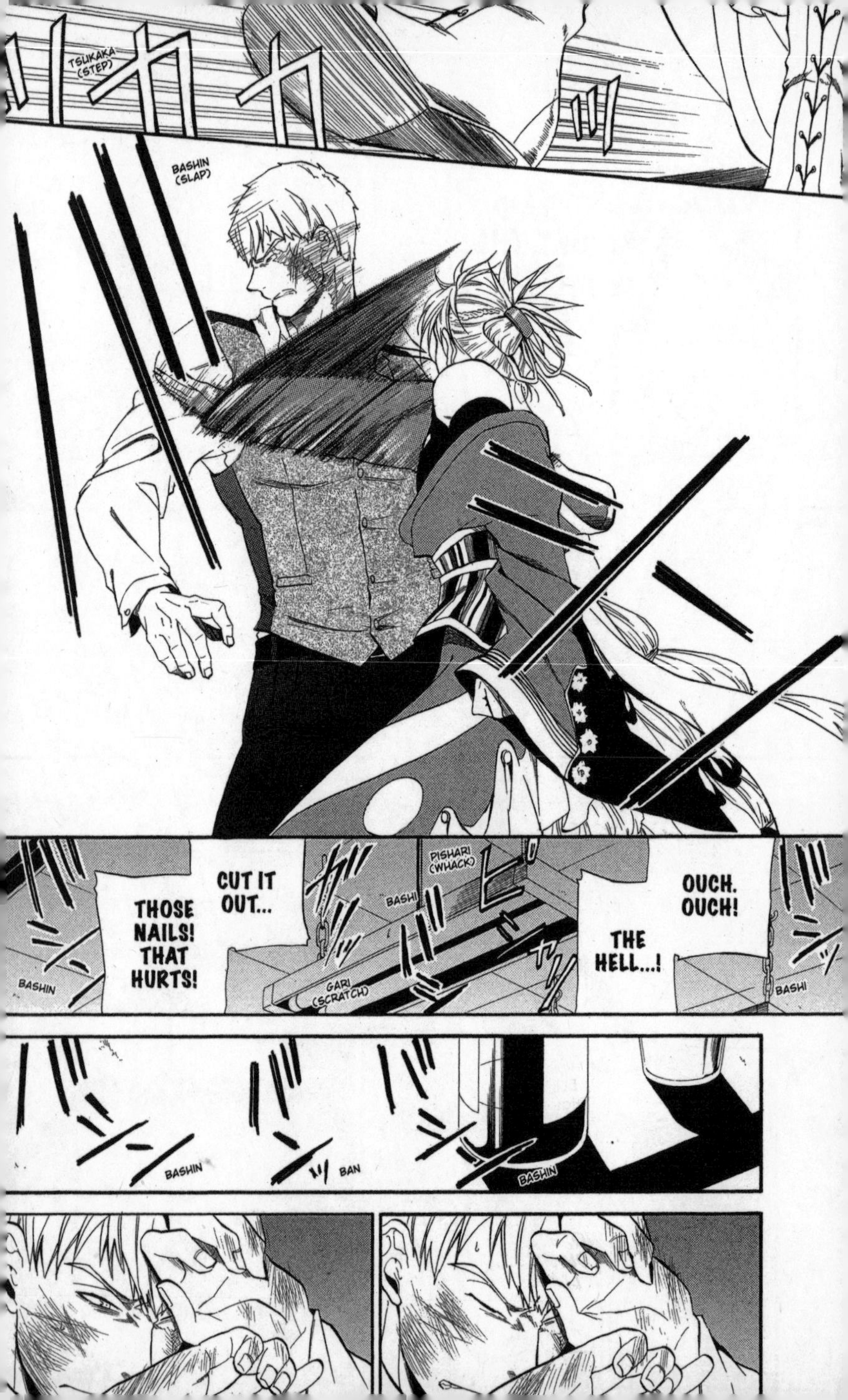
TSUKAKA (STEP)
BASHIN (SLAP)
BASHI
OUCH. OUCH!
THE HELL...!
PISHARI (WHACK)
BASHI
GARI (SCRATCH)
CUT IT OUT...
THOSE NAILS! THAT HURTS!
BASHIN
BASHIN
BAN
BASHIN

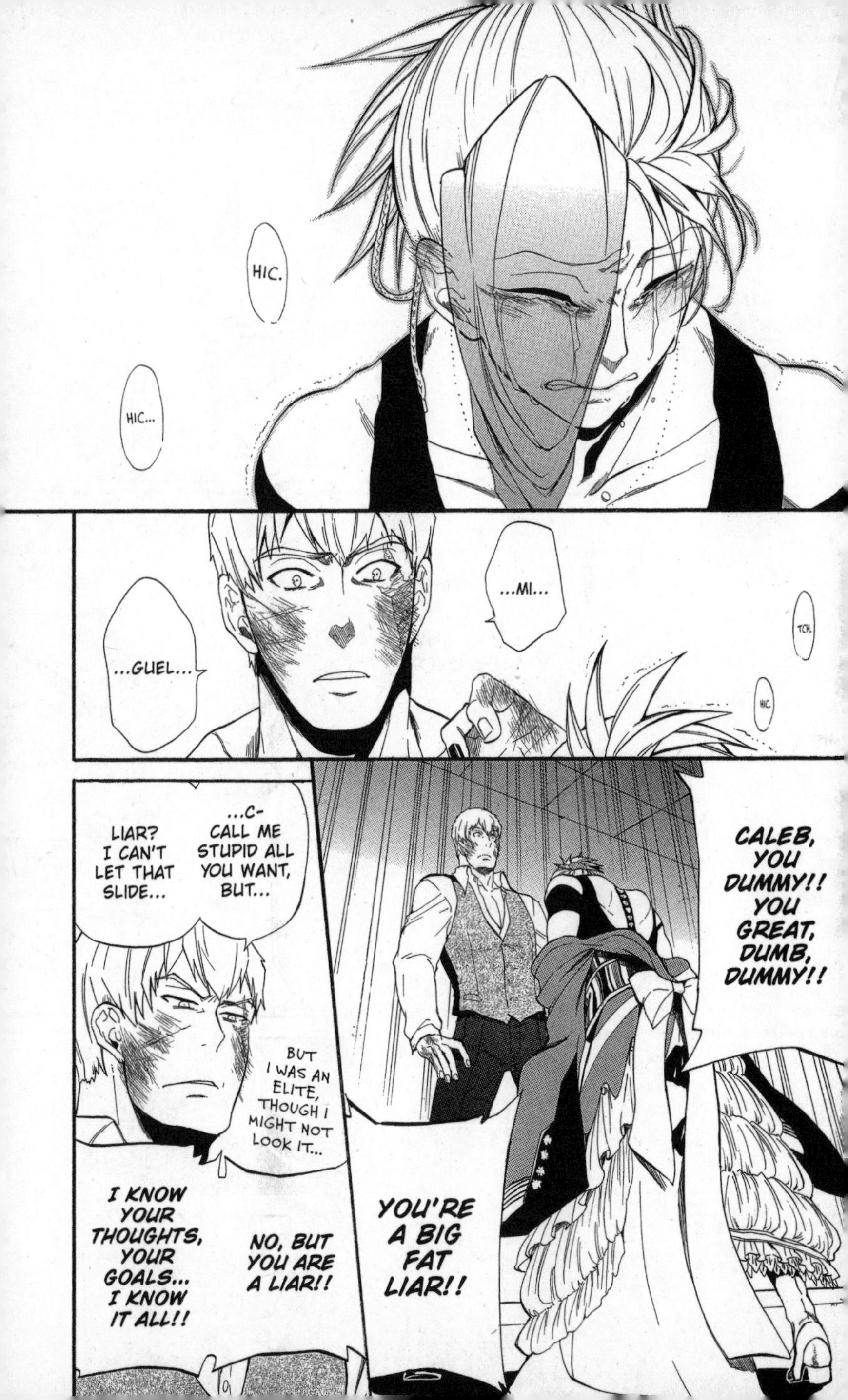
HIC.
HIC...
TCH.
HIC.
...MI...
...GUEL...
CALEB, YOU DUMMY!! YOU GREAT, DUMB, DUMMY!!
YOU'RE A BIG FAT LIAR!!
...C- CALL ME STUPID ALL YOU WANT, BUT...
LIAR? I CAN'T LET THAT SLIDE...
BUT I WAS AN ELITE, THOUGH I MIGHT NOT LOOK IT...
NO, BUT YOU ARE A LIAR!!
I KNOW YOUR THOUGHTS, YOUR GOALS... I KNOW IT ALL!!

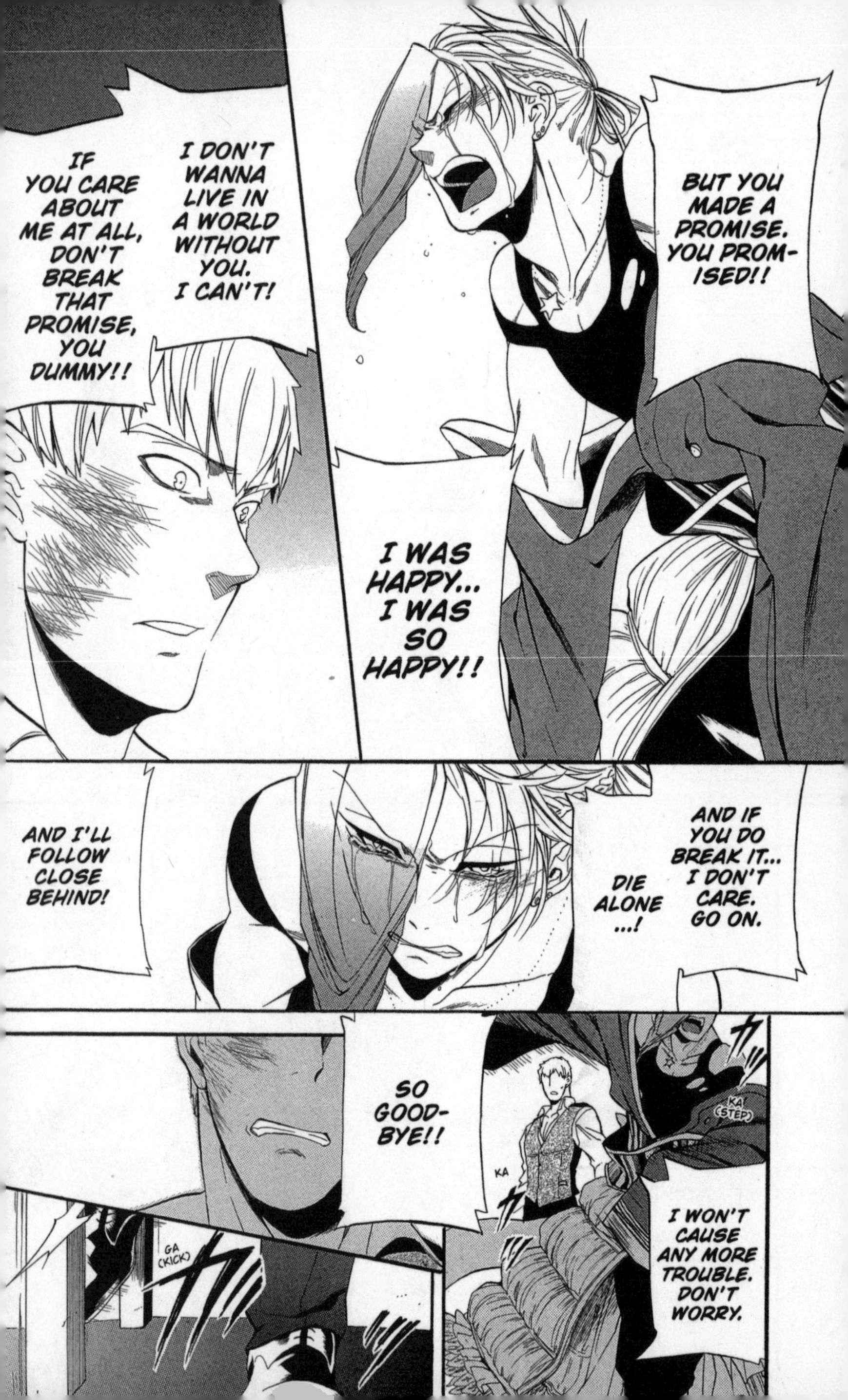
BUT YOU MADE A PROMISE. YOU PROMISED!!
I WAS HAPPY... I WAS SO HAPPY!!
I DON'T WANNA LIVE IN A WORLD WITHOUT YOU. I CAN'T!
IF YOU CARE ABOUT ME AT ALL, DON'T BREAK THAT PROMISE, YOU DUMMY!!
AND IF YOU DO BREAK IT... I DON'T CARE. GO ON.
DIE ALONE ...!
AND I'LL FOLLOW CLOSE BEHIND!
KA (STEP)
KA
I WON'T CAUSE ANY MORE TROUBLE. DON'T WORRY.
SO GOOD-BYE!!
GA (KICK)
...

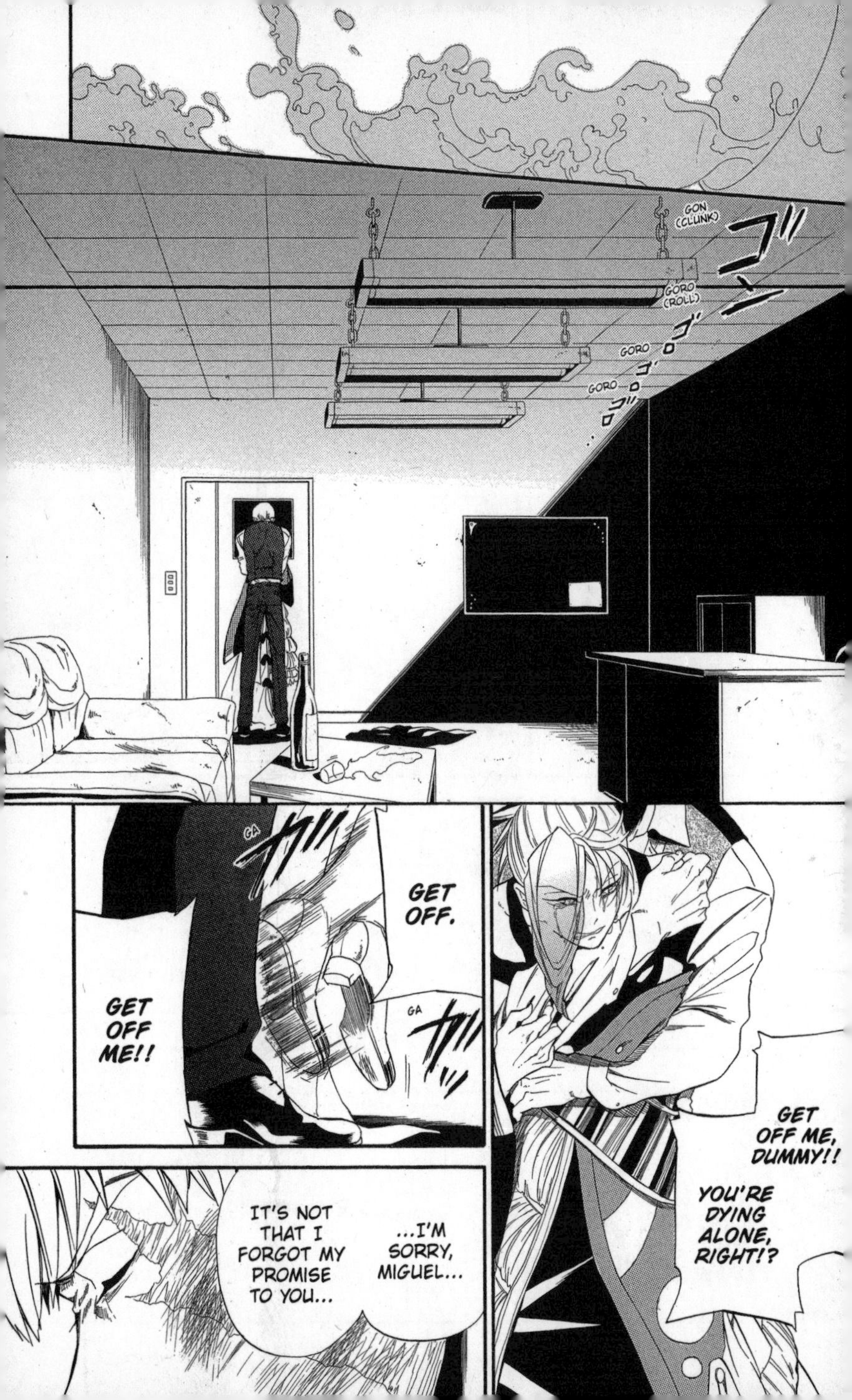
GON (CLUNK)
GORO (ROLL)
GORO
GORO
GA
GET OFF.
GET OFF ME!!
GA
GET OFF ME, DUMMY!!
YOU'RE DYING ALONE, RIGHT!?
...I'M SORRY, MIGUEL...
IT'S NOT THAT I FORGOT MY PROMISE TO YOU...

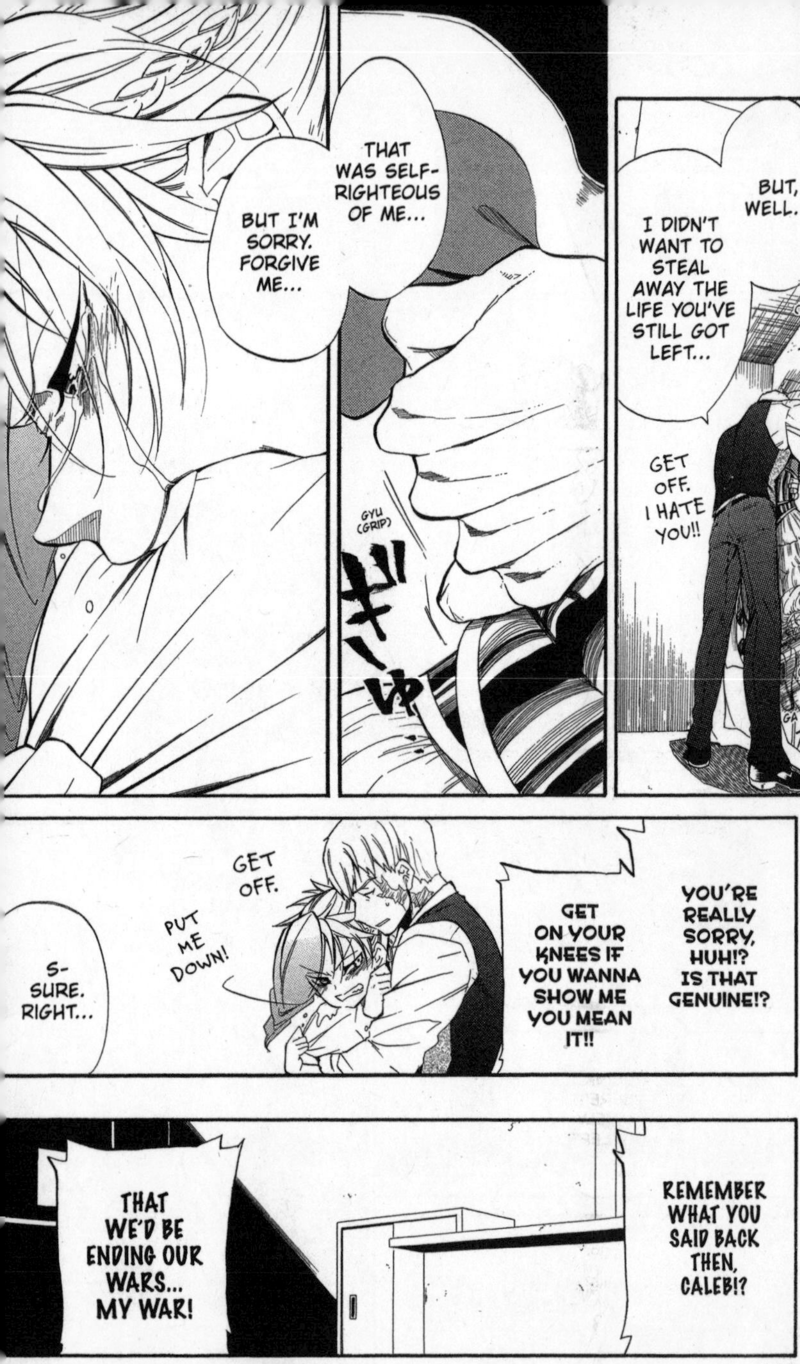

BUT, WELL...
I DIDN'T WANT TO STEAL AWAY THE LIFE YOU'VE STILL GOT LEFT...
GON (WHACK)
GO
GET OFF. I HATE YOU!!
GA (KICK)
GA
THAT WAS SELF-RIGHTEOUS OF ME...
GYU (GRIP)
BUT I'M SORRY. FORGIVE ME...
YOU'RE REALLY SORRY, HUH!? IS THAT GENUINE!?
GET ON YOUR KNEES IF YOU WANNA SHOW ME YOU MEAN IT!!
GET OFF.
PUT ME DOWN!
S-SURE. RIGHT...
REMEMBER WHAT YOU SAID BACK THEN, CALEB!?
THAT WE'D BE ENDING OUR WARS... MY WAR!

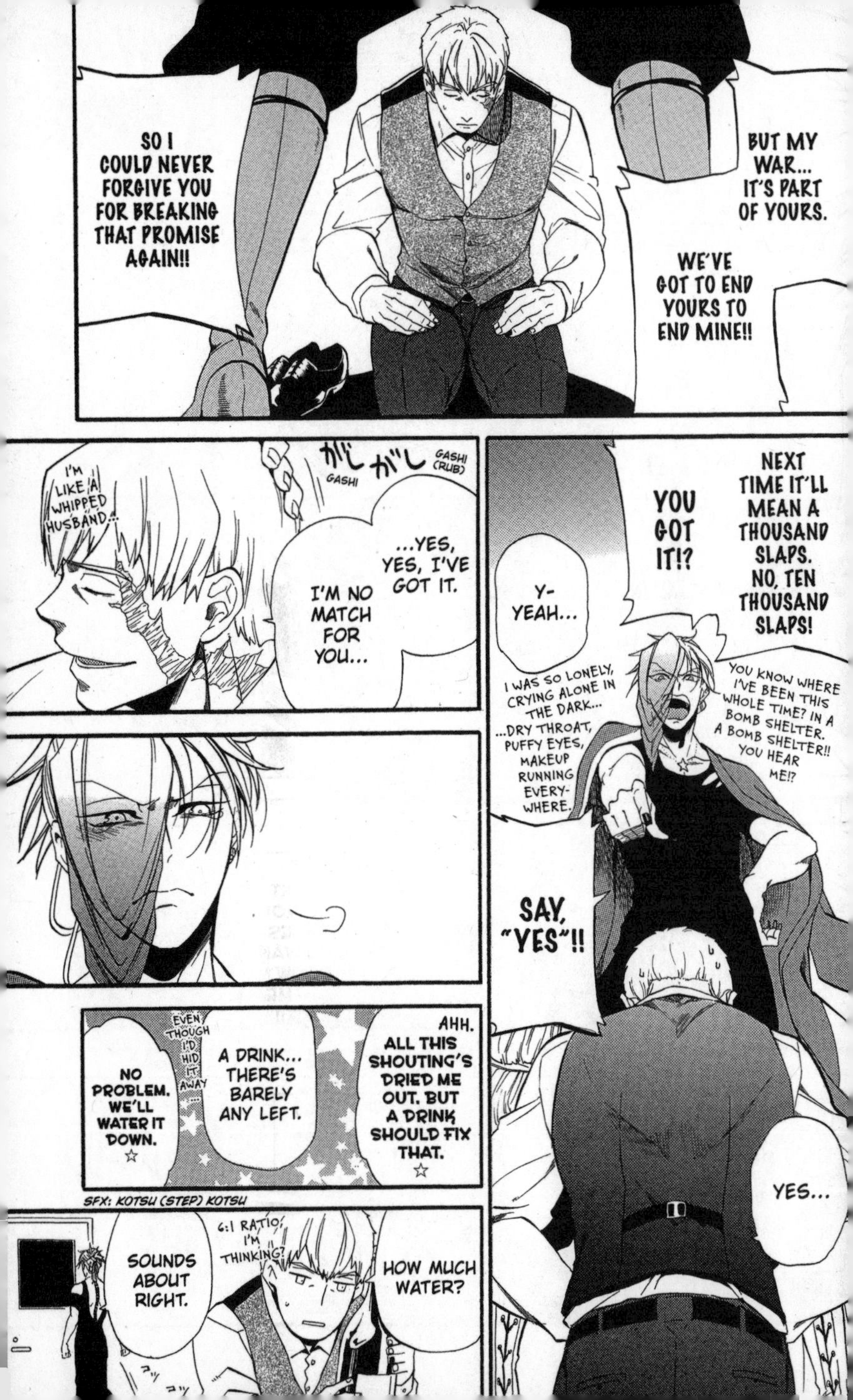
BUT MY WAR... IT'S PART OF YOURS.
WE'VE GOT TO END YOURS TO END MINE!!
SO I COULD NEVER FORGIVE YOU FOR BREAKING THAT PROMISE AGAIN!!
NEXT TIME IT'LL MEAN A THOUSAND SLAPS. NO, TEN THOUSAND SLAPS!
YOU GOT IT!?
Y-YEAH...
YOU KNOW WHERE I'VE BEEN THIS WHOLE TIME? IN A BOMB SHELTER. A BOMB SHELTER!! YOU HEAR ME!?
I WAS SO LONELY, CRYING ALONE IN THE DARK... ...DRY THROAT, PUFFY EYES, MAKEUP RUNNING EVERYWHERE.
SAY, "YES"!!
YES...
GASHI GASHI (RUB)
...YES, YES, I'VE GOT IT.
I'M NO MATCH FOR YOU...
I'M LIKE A WHIPPED HUSBAND...
AHH. ALL THIS SHOUTING'S DRIED ME OUT. BUT A DRINK SHOULD FIX THAT. ☆
A DRINK... THERE'S BARELY ANY LEFT.
EVEN THOUGH I'D HID IT AWAY...
NO PROBLEM. WE'LL WATER IT DOWN. ☆
SFX: KOTSU (STEP) KOTSU
HOW MUCH WATER?
6:1 RATIO, I'M THINKING?
SOUNDS ABOUT RIGHT.

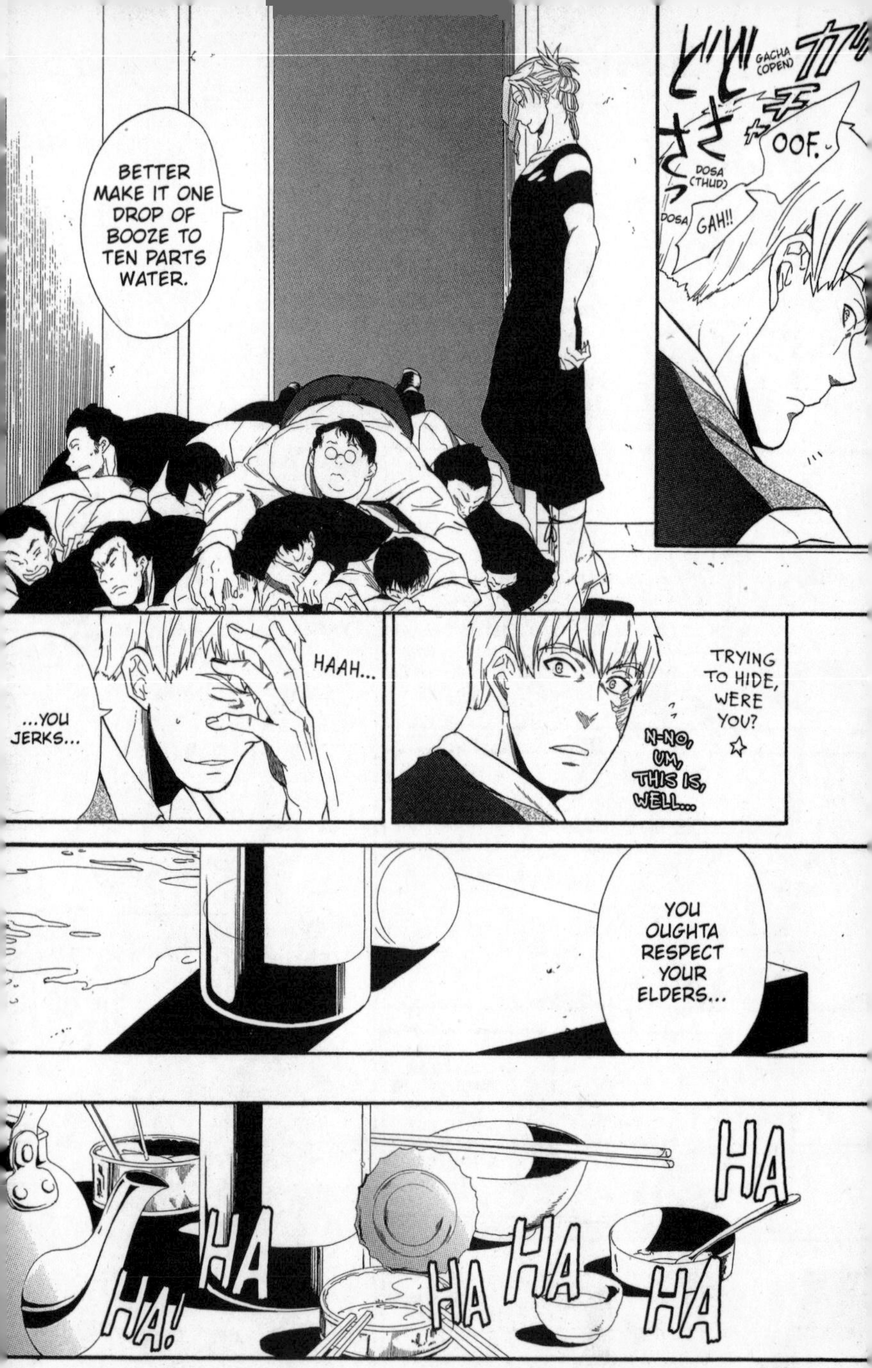
GACHA (OPEN)
OOF.
DOSA (THUD)
DOSA
GAH!!
BETTER MAKE IT ONE DROP OF BOOZE TO TEN PARTS WATER.
TRYING TO HIDE, WERE YOU? ☆
N-NO, UM, THIS IS, WELL...
HAAH...
...YOU JERKS...
YOU OUGHTA RESPECT YOUR ELDERS...
HA
HA
HA HA HA
HA
HA!

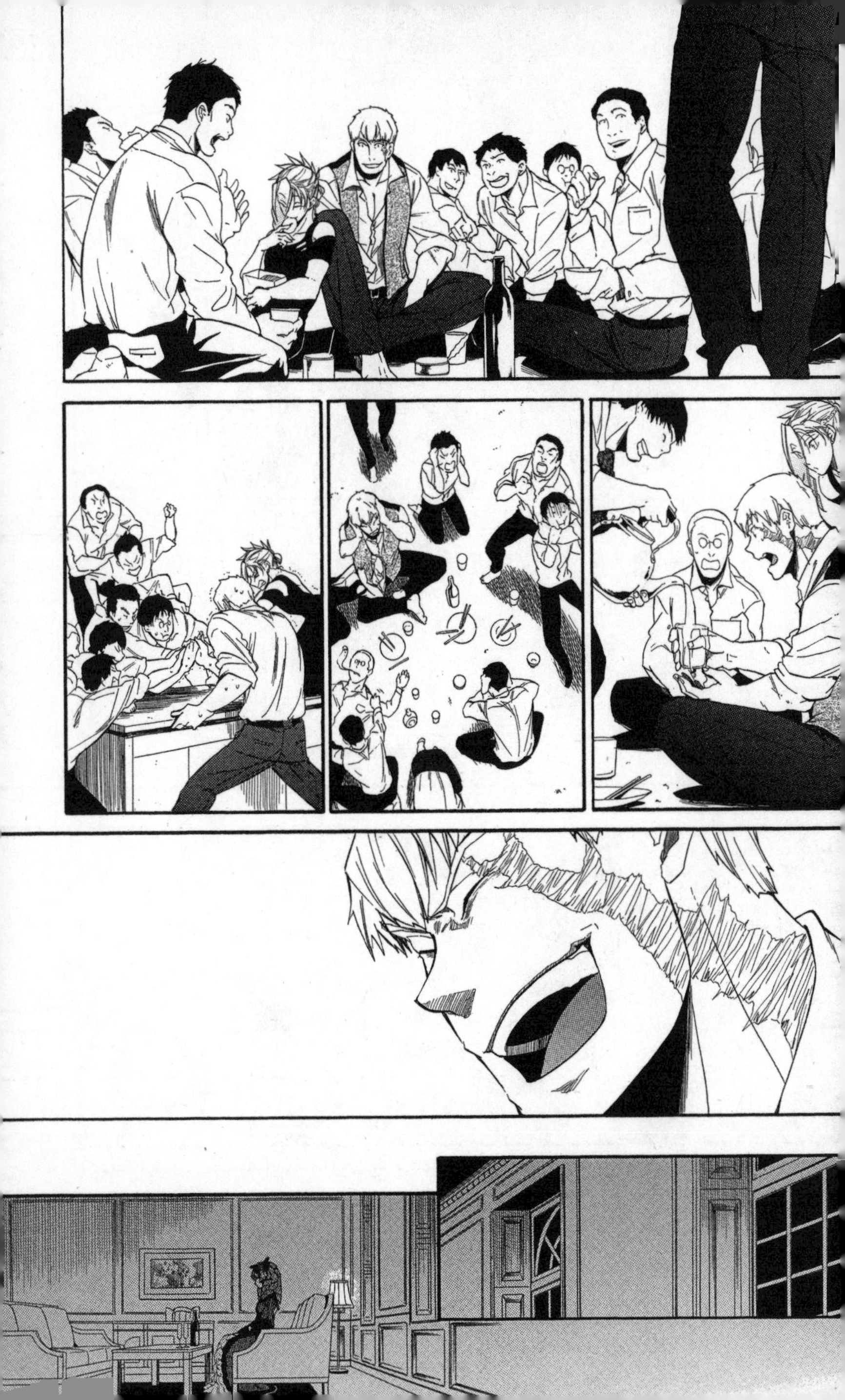

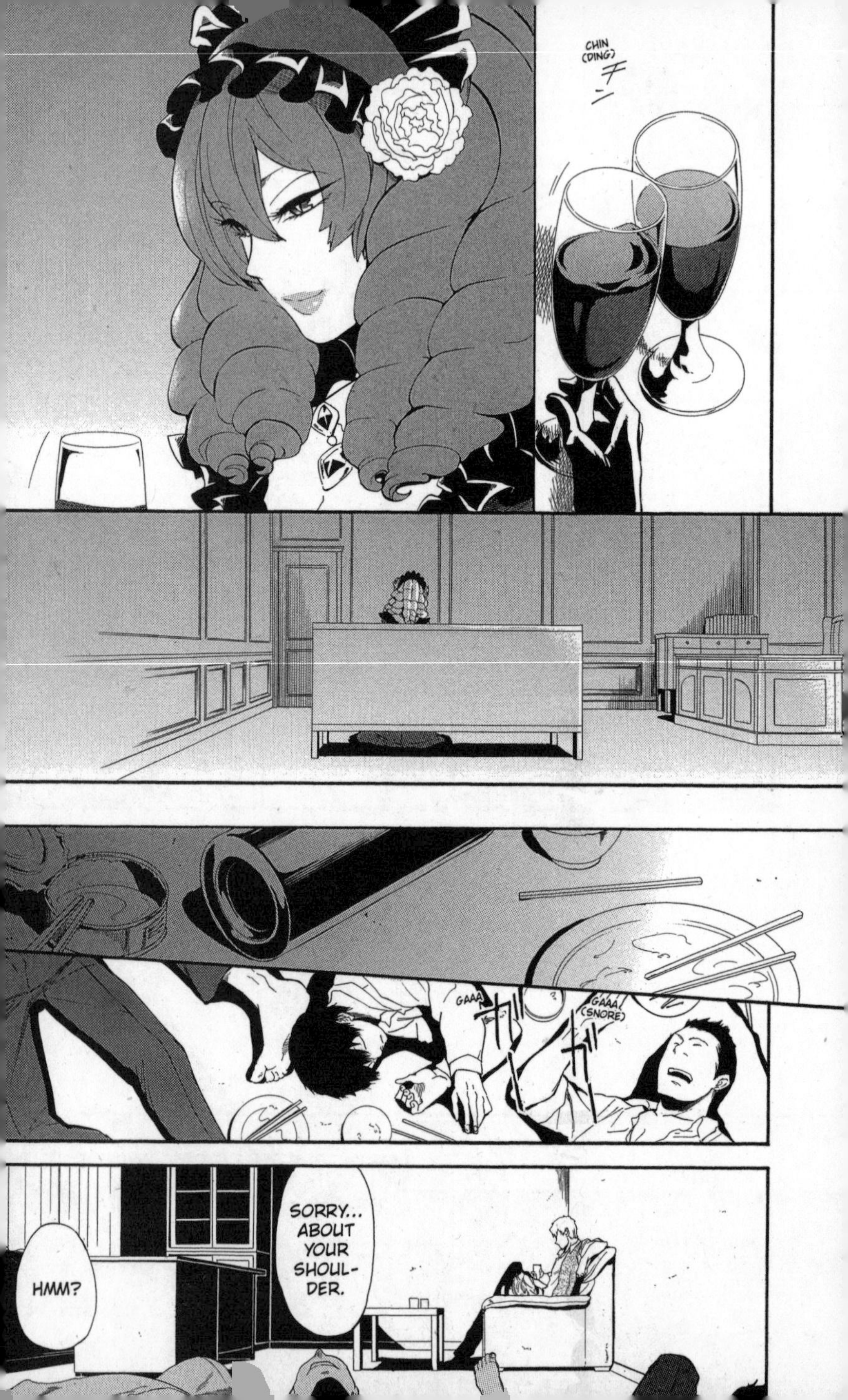
CHIN (DING)
GAAA (SNORE)
GAAA
SORRY... ABOUT YOUR SHOUL-DER.
HMM?

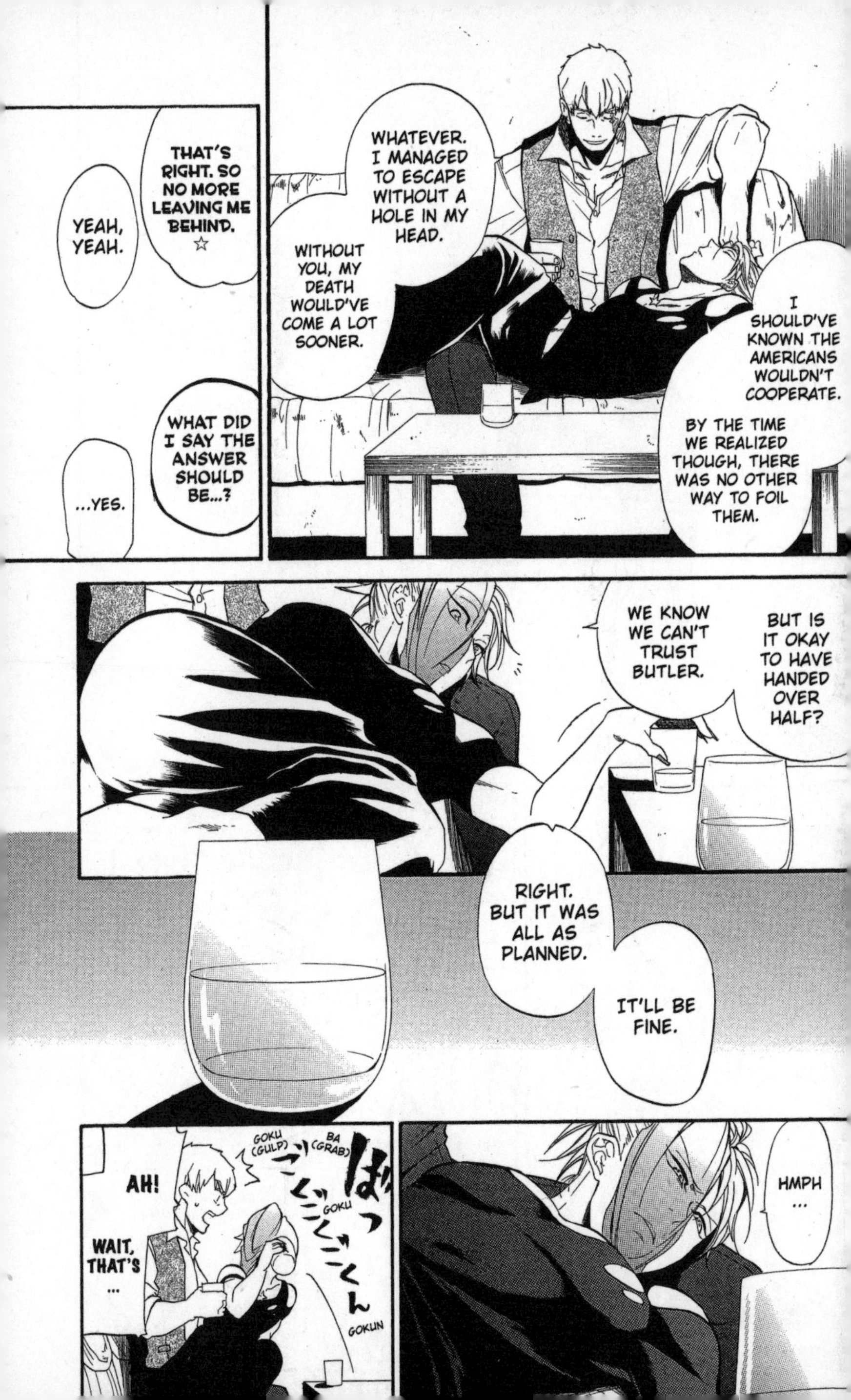
WHATEVER. I MANAGED TO ESCAPE WITHOUT A HOLE IN MY HEAD.
WITHOUT YOU, MY DEATH WOULD'VE COME A LOT SOONER.
I SHOULD'VE KNOWN THE AMERICANS WOULDN'T COOPERATE.
BY THE TIME WE REALIZED THOUGH, THERE WAS NO OTHER WAY TO FOIL THEM.
THAT'S RIGHT. SO NO MORE LEAVING ME BEHIND. ☆
YEAH, YEAH.
WHAT DID I SAY THE ANSWER SHOULD BE...?
...YES.
WE KNOW WE CAN'T TRUST BUTLER.
BUT IS IT OKAY TO HAVE HANDED OVER HALF?
RIGHT. BUT IT WAS ALL AS PLANNED.
IT'LL BE FINE.
HMPH ...
BA (GRAB)
GOKU (GULP)
GOKU
GOKUN
AH!
WAIT, THAT'S ...

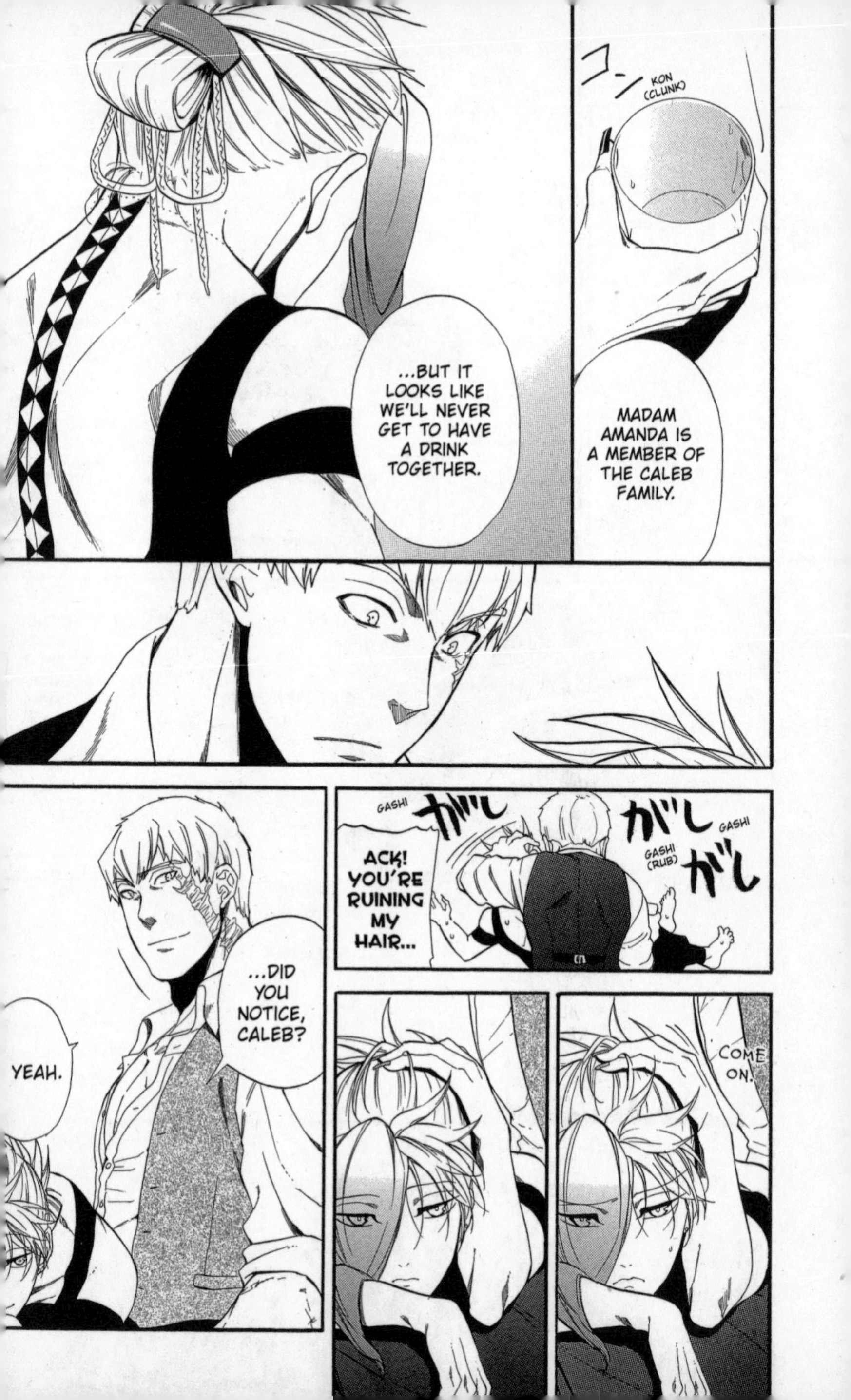

KON (CLUNK)
MADAM AMANDA IS A MEMBER OF THE CALEB FAMILY.
...BUT IT LOOKS LIKE WE'LL NEVER GET TO HAVE A DRINK TOGETHER.
がし
GASHI
がし
GASHI
がし
GASHI (RUB)
ACK! YOU'RE RUINING MY HAIR...
COME ON.
...DID YOU NOTICE, CALEB?
YEAH.

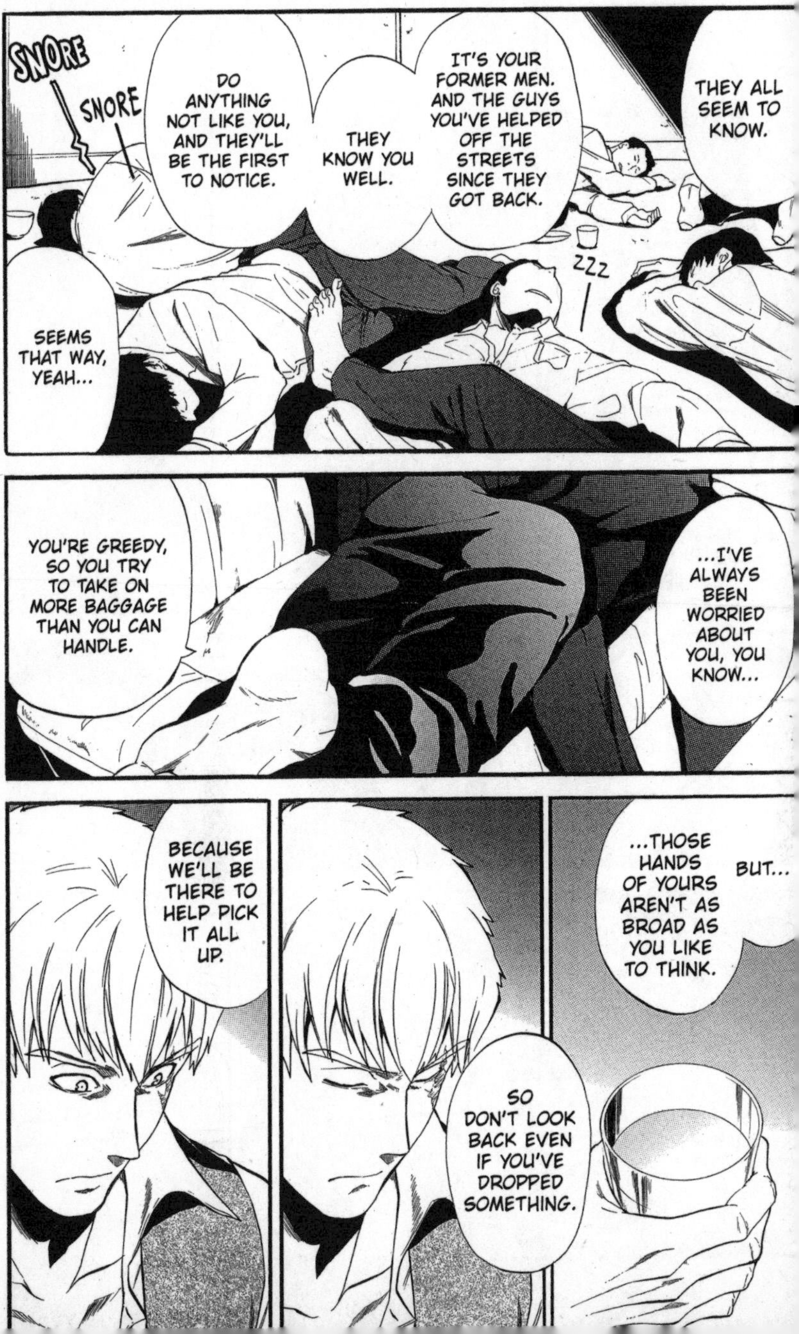
THEY ALL SEEM TO KNOW.
IT'S YOUR FORMER MEN. AND THE GUYS YOU'VE HELPED OFF THE STREETS SINCE THEY GOT BACK.
THEY KNOW YOU WELL.
DO ANYTHING NOT LIKE YOU, AND THEY'LL BE THE FIRST TO NOTICE.
ZZZ
SNORE
SNORE
SEEMS THAT WAY, YEAH...
...I'VE ALWAYS BEEN WORRIED ABOUT YOU, YOU KNOW...
YOU'RE GREEDY, SO YOU TRY TO TAKE ON MORE BAGGAGE THAN YOU CAN HANDLE.
BUT...
...THOSE HANDS OF YOURS AREN'T AS BROAD AS YOU LIKE TO THINK.
SO DON'T LOOK BACK EVEN IF YOU'VE DROPPED SOMETHING.
BECAUSE WE'LL BE THERE TO HELP PICK IT ALL UP.

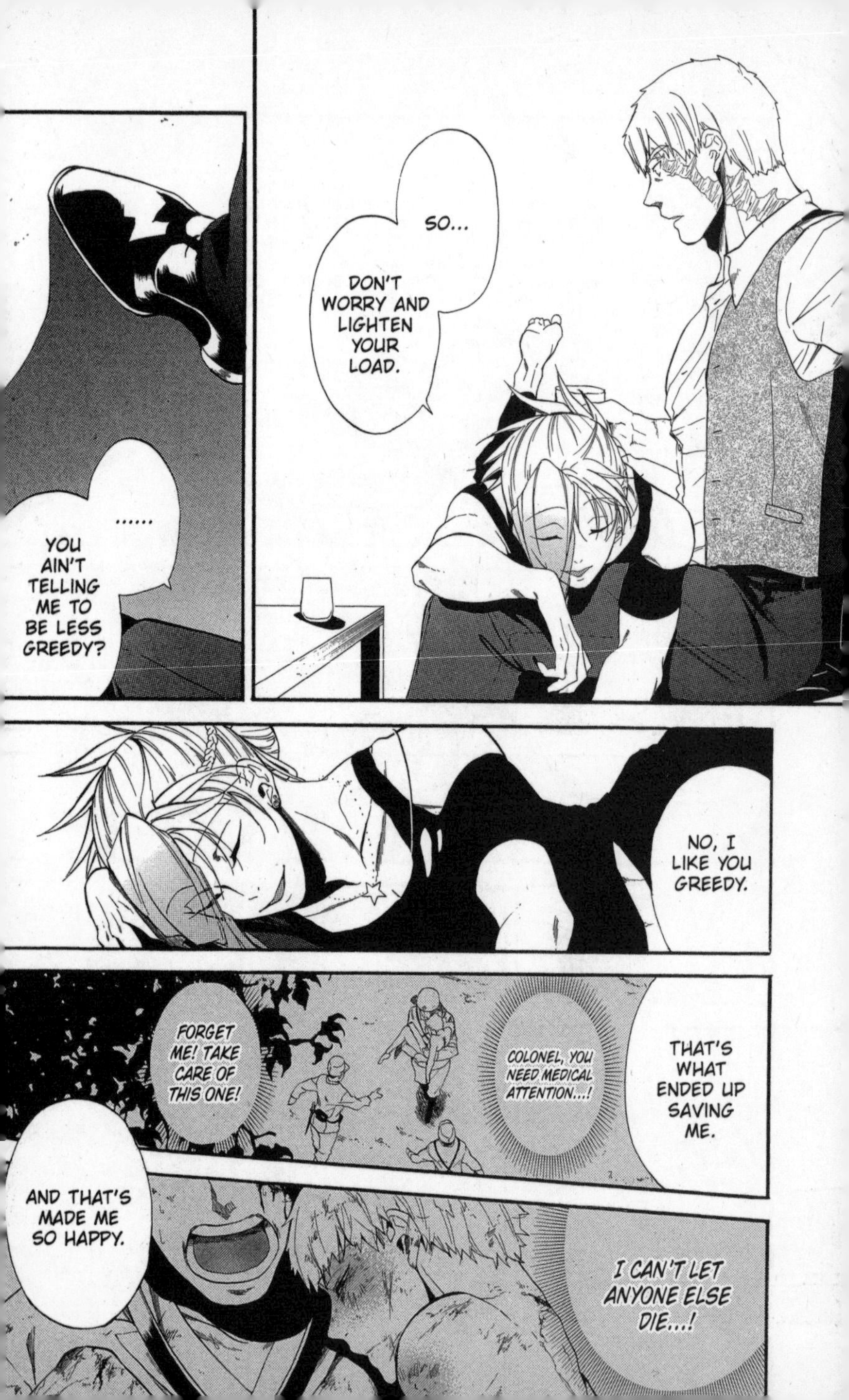
SO...
DON'T WORRY AND LIGHTEN YOUR LOAD.
......
YOU AIN'T TELLING ME TO BE LESS GREEDY?
NO, I LIKE YOU GREEDY.
THAT'S WHAT ENDED UP SAVING ME.
COLONEL, YOU NEED MEDICAL ATTENTION...!
FORGET ME! TAKE CARE OF THIS ONE!
I CAN'T LET ANYONE ELSE DIE...!
AND THAT'S MADE ME SO HAPPY.

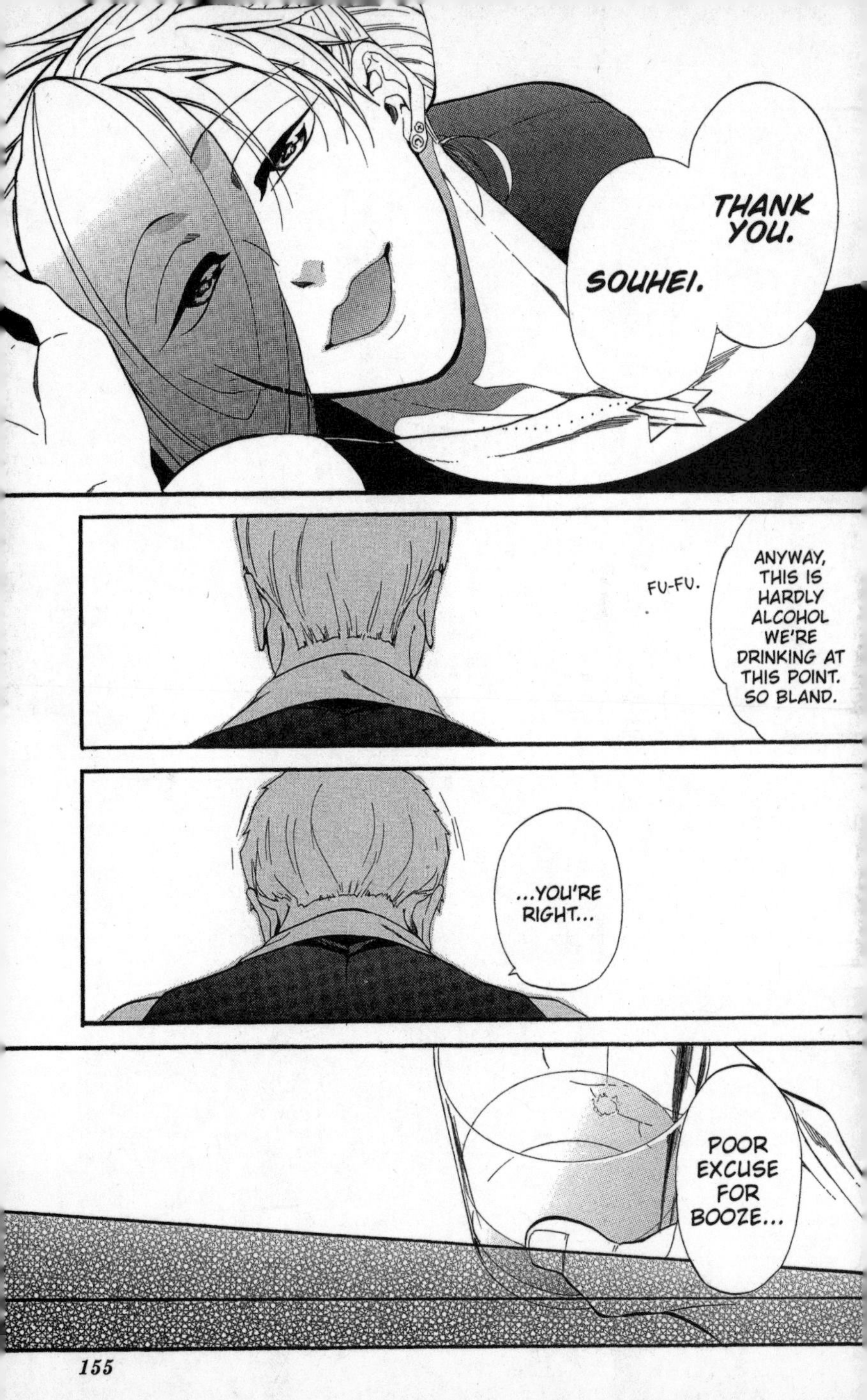
THANK YOU.
SOUHEI.
ANYWAY, THIS IS HARDLY ALCOHOL WE'RE DRINKING AT THIS POINT. SO BLAND.
FU-FU.
...YOU'RE RIGHT...
POOR EXCUSE FOR BOOZE...

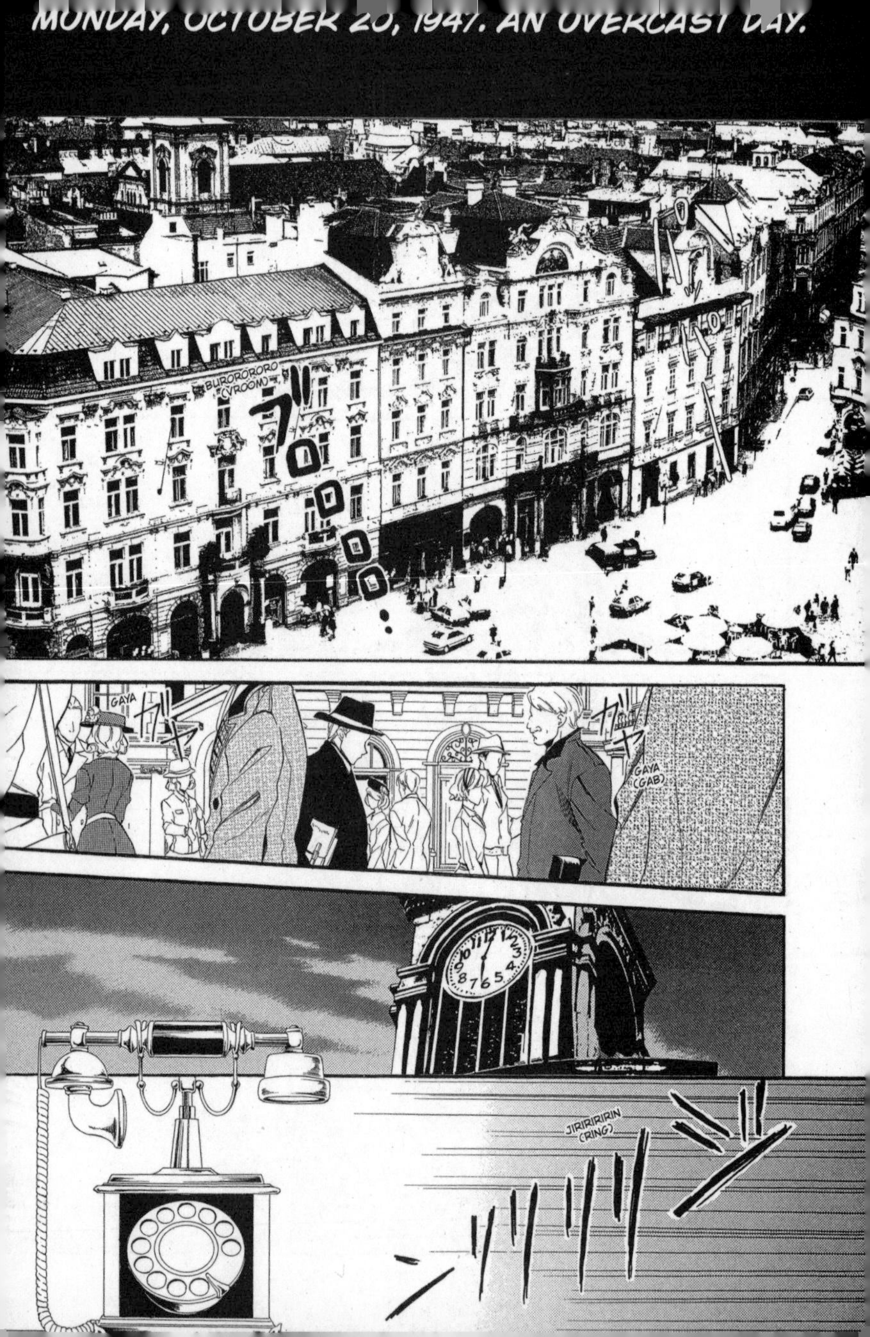
MONDAY, OCTOBER 20, 1947. AN OVERCAST DAY.
BURORORORO (VROOM)
GAYA
GAYA (GAB)
JIRIRIRIRIN (RING)

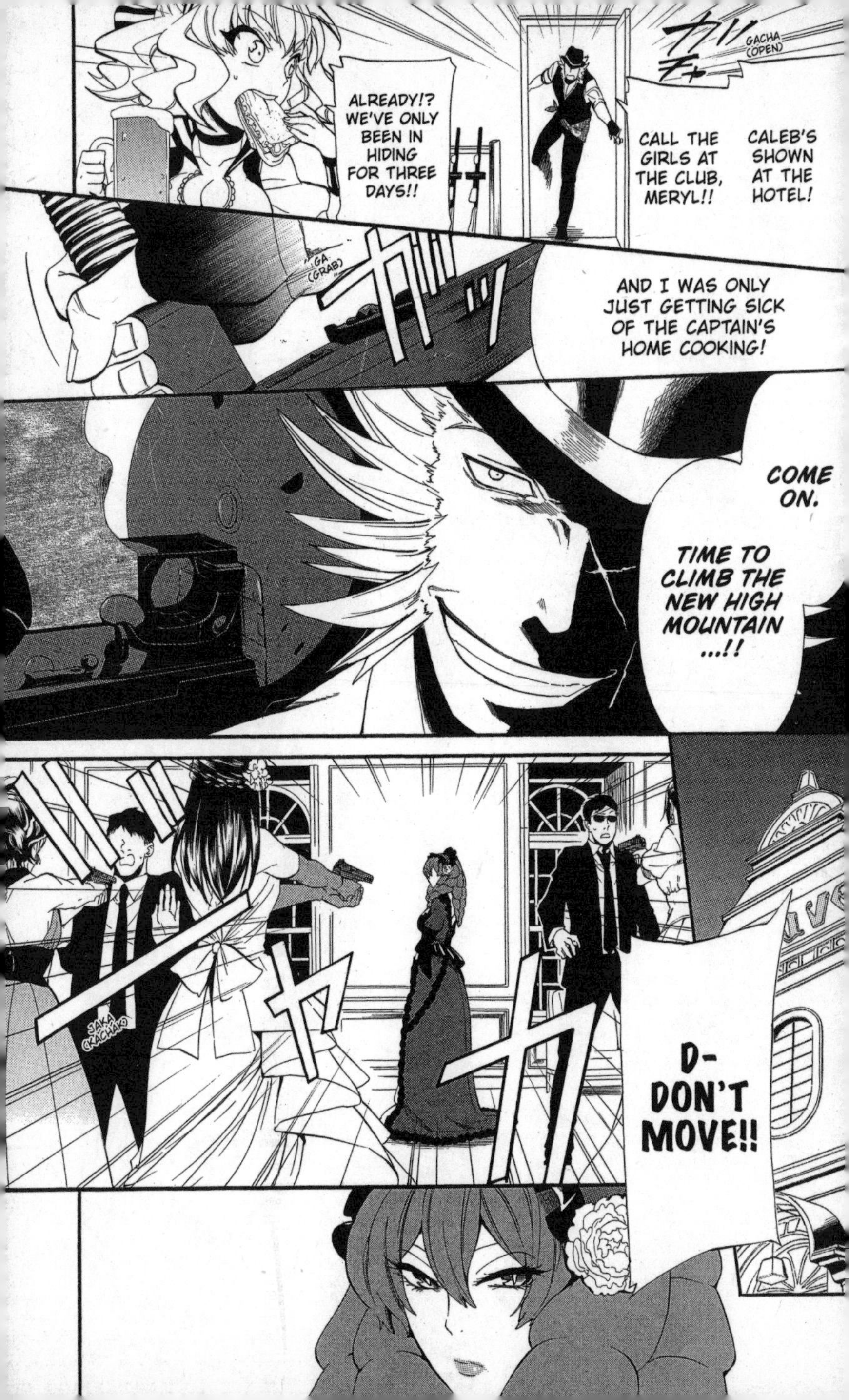
GACHA (OPEN)
CALEB'S SHOWN AT THE HOTEL!
CALL THE GIRLS AT THE CLUB, MERYL!!
ALREADY!? WE'VE ONLY BEEN IN HIDING FOR THREE DAYS!!
AND I WAS ONLY JUST GETTING SICK OF THE CAPTAIN'S HOME COOKING!
GA (GRAB)
COME ON.
TIME TO CLIMB THE NEW HIGH MOUNTAIN ...!!
D-DON'T MOVE!!
JAKA (KACHAK)

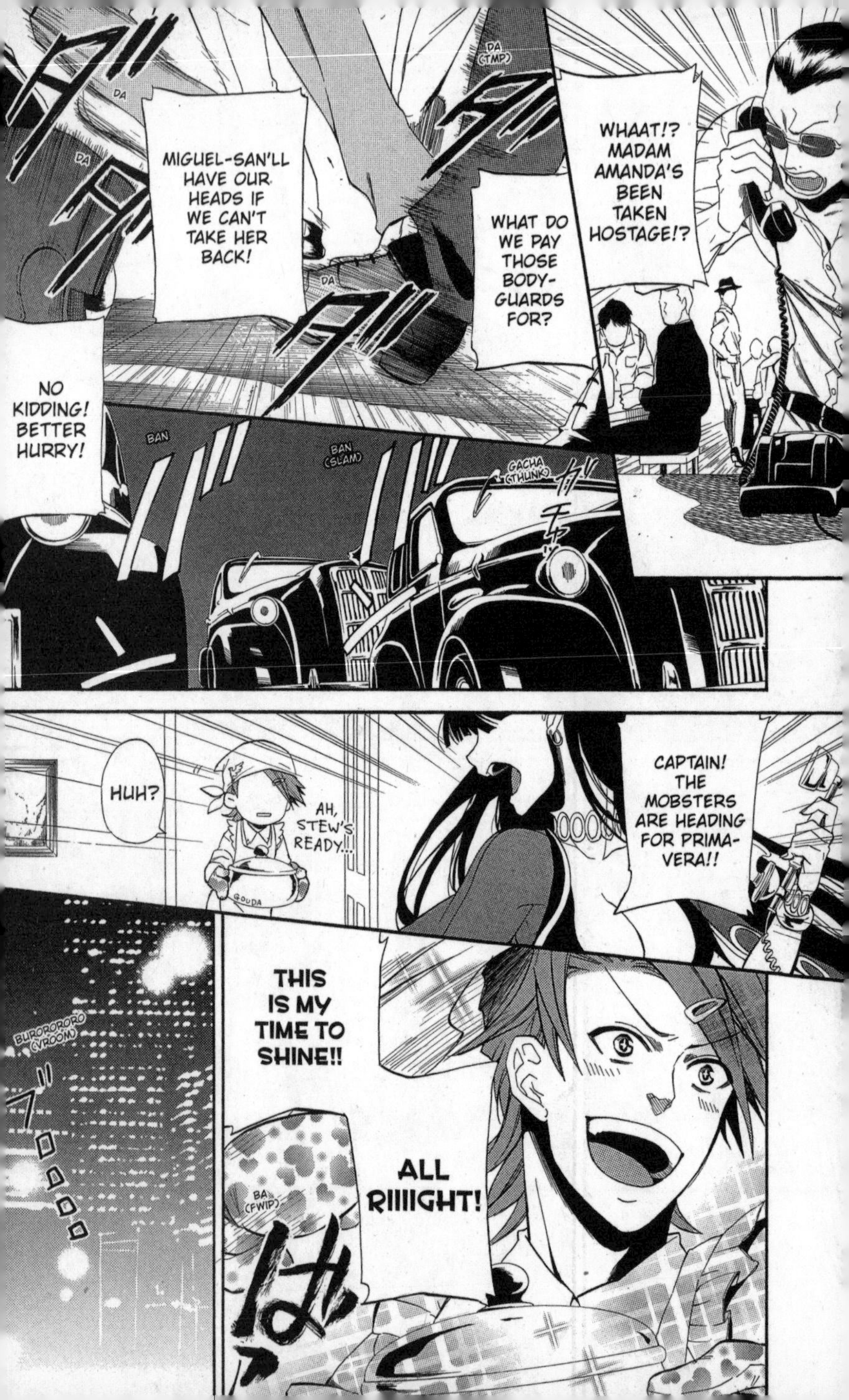
WHAAT!? MADAM AMANDA'S BEEN TAKEN HOSTAGE!?
WHAT DO WE PAY THOSE BODY-GUARDS FOR?
DA (TMP)
DA
DA
DA
MIGUEL-SAN'LL HAVE OUR HEADS IF WE CAN'T TAKE HER BACK!
NO KIDDING! BETTER HURRY!
GACHA (THUNK)
BAN (SLAM)
BAN
CAPTAIN! THE MOBSTERS ARE HEADING FOR PRIMA-VERA!!
AH, STEW'S READY...
HUH?
GOUDA
THIS IS MY TIME TO SHINE!!
ALL RIIIIGHT!
BA (FWIP)
BURORORORO (VROOM)

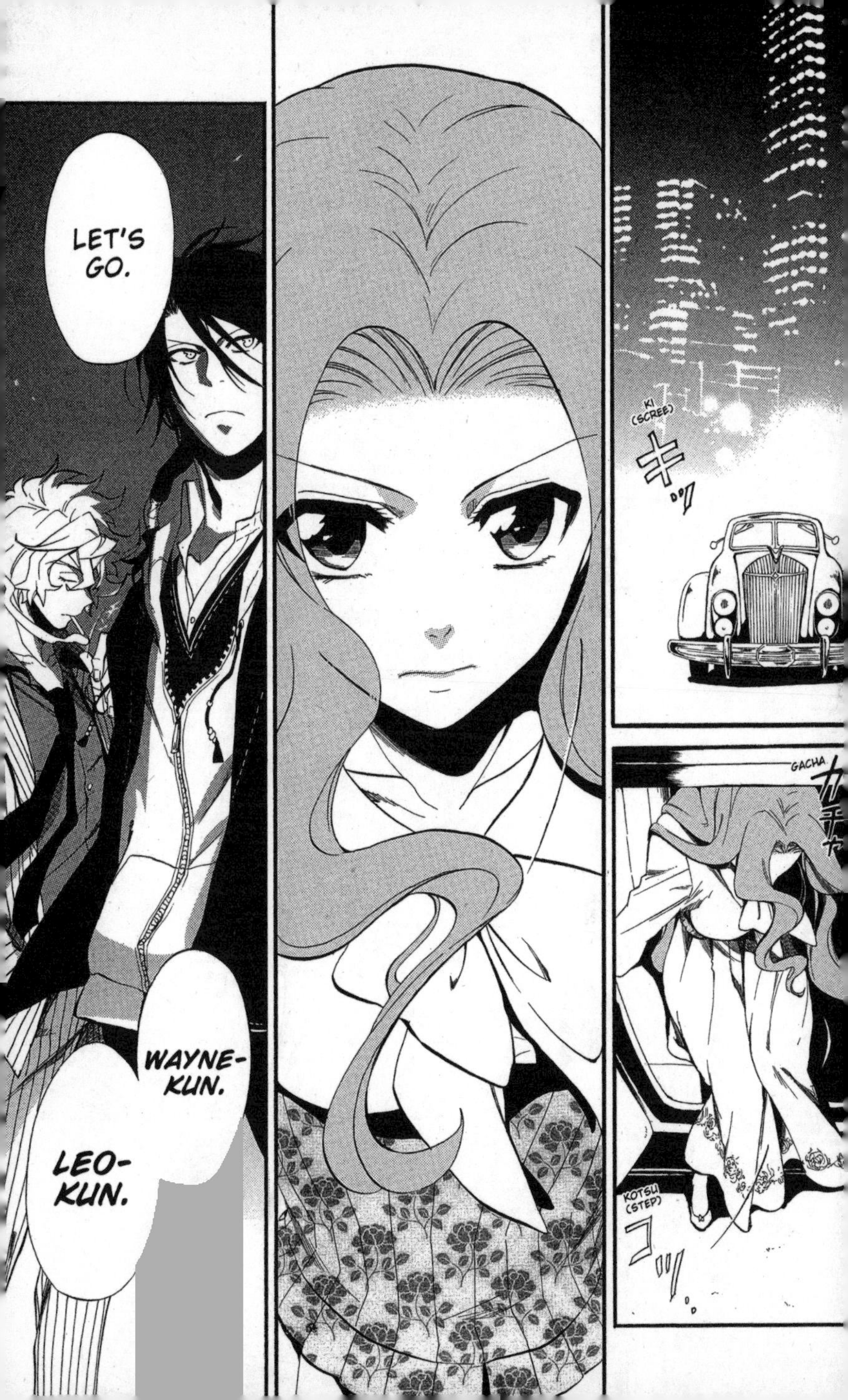

KI (SCREE)
GACHA
KOTSU (STEP)
LET'S GO.
WAYNE-KUN.
LEO-KUN.

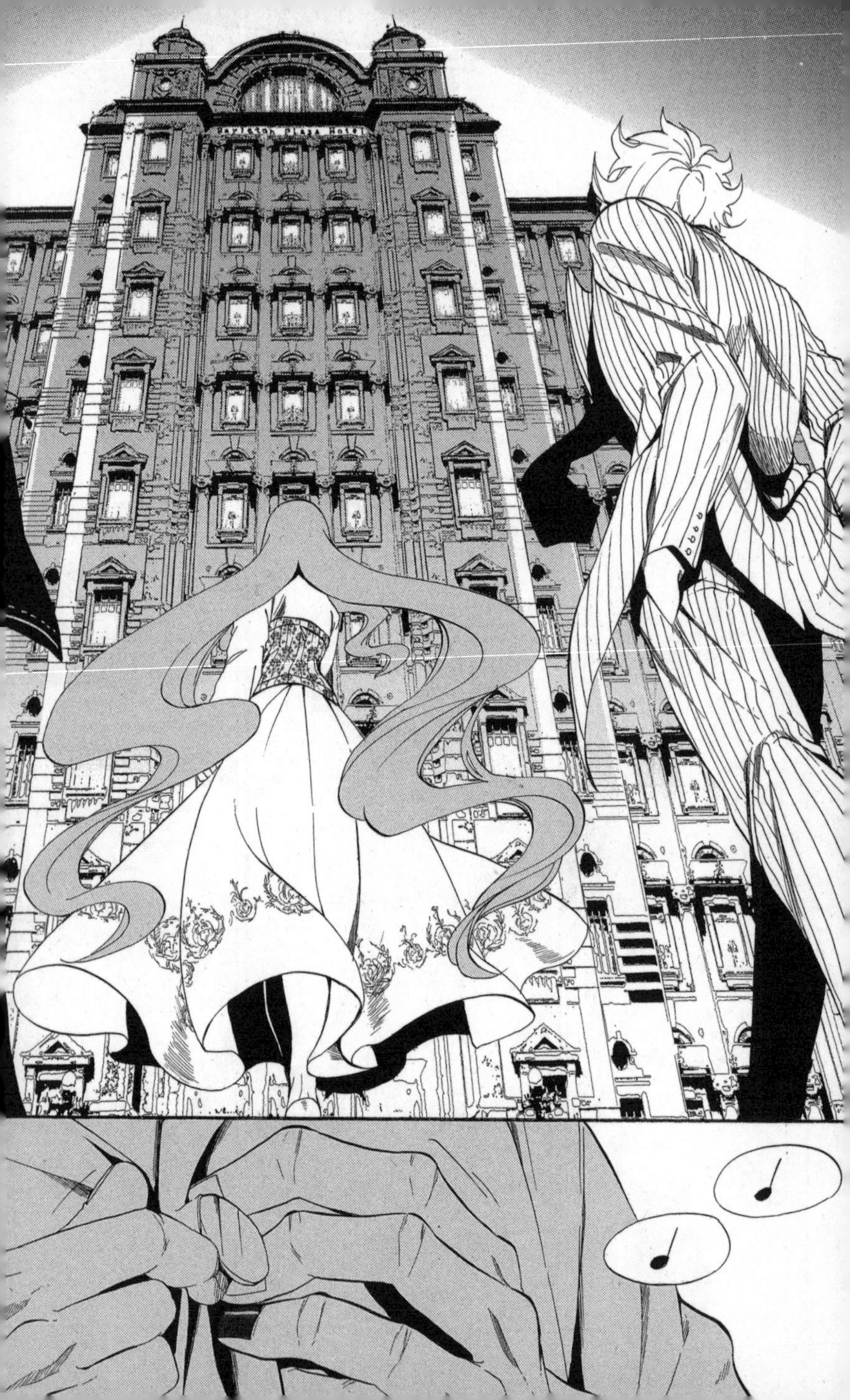
PLAZA HOTEL

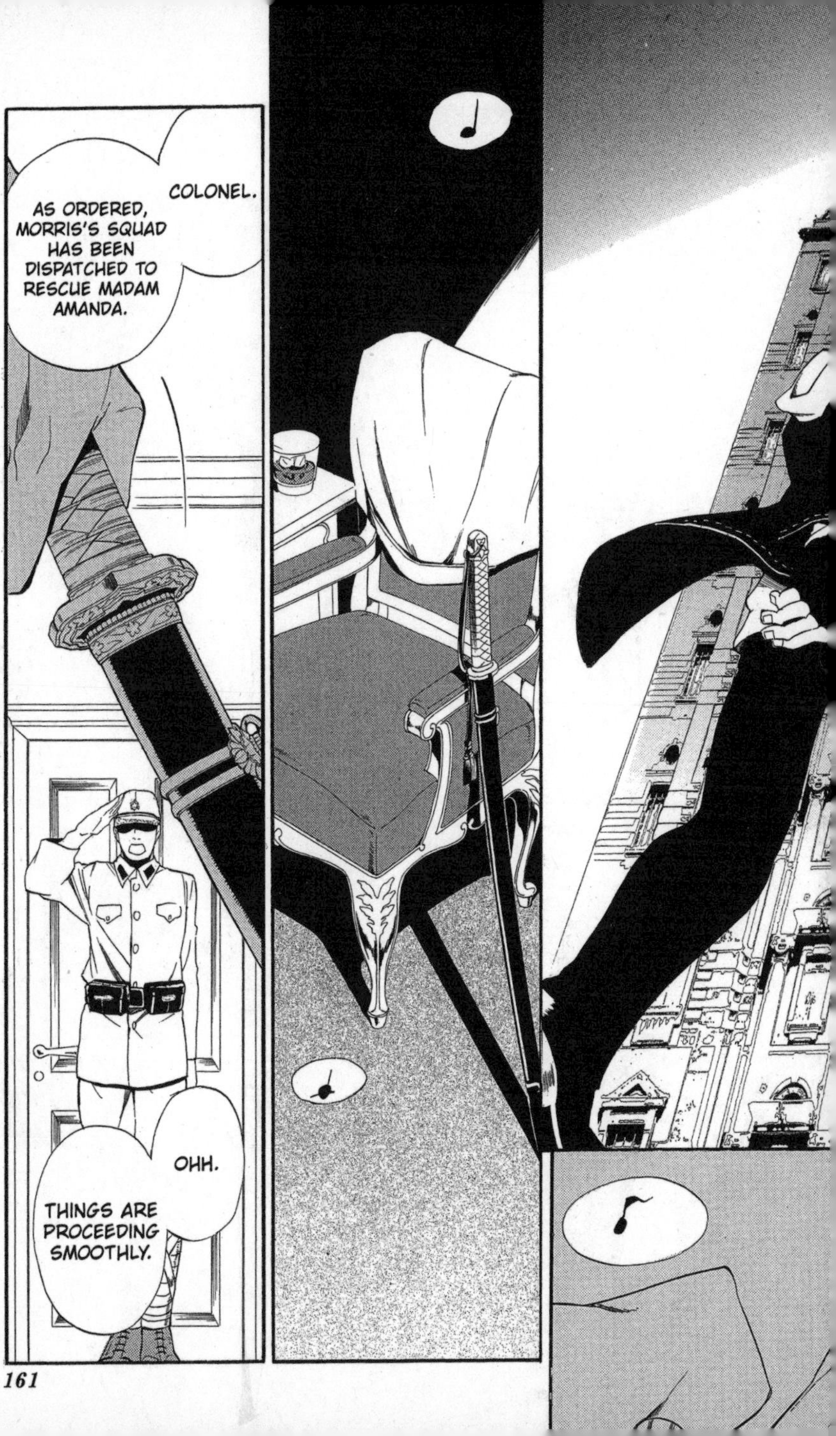
COLONEL.
AS ORDERED, MORRIS'S SQUAD HAS BEEN DISPATCHED TO RESCUE MADAM AMANDA.
OHH.
THINGS ARE PROCEEDING SMOOTHLY.

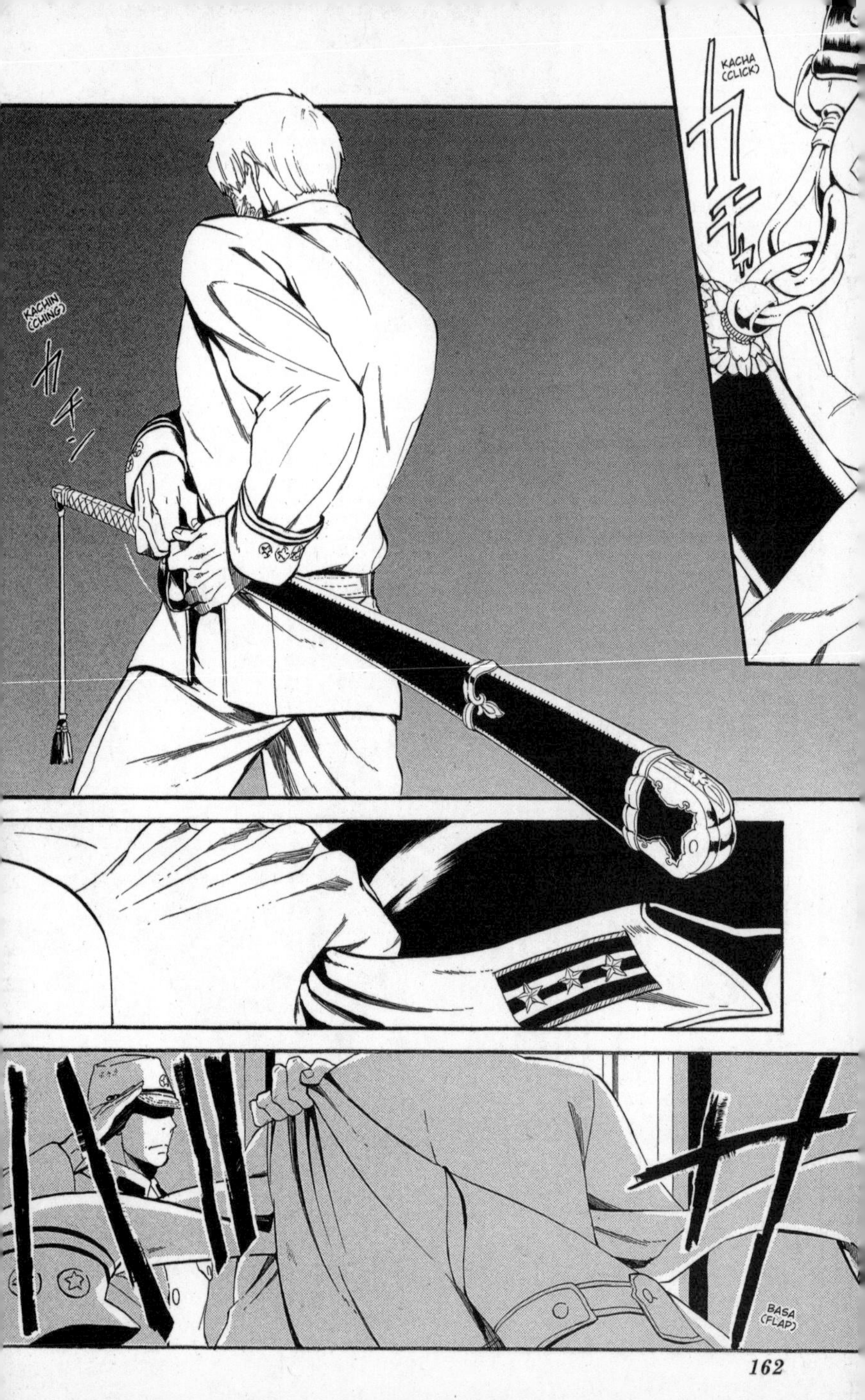
KACHA
(CLICK)
カチャ
KACHIN
(CHING)
カチーン
BASA
(FLAP)

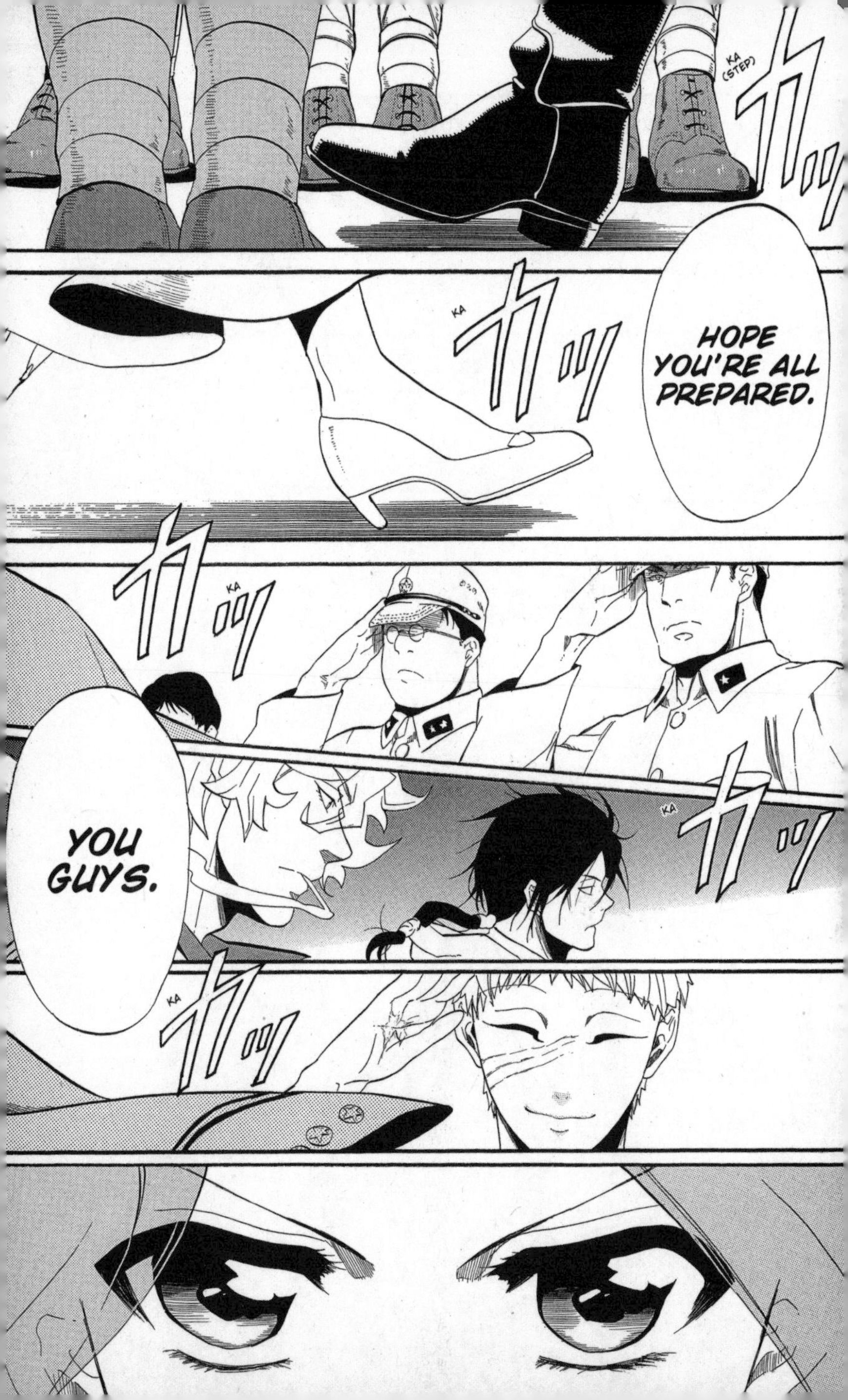

KA (STEP)
カッ
HOPE YOU'RE ALL PREPARED.
KA
カッ
KA
カッ
KA
カッ
YOU GUYS.
KA
カッ

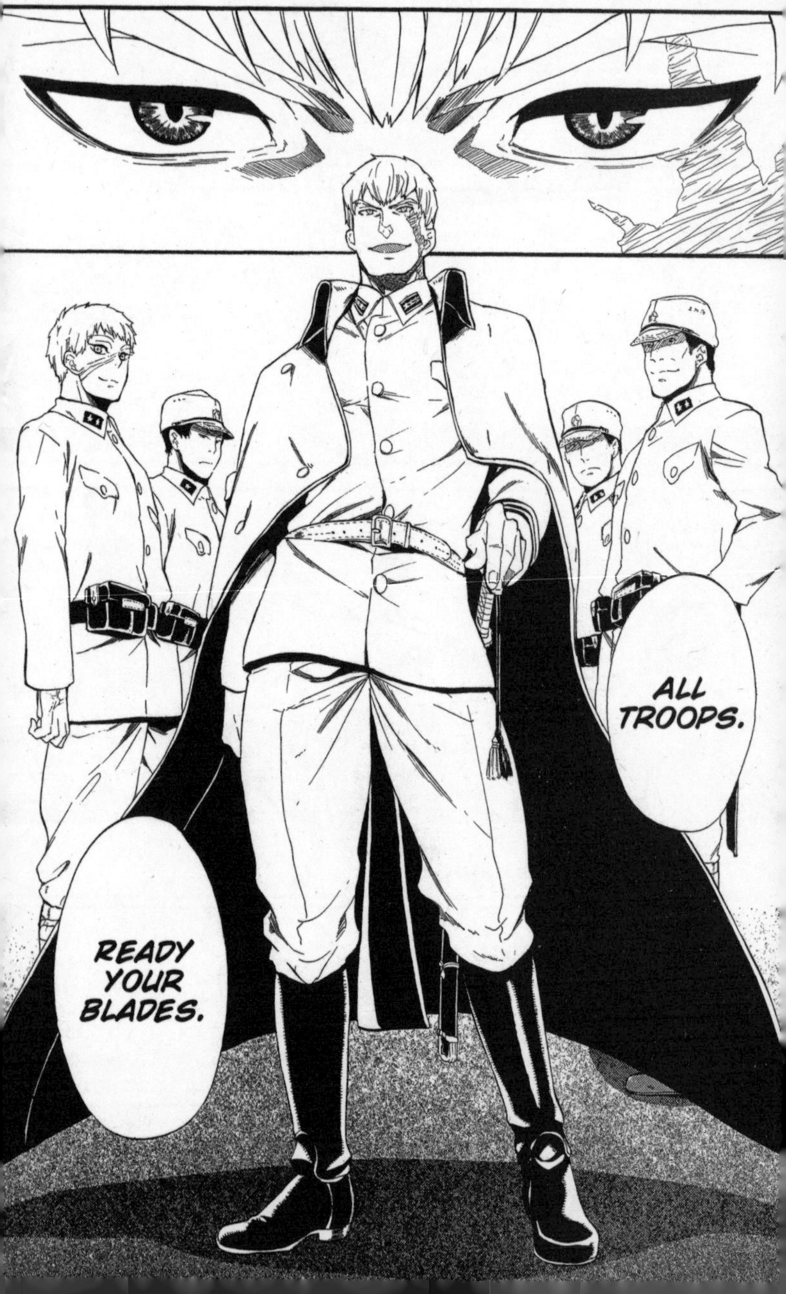
ALL TROOPS.
READY YOUR BLADES.

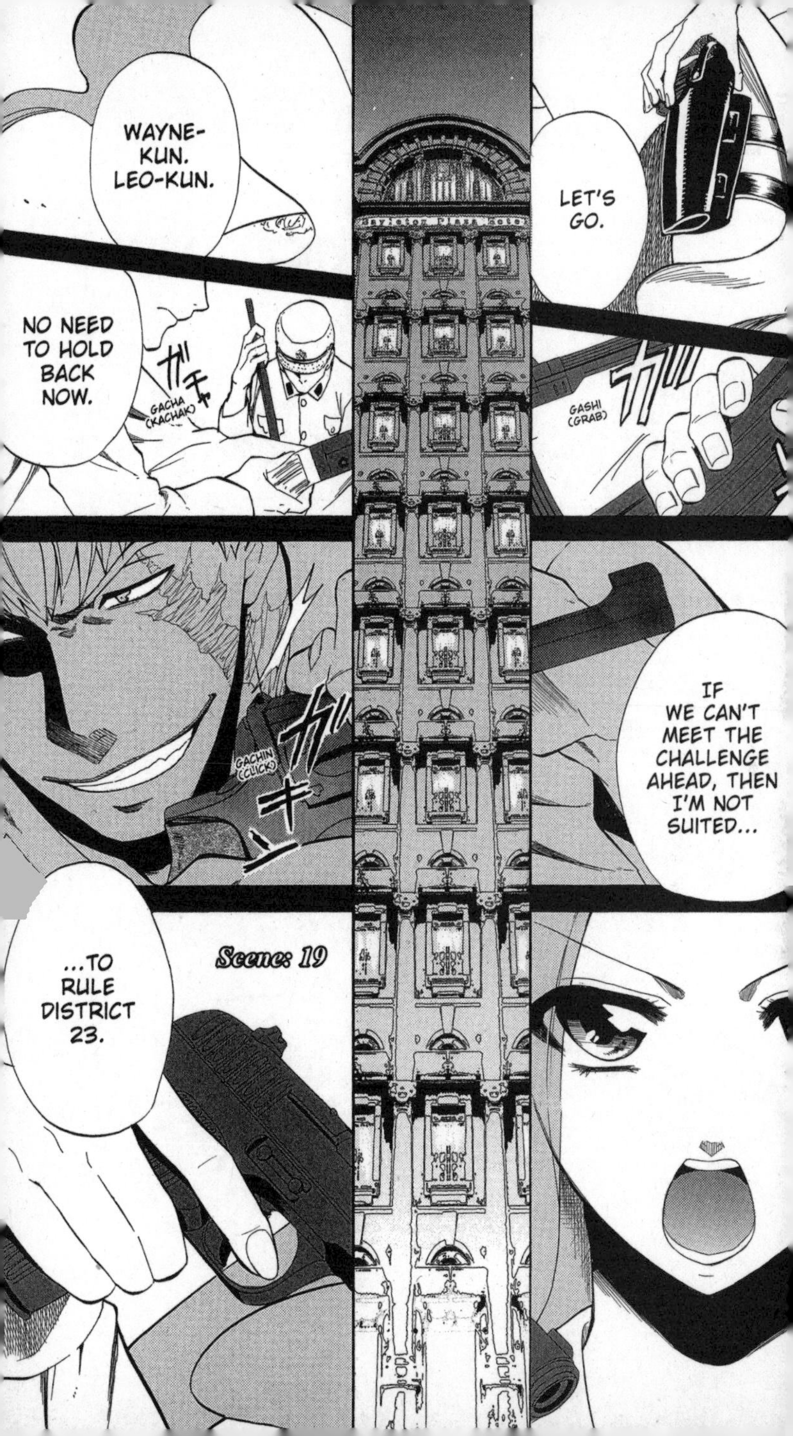
LET'S GO.
GASHI (GRAB)
WAYNE-KUN. LEO-KUN.
NO NEED TO HOLD BACK NOW.
GACHA (KACHAK)
IF WE CAN'T MEET THE CHALLENGE AHEAD, THEN I'M NOT SUITED...
GACHIN (CLICK)
...TO RULE DISTRICT 23.
Scene: 19

Scene: 19

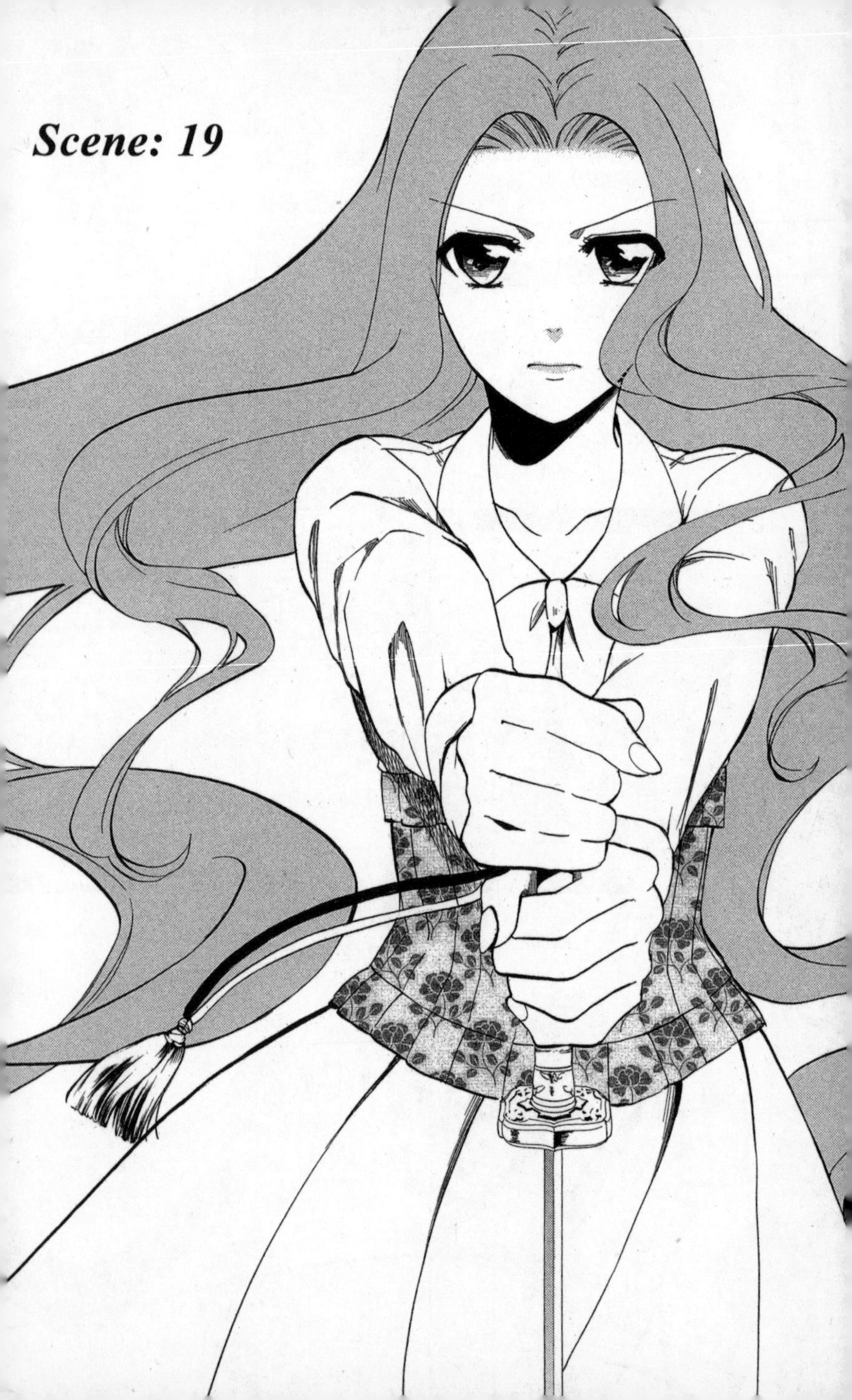

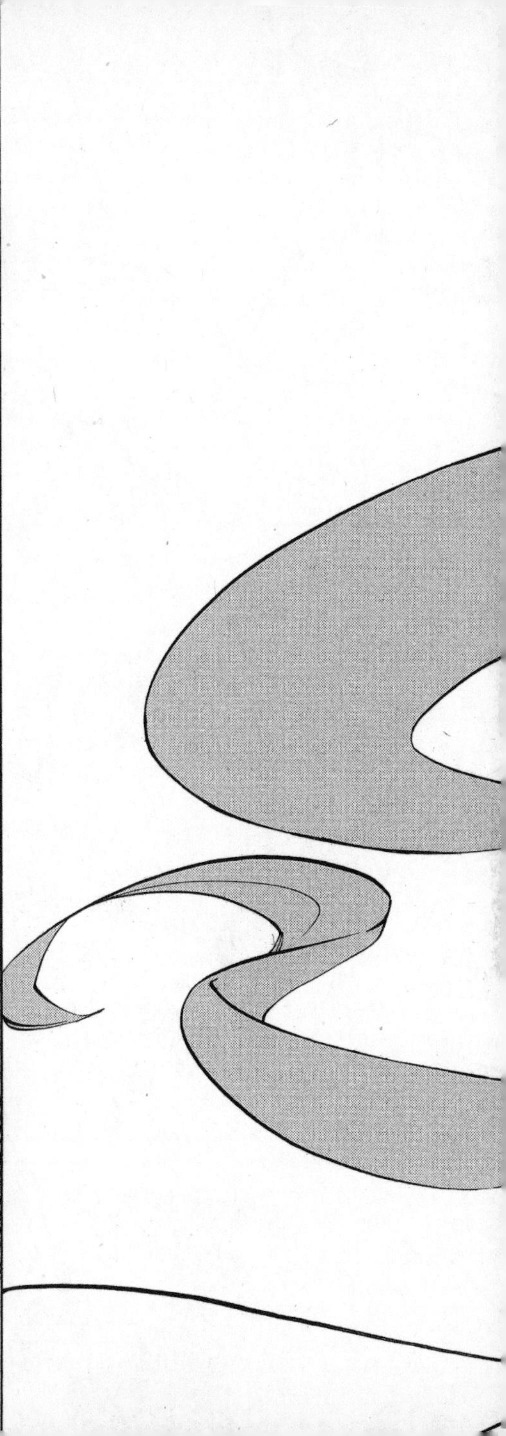

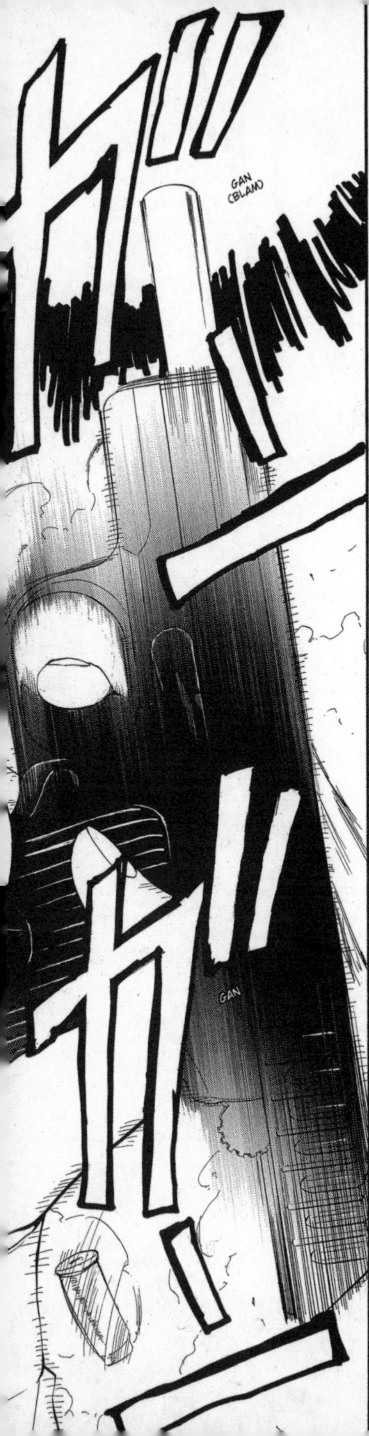
GAN
(BLAM)
GAN

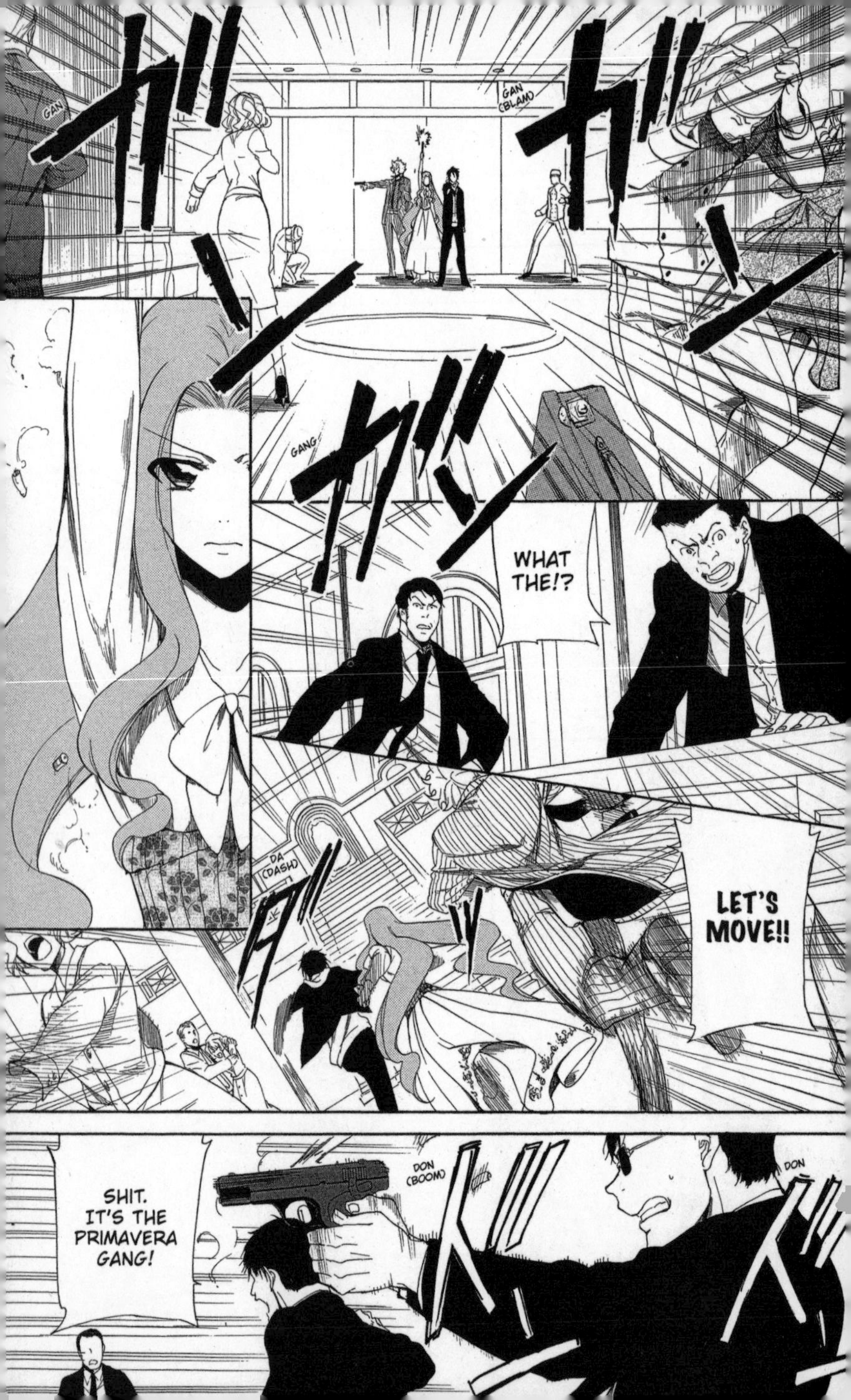
GAN (BLAM)
GAN
GANG
WHAT THE!?
LET'S MOVE!!
DA (DASH)
DON
DON (BOOM)
SHIT. IT'S THE PRIMAVERA GANG!

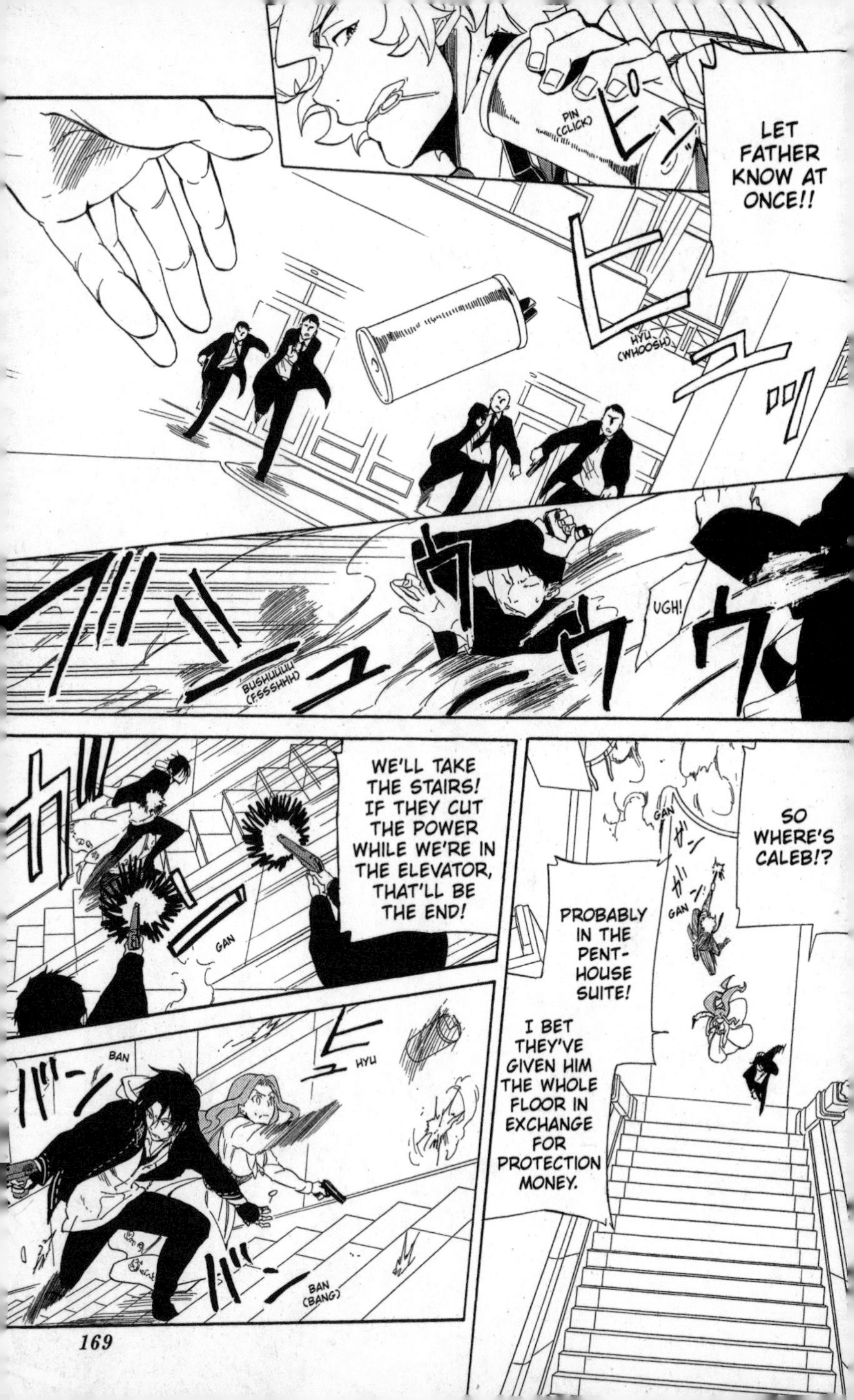
LET FATHER KNOW AT ONCE!!
PIN (CLICK)
HYU (WHOOSH)
UGH!
BUSHUUUU (FSSSHHH)
SO WHERE'S CALEB!?
PROBABLY IN THE PENT-HOUSE SUITE!
I BET THEY'VE GIVEN HIM THE WHOLE FLOOR IN EXCHANGE FOR PROTECTION MONEY.
GAN
GAN
WE'LL TAKE THE STAIRS! IF THEY CUT THE POWER WHILE WE'RE IN THE ELEVATOR, THAT'LL BE THE END!
GAN
HYU
BAN
BAN (BANG)

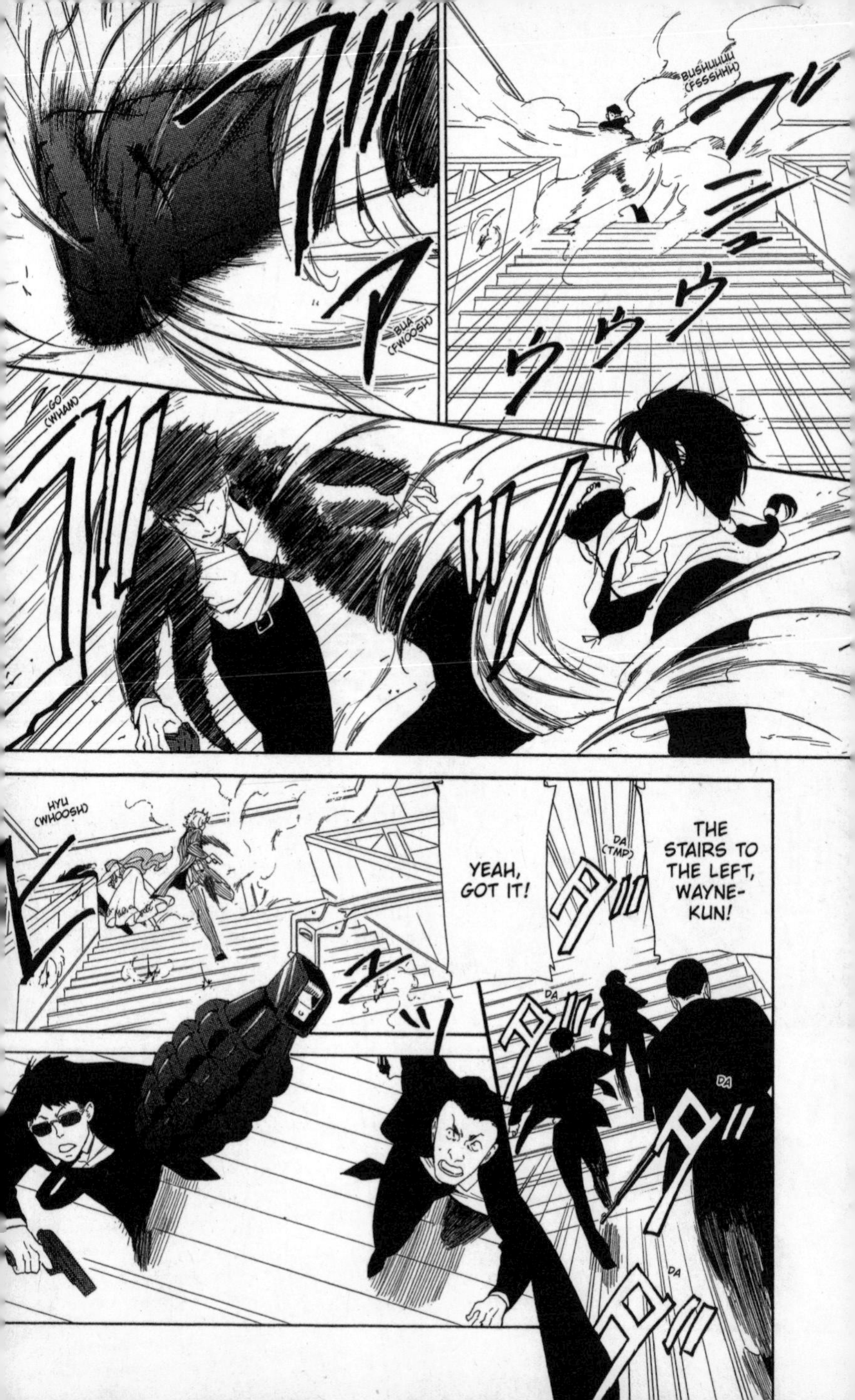
BUSHUUUU (FSSSHHH)
BUA (FWOOSH)
GO (WHAM)
THE STAIRS TO THE LEFT, WAYNE-KUN!
YEAH, GOT IT!
DA (TMP)
HYU (WHOOSH)
DA
DA
DA

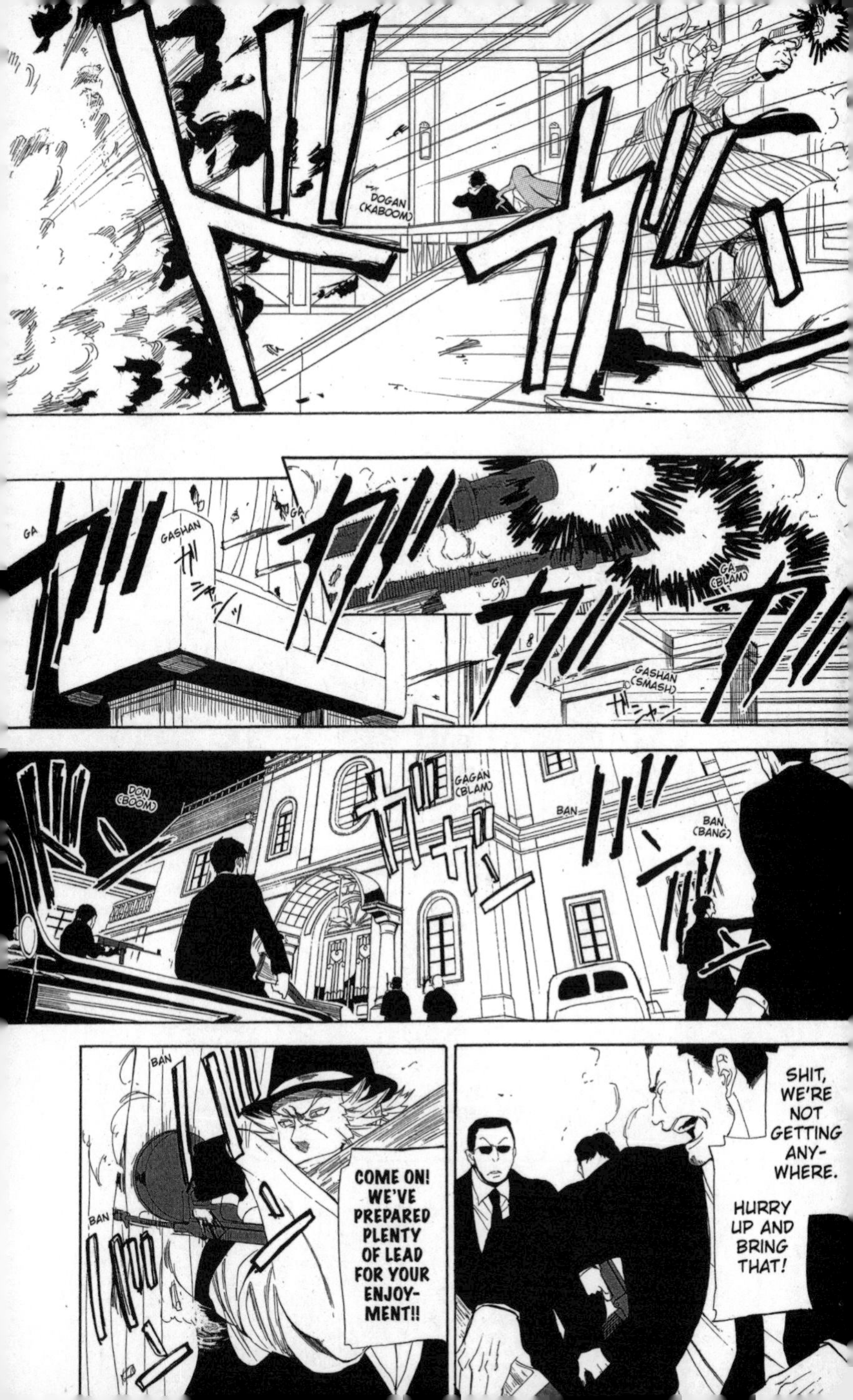
DOGAN (KABOOM)
GA (BLAM)
GASHAN (SMASH)
GA
GA
GASHAN
GA
BAN (BANG)
BAN
GAGAN (BLAM)
DON (BOOM)
SHIT, WE'RE NOT GETTING ANYWHERE.
HURRY UP AND BRING THAT!
BAN
COME ON! WE'VE PREPARED PLENTY OF LEAD FOR YOUR ENJOYMENT!!
BAN

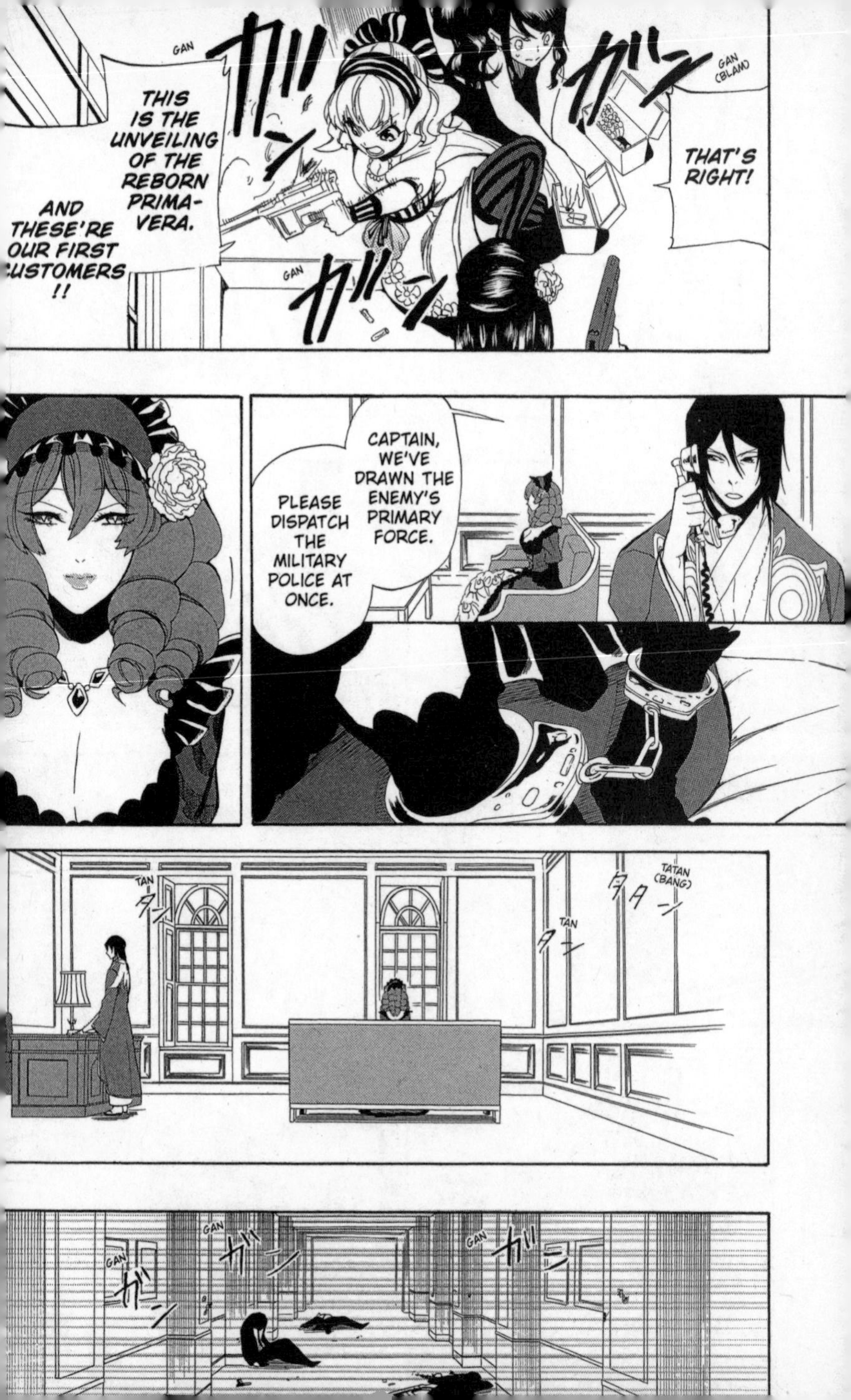

GAN (BLAM)
THAT'S RIGHT!
GAN
THIS IS THE UNVEILING OF THE REBORN PRIMA-VERA.
AND THESE'RE OUR FIRST CUSTOMERS!!
GAN
CAPTAIN, WE'VE DRAWN THE ENEMY'S PRIMARY FORCE.
PLEASE DISPATCH THE MILITARY POLICE AT ONCE.
TATAN (BANG)
TAN
TAN
GAN
GAN
GAN

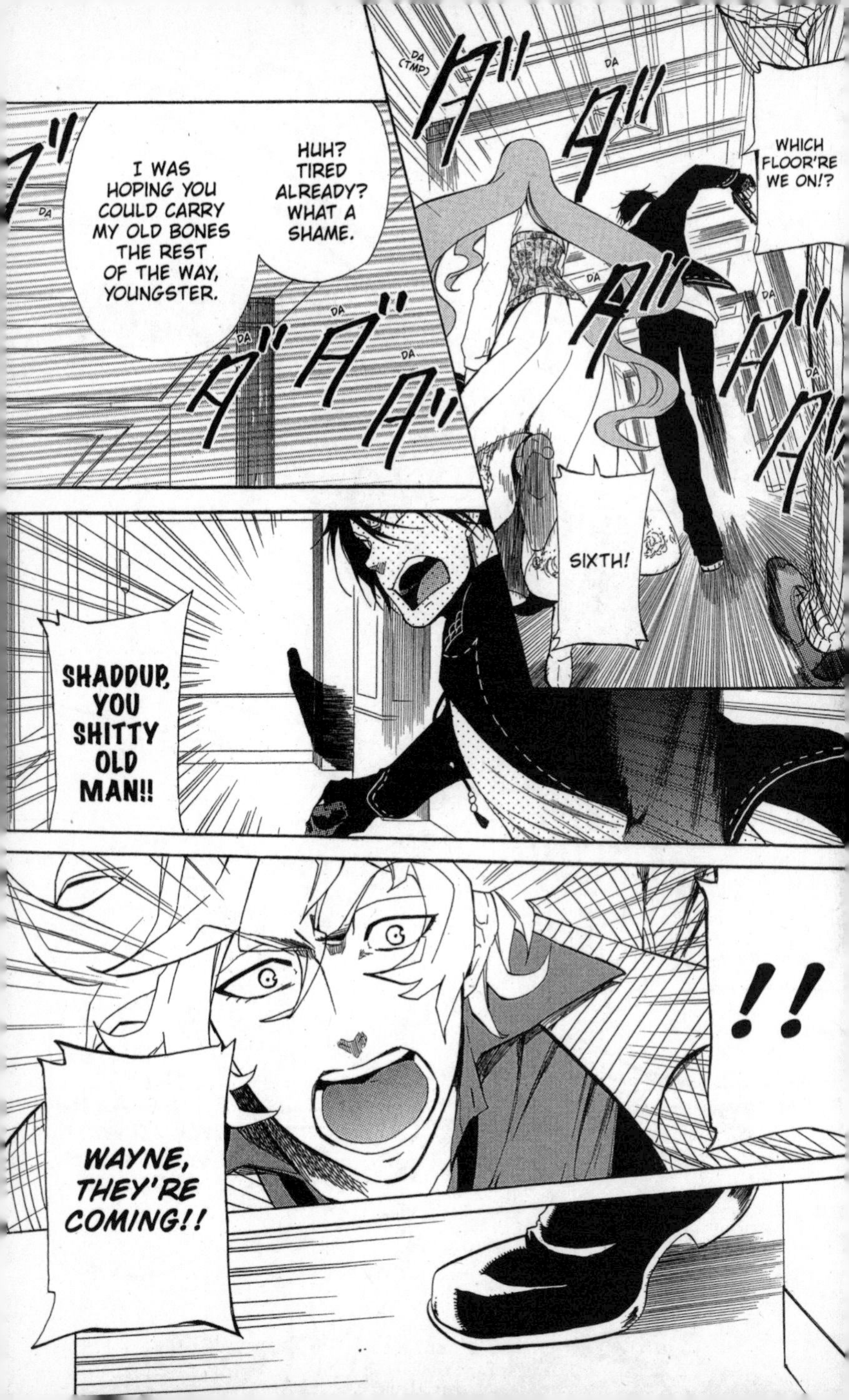
DA (TMP)
DA
WHICH FLOOR'RE WE ON!?
DA
DA
DA
SIXTH!
HUH? TIRED ALREADY? WHAT A SHAME.
I WAS HOPING YOU COULD CARRY MY OLD BONES THE REST OF THE WAY, YOUNGSTER.
DA
DA
DA
SHADDUP, YOU SHITTY OLD MAN!!
!!
WAYNE, THEY'RE COMING!!

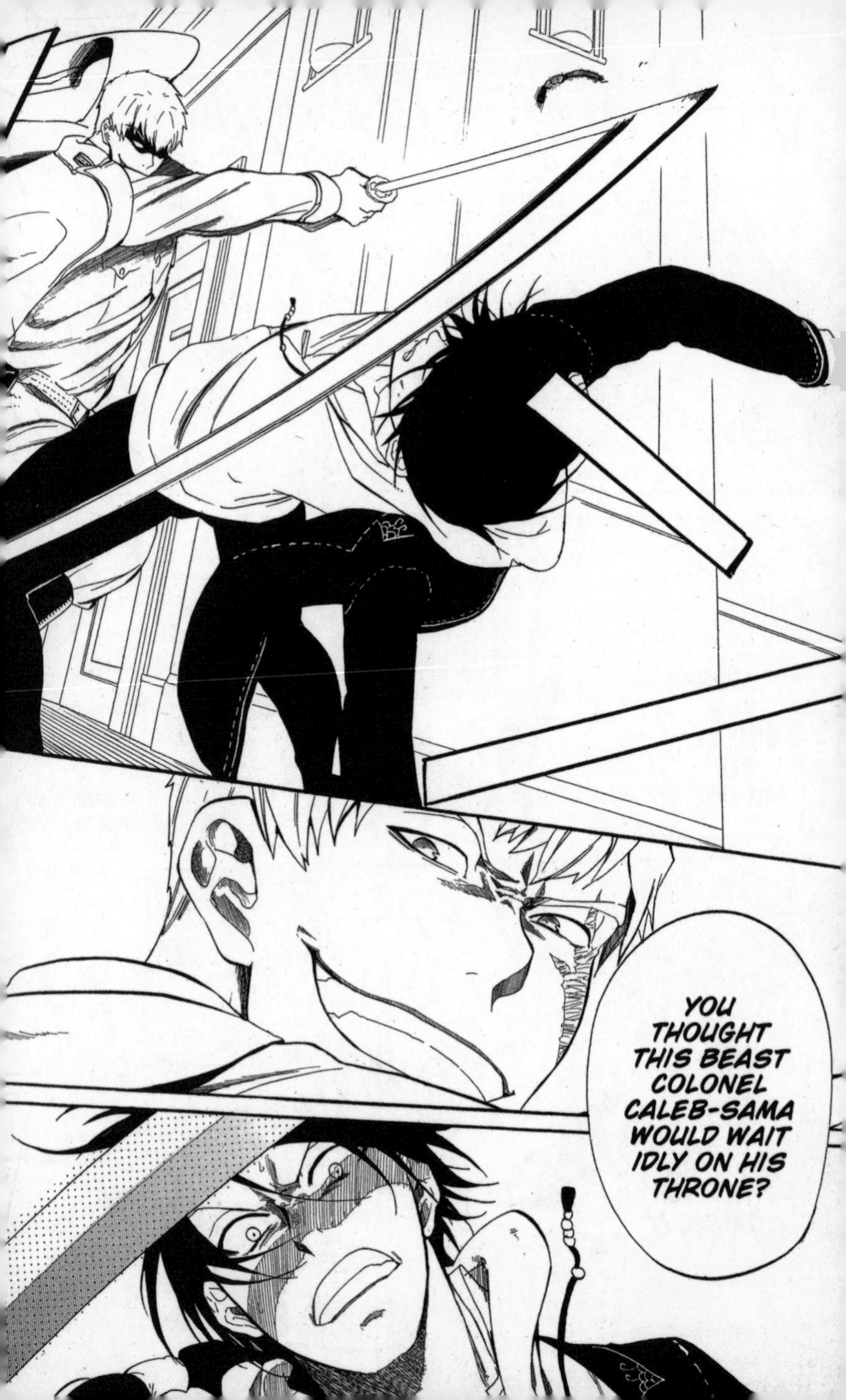
YOU THOUGHT THIS BEAST COLONEL CALEB-SAMA WOULD WAIT IDLY ON HIS THRONE?

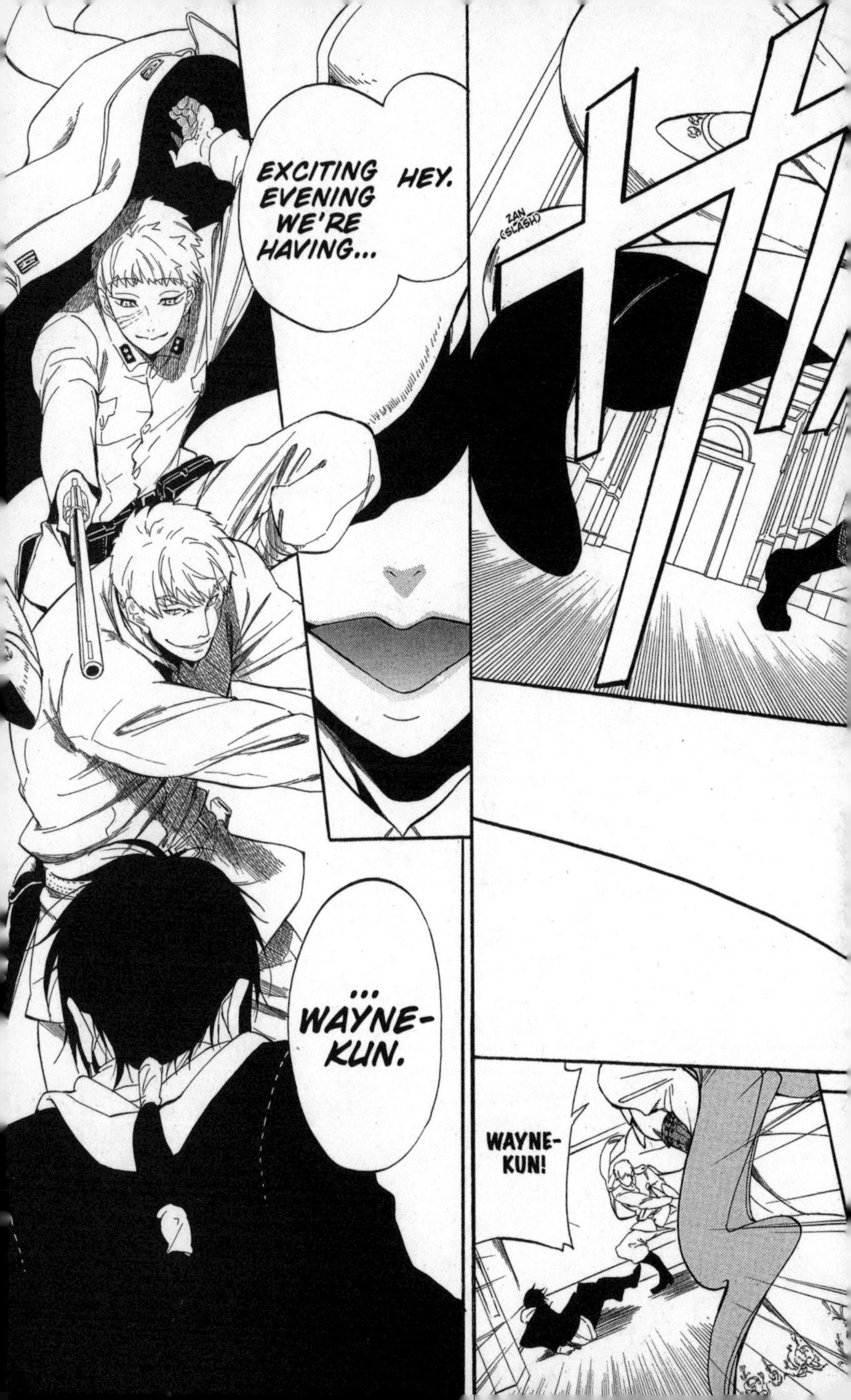
ZAN (SLASH)
WAYNE-KUN!
HEY. EXCITING EVENING WE'RE HAVING...
...WAYNE-KUN.

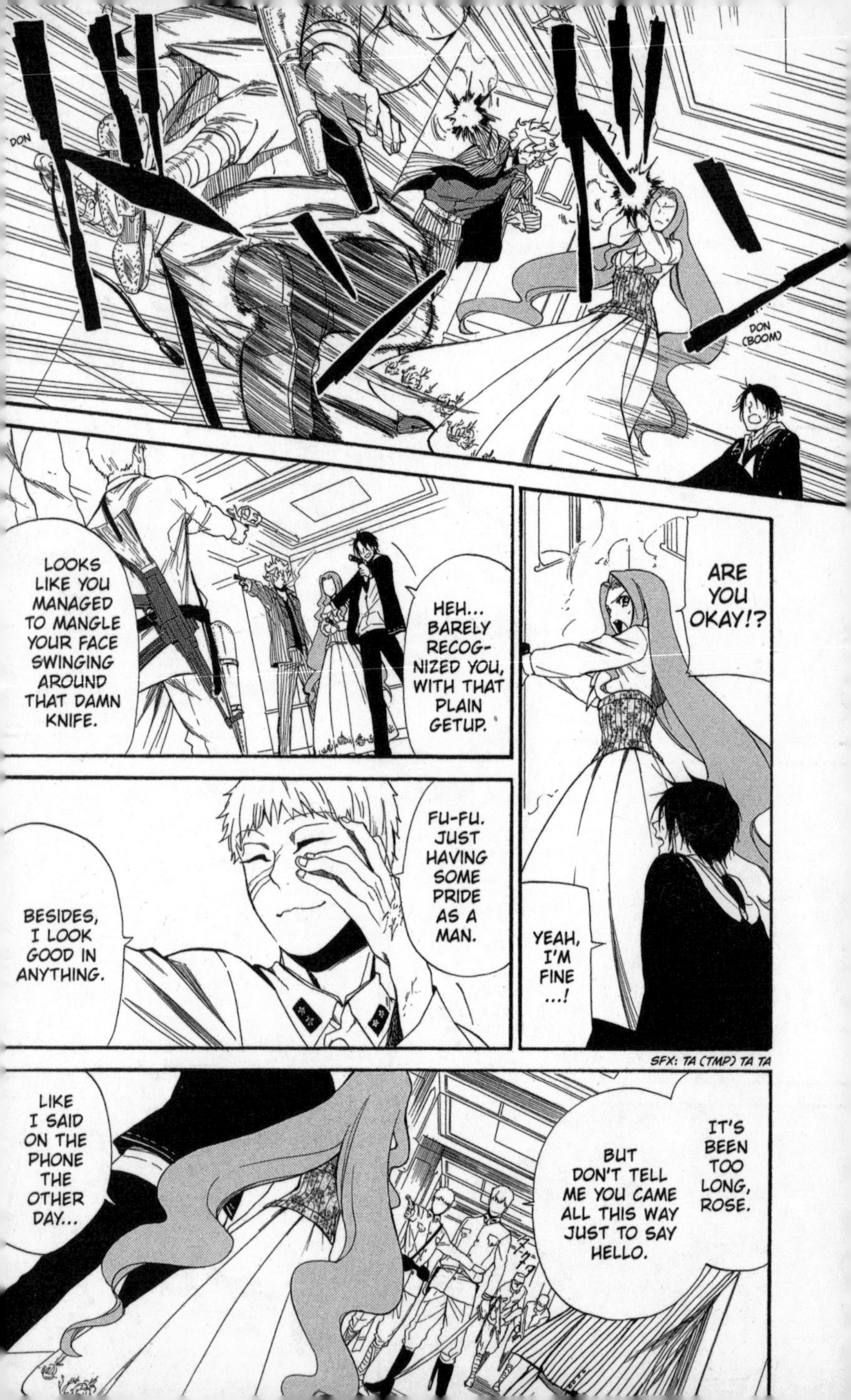
DON (BOOM)
DON
ARE YOU OKAY!?
YEAH, I'M FINE ...!
HEH... BARELY RECOGNIZED YOU, WITH THAT PLAIN GETUP.
LOOKS LIKE YOU MANAGED TO MANGLE YOUR FACE SWINGING AROUND THAT DAMN KNIFE.
FU-FU. JUST HAVING SOME PRIDE AS A MAN.
BESIDES, I LOOK GOOD IN ANYTHING.
SFX: TA (TMP) TA TA
IT'S BEEN TOO LONG, ROSE.
BUT DON'T TELL ME YOU CAME ALL THIS WAY JUST TO SAY HELLO.
LIKE I SAID ON THE PHONE THE OTHER DAY...

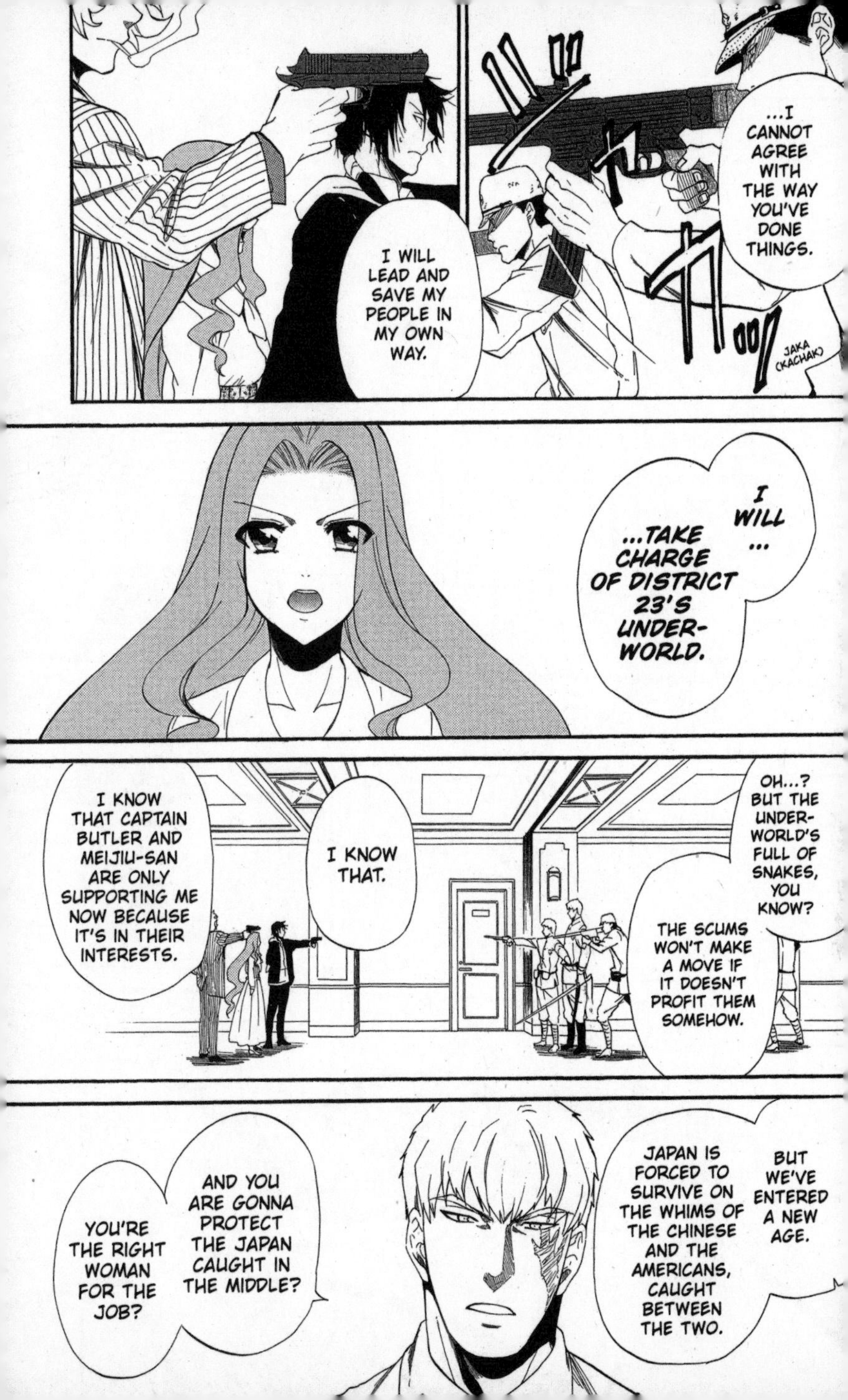
...I CANNOT AGREE WITH THE WAY YOU'VE DONE THINGS.
JAKA (KACHAK)
I WILL LEAD AND SAVE MY PEOPLE IN MY OWN WAY.
I WILL...
...TAKE CHARGE OF DISTRICT 23'S UNDER-WORLD.
OH...? BUT THE UNDER-WORLD'S FULL OF SNAKES, YOU KNOW?
THE SCUMS WON'T MAKE A MOVE IF IT DOESN'T PROFIT THEM SOMEHOW.
I KNOW THAT.
I KNOW THAT CAPTAIN BUTLER AND MEIJIU-SAN ARE ONLY SUPPORTING ME NOW BECAUSE IT'S IN THEIR INTERESTS.
BUT WE'VE ENTERED A NEW AGE.
JAPAN IS FORCED TO SURVIVE ON THE WHIMS OF THE CHINESE AND THE AMERICANS, CAUGHT BETWEEN THE TWO.
AND YOU ARE GONNA PROTECT THE JAPAN CAUGHT IN THE MIDDLE?
YOU'RE THE RIGHT WOMAN FOR THE JOB?

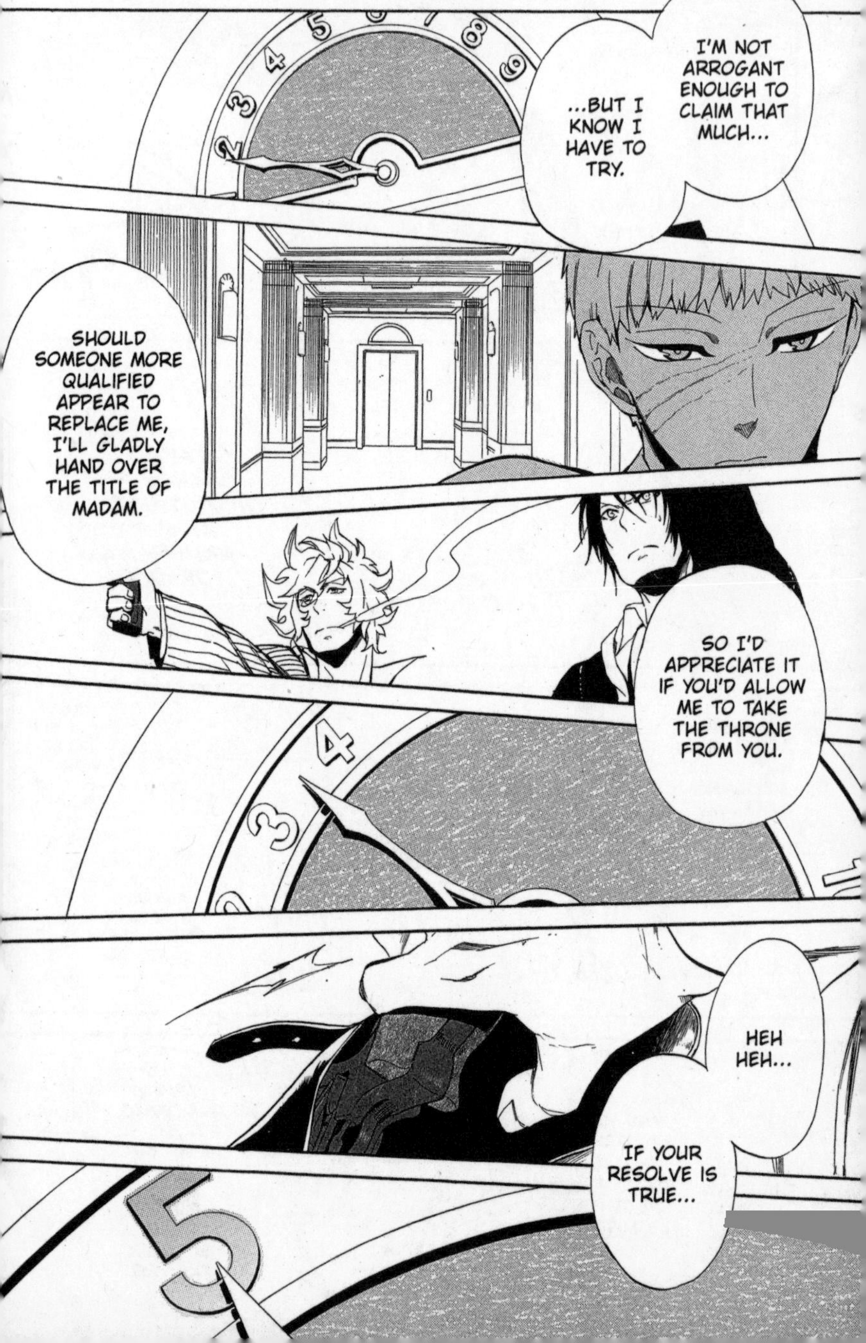

I'M NOT ARROGANT ENOUGH TO CLAIM THAT MUCH...
...BUT I KNOW I HAVE TO TRY.
SHOULD SOMEONE MORE QUALIFIED APPEAR TO REPLACE ME, I'LL GLADLY HAND OVER THE TITLE OF MADAM.
SO I'D APPRECIATE IT IF YOU'D ALLOW ME TO TAKE THE THRONE FROM YOU.
HEH HEH...
IF YOUR RESOLVE IS TRUE...

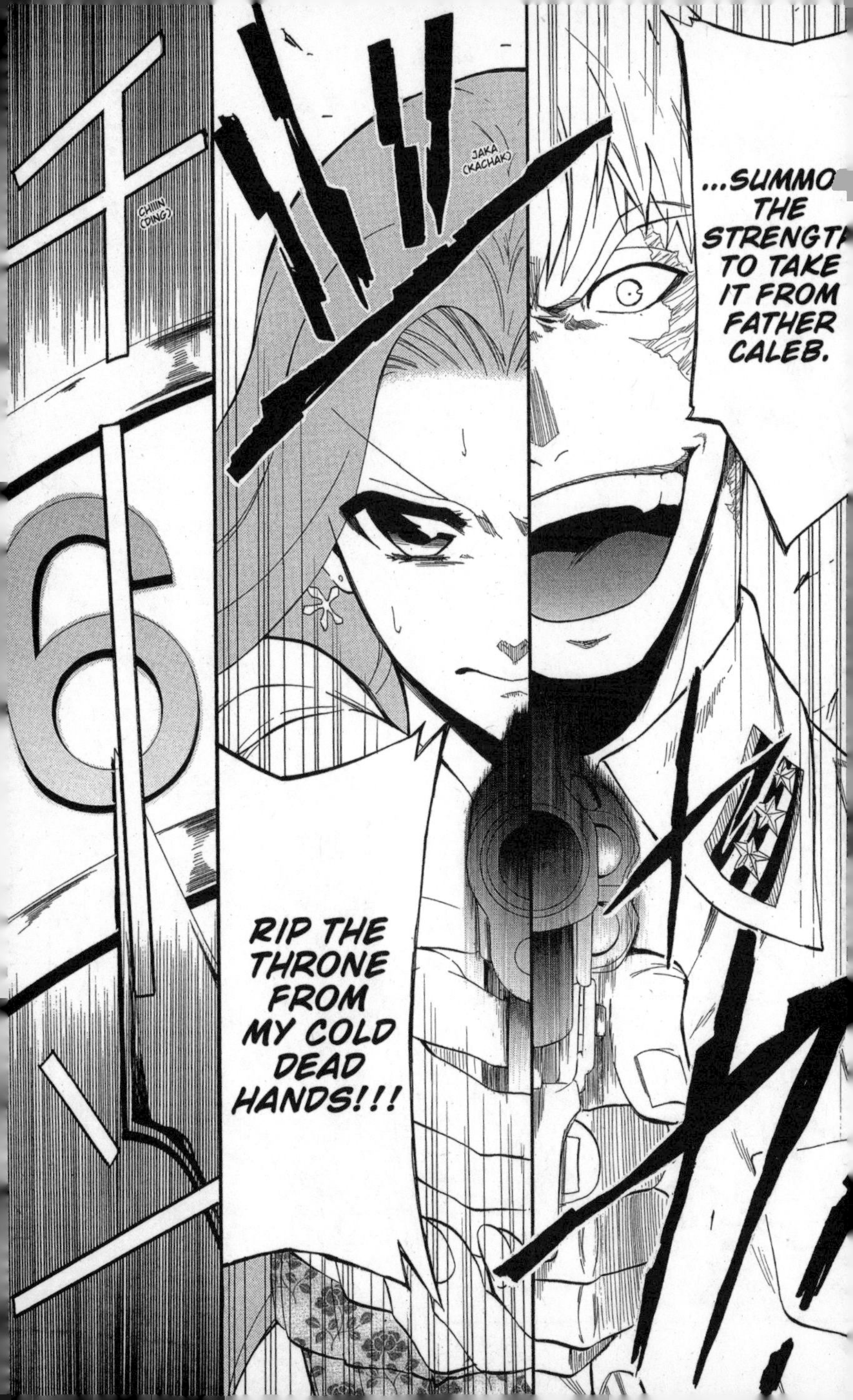
...SUMMO THE STRENGT TO TAKE IT FROM FATHER CALEB.
JAKA (KACHAK)
RIP THE THRONE FROM MY COLD DEAD HANDS!!!
CHIIIN (DING)

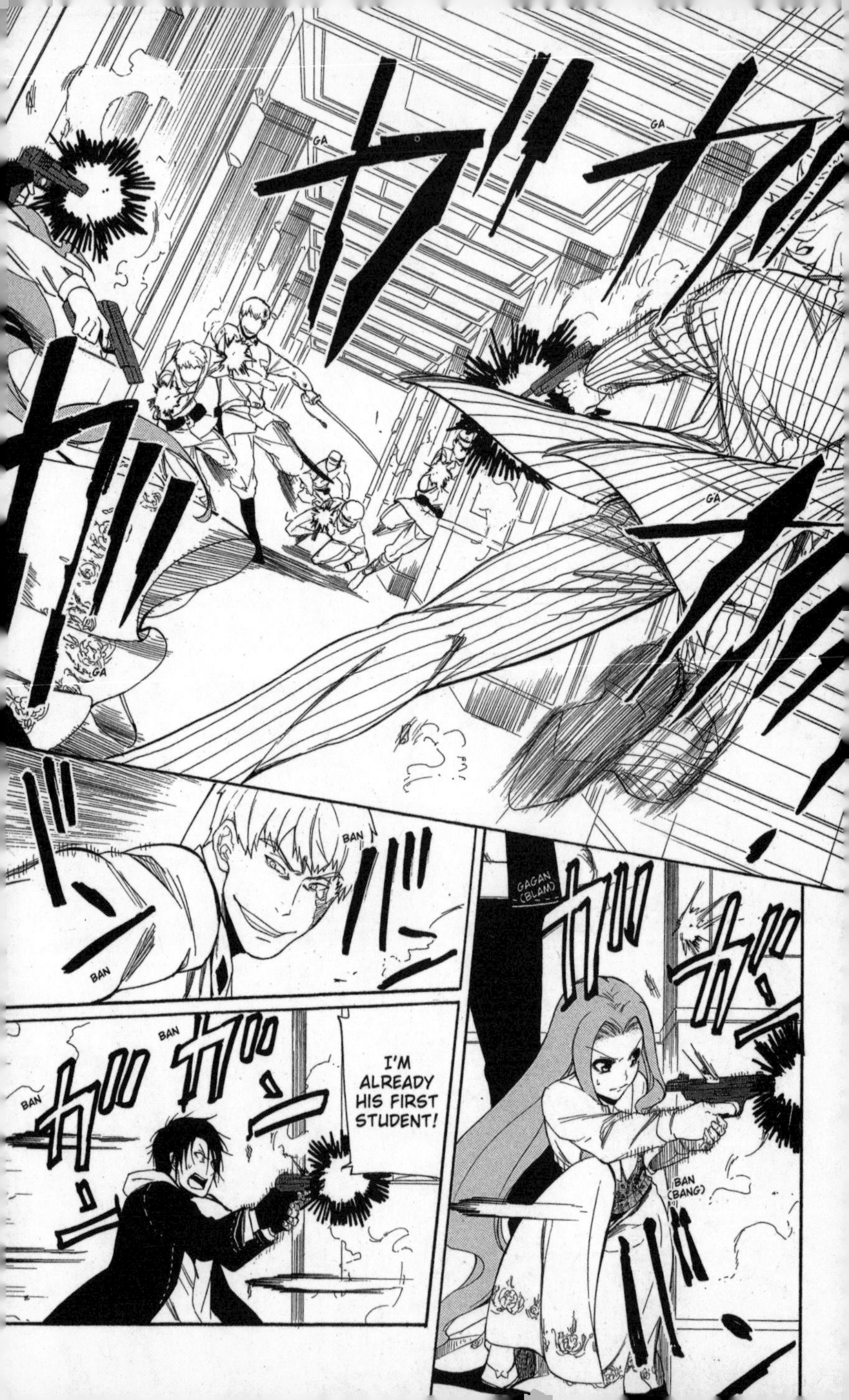
GA
GA
GA
GA
GAGAN (BLAM)
BAN (BANG)
BAN
BAN
BAN
BAN
I'M ALREADY HIS FIRST STUDENT!

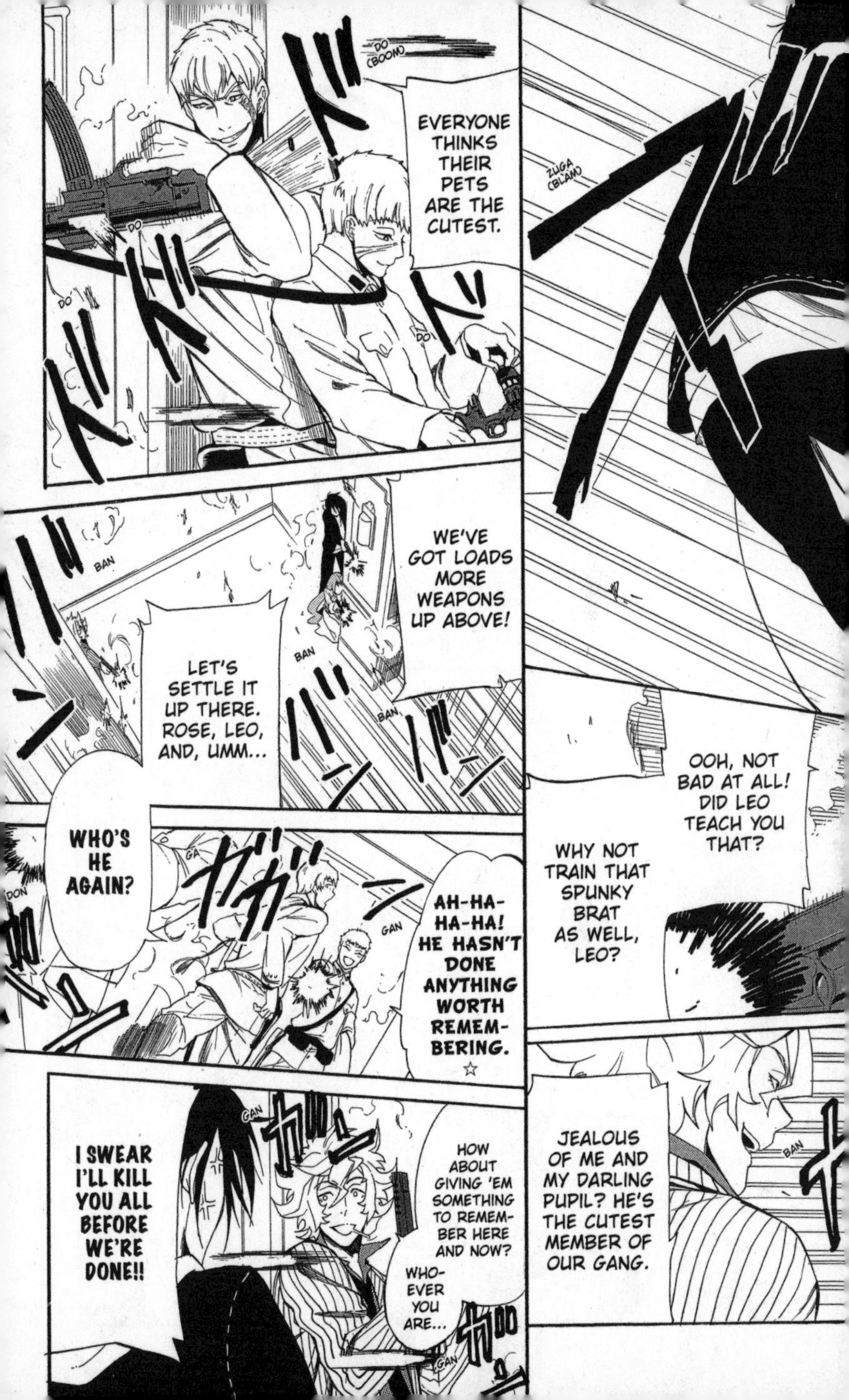
ZUGA (BLAM)
DO (BOOM)
EVERYONE THINKS THEIR PETS ARE THE CUTEST.
DO
DO
DO
WE'VE GOT LOADS MORE WEAPONS UP ABOVE!
BAN
LET'S SETTLE IT UP THERE. ROSE, LEO, AND, UMM...
BAN
BAN
OOH, NOT BAD AT ALL! DID LEO TEACH YOU THAT?
WHY NOT TRAIN THAT SPUNKY BRAT AS WELL, LEO?
AH-HA-HA-HA! HE HASN'T DONE ANYTHING WORTH REMEMBERING. ☆
GAN
GA
WHO'S HE AGAIN?
DON
JEALOUS OF ME AND MY DARLING PUPIL? HE'S THE CUTEST MEMBER OF OUR GANG.
BAN
HOW ABOUT GIVING 'EM SOMETHING TO REMEMBER HERE AND NOW?
WHO-EVER YOU ARE...
GAN
GAN
I SWEAR I'LL KILL YOU ALL BEFORE WE'RE DONE!!

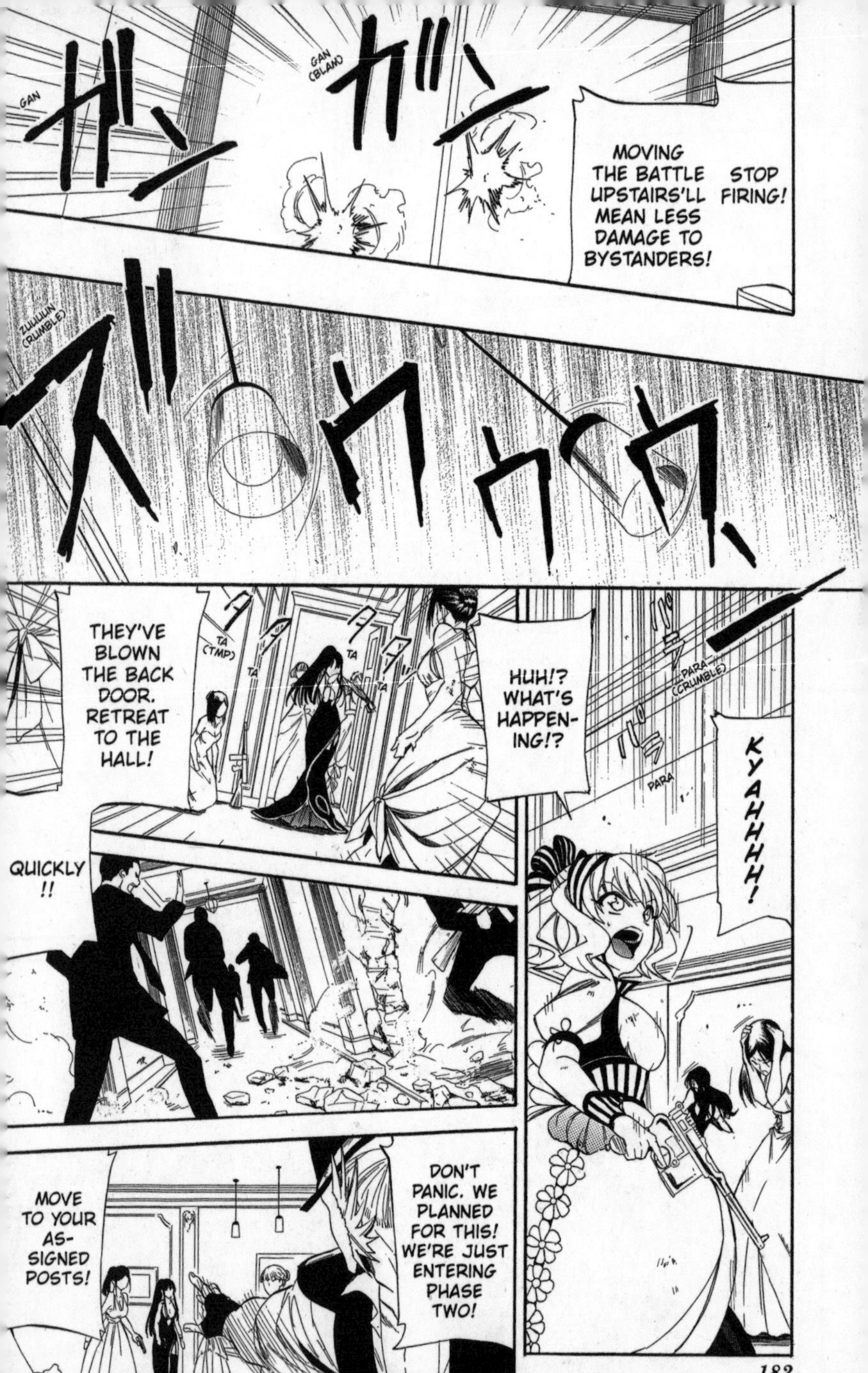
STOP FIRING!
MOVING THE BATTLE UPSTAIRS'LL MEAN LESS DAMAGE TO BYSTANDERS!
GAN (BLAM)
GAN
ZULUUUN (CRUMBLE)
PARA (CRUMBLE)
KYAHHHH!
PARA
...
HUH!? WHAT'S HAPPEN-ING!?
TA
TA (TMP)
TA
THEY'VE BLOWN THE BACK DOOR. RETREAT TO THE HALL!
QUICKLY !!
DON'T PANIC. WE PLANNED FOR THIS! WE'RE JUST ENTERING PHASE TWO!
MOVE TO YOUR AS-SIGNED POSTS!

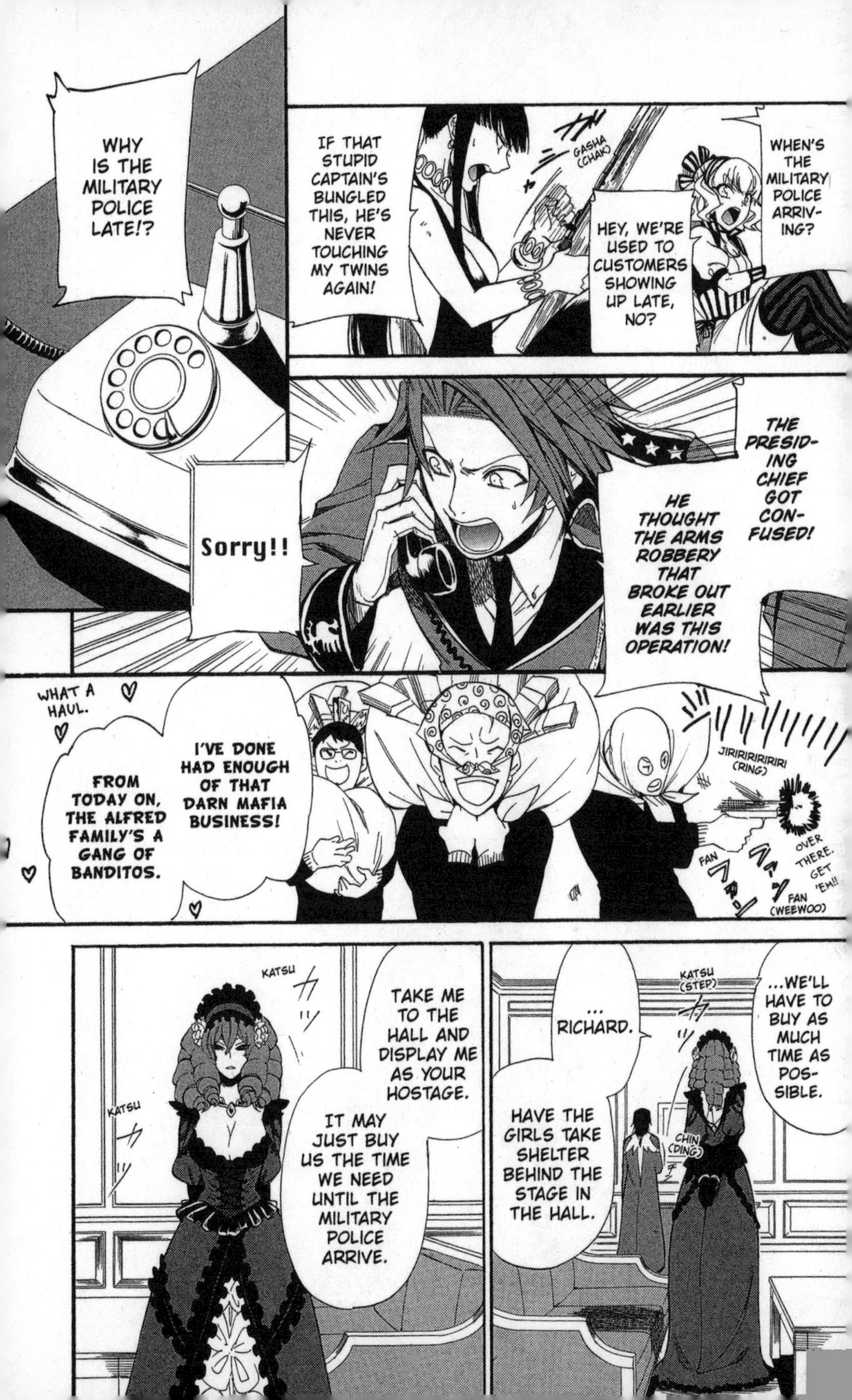
WHEN'S THE MILITARY POLICE ARRIV-ING?
HEY, WE'RE USED TO CUSTOMERS SHOWING UP LATE, NO?
GASHA (CHAK)
IF THAT STUPID CAPTAIN'S BUNGLED THIS, HE'S NEVER TOUCHING MY TWINS AGAIN!
THE PRESID-ING CHIEF GOT CON-FUSED!
HE THOUGHT THE ARMS ROBBERY THAT BROKE OUT EARLIER WAS THIS OPERATION!
Sorry!!
WHY IS THE MILITARY POLICE LATE!?
JIRIRIRIRIRIRI (RING)
OVER THERE. GET 'EM!!
FAN FAN (WEEWOO)
I'VE DONE HAD ENOUGH OF THAT DARN MAFIA BUSINESS!
FROM TODAY ON, THE ALFRED FAMILY'S A GANG OF BANDITOS.
WHAT A HAUL.
...WE'LL HAVE TO BUY AS MUCH TIME AS POS-SIBLE.
KATSU (STEP)
... RICHARD.
CHIN (DING)
HAVE THE GIRLS TAKE SHELTER BEHIND THE STAGE IN THE HALL.
KATSU
TAKE ME TO THE HALL AND DISPLAY ME AS YOUR HOSTAGE.
IT MAY JUST BUY US THE TIME WE NEED UNTIL THE MILITARY POLICE ARRIVE.
KATSU

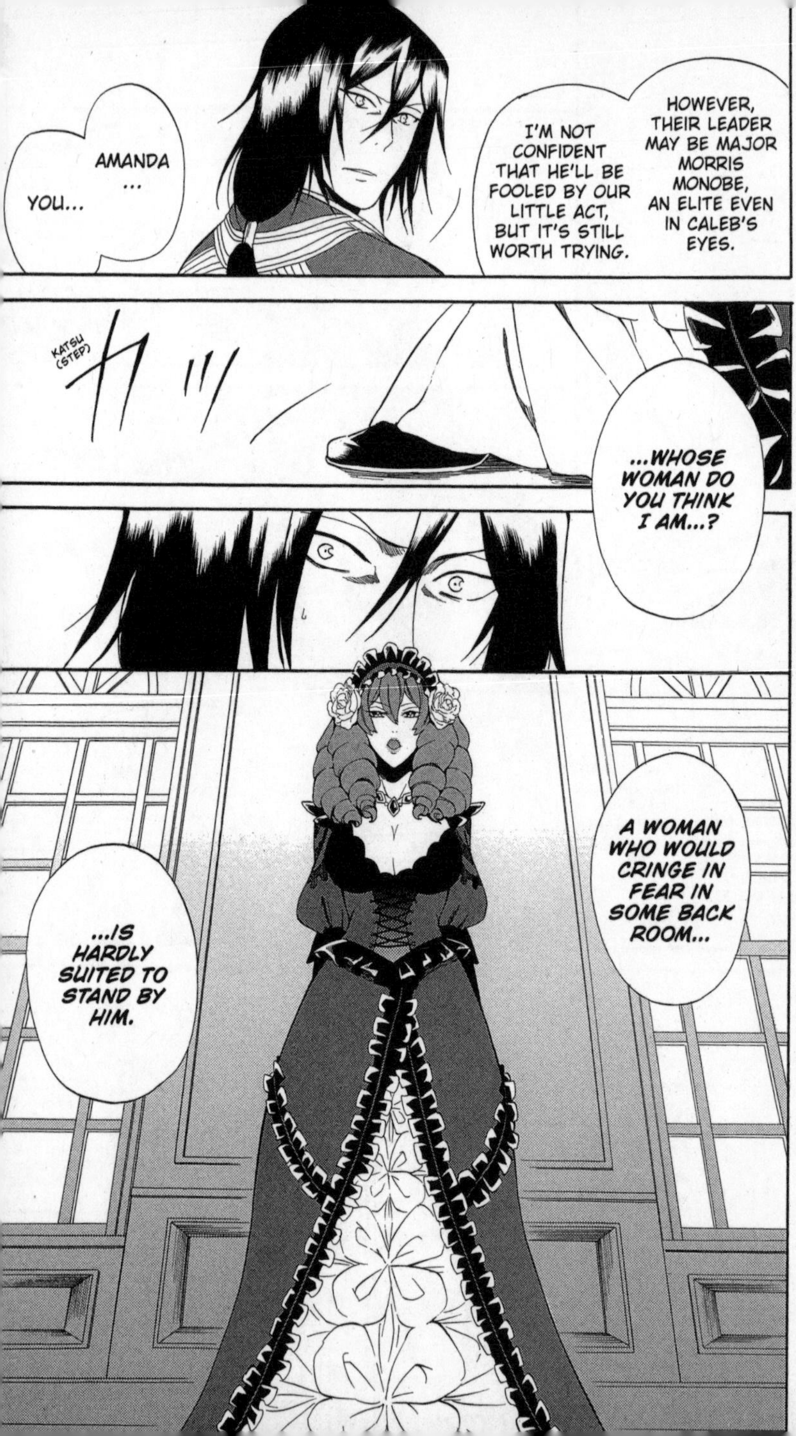
HOWEVER, THEIR LEADER MAY BE MAJOR MORRIS MONOBE, AN ELITE EVEN IN CALEB'S EYES.
I'M NOT CONFIDENT THAT HE'LL BE FOOLED BY OUR LITTLE ACT, BUT IT'S STILL WORTH TRYING.
AMANDA ... YOU...
KATSU (STEP)
...WHOSE WOMAN DO YOU THINK I AM...?
A WOMAN WHO WOULD CRINGE IN FEAR IN SOME BACK ROOM...
...IS HARDLY SUITED TO STAND BY HIM.

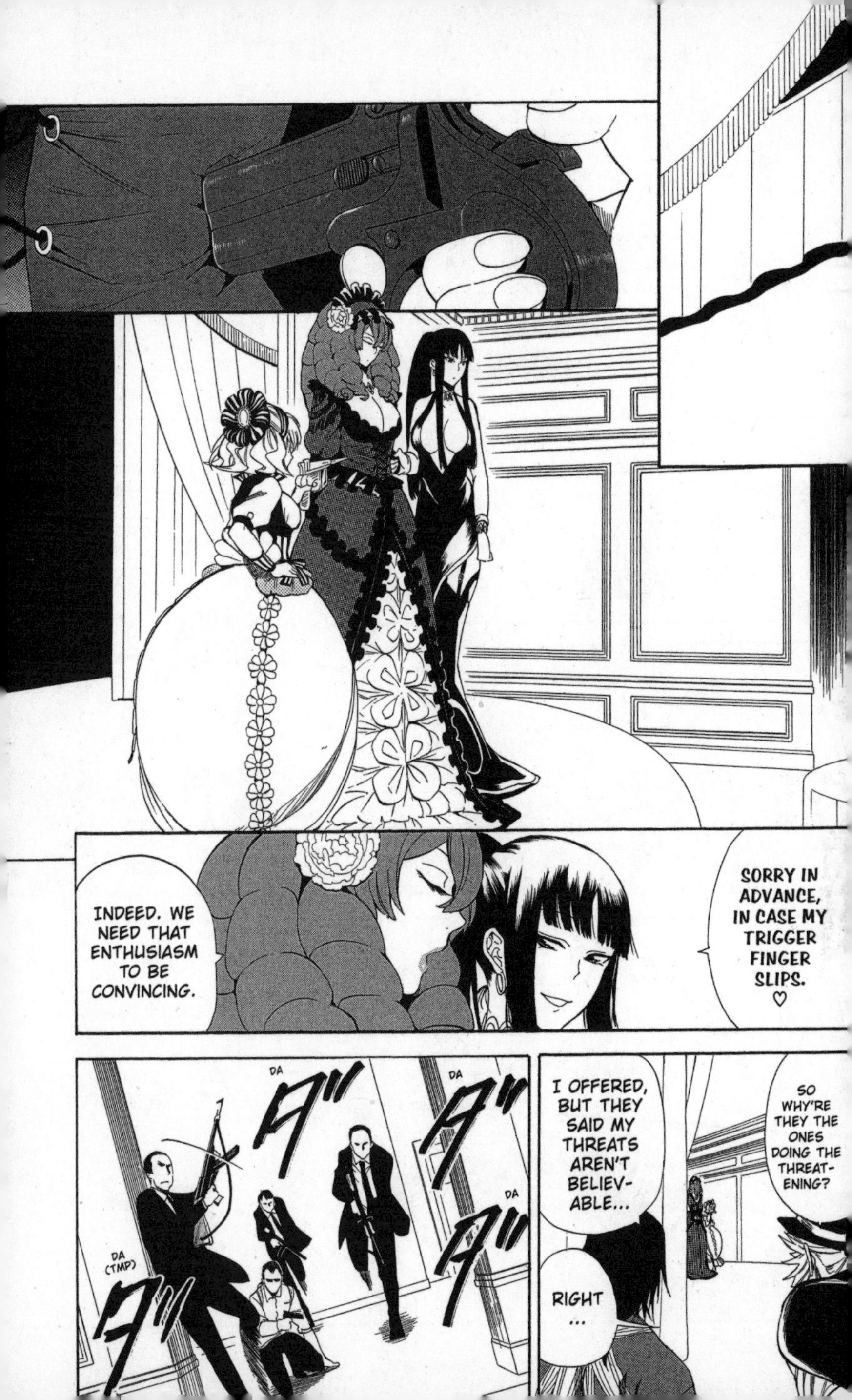
SORRY IN ADVANCE, IN CASE MY TRIGGER FINGER SLIPS. ♡
INDEED. WE NEED THAT ENTHUSIASM TO BE CONVINCING.
SO WHY'RE THEY THE ONES DOING THE THREAT-ENING?
I OFFERED, BUT THEY SAID MY THREATS AREN'T BELIEV-ABLE...
RIGHT ...
DA
DA
DA
DA (TMP)

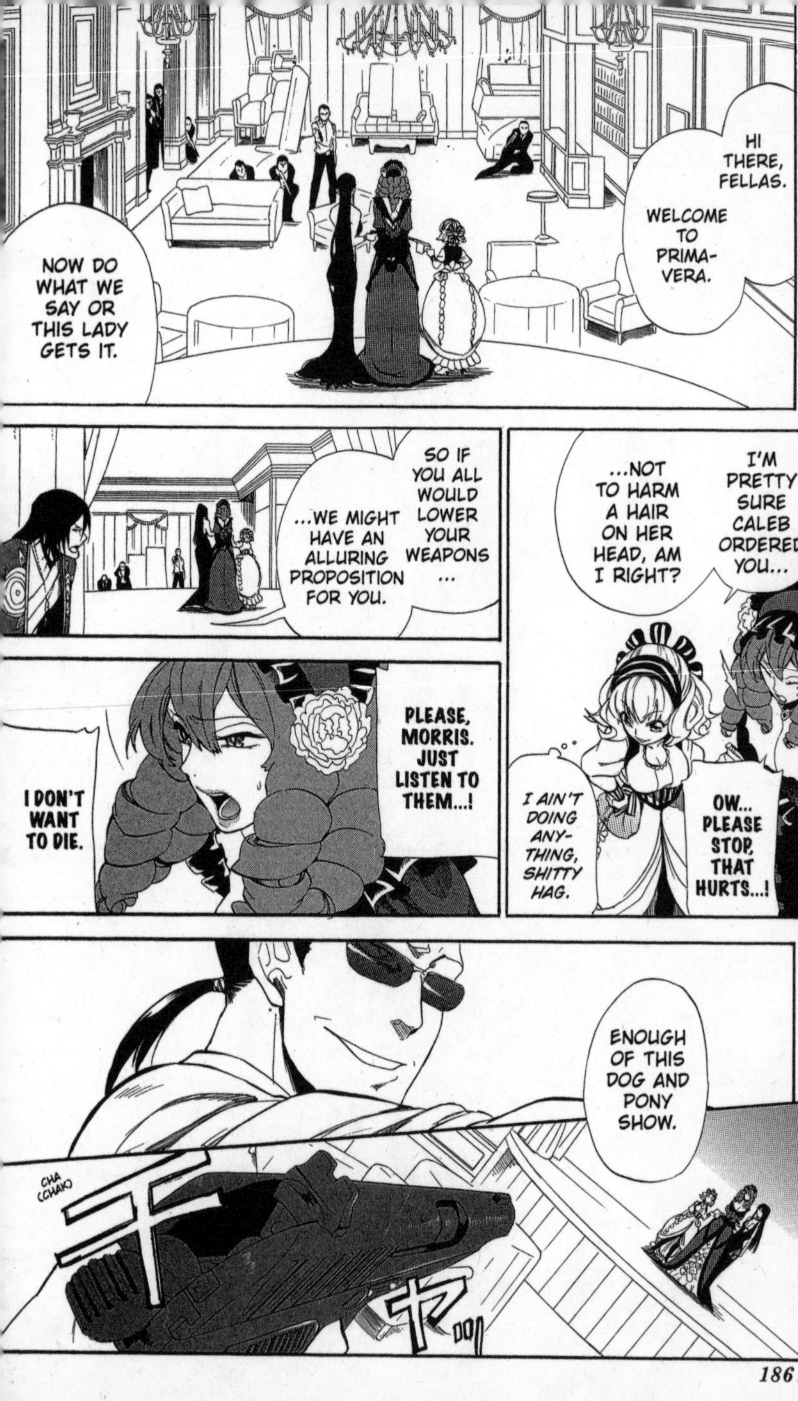
HI THERE, FELLAS.
WELCOME TO PRIMAVERA.
NOW DO WHAT WE SAY OR THIS LADY GETS IT.
I'M PRETTY SURE CALEB ORDERED YOU...
...NOT TO HARM A HAIR ON HER HEAD, AM I RIGHT?
OW... PLEASE STOP, THAT HURTS...!
I AIN'T DOING ANYTHING, SHITTY HAG.
SO IF YOU ALL WOULD LOWER YOUR WEAPONS...
...WE MIGHT HAVE AN ALLURING PROPOSITION FOR YOU.
PLEASE, MORRIS. JUST LISTEN TO THEM...!
I DON'T WANT TO DIE.
ENOUGH OF THIS DOG AND PONY SHOW.
CHA (CHAK)

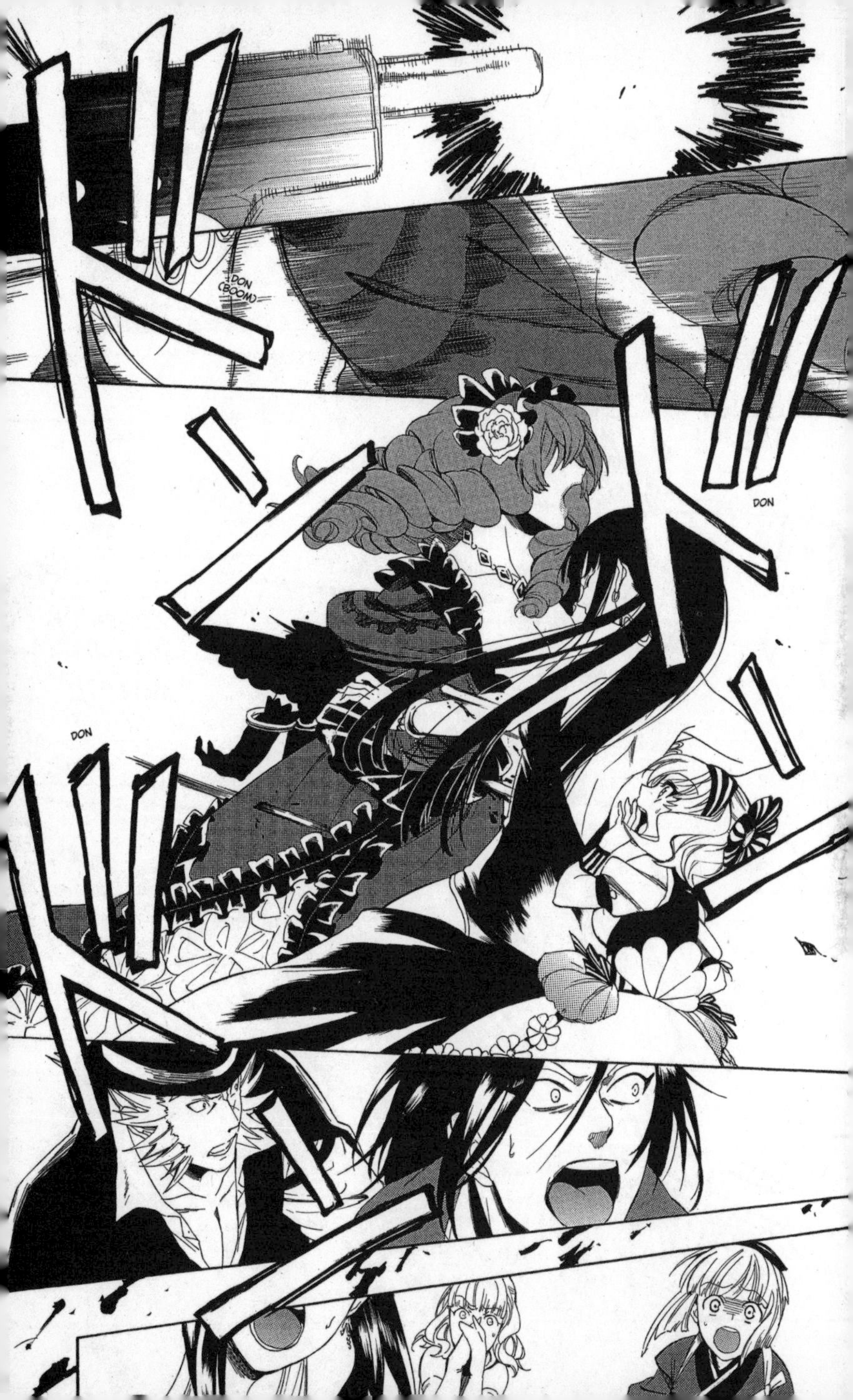
DON
(BOOM)
DON
DON

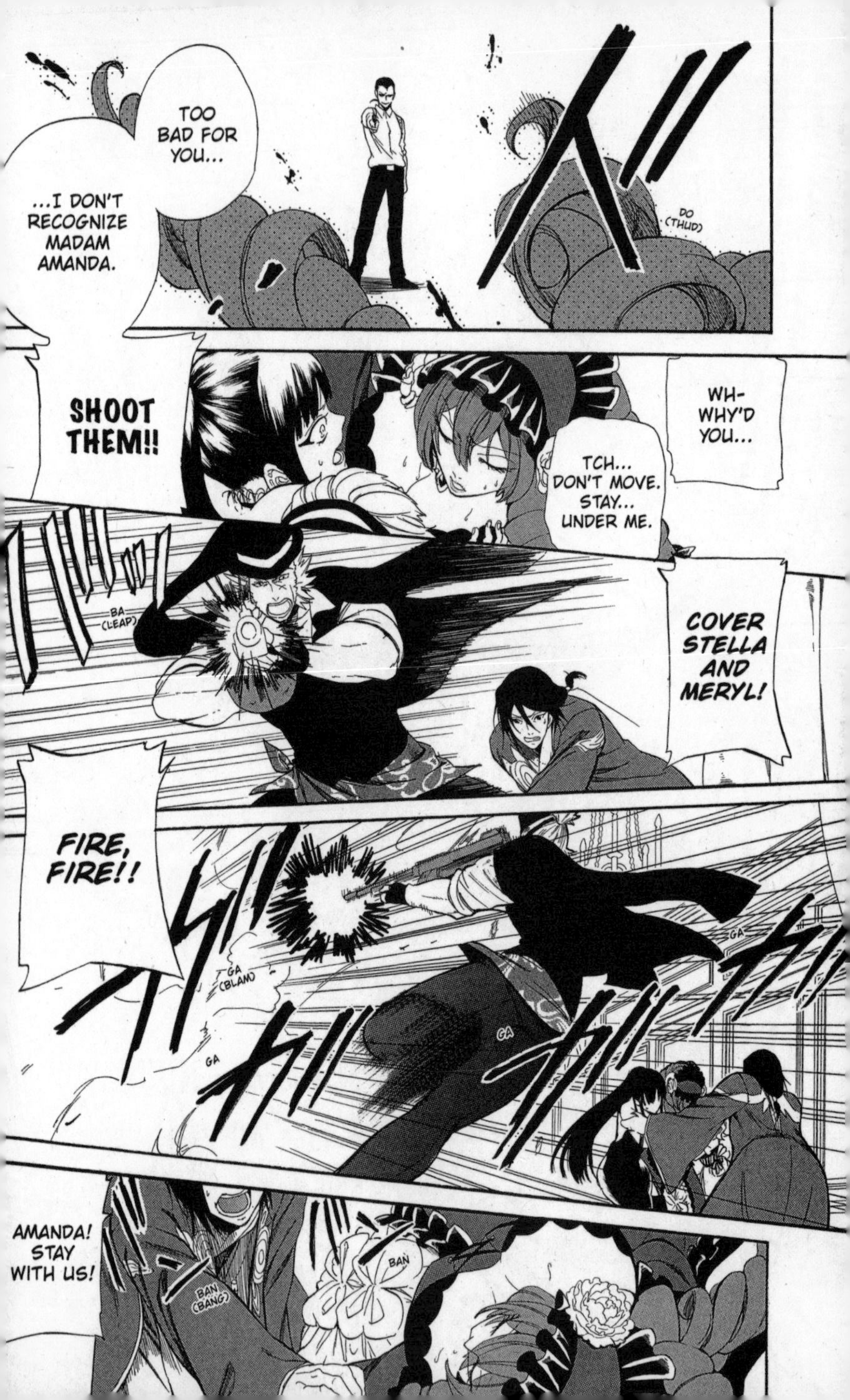
TOO BAD FOR YOU...
...I DON'T RECOGNIZE MADAM AMANDA.
DO (THUD)
WH- WHY'D YOU...
TCH... DON'T MOVE. STAY... UNDER ME.
SHOOT THEM!!
COVER STELLA AND MERYL!
BA (LEAP)
FIRE, FIRE!!
GA
GA
GA (BLAM)
GA
AMANDA! STAY WITH US!
BAN
BAN (BANG)

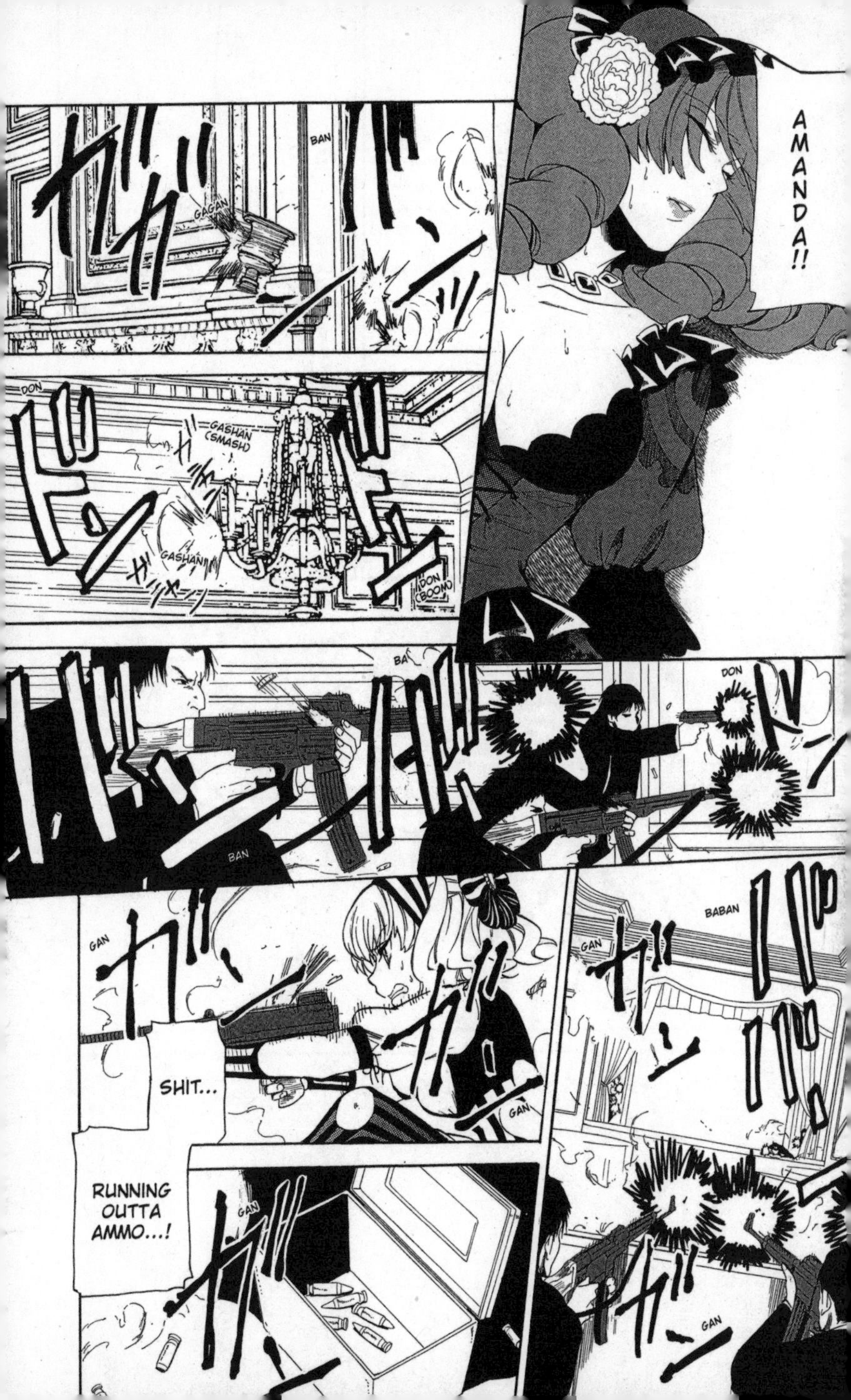
AMANDA!!
BAN
GAGAN
GASHAN (SMASH)
DON
GASHAN
DON (BOOM)
DON
BA
BAN
BABAN
GAN
GAN
GAN
SHIT...
GAN
RUNNING OUTTA AMMO...!
GAN

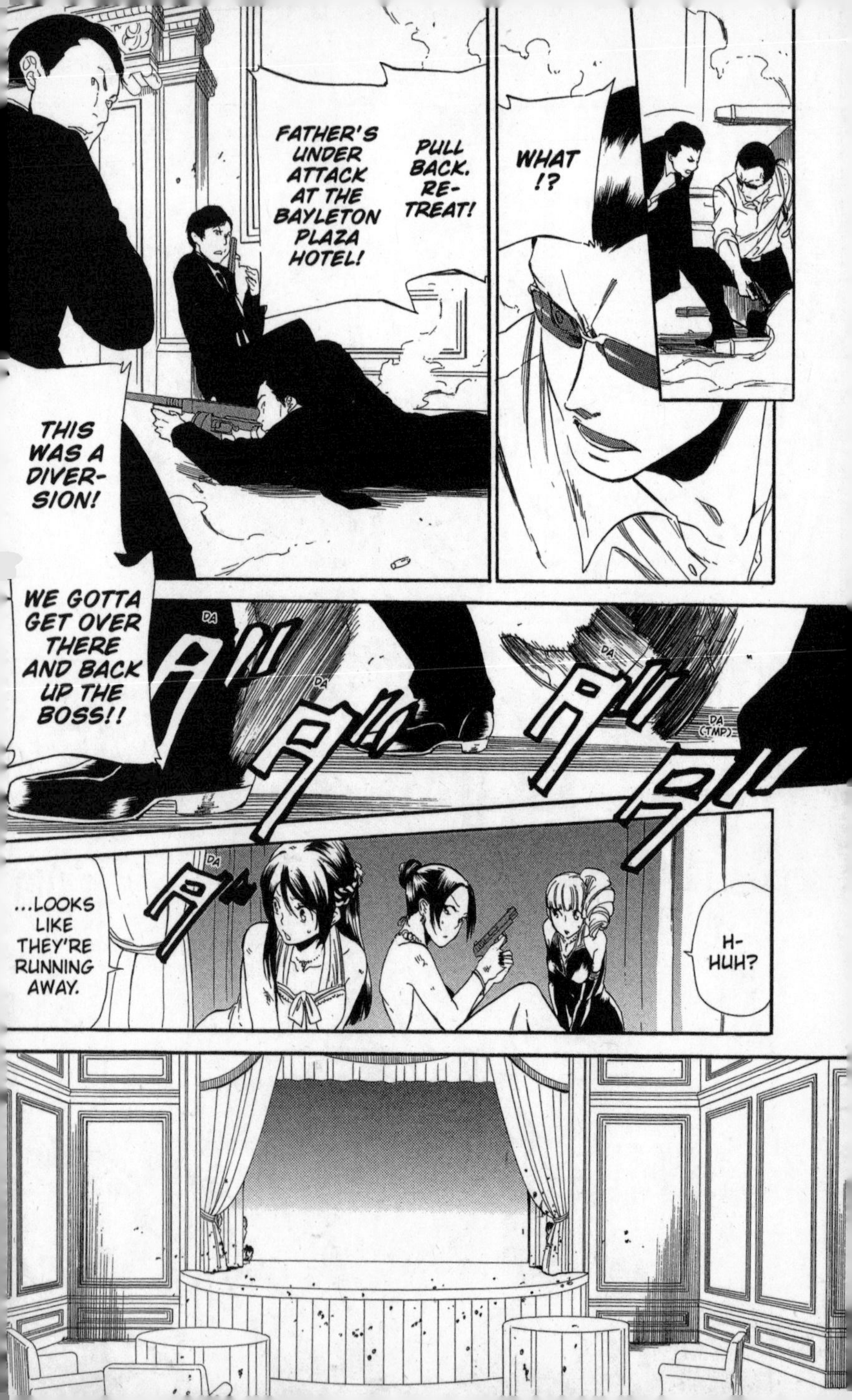
WHAT!?
PULL BACK. RE-TREAT!
FATHER'S UNDER ATTACK AT THE BAYLETON PLAZA HOTEL!
THIS WAS A DIVERSION!
DA
DA
DA
DA (TMP)
WE GOTTA GET OVER THERE AND BACK UP THE BOSS!!
H-HUH?
DA
...LOOKS LIKE THEY'RE RUNNING AWAY.

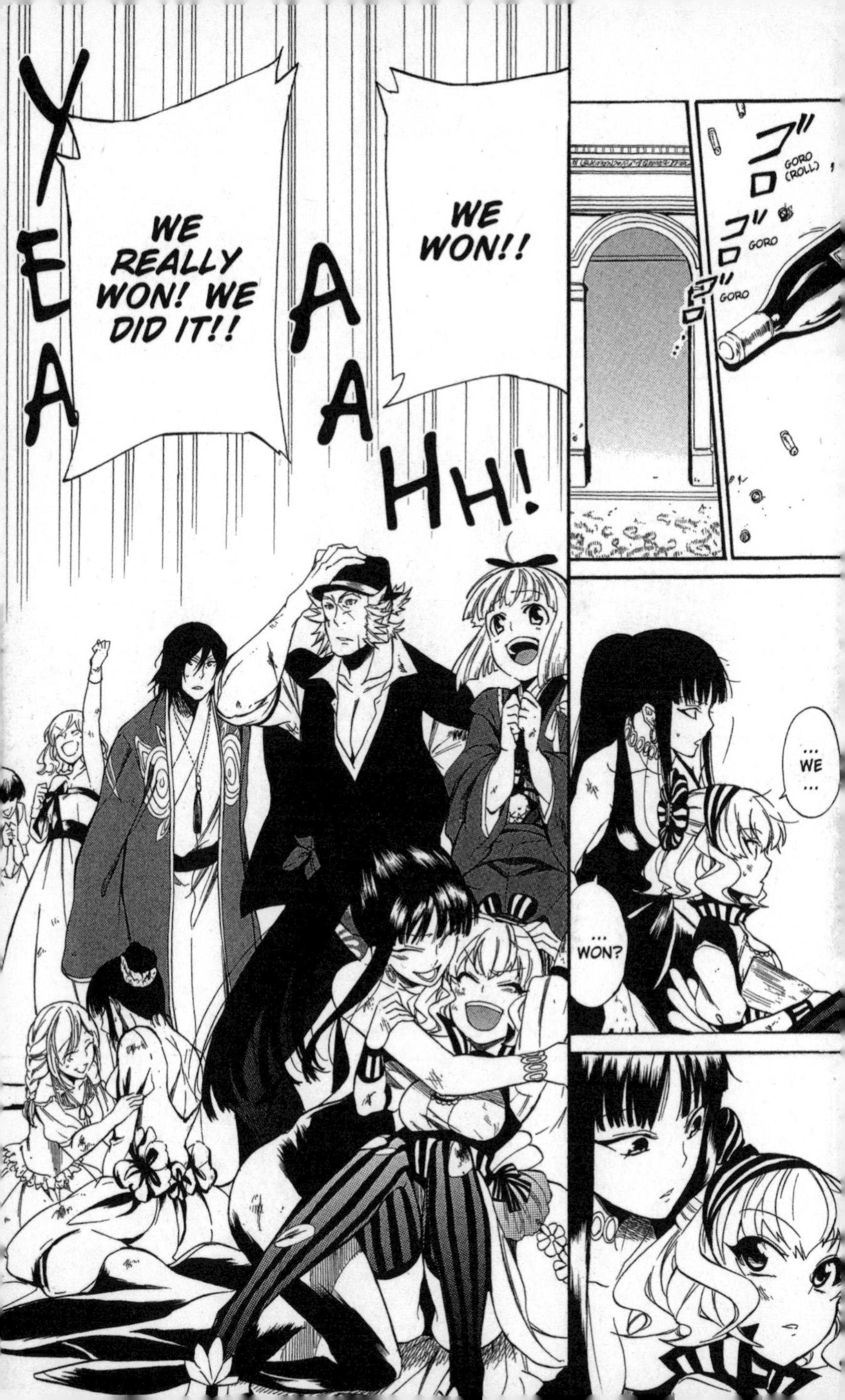
ゴロ GORO (ROLL)
ゴロ GORO
ゴロ GORO
...WE...
...WON?
WE WON!!
YEAAAHH!
WE REALLY WON! WE DID IT!!

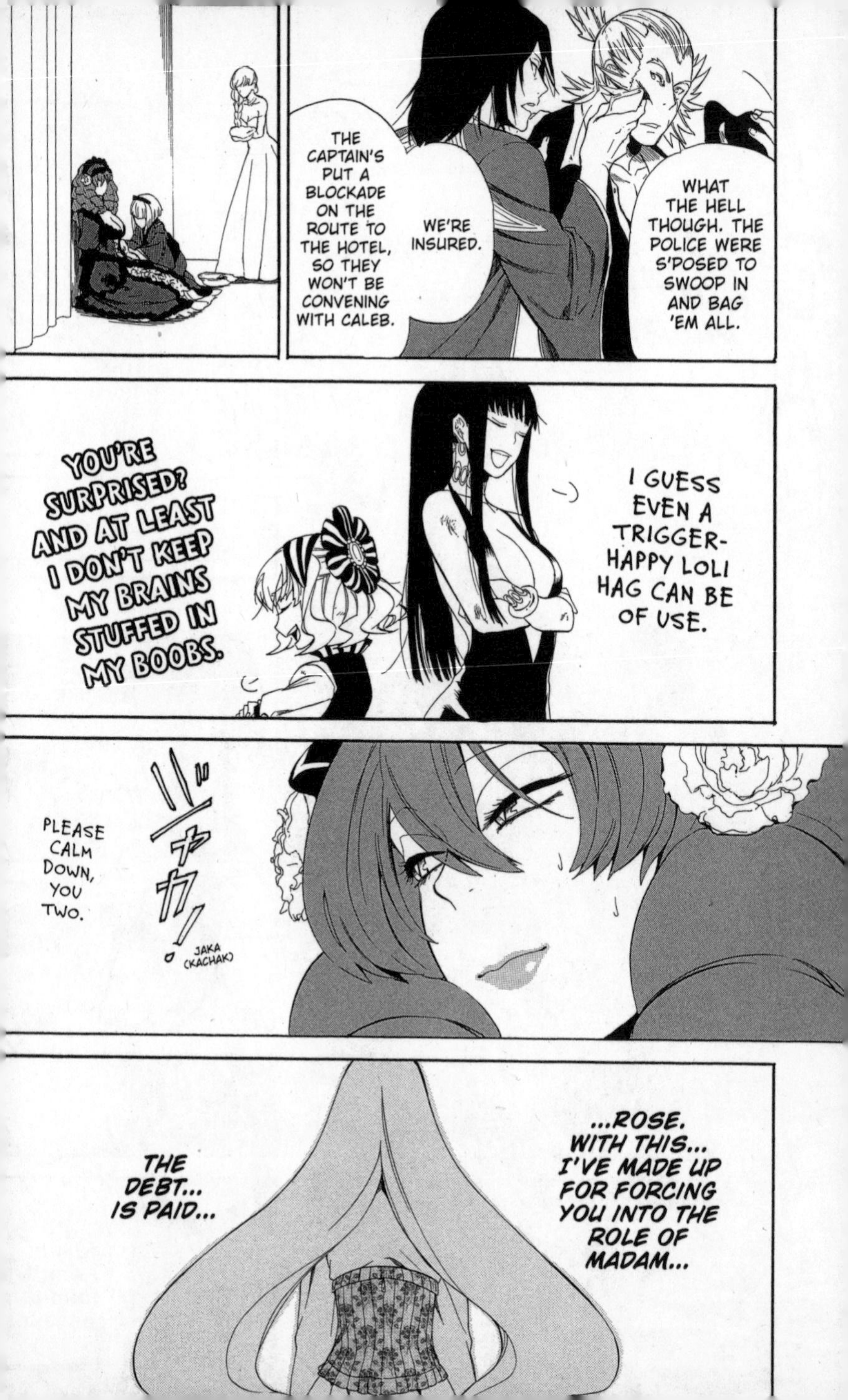
WHAT THE HELL THOUGH. THE POLICE WERE S'POSED TO SWOOP IN AND BAG 'EM ALL.
WE'RE INSURED.
THE CAPTAIN'S PUT A BLOCKADE ON THE ROUTE TO THE HOTEL, SO THEY WON'T BE CONVENING WITH CALEB.
I GUESS EVEN A TRIGGER-HAPPY LOLI HAG CAN BE OF USE.
YOU'RE SURPRISED? AND AT LEAST I DON'T KEEP MY BRAINS STUFFED IN MY BOOBS.
JAKA (KACHAK)
PLEASE CALM DOWN, YOU TWO.
...ROSE. WITH THIS... I'VE MADE UP FOR FORCING YOU INTO THE ROLE OF MADAM...
THE DEBT... IS PAID...

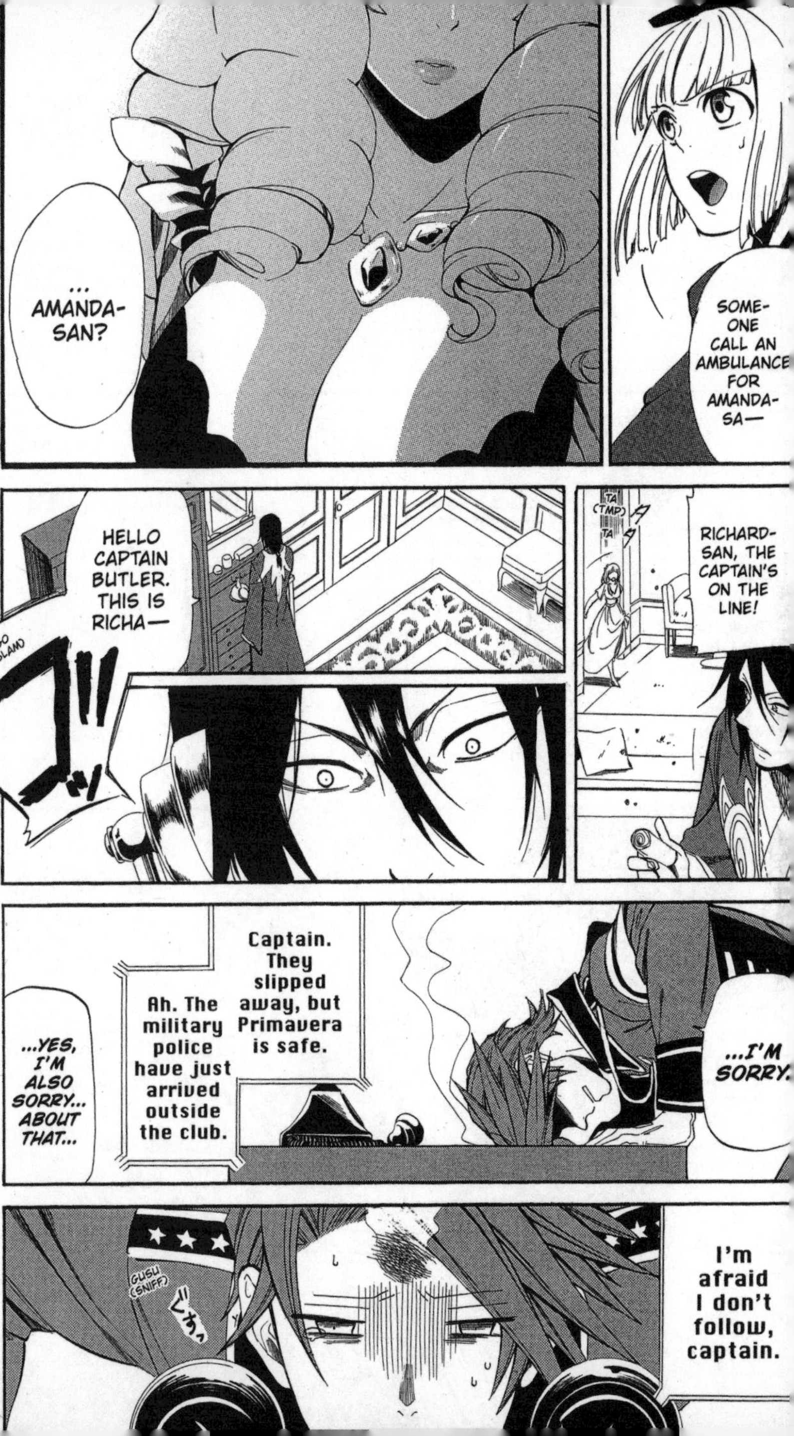
SOME-ONE CALL AN AMBULANCE FOR AMANDA-SA—
... AMANDA-SAN?
TA (TMP) TA
RICHARD-SAN, THE CAPTAIN'S ON THE LINE!
HELLO CAPTAIN BUTLER. THIS IS RICHA—
GO (SLAM)
...I'M SORRY.
Captain. They slipped away, but Primavera is safe.
Ah. The military police have just arrived outside the club.
...YES, I'M ALSO SORRY... ABOUT THAT...
I'm afraid I don't follow, captain.
GUSU (SNIFF)

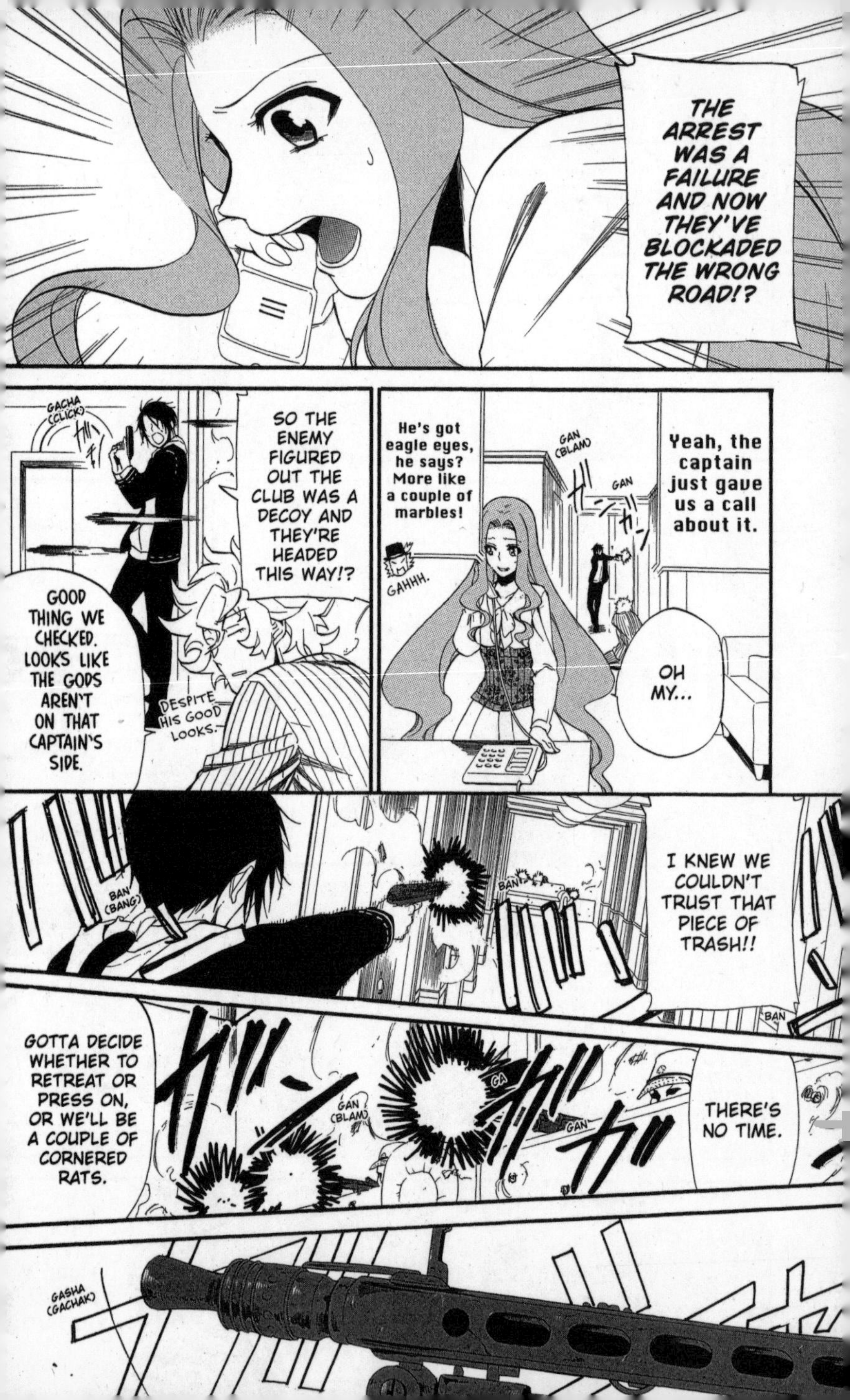
THE ARREST WAS A FAILURE AND NOW THEY'VE BLOCKADED THE WRONG ROAD!?
Yeah, the captain just gave us a call about it.
GAN (BLAM)
GAN
He's got eagle eyes, he says? More like a couple of marbles!
GAHHH.
OH MY...
SO THE ENEMY FIGURED OUT THE CLUB WAS A DECOY AND THEY'RE HEADED THIS WAY!?
GACHA (CLICK)
GOOD THING WE CHECKED. LOOKS LIKE THE GODS AREN'T ON THAT CAPTAIN'S SIDE.
DESPITE HIS GOOD LOOKS.
I KNEW WE COULDN'T TRUST THAT PIECE OF TRASH!!
BAN
BAN (BANG)
BAN
THERE'S NO TIME.
GAN
GA
GAN (BLAM)
GOTTA DECIDE WHETHER TO RETREAT OR PRESS ON, OR WE'LL BE A COUPLE OF CORNERED RATS.
GASHA (GACHAK)

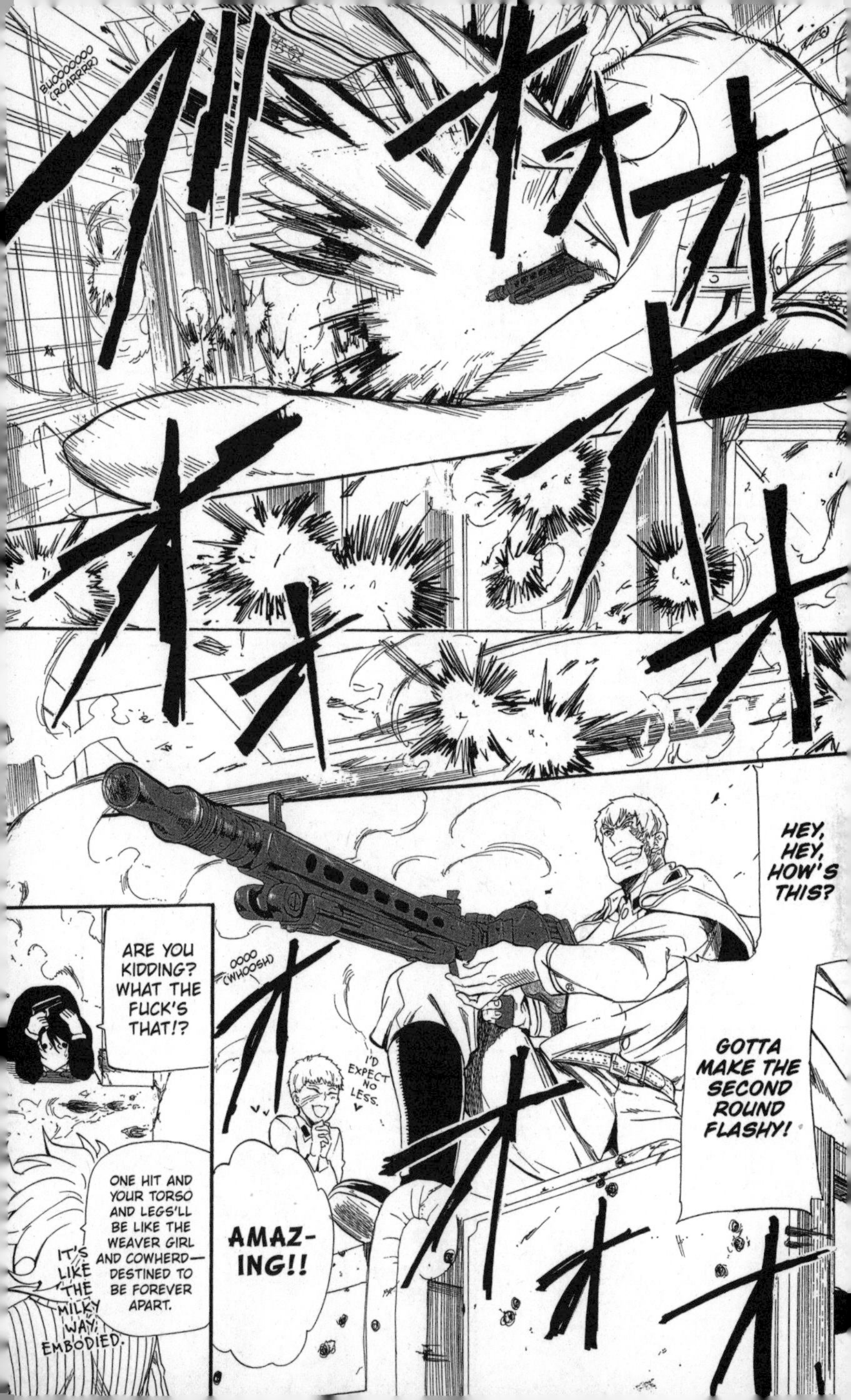
BUOOOOOOO (ROARRRR)
HEY, HEY, HOW'S THIS?
GOTTA MAKE THE SECOND ROUND FLASHY!
OOOO (WHOOSH)
I'D EXPECT NO LESS.
AMAZ-ING!!
ARE YOU KIDDING? WHAT THE FUCK'S THAT!?
ONE HIT AND YOUR TORSO AND LEGS'LL BE LIKE THE WEAVER GIRL AND COWHERD— DESTINED TO BE FOREVER APART.
IT'S LIKE THE MILKY WAY EMBODIED.

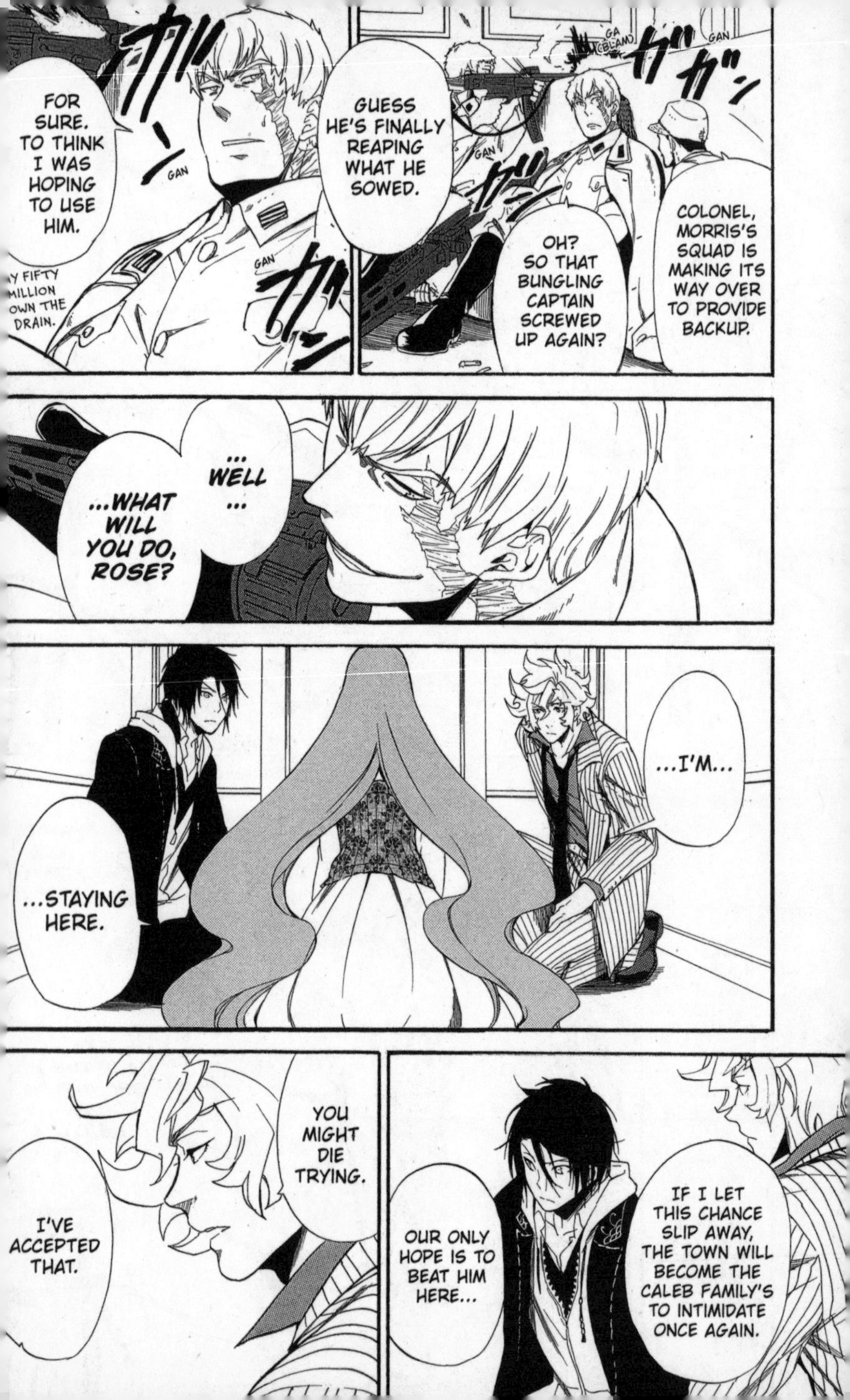
GA (BLAM)
GAN
GAN
COLONEL, MORRIS'S SQUAD IS MAKING ITS WAY OVER TO PROVIDE BACKUP.
OH? SO THAT BUNGLING CAPTAIN SCREWED UP AGAIN?
GUESS HE'S FINALLY REAPING WHAT HE SOWED.
GAN
GAN
FOR SURE. TO THINK I WAS HOPING TO USE HIM.
Y FIFTY MILLION OWN THE DRAIN.
...WELL...
...WHAT WILL YOU DO, ROSE?
...I'M...
...STAYING HERE.
IF I LET THIS CHANCE SLIP AWAY, THE TOWN WILL BECOME THE CALEB FAMILY'S TO INTIMIDATE ONCE AGAIN.
OUR ONLY HOPE IS TO BEAT HIM HERE...
YOU MIGHT DIE TRYING.
I'VE ACCEPTED THAT.

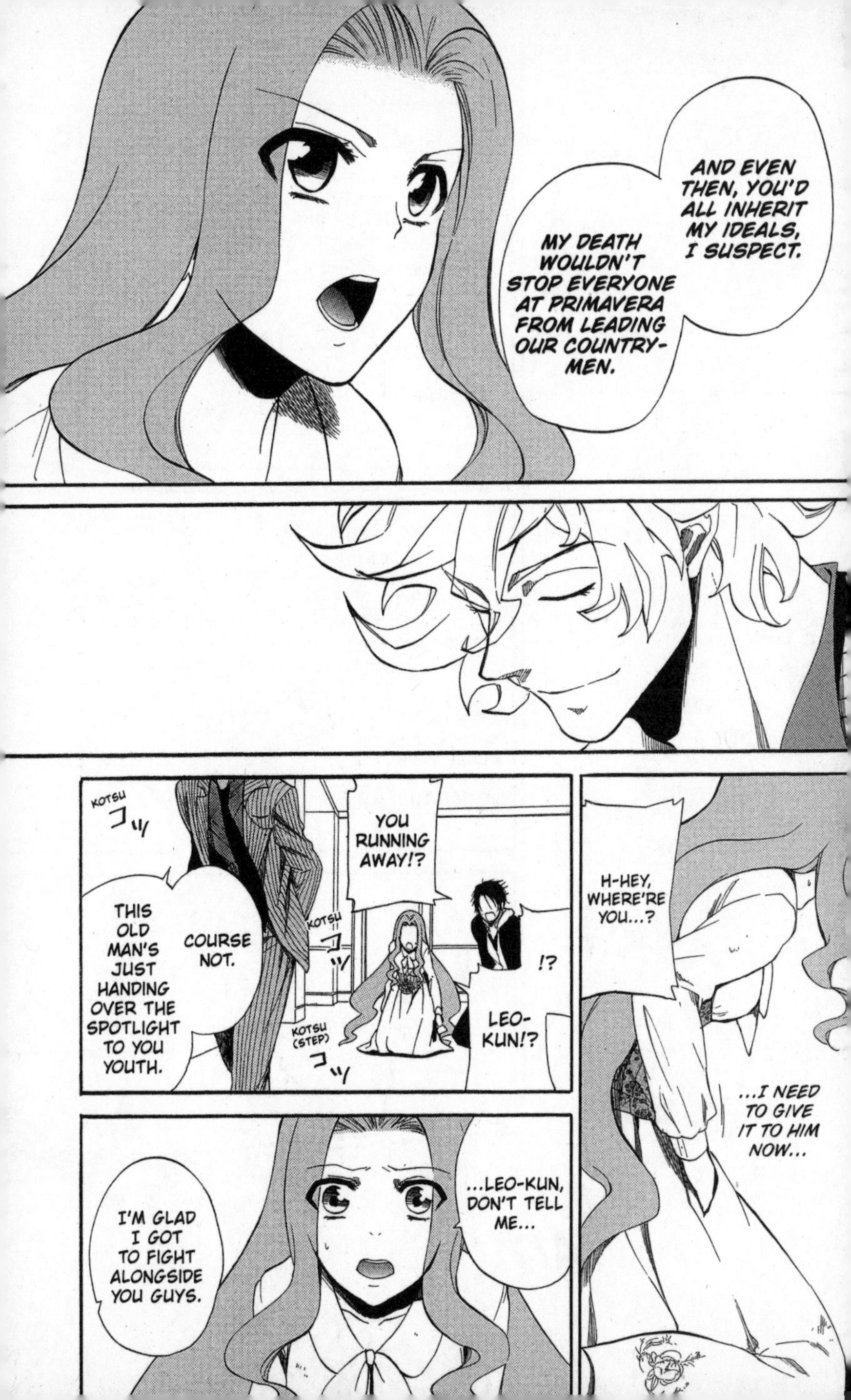
MY DEATH WOULDN'T STOP EVERYONE AT PRIMAVERA FROM LEADING OUR COUNTRYMEN.
AND EVEN THEN, YOU'D ALL INHERIT MY IDEALS, I SUSPECT.
H-HEY, WHERE'RE YOU...?
...I NEED TO GIVE IT TO HIM NOW...
YOU RUNNING AWAY!?
!?
LEO-KUN!?
KOTSU
コツ
KOTSU
コツ
COURSE NOT.
THIS OLD MAN'S JUST HANDING OVER THE SPOTLIGHT TO YOU YOUTH.
KOTSU (STEP)
コツ
...LEO-KUN, DON'T TELL ME...
I'M GLAD I GOT TO FIGHT ALONGSIDE YOU GUYS.

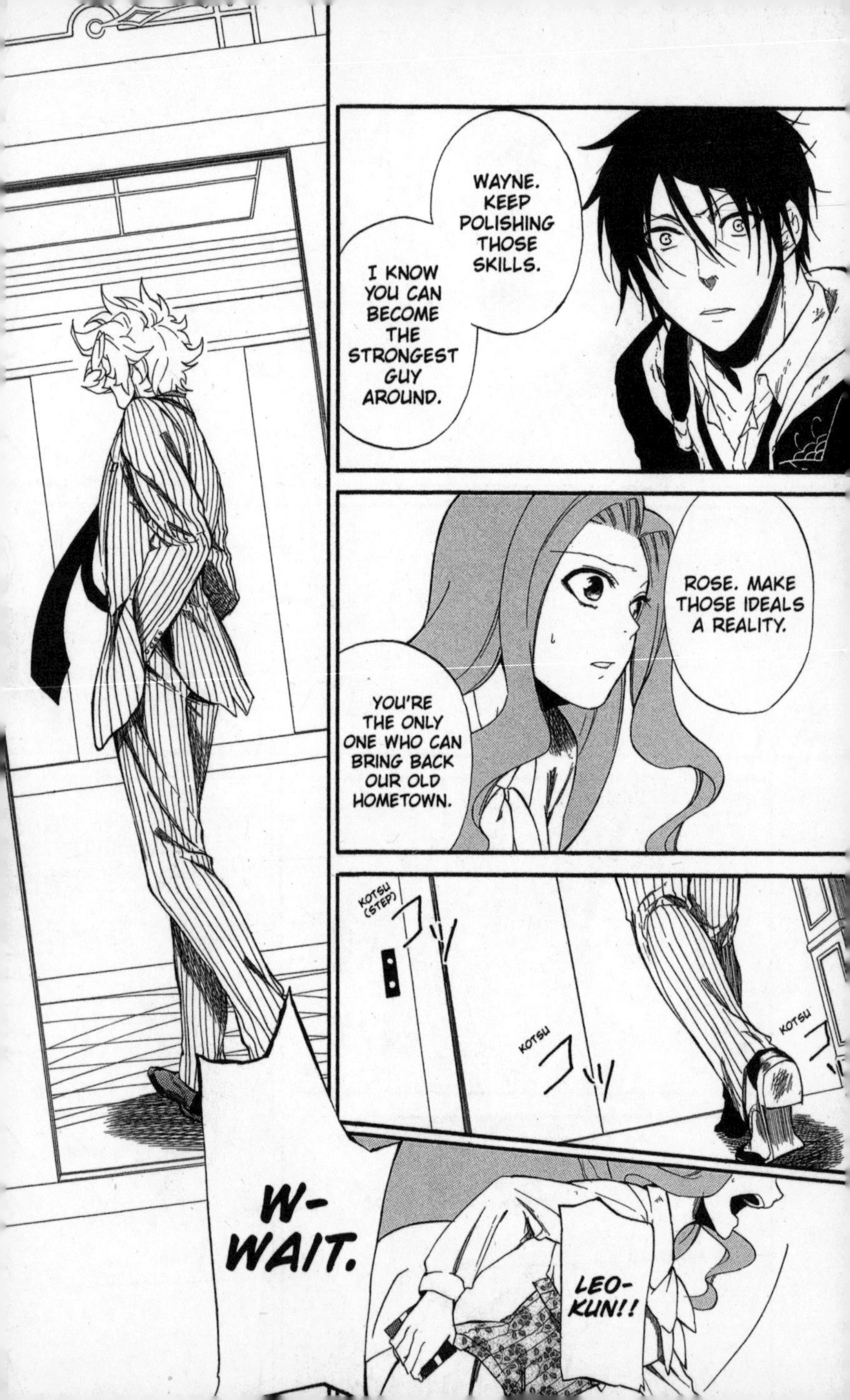
WAYNE. KEEP POLISHING THOSE SKILLS.
I KNOW YOU CAN BECOME THE STRONGEST GUY AROUND.
ROSE. MAKE THOSE IDEALS A REALITY.
YOU'RE THE ONLY ONE WHO CAN BRING BACK OUR OLD HOMETOWN.
KOTSU (STEP)
KOTSU
KOTSU
W-WAIT.
LEO-KUN!!

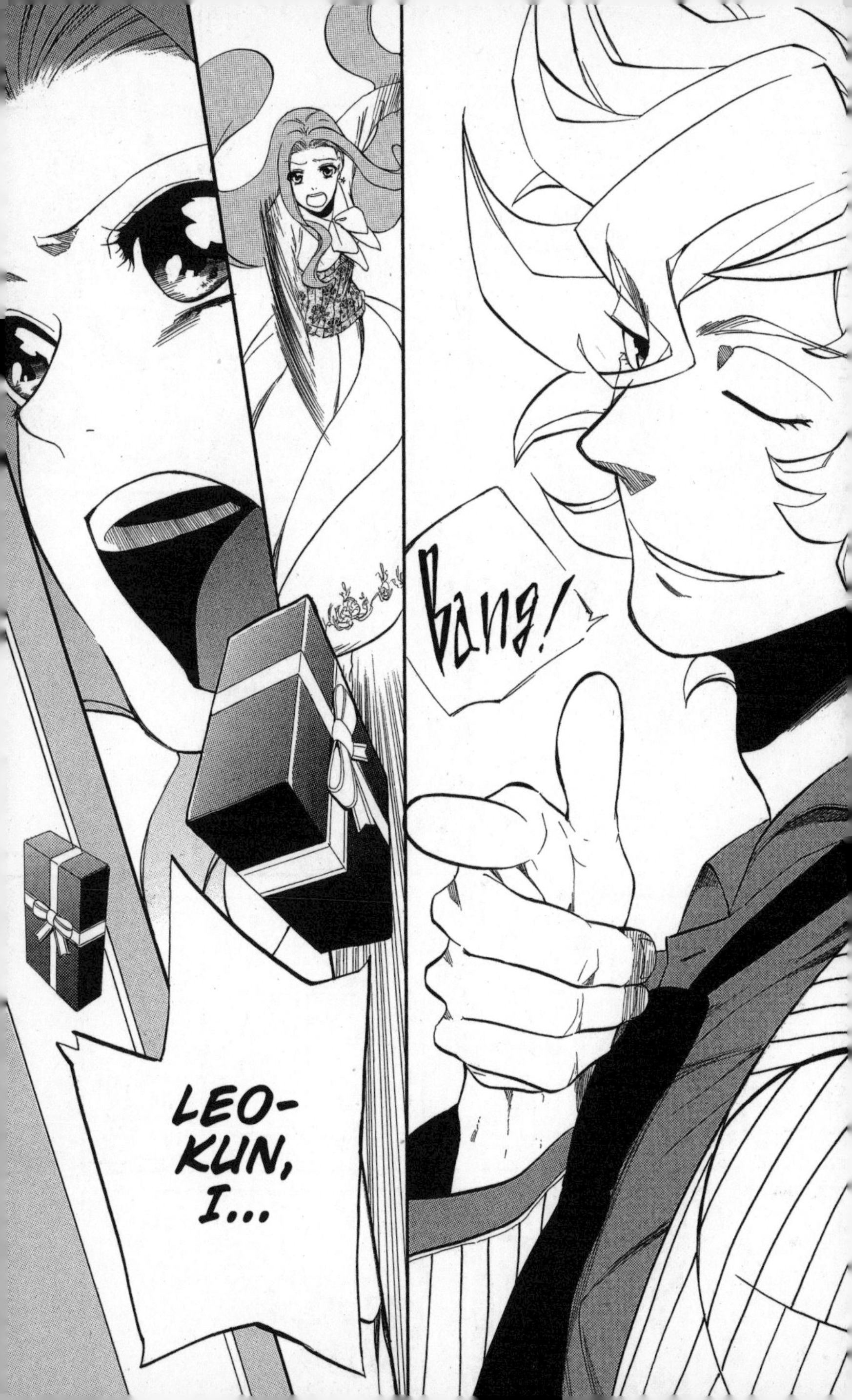
Bang!
LEO-KUN, I...

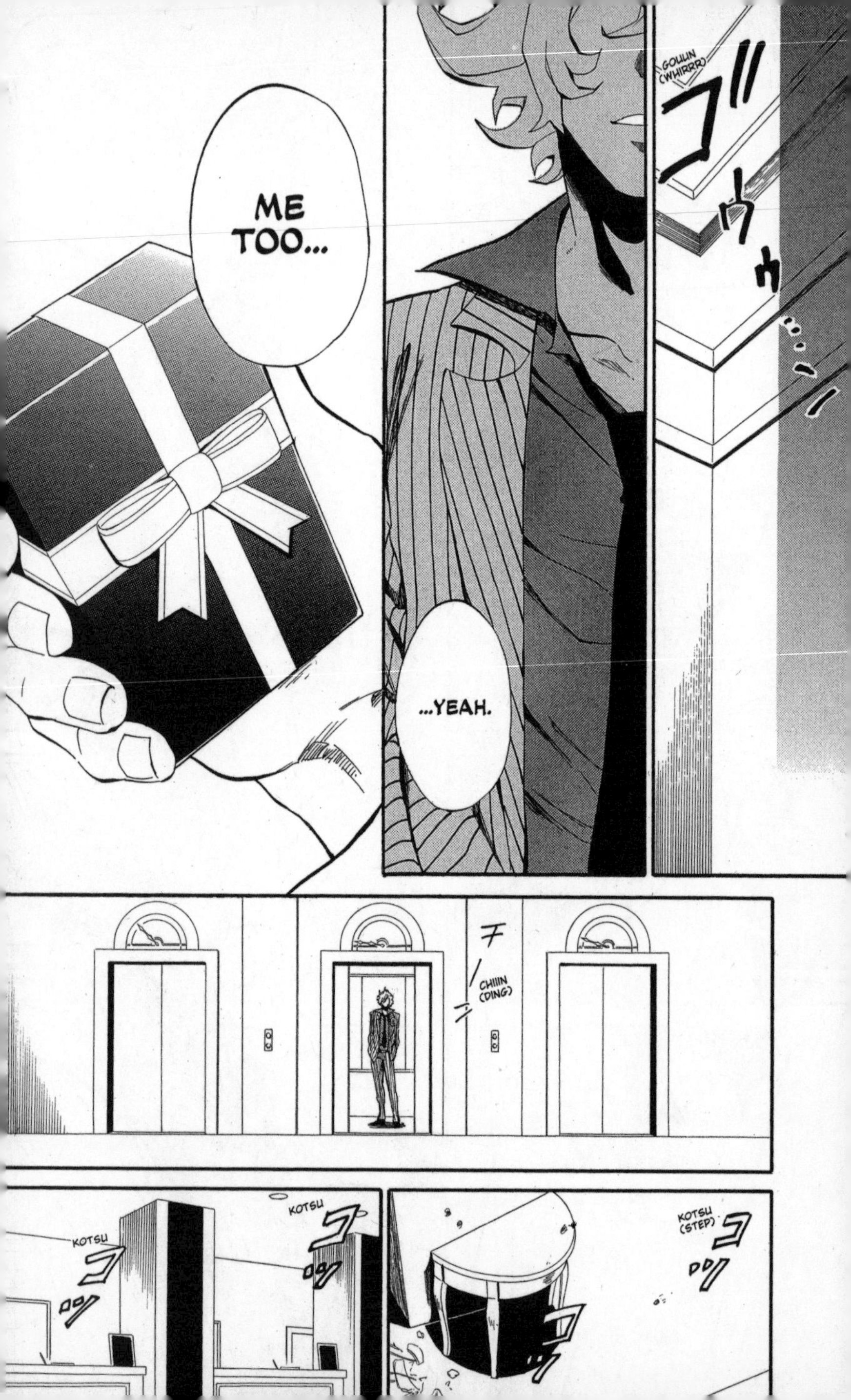
GOUUN (WHIRRR)
...YEAH.
ME TOO...
CHIIIN (DING)
KOTSU (STEP)
KOTSU
KOTSU

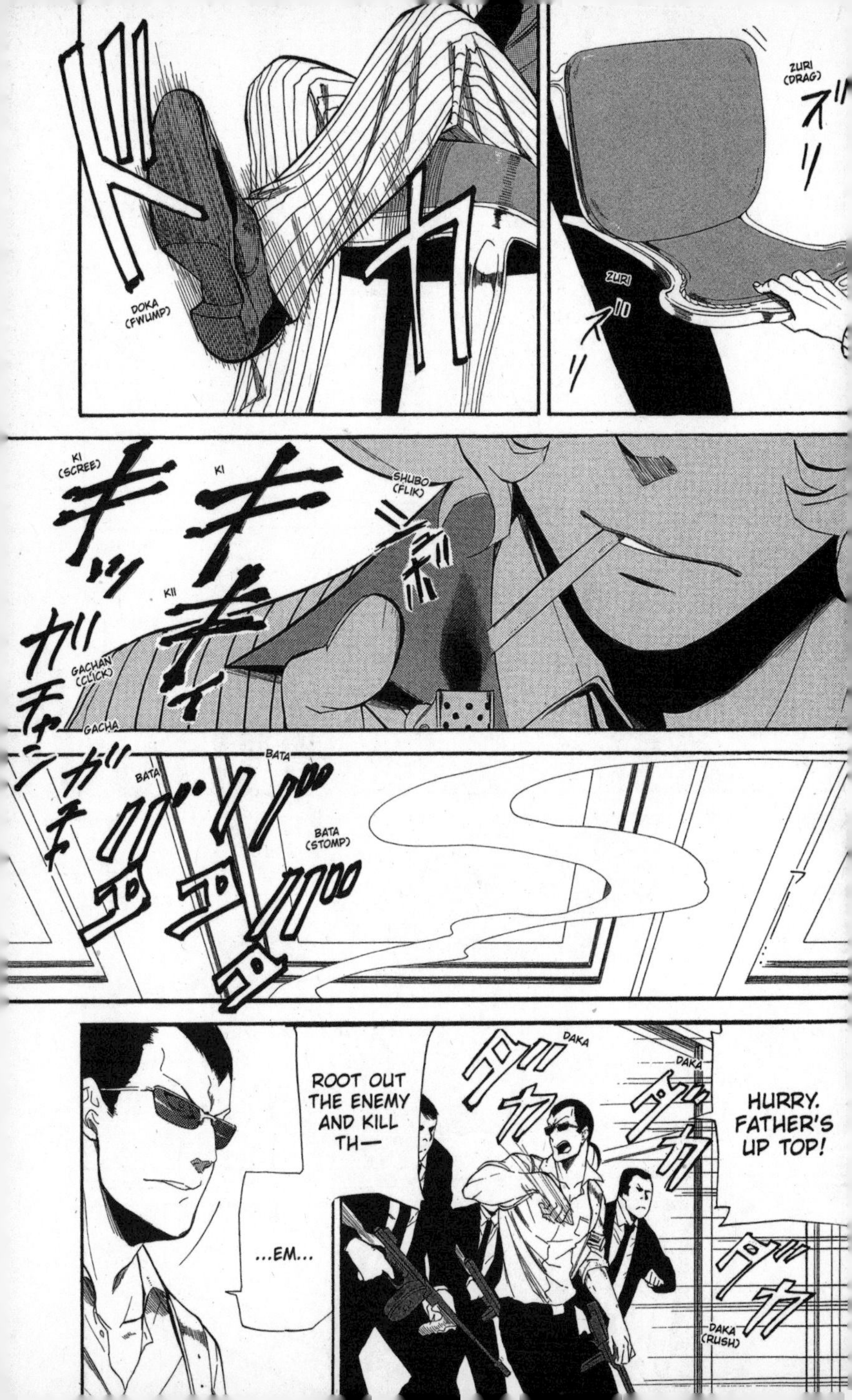
ZURI (DRAG)
ZURI
DOKA (FWUMP)
SHUBO (FLIK)
KI
KI (SCREE)
KII
GACHAN (CLICK)
GACHA
BATA
BATA (STOMP)
BATA
HURRY. FATHER'S UP TOP!
DAKA
DAKA
DAKA (RUSH)
ROOT OUT THE ENEMY AND KILL TH—
...EM...

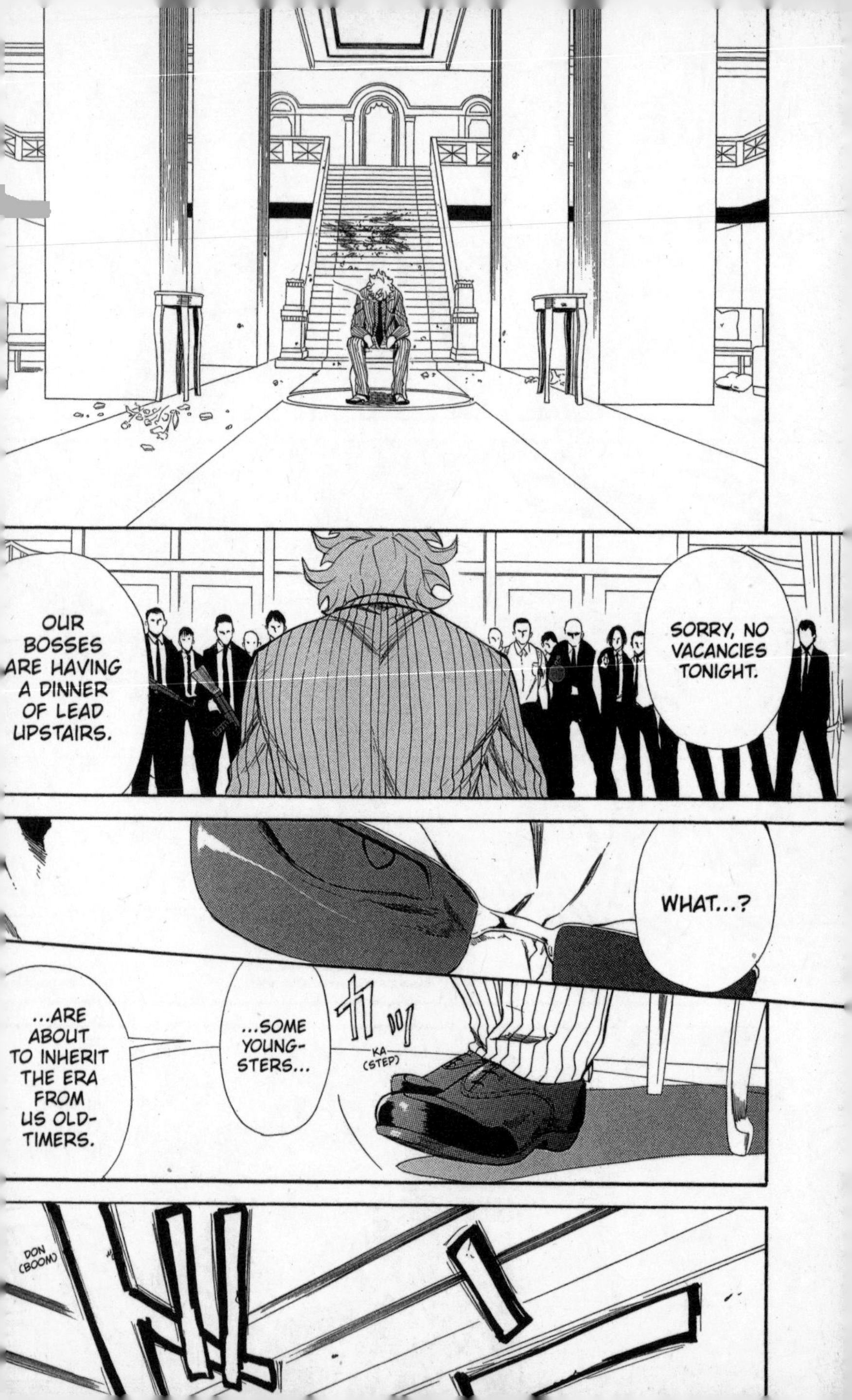
SORRY, NO VACANCIES TONIGHT.
OUR BOSSES ARE HAVING A DINNER OF LEAD UPSTAIRS.
WHAT...?
KA (STEP)
...SOME YOUNG-STERS...
...ARE ABOUT TO INHERIT THE ERA FROM US OLD-TIMERS.
DON (BOOM)

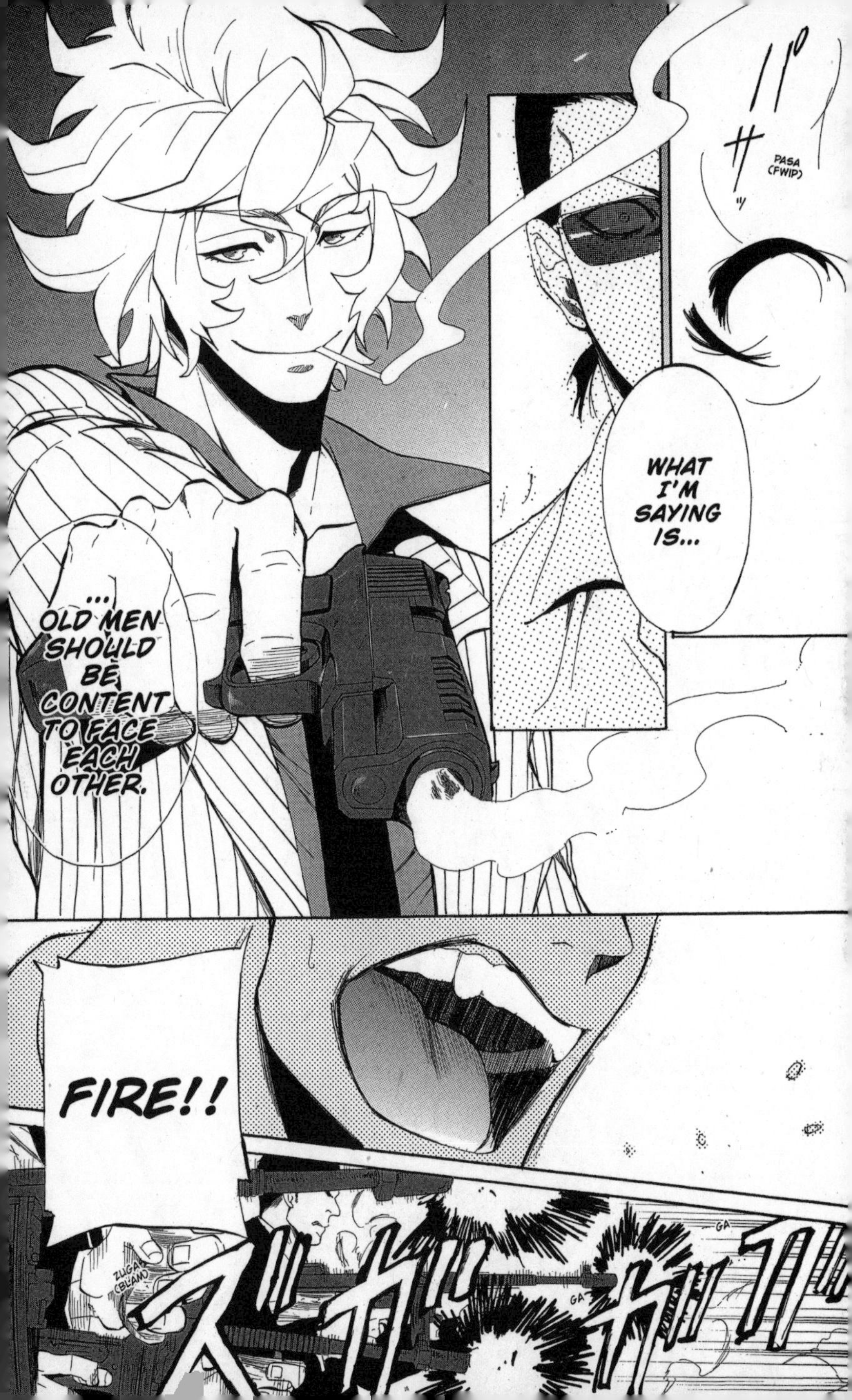
PASA (FWIP)
WHAT I'M SAYING IS...
...OLD MEN SHOULD BE CONTENT TO FACE EACH OTHER.
FIRE!!
GA
GA
ZUGA (BLAM)

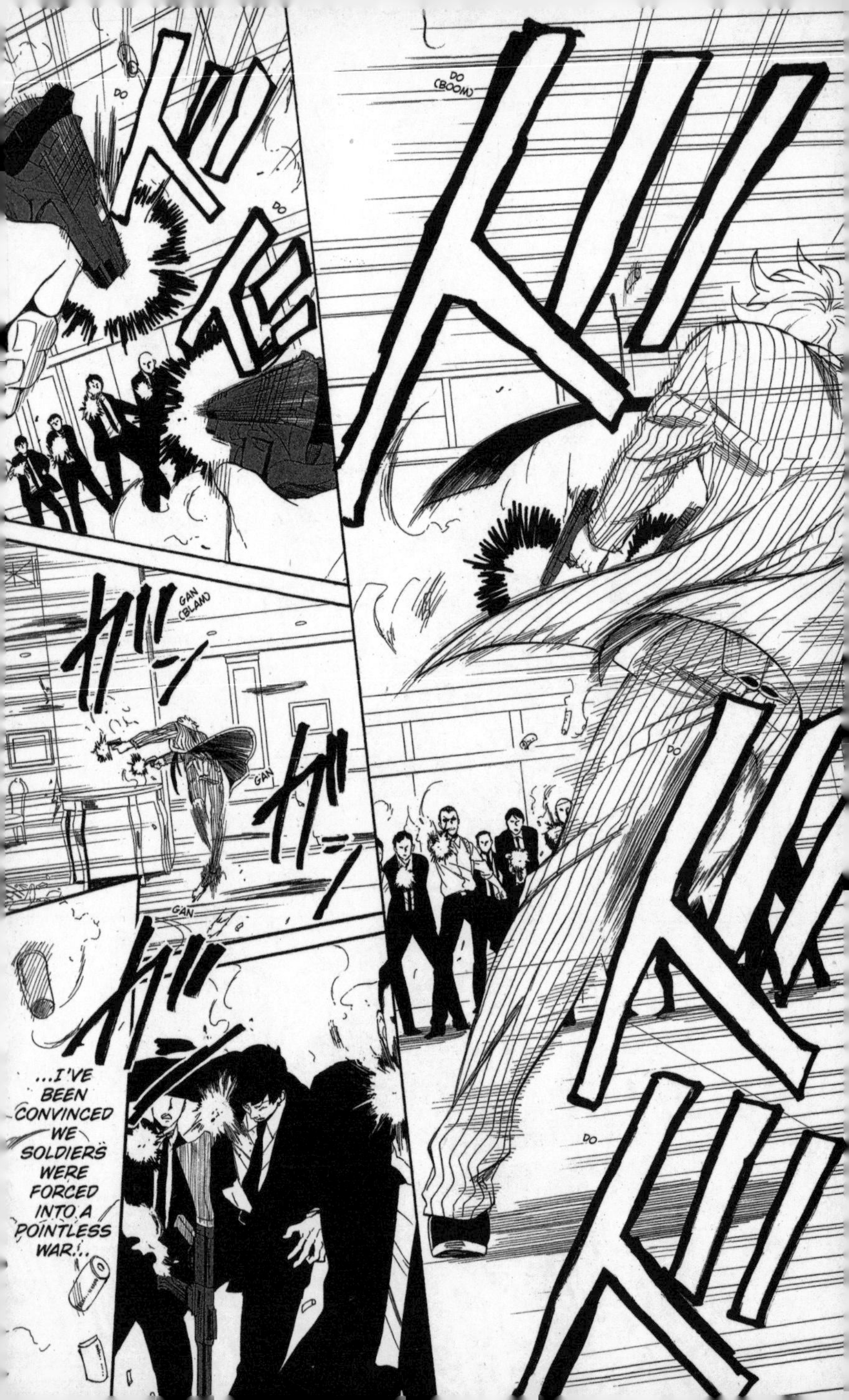
DO (BOOM)
DO
DO
DO
DO
GAN (BLAM)
GAN
GAN
...I'VE BEEN CONVINCED WE SOLDIERS WERE FORCED INTO A POINTLESS WAR...

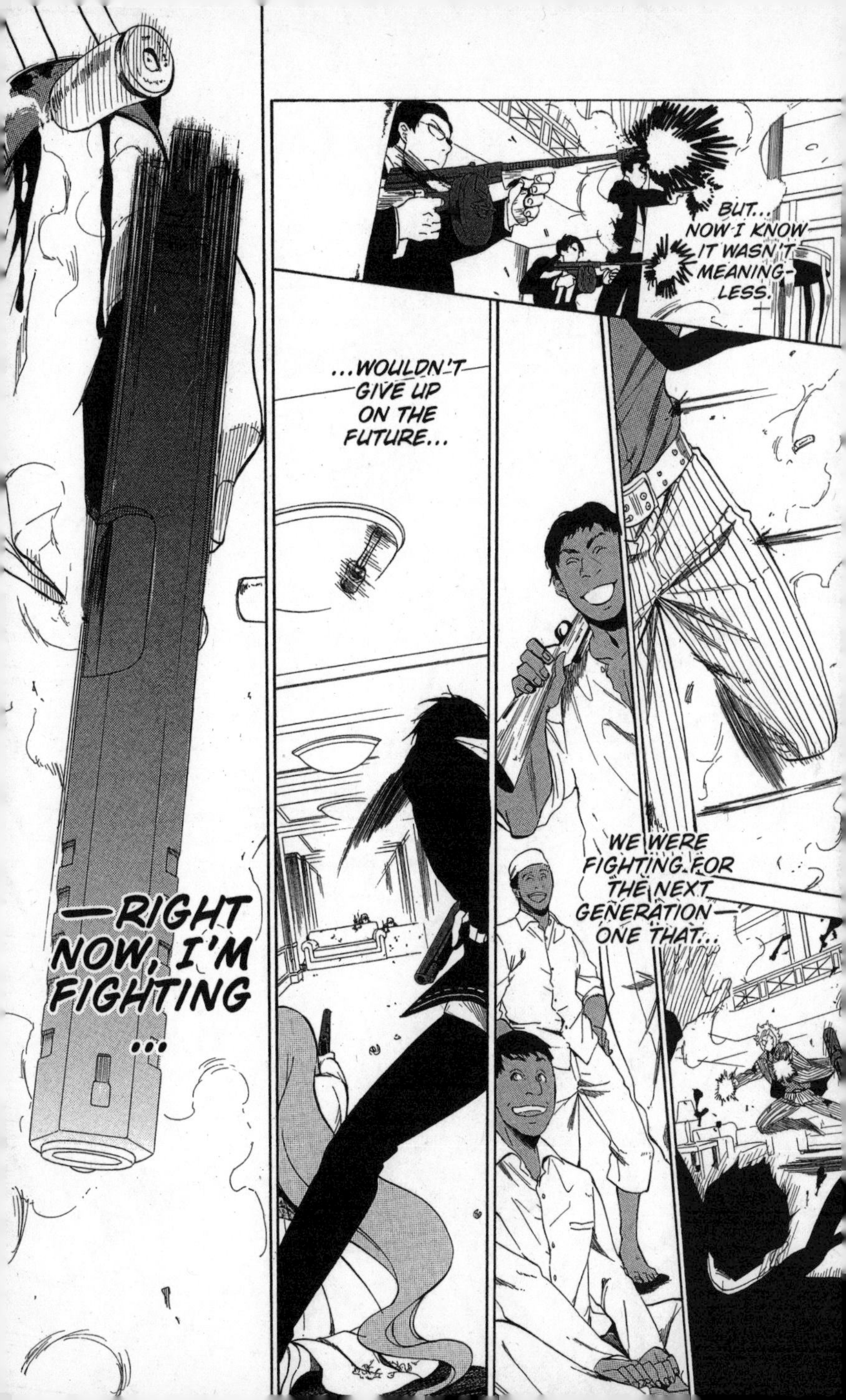
BUT... NOW I KNOW IT WASN'T MEANING-LESS.
WE WERE FIGHTING FOR THE NEXT GENERATION—ONE THAT...
...WOULDN'T GIVE UP ON THE FUTURE...
—RIGHT NOW, I'M FIGHTING...

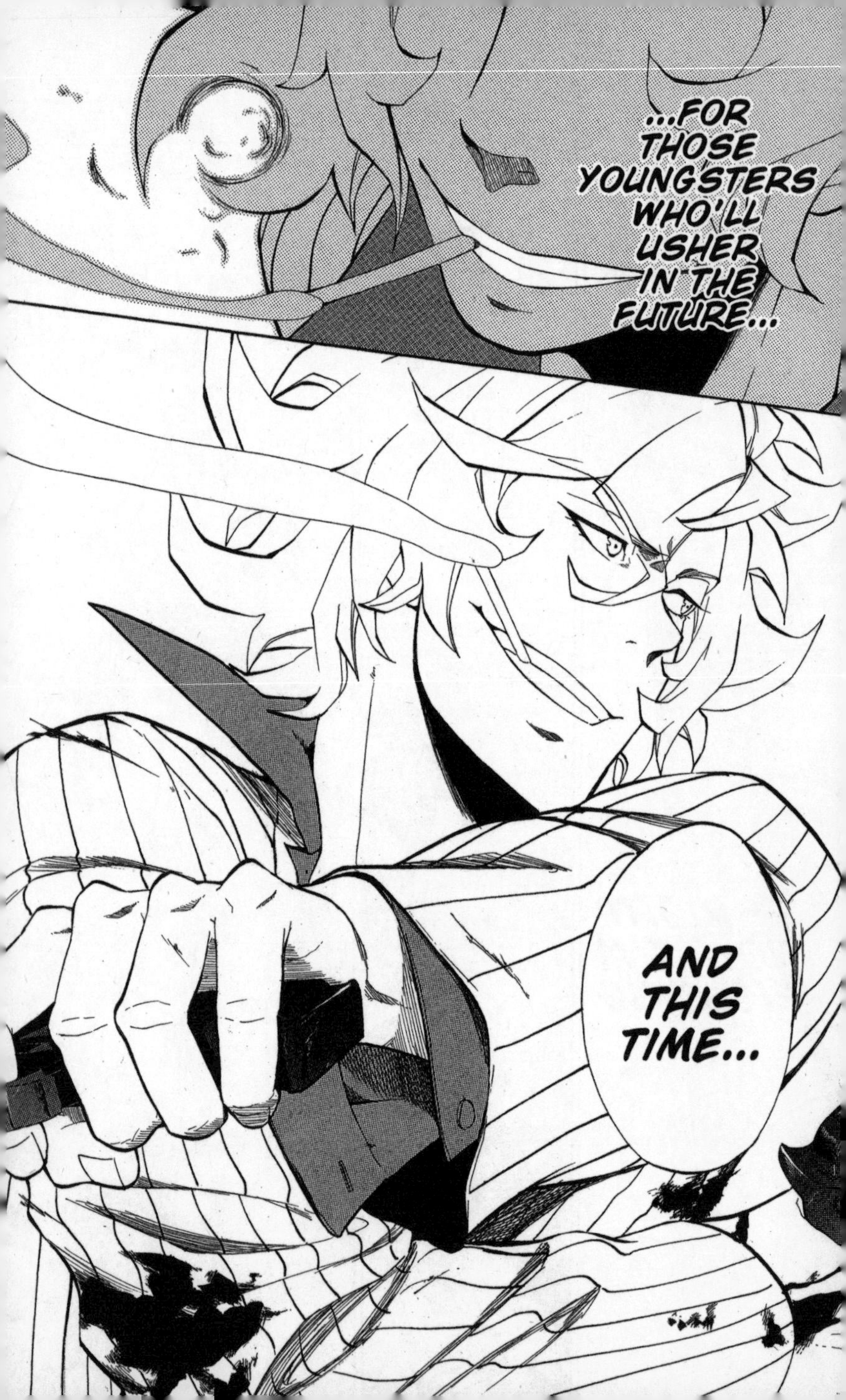
...FOR THOSE YOUNGSTERS WHO'LL USHER IN THE FUTURE...
AND THIS TIME...

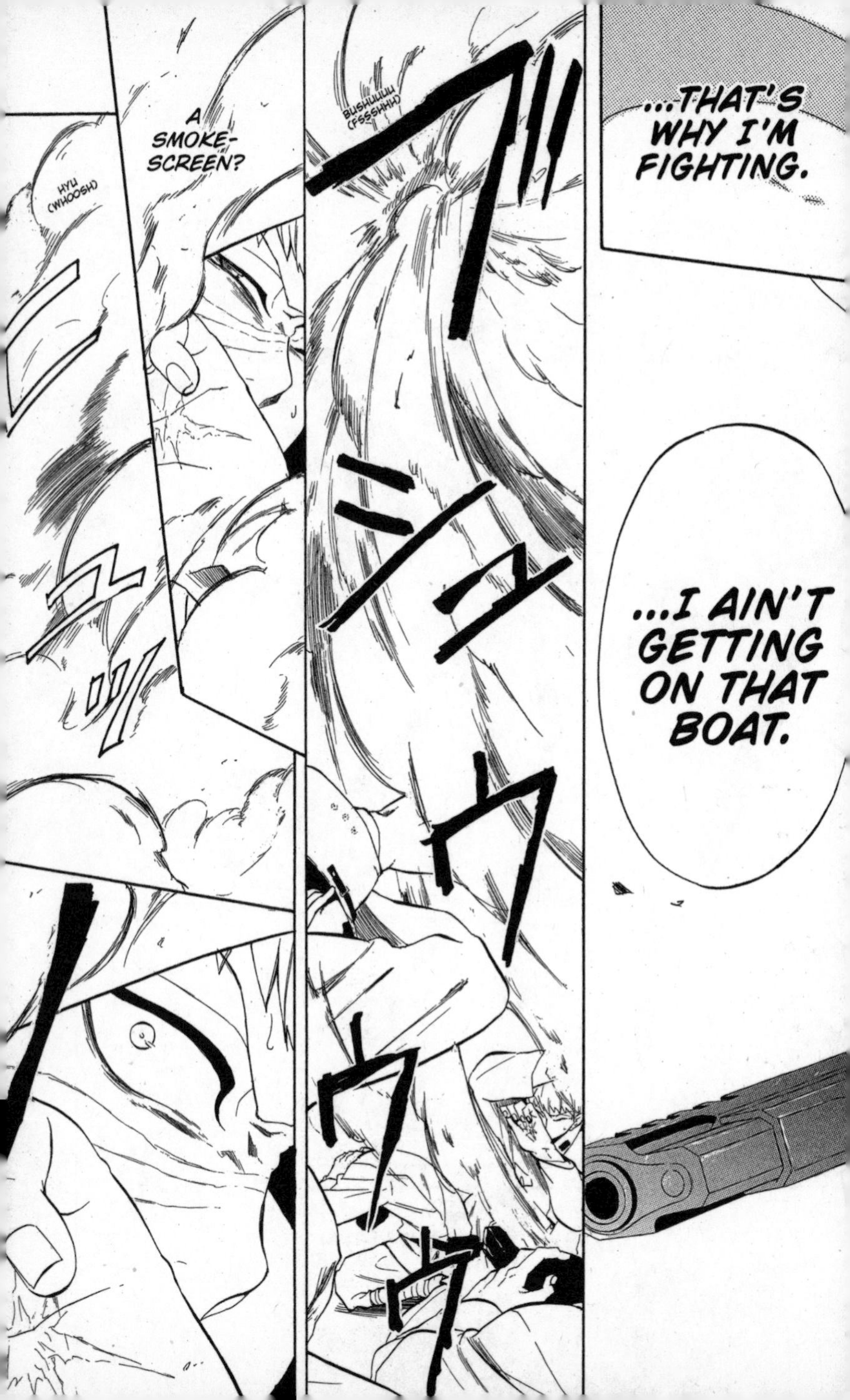

...THAT'S WHY I'M FIGHTING.
...I AIN'T GETTING ON THAT BOAT.
BUSHUUUUU (FSSSHHH)
A SMOKE-SCREEN?
HYU (WHOOSH)

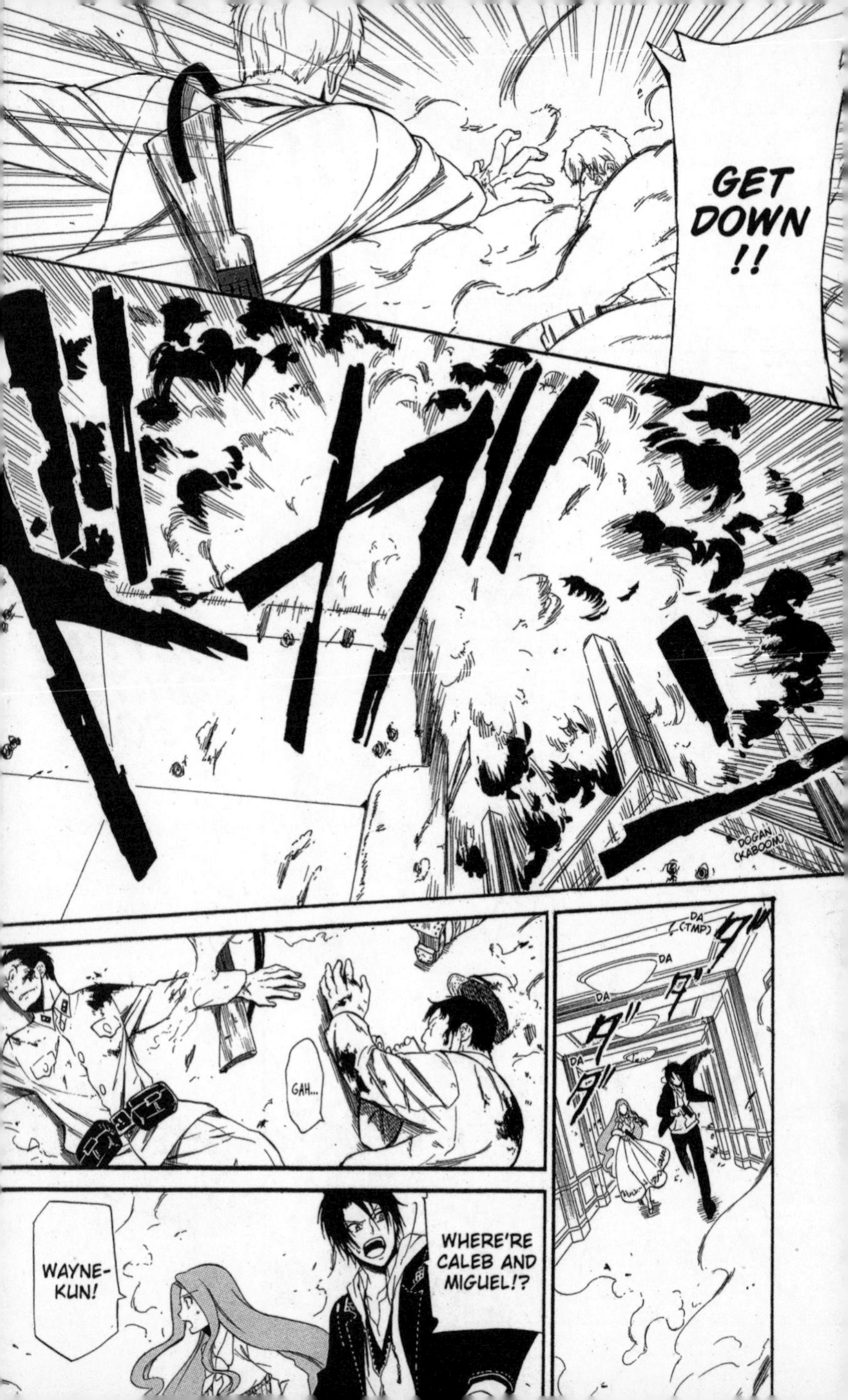
GET DOWN!!
DOGAN (KABOOM)
DA (TMP)
DA
DA
DA
GAH...
WHERE'RE CALEB AND MIGUEL!?
WAYNE-KUN!

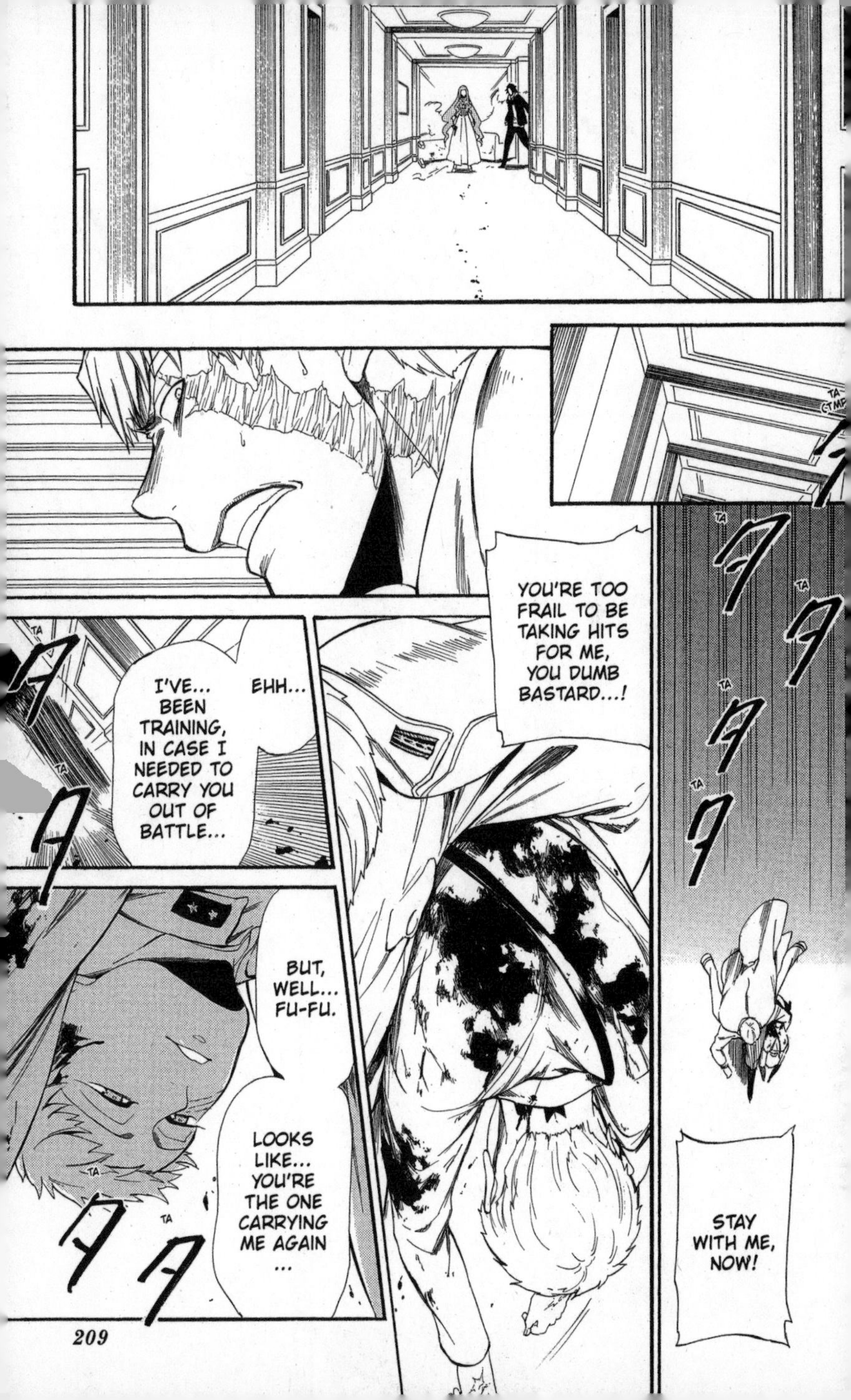
TA
TMP
TA
TA
TA
TA
STAY WITH ME, NOW!
YOU'RE TOO FRAIL TO BE TAKING HITS FOR ME, YOU DUMB BASTARD...!
EHH...
I'VE... BEEN TRAINING, IN CASE I NEEDED TO CARRY YOU OUT OF BATTLE...
TA
TA
BUT, WELL... FU-FU.
LOOKS LIKE... YOU'RE THE ONE CARRYING ME AGAIN ...
TA
TA

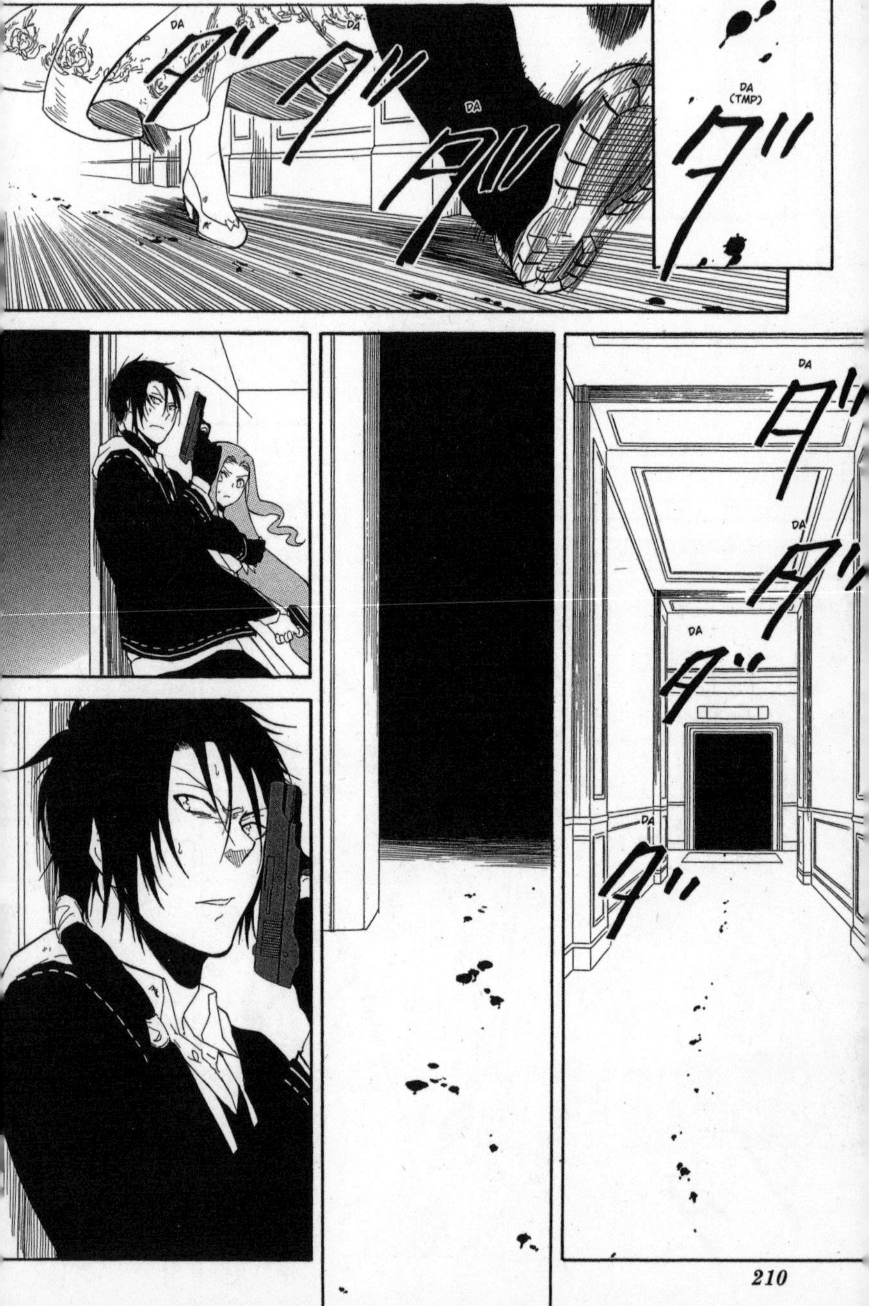
DA
(TMP)
DA
DA
DA
DA
DA
DA
DA

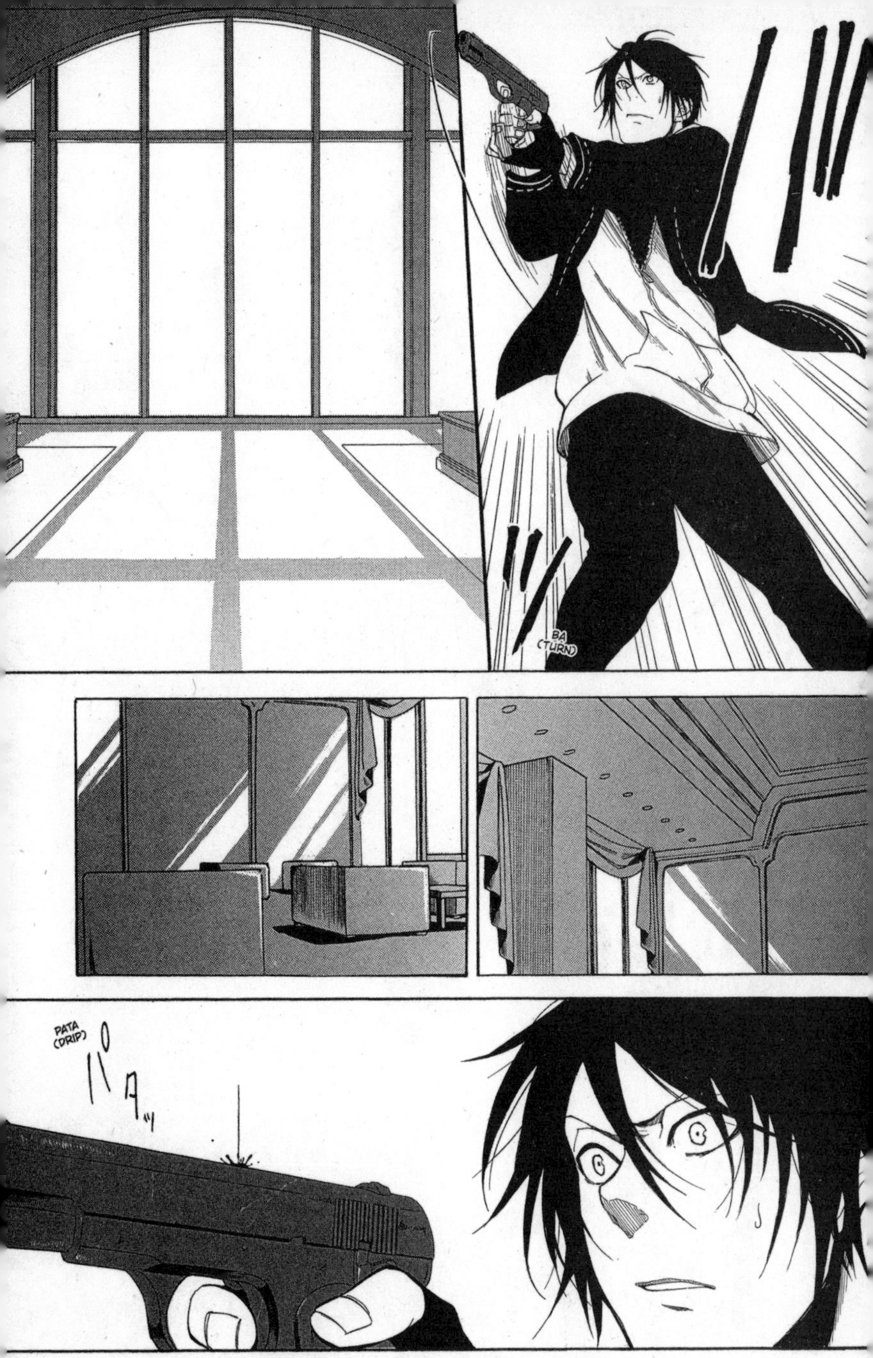
BA
(TURN)
PATA
(DRIP)
パタッ

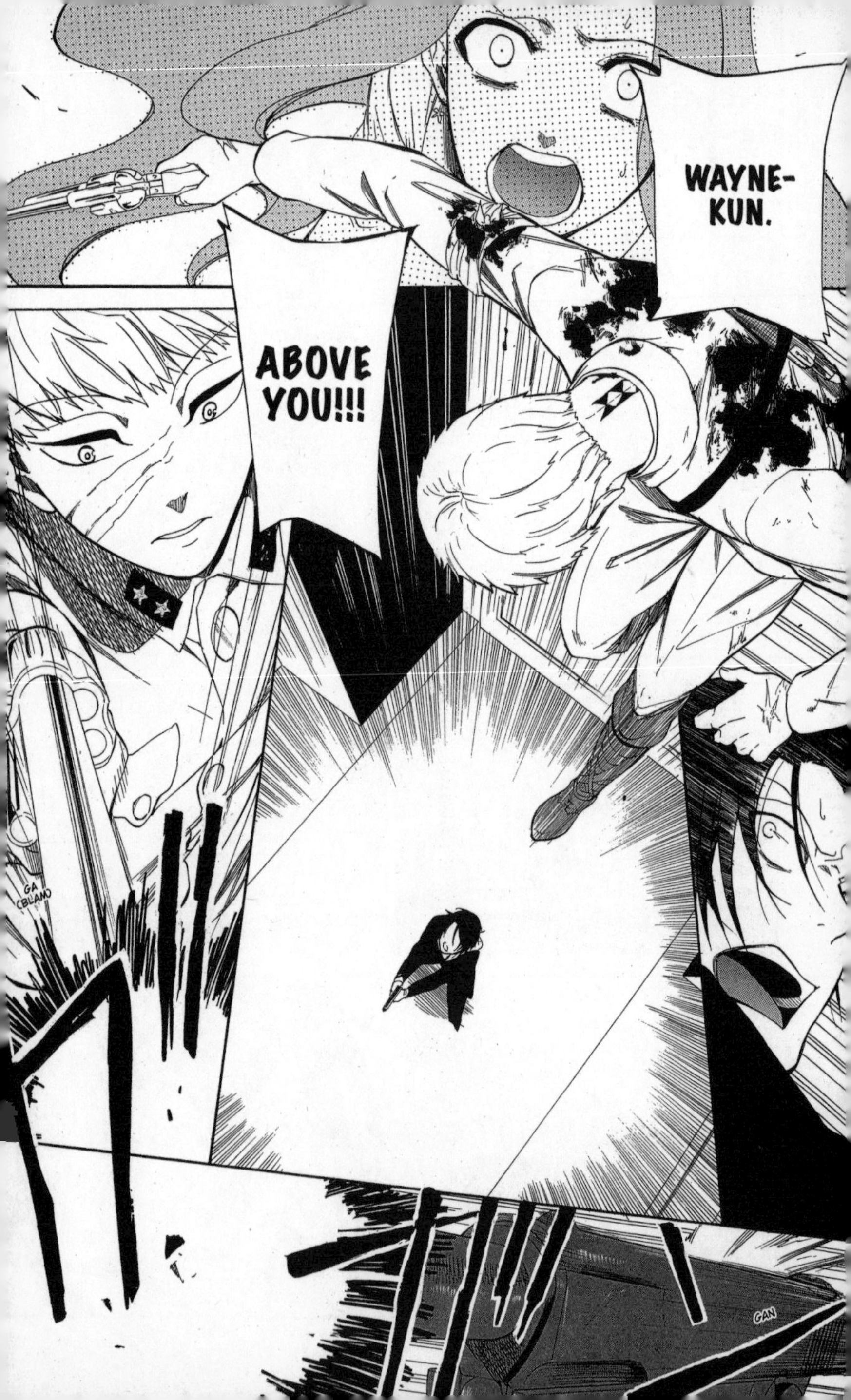
WAYNE-KUN.
ABOVE YOU!!!
GA (BLAM)
GAN

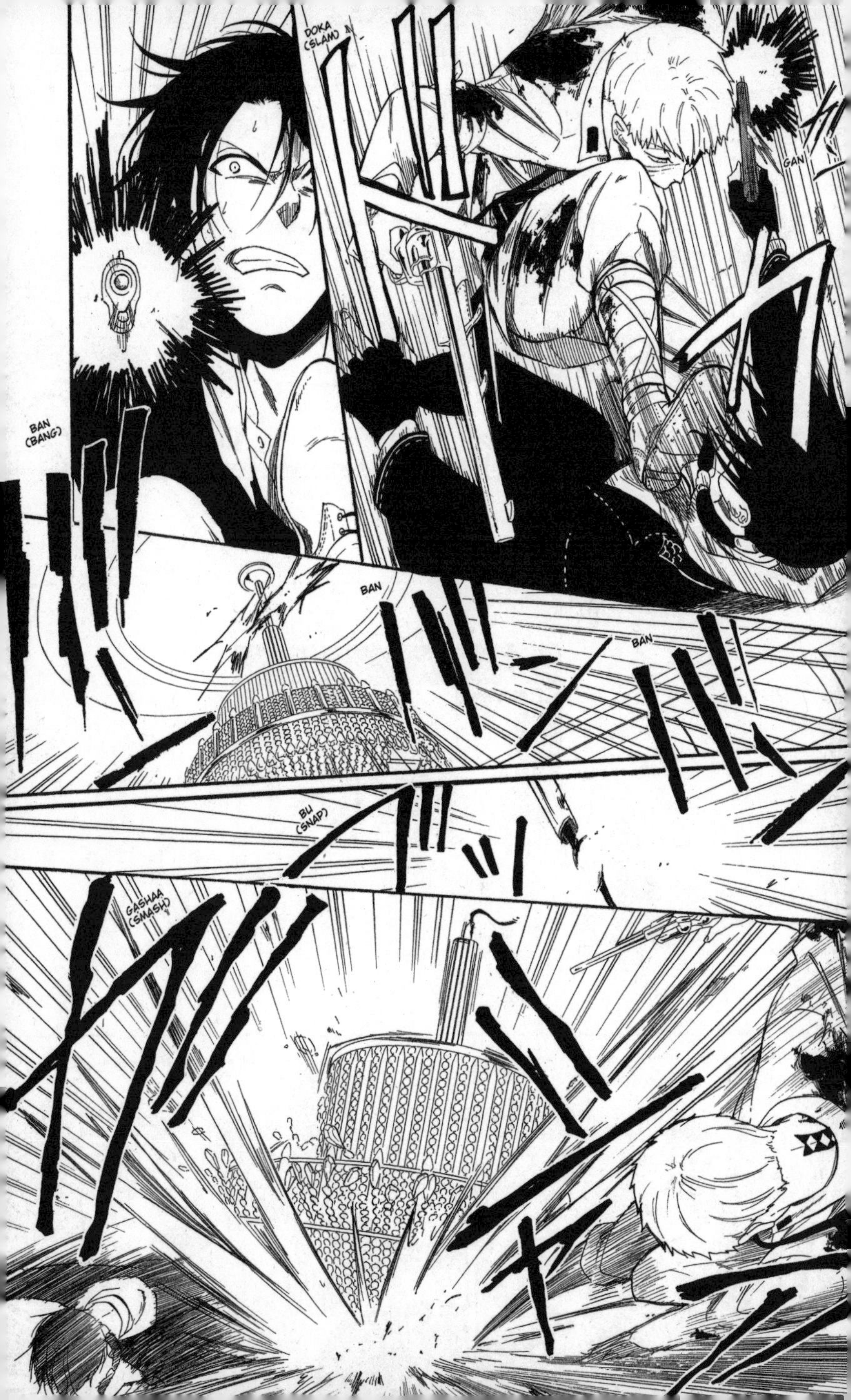
DOKA (SLAM)
GAN
BAN (BANG)
BAN
BAN
BU (SNAP)
GASHAA (SMASH)

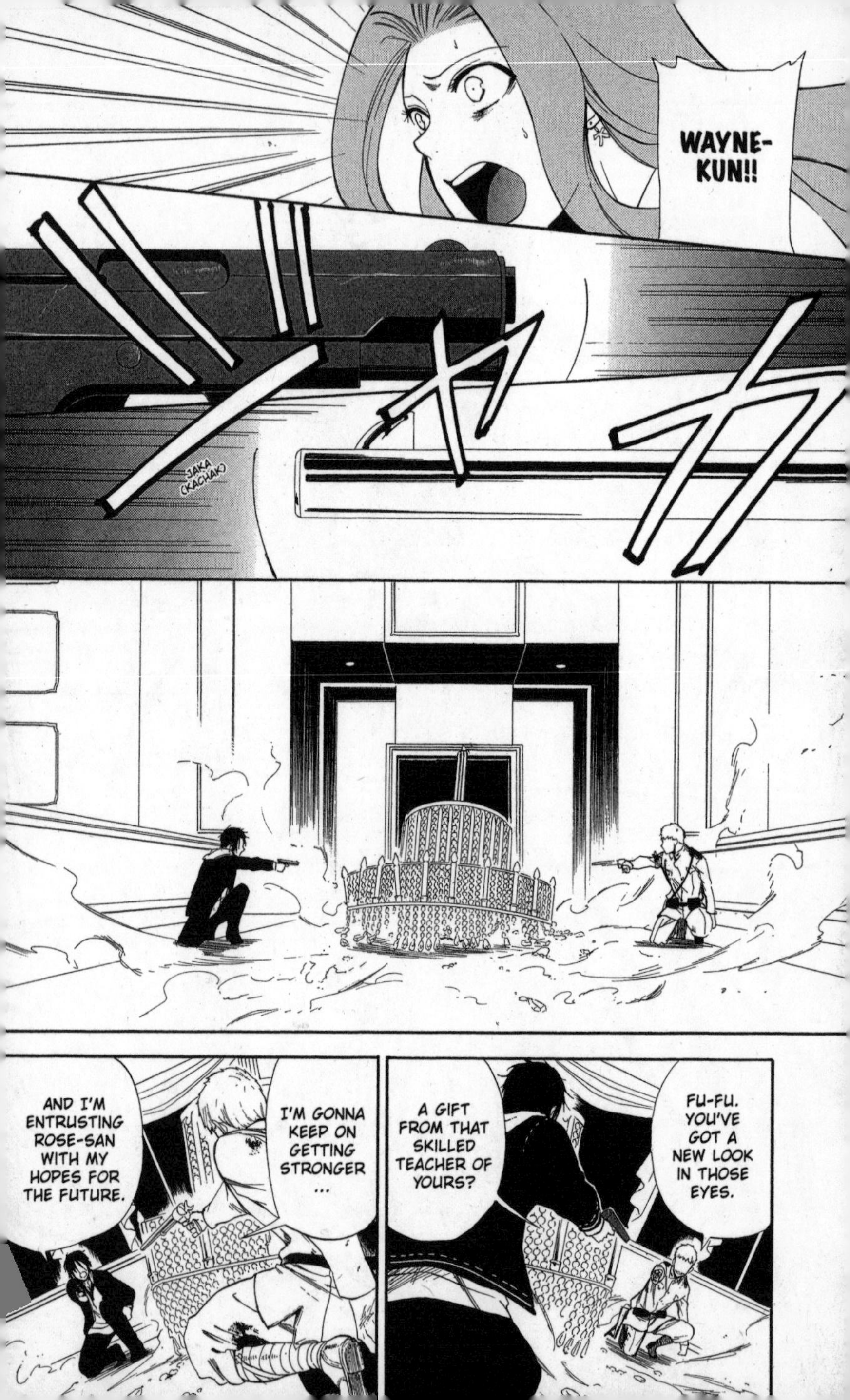
WAYNE-KUN!!
JAKA (KACHAK)
FU-FU. YOU'VE GOT A NEW LOOK IN THOSE EYES.
A GIFT FROM THAT SKILLED TEACHER OF YOURS?
I'M GONNA KEEP ON GETTING STRONGER...
AND I'M ENTRUSTING ROSE-SAN WITH MY HOPES FOR THE FUTURE.

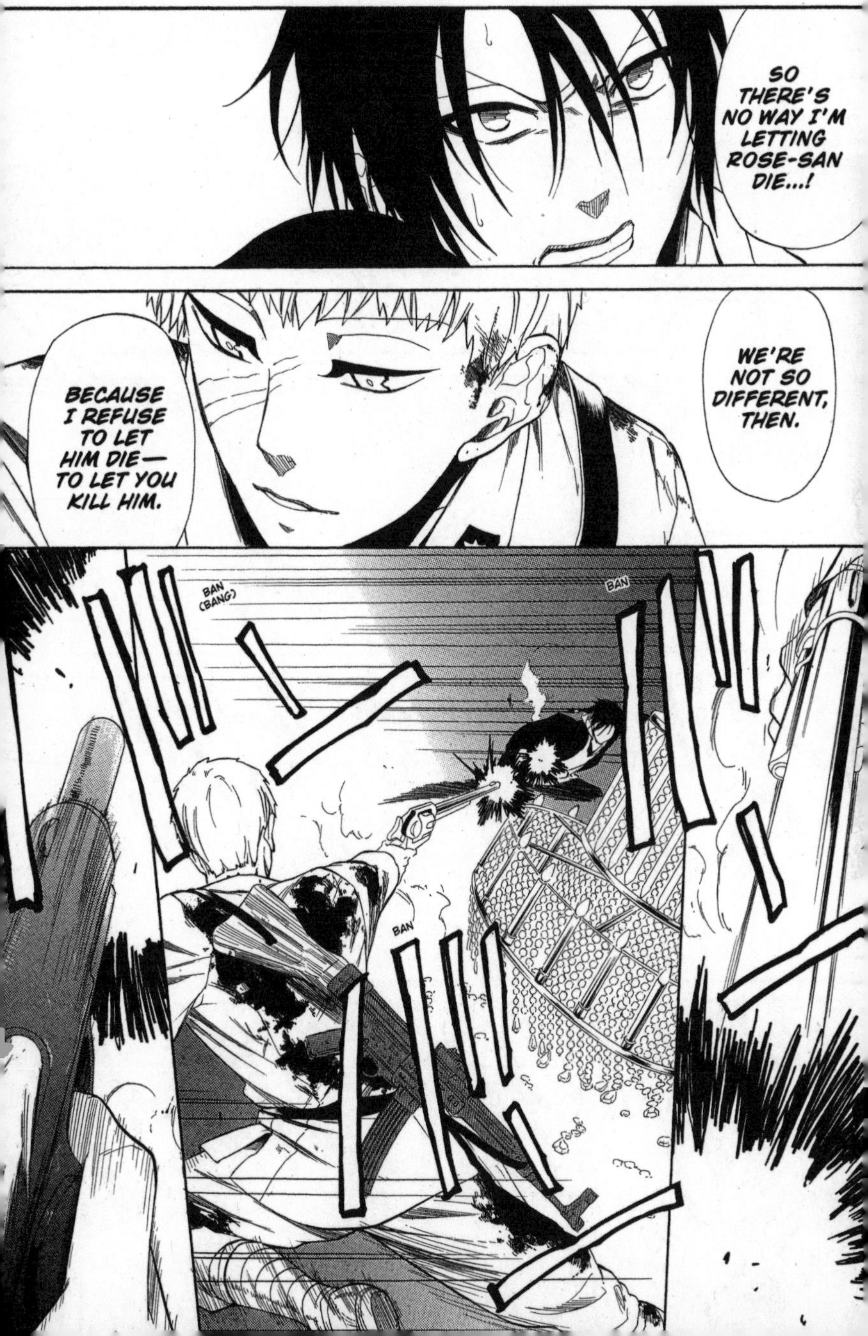
SO THERE'S NO WAY I'M LETTING ROSE-SAN DIE...!
WE'RE NOT SO DIFFERENT, THEN.
BECAUSE I REFUSE TO LET HIM DIE— TO LET YOU KILL HIM.
BAN
BAN (BANG)
BAN

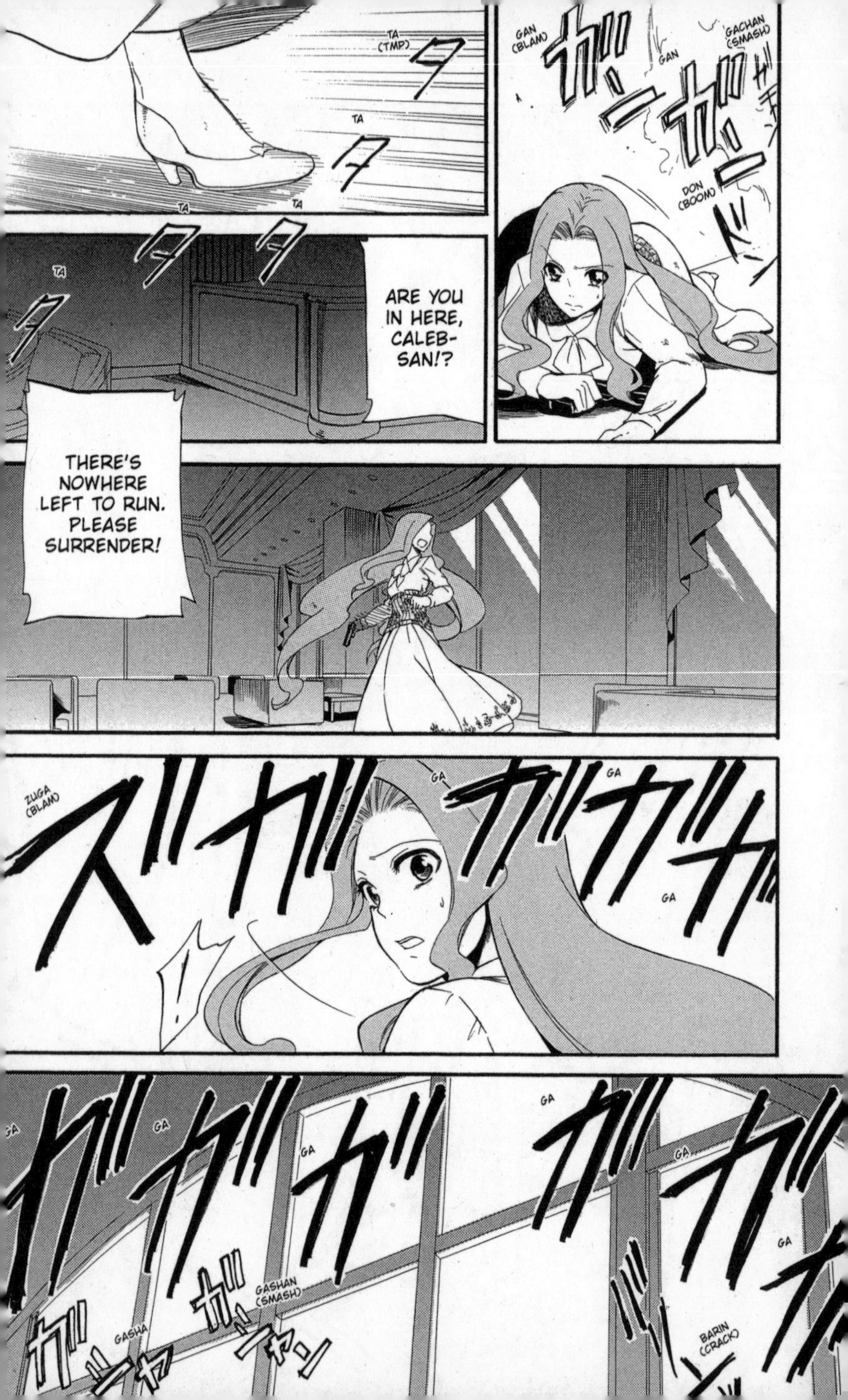
GAN (BLAM)
GAN
GACHAN (SMASH)
DON (BOOM)
TA (TMP)
TA
TA
TA
TA
ARE YOU IN HERE, CALEB-SAN!?
THERE'S NOWHERE LEFT TO RUN. PLEASE SURRENDER!
GA
GA
GA
ZUGA (BLAM)
GA
GA
GA
GA
GA
BARIN (CRACK)
GASHAN (SMASH)
GASHA

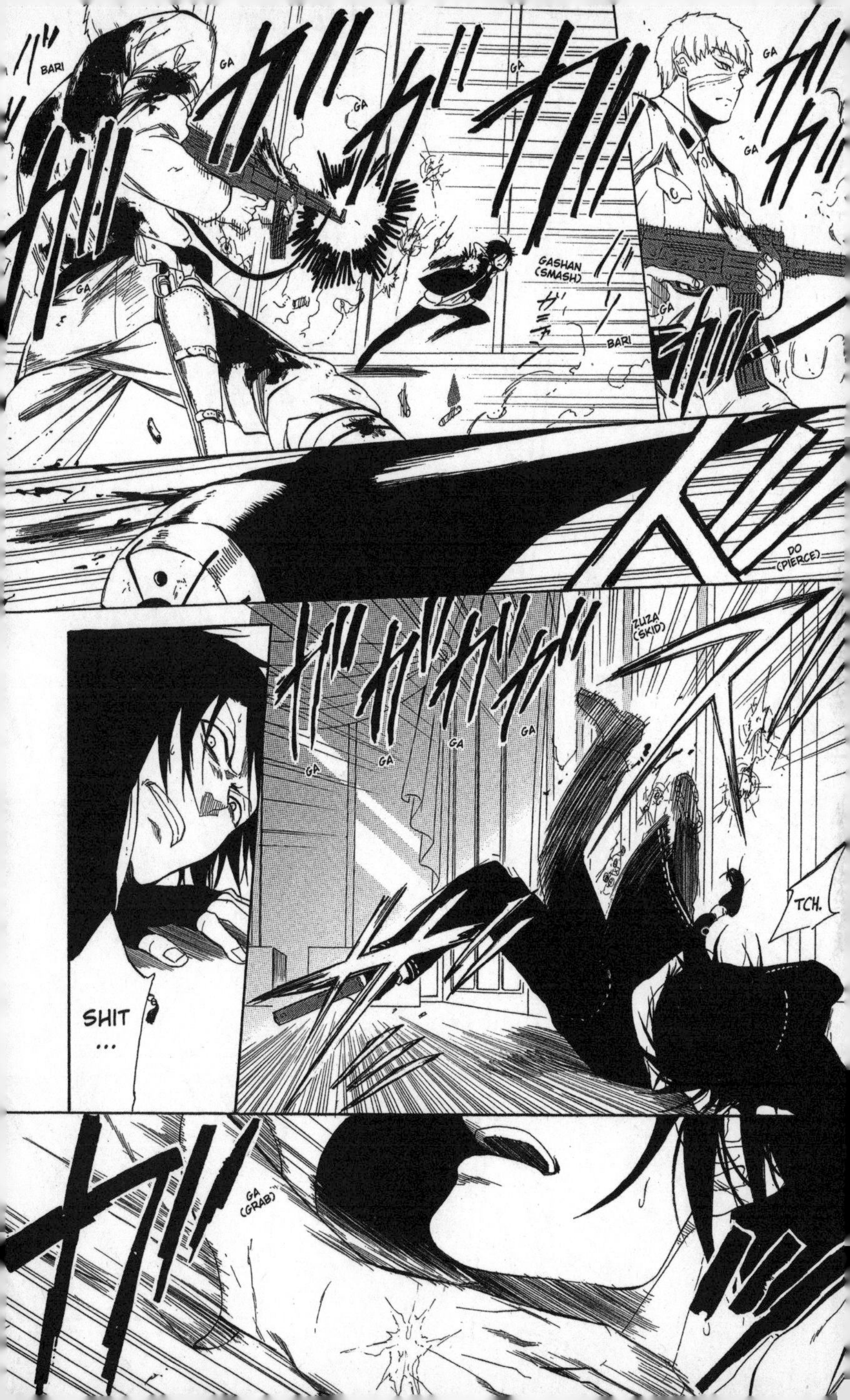
GA
GA
GA
GASHAN (SMASH)
BARI
GA
GA
BARI
GA
GA
DO (PIERCE)
TCH.
ZUZA (SKID)
GA
GA
GA
GA
SHIT ...
GA (GRAB)

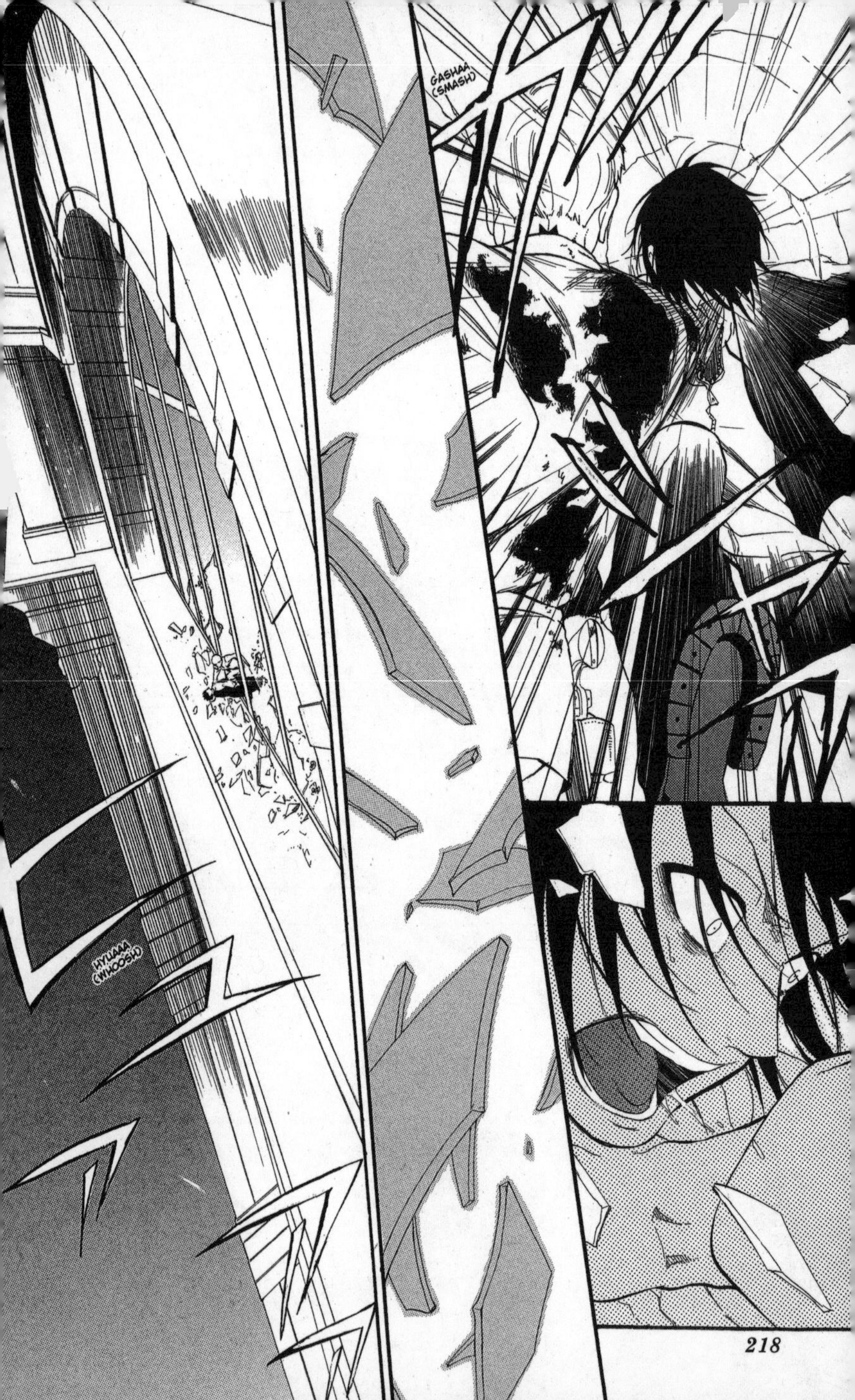
GASHAA (SMASH)
HYUAAA (WHOOSH)

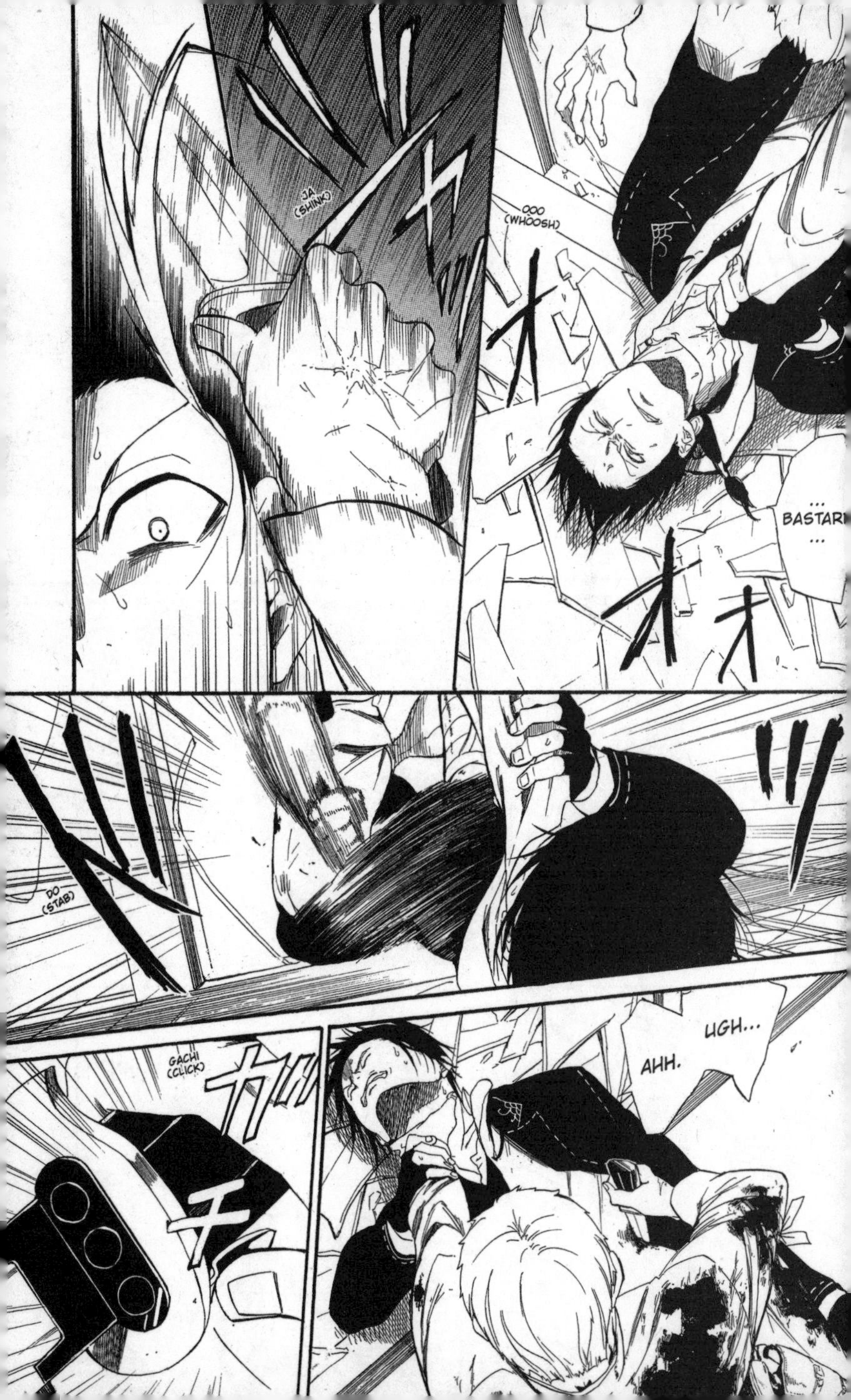
OOO (WHOOSH)
... BASTAR ...
JA (SHINK)
DO (STAB)
UGH...
AHH.
GACHI (CLICK)

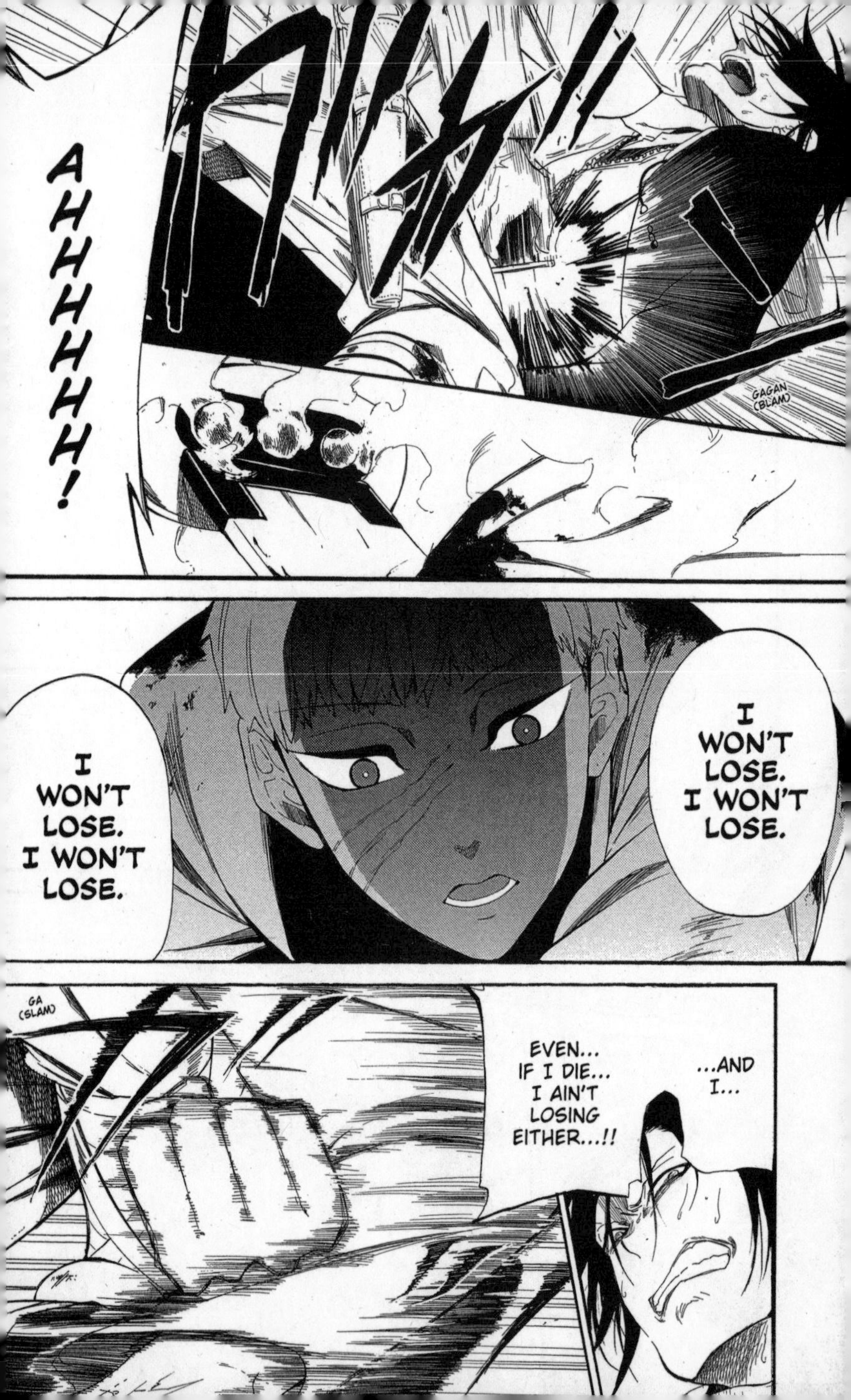
GAGAN (BLAM)
AHHHHHHH!
I WON'T LOSE. I WON'T LOSE.
I WON'T LOSE. I WON'T LOSE.
...AND I...
EVEN... IF I DIE... I AIN'T LOSING EITHER...!!
GA (SLAM)

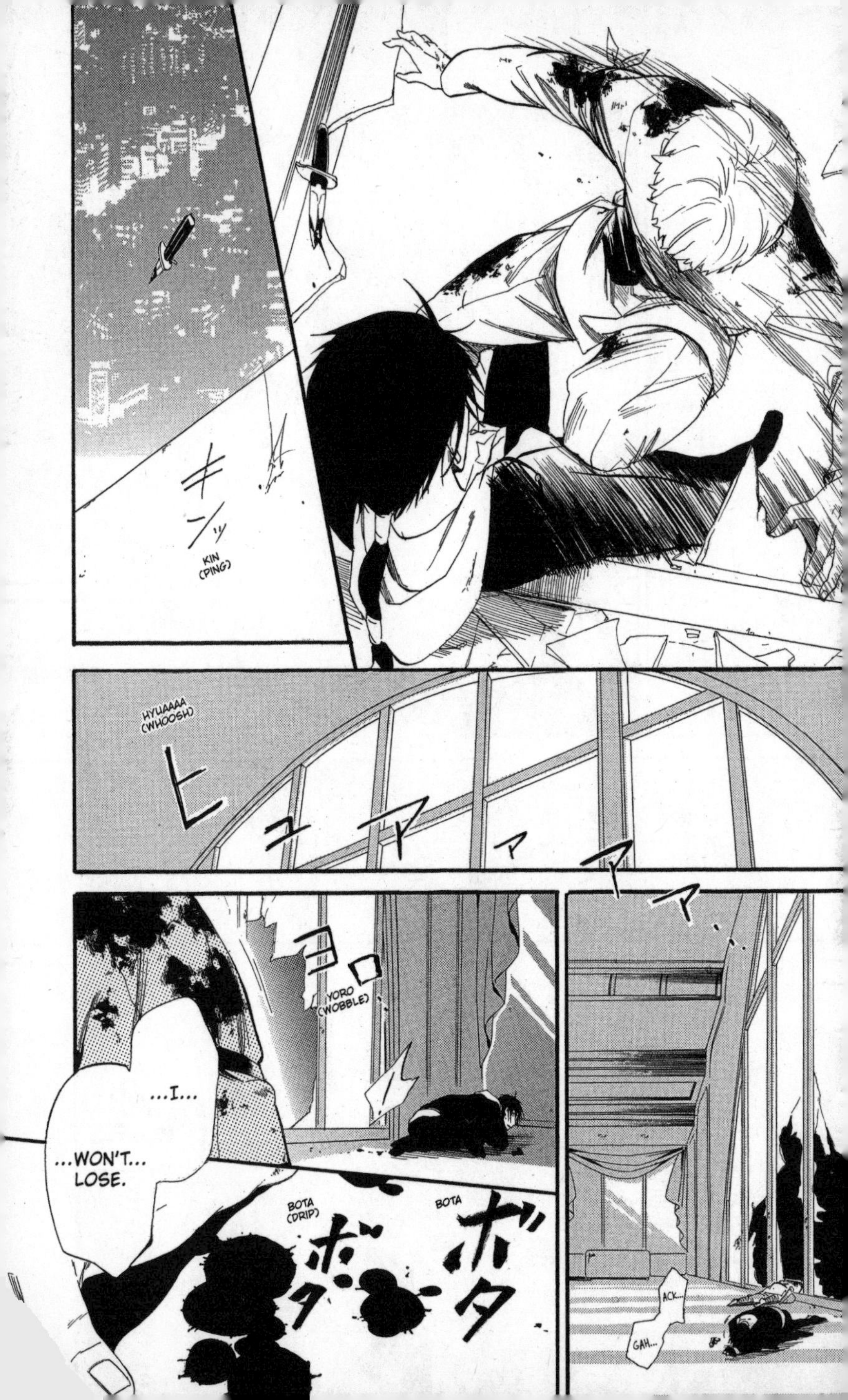
キンッ
KIN (PING)
HYUAAAA (WHOOSH)
ヒュアァァ
ACK...
GAH...
ヨロ
YORO (WOBBLE)
...I...
...WON'T... LOSE.
BOTA
ボタ
BOTA (DRIP)
ボタ

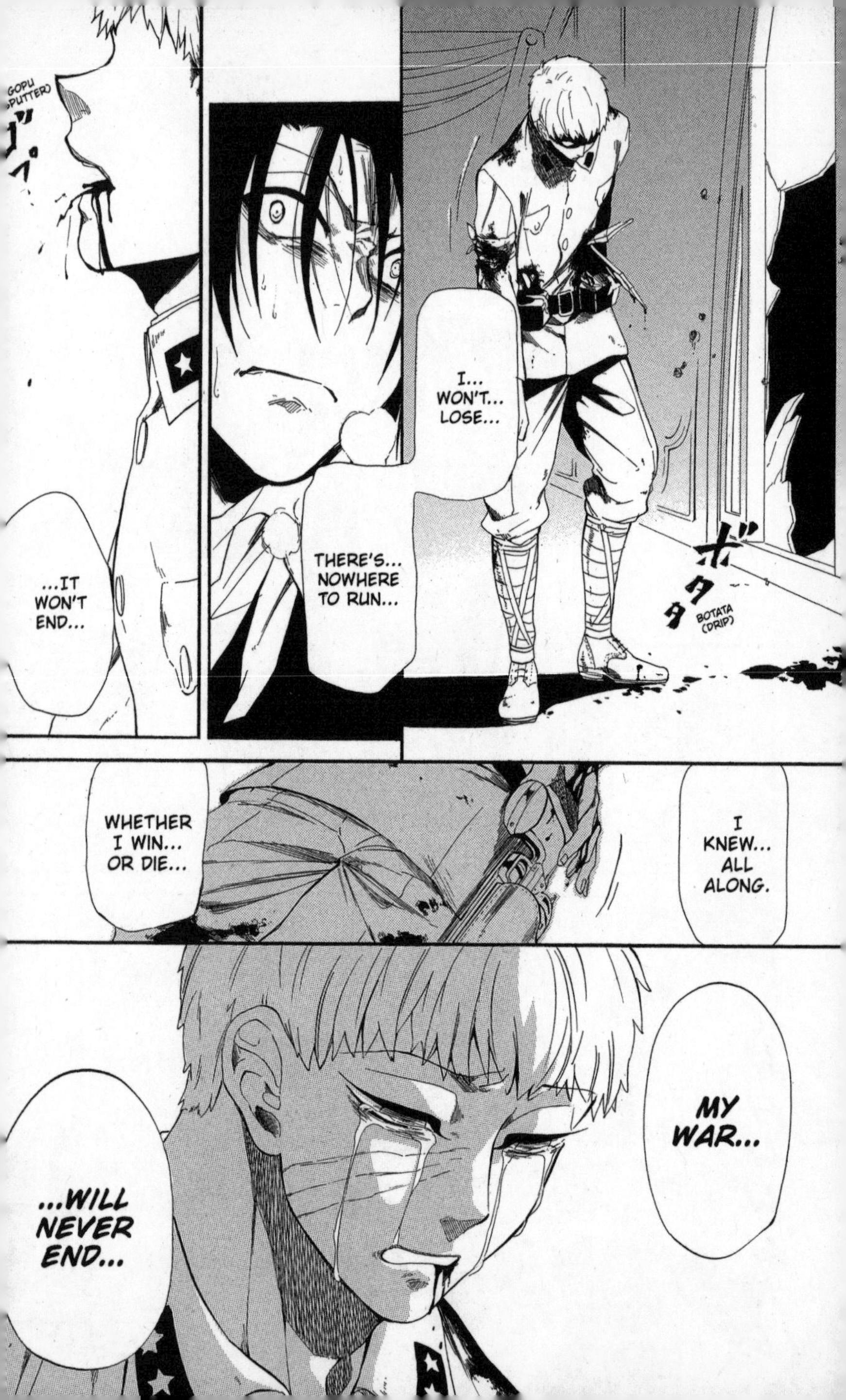
I... WON'T... LOSE...
ボタタ
BOTATA (DRIP)
THERE'S... NOWHERE TO RUN...
ゴプ
GOPU (SPUTTER)
...IT WON'T END...
I KNEW... ALL ALONG.
WHETHER I WIN... OR DIE...
MY WAR...
...WILL NEVER END...

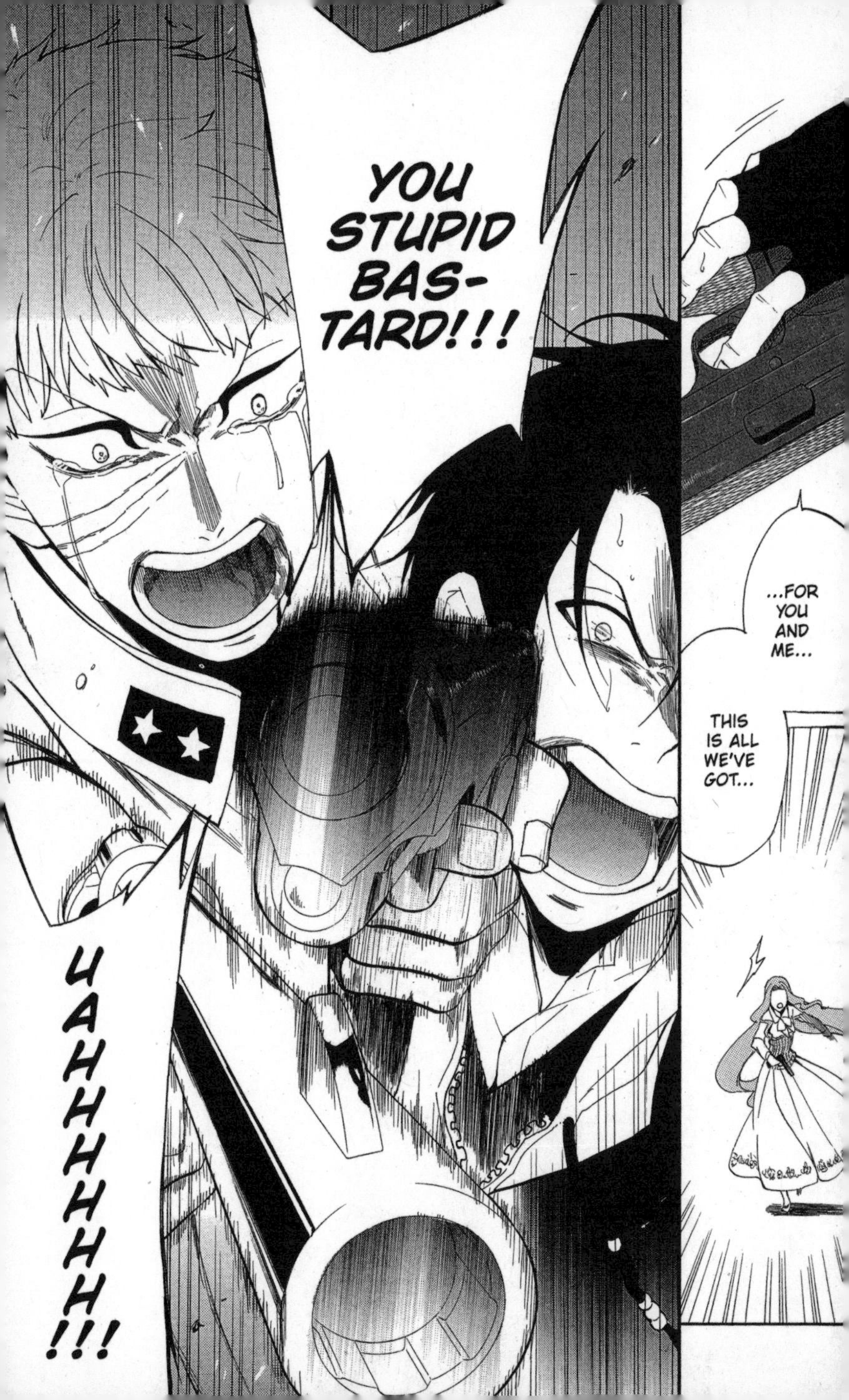
...FOR YOU AND ME...
THIS IS ALL WE'VE GOT...
YOU STUPID BAS-TARD!!!
UAHHHHHH!!!

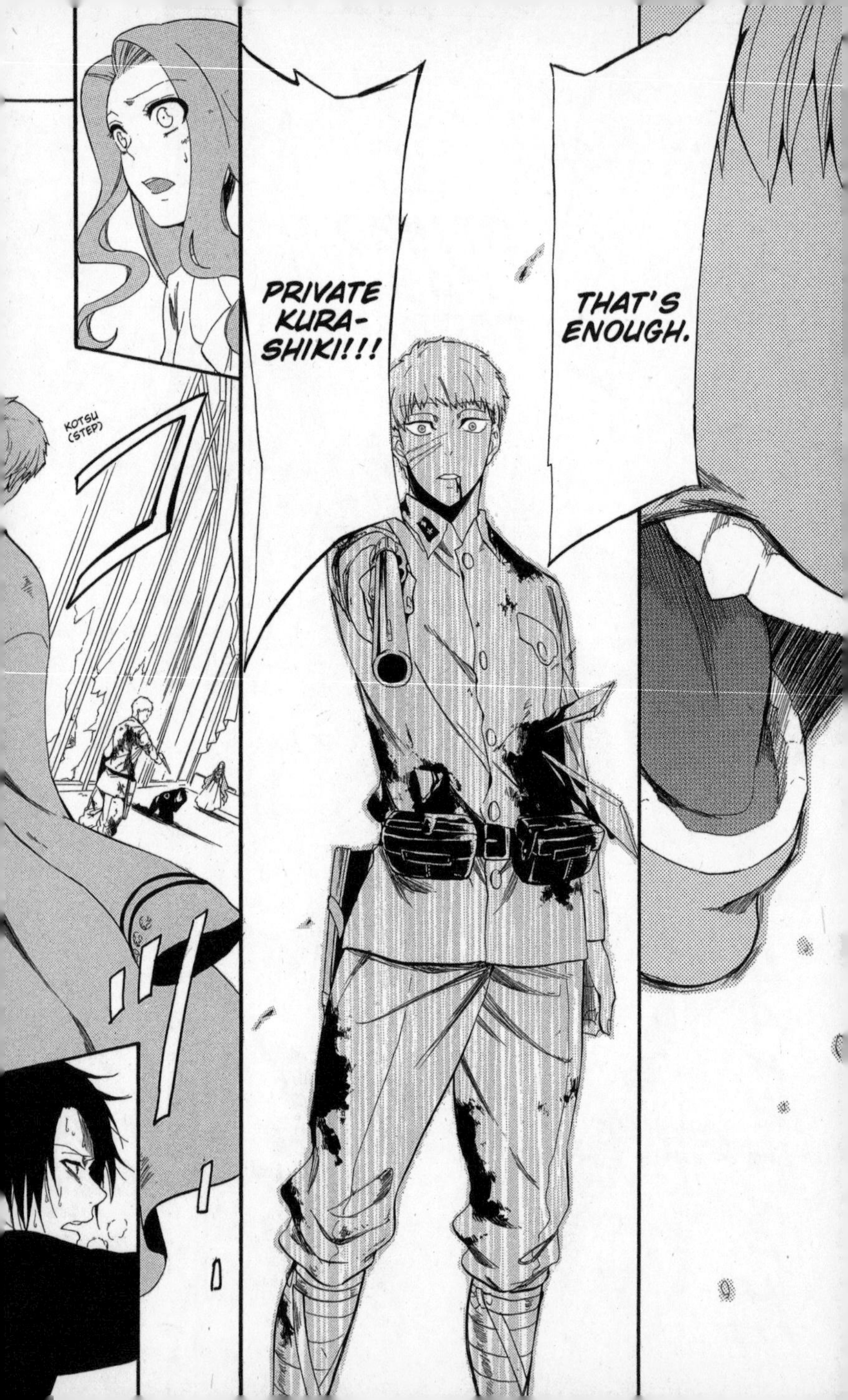
THAT'S ENOUGH.
PRIVATE KURA-SHIKI!!!
KOTSU (STEP)

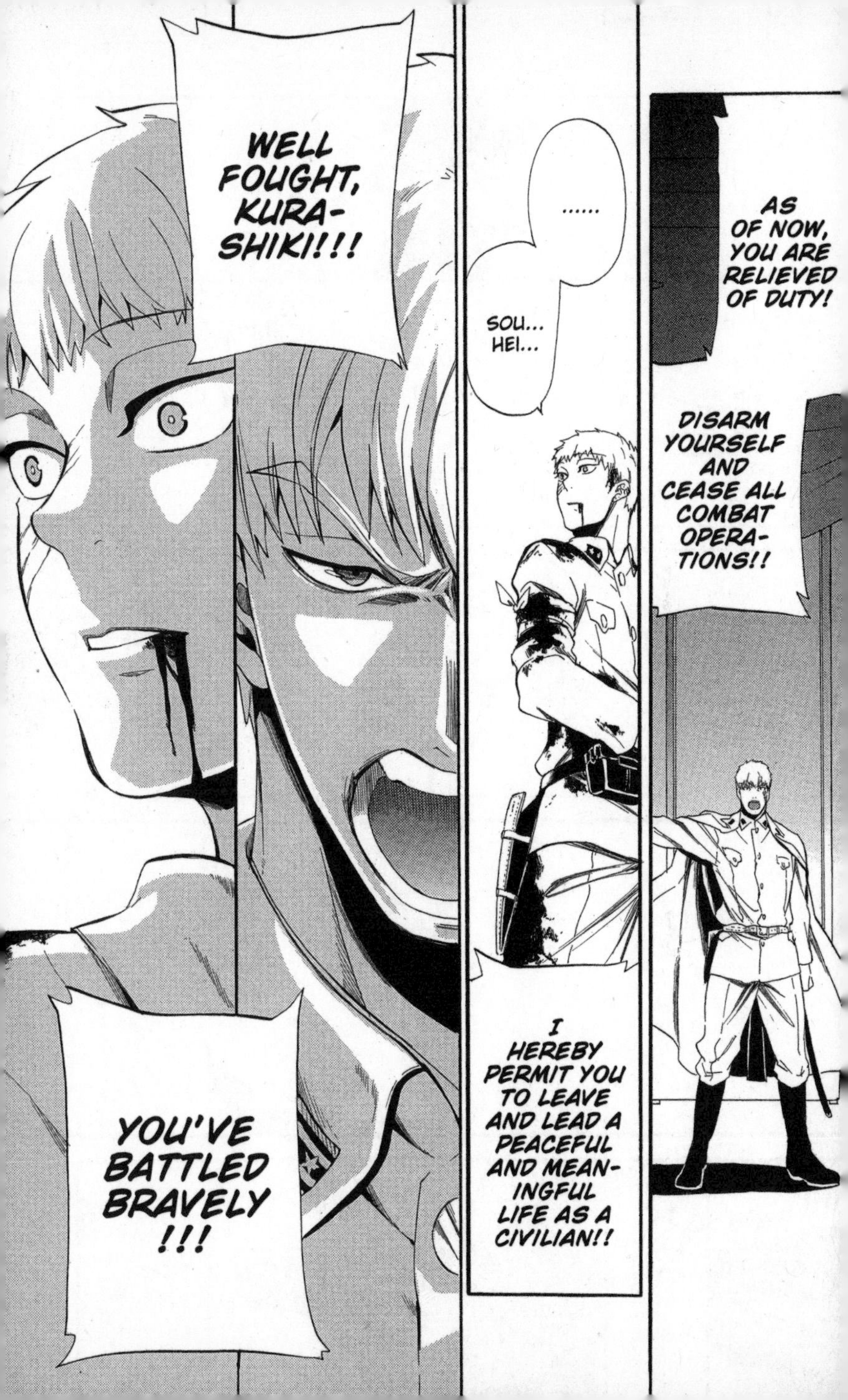
AS OF NOW, YOU ARE RELIEVED OF DUTY!
DISARM YOURSELF AND CEASE ALL COMBAT OPERATIONS!!
......
SOU... HEI...
I HEREBY PERMIT YOU TO LEAVE AND LEAD A PEACEFUL AND MEANINGFUL LIFE AS A CIVILIAN!!
WELL FOUGHT, KURASHIKI!!!
YOU'VE BATTLED BRAVELY!!!

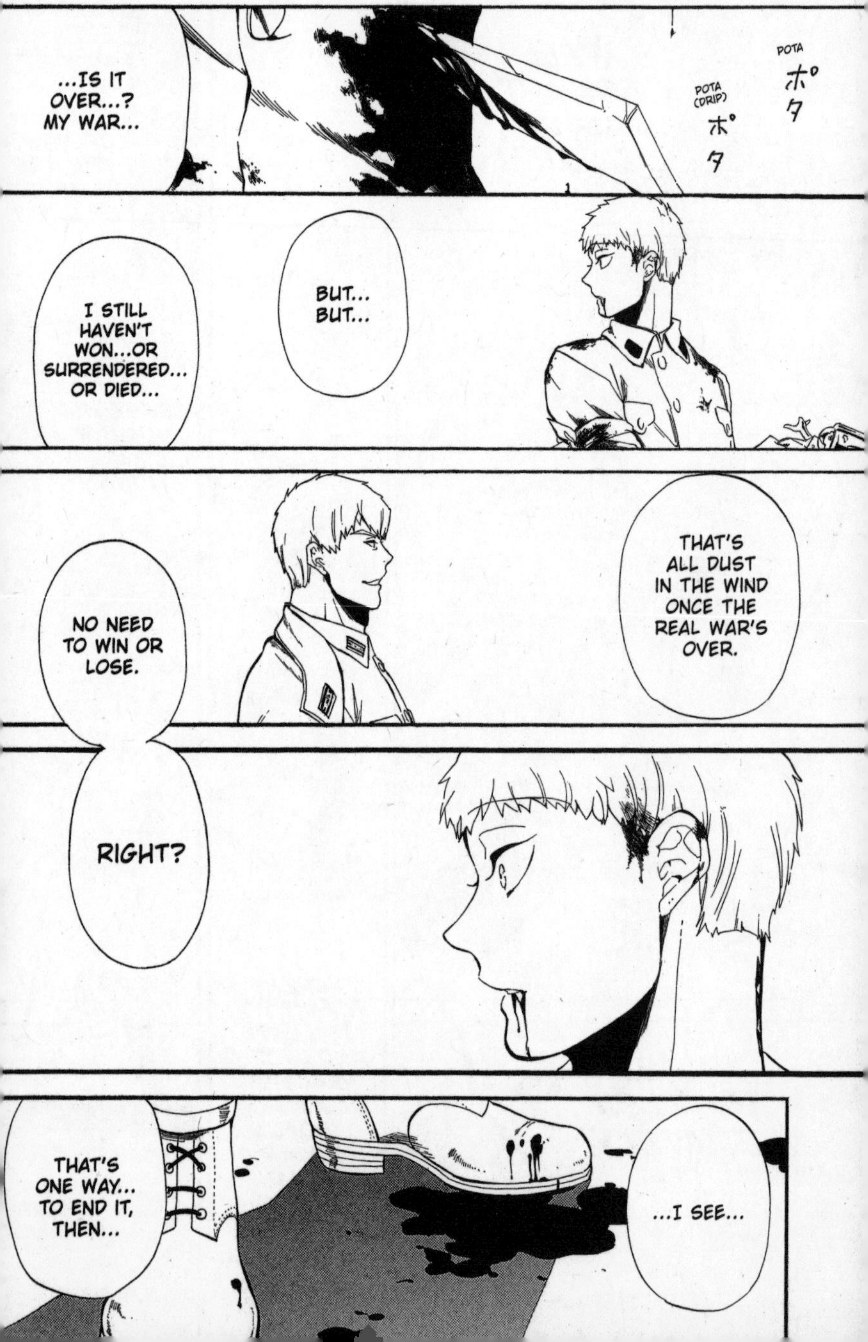
POTA ポタ
POTA (DRIP) ポタ
...IS IT OVER...? MY WAR...
BUT... BUT...
I STILL HAVEN'T WON...OR SURRENDERED... OR DIED...
THAT'S ALL DUST IN THE WIND ONCE THE REAL WAR'S OVER.
NO NEED TO WIN OR LOSE.
RIGHT?
...I SEE...
THAT'S ONE WAY... TO END IT, THEN...

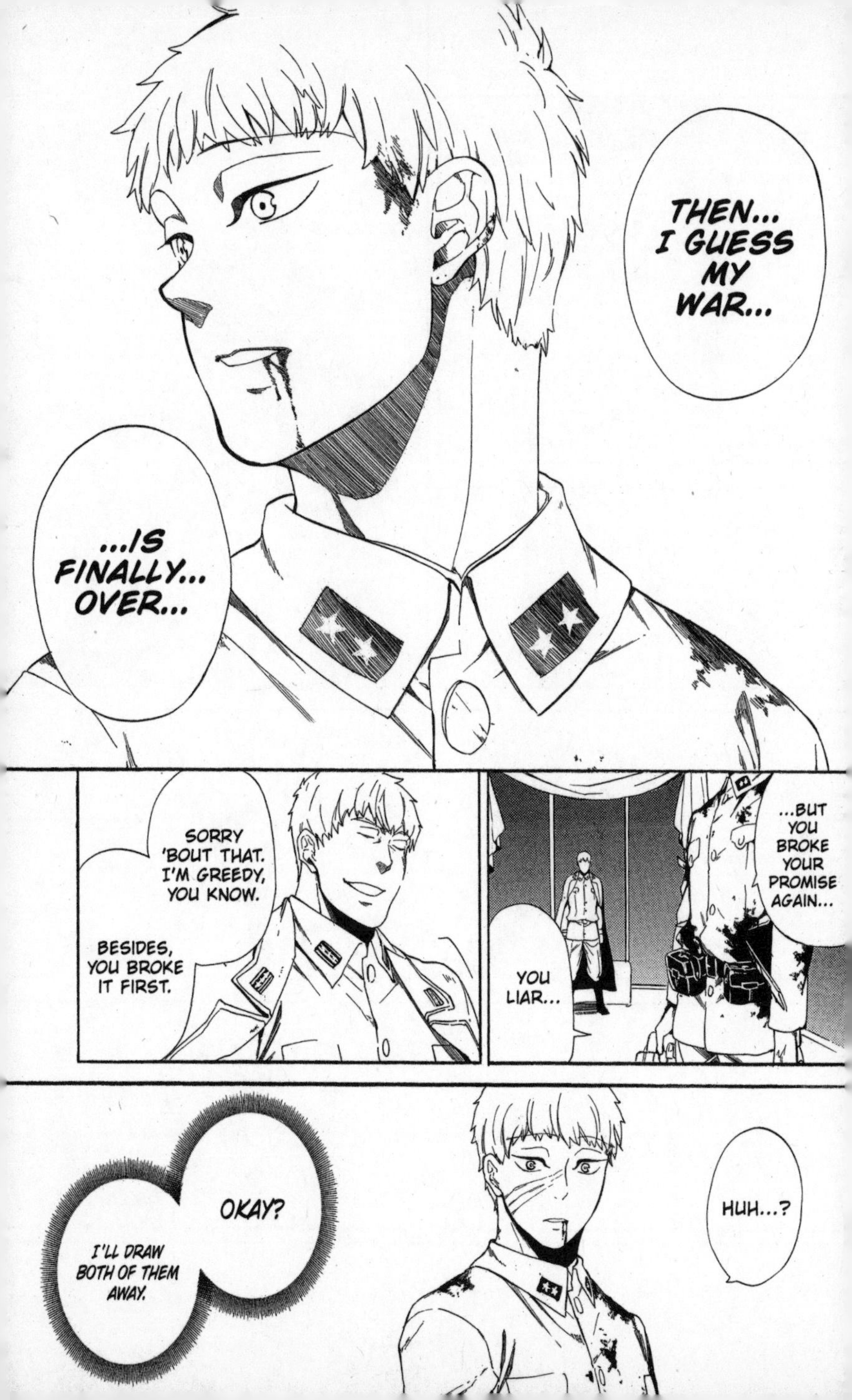
THEN... I GUESS MY WAR...
...IS FINALLY... OVER...
...BUT YOU BROKE YOUR PROMISE AGAIN...
YOU LIAR...
SORRY 'BOUT THAT. I'M GREEDY, YOU KNOW.
BESIDES, YOU BROKE IT FIRST.
HUH...?
I'LL DRAW BOTH OF THEM AWAY.
OKAY?

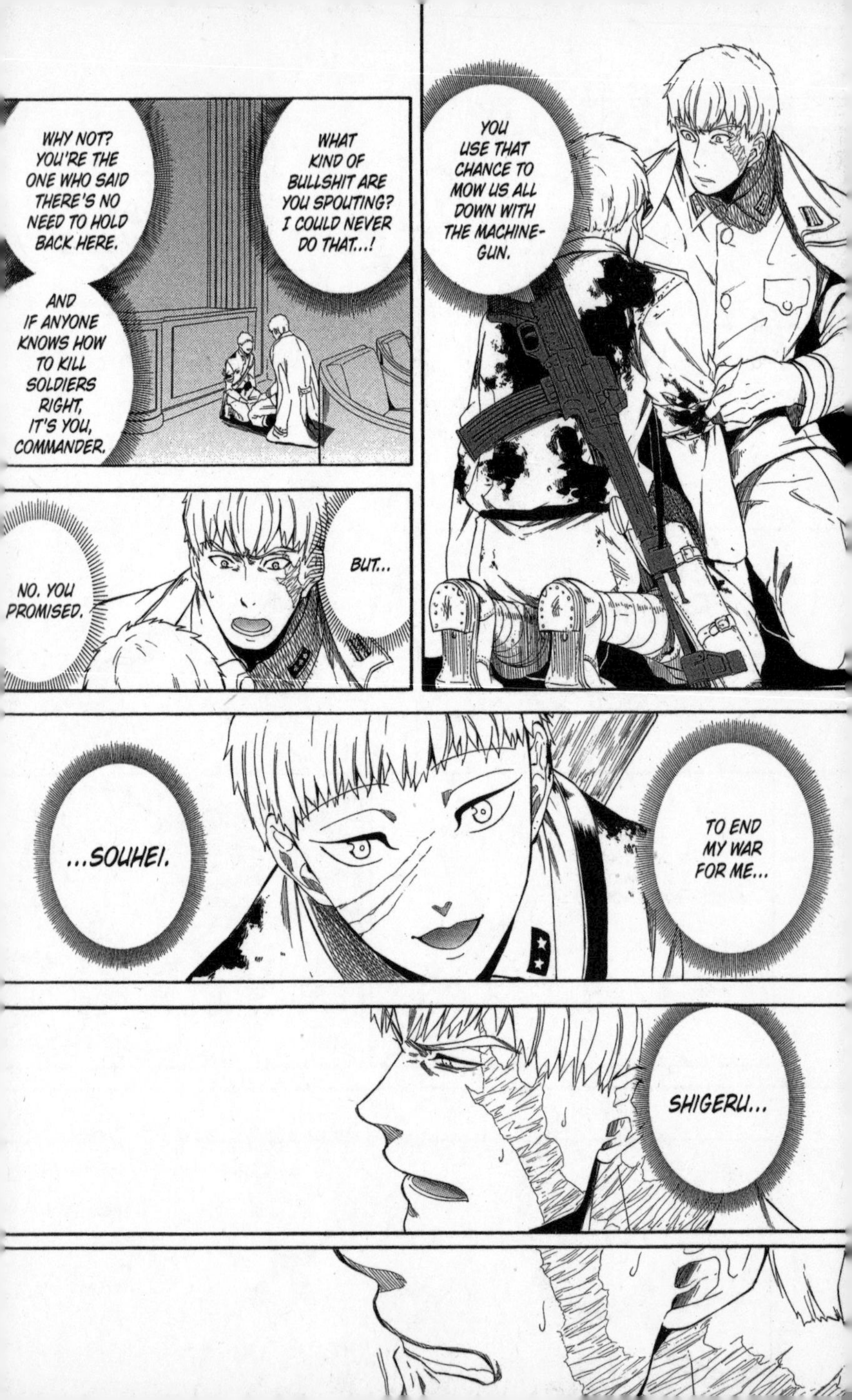
YOU USE THAT CHANCE TO MOW US ALL DOWN WITH THE MACHINE-GUN.
WHAT KIND OF BULLSHIT ARE YOU SPOUTING? I COULD NEVER DO THAT...!
WHY NOT? YOU'RE THE ONE WHO SAID THERE'S NO NEED TO HOLD BACK HERE.
AND IF ANYONE KNOWS HOW TO KILL SOLDIERS RIGHT, IT'S YOU, COMMANDER.
BUT...
NO. YOU PROMISED.
TO END MY WAR FOR ME...
...SOUHEI.
SHIGERU...

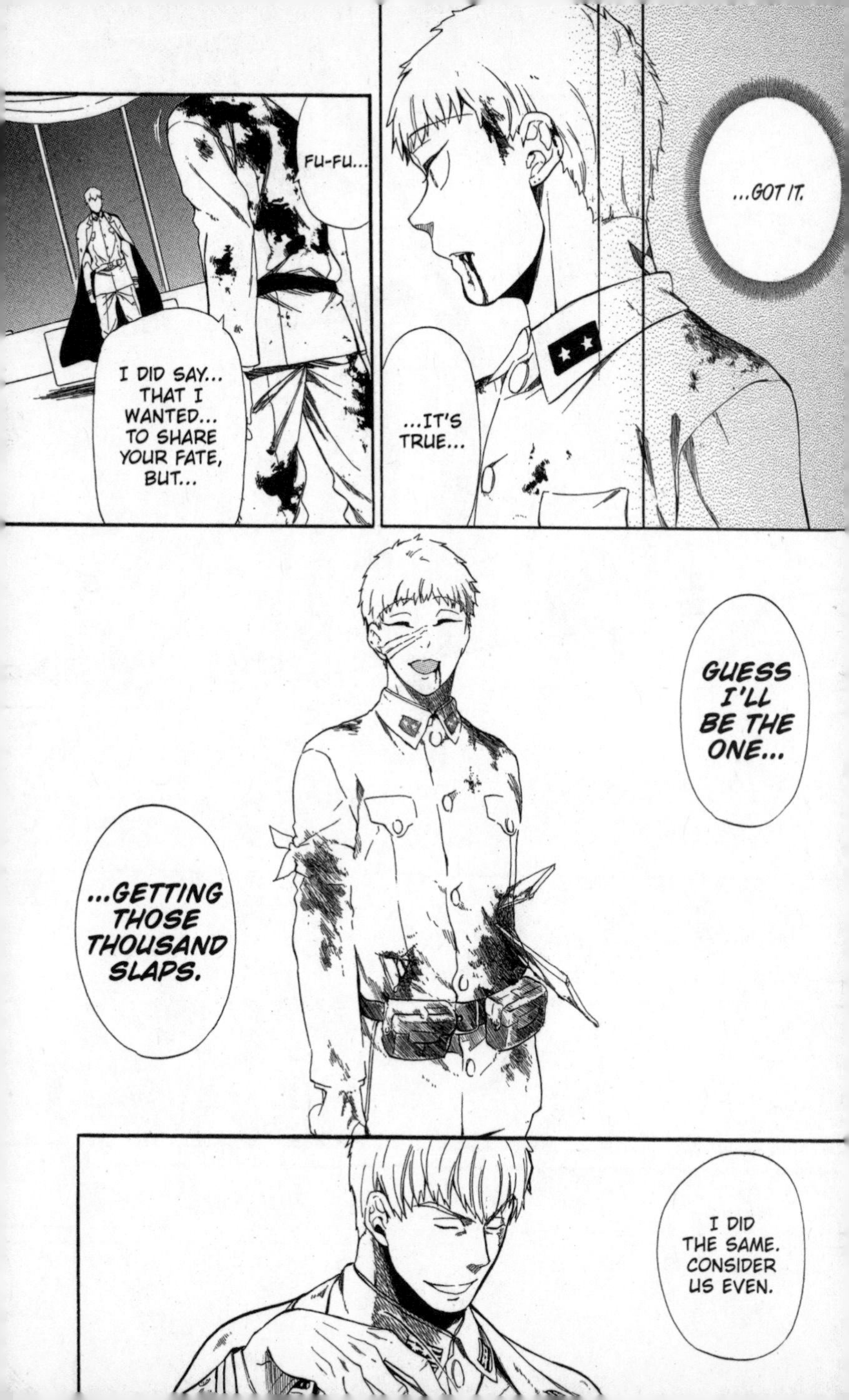
...GOT IT.
...IT'S TRUE...
FU-FU...
I DID SAY... THAT I WANTED... TO SHARE YOUR FATE, BUT...
GUESS I'LL BE THE ONE...
...GETTING THOSE THOUSAND SLAPS.
I DID THE SAME. CONSIDER US EVEN.

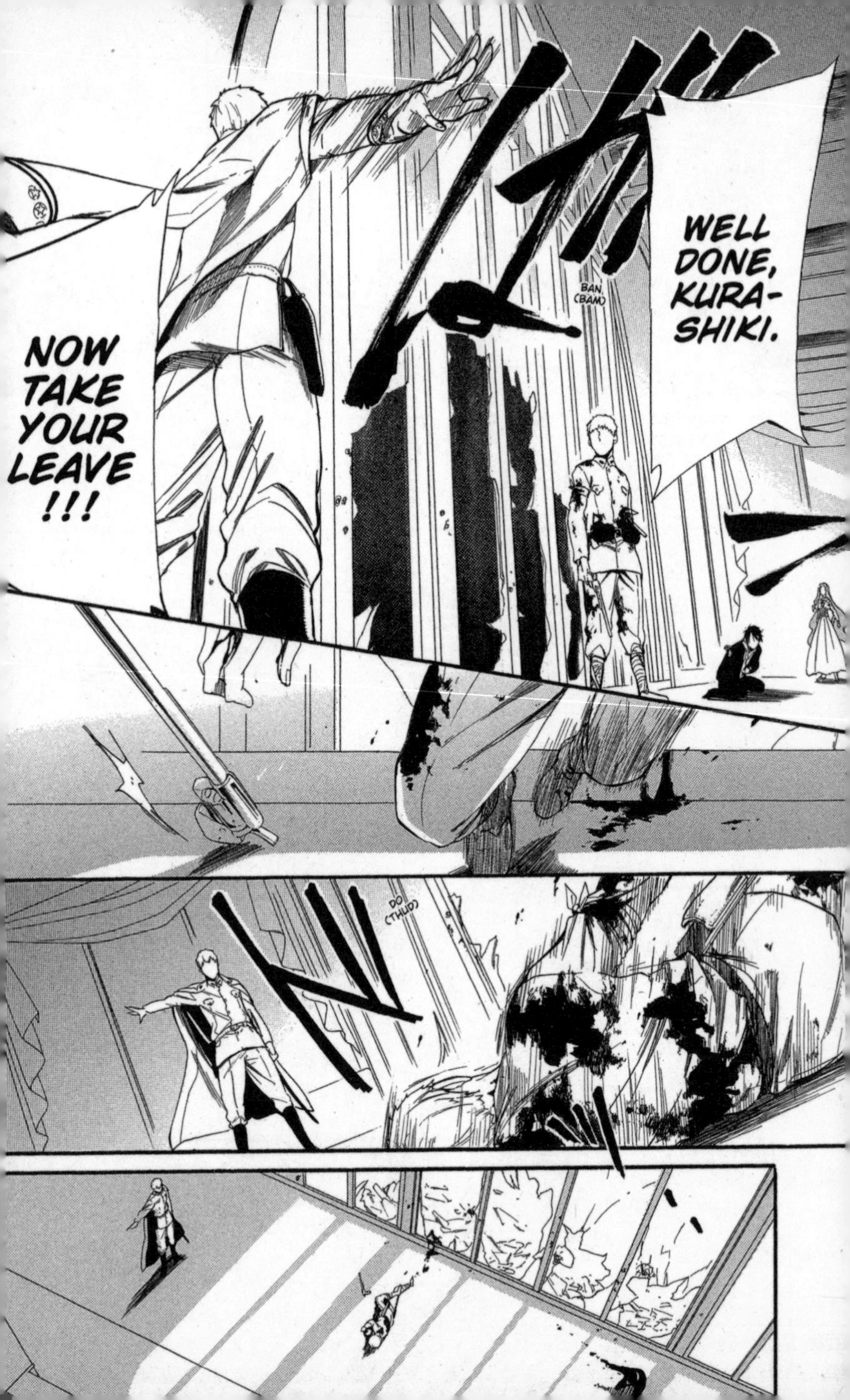
WELL DONE, KURA-SHIKI.
BAN (BAM)
NOW TAKE YOUR LEAVE!!!
DO (THUD)

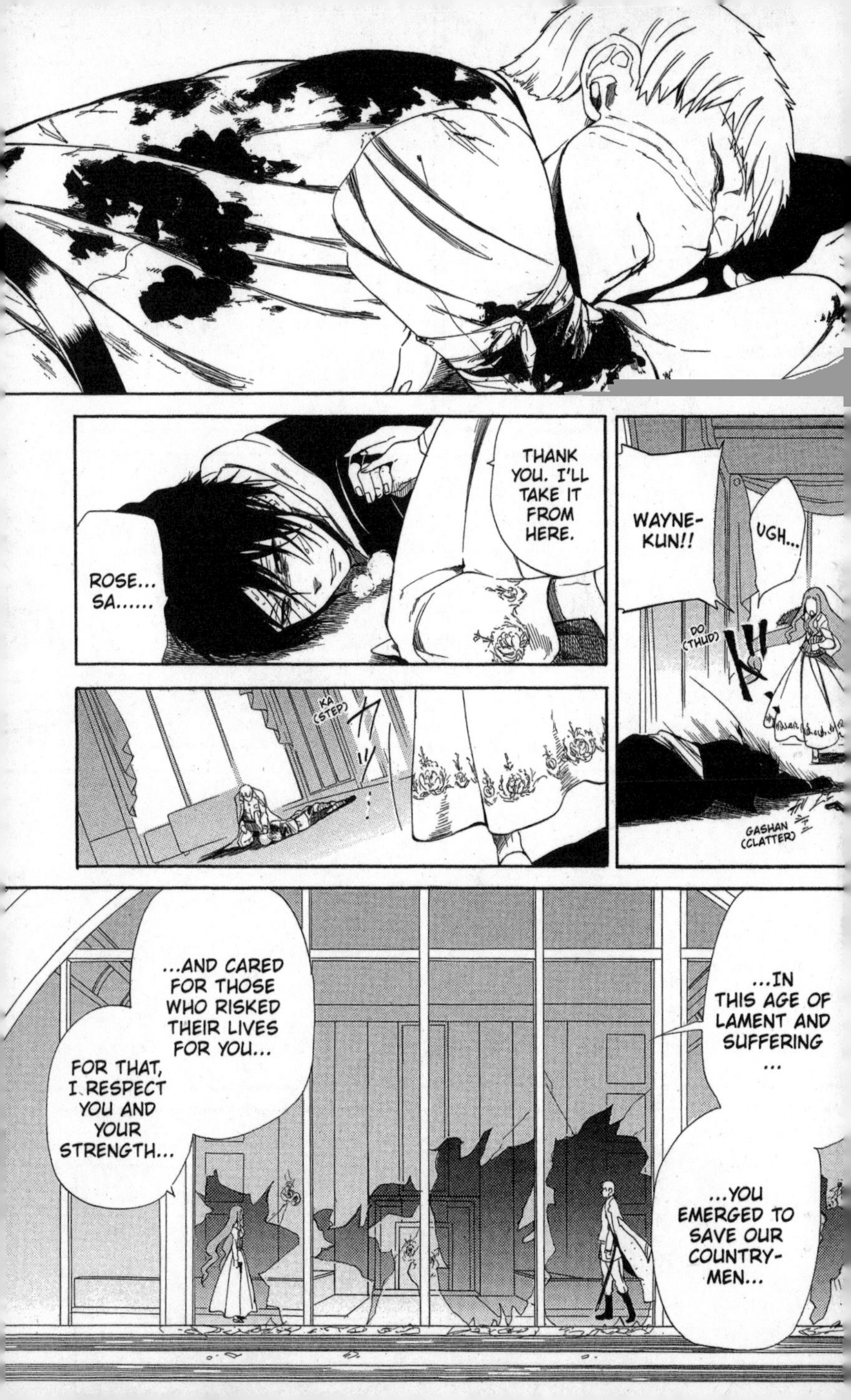
UGH...
WAYNE-KUN!!
DO (THUD)
GASHAN (CLATTER)
THANK YOU. I'LL TAKE IT FROM HERE.
ROSE... SA......
KA (STEP)
...IN THIS AGE OF LAMENT AND SUFFERING...
...YOU EMERGED TO SAVE OUR COUNTRYMEN...
...AND CARED FOR THOSE WHO RISKED THEIR LIVES FOR YOU...
FOR THAT, I RESPECT YOU AND YOUR STRENGTH...

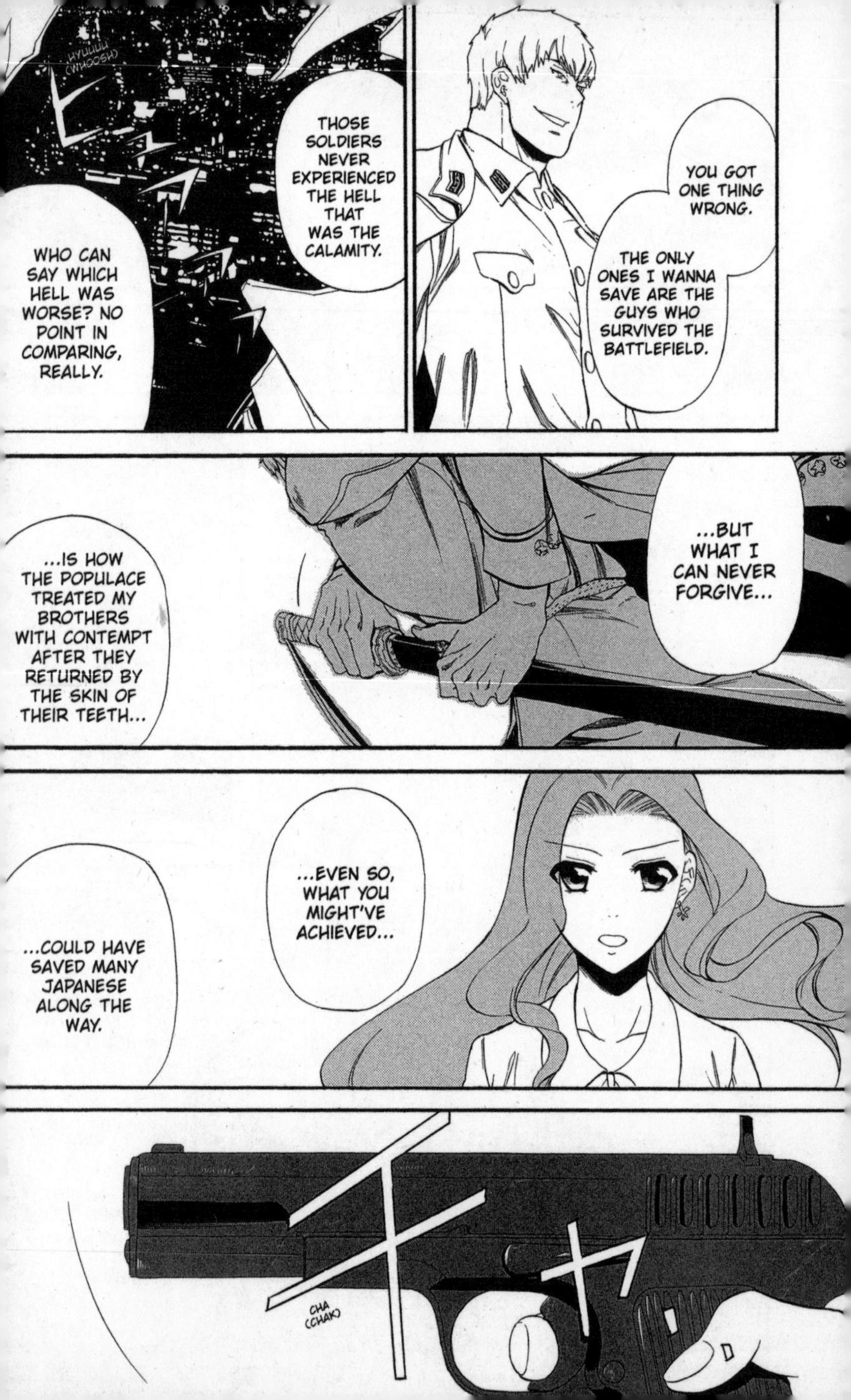
YOU GOT ONE THING WRONG.
THE ONLY ONES I WANNA SAVE ARE THE GUYS WHO SURVIVED THE BATTLEFIELD.
THOSE SOLDIERS NEVER EXPERIENCED THE HELL THAT WAS THE CALAMITY.
HYUUUU (WHOOSH)
WHO CAN SAY WHICH HELL WAS WORSE? NO POINT IN COMPARING, REALLY.
...BUT WHAT I CAN NEVER FORGIVE...
...IS HOW THE POPULACE TREATED MY BROTHERS WITH CONTEMPT AFTER THEY RETURNED BY THE SKIN OF THEIR TEETH...
...EVEN SO, WHAT YOU MIGHT'VE ACHIEVED...
...COULD HAVE SAVED MANY JAPANESE ALONG THE WAY.
CHA (CHAK)

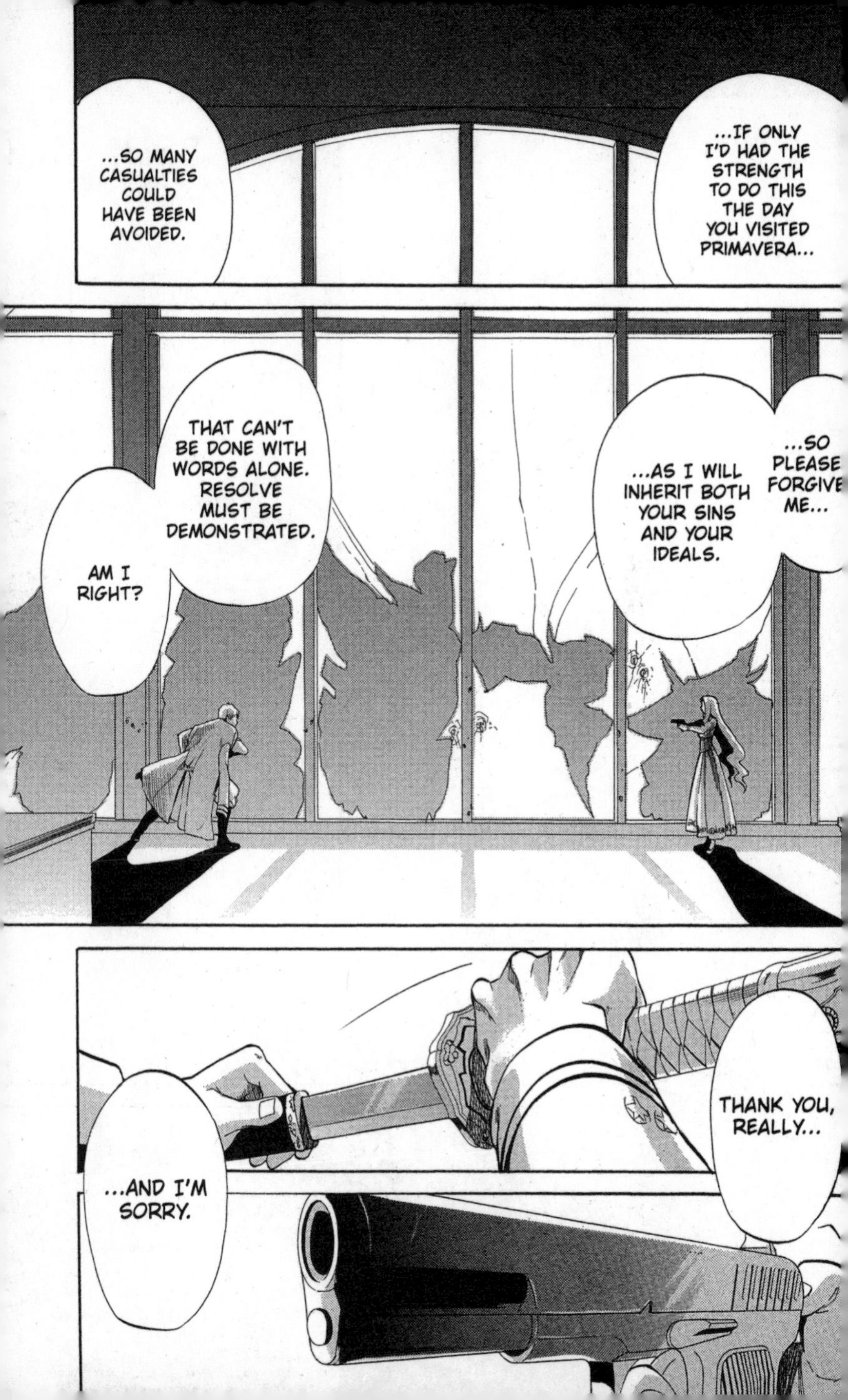
...IF ONLY I'D HAD THE STRENGTH TO DO THIS THE DAY YOU VISITED PRIMAVERA...
...SO MANY CASUALTIES COULD HAVE BEEN AVOIDED.
...SO PLEASE FORGIVE ME...
...AS I WILL INHERIT BOTH YOUR SINS AND YOUR IDEALS.
THAT CAN'T BE DONE WITH WORDS ALONE. RESOLVE MUST BE DEMONSTRATED.
AM I RIGHT?
THANK YOU, REALLY...
...AND I'M SORRY.

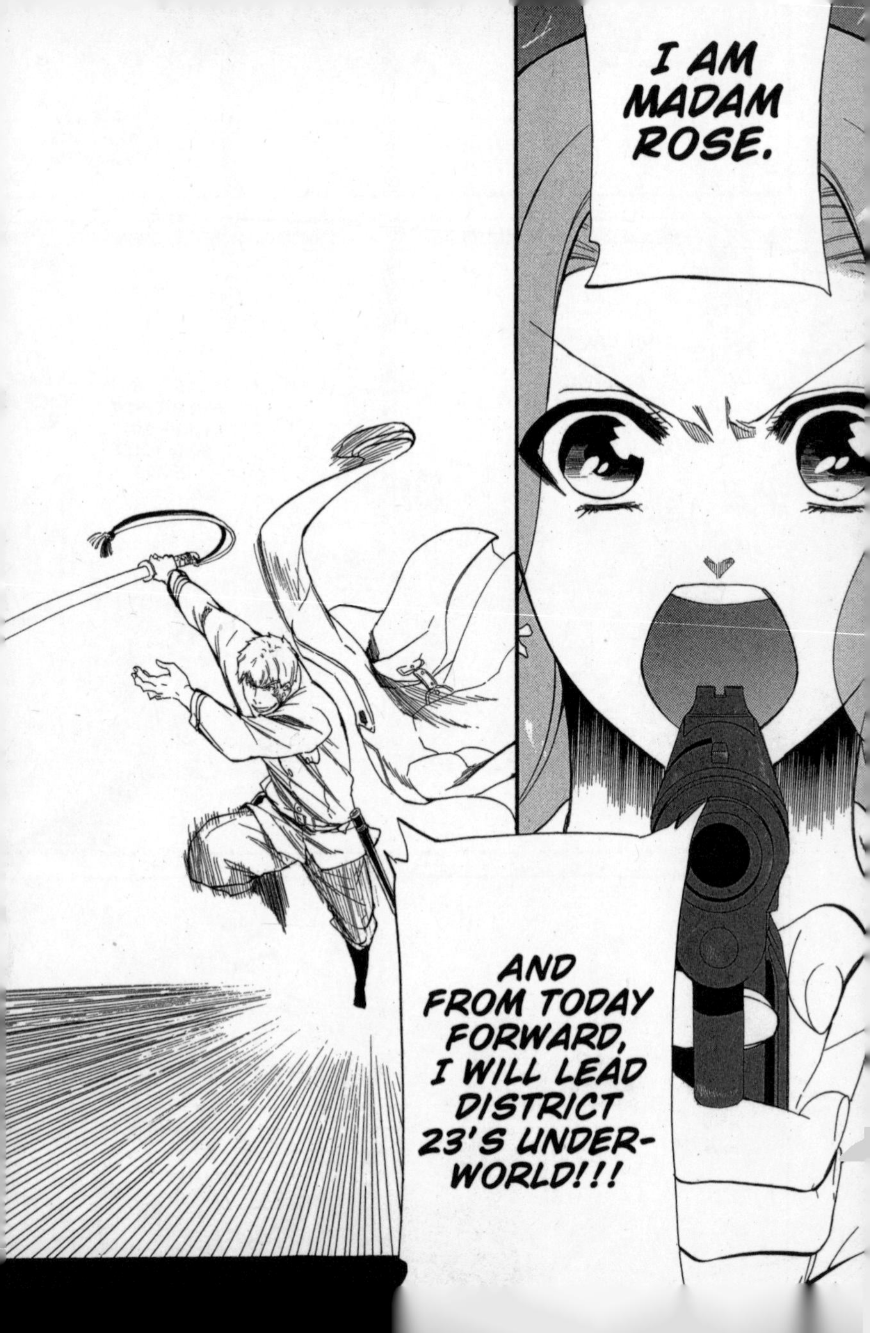
I AM MADAM ROSE.
AND FROM TODAY FORWARD, I WILL LEAD DISTRICT 23'S UNDER-WORLD!!!

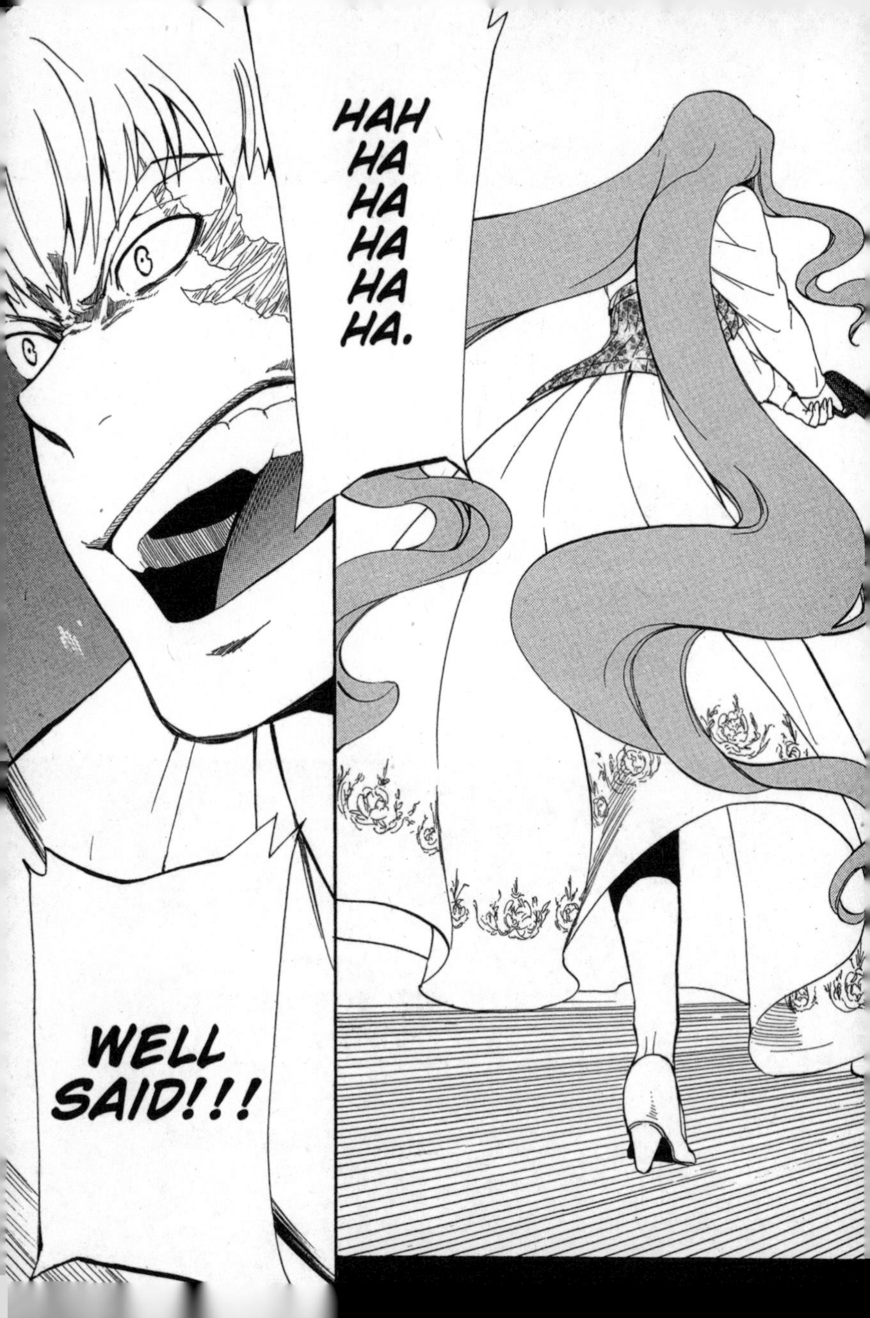
HAH HA HA HA HA HA.
WELL SAID!!!

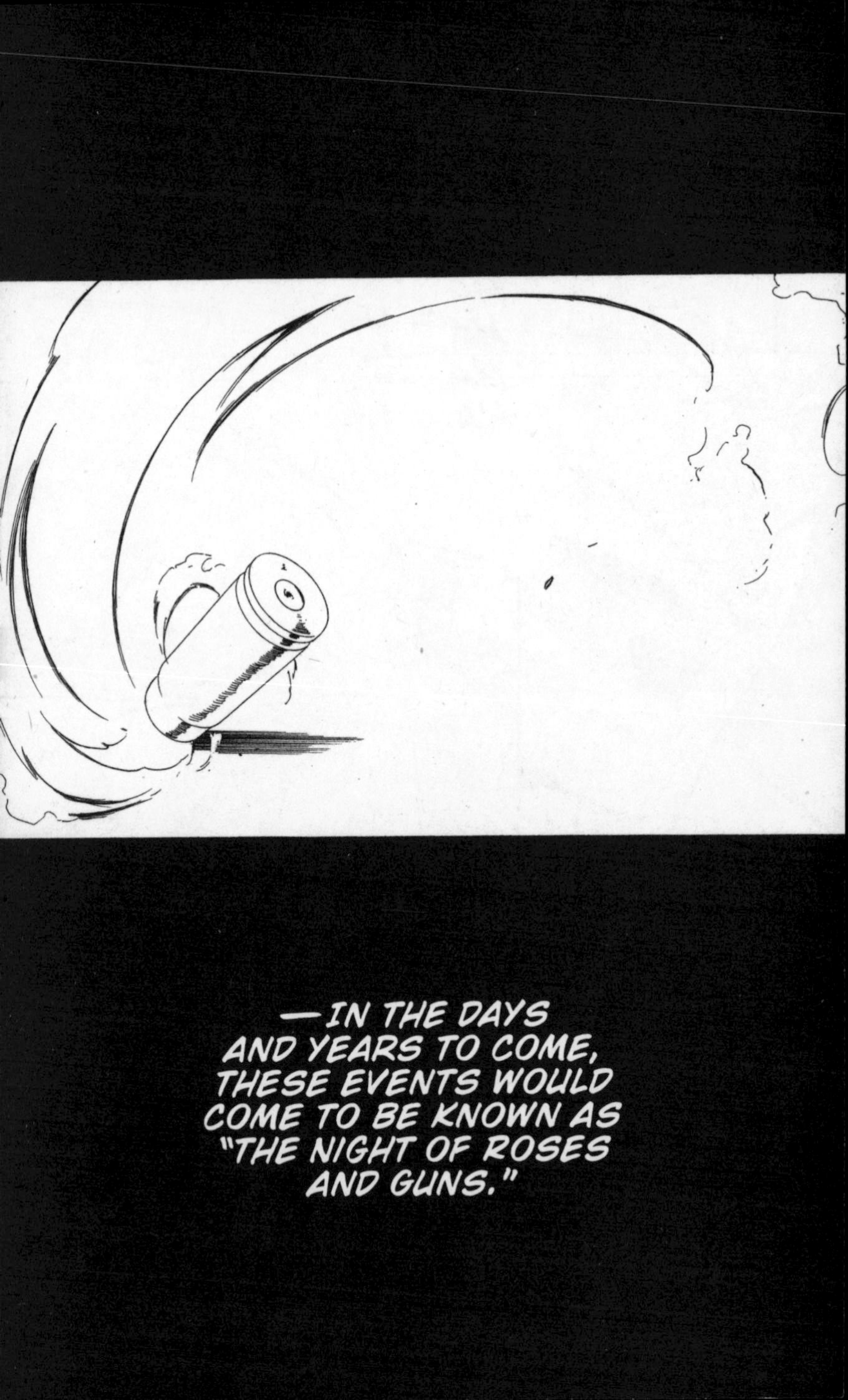
—IN THE DAYS AND YEARS TO COME, THESE EVENTS WOULD COME TO BE KNOWN AS "THE NIGHT OF ROSES AND GUNS."

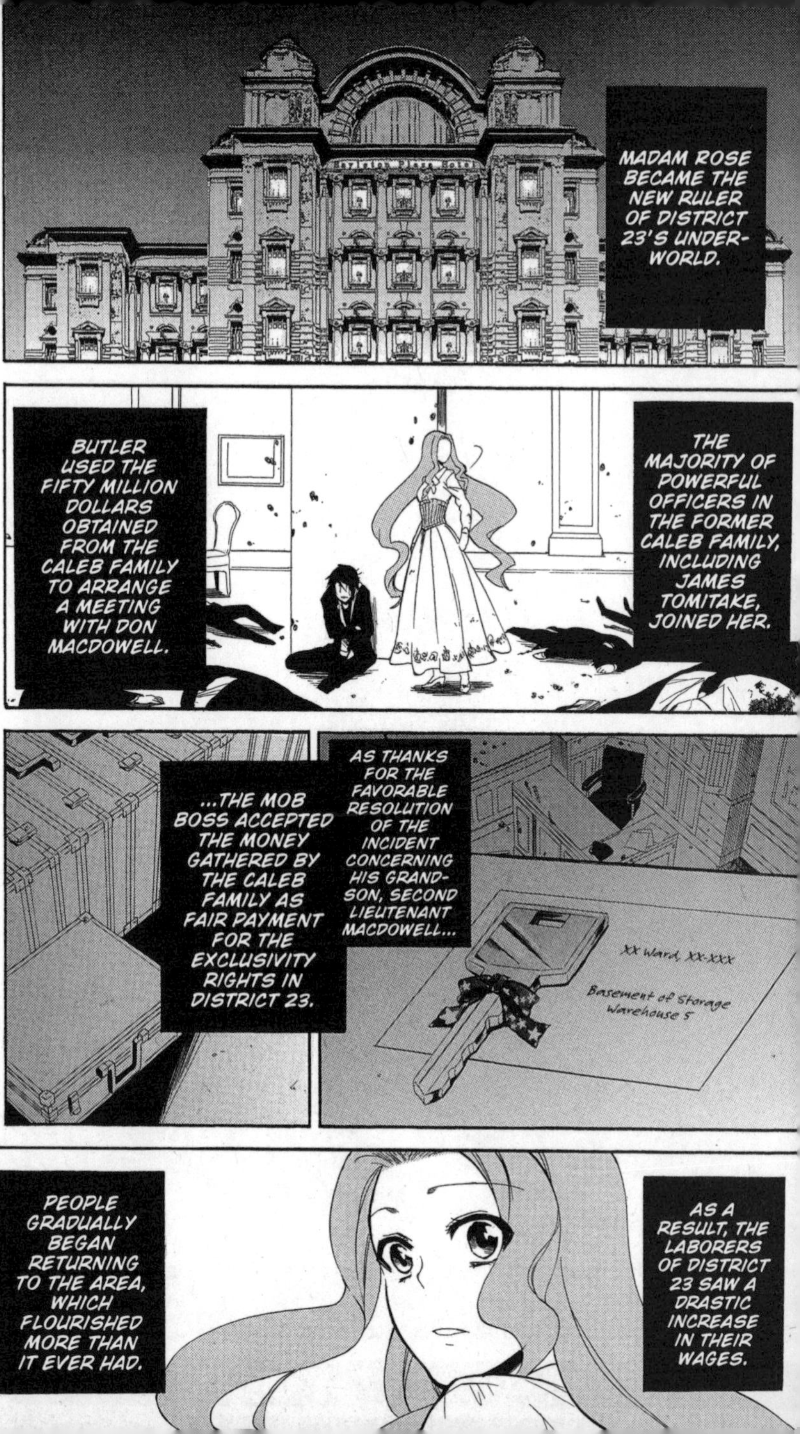
MADAM ROSE BECAME THE NEW RULER OF DISTRICT 23'S UNDER-WORLD.
THE MAJORITY OF POWERFUL OFFICERS IN THE FORMER CALEB FAMILY, INCLUDING JAMES TOMITAKE, JOINED HER.
BUTLER USED THE FIFTY MILLION DOLLARS OBTAINED FROM THE CALEB FAMILY TO ARRANGE A MEETING WITH DON MACDOWELL.
AS THANKS FOR THE FAVORABLE RESOLUTION OF THE INCIDENT CONCERNING HIS GRAND-SON, SECOND LIEUTENANT MACDOWELL...
XX Ward, XX-XXX
Basement of Storage Warehouse 5
...THE MOB BOSS ACCEPTED THE MONEY GATHERED BY THE CALEB FAMILY AS FAIR PAYMENT FOR THE EXCLUSIVITY RIGHTS IN DISTRICT 23.
AS A RESULT, THE LABORERS OF DISTRICT 23 SAW A DRASTIC INCREASE IN THEIR WAGES.
PEOPLE GRADUALLY BEGAN RETURNING TO THE AREA, WHICH FLOURISHED MORE THAN IT EVER HAD.

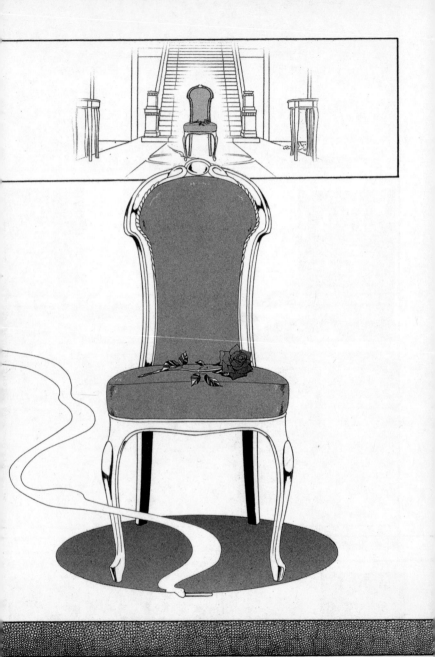

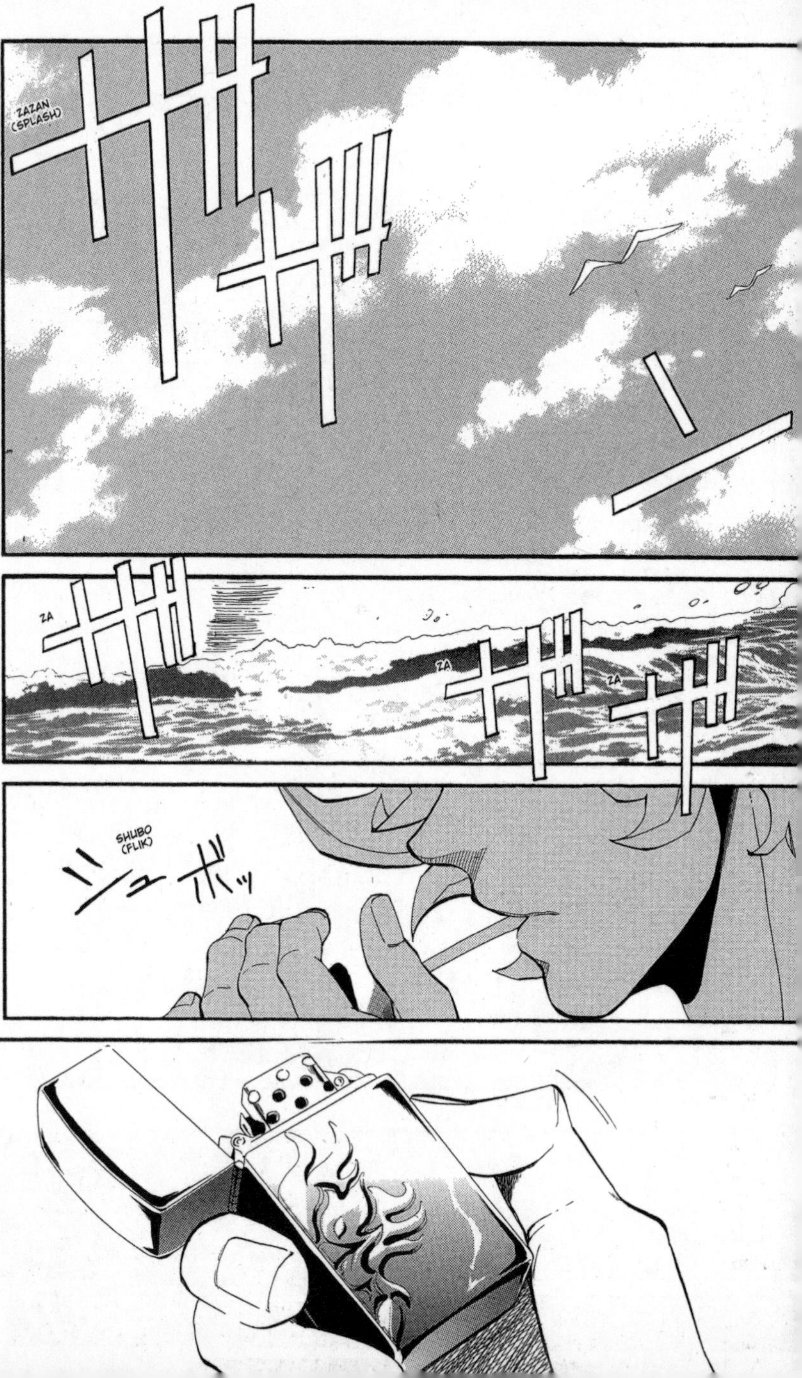
ZAZAN (SPLASH)
ザザザーン
ZA
ZA
ZA
ザザザ
SHUBO (FLIK)
シュボッ

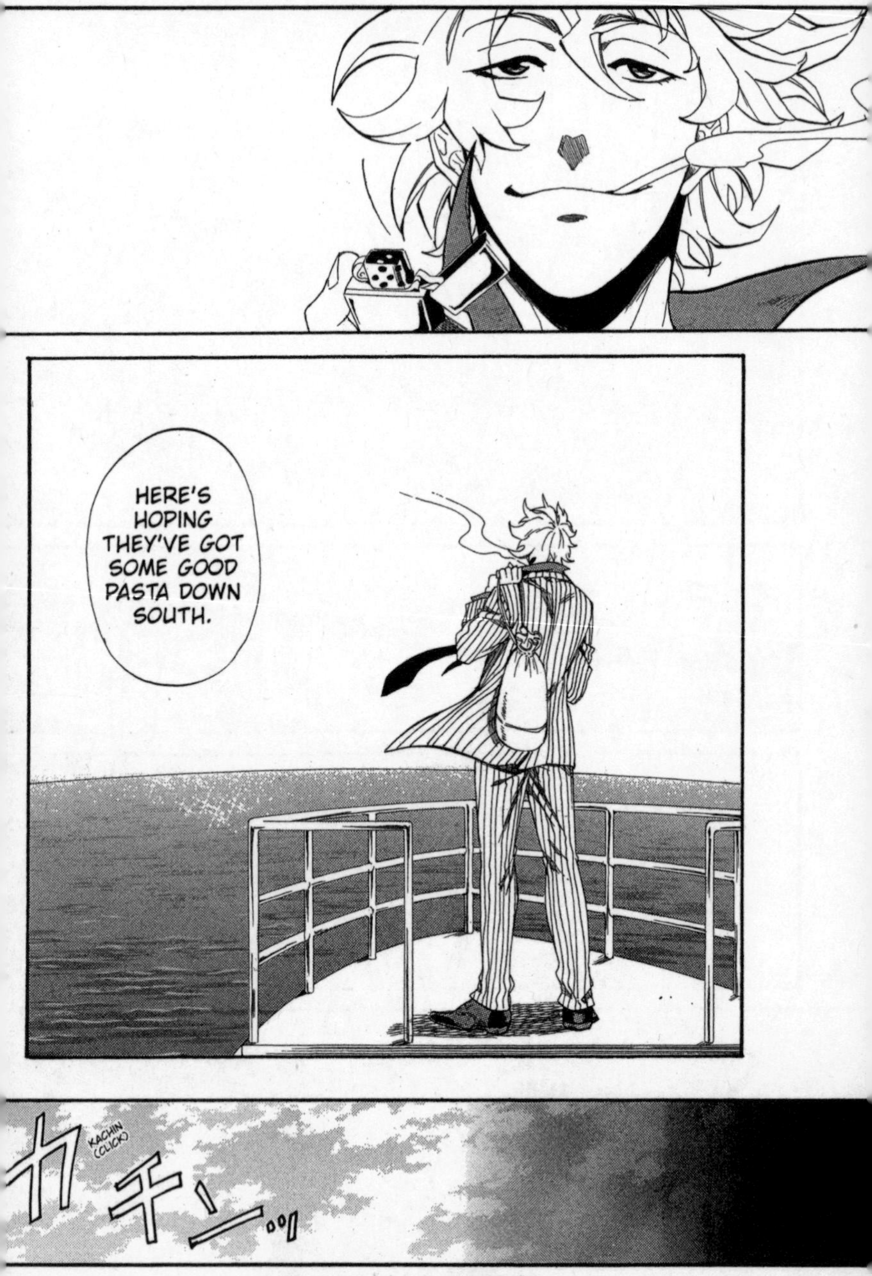
HERE'S HOPING THEY'VE GOT SOME GOOD PASTA DOWN SOUTH.
KACHIN (CLICK)

ROSE GUNS DAYS Season 1 END

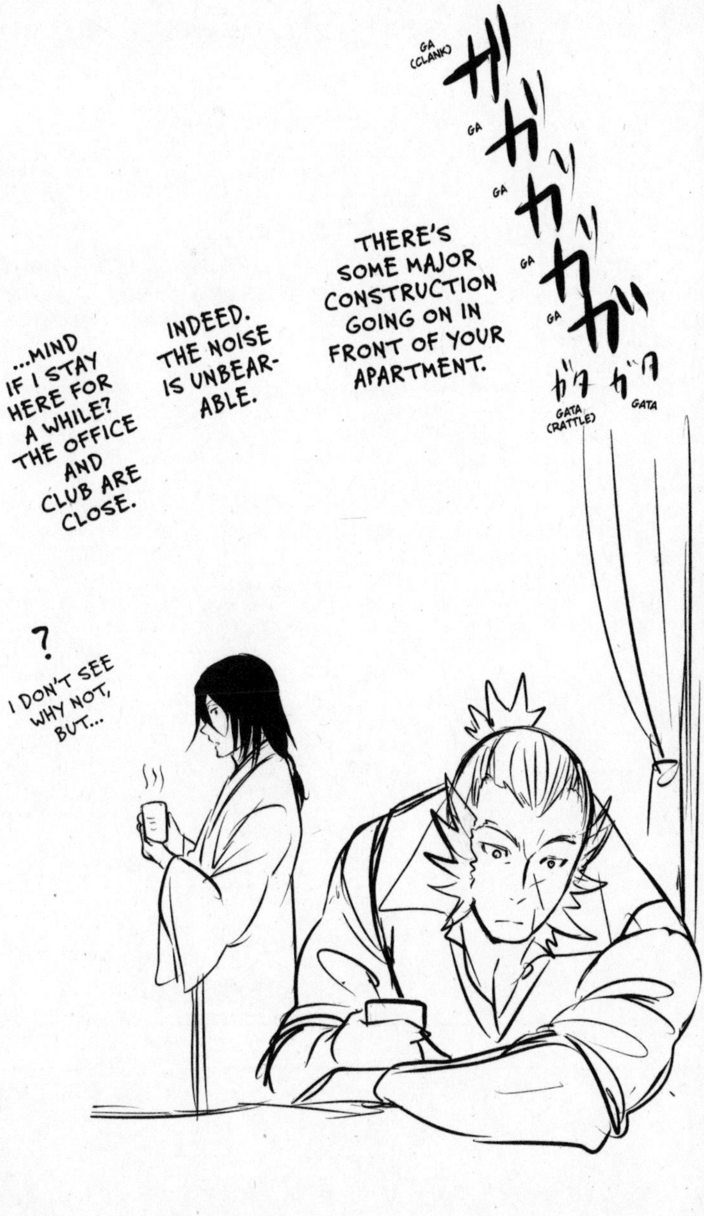

ガ
GA (CLANK)
ガ
GA
ガ
GA
ガ
GA
ガ
GA
ガタ
GATA (RATTLE)
ガタ
GATA
THERE'S SOME MAJOR CONSTRUCTION GOING ON IN FRONT OF YOUR APARTMENT.
INDEED. THE NOISE IS UNBEAR-ABLE.
...MIND IF I STAY HERE FOR A WHILE? THE OFFICE AND CLUB ARE CLOSE.
?
I DON'T SEE WHY NOT, BUT...

ABOUT ROSE GUNS DAYS SEASON 1

The Incredible Power of the Pen!

From the original writer and supervisor Ryukishio7

Hey! Ryukishio7, here.

How did you like Rose Guns Days Season 1? It showcases the meeting between Leo and Rose and marks the start of this post-war underworld epic, and I want to applaud Soichiro-sensei from the bottom of my heart for using his incredible power of the pen to bring it to life!

In the manga version of Season 1, he's managed to portray the charm of each and every character—even those who didn't get as much of a chance to shine in the original work. It's been done in such a way that even those who've played the original should find this a new and exciting read.

Again, I have to thank Soichiro-sensei for his hard work! He managed to preserve the integrity of the original while finding just the right way to portray it in manga form.

I'm so glad that the opening to the long tale of Rose Guns Days has been faithfully recreated in his magnificent art style!

As the original author, getting to experience this manga interpretation was really fun, because it felt like I was just another reader. Getting a peek at Soichiro-sensei's rough drafts was always a blast. I'm honestly a little sad that it's all over now, and I'd love another chance to work with him! Thanks again for everything!

BONUS

A LITTLE MEETING

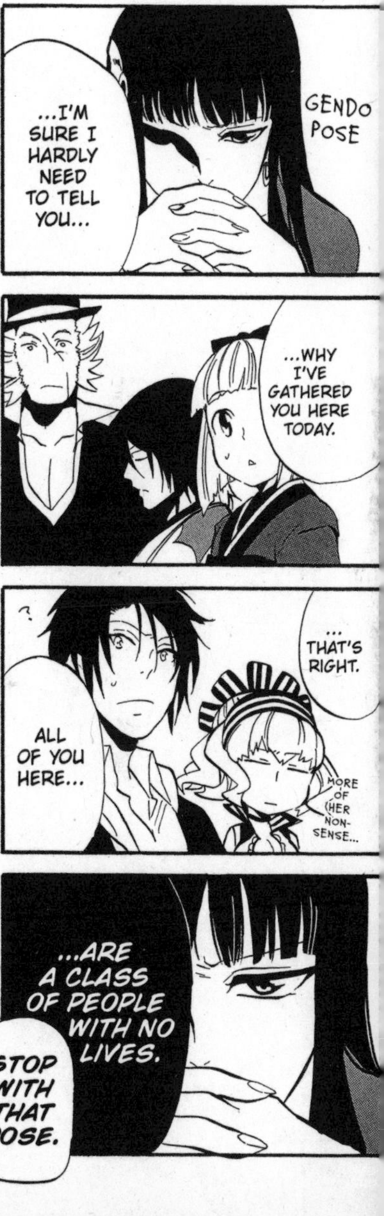
GENDO POSE
...I'M SURE I HARDLY NEED TO TELL YOU...
...WHY I'VE GATHERED YOU HERE TODAY.
...THAT'S RIGHT.
?
ALL OF YOU HERE...
MORE OF (HER NON-SENSE...
...ARE A CLASS OF PEOPLE WITH NO LIVES.
STOP WITH THAT POSE.

THE SIZE OF ONE'S HEART

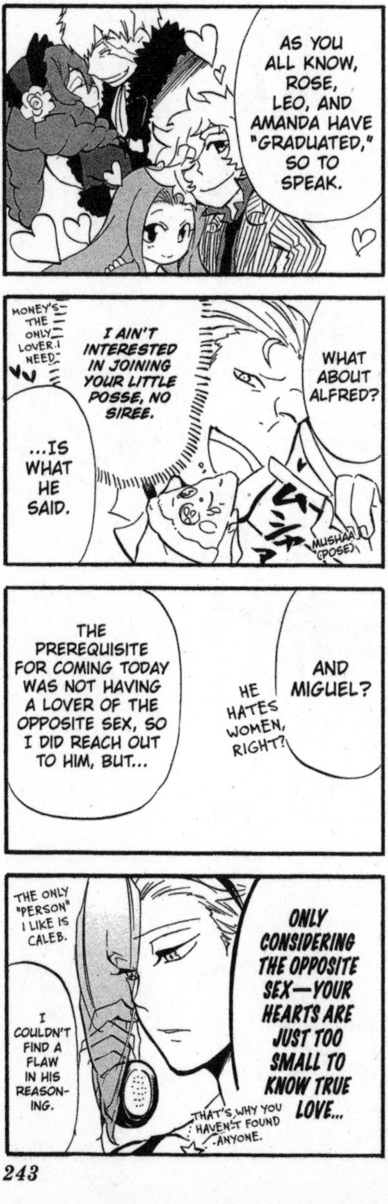
AS YOU ALL KNOW, ROSE, LEO, AND AMANDA HAVE "GRADUATED," SO TO SPEAK.
WHAT ABOUT ALFRED?
I AIN'T INTERESTED IN JOINING YOUR LITTLE POSSE, NO SIREE.
MONEY'S THE ONLY LOVER I NEED
...IS WHAT HE SAID.
MUSHAA (POSE)
AND MIGUEL?
HE HATES WOMEN, RIGHT?
THE PREREQUISITE FOR COMING TODAY WAS NOT HAVING A LOVER OF THE OPPOSITE SEX, SO I DID REACH OUT TO HIM, BUT...
ONLY CONSIDERING THE OPPOSITE SEX—YOUR HEARTS ARE JUST TOO SMALL TO KNOW TRUE LOVE...
THE ONLY "PERSON" I LIKE IS CALEB.
THAT'S WHY YOU HAVEN'T FOUND ANYONE.
I COULDN'T FIND A FLAW IN HIS REASONING.

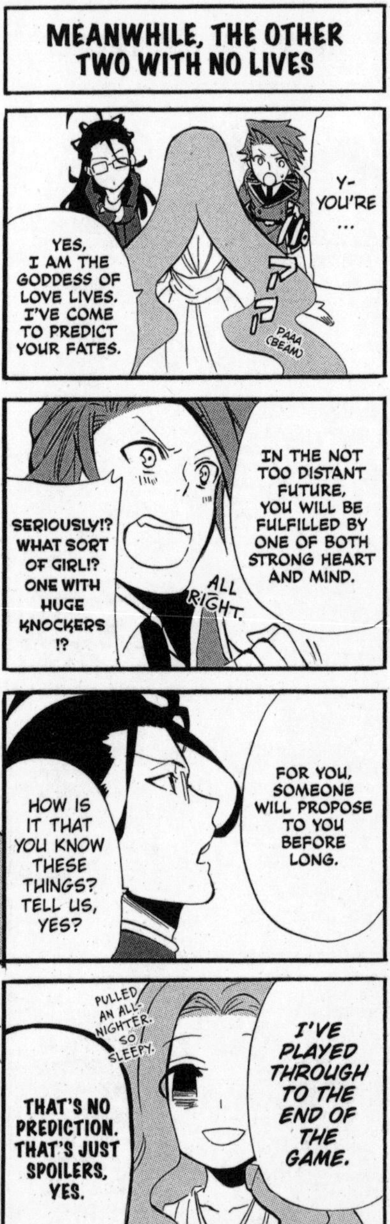
MEANWHILE, THE OTHER TWO WITH NO LIVES
Y-YOU'RE...
YES, I AM THE GODDESS OF LOVE LIVES. I'VE COME TO PREDICT YOUR FATES.
PAAA (BEAM)
IN THE NOT TOO DISTANT FUTURE, YOU WILL BE FULFILLED BY ONE OF BOTH STRONG HEART AND MIND.
ALL RIGHT.
SERIOUSLY!? WHAT SORT OF GIRL!? ONE WITH HUGE KNOCKERS!?
FOR YOU, SOMEONE WILL PROPOSE TO YOU BEFORE LONG.
HOW IS IT THAT YOU KNOW THESE THINGS? TELL US, YES?
I'VE PLAYED THROUGH TO THE END OF THE GAME.
PULLED AN ALL-NIGHTER. SO SLEEPY.
THAT'S NO PREDICTION. THAT'S JUST SPOILERS, YES.

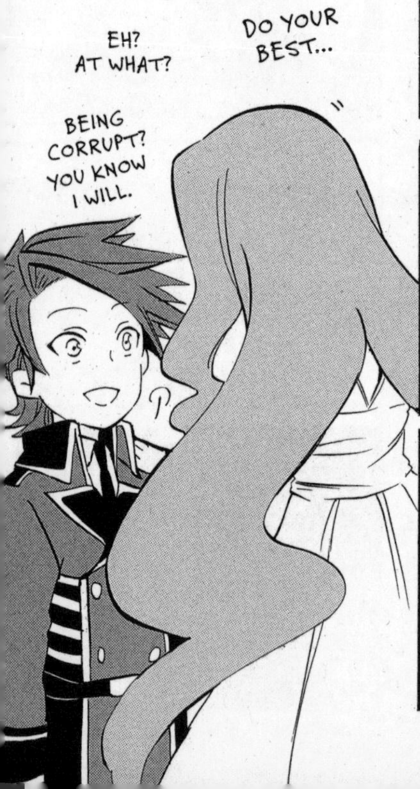
DO YOUR BEST...
EH? AT WHAT?
BEING CORRUPT? YOU KNOW I WILL.

THE ENEMY WITHIN...

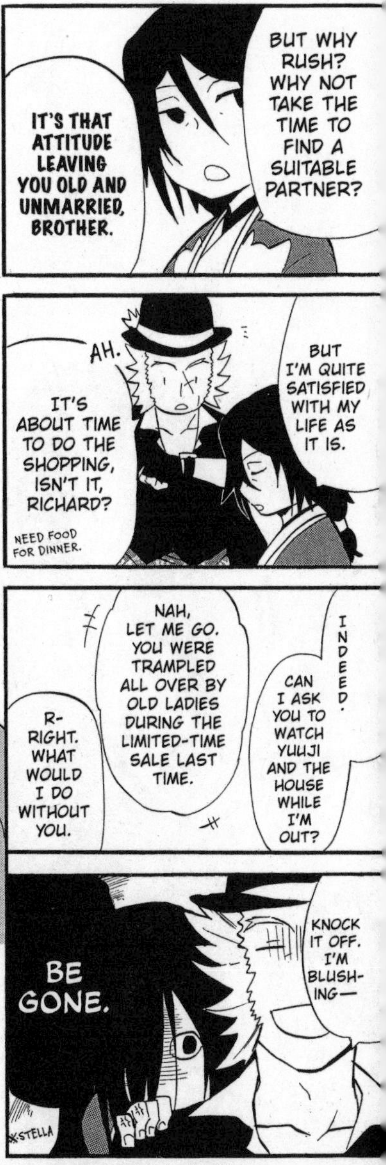
BUT WHY RUSH? WHY NOT TAKE THE TIME TO FIND A SUITABLE PARTNER?
IT'S THAT ATTITUDE LEAVING YOU OLD AND UNMARRIED, BROTHER.
BUT I'M QUITE SATISFIED WITH MY LIFE AS IT IS.
AH.
IT'S ABOUT TIME TO DO THE SHOPPING, ISN'T IT, RICHARD?
NEED FOOD FOR DINNER.
INDEED.
CAN I ASK YOU TO WATCH YUUJI AND THE HOUSE WHILE I'M OUT?
NAH, LET ME GO. YOU WERE TRAMPLED ALL OVER BY OLD LADIES DURING THE LIMITED-TIME SALE LAST TIME.
R-RIGHT. WHAT WOULD I DO WITHOUT YOU.
KNOCK IT OFF. I'M BLUSHING—
BE GONE.
※STELLA

YOU'RE LIKE A HOUSEWIFE.

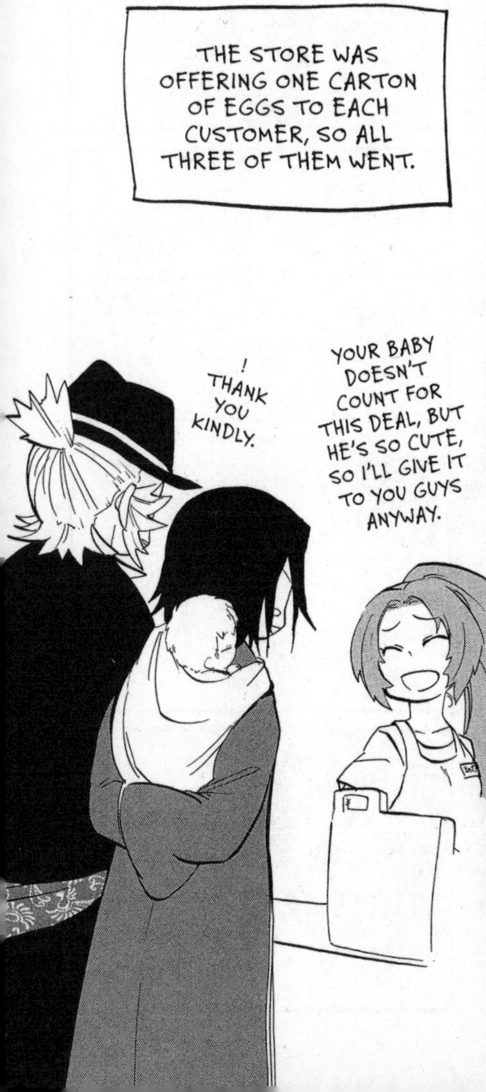
THE STORE WAS OFFERING ONE CARTON OF EGGS TO EACH CUSTOMER, SO ALL THREE OF THEM WENT.
YOUR BABY DOESN'T COUNT FOR THIS DEAL, BUT HE'S SO CUTE, SO I'LL GIVE IT TO YOU GUYS ANYWAY.
! THANK YOU KINDLY.

THE MESSIAH WITH A LOVE LIFE

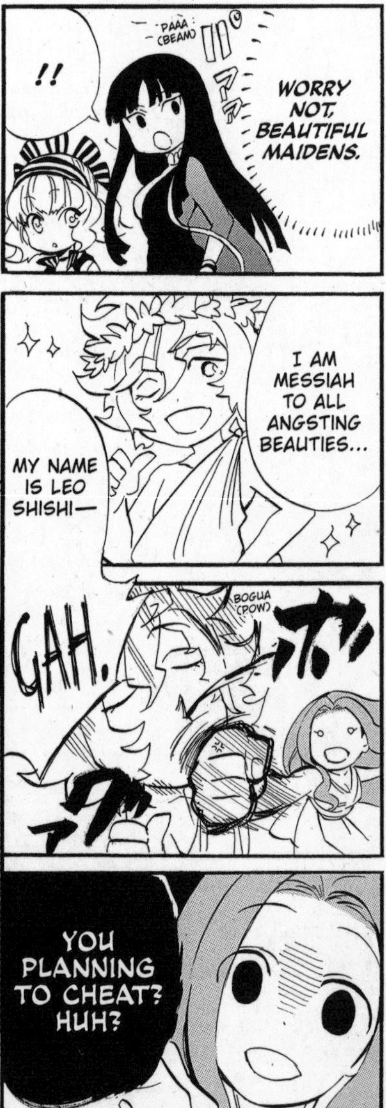
PAAA (BEAM)
WORRY NOT, BEAUTIFUL MAIDENS.
!!
I AM MESSIAH TO ALL ANGSTING BEAUTIES...
MY NAME IS LEO SHISHI—
BOGUA (POW)
GAH.
YOU PLANNING TO CHEAT? HUH?

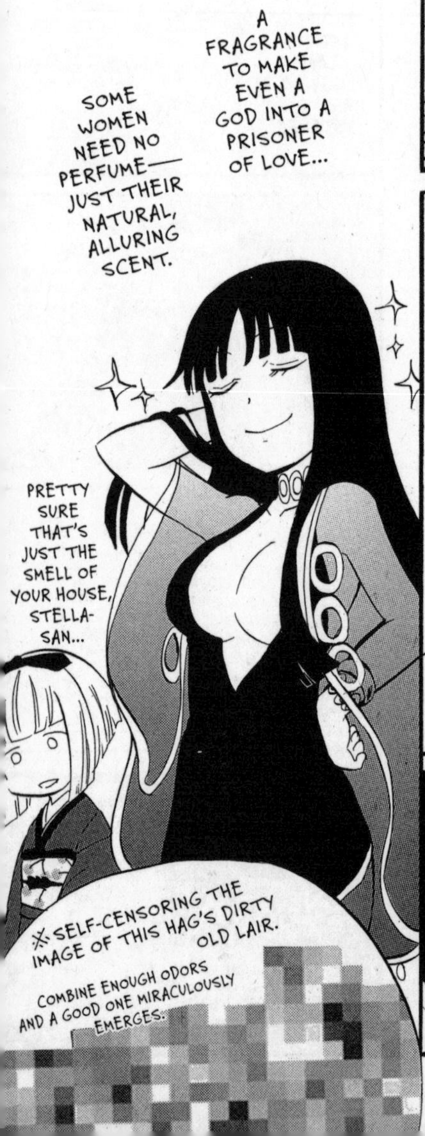
A FRAGRANCE TO MAKE EVEN A GOD INTO A PRISONER OF LOVE...
SOME WOMEN NEED NO PERFUME— JUST THEIR NATURAL, ALLURING SCENT.
PRETTY SURE THAT'S JUST THE SMELL OF YOUR HOUSE, STELLA-SAN...
※SELF-CENSORING THE IMAGE OF THIS HAG'S DIRTY OLD LAIR.
COMBINE ENOUGH ODORS AND A GOOD ONE MIRACULOUSLY EMERGES.

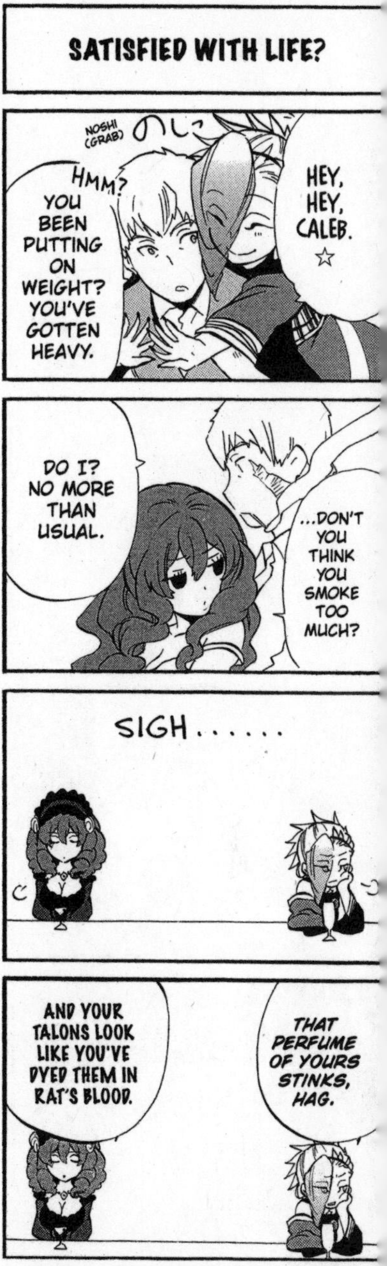
SATISFIED WITH LIFE?
NOSHI (GRAB)
HEY, HEY, CALEB. ☆
HMM? YOU BEEN PUTTING ON WEIGHT? YOU'VE GOTTEN HEAVY.
...DON'T YOU THINK YOU SMOKE TOO MUCH?
DO I? NO MORE THAN USUAL.
SIGH......
THAT PERFUME OF YOURS STINKS, HAG.
AND YOUR TALONS LOOK LIKE YOU'VE DYED THEM IN RAT'S BLOOD.

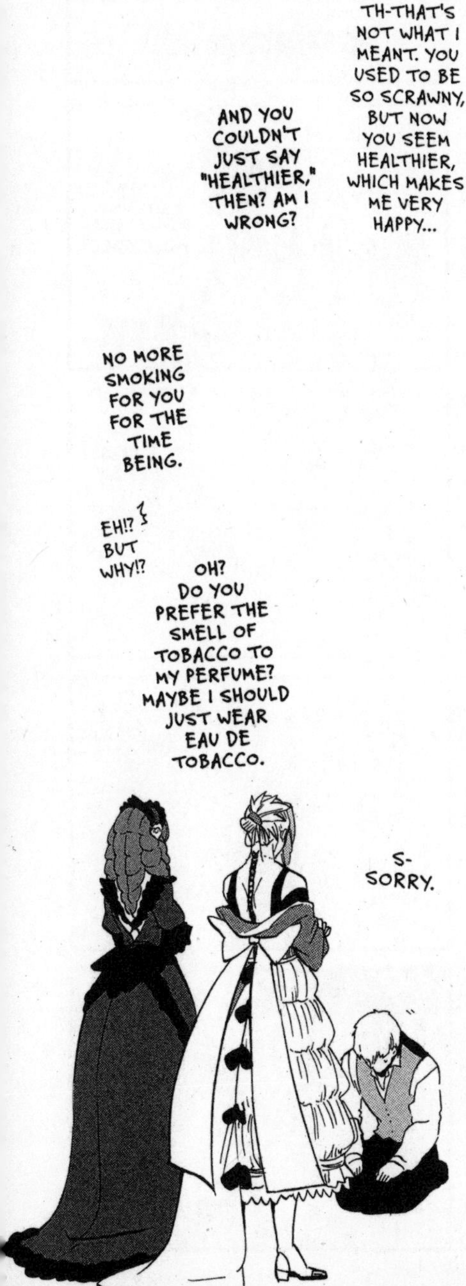
TH-THAT'S NOT WHAT I MEANT. YOU USED TO BE SO SCRAWNY, BUT NOW YOU SEEM HEALTHIER, WHICH MAKES ME VERY HAPPY...
AND YOU COULDN'T JUST SAY "HEALTHIER," THEN? AM I WRONG?
NO MORE SMOKING FOR YOU FOR THE TIME BEING.
EH!? BUT WHY!?
OH? DO YOU PREFER THE SMELL OF TOBACCO TO MY PERFUME? MAYBE I SHOULD JUST WEAR EAU DE TOBACCO.
S-SORRY.

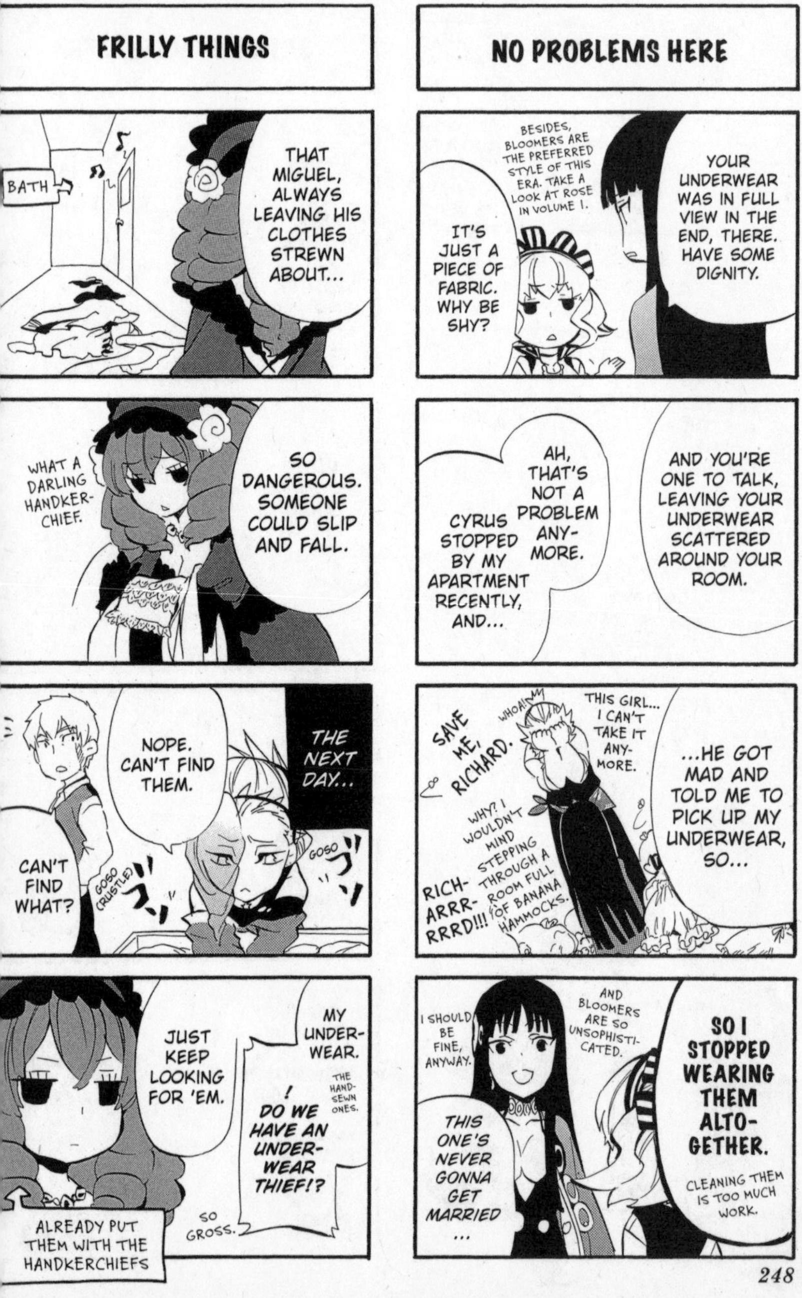
NO PROBLEMS HERE
YOUR UNDERWEAR WAS IN FULL VIEW IN THE END, THERE. HAVE SOME DIGNITY.
BESIDES, BLOOMERS ARE THE PREFERRED STYLE OF THIS ERA. TAKE A LOOK AT ROSE IN VOLUME 1.
IT'S JUST A PIECE OF FABRIC. WHY BE SHY?
AND YOU'RE ONE TO TALK, LEAVING YOUR UNDERWEAR SCATTERED AROUND YOUR ROOM.
AH, THAT'S NOT A PROBLEM ANYMORE.
CYRUS STOPPED BY MY APARTMENT RECENTLY, AND...
...HE GOT MAD AND TOLD ME TO PICK UP MY UNDERWEAR, SO...
THIS GIRL... I CAN'T TAKE IT ANYMORE.
WHOA!
SAVE ME, RICHARD.
WHY?! I WOULDN'T MIND STEPPING THROUGH A ROOM FULL OF BANANA HAMMOCKS.
RICH-ARRR-RRRD!!!
SO I STOPPED WEARING THEM ALTOGETHER.
CLEANING THEM IS TOO MUCH WORK.
AND BLOOMERS ARE SO UNSOPHISTICATED.
I SHOULD BE FINE, ANYWAY.
THIS ONE'S NEVER GONNA GET MARRIED...
FRILLY THINGS
THAT MIGUEL, ALWAYS LEAVING HIS CLOTHES STREWN ABOUT...
BATH
SO DANGEROUS. SOMEONE COULD SLIP AND FALL.
WHAT A DARLING HANDKERCHIEF.
THE NEXT DAY...
GOSO
NOPE. CAN'T FIND THEM.
GOSO (CRUSTLE)
CAN'T FIND WHAT?
MY UNDERWEAR.
THE HAND-SEWN ONES.
DO WE HAVE AN UNDERWEAR THIEF!?
JUST KEEP LOOKING FOR 'EM.
SO GROSS.
ALREADY PUT THEM WITH THE HANDKERCHIEFS

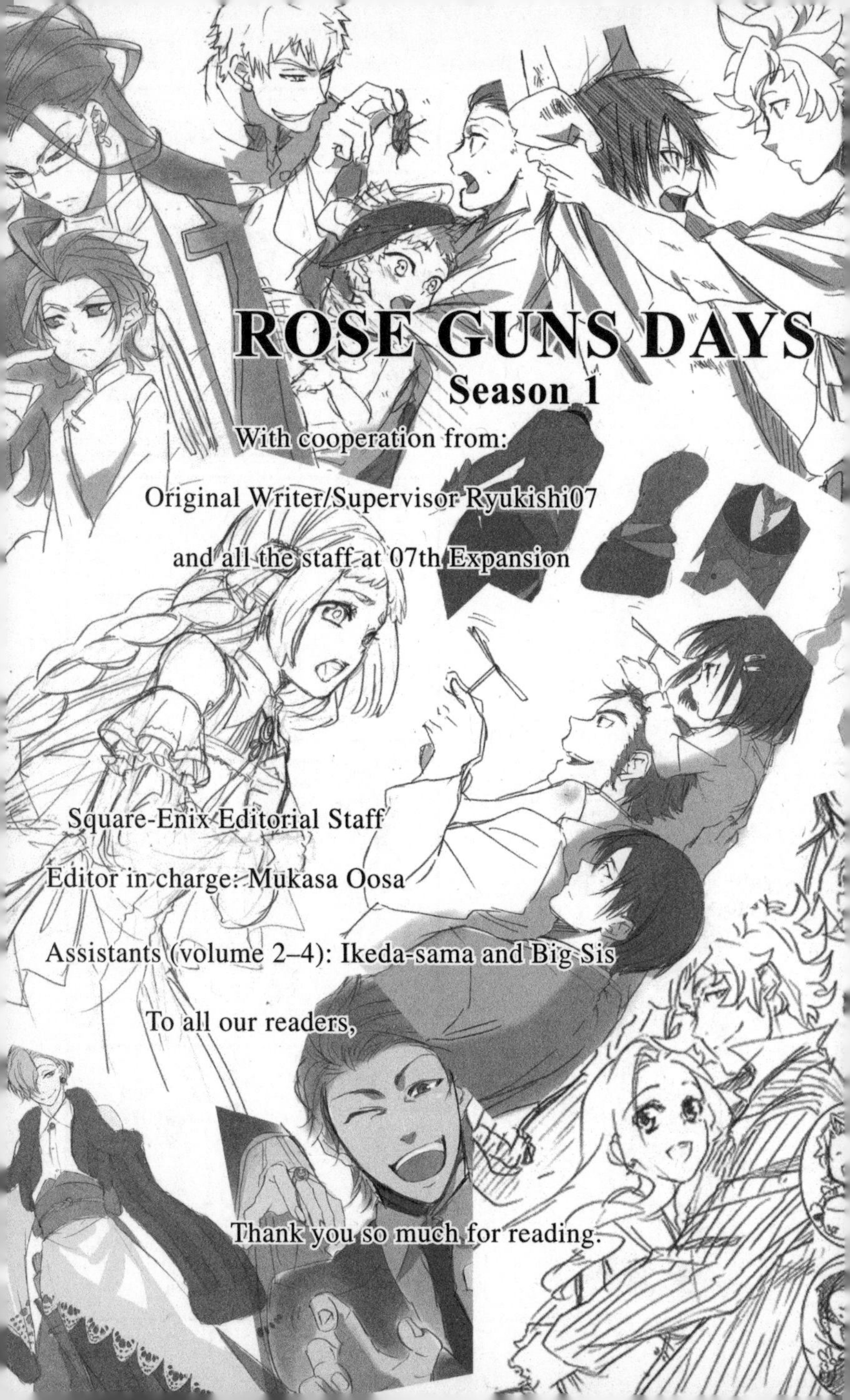

ROSE GUNS DAYS

Season 1

With cooperation from:

Original Writer/Supervisor Ryukishi07

and all the staff at 07th Expansion

Square-Enix Editorial Staff

Editor in charge: Mukasa Oosa

Assistants (volume 2–4): Ikeda-sama and Big Sis

To all our readers,

Thank you so much for reading.

BONUS CONTENT FROM UNDER THE JACKET OF VOLUME 4!

I TRIED IT OUT

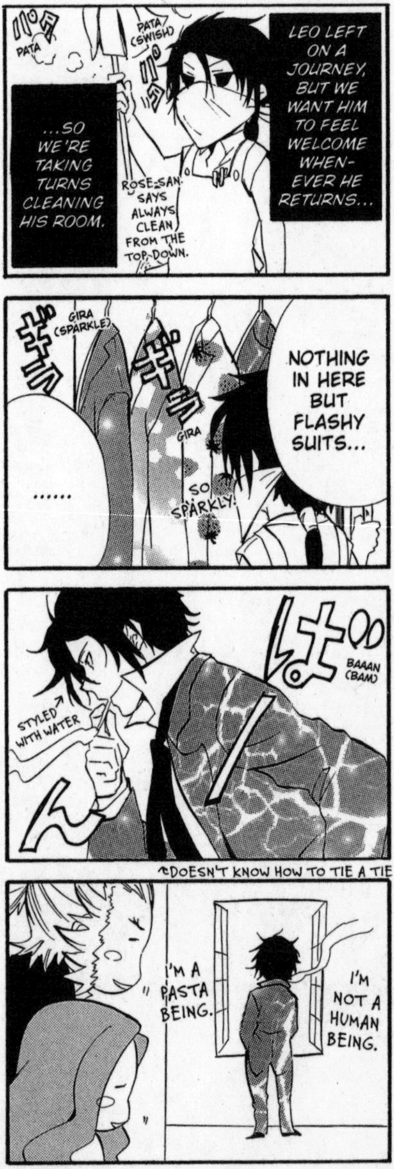
LEO LEFT ON A JOURNEY, BUT WE WANT HIM TO FEEL WELCOME WHENEVER HE RETURNS...
PATA (SWISH)
PATA
...SO WE'RE TAKING TURNS CLEANING HIS ROOM.
ROSE-SAN SAYS ALWAYS CLEAN FROM THE TOP DOWN.
NOTHING IN HERE BUT FLASHY SUITS...
GIRA (SPARKLE)
GIRA
SO SPARKLY.
......
BAAAN (BAM)
STYLED WITH WATER
DOESN'T KNOW HOW TO TIE A TIE
I'M NOT A HUMAN BEING.
I'M A PASTA BEING.

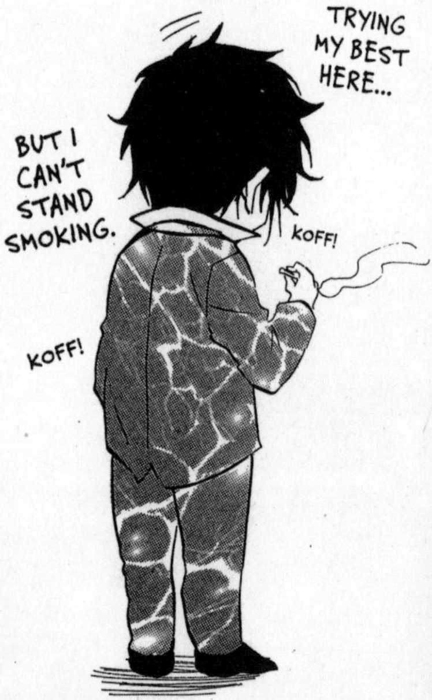
TRYING MY BEST HERE...
BUT I CAN'T STAND SMOKING.
KOFF!
KOFF!

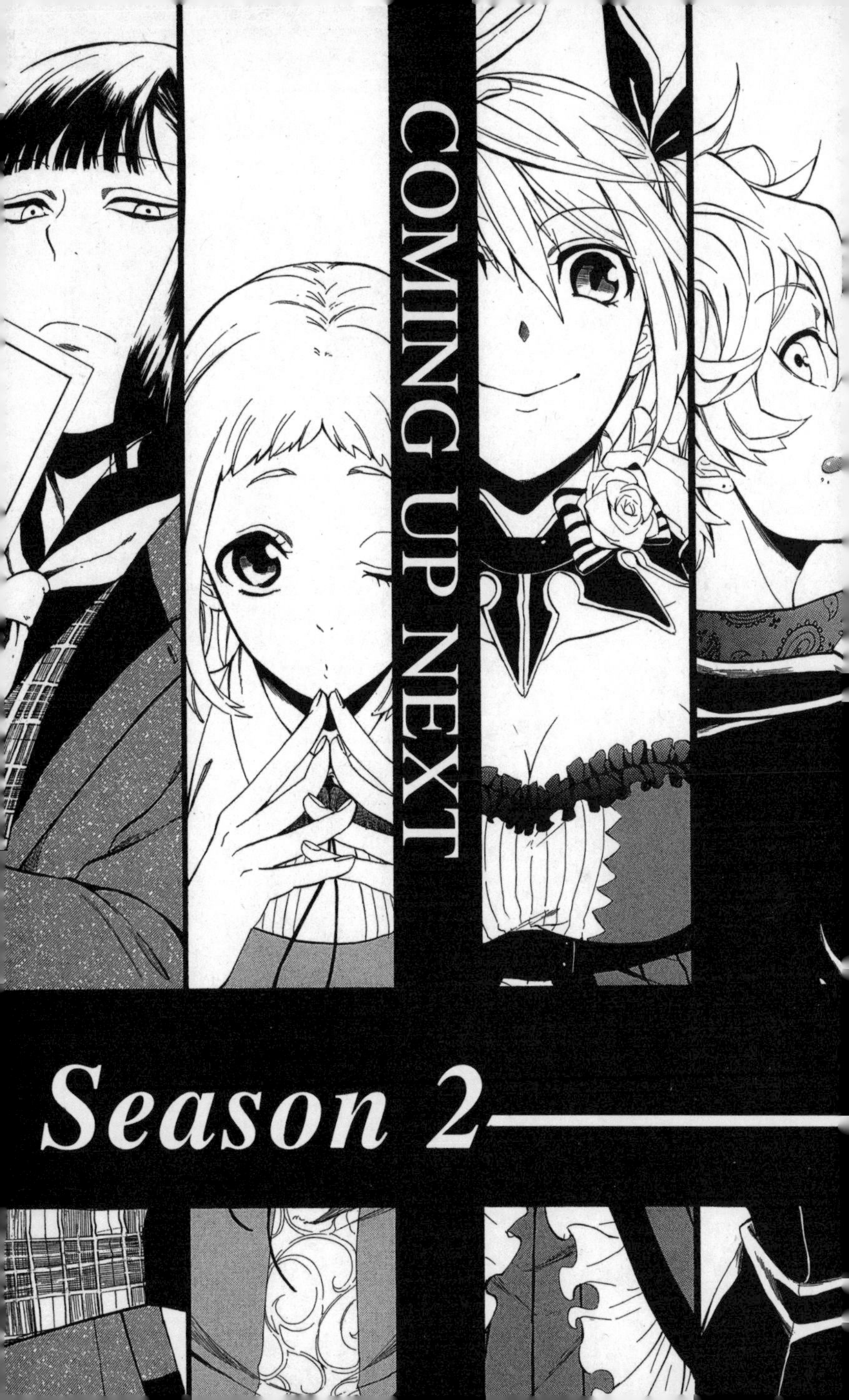
COMING UP NEXT
Season 2

TRANSLATION NOTES

COMMON HONORIFICS

no honorific: Indicates familiarity or closeness; if used without permission or reason, addressing someone in this manner would constitute an insult.

-san: The Japanese equivalent of Mr./Mrs./Miss. If a situation calls for politeness, this is the fail-safe honorific.

-sama: Conveys great respect; may also indicate that the social status of the speaker is lower than that of the addressee.

-kun: Used most often when referring to boys, this indicates affection or familiarity. Occasionally used by older men among their peers, but it may also be used by anyone referring to a person of lower standing.

-chan: An affectionate honorific indicating familiarity used mostly in reference to girls; also used in reference to cute persons or animals of either gender.

-senpai: A suffix used to address upperclassmen or more experienced coworkers.

PAGE 44

Here, Soichiro explains a printing error in the original magazine publication. The kanji shown in the third panel (in his own rough handwriting) is correct, "eagle," but what ended up getting printed in the magazine was the very similar kanji for "hawk," shown in the second panel.

PAGE 157

Cyrus's line refers to a real mountain in Taiwan called "Niitakayama" (or "new high mountain") by the Japanese. But the line itself is a reference to the infamous secret code—*"Niitakayama Nobore"* ("Climb the new high mountain")—that signaled the Japanese carrier fleet to begin its attack on Pearl Harbor.

PAGE 195

The weaver girl and the cowherd refers to love story between Vega and Altair, the stars central to the Chinese Qixi Festival—which in turn inspired Japan's Tanabata Festival. Vega and Altair were heavenly star-crossed lovers separated by the Milky Way, allowed to meet only once a year on the seventh day of the seventh month.

ROSE GUNS DAYS

Season 1

PAGE 228

Note that the Japanese pronunciation of "**Miguel**" (Migeru) contains the same "-*geru*" as the character's Japanese name, revealed in this volume as Shigeru. Similarly, we have Keireiji becoming Caleb (Keirebu), Saimura becoming Cyrus (Sairasu), Sumiko becoming Stella (Sutera), Kurosaki becoming Claudia (Kuroodia), Amamiya becoming Amanda, and so on. Rose and Leo's chosen English names operate on meaning rather than phonetics, as the "*bara*" in Rose's last name, Haibara, actually means "rose," and the "*shishi*" in Shishigami means "lion."

PAGE 243

Stella's "**Gendo**" pose is a reference to Gendo Ikari of Hideaki Anno's *Neon Genesis Evangelion*. The character is known for tenting his fingers in front of his mouth in that manner—so much so that the pose is colloquially referred to by his name.

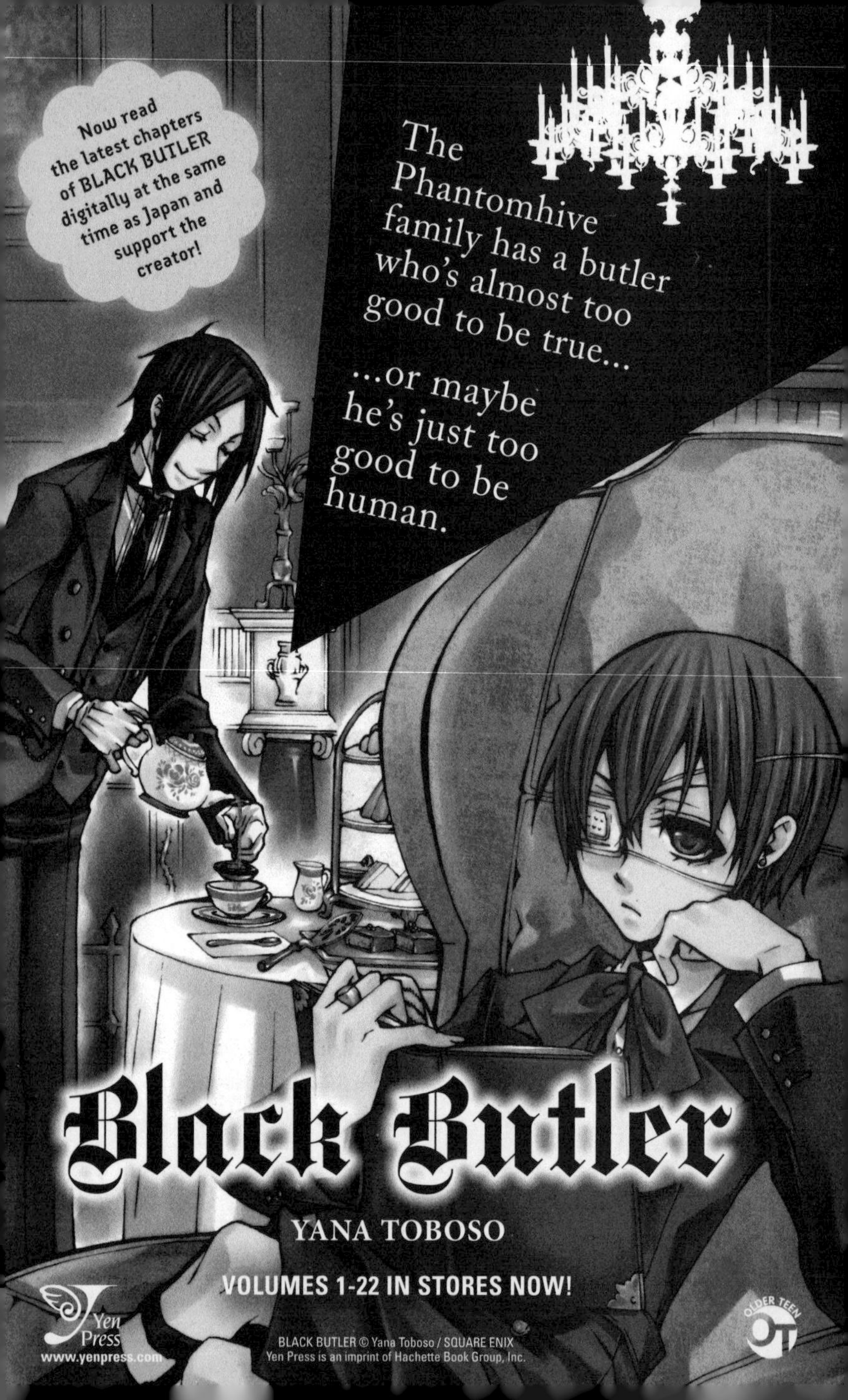
Now read the latest chapters of BLACK BUTLER digitally at the same time as Japan and support the creator!
The Phantomhive family has a butler who's almost too good to be true...
...or maybe he's just too good to be human.
Black Butler
YANA TOBOSO
VOLUMES 1-22 IN STORES NOW!
Yen Press
www.yenpress.com
BLACK BUTLER © Yana Toboso / SQUARE ENIX
Yen Press is an imprint of Hachette Book Group, Inc.
OLDER TEEN
OT

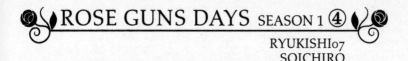

ROSE GUNS DAYS SEASON 1 ④

RYUKISHI07
SOICHIRO

Translation: Caleb D. Cook • Lettering: Katie Blakeslee and Lys Blakeslee

This book is a work of fiction. Names, characters, places, and incidents are the product of the author's imagination or are used fictitiously. Any resemblance to actual events, locales, or persons, living or dead, is coincidental.

ROSE GUNS DAYS Season 1 vol. 4
© RYUKISHI07 / 07th Expansion
© 2014 Soichiro / SQUARE ENIX CO., LTD.
First published in Japan in 2014 by SQUARE ENIX CO., LTD.
English translation rights arranged with SQUARE ENIX CO., LTD.
and Hachette Book Group through Tuttle-Mori Agency, Inc.

Translation © 2016 by SQUARE ENIX CO., LTD.

Yen Press
Hachette Book Group
1290 Avenue of the Americas
New York, NY 10104

www.hachettebookgroup.com
www.yenpress.com

Yen Press is an imprint of Hachette Book Group, Inc.
The Yen Press name and logo are trademarks of Hachette Book Group, Inc.

The publisher is not responsible for websites (or their content) that are not owned by the publisher.

Library of Congress Control Number: 2016932697

First Yen Press Edition: June 2016

ISBN: 978-0-316-39154-2

10 9 8 7 6 5 4 3 2 1

BVG

Printed in the United States of America